St. Louis Catholic Parish
Fond du Lac, Wisconsin
Répertoire of Baptisms, Marriages, & Burials
1850-1920

Compiled by Kateri (Teri) Dupuis, Don Cayen

and the

French Canadian/Acadian Genealogists of Wisconsin

Published for Clearfield Company by
Genealogical Publishing Company
Baltimore, Maryland
2010

ISBN 978-0-8063-5478-1

Made in the United States of America

Dedication

"This work is dedicated to the memory of the
Catholic pioneers of the Fond du Lac, Wisconsin area and
to the missionaries who served them."

TABLE OF CONTENTS

ACKNOWLEDGMENTS

This project is the work of many people, all of whom have made important contributions. First mention goes to the extractors, who had the tedious and eye-straining work of deciphering the original handwritten records. The extractors were Joyce Banachowski, Don Cayen, Audrey Cayo, Mary Dunsirn, Kateri (Teri) Dupuis, Barbara Glassel, F. Barton Jacques, Ray Lusty, Patricia Ustine, and Susan White. The extracted information was compared by Don Cayen, Janet Dupuis Cox, Kateri (Teri) Dupuis, Sue Holton, Maxine Plasa, and Celeste Dupuis Walsh.

The typists did invaluable work keying the data into the Excel spreadsheet. Like all of the extractors and comparers, most of the typists were volunteers. However, due to certain circumstances, a few of the typists were paid a small amount, as is indicated by a "+". The typists were: Wil Brazeau, Joyce Dreischmeier+, Kateri (Teri) Dupuis, Rachelle Dupuis+, Cindy Koschmann, Steve McKay, Susan Ojala Myers+, Ruth Paulsen, and Judy Vezzetti.

Proofreaders of the various versions of the manuscript were Joyce Banachowski, Don Cayen, Marilyn Cayen, Kateri (Teri) Dupuis, and Patricia Ustine.

All the best intentions still require money to cover necessary expenses.. The project team was very fortunate to receive a major contribution from Dawn Snow. Joyce Banachowski, Marilyn Bourbonais, Judith Edholm, Patricia Geyh, Sue Holton, Nancy Kerr Reed, and Darlene Wnuk also made generous contributions.

A special note of gratitude goes to Mr. James Hansen of the Wisconsin Historical Society for his encouragement and advice regarding this project. Thanks to Mr. Hansen, this Répertoire contains information on early Catholic settlers in the Fond du Lac area that are from the records of St. John Catholic Church in Little Chute, Wisconsin.

This project could not have been accomplished without the expert help and patience of Jason Pettit of Pettit Media, LLC of Fond du Lac, Wisconsin (www.pettitmedia.com). Jason adapted the genealogy program "The Next Generation of Genealogy Sitebuilding" to the needs of this project. His work included building the on-line database and the printing format for this Répertoire, all at a very reasonable cost to the French Canadian/Acadian Genealogists of Wisconsin (FCGW). When other commitments forced Jason to leave this project, Michael V. Loser graciously stepped in to lend his expertise to complete the database.

The French Canadian/Acadian Genealogists of Wisconsin gratefully acknowledge John Grignon of Grignon Advertising, Milwaukee, Wisconsin. John redesigned the FCGW logo to its present enhanced form.

INTRODUCTION

This Répertoire of the baptisms, confirmations, marriages, and burials performed at St. Louis Catholic Church in Fond du Lac, Wisconsin, is the result of a major project undertaken by the French-Canadian/Acadian Genealogists of Wisconsin (www.fcgw.org). The time period for all the events is from its formation in 1847 to 1920. The first event actually recorded in the Church, however, occurred in 1850. Thus, it is important to realize that this Répertoire represents original records that were created by several priests and/or other transcribers over a period of 70 years.

Handwriting legibility of the original records varied widely, some indecipherable, some illegible and some faded. It is often difficult and sometimes impossible to discern, for both upper and lower case, between the letters a and o, e and i, l and t, g and y, u and v, m and n, u and n. Not only names, but also dates in some instances are almost impossible to ascertain with certainty. Hence, users of this Répertoire need to use creative thinking regarding the spellings of names. A few examples of some original handwritten marriage records are given in Appendix A.

The original record books are kept at the Archives of the Catholic Archdiocese of Milwaukee, Wisconsin. The books are generally in poor condition. Some pages have ink splotches that make it impossible to know what information is hidden.

In most instances, the records are written in Latin. Margin notations are usually in French. For convenience, a list of common Latin names and their French and English equivalents is presented in Appendix B of this Répertoire.

It appears from the original records that all the entries were written only by priests or other transcribers. The project team found no instance in which another participant in an event, such as a godparent at a baptism or a spouse at a wedding, signed the record.

The original records were filmed by both the Milwaukee Archdiocese and by the Church of Jesus Christ of Latter Day Saints. The film numbers are 1862602 and 1862866. It is unfortunate that numerous pages of the films are faulty at their bottom margins. In some cases the lower margins are cut off. In other pages, the lower margins are "black" from excess light entering the camera. In both situations, it is difficult at best and impossible in some instances to read the entries at the bottoms of the pages from the films.

In the original baptism records, three sets of entries, each containing a few dozen baptisms, are written in three different handwritings, but all three sets are under the name of a same priest. The multiple entries often have slightly different spellings of the names (Martin, Marten). There are also some multiple entries for the marriages and burials of some persons. The multiple entry situation is more common for baptisms than for marriages and burials. In this Répertoire, those entries marked with a single asterisk (*) indicate multiple entries for the same person.   One can only speculate as to the reason the records contain multiple entries.

The priests (and copyists) were highly creative in their spellings. One priest, for example, spelled his own name differently in different records. The use of apostrophes (Obryan, O'bryan) was inconsistent, as was the form of the prefix "Mc" (Mccarthy, MCCarthy). Given names varied considerably. "Elizabeth" could be "Elisabeth," "Elazabet," "Elisabeh," "Ellesbet," and several more. "Margaret", "Catherine", and "Bridget" are three other names whose spellings were limited only by the imaginations of the recorders. The endings of Latin given names were inconsistent. Some Latin masculine names do have feminine endings, e. g., Baptista, Andrea. The spellings are presented as they appear in the records. (The Latin names in Appendix B illustrate common Latin spellings.) First-name abbreviations sometimes give only hints of what the real name was intended to be: "Cath," "Philome."

Another major problem is that the records are incomplete. There are no records for the years 1910-1918. A diligent search of the Milwaukee Archdiocese Archives with the help of the archivist, Shelly Solberg, failed to uncover the missing records. Again, one must resort to speculation for explaining why the records are missing.

The original records contain the names of priests "L. Dael" and "L. Dale." A check of the Archdiocese Archives was unsuccessful in determining whether there were two priests or one. The names given in the database and are as they are spelled in the records.

A list of names appears in the original records at pages in front of the pages containing the baptisms for the year 1857. There was no explanation for the list. Perhaps it was the names of children making their First Holy Communion. Perhaps it is a list of persons being confirmed. The list is included in this Répertoire at Appendix C.

The original records contain a few lists of persons who received the sacrament of Confirmation. The lists are relatively short and cover only the years 1857, 1882, 1886, 1891, 1894, 1897, 1899, and 1918. The information is sketchy, but it may give some leads to persons who were associated with St. Louis Parish during its early years. The list of all persons confirmed is presented in Appendix D.

During the course of this project, the project team contacted Mr. James Hansen of the Wisconsin Historical Society. Mr. Hansen informed the project team that the records of early Catholic residents of the Fond du Lac area prior to the founding of St. Louis Church were kept at St. John Catholic Church in Little Chute, Wisconsin. Mr. Hansen extracted those records and graciously shared them with the project team. This Répertoire contains the pertinent information from the records of St. John Catholic Church in Little Chute, Wisconsin, at page xvi below.

The original records contain a very curious letter. It was written by the Federal Bureau of Investigation and signed by J. Edgar Hoover. The letter apparently is in reply to a request by a member of St. Louis Church for assistance in reading faded script on a document. Mr. Hoover was unable to provide any specific help to the faded document problem. The letter is shown in Appendix E.

HISTORY OF ST. LOUIS CHURCH

In 1847, Fond du Lac was a village of 519 settlers. The following year, Wisconsin was to become a state. Father Caspar Rehrl was one of the missionary priests who served the communities of Fond du Lac, Washington, Calumet, and Sheboygan counties. In 1847-1848, he, with thirty people, met to form a parish in Fond du Lac. In 1848, the parish was formed and named St. Louis. It was so named in honor of the crusader, Louis IX, who ruled France from 1214-1270.

Since St. Louis was the first Catholic parish in the Fond du Lac area, it initially included outlying areas. The title page of the first book of baptism records from 1850 states that St. Louis Parish included Eden, Eldorado, and Byron. For convenience in determining some of the various locations mentioned in the records, maps showing the townships of Fond du Lac County as well as the counties of the state of Wisconsin are included in this Répertoire at Appendix F.

The French were a majority of the early parishioners, followed by the Irish and German populations. As time went on and with new migrations, many other ethnic groups would become a part of the St. Louis Parish. The first chapel was located on the corner of Marr and Second Streets. The land had been purchased earlier by Father Florimond Bonduel, a Belgian territorial missionary. He deeded the land to the Milwaukee diocese. Originally a wooden structure, the chapel would undergo a number of changes and renovations in the years to come.

In 1850 Father Anthony Godfert was named the first resident pastor. He served from 1850-1853, when he returned to missionary work. Father Louis Dael replaced him.

By 1854, the parish had about 2,000 members of a variety of ethnic backgrounds — some wanting to form and attend new parishes of their own ethnic background. In 1855, the first group to leave was the Irish to form St. Patrick's Church. In 1857, a German Catholic school opened, and in 1866, the German parishioners began construction of St. Mary's Church.

In 1860, Father John C. Perrodin, ordained in France, replaced Father Dael. Almost immediately he sought permission to organize a French congregation. In 1862, it was agreed to, but the Civil War and scarce money and building supplies held up the project until 1868 when a stone structure would begin to be constructed. A bell had been purchased and placed in the tower of the original chapel. In 1864 the chapel bell was moved to the site of the new French church, which retained the name St. Louis. The original parish was renamed St. Joseph. The new church would be located at the corner of Follett and Bannister (now Macy) streets. In 1870, the church was not yet completed, but on 25 December 1870 Father Perrodin said the first Mass for French parishioners at their new location. Officially, the parishioners moved to their new site in 1871. On 7 June 1873, Father Perrodin died; Father George Willard replaced him.

Between 1874-1888 a new St. Joseph Church (the former St. Louis Chapel) was built. When the basement was completed, services were held there. The 7 May 1874 *Fond du Lac Journal* stated that Bishop Henni planned to visit the city on 21 June 1874 to lay the cornerstone of the new building. The old mission chapel was still in use at this time and was used until the basement of the new church could be used. On 5 December 1875 the first Mass was scheduled in the basement church. On 24 March 1888, just a few finishing touches had to be completed on the new church. The original chapel was sold at public auction after the basement church was completed. The altar was cut in pieces and given to the parishioners as keepsakes or souvenirs.

In July 2000, St. Louis Parish merged with five other Catholic parishes in Fond du Lac to create Holy Family Catholic Church. Services continued to be held in St. Louis Church until the closing Mass on August 25, 2005. At that time, the church building was put on the market for sale. A large crucifix that hung behind the altar was removed and installed on the altar of the new St. John Vianney Church in Rio Rancho, New Mexico. The project team took photographs of the stained glass windows, which may be seen at www.fcgw.org. The windows clearly showed the names of prominent early parishioners. The names are as follows:

> Rev. J. C. Perrodin
> Mme. Jos. Mitchell
> Mr. et Mme. T. Chapleau
> Mr. et Mme. C. E. Errard
> Société St. Jean Baptiste
> Mr. et Mme. F. Lauson
> Mr. & Mrs. H. Boyle
> Nap. Z. & P. T. Corbeille
> F. F. Duffy
> J. H. McCrory
> Mr. et Mme. P. Beaudreau

The church building was purchased by a local sporting goods business, which planned to remodel the building. During the night of March 19-20, 2007, disaster stuck. St. Louis church was destroyed by fire. The owner pulled down the walls and steeples that remained standing. A new building containing the sporting goods store now occupies the site.

Before St. Louis Church was founded, the records of Catholic residents in the Fond du Lac area were kept at St. John Catholic Church in Little Chute, Wisconsin. Extracts of those very early records are included in this Répertoire.

At the time St. Patrick's Church was founded, some early events of the new St. Patrick parishioners were performed at St. Louis. Those events are among the records of St. Louis Church and are included in this Répertoire. This may be important for researchers looking into early St. Patrick's records. The same might be true for early events of St. Mary's (German) parishioners, but such is not as clear from the St. Louis records as it is for St. Patrick's parishioners.

The original records contain a list of persons who were present at a ceremony held August 29, 1897, at which a school bell was blessed. The list is as follows:

Blessing of School Bell 29-AUG-1897

Persons present	Date
Venne, Louis & wife	29-AUG-1897
Chapleau, Toussaint & wife	29-AUG-1897
Marcoux, Frank & wife	29-AUG-1897
Sénécal, Ovide & wife	29-AUG-1897
Corbeille, N. Z. & wife	29-AUG-1897
Langlois, Vital & wife	29-AUG-1897
Lyonais, Come & wife	29-AUG-1897
Balthazar, J. Bapt. & wife	29-AUG-1897
Pingair, Eugène & wife	29-AUG-1897
Brunet, Gédéon & daughter	29-AUG-1897
Beaudreault, Placide & wife	29-AUG-1897
Gagnier, Edouard & wife	29-AUG-1897

METHODOLOGY

The project of creating this Répertoire included extracting data from paper copies made from films of the original hand-written records. Because of the great difficulty in reading some of the handwritings, the information of each record was extracted independently by two persons. A third person compared the two extractions with the original records and decided which extraction, if either, more accurately represented the original record. The extracted information as finally determined to be the most accurate was entered as data into an Excel spreadsheet computer program. All the data in the spreadsheet was then proofread against the extracted information that was determined to be the most accurate. The data on the spreadsheet was imported into a web-based database for on-line searching. The searchable database is available only to FCGW members. The FCGW web site www.fcgw.org gives information on membership. This Répertoire is printed from the on-line database.

Many records contain more information than can easily fit into a printed format. Such information was entered into a "Note" in the database for the corresponding record. Researchers are encouraged to study the "Note" for each record, because the "Notes" contain some very interesting and often helpful information. For example, some marriage records give the parishes in Canada from which the bride and/or groom emigrated.

To make this Répertoire, as well as the on-line database, useful to researchers despite the problems with the original records, the project team established several conventions. A description and discussion of the conventions, which sometimes overlap each other, follow.

1. Standardized spelling
   a. Apostrophes are used or not used as they appear in the records (O'bryan, Obryan).
   b. "Mc" is used. No space is used between "Mc" and the rest of the name (McCarthy).
   c. Only one spelling is given for each priest.
   d. The Latin endings "oe" and "ae" are not used. For example, "Mariae" is shown as "Maria".

2. The spellings are shown in this Répertoire as accurately as can be determined from the original records. That is to say, this Répertoire does not contain copying or spelling errors. Where one or more letters is completely indeterminable from a record, a "-" is used to indicate those letters. Examples are "Je-m-" and "-erina." It is therefore unnecessary to use, and the Répertoire does not contain, the symbol "sic." This convention avoids the project team from being arbiters of what are the "correct" spellings and from making any assumptions regarding spellings. Exceptions to the foregoing are obvious names where only one letter is indecipherable. For example, if the record reads "Catheri-a", this Répertoire will show "Catherina."

3. In some records, one or more dates are incomplete or are indecipherable. In those cases, the date(s) is left blank. A researcher must go to the "Note" of that record in the database in order to find the explanation of the problem date(s).

4. To satisfy the field requirements for the database, it was necessary to add hyphens in certain instances where hyphens do not appear in the original records:
    a. To indicate missing or indecipherable letters in a name (see Paragraph 2 above.)
    b. In all records listing parents and/or witnesses, to connect first and second given names of the parent and/or witness in order to distinguish the given names from the surname. For example, a parent shown as "Anna Celina Levesque" in a record is shown in this Répertoire as "Anna-Celina Levesque."
    c. In all records listing parents and/or witnesses, to connect first and second words of a surname of the parent and/or witness in order to distinguish the words of the surname from the given name. For example, "Armina St. Antoine" in a record is shown in this Répertoire as "Armina St.-Antoine."
    d. To indicate dit names. "Meunier dit LaPierre" in a record is shown as "Meunier-LaPierre" in this Répertoire.
    e. To indicate a married woman's maiden name. "Moquin née Roi" in a record is shown in this Répertoire as "Roi-Moquin."
    A researcher must consider the context of the name in order to determine the meaning of the hyphen.

5. Where the priest entered a feast day, such as Easter or Corpus Christi, as the date, the project team used internet sources to find the actual date.

6. In a few records, the date(s) is known but is obviously incorrect.
    a. One example is an inherently incorrect date, such as "April 31." In those cases, the date is left blank (because of database requirements). A double asterisk "**" is placed after the name of the person to alert researchers of the date problem. The researcher must check the "Note" in the database for that record.
    b. Other examples are a baptism date earlier than a birth date and a burial date earlier than a death date. In those instances, the dates are presented in this Répertoire as they appear in the record. A double asterisk "**" is placed after the name of the person to alert researchers of the date problem. The researcher must check the "Note" in the database for that record for any available information about the date problem.

SUGGESTIONS FOR USE

It is important for researchers to check the dates in this Répertoire and the on-line database to verify multiple entries for the same event. Such multiple baptism, marriage, and burial entries are indicated by an "*". Researchers should be aware of the variant spellings that exist in the Répertoire and database for such multiple entries. Problem dates are marked with "**" and should be checked in the database notes.

Researchers who want information beyond what is in this Répertoire are encouraged to view the on-line database at the web-site www.fcgw.org, available only wwith FCGW Membership. The database is searchable. However, because of the variable spellings used for family names, it will be difficult to search the database by name. For example, "Boudrieaux," "Beaudreault," "Beaudreau" are all found in the records. A researcher must be flexible when it comes to searching, e. g., "Levy" and "Levi"; "McTevy" and "McLevy."

The project team has retained a film of the original records. If researchers require more information than is available either in the Répertoire or on the web-site, they may make arrangements to view the film by contacting the project team of the French-Canadian/Acadian Genealogists of Wisconsin. Alternately, of course, the researcher may contact the Milwaukee Archdiocese or obtain films 1862602 and 1862866 through a Family History Center of the Church of Jesus Christ of Latter Day Saints.

Researchers should keep in mind the lack of any records for the years 1910-1918. Civil records of births, marriages, and deaths during those years may be available at the office of the Fond du Lac County Register of Deeds. (In Wisconsin, civil registrations of births, marriages, and deaths were required starting in 1907.)

Concerning burials, researchers will notice that many early burials occurred in St. Charles and Taycheedah cemeteries. Those two cemeteries are located about one-third mile apart on the same rural road in the Town of Taycheedah. The first burial in Taycheedah cemetery occurred in 1852. St. Charles was formally established in 1863 and was considered to be the "Catholic" cemetery. Researchers are advised to look at St. Charles if a record indicates that burial took place in "Taycheedah."

EARLIEST RECORDS OF CATHOLIC RESIDENTS IN THE FOND DU LAC AREA

Fond du Lac Records at Little Chute

The following baptisms were extracted from the records of St. John Nepomucene Catholic Church, Little Chute, Wisconsin, 1826-1851, by James L. Hansen, FASG.

10-SEP-1842 at Fond du Lac, Isodore, son of Rodori [Robert] Ebert and Florence Genar; sponsors Isodore Genar and Sophie Sir.

10-SEP-1842 at Fond du Lac, Henry, Francois and Joseph, sons of Joseph Roy and Dina Roy; sponsors Herman [Prob. Hermengilde] St. Marie, Paul Tibo, Odile St. Marie.

26-JAN-1843 at Fond du Lac, Hortense Amable Elphege, daughter of Amable Brouillard and Oportune St. Marie; sponsors Raphael St. Marie and Marie Cardinal.

26-JAN-1843 at Fond du Lac, Narcisse, son of Paul Coillier and Marie Ann Douville; sponsors Pierre le For and Odile St. Marie.

26-JAN-1843 at Fond du Lac, Philomene, daughter of Theodore Chenar and Sophie Cyr; sponsors Luke Labor and Elisabeth LaBord.

13-FEB-1843 at Fond du Lac, Marguerite, daughter of Paul Tibeau and Marie Plan; sponsors Luc Laborde and Liset Beauprè.

29-JUN-1843 at Fond du Lac, Marie Anne, daughter of William La Londe and Susanna Lyens?; sponsors Amable Broullard and Josette Beaupré.

29-JUN-1843 at Fond du Lac, Louis, son of Luc Laborde and Josette Beaupre; sponsors Louis Beaupre and Angelique Belchair.

10-JUN-1844 at Fond du Lac, Augustin, son of Louis Porlier and Sophie Grignon; sponsors Augustin Grignon and Marie Grignon.

10-JUN-1844 at Fond du Lac, Louis, son of William La Londe and Susanna Tutjens; sponsor Louis Dupre.

10-JUN-1844 at Fond du Lac, James and Urban, twin sons of Conrad Coen and Catherine Coen; sponsors Joseph Beter, Agathe Porlier, Augustin Grignon, and Sophie Porlier.

14-FEB-1845 at Fond du Lac, Marie Josephe daughter of John Joseph Raher? and Anna Wales; sponsors Joseph Lauder? and Marie Wollerheim.

14-FEB-1845 at Fond du Lac, Julia, daughter of Isidore Me[ad?] and Sophie Sir; sponsors Paul Tibeau and Julie le Mier.

14-FEB-1845 at Fond du Lac, Teatis, daughter of Paul Cajé and Marie Douville; sponsors Francois Roy and Marie Le Mier.

14-FEB-1845 at Fond du Lac, Pelagie, daugher of Amable Broullard and Oportune St. Marie; sponsors Hermegil St. Marie and Catherine Dousman.

14-FEB-1845 at Fond du Lac, Peter, son of Robert Eber and Florence Sir; sponsors Francois Le Roy and Marie Le Mier.

14-FEB-1845 at Fond du Lac, Andrew, son of John Gibson and Marie Gibson; sponsors Luc Labord and Agathe Porlier.

The priest recording these events was Father Theodore J. Van den Broek.

St. Louis Catholic Parish
Fond du Lac, Wisconsin

Baptisms 1850-1920

Surname	Given Name	Birth	Baptism	Parents	Godparents
------	Helenam		25-FEB-1854	Cornelii ------/Julia Carton	T Clark/M. Mullen
------	------nam	06-JUL-1879	20-JUL-1879	Eduard------/Edessa Pariseau	J. Lefouré/E Gagnier
------	Catherine Lorette		08-DEC-1878		
------	Elizabeth	10-SEP-1899	09-JAN-1900		Joannes-Baptista Beaudry/Ursula Charron
------	Eugene		20-AUG-1872		
------	Franciscum				
------	Georgium	09-MAR-1866	11-MAR-1866		
------	Georgium	21-JUL-1861	11-AUG-1861	Georgii ------/Maria ------	M. Portten/A. Kennaady
------	Jean-----etium Hilarium		05-JUL-1881	Georgio Gosseln/Lou----sa Leduc	Franciscus Rondeau/Josephina Rondeau
------	Joannem Henricum	05-SEP-1877	20-SEP-1877		J. Dumond/M. Dumond
------	Josephum		11-JAN-1874	Joseph ------/Maria Dufresne	Joseph Lepine/Josephine Lepine
------	Josephum Herminium	07-JAN-1874	12-JAN-1874	Amabilis ------/Ludovica Chef	------ Chef/------na Chef
------	Maria				
------	Mariam	03-NOV-1851	03-SEP-1852	Josephi ------/Cordelia ------	P. Keating/M Beaudriaux
------	Mariam	20-AUG-1877	01-SEP-1877	------/Anna Tinter	L. Lecadie/------ ------
------	Mariam Josephinam	03-MAR-1874	07-APR-1874	Caroli ------/Antoni Trappman	------/Nely Oconnor
------	Mariam Mercedem	16-JAN-1882	18-JAN-1882		Eugenius Pinget/Eugenia Pinget
------	Mariam Olisam	08-FEB-1866	11-MAR-1866		
------	Mariam Virginiam	17-OCT-1873	18-OCT-1873	Olivarii ------/Alphonsina Agagner	Joseph Papineau/Maria Agagné
------	Mary				
------	Michael				
------	Petrum	02-FEB-1893	18-SEP-1881	Petro Lécuyer/Carolina Lefort	Josephus Nospre/Genofera Bastien
------	Pfetner		09-FEB-1893	Philippi Pfetner/Malvina Duford	------/------ ------
------	Rosam	03-APR-1860	29-APR-1860	Wenzel ------/Margeret------	
------	Sybilla				
------*	------	09-APR-1860	19-MAY-1860	Joannis ------/Margetha ------	Thomas ------/------ ------
------*	Alexander				
------*	Charle				
------*	Joannes		29-APR-1860		
------*	Maria Rosa Francesca				
------*	Mary				
------*	Mary Elizabeth				
------*	Sera G-----am	22-FEB-1860	25-APR-1860	------ ------/------ Keny	------/------ Maria ------
-----cott	Philomenam	25-NOV-1873	25-NOV-1873	Guilielmi ------cott/Philomena Odet	Georgius Odet/Julia Odet
-----ma-*	H-----um	23-JUL-1858	25-JUL-1858	Heromimi ------ma-/Asilite To-----	Joseph Petit/Ed--- Belhumeur
-----sept	Marie	23-SEP-1855	26-AUG-1855	Joseph ------sept/Josephina Vernuf	L ---net/M Doulaine
---Deaux*	Cyprianus		10-AUG-1856	Niel ----Deaux/Margert Bodien	------ peau/M Just
----rrly	------ina		24-AUG-1856	------rrly ------/------ Maria Gul--glogen	------ Harpin/------ ------
----tins*	Rose				
---é--s*	Catharine				
--eld*	Maria Eugenia	20-NOV-1856	20-DEC-1856	Patrick ---eld/Brigth ---isin	P. Kelly/------sson
--eran*	Jocobus	22-MAY-1858	29-MAY-1858	William ---eran/Chaterina Lienschs	John Lis---/Brigetha Ocennel
-etti-*	Joseph				
---ich	Margeta Eugenia	07-SEP-1857	13-SEP-1857	James ---ich/Margita Galligan	J Galligan/B.------n
---illen*	Margarita	04-MAY-1857	16-MAY-1857	------illen/Matilda Mccomb	J.McKalon/M. McCormit
----tt	Helenam		29-DEC-1863	Jacobi ----tt/Christina ---tt	N Reinhart/M. Reinhart
---lier*	Melina	10-JAN-1856	12-JAN-1856	Noel ---lier/Leu-da Pariso	R. Marrais/P. Pariso
---ly*	Cecilia	03-FEB-1858	07-FEB-1858	Patrick ---ly/Maria Hogan	Patrick Caffy/Anna Flannigan
---quer	Mariam ---tina	16-JUL-1873	20-JUL-1873	Da-----quer/Philomena Pellan	Adolphus Pellan/Edena Pellan

3

Surname	Given Name	Birth	Baptism	Parents	Godparents
---u---	Michaelis		19-MAR-1856	Michael -u--/Hanna Connel	J. -----/M Wels--
--alt*	Joannem	23-NOV-1858	28-NOV-1858	Bernard --alt/Elisalte Crammer	Joanns Herss/Babera Gibel
--bord	Marselle	22-JUL-1875	25-JUL-1875	Messael Roy/Chna Moran	Francis Marcou/Cathaia Kelly
--d	Narsis	12-OCT-1876	24-DEC-1876	Joseph --d/Lousa Burchau	D. Bodet/E Gosselin
--dden*	Petrus	19-JUL-1857	19-JUL-1857	Dens --dden/Brigta ---sy	J -----/M. -----
--entz	Gilbertum Laurentium	28-NOV-1906	02-DEC-1906	Francisco --enz/Exilda Corbeille	Nopoleo Corbeille/Melinda Lebeau-Corbeille
--h--t*	Marie Philomna	02-APR-1858	16-MAY-1858	Alexander --h--t/Berrandna Tirion	Andrea Peron/Maria Peron
--l-fer*	John				
--ten*	Joannem	23-SEP-1855	11-NOV-1855	Danelis --ten/Maria Carmel	G. Flannigan/M Cranmal
--llivan*	Annam	16-OCT-1859	31-OCT-1859	Jacobi Sullivan/Marie Singer	T Gennaly/M. Garrelhy
--rland*	Josephum	05-SEP-1837	12-SEP-1858	Joseph --rland/Delmina Baltazar	Michel Baltazar/Julia Baltazar
--veu	Mariam Rosam		15-FEB-1874	Stanslai --veu/Emilia Jolly	Carolus Jolly/---esa Jolly
--ac-rmon	Joannem Levit-	25-FEB-1860	13-JUL-1862	Davidis -ac-rmon/Regina -ac-rmon	L. Vadney/M. -----
--agan*	Franciscum	01-NOV-1859	10-NOV-1859	Michaeli -agan/Elena McGinis	F. H-i--/M. Hemery
--anly*	Ellina		22-FEB-1858	Patrick -anly/Brigta ---ly	Pn-k Huges/Brigita Marten
--anneau*	Philomina	14-OCT-1857	25-OCT-1857	Perre -anneau/Clementina Beaudien	L Duranseau/J Mobiliant
--annigan*	Maria Anna	14-FEB-1858	18-FEB-1858	Joseph -annigan/Bigeta Loi-an	James Bakn/Mia Schea
--ed-reed*	Theresia	12-JAN-1857	12-JAN-1857	Andrus -ed-reed/Marianna Lourens	M. Seefur/A. Chaterina
--emlois*	Emiliam	10-MAY-1860	27-MAY-1860	Constantus -emlois/N Devilers	---dus Dupea/Emlie Vernais
--errier	Guillelmum	12-MAY-1861	27-MAY-1861	Patricu --errier/Bridgitta --errier	H Harrigan/B. Harrigan
--f--*	Alice	18-NOV-1858	18-NOV-1858	John -f--/Helene Kane	---mes Duffy/Mary Duffy
--h-n--*	Al--etum	22-SEP-1858	23-SEP-1858	Baptista -h-n--/Rosatha Hubert	Antum Ysi---/Col-ta -iera
--han*	Chaterina	21-MAR-1857	30-MAR-1857	Pa--h -ham/Honore Conner	J Hennelan/----- -----
--inna*	Maria	27-MAR-1857	27-MAR-1857	James Innar/Cath Nery	M D---le/M Nery
--inny*	Elisa Eugenia	13-AUG-1857	16-AUG-1857	John -inny/Marie -a-hy	J G---an/M. Y---h
--lama-*	Mariam ---Ifenam		05-SEP-1858	Gulm -lama--/Ma--- Mage-ho	Jocobus Rayly/Thoam Ry---
--ockway	Petrus Samuelem	29-JAN-1867	03-FEB-1867	Benjamm -ockway/Ludovica -ockway	C. Rulo/M Mayo--
--ogesan	Margetam	15-MAY-1860	25-MAY-1860	Patric--- -ogesan/Elisabeth McClain	Michel Kelly/Ma--- Kerry
--olan*	Marguerite	18-JAN-1858	07-FEB-1858	Peter-olan/Catherine Donneley	Peter Dun/Mary Higgins
--on*	Richard	07-MAR-1858	29-MAY-1858	--turns -on/Anastasia Phalan	William Phalan/Margeta Nortan
--onneley*	Joannem	17-SEP-1858	19-SEP-1858	Jacobi -onmeley/Marie -----	Micheli -orkcg/Catharina -hakey
--onnick*	Mariam	28-AUG-1858	13-SEP-1858	Fede--- -onnick/Marise Francia Burgers	-----/Maria Chamber
--ou---	Carolum Eduardum	04-NOV-1870	22-OCT-1871	Eduardi -ou---/Anna -ou---	Petrus Bessete/Maria Bessete
--ouly	Marguerite	09-NOV-1850	19-NOV-1850	Charles -ouly/Lucie St T-----	M. St.-Anthony/D. Benoit
--ran-*	Hellena		19-MAY-1856	-----ran-/Margrit Crimmer	J Crimmer/ - Lo-s-
--rbai--*	Mariam Lousam	17-APR-1858	26-FEB-1860	-----rbai--/Maria-Theresa Snesens	Francois L'Orge/Mart--- -------
--uick*	Maria Eugenia	15-JAN-1861	16-MAY-1858	Peter -uick/Anna Gaffeny	Patrick Gaffeny/Honnora Melay
Aarons	Jacobum	09-APR-1850		Pharone Aarons/Rachel Lyons	Rev.Francis-R DeBeaumont/Virgnia Cotte-Mayar
Ab-----	Tharsila	02-JUL-1863	12-DEC-1850	Peter Descoteaux/Mary Wheeler	P. Harnois/M Descoteaux
Abel	Nicholaum	25-FEB-1866	31-JUL-1863	Joanns Abel/Maria Abel	N. Abel/M. Abel
Abeler	Barbaram	29-NOV-1854	28-FEB-1866	Petri Abeler/Maria Abeler	A Reichling/B Hartzeim
Al---t	Margartam	10-NOV-1874	24-DEC-1854	Chryst--- Al---t/Margarta Peron	H Peron/M Aurel
Alane	Jocobum Andream	19-JUL-1872	22-NOV-1874	Francisci Alane/Josephna Buschar	Jocobus Alane/Judit Hennard
Alar	Adeliam	31-AUG-1870	21-JUL-1872	Caroli Alar/Emilia Alar	Isidorus Pratt/Philomeno Marcou
Alard	Emmam	11-SEP-1885	11-SEP-1870	Caroli Alard/Emilia Donat	Josephus Alard/Domitilla Alard
Allan	Carolum Theophilum	25-DEC-1882	13-SEP-1885	Carolo Allain/Edessea Pellant	Theophilus Allan/Louisa Roy
Allaun	Juliam Elizabeth	01-SEP-1884	31-DEC-1882	Francisco Allan/Josephna Bouchard	Franciscus Boucher/Judith Bessette
Allann	Mariam Lousam	23-MAR-1877	02-SEP-1884	Carolo Allaun/Edesia Pellant	Alexander Edoun/Maria Beaupre
Allard	Evam		25-MAR-1877	Caroli Allard/Em Dolla--	J. Vane/E. Donnet

4

Surname	Given Name	Birth	Baptism	Parents	Godparents
Allen	Sarah Ellen	26-AUG-1850	02-SEP-1850	Richard Allen/Elizabeth Allen	R Allen/S. -----
Altero	Brigittam	06-AUG-1883	11-AUG-1883	Ludovico Altera/Maria Gilligan	Patricius -----/Elizabeth Owens
Amdan*	Brigta	21-SEP-1855	15-OCT-1855	Philipi Amdan/----- Ward	B Amdan/L. McGrath
Amel	Hazel Helenam	11-JUN-1906	01-JUL-1906	Eduardo Amel/Eleena Devillers	Theophilus Devillers/Stella Devillers
Amel	Mariam Leonam Glendolam	22-NOV-1904	05-DEC-1904	Eduardi Amel/Nellie Devillers	Amabilis Gervais/Maria Laberge-Devillers
Amel	Mariam Leoniam Blantolam	02-NOV-1904	05-DEC-1904	Eduardi Amel/Nellie Devillers	Amabilis Gervais/Maria Laberge-Devillers
Amour	Philomenam L'Etourneauu	09-MAR-1876	19-MAR-1876	Pascal L'Etourneauu-Amour/Marie Bomgard	P. Amour/L. Sorrell
Annan*	Vicentius	02-SEP-1859	25-SEP-1859	Antoni Annam/Maria Ev---	V. Rius/E. Rius
Annan	Joannem	12-JAN-1864	30-JAN-1864	Antoni Annan/Maria-Annan	J Hirsh/A. Hirsh
Annan*	Elisabetham	13-SEP-1857	27-SEP-1857	Antonus Annan/Eva -ears	J. Hi---/E. Hi---
Annan*	Elsabet	13-SEP-1857	27-SEP-1857	Antone Annan/Eva Ohernhears	J Hiers/E. Hiers
Annan*	Vincent				
Annean*	Philomenam	14-OCT-1857	25-OCT-1857	Petrus Annean/Clementa Beaulieu	L Duranseau/J. Mobiliant
Arboreaux	Josephum	21-NOV-1854	10-DEC-1854	Francisci Arboreaux/Adela Felbert	I St-Antone/J Lebeau
Archambeau	Achlem		30-OCT-1870	Hermangilda Archambeau/Julia-A. Archambeau	Isaaus Fernet/Mathilda -----
Archambeau	Josephum	07-APR-1872	12-MAY-1872	Hermini Archambeau/Julianna Archambeau	Franciscus Beaudrieau/Delphina Fernet
Archambeault	Juliam Eleonoram	04-APR-1882	16-APR-1882	Ludovico Archambeault/Lucia Letourneau	Moises Tremblay/Leonora Lajeunesse
Archambeault	Victorem Zephirum	02-AUG-1879	13-AUG-1879	Ludovico Archambeault/Lucia Letourneau	P. Letourneau/S Bissmonette
Ardelle	Marguerltam	21-AUG-1852	26-OCT-1852	Richardi Ardelle/Maria Doroghty	P Manahan/M. Manahan
Aritar*	Mariah	03-SEP-1856	07-SEP-1856	Perri Melansons/Usseu Bodrieau	A. Duclean/L. Gautier
Armand*	Elsabeh	11-SEP-1855	12-SEP-1855	Peter Armand/Maria Sillia	J Crammers/E. Serwe
Armond*	Elisabetham	11-SEP-1855	12-SEP-1855	Petri Armond/Maria Silla	J. Crammer/E. Serwe
Arrmond*	Peter				
Arrmond*	Petrum	19-AUG-1859	21-AUG-1859	Petri Arrmond/Margerethe Sullivan	P. Prester/S. Serwe
Aspator	Josephum Ludovicum	30-JAN-1897	21-FEB-1897	Petro Aspator/Maria Skaf	Josephus Ferres/Anna Casel
Aspatore	Ludovicum Geogium	06-APR-1905	16-APR-1905	Petro Aspatore/Maria Skaf	Shaker Faris/Scltaney Skaf
Aspetore	Mariam Louisa	07-SEP-1906	09-SEP-1906	Petro Aspartore/Maria Scaff	Shaker Faris/Siltaney Humsay
Aspetore	Joannem	25-JUN-1903	05-JUL-1903	Petro-J Aspetore/Maria Schaff	Sheker Ferres/Anna As-off
Aspitore	Ludovicum Georgium	05-APR-1905	16-APR-1905	Petri-J Aspitore/Maria Skaff	Shaker Faris/Seltaney Skaff
Attr-	Jaco-um	22-DEC-1876		Lous Attr-/Maria Gilliam	P McGrigrigan/A. Hi-ky
Auchen	Clayton Arthurum	30-MAY-1909	06-JUN-1909	Alfredo Aucheu/Della LeMieux	A C Beaudreau/Exilda Lemieux
Auchue	Lavern Alfredum	22-JUN-1905	25-JUN-1905	Alfredo Aucheu/Della LeMieux	Antonus LeMieux/Rosa LeMieux
Auchue	Valora Lucine	16-APR-1920	25-APR-1920	Fred Auchue/Delphinc LeMieux	Jeremiah LeMieux/Julia Perry
Auclaire	Joannem Fredericum	12-MAR-1874	22-MAR-1874	Frederca Auclaire/Joanna Smith	J. Baptista Charette/Fe--- Lemoine
Audet	Georgium Willard	02-DEC-1888	09-DEC-1888	Georgio Audet/Ludovica Lavigne	Panagius Chapleau/Virginia Audet
Audet	Gertrudam Marguritam	27-AUG-1890	07-SEP-1890	Georgio Audet/Louisa Lavigne	Georgius Langlois/Emelia Duquet
Audet	Josephum	18-DEC-1891	03-JAN-1892	Georgio Audet/Ludovica Lavigne	Josephus Moquin/Vitalina Audet
Audet	Mariam Genofevam	08-MAY-1893	28-MAY-1893	Georgio Audet/Ludovica Lavigne	Evaristus Beaudette/Cordelia Audet
Auger	Edessam	20-JUN-1864	20-JUN-1864	Leandri Auger/Esthera Auger	S Joubert/L. Gosselm
Auger	Josephne Jesse	25-APR-1880	02-MAY-1880	Andrea Auger/Alida Harnois	N Auger/E. Harnois
Auger	Mariam Edessam Laurattam	24-MAY-1883	05-JUL-1883	Adréa Auger/Alida Harnois	Gulielmus Baudet/Lousa Auger
Auger	Mariam Ludovicam	13-AUG-1862	14-AUG-1862	Leandri Auger/Estera Auger	A Grizet/M. Morin
B---*	Dougherty				
B-ar*	Olivina	12-SEP-1857	24-SEP-1857	Jam--- B-ar/Lusia Potet	P Eculer/M. Shinard
B--le-*	Mathilda				
B-lly*	Mariam Annam	26-JAN-1857	02-FEB-1857	Aug B-lly/Nansi Dunsy	P Quen/R Donly
Ba-comb	Carolum Henricum	29-AUG-1872	15-SEP-1872	Henrici Ba-comb/Isabella Ba-comb	Narcissus Strong/Aurelia Trahant
Ba-e-*	Anna Elisabetha	07-JUL-1858	10-JUL-1858	James Ba-e-/Brigetha Murphy	William Murphy/Brigetha Hannegan
Bacon	Mariam	25-MAR-1861	31-MAR-1861	Jacobi Bacon/Bridgitta Bacon	T Moore/M. Moore

5

Surname	Given Name	Birth	Baptism	Parents	Godparents
Bacon*	Annam Mariam	07-JUL-1858	10-JUL-1858	Jacobi Bacon/Bridgitta Murphy	G Murphy/B. Ha--igan
Baillargeon	Georgium	06-JAN-1867	13-JAN-1867	Huberti Baillargeon/Eulalia Baillargeon	J. Real/R. Baillargeon
Baillargeon	Josephinam Phoebeam	02-MAR-1886	11-APR-1886	Josepho Baillargeon/Josephina Demarais	Antonius Desmarais/Adelaida Lamontagne
Baillargeon	Paulum Josephum	19-APR-1881	24-APR-1881	Josepho Baillargeon/Aurelia Landerman	M. Moqun/A. Moqun
Bauryer	George Thomas	08-OCT-1859	30-OCT-1859	Pat. Bairyer/Mary Matthew	Richard Matthew/Mary -----
Baker	Henricum	29-APR-1854	13-MAY-1854	Henrici Baker/Maria Gill	M Gill/B. Dallen
Baker*	Anna Emla	19-JUL-1856	26-JUL-1856	Mat Baker/Maria Liens	J. Pilant/A. Sch--d
Baker*	Annam Emiliam	19-JUL-1856	26-JUL-1856	Math Baker/Maria Liens	J Picart/A. Chenard
Baillargeon	Henreliam Cleopatram	01-SEP-1879	02-SEP-1879	Josepho Baillargeon/Henrelia Landermann	L. Landerman/H Landerman
Baltazar	Josephum	08-OCT-1876	21-OCT-1876	Baptis Baltazar/Maria Marco	M. Lebeau/M. Marcou
Baltazar	Josephum Joannem	22-OCT-1878	22-OCT-1878	Joannis-Bapt Baltazar/Armine Marcou	M. Baltazar/P. Robert
Baltazar	Mariam Herminam	09-SEP-1874	13-SEP-1874	Joannis-Baptista Baltazar/Hermina Marcou	Jeremius Marcou/Rosalia Balthazar
Baltazar	Mariam Josephinam	22-JUL-1879	27-JUL-1879	Michaeli Baltazar/Philomena Robert	F. Robert/M Robert
Baltazar	Mariam Julianam	14-JUN-1876	18-JUN-1876	Batis Baltazar/Amina Marco	B. Baltazar/ wife
Baltazar	Welliam	05-OCT-1878	12-OCT-1878	Martini Baltazar/--dreth Vernet	I. Vernete/S. Baltazar
Baltazar*	Carolum	26-DEC-1856	27-DEC-1856	Caroli Baltazar/Demilina Benoit	M. Baltazar/M Delavaline
Baltazar*	Charolus	26-DEC-1856	27-DEC-1856	Charles Baltazar/Domitila Benoit	M. Baltazar/M. Delavaline
Baltazar*	Julinam	24-MAY-1860	15-JUL-1860	Monse Baltazar/Josehte Leblanc	Joseph Berlant/Elmira Berlant
Baltazar*	Rosalia	02-AUG-1857	23-AUG-1857	Michel Baltazar/Rosalia ---any	J. L'ossiler/J. Bultazar
Balthasard	Theodorem Michaelem	28-JUN-1884	29-JUN-1884	Theodore Balthasard/Hermine Saint-Antoine	Michael Balthasard/Philomene Robert
Balthazar	Agnetem Ceciliam	08-AUG-1909	19-SEP-1909	Ludovico Balthazar/Emilina Robert	Joannes McCasy/Josephina Robert-McCasy
Balthazar	Alexandrum		12-APR-1868	Baptista Balthazar/Maria Balthazar	Josephus Loisele/Hermina Balthazar
Balthazar	Alfredum	02-DEC-1884	10-DEC-1884	Alfredo Balthazar/Delima Pratte	Ludovicus Balthazar/Emelia Robert
Balthazar	Benjaminem	28-MAY-1891	30-MAY-1891	Julien Balthazar/Margarita Lajeunesse	Theodorus Balthazar/Annmia St.-Antoine
Balthazar	Blancam Emeliam	02-JUN-1886	06-JUN-1886	Martino Balthazar/Tarsilla Frenette	Josephus Pariseau/Maria Gilman
Balthazar	Carolum	22-MAR-1863	26-MAR-1863	Moyse Balthazar/Josepha Balthazar	H. Lajeunesse/E. Gayet
Balthazar	Eduardum	11-MAR-1887	11-MAR-1887	Alfredo Balthazar/Delima Pratte	Isidarus Pratte/Philumena Marcoux
Balthazar	Eleonoram	25-JAN-1869	31-JAN-1869	Josephi Balthazar/Marguaritam Balthazar	Henricus Lajeunesse/Eleonora Lajeunesse
Balthazar	Emiliam Mariam	14-JUL-1866	15-JUL-1866	Baptista Balthazar/Herminia Balthazar	M. Balthazar/R. Bla--
Balthazar	Ernestum	25-NOV-1890	30-NOV-1890	Martino Balthazar/Tharsilla Frenette	Alfredus Balthazar/Rosa-Delma Pratte
Balthazar	Eugenium	12-JAN-1867	13-JAN-1867	Ludovico Balthazar/Emelia Robert	I. Surprenant/H. Marcou
Balthazar	Eugenum	01-JUL-1904	04-SEP-1904	Ludovico Balthazar/Emelina Robert	G. Beaudin/J. Balthazar
Balthazar	Franciscum	05-APR-1873	12-APR-1873	Georgio Balthazar/Ezilda Venne	Joannes Marcou/Honora Lepine
Balthazar	Franciscum Albertum	07-DEC-1896	14-DEC-1896	Juliano Balthazar/Marguerita Lajeunesse	Franciscus Marcoux/Maria Lajeunesse
Balthazar	Franciscum Elmer	16-NOV-1898	19-NOV-1898	Gulielmo Balthazar/Ida Letourneau	Josephus Diette/Elisa Letourneau
Balthazar	Franciscum Genofevam	10-FEB-1899	19-FEB-1899	Ludovico Balthazar/Emelia Robert	Georgius Robert/Josephina Rondeau
Balthazar	Franciscum Ludovicum	01-JUL-1904	04-SEP-1904	Ludovico Balthazar/Emelina Robert	Franciscus Dellger/Maria Tice
Balthazar	Franciscum Rollandum	13-JAN-1903	18-JAN-1903	Georgio Balthazar/Estella Atkinson	Ludovicus Balthazar/Estella Atkinson
Balthazar	Georgium	23-JUL-1871	23-JUL-1871	Baptista Balthazar/Hermina Balthazar	Franciscus Marcou/Emilia Marcou
Balthazar	Georgium David	10-JUL-1905	17-JUL-1905	Georgio Balthazar/Exilda Venne	Julianus Balthazar/Margarita Balthazar
Balthazar	Gerald William	05-NOV-1919	07-NOV-1919	William Balthazar/Ida Blackbird	Joseph Errard/Mrs.-Joseph Errard
Balthazar	Gilbertum	18-AUG-1890	24-AUG-1890	Alfredo Balthazar/Delima Pratte	Albertus Petters/Sophia Balthazar
Balthazar	Guillelmum	23-SEP-1871	15-OCT-1871	Baptri Balthazar/Maria Balthazar	Joannis-M. Marlou/Julia Loisele
Balthazar	Helenam	06-FEB-1871	15-FEB-1871	Josephi Balthazar/Marguaritta Gayet	Franciscus Gayete/Delma Beaudin
Balthazar	Henricum	02-FEB-1889	07-FEB-1889	Michaele Balthazar/Philumena Robert	Theodorus Balthazar/Hermina St -Antoine
Balthazar	Ireneam	10-OCT-1896	18-OCT-1896	Martino Balthazar/Tarzila Frenet	Albertus Petters/Sophia Balthazar
Balthazar	Isabellam	18-MAR-1883	22-MAR-1883	Martino Balthazar/Tharzila Frenette	Franciscus Beaudrault/Alphea Frenette
Balthazar	Joannem	09-FEB-1864	28-FEB-1864	Baptista Balthazar/Maria Balthazar	F. Marcou/J. Lebeau
Balthazar	Joannem Baptistam	22-MAR-1865	02-APR-1865	Josephi Balthazar/Marguarita Balthazar	J. Balthazar/----- ---

6

Surname	Given Name	Birth	Baptism	Parents	Godparents
Balthazar	Joannem Baptistam Alden	12-JUL-1904	03-AUG-1904	Juliano Balthazar/Margarita Lajeunesse	Joannes-Baptista Balthazar/Josephina Desuarais
Balthazar	Joannem Baptistam Frederi	31-DEC-1905	04-MAR-1906	Ludovico Balthazar/Emilio Robert	Joannas-B Balthazar/Josephina Desmarais-Balthaza
Balthazar	Joannem Clayton	31-DEC-1909	23-JAN-1910	Gulielmo-Henrico Balthazar/Ida LeTourneau	Josephieso Balthazar/Flora LeTourneau
Balthazar	Joannem Franciscum	13-SEP-1896	20-SEP-1896	Georgio Balthazar/Exilda Venne	Joannes-Baptista Balthazar/Henrica Rondeau
Balthazar	Josephum	13-SEP-1880	20-SEP-1880	Justino Balthazar/Tharsilla Freuet	J. Balthazar/M Hubert
Balthazar	Josephum	02-MAR-1862	27-APR-1862	Josephi Balthazar/Marguarita Balthazar	M. Balthazar/R. Plat-t-
Balthazar	Josephum Albertum	24-MAR-1892	29-MAR-1892	Theodore Balthazar/Armina St.-Antoine	Joannes Balthazar/Hermina Balthazar
Balthazar	Josephum Arnoldum	09-APR-1907	21-APR-1907	Goergio Balthazar/Exilda Venne	Alexander Goyette-Jr./Hermine Balthazar-Goyette
Balthazar	Josephum Arthurum	22-DEC-1892	25-DEC-1892	Juliano Balthazar/Margaritta Lajeunesse	Alexander Marcoux/Eleonora Lajeunesse
Balthazar	Josephum Eduardum	10-APR-1902	13-APR-1902	Josepho Balthazar/Philumena Letourneau	Josephus Diette/Elizabeth Letourneau
Balthazar	Josephum Georgium Malac	04-AUG-1899	08-AUG-1899	Juliano Balthazar/Margarita Lajeunesse	Georgius Gardon/Sara Balthazar
Balthazar	Josephum Gulielmum Clar	17-DEC-1900	23-DEC-1900	Gulielmo Balthazar/Ida Letourneau	Joannes Balthazar/Emelia Lebeau
Balthazar	Josephum Leonem	10-MAY-1889	18-MAY-1889	Ludovico Balthazar/Emma Robert	Michael Balthazar/Philumena Robert
Balthazar	Josephum Michaelum	13-OCT-1882	15-OCT-1882	Michaele Balthazar/Philumena Robert	Joannes-Baptista Balthaar/Armina Marcoux
Balthazar	Josephum Royal Laverne	13-APR-1908	03-MAY-1908	Gulielmo-H. Balthazar/Ida Letourneau	Ernestus Balthazar/Melinda Balthazar
Balthazar	Josephum W	26-MAR-1893	30-MAR-1893	Alfredi Balthazar/Delima Pratte	Georgius Gardon/Sara Balthazar
Balthazar	Julianum	25-MAY-1864	25-MAY-1864	Michaelis Balthazar/Rosalia Balthazar	J Balthazar/H. Balthazar
Balthazar	Lauram Mariam	24-MAY-1890	03-JUN-1890	Theodoro Balthazar/Hermina Robert	Ludovicus Balthazar/Emelina Robert
Balthazar	Laurentium Henricum	29-NOV-1897	26-DEC-1897	Georgii Balthazar/Ezilda Venne	Michael Balthazar/Elizabeth Dufresne
Balthazar	Leonem Paulum	09-JUL-1900	14-JUL-1900	Georgio Balthazar/Ezilda Venne	Vatalis Langlois/Emelia Balthazar
Balthazar	Luciam Gordon	15-NOV-1881	27-NOV-1881	Georgio Gordon/Barbara Balthazar	Alfredus Balthazar/Delima Pratte
Balthazar	Ludovicum	07-APR-1883	09-APR-1883	Joanne-Baptista Balthazar/Armina Marcoux	Ludovicus Balthazar/Emelia Balthazar
Balthazar	Ludovicum	12-MAR-1873	20-MAR-1873	Josephi Balthazar/Marguarita Balthazar	Ludovicus Balthazar/Eleonora Lajeunesse
Balthazar	Ludovicum Oliverum	07-NOV-1887	10-NOV-1887	Ludovico Balthazar/Emma Robert	Franciscus Robert/Maria Beaudoin
Balthazar	Marcellinam	19-MAY-1866	03-JUN-1866	Joannis-Baptista Balthazar/Maria Balthazar	F. Marcou/J. Loiselle
Balthazar	Mariam	20-AUG-1883	25-AUG-1883	Alfredo Balthazar/Delima Pratte	Martinus Balthazar/Tharzillus Frenette
Balthazar	Mariam	17-DEC-1862	01-JAN-1863	Joannis Balthazar/Eliz. Balthazar	P. Bourasseau/M. Bourasseau
Balthazar	Mariam	02-MAY-1881	04-MAY-1881	Teodore Balthazar/Armina St.-Antoine	I. St.-Antoine/J. Lebeau
Balthazar	Mariam	04-NOV-1895	06-NOV-1895	Guelielmo Balthazar/Adea Letourneau	Joannes Balthazar/Maria Marcoux
Balthazar	Mariam Agnetem	22-NOV-1882	26-NOV-1882	Joanne-Baptista Balthazar/Mary-Marose Lamar	Abertus Peters/Sophia Balthazar
Balthazar	Mariam Alsam	17-APR-1894	28-APR-1894	Theodore Balthazar/Hermina St.-Antoine	Alfredus Balthazar/Delima Pratte
Balthazar	Mariam Celinam	22-MAR-1863	26-MAR-1863	M. Balthazar/J Balthazar	B. Marco/M. Marco
Balthazar	Mariam Edessam	23-AUG-1885	30-AUG-1885	Michaele Balthazar/Philumena Robert	Ludovicus Balthazar/Emelina Robert
Balthazar	Mariam Eleonoram Mabel	25-AUG-1894	30-AUG-1894	Juliano Balthazar/Margaritta Lajeunesse	Michael Balthazar/Philumena Robert
Balthazar	Mariam Elisam	05-MAR-1886	14-MAR-1886	Theodore Balthazar/Hermina St.-Antoine	Julianus Balthazar/Margaritta Lajeunesse
Balthazar	Mariam Emelinam	09-APR-1893	12-APR-1893	Ludovico Balthazar/Emilina Robert	Theodorus Balthazar/Hermina St.-Antoine
Balthazar	Mariam Esther	07-MAY-1885	09-MAY-1885	Joanne-Baptista Balthazar/Hermina Marcoux	Josephus Goyette/Magdalena Lavallie
Balthazar	Mariam Genovefam	29-JUN-1901	29-JUN-1901	Joanne-Baptista Balthazar/Emelia Lebeau	Moises Lebeau/Angela Mecier
Balthazar	Mariam Gratosam	19-NOV-1900	25-NOV-1900	Josepho Balthazar/Philumena Letourneau	Paschalis Letourneau/Marra Baumhar
Balthazar	Mariam Idam	01-JUN-1882	06-JUN-1882	Theodore Balthazar/Hermina St.-Antoine	Joannes-Baptista Balthazar/Herminne Marcoux
Balthazar	Mariam Josephinam	05-DEC-1884	17-DEC-1884	Joane-Baptista Balthazar/Maria Marcoux	Franciscus Robert/Marcellina Balthazar
Balthazar	Mariam Malvinam	22-DEC-1880	25-DEC-1880	Joanne-Baptista Balthazar/Armina Marcoux	T. Balthazar/A. St.-Antoine
Balthazar	Mariam Melinam	27-FEB-1890	23-MAR-1890	Joanne-Baptista Balthazar/Maria Marcoux	Jeremias Marcoux/Sophia Miné
Balthazar	Mariam Olivinam	02-DEC-1869	01-JAN-1870	Baptista Balthazar/Hermina Marcou	Franciscus Marcou/Josephina Roi
Balthazar	Mariam Olivinam	16-AUG-1867	25-AUG-1867	Joannis-Baptista Balthazar/Herminia Balthazar	F. Marcou/E. Cyr
Balthazar	Mariam Thelman Theresam	09-JAN-1907	13-JAN-1907	Gulielmo Balthazar/Eva Welling	Peter Welling/Theresa Frenette-Balthazar
Balthazar	Mariam Zocam	27-SEP-1891	04-OCT-1891	Ludovico Balthazar/Emelia Lajeunesse	Franciscus Robert/Marcellina Balthazar
Balthazar	Martinum	29-NOV-1874	06-DEC-1874	Joanis Baltazar/Maria Marcou	Joannes B. Baltazar/Ellena Marcou
Balthazar	Martinum Raymundum	25-FEB-1909	28-FEB-1909	Gulielmo Balthazar/Eva Welling	Martinus Balthazar/Maria-Anna Toney-Welling

7

Surname	Given Name	Birth	Baptism	Parents	Godparents
Balthazar	Melnam	10-FEB-1888	15-FEB-1888	Theodoro Balthazar/Hermina St -Antoine	Martinus Balthazar/Tharsila Frenette
Balthazar	Michaelem	17-MAR-1864	20-MAR-1864	Josephi Balthazar/Marguarttha Balthazar	J Gayet/P Thibodeau
Balthazar	Nataliam	11-MAR-1887	11-MAR-1887	Alfredo Balthazar/Delima Pratte	Josephus Balthazar/Sophia Manny
Balthazar	Noe Henricum	03-FEB-1889	05-FEB-1889	Juliano Balthazar/Margaritta Lajeunesse	Henricus Lajeunesse/Eleonora Goyette
Balthazar	Philumenam Maud	19-DEC-1896	27-DEC-1896	Gulielmo Balthazar/Ida Letourneau	Pascals Letourneau/Maria Baumhart
Balthazar	Rosam Olivinam	23-MAR-1901	31-MAR-1901	Juliano Balthazar/Margarita Lajeunesse	Generosus Lajeunesse/Olivina Balthazar
Balthazar	Sophiam Hermmnam		26-APR-1868	Caroli Balthazar/Mathilda Balthazar	Michael Balthazar/Sopha Balthazar
Balthazar	Virgina	06-APR-1919	18-OCT-1919	Ernest Balthazor/Mate Lange	------/Irene-Maraja Balthazor
Balthazar	W M		05-OCT-1878	Martin Balthazar/Thursa Furnett	
Balthazar	Walter Earl Josephum	31-JAN-1906	04-FEB-1906	Gulielmo Balthazar/Ida LeTourneau	Georgius Flood/Maria Balthazar-Hogey
Balthazar	Zoahm	08-DEC-1869	16-JAN-1870	Baptista Balthazar/Marra Marcou	Martinus Balthazar/Olivina Marcou
Balthazar*	Mathilda	26-MAY-1858	10-JUN-1858	M----- Balthazar/Josephte Lebl----	Joseph Goyeth/Jule Balthazar
Balthazar*	Mathilda	25-MAY-1858	10-JUN-1858	Moysis Balthazar/Josepha Lebeau	J. Gayet/J Balthazar
Balthazar*	Rosalam	02-AUG-1857	23-AUG-1857	Michaeli Balthazar/Rosala Plany	J. Osseler/P. Balthazar-Marcoux
Balthazar**	Mariam Emeliam	24-NOV-1880	01-NOV-1880	Joanne-Baptista Balthazar/----- -----	I. St.-Antoine/J Lebeau
Balthazor*	Julianne				
Banek*	Mariam Eugenıam	17-APR-1858	16-MAY-1858	Petri Banek/Anna Gaffeny	P. Gaffeny/H. Mel-y
Bannan	Jacobum	28-MAY-1852	11-JUL-1852	----- Bannan/----- Bannan	M. Mccallogh/C. Clotch
Barbeau	Adelaidam	08-JUN-1872	09-JUN-1872	Isaia Barbeau/Eulalia Barbeau	Josephus Maas/Sophia Lefeve
Barbeau	Annam Theresiam	06-JAN-1897	06-JAN-1897	Levi Barbeau/Celina Leveque	Petrus Barbeau/Ezild Moquin
Barbeau	Dorotheam Julian	25-MAY-1909	13-JUN-1909	Ludovico Barbeau/Eugenia Krisol	Martinus Schoblacku/Julia Krisal-Schoblacke
Barbeau	Fabianum	01-MAY-1900	20-MAY-1900	Levi Barbeau/Celna Leveque	Franciscus-Walter Barbeau/Maria-Clara Barbeau
Barbeau	Ludovicum	17-JAN-1872	19-JAN-1872	Petri Barbeau/Philomna Barbeau	Gilbertus Suprenant/Dina Dupus
Barbeau	Mariam Claram	17-OCT-1881	22-OCT-1881	Petro Barbeau/Ezilda Maqun	Petrus Barbeau/Philomena Charron
Barbeau	Mariam Ettam		07-FEB-1891	Levi Barbeau/Celna Lrvigne	Petrus Barbeau/Philomena Charon
Barbeau	Mariam Melerinam	29-APR-1874	29-APR-1874	Petri Barbeau/Philomen Charron	Isaia Langlois/Adéla -----
Barbeau	Melinam Esmeraldam	27-SEP-1892	02-OCT-1892	Levi Barbeau/Celina Lévêque	Nehemas Moquin/Melina Barbeau
Barbeau	Normanum Hermanum	26-AUG-1905	03-SEP-1905	Ludovico Barbeau/Eugenia Kreisel	Hermanus Kreisel/Philomena Charron-Barbeau
Barbo	Mariam Angelicam	04-OCT-1877	24-OCT-1877	Petri Barbo/Philamena Sharon	J. Dupuis/----- Dupuis
Barbow	Charles A	06-MAY-1896	13-FEB-1920	Leverett Barbow/Ella Chase	-----/Lena Perron
Barete	Ludovicum Isidorum	08-SEP-1871	12-SEP-1871	Eduardi Barete/Emilia Ebert	Ludovicus Molheur/Felicité Cyr
Bargon*	Joannes	18-AUG-1857	01-OCT-1857	Thimuty Bargon/Honnora Bays	C. Gillan/E. Bays
Barnès	Guillelmum	23-JUL-1863	26-JUL-1863	Thoma Barnès/Catharina Barnès	T Barnès/M. Murry
Barnès	Mariam	18-NOV-1861	24-NOV-1861	Francisci Barnès/Bridgetta Barnès	M. Mullen/S. Waters
Barnès	Michaelem Josephum	30-JUL-1863	02-AUG-1863	Francisci Barnès/Bridgitta Barnès	F Rodgers/C Rodgers
Barret	Eugenıam	13-SEP-1863	26-SEP-1863	Eduardi Barret/Amelia Barret	I. Ebert/M. Ebert
Barret*	Ellen Carolina				
Barret*	Helenam Carolinam	15-JAN-1855	12-JUN-1859	Ludovici Barret/Maria Furlong	J Furlong/P Barret
Barret*	Maria Florentia				
Barret*	Mariam Florentiam	09-FEB-1859	24-FEB-1859	Eduardi Barret/Emilie Hubert	I. Hubert/-. Surpurant
Barrete	Petrum	06-APR-1868	12-APR-1868	Petri Barrete/Emilie-Anna Barrete	Vitalis Langlois/Flavia Langlois
Barrett	Ema Elisabeth	07-OCT-1876	01-NOV-1876	Eduardi Barrett/Emelia Hebbert	N Bessett/M. -i-
Barrett	Joannem Edwardum		28-JUL-1861	Edwardi Barrett/Emilia Barrett	J. Perradis/S. Chenar
Barrett*	John				
Barrette	Edwardum Alphonsum	06-APR-1866	22-APR-1866	Edwardi Barrette/Emilia Barrette	A Snow/F Ebert
Barrette	Mariam Laurentiam	02-JUN-1874	24-JUN-1874	Edwardi Barrette/Emilia -l--	Franciscus Marcou/Emilia Marcou
Barry	Elizabetham		01-NOV-1863	Thoma Barry/Elizabetha Barry	J O'Brien/J. O'Connel
Barry	Ludovicum Emericum El----	18-NOV-1886	18-SEP-1887	Gulielmo Barry/Adea Gervais	Emericus Gervais/Olivina Charron
Barry	Mary Eugenia				

Surname	Given Name	Birth	Baptism	Parents	Godparents
Barry	Thomam	23-FEB-1862	23-FEB-1862	Thoma Barry/Elizabeth Barry	J. Gallagher/M. Brown
Bartlett	Aliciam Marguaritam		03-NOV-1861	Jacobi Bartlet/Anna Quinn	R. Quinn/M McTeavy
Basquin	Mariam Marguaritam	08-JUN-1865	11-JUN-1865	Antoni Basquin/Marguarita Rondeau	J. Duquete/C Chef
Basset	Allen Edunum		18-APR-1872	Edumo-B. Basset/Maria E. Devillers	Joannes Hartnet/----- -----
Basset	Annam Mariam	05-MAY-1878	05-MAY-1878	Israel Basset/----- Chinard-Snow	J Basset/S Bassett
Basset	Emmam Sophiam	25-AUG-1866	09-SEP-1866	Israelis Basset/Julia Basset	C. Bassete/M. Gobet
Basset	Franciscum	16-MAR-1876	26-MAR-1876	Joseph Basset/Marie Bray	F Bisset/L. Bisset
Bassete	Franciscum Xavierium	17-APR-1865	30-APR-1865	Israelis Bassete/Julia Snow	A Chenar/E. Molheur
Bassete	Petrum	23-APR-1867	19-MAY-1867	Ambrosi Bassete/Magdalena Bassete	J. Balthazar/J. Surprenant
Bassete*	Joseph				
Bassett	Mathildam	08-SEP-1860	09-AUG-1863	Davidis Bassett/Aurelia Bassett	P Boitun/P. Odet
Bassett	Paulum	19-JUN-1863	09-AUG-1863	Davidis Bassett/Aurelia Bassett	O Tontan/M Monitier
Bassette	Arlinam Adelinam		11-OCT-1863	Ambrosi Bassete/Magdalena Bassett	T Thibaudeau/R. Gayet
Bassette	Georgium Israelem	21-JAN-1863	08-FEB-1863	Isaac Bassette/Julia Bassette	----- Snow/H Marco
Bassette	Marguaritam		28-OCT-1860	Ambrosei Bassette/Magdalena Bassette	I. Chenar/M. Gayet
Bassette	Melinam	02-JUN-1862	06-JUL-1862	Ambrosi Bassette/Magdalena Bassette	F. Gayet/L. Beaudriau
Bassien	Maria Anna	31-MAY-1879	01-JUN-1879	Joh.-Bapt Bassien/Ursula Ven	G Derochelle/L Ven
Bastian	Eduardum	22-APR-1877	22-APR-1877	Antoni Bastian/Margeret Rando	M. Menbleau/ (wife)
Bastian	Eulaliam	16-AUG-1905	20-AUG-1905	Pacifico Bastian/Adela Robidoux	Albertus Brucker/Maria-Anna Bastian-Brucker
Bastien	Alexandrum	21-MAY-1868	24-MAY-1868	Petri Bastien/Philomena Bastien	Petrus Annan/ Dyonisia
Bastien	Eduardum Edgardum Franc	16-JAN-1903	18-JAN-1903	Eugenio Bastien/Agnete Dufresne	Arthurus Venne/Maria Dufresne
Bastien	Emiliam	16-MAR-1864	20-MAR-1864	Antoni Bastien/Marguarita Bastien	Petrus Chef/Christina Chef
Bastien	Eugeniam Leoniam	18-APR-1904	24-APR-1904	Pacifico Bastien/Adela Robidoux	Jacobus Waltz/Albertus Dufresne
Bastien	Genofevam Agnetem	09-MAR-1897	09-MAR-1897	Eugenio Bastien/Agnete Dufresne	Andreas Bastien/Graciosa Dufresne
Bastien	Georginam	13-JUN-1869	20-JUN-1869	Antonni Bastien/Marguarita Rondeau	Alvida Rondeau/Maria Rondeau
Bastien	Hubertum Adolphum	01-JAN-1900	01-JAN-1900	Pacifico Bastien/Adela Robidoux	Josephus Diedrich/Anna Frank
Bastien	Joannem Baptistam		08-FEB-1874	J.-Baptista Bastien/----- Elis Veine	Moyses Bastien/Sophia Veine
Bastien	Joannem Ludovicum Clare	22-MAR-1901	24-MAR-1901	Pacifico Bastien/Adela Rabidoux	Joannes Rabidoux/Josephina Rabidoux
Bastien	Josephum Eduardum Wilfr	20-MAR-1871	20-MAR-1871	Joannis-Baptista Bastien/Rachelis Bastien	Franciscus-Eduardus Veine/Rosalia Veine
Bastien	Josephum Eugenium	14-SEP-1868	14-SEP-1868	Joannis-Baptista Bastien/Rachelis Bastien	Augustus Landreman/Theresa Joli
Bastien	Josephum Marcum Eugeni	07-JAN-1901	12-JAN-1901	Eugenio Bastien/Agnete Dufresne	Stephanis Dufresne/Heloisa Lebeau
Bastien	Josephum Pacificum	24-SEP-1898	26-SEP-1898	Pacifico Bastien/Adela Robidoux	Josephus Robidoux/Herminia Pellant
Bastien	Josephum Parsefium	28-JUL-1875	29-JUL-1875	Joannes-Bapt. Bastien/Rosshelle Verne	Leander Landermann/----- Landermann
Bastien	Lucreciam Ludovicam	11-DEC-1902	14-DEC-1902	Pacifico Bastien/Maria-Adela Robidoux	Franciscus Boyer/Maglorium Robidoux
Bastien	Marguaritam	18-JUL-1871	21-JUL-1871	Antoni Bastien/Marguarita Rondeau	Baptista Rondeau/Julia-Anna Chef
Bastien	Mariam Alexiam	09-JUL-1872	10-JUL-1872	J.-Bta. Bastien/Rachelis Bastien	Paulus Sauvé/Marguarita Venne
Bastien	Mariam Elodiam	31-MAY-1881	01-JUN-1881	Joanne-Baptista Bastien/Rachel Bastien	Paulum Sau--/Margarittam Venne
Bastien	Mariam Josephum	12-NOV-1866	13-NOV-1866	Baptista Bastien/Rachaelis Veine	F. Veine/M. Landreman
Bastien	Mariam Rachelem Eugenia	03-JAN-1870	03-JAN-1870	Joannis-Baptista Bastien/Rachelis Verne	Eucildus Veine/Adelina Borage
Bastien	Wilfredum Leonardum	24-AUG-1895	25-AUG-1895	Wilfredus Bastien/Martha Dufresne	Franciscus Dufresne/Elisa Ste.-Marie
Batal	Joannem	24-JUN-1905	16-JUL-1905	Habib Batal/Najibe Galeh	Michael Galeh/Martha Batal
Batter	Rosnam	19-NOV-1852	19-FEB-1854	Jacobi Batter/Maria Bilhlan	M Hermiller/T Hermiller
Baudoun	Mariam Elizabeth	21-FEB-1874	01-MAR-1874	Isidori Baudoin/Philomena Moleure	Christophorus Letourneau/Maria Letourneau
Baudrio	Mariam Emam	24-NOV-1873	30-NOV-1873	Laurentii Baudrio/Sophia Braut	Joseph Lepine/Sophia Baudrio
Baudry	Martialem Ovidem	28-JUL-1904	02-SEP-1904	Martiali Baudry/Ida-Anna Bechand	Ovides Baudry/Clara Elizabeth Jacoby
Bauer	Hermanum	24-JUN-1861	27-OCT-1861	Christiani Bauer/Maria-Anna Bauer	M. Straas/A Everling
Bayen*	Joannem Martinum	11-AUG-1859	14-AUG-1859	Michaelis Bayen/Maria Corrigan	G. Bermingham/----- Bermingham
Bazinet	Albertum	14-FEB-1883	22-APR-1883	Josepho Bazinet/Louisa Fluet	Nicholaus Lamanche/Mercelline Livernois
Bazinet	Mariam Louisam	24-NOV-1880	12-DEC-1880	Josepho Bazinet/Louise Fluet	M. Fitzsimmons/A. Prassiter

9

Surname	Given Name	Birth	Baptism	Parents	Godparents
Be--el*	Eduard	04-APR-1858	11-APR-1858	William Be--el/Mariam Sloon	Michel Kieru-/Maria Cl-ny
Be-ch-*	Miriam Elisath	20-SEP-1859		German Be-ch-/Anna Pellet	C Allart/----- Allart
Beaud-----	Joseph Olivarium	10-JUL-1874	08-AUG-1874	Olivarii Beaud--/Julia Bessette	Petrus Beaud--/Sophia Bessette
Beaudau	------	17-JUN-1874	17-JUN-1874	J B. Beaudau/Maria Chef	Amabilis Gervais/Philomena Gervais
Beaudet	Franciscum Davidem	16-MAY-1889	19-MAY-1889	Evarito Beaudet/Alma Carbonneau	Benjamin Beaudet/Alma Lanthier
Beaudet	Mariam Almam	07-SEP-1884	16-SEP-1884	Evaristo Baudet/Maria-Alma Carbonneau	Adolphus Baudet/Domitilda Carbonneau
Beaudette	Mariam Ellam	07-OCT-1887	18-OCT-1887	Evaristo Beaudette/Emma Carbonneau	Mauritus McGown/Lousa Corbonneau
Beaudette	Valentinum Pearlie	14-FEB-1892	20-FEB-1892	Evaristo Beaudette/Emma Carbonneau	Alexander Marcoux/Arzelia Beaudreault
Beaudin	Carolum Emeritum	24-FEB-1864	27-FEB-1864	Caroli Beaudin/Edessa Beaudin	J Joubert/L Joubert
Beaudin	Carolum Reyonolds	03-MAY-1907	12-MAY-1907	Ludovico Beaudin/Exidla Deroum	Isidorum Hebert/Julia Caron
Beaudin	Delphnam	06-JAN-1866	10-JUN-1866	Juliani Beaudin/Ludovica Beaudin	J Joubert/L Joubert
Beaudin	Edessam	16-JUL-1866	16-JUL-1866	Caroli Beaudin/Edessa Beaudin	J Beaudin/L. Norandin
Beaudin	Franciscum Xaverum	20-NOV-1865	28-NOV-1865	Guillelmi Beaudin/Julia Beaudin	F. Gayet/L. Beaudin
Beaudin	Georgium Henricum		25-OCT-1863	Guillelmi Beaudin/Julia Beaudin	M Balthazar/L Normandin
Beaudin	Helenam	22-OCT-1864	12-DEC-1864	Michaelis Beaudin/Maria Beaudin	G Beaudin/L. Normandin
Beaudin	Henricum	05-FEB-1904	19-FEB-1904	Ludovico Beaudin/Ezilda Derouin	Oliverus Lapalme/Mathilda Derouin
Beaudin	Joannem Glen	23-AUG-1900	02-SEP-1900	Joanne-Baptista Beaudin/Maria-Francisca Lucier	Joannes Lucier/Clara Lucier
Beaudin	Josephum Ludovicum Elise	21-SEP-1898	02-OCT-1898	Ludovicus Turenore/Delia Juneau	Ludovicus Turenore/Delia Juneau
Beaudin	Julianum	15-MAR-1868	17-MAR-1868	Juliani Beaudin/Ludovica Beaudin	Carolus Beaudin/Edessa Beaudin
Beaudin	Justnam	13-APR-1862	27-APR-1862	Guillelmi Beaudin/Julia Beaudin	G Beaudin/R. Leblanc
Beaudin	Mariam Adelaidam	10-JUL-1862	17-AUG-1862	Guillelmi Beaudin/Ludovica Beaudin	J. Beaudin/R. Gayet
Beaudin	Mariam Amandam	31-MAY-1901	14-JUN-1901	Ludovico Beaudin/Ezilda Derouin	Achilleus Beaudin/Maria Beaudin
Beaudin**	Adeliam	25-JUN-1866	03-JUN-1866	Isidori Beaudin/Germana Beaudin	L Molheur/F. Cyr
Beaudoin	Felicitatem	14-SEP-1860	14-SEP-1860	Isidori Beaudoin/Philomena Beaudoin	J Touchete/A. Mathews
Beaudoin	Isidorum Hilarium	26-DEC-1870	06-JAN-1871	Isidori Beaudoin/Philomena Beaudoin	Hilarus Landreman/Felicitas Malheur
Beaudoin	Ludovicam	20-MAR-1864	27-APR-1864	Julii Beaudoin/Ludovica Beaudoin	N. Jubert/A. Beaudoin
Beaudoin	Mariam Marguaritam	09-OCT-1864	11-OCT-1864	Theodori Beaudoin/Philomena Beaudoin	F Robert/M. Robert
Beaudoin	Mariam Marguaritam		25-MAY-1862	Isidori Beaudoin/Philomena Beaudoin	J. Boreman/F Cyr
Beaudoin	Philomenam	14-SEP-1860	14-SEP-1860	Isidori Beaudoin/Philomena Beaudoin	M. Marcott/J Mosquin
Beaudreau	Edwinum Willard Adolph	13-OCT-1904	13-NOV-1904	Adolpho Beaudreau/Maria Burgess	Alec-L Marcoe/Orzelia Beaudreau-Marcoe
Beaudreau	Ernestum Alfredum	01-FEB-1909	07-FEB-1909	A C. Beaudreau/Exilda Lemieux	Alfredus Auchen/Della LeMieux-Auchen
Beaudriaux	Margaritam Olivam	29-OCT-1903	01-NOV-1903	Asa Beaudreau/Ezilda Lemeux	Israel Lemieux/Emma Beaudreau
Beaudreau	Nedwin Willard Adolphum	13-OCT-1904	13-NOV-1904	Adolfo Beaudreau/Maria Burgess	Alexander Marcoux/Orzelia Beaudreau-Marcoux
Beaudreau	Theodorum Laurentium	31-JAN-1906	04-FEB-1906	A C. Beaudreau/Exilda LeMieux	Josephus Dubois/Cedulla Beaudrea-Dubois
Beaudreau-Marc	Purl Laurantium	25-DEC-1880	18-OCT-1908	Mederico Beaudreau/Clementia Larose	Alexander Marcoux/Orzelia Beaudreau-Marcoux
Beaudreault	Leonem Asa Hieronimum	14-OCT-1902	16-OCT-1902	Asa Beaudreault/Ezilda Lemieux	Jeremias Lemieux/Rosa Lemieux
Beaudrau	Jacobum Segastum	15-NOV-1862	23-NOV-1862	Davidis Beaudriau/Anna Beaudriau	F Beaudrau/C Daugherty
Beaudriau	Mathildam Theodosiam	06-OCT-1862	19-OCT-1862	Laurentii Beaudriau/Sophia Beaudriau	D. Beaudrau/A Meunier
Beaudraux	John Henry	18-FEB-1852	18-APR-1852	David Beaudraux/Ann Calleghan	P. Dufresne/L. Meunier
Beaudrieau	Adelaidam Leoniam	25-MAY-1862	24-AUG-1862	Francisci Mederici/Clementa Beaudriau	L. Beaudriau/A. Gauthier
Beaudrieau	Anaclitum Herculanum	06-MAY-1871	14-MAY-1871	Laurentii Beaudreau/Sophia Bron	E Lyonnais/M. Leduc
Beaudreau	Annam Deliam	12-DEC-1867	29-DEC-1867	Israelis Beaudreau/Catharina Beaudreau	N Lyonnais/C. Beaudreau
Beaudreau	Corneliam Clementiam	28-MAY-1863	03-APR-1863	Mederici Beaudreau/Clementia Beaudrieau	C. Lyonnais/S Brico
Beaudrieau	Edwardum Laurentium		01-APR-1866	Israelis-C Beaudrieau/Catharina-A Beaudreau	L Beaudreau/S. Brion
Beaudrieau	Georgium Augustum	17-DEC-1864	17-DEC-1864	Davidis Beaudrieau/Anna Beaudrieau	E Lyonnais/M. Leduc
Beaudreau	Georgium Edwardum	20-AUG-1860	09-SEP-1860	Davidis Beaudrieau/Anna Beaudreau	B. Harican/M. McDermott
Beaudrieau	Jacobum Albertum	04-NOV-1862	09-NOV-1862	Israelis Beaudrieau/Catharina Beaudrieau	F. Beaudrieau/A. Mulony
Beaudreau	Josephum Ebenezerum	20-APR-1865	23-APR-1865	Laurentii Beaudrieau/Sophia Beaudreau	C Lyonnais/C. Lyonnais
Beaudreau	Moysem Franciscum		05-NOV-1865	Francisci-Meder Beaudrieau/Clementina Beaudrie	A Florent/L. Beaudrieau

Surname	Given Name	Birth	Baptism	Parents	Godparents
Beaudreaux	Cordelia	27-DEC-1851	01-JAN-1852	Lawrence Beaudreaux/Sophie Brion	H Desnoyers/C. Baudriaux
Beaudreaux	Francois Israel	20-FEB-1858	23-FEB-1858	David Beaudreaux/Ann Calaghan	Charles Miller/Julie Beaudrieaux
Beaudreaux	Laurentium Delphinum	04-FEB-1868	01-MAR-1868	Laurentin Beaudrieaux/Sophia Beaudrieaux	Albertus Florant/Anna Fenet
Beaudrieux	Luciam Annam	19-JUN-1864	17-JUL-1864	Francisci Beaudrieux/Clementia Beaudrieux	M L----e/J Leduc
Beaudry	Evam	25-JUN-1890	10-AUG-1890	Carolo Beaudry/Maria-Anna Faschant	Georgius Abel/Dyonisia Beaudry
Beaudry	Josephum Benoni	28-MAR-1889	31-MAR-1889	Treffleo Beaudry/Ursula Charron	Pascholis Dufresne/Sara St. Marie
Beaudry	Mariam Annam	13-SEP-1879	28-SEP-1879	Treffleo Beaudry/Ursula Charon	J Moquin/P Charon
Beaudry	Mariam Clarindam	11-DEC-1881	11-DEC-1881	Treffleo Beaudry/Ursula Charron	Petrus Barbeau/Ezilda Maquin
Beaudry	Sharon Levy Ovid	24-DEC-1902	13-AUG-1905	David Beaudry/Antonia Bernne	Ovid Beaudry/----- -----
Beaulieu	Hubertum	02-JUN-1869	03-JUL-1869	Johannis Beaulieu/Exilda Ducharme	Hubertus Leduc/Merentia Beaulieu
Beaumar	Luciam	25-JUN-1864	24-JUL-1864	Abrahami Beaumar/Osidia Beaumar	F. Gayet/J. Beaumar
Beaumar	Marguaritam	02-JUN-1861	02-JUN-1861	Abraham Beaumar/Josepha-Eneta Beaumar	P. Létourneau/M. Beaumar
Beaumar	Ositam	15-SEP-1866	06-OCT-1866	Abrahami Beaumar/Osita Beaumar	E. John/M. Jolin
Beaumar*	Hemilnam Ameliam	18-JUL-1858	25-JUL-1858	Abrahams Beaumar/Osita Detugan	J Petit/H Lemr----
Beaupré	Joseph David Francois	15-AUG-1879	17-AUG-1879	Petro Beaupré/Eddessa Pellond	F. Pellond/J. Pellond
Beaupré	Josephum Edmundum	10-AUG-1875	15-AUG-1875	Narsisi Beaupré/Josephina Prefontaine	Adelar Beaupré/Anna Gilbou
Beaupre	Mariam Amandam Adelam		31-AUG-1881	Petro Beaupre/Edessa Pelland	Napoleo Julien/Adela Pelland
Beauregard	Josephinam	29-APR-1870	01-MAY-1870	Caroli Beauregard/Salomé Beauregard	Hubertus Baillargeon/Eulalia Baillargeon
Beauregard	Ludgerium	14-DEC-1871	17-DEC-1871	Caroli Beauregard/Soloma Beauregard	Ludgerius Préfontaine/Melina Deno
Bech*	Peter S.				
Bechaud	Philum Adolphum	30-JUL-1854	23-NOV-1854	Joannis Bechaud/Maria Tellmann	T G---s
Beck	Ludovicum Clarentium	28-OCT-1895	10-NOV-1895	Josepho Beck/Georgina Roy	Stephanum Beck/Clementina Beck
Becker	Aloysium Jacobum	01-MAY-1866	13-MAY-1866	Theodori Becker/Elizabetha Becker	A. Martz/G Wolf
Becker	Christophorum Albertum	21-MAR-1864	27-MAR-1864	Alberti Becker/Maria Becker	C. Serwe/M. Olinger
Becker	Mariam Elizabetham	09-OCT-1861	13-OCT-1861	Alberti Becker/Maria Becker	J Serwe/A. Serwe
Beeson	Mariam Annam		02-APR-1861	Joannis Beeson/Elizabetha Beeson	M. Beeson/----- -----
Berns*	John Edward	19-MAY-1857	04-NOV-1858	John Beirns/Lucie Rand----	Thos Beirns/Sarah Nicholas
Berns*	John Edward				
Berns*	Mary	17-MAY-1858	04-NOV-1858	Thomas Berns/Elizabeth Stein	John Beirns/Mary Ann Linch
Berns*	Mary				
Beker*	Antonium	12-AUG-1855	26-AUG-1855	Jacobi Beker/Maria Buchelaer	A. Coell/M. Stephani
Belami	James Niel	29-JUN-1856	05-JUL-1856	Michel Belami/Ellisabeth Belami	A. Chasman/----- -----
Belhomeu	Mariam	08-MAR-1854	09-MAR-1854	Francisci Belhomeu/Maria Petit	L Petit/-. Maram
Belhumeur	Josephum	08-SEP-1852	26-SEP-1852	Francisci Belhumeur/Maria Petit	L Petit/E. Leonard
Belhumeur*	Virginam	02-SEP-1859	08-SEP-1859	Francisci Belhumeur/Maria Petit	G. Ouellet/V. Petit
Bellangemyer	Petrum Ludovicum	12-JUL-1868	27-JAN-1875	Petri Bellangemyer/Lina Ebber	Michaelis Satuaire/Mathilda Ebber
Bellanger	Carolum	18-JUN-1861	30-JUN-1861	Caroli Bellanget/Elizabetha Bellanger	A Tiffan/----- -----
Bellanger	Elizam	27-JUL-1865	07-AUG-1865	Petri Bellanget/Lina Bellanger	E. Oreal/A. Cren
Bellanger	Mariam	25-MAR-1867	17-APR-1867	Petri Bellanger/Lina Ebert-Bellanger	C. Nolin/S. Loiron
Bellanger	Petrum	30-MAY-1862	02-JUN-1862	Eusebii Bellanger/Josepha Bellanger	L. Brico/G. Meunier
Bellanger*	Mariam	14-MAY-1857	28-JUN-1857	Josephi Bellanger/Josephina Gabrieaux	F Deroché/F. Bellanga
Beller*	Antonius	12-AUG-1855	26-AUG-1855	Jacobus Beller/Maria Buchelaer	A. Coll/M Stephanie
Bellerive	----	23-AUG-1906	23-AUG-1906	Phillippo-L. Bellerive/Odelia Brulotte	
Bellerive	Josephum Remigium	01-OCT-1909	27-OCT-1909	Philippo Bellerive/Odelia Brulotte	Goergius Bellerive/Leda Bellerive
Bellerive	Ludovicum Andream	18-OCT-1907	10-NOV-1907	Philippo-L. Bellerive/Odelia Brulotte	Franciscus Bellerive/Emma Beaudette
Bellimeur	Edwardum	02-JUN-1866	17-JUN-1866	Francisci Bellimeur/Zoah Bellimeur	E. Bernier/M. Dufresne
Bellimeur	Elmiram	16-APR-1865	26-APR-1865	Francisci Bellimeur/Zoah Bellimeur	H. Pariso/O. Pariso
Bellimeur	Emiliam	08-NOV-1863	29-NOV-1863	Francisci Bellimeur/Zoah Bellimeur	J Petit/E. Bellimeur
Bellimeur	Juliam	27-AUG-1861	08-SEP-1861	Francisci Bellimeur/Zoeh Bellimeur	L. Durocher/M. Dufresne

11

Surname	Given Name	Birth	Baptism	Parents	Godparents
Bellmeur	Olivinam	20-OCT-1862	26-OCT-1862	Francisci Bellimeur/Zoah Dufresne	O Dufresne/O. Meunier
Bellimeur	Zoahm	05-OCT-1867	10-NOV-1867	Francisci Bellimeur/Zoah Bellimeur	F. Dufresne/E. Ste.-Marie
Bellimeur*	Virginia				
Bellonger*	Marie	12-MAY-1857	28-JUN-1857	Eseph Bellonger/Josept Gabriaux	F. Deruché/F. Bellanger
Belmer	Francescam Golde	17-AUG-1902	24-AUG-1902	Henrico Belmer/Malvina Balthazar	Georgius Balthazar/Ezilda Venne
Belmer	Mariam Noelam Louella	10-JUN-1901	13-JUN-1901	Henrico Belmer/Malvina Balthazar	Generosus Lajeunesse/Olivina Balthazar
Benett*	Joannem		26-OCT-1858	--han-nus Benett/Maria Kelly	John Kelly/Caterna Kelly
Benner	Joannem	28-DEC-1862	04-JAN-1863	Henrici Benner/Sarah Benner	J. Wagner/A. Murphy
Benner*	Anna	12-SEP-1855	16-SEP-1855	Hennory Benner/Sera McKein	P Mayer/S. Chnnere
Benner*	Annam	12-SEP-1855	16-SEP-1855	Nimci Benner/Sera Mckein	P. Mayer/S Snow
Benoit*	Maria Ludovica	14-JUN-1857	02-JUL-1857	Julien Benoit/Cloaline Cayher	J Delaine/M. Birouseaux
Benoit*	Mariam Ludevicam	14-JUN-1857		Julii Benoit/Carolna Cahier	F. Dulai--/M. Boraseaux
Benot---*	Sera		12-JUL-1860	---- Bent--/S. Mi---en	M. ---nall/E. ---nall
Benton**	Sera	05-AUG-1860	12-AUG-1860	Lin--- Benton/Sera Mi-l-n	Marta Wall/Ed--- Wall
Bergan*	Maria Ellen	12-NOV-1857	19-NOV-1857	Michel Bergan/Maria Korgan	J. Knicht/M. Gruin
Bergan	Timotheum	26-MAR-1853	17-MAY-1853	Michaelis Bergan/Julia Glassy	T Bergan/-. Kennedy
Bergan*	Joannem	18-AUG-1857	01-OCT-1857	Thimotie Bergan/Honnora Bays	C Gillan/E. Bays
Bergan*	Margetham	14-FEB-1860	17-MAR-1860	Michaelis Bergan/Julia Closset	Michaelis McManmgan/Julie McManmgan
Bergan*	Mariam Elenam	12-NOV-1857	19-NOV-1857	Michaelis Bergan/Maria Kerigan	J. Petit/M. G----
Bergeron	Oliviam Victoriam	25-SEP-1867	29-SEP-1867	Olivieri Bergeron/Mathld Bergeron	N. Marion/S. Therien
Berigan*	Marguaret				
Berl	Lucam	29-AUG-1852	16-SEP-1852	Baptista Berl/Precilla Provot	E. Juneau/H. Juneau
Berlan*	Joseph				
Berland*	Matildam	28-MAY-1860	17-JUN-1860	Josephi Berland/Edemunda Baltazar	Jorgeus Ollet/Rosalia Baltazar
Berlant	Josephina	02-SEP-1874	07-SEP-1874	----- -----/Maria Berlant	Joseph Loiselle/Sophia Breva-t
Bermans	Barbaram	05-AUG-1864	07-AUG-1864	Josephi Bermans/Catharna Bermans	S. Tell/B. Grimm
Bermigham	James	04-JUN-1857	07-JUN-1857	Garret Bermigham/Anna ------	W. Flanigan/M. Canal
Berneche	Alfredum	01-MAR-1903	12-MAR-1903	Davde Berneche/Albina Aubry	Michael Ryaume/Philumena Charron
Berneche	Victorinam	11-DEC-1900	25-DEC-1900	Davide-Adelarno Berneche/Albina Aubry	Amabilis Gervais/Philumena Chef
Bernier	Edessam	18-SEP-1869	31-OCT-1869	Edwardi Bernier/Emilia Bernier	Paulus Gagner/Electrea Bernier
Bernier	Guillelmum Eduardum	25-MAR-1872	31-MAR-1872	Eduardi Bernier/Emilia Bernier	Guillelmus Blair/Clotilda Gagner
Berns	Claresa Mary	14-FEB-1849	24-JUN-1852	John Berns/Lucy Randal	
Berns	Lucian	28-JAN-1851	24-JUN-1852	John Berns/Lucy Randal	W. Wilson/M. Berns
Berrigan	Joannam	01-OCT-1860	18-OCT-1860	Timothei Berrigan/Anna Berrigan	R. Kennedy/J. Kennedy
Berrigan	Joannem	27-AUG-1862	14-OCT-1862	Michaelis Berrigan/Julia Berrigan	J Mckell--/M. Morton
Berry	Genovefam Adelaidam	20-MAR-1890	20-APR-1890	Gulielmo Berry/Adela Gervais	Petrus Barbeau/Ezilda Barbeau
Berry	Ivam Ethel Mariam	28-NOV-1888	24-MAR-1889	Gulielmo Berry/Adela Gervais	Gilbertus Surprenant/Zoe Barbeau
Berry	Mariam Edm--dy		10-OCT-1854	Kerry Berry/Maria Donovan	D. Kennel/E. Murphy
Berry	Mariam Stellam	08-OCT-1881	07-MAR-1882	Gulielmo Berry/Maria Gervais	Narcissus Gervais/Adela Gervais
Berry	Neo Eduard	27-APR-1880	17-MAY-1880	Gulielmo Berry/Ada Gervais	J. Moquin/M. Moquin
Berry*	Rubiam Sophiam Adelam	11-FEB-1894	18-FEB-1894	Gulielmo Berry/Adea Gervais	Telesphorus Gervais/Melina Beauregard
Berry*	Maria Sera Annam	22-SEP-1858	17-OCT-1858	Cha--- Berry/Elisaht Galliger	Caroli Janzen/Maria O'---gan
Berry*	Sarah Anne				
Bet	Euphemiam	28-APR-1862	22-JUN-1862	Joanns Bert/Catharina Bert	J Tierney/C. Tierney
Bertrand	Florentiam	10-FEB-1871	05-MAR-1871	Maxımı Bertrand/Clarissa Bertrand	Josephus Baillargeon/Auralia Leclèrc
Bertrand	Franciscam Lousam	10-FEB-1883	25-FEB-1883	Joanne-Napoleone Bertrand/Audilia Leduc	Antonius Charron/Virginia Le----
Bertrand	Franciscum Simeonem	13-JUN-1869	20-JUN-1869	Maximi Bertrand/Clarissa Bérubé	Franciscus Roi/Julia Roi
Bertrand	Irenam Margaritam	05-MAR-1892	27-MAR-1892	Joanne-Napoleone Bertrand/Odelia Leclerc	Josephus Moqun/Elmer--- Lefort
Bertrand	Joannem Arthurum	11-SEP-1896	08-DEC-1896	Ludovico Bertrand/Ella Jacobs	Joannes Bertrand/Della Leclerc

Surname	Given Name	Birth	Baptism	Parents	Godparents
Bertrand	Josephum	14-MAR-1873	21-MAR-1873	Maximi Bertrand/Clarisse Bérubé	Josephus Leclerc/Ludovica Leclerc
Bertrand	Josephum Guilielmum Edua	31-MAR-1885	19-APR-1885	Joanne-Napoleone Bertrand/Eulalia Leclerc	Gilbertus Surprenant/Mathilde Barbeau
Bertrand	Mathldam Clarissam	25-JUN-1867	30-JUN-1867	Maximi Bertrand/Clarissa Bertrand	H.Baillargeon/ M Baillargeon
Bertrand	Maud Merandam	23-MAR-1890	06-APR-1890	Joanne-Napoleone Bertrand/Odelia Leclar	Gadeo Brunet/Zoe Barbeau
Bertrand	Odilon Napolion	14-MAR-1875	23-MAR-1875	Maximi Bertrand/Clarista Burbé	Joannis-Napolien Bertrand/Oliv--- Plouf
Bertrant	Ludovicum Napolion	15-APR-1876	16-APR-1876	Joannis-Napolion Bertrant/Odilia Declaire	M. Bertrant/E. Berbie
Bertrant*	Mariam	21-DEC-1856	21-DEC-1856	Josephi Bertrant/Delm--- Baltazar	M Baltazar/J Deblanc
Besette	Israelem Lafayette	06-JAN-1881	11-JAN-1881	Cyrillo Bessette/Rosa-Delma Leduc	L. Mangin/L Leduc
Besset	Ludovicum Philipum	08-JUL-1877	08-JUL-1877	Cerıl Besset/Denmor Leduc	F. Bouche/ wife
Bessete	Alphonsum Fredericum	05-JUL-1868	06-JUL-1868	Israli Basset/Julia Snow	Franciscus Bessete/Emilia Snow
Bessete	Fredericum	07-NOV-1868	16-NOV-1868	Petri Bessete/Rosalia Thibodeau	Petrus Bessete/Sophia Beaulieu
Bessete	Isidorum	28-JUL-1871	05-AUG-1871	---- Bessete/Julia Snow	Theo----- Rıeve/----- Rıeve
Bessete	Mariam Josephinam	26-AUG-1870	04-SEP-1870	Josephi Bessete/Maria Bessete	Petrus Bessete/Sophia Beaulieu
Bessete	Rosam Annam	25-NOV-1872	08-DEC-1872	Petri Bessete/Rosalia Thibodeau	Josephus Bessete/Maria Bré
Bessett	Carolus	22-APR-1879	24-APR-1879	C.yrilli Bessett/Amou- Leduc	C. Errard/D Leduc-Errard
Bessette	Carolum	19-NOV-1865	19-NOV-1865	Ambrosn Bessette/Magdalena Gayet	C. Gayet/E. Surprenant
Bessette	Josephum Ludgerum	21-NOV-1880	22-NOV-1880	Israel Bessette/Julia Chenard	F. Boucher/J. Bessette
Bessette	Mariam Joannam	26-FEB-1874	01-MAR-1874	Israelie Bessette/Julia Chenard	P----- Bussonette/Sophia Buissonette
Beuendle	Franciscum Jacobum Walt	30-JUN-1887	28-AUG-1887	Jacobo Buendle/Sophia Miller	Alphonsus Chenart/Sophia Chenart
Bi--l	Mariam Ediiam	15-MAR-1877	29-MAR-1877	William Bi--i/M--- July	L. Brunet/E. Joly
Bib*y	Josept	06-FEB-1857	07-FEB-1857	Ambrose Biby/Madelana Gayet	I. Leprenant/J. Gayet
Bibeau	Ludovicum Guilielmum	28-JAN-1872	04-FEB-1872	Henrici Bibeau/Angela Cartier	Carolus Tremblé/Clementia Tremblé
Bibeau*	Maria	18-JUL-1855	09-AUG-1855	Joseph Lebeau/Adelina Bissept	I. St-Antone/J. Bıbeau
Biby*	Emelına	06-FEB-1857	07-FEB-1857	Ambrose Biby/Madelana Gayet	J. Oillet/M. Lavalé
Billchuck	Mariam Larndam	14-JUN-1906	09-JUL-1906	Francisco Billchuck/Martha Kozprovick	Henricus Gutranter/Lalie Billchuck
Bird	Albam Mariam	03-JUL-1918	01-SEP-1918	Leone Brrd/Gratia Tomies	Ludovicus Bırd/Emily Degner-Bird
Bird	Annam	04-FEB-1853	13-MAR-1853	Michaelis Bird/Maria Stanton	J. Lyman/M. Lassy
Bird	Carolum Ephrem Leonem	22-NOV-1904	27-NOV-1904	Leone Brrd/Grace Townes	Carolus Bırd/Martha Becaw
Bird-L'Oiseau	Carolam Ephrem Leonem	22-NOV-1904	27-NOV-1904	Leone Bird-L'Oiseau/Gratia Tomies	Carolus Bird/Martha Besaw
Bırsau	Jocobum Ludovicum		25-SEP-1875	Olivier Birsau/Maria L'Oiseau	C. L'Oiseau/M Bırsau
Bırsept	Emelinam	06-FEB-1857	07-FEB-1857	Ambrose Bırsept/Magdalena Gayet	G. Ollet/M. Delavalle
Bırsept*	Josephum	06-FEB-1857	07-FEB-1857	Ambrose Bırsept/Magdolanı Gayet	I Surprenant/J Gayet
Bissant	Burté Jessé	12-APR-1875	05-MAY-1875	Martini Bisson/Julia Beard	Will Beard/Louise Gother
Bissept	Josephum	17-JAN-1859	23-JAN-1859	Abrascı Bissept/Madalena Gayet	J. Gayet/P. Thıbadeau
Bissept	Julıam Idam	26-MAY-1876	28-MAY-1876	Israel Bissept/Julia Shunard-Snow	L. Chunard/B. Balta-al
Bissept	Julian Idam	30-MAY-1875	07-JUN-1875	Isaelis Bissept/Julia Chunard	Francois Meller/----- Meller
Bıssept*	Josephum	17-JAN-1859	23-JAN-1859	Abrasi- Bissept/Madalena Gayet	Josephus Gayet/Philomena Tibodeau
Bisson	Eduardum Ludovicum	11-JUL-1875	21-DEC-1875	Ludovici Bi-son/Elena Hogan	F. Bi-son/ (wife)
Bisson	Emmam Ludovicam		20-JUN-1869	Martini Bisson/Julia Bid	Narcissus Trahant/Maria Trahant
Bisson	Franciscum Xaverum	25-APR-1867	05-MAY-1867	Martini Bisson/Julia Bisson	F. Bisson/E. Vient
Bisson	Guilielmum Eduardum	08-AUG-1871	03-JUL-1871	Martini Bisson/Julia Besson	Joannes Bird-Loiseau/Josepha Bisson
Bisson	Guilielmum Roy	23-JAN-1904	03-APR-1904	Gulielmo Bisson/Helena Gauthier	Narcissus Dinelle/Ida Gauther
Bisson	Harvy Dale Sylvestrum	14-OCT-1905	05-NOV-1905	Gulielmo Bisson/Nellie Gauthier	Martinus Bisson/Emma Bisson-Trilbey
Bisson	Martinum Edwardum	28-SEP-1873	16-NOV-1873	Martini Bisson/Julia Loison	Ludovicus Bisson/Maria Bisson
Bisson	Violam		17-JUN-1883	Martino Bisson/Julia Loscau	David Chaperon/Della Loseau
Bissonet	Aurelıam	30-JAN-1872	04-FEB-1872	Davidis Bissonet/Lucia Bissonet	Carolus Tremblé/Sophia Tremblé
Bissonet	Davidem	01-JUN-1869	06-JUN-1869	Davidus Bissonet/Lucia Bissonet	Narcissus Gayet/Phoebe Bissonet
Bıssonet	Mariam Clotıldam	06-MAR-1870	06-MAR-1870	Noelis Bissonet/Sophia Bissonet	Ludovicus Gayet/Emerentia D-----
Bıssonet	Mariam Delphinam	06-MAR-1870	06-MAR-1870	Noelis Bissonet/Sophia Bissonet	Elias Chapman/Phlomina Chapman

13

Surname	Given Name	Birth	Baptism	Parents	Godparents
Bissonet	Mariam Marcelinam	02-JUL-1870	04-JUL-1870	Davidis Bissonet/Lucia Bissonct	----- Letourneau/Sophia Bissonet
Bissonnet	Franciscum Philipum	21-FEB-1876	19-MAR-1876	Joseph Bissonnet/Ludovica Gollet	P. Bissonnet/ wife
Bisycpt	Ambrosum	21-APR-1855	21-APR-1855	Ambrosi Bisycpt/Magdalena Gaget	A. Gaget/D Gaget
Bitel*	Eduardum	04-APR-1858	11-APR-1858	Wellihelm Bitel/Maria Sloon	M. Kerran/M. Claury
Bl----*	Mariam Helenam	04-SEP-1858	05-SEP-1858	Guillelmi Bl----/Marguarta Norton	J Reyly/H -
Black	Joannem	18-JUN-1854	25-DEC-1854	Joannis Black/Esther Hudpaus	J. Black/C. McWigan
Black	Mariam Joannam	05-AUG-1852	21-SEP-1852	Jacobi Black/Ester Hutchinons	P Flanegan/C Flanegan
Blake	Joannem Thomam	05-OCT-1862	12-OCT-1862	Guillelmi Blake/Catharina Blake	B. Lawton/M Lynch
Blo-d*	Thomas		19-AUG-1855	James Blo-d/Mary Ka--	P Blo-d/M. Lary
Bloed*	Thomam	10-AUG-1855	19-AUG-1855	Petrus Bloed/Maria Cary	P. Bloed/M Lary
Blondeau	Ludovicum	30-JAN-1866	27-MAY-1866	Francisci Blondeau/Elizabetha Blondeau	B. Chaunière/R Ebert
Blondin	Elizabetham	15-JUL-1871	30-JUL-1871	Francisci Blondin/Elizabetha Gauchere	----- -----/Maria Ca----
Blondin	Emiliam	16-MAR-1868	16-MAR-1868	Francisci Blondin/Elizabetha Gauthier	----- -----/Emilia Odete
Blut*	Pierce	19-APR-1859	19-APR-1859	Thos. Blut/Mary Lary	A. Dungan/M. Dumgan
Bluit*	Pierce				
Bock	Carolum	17-FEB-1866	07-OCT-1866	Christiani Bock/Maria Bock	G Fisher/M. Stratz
Bock	Julium	16-JUL-1864	07-OCT-1866	Christiani Bock/Maria Bock	M. Stratz/M. Werlng
Bockkeless*	Anges	21-APR-1855	08-DEC-1855	Joannes Bockkeless/Jannan Keppers	E. Devin/----- -----
Boda	Irene Elizabeth	02-SEP-1920	19-SEP-1920	Joseph-Levy Boda/Dora-Marianne Reichelt	Adolphe Bastien/Geneveve Moquin
Bodamaer*	Sophia Mathilda Lousa				
Bodemaer*	Lousa		17-JAN-1859	Philippe Bodemaer/Mary Clay	
Bodemaer*	Matilda		17-JAN-1859	Philippe Bodemaer/Mary Clay	
Bodemaer*	Sophia		17-JAN-1859	Philippe Bodemaer/Mary Clay	----- -----/----- -----
Bodeman*	Lousa		17-JAN-1859	Phillippe Bodeman/Mary Clay	----- -----/----- -----
Bodeman*	Mathilda		17-JAN-1859	Phillippe Bodeman/Mary Clay	----- -----/----- -----
Bodeman*	Sophia		17-JAN-1859	Phillippe Bodeman/Mary Clay	----- -----/----- -----
Bodet	Leo Ludovicus	22-NOV-1879	07-DEC-1879	Agile Bodet/Ludovica Beaudet	D. Beaudet/A. Gauthier
Bodin	Josephum	01-MAY-1878	05-MAY-1878	Josephi Bodin/Ellia Carbena	F. Corbono/M. Bodet
Bodin*	Cl--bia	27-SEP-1857	28-SEP-1857	Jacobus Bodin/Marie L---din	P. Garro/C. Br---
Bodin*	Clementiam	27-SEP-1857	28-SEP-1857	Jocobi Bodin/--o-isa L'Armodin	P. Garron/C Bricau
Bodin*	Franciscum Regis	08-APR-1856	24-APR-1856	Jacobi Bodin/Louisa Larmeny	P. Gou--/M. Menard
Bodin*	Francois Regis	09-APR-1856	24-APR-1856	Jocobus Bodin/Eloise L-miný	P. G---e/M. Minard
Bodoit	Mariam Diliam		01-SEP-1876	Isedore Bodot/Philome Malheur	J. Malheur/ wife
Bodou	Franciscum Xavierum	17-JUL-1873	27-JUL-1873	Francisci Bodou/Octavia Edoun	Joseph Lepine/Josephne Bodou
Bodrieau*	Georgium	21-MAR-1857	27-MAR-1857	Joannis Bodrieau/Sophia Shenard	I. Snow/S. In--
Bodrieau*	Ignace Israel				
Bodrieau*	Jorge	18-MAR-1857	27-MAR-1857	John Bodrieau/Sophe Shinard	I ---nar/S Sir
Bodrieaux*	Maria Eulalia				
Bodrieaux*	Maria Serina	19-JUN-1856	13-AUG-1856	Joseph Bodrieau/Melvina Cavaler	A Ducleau/J Bodrieau
Bodrieaux	Arietam	04-AUG-1853	21-AUG-1853	Laurenti Bodrieaux/Sophia Reigner	J. Jubert/A. Reigner
Bodrieaux	David	24-DEC-1855	28-DEC-1855	David Bodrieaux/Anna Galligan	A Debeau/L Bodrieaux
Bodrieaux	Lousam	02-FEB-1854	05-FEB-1854	Davidis Bodrieaux/Anna Calliar	L Bodrieaux/S Raihl
Bodrieaux*	Ignatium Israel	04-SEP-1858	09-OCT-1858	Lairentis Bodrieaux/Sophia Brion	Israel Hebert/Louisa Bodrieaux
Bodrieaux*	Mariam Serinam	19-JUN-1856	13-AUG-1856	Josephi Bodrieaux/Madalena Cavalier	A Lebeau/J Bodrieaux
Bodreaux*	Nestor Hilarus	23-OCT-1857	25-OCT-1857	Laurentius Beaudreaux/Sophia Brion	H. Leduc/S. Poderet
Bodreaux*	Nestorem Hilarium	23-OCT-1857	25-OCT-1857	Laurentii Bodrieaux/Sophia Bron	H. Leduc/S. Poderet
Bodreaux*	Sophiam	19-OCT-1855	30-OCT-1855	Laurentii Bodrieaux/Sophia Bron	M Bodrieaux/S. Bron
Bodrieux*	Mariam Evelina	24-MAY-1860	27-MAY-1860	Laurentius Bodrieux/Sophia Brion	Noe Sersi/Brix Bodrieau
Bodrieux*	Sophia	15-OCT-1855	30-OCT-1855	Laurentius Bodrieux/Sophie Bron	M. Bodrieau/S Bron

14

Surname	Given Name	Birth	Baptism	Parents	Godparents
Bodrio	Mariam	20-MAR-1863	31-DEC-1873	Joseph Bodrio/Herminia Pellan	Damasi Trottier/Philomena Trottier
Boeck	Josephum	21-APR-1855	01-APR-1863	Christian Boeck/Maria-Anna Boeck	M. Stre--/B Hurlings
Boeckkelers*	Agnes	21-DEC-1858	08-DEC-1855	Joannis Boekkelers/Joanna Kippers	------/E Devin
Boes--d--*	Joannem	20-DEC-1859	26-DEC-1858	Joannis Boes--d--/Sophie Chmard	Cho-ilus Chenard/Sophie Pellant
Bohem*	Cecilia	12-APR-1896	14-FEB-1860	Joannes Bohem/Catherina Gary	Terrence McCoy/Maria-Anna Ferguson
Bohemier	Mariam Annam Claram	23-SEP-1857	02-JUN-1896	Josepho-Eugenio Bohemier/Anna Bellam	Franciscus Marcoux/Josephina Roy
Bohen	John		16-OCT-1857	Peter Bohen/Alice Hennessey	M-C Dillon/Marguerite Fitzgerald
Bohen*	Cecilia				
Boisledeau*	------	04-APR-1859	22-MAY-1859	Joannis Boisledeau/Lucia Terry	T. Stantam/A. Stantam
Boisledeau*	Ludovicum	04-APR-1859	22-MAY-1859	Joannis Boisledeau/Lucia Terry	F Royer/J. Ludovicam
Boisson	Franciscum Oliverum	18-AUG-1873	15-AUG-1873	Olivarii Boisson/Maria Loizeau	Ludovicus Boisson/Milia Trahant
Boisvert	Elizabetham	09-MAR-1867	28-APR-1867	Thoma Boisvert/Ludovica Boisvert	F. Blondin/E. Gauthier
Boisvert	Hypolitum	02-MAY-1861	16-JUN-1861	Thoma Boisvert/Ludovica Boisvert	H. Ebert/E. Letourneau
Boisvert	Ludovicam		15-AUG-1862	Thoma Boisvert/Ludovica Boisvert	L Petit/F Morel
Boisvert	Theophilum	23-MAR-1864	22-MAY-1864	Thoma Boisvert/Ludovica Boisvert	F. Robert/M. Robert
Boisvin	Georgium	02-JUN-1873	22-JUN-1873	Antoni Boisvin/Amablia Hurto	Georgius Oudet/Julia --gent
Boisvin	Wilham		03-JUN-1877	Antoni Boisvin/Amabelis Gurto	J Boisledueduc/ wife
Boivin	Helenam Estheram		26-APR-1868	Antonii Boitvin/Amata Bottvin	Xaverus Hurtot/Magdalena Boitvin
Boivin	Adeliam Emeliam	11-JAN-1880	29-MAR-1880	Josepho Boivin/Maria Boivin	G. Boivin/P. Brodeur
Boivin	Albertum Leonem	11-FEB-1891	14-FEB-1891	J.B Boivin/Josephina Dufort	Petrus Lepine/Josephina Corbeille
Boivin	Caram Solomi	13-NOV-1870	20-NOV-1870	Antoni Boivin/Amata Hurteau	Josephus Rabidou/Aurelia Boivin
Boivin	Catharina	13-MAY-1888	27-MAY-1888	Ludovico Boivin/Ursa Roches	------/Catharina Turney
Boivin	Emmam Rosaliam	01-MAR-1906	03-MAR-1906	Georgio Boivin/Julia Turcotte	------/Maria Turcotte-Hurteau
Boivin	Josephum		04-OCT-1883	Joanne-Baptista Boivin/Josephina Dufort	Antonius Boivin/Annabilis Boivin
Boivin	Kenneth Solvinium Georgi	16-FEB-1909	21-FEB-1909	Georgio Boivin/Julia Turcotte	Cyrillus-Solvinia Dufort/Salome Boivin-Dufort
Boivin	Mabel Josephinam	28-MAY-1885	31-MAY-1885	Joanne-Baptista Boivin/Josephina Dufort	Antonus Lamontagne/Magdalena Boivin
Boivin	Mariam Lucindam	05-MAR-1889	27-APR-1889	Joanne-Baptista Boivin/Josephina Dufort	Cyrillus Corbeille/Anastasia Dufort
Boivin	Phulumenam Ursulam	04-JUL-1904	05-JUL-1904	Georgio Boivin/Julia Turret	Ludovicus Boivin/Philumena Coté
Bolan	Augustam Julianam		05-MAY-1861	Ludovici Bolan/Frederica -ock	M. Manegan/A. Schmit
Bolduc	Elizabetham	29-DEC-1867	26-JAN-1868	Joannis Bolduc/Lucia Bolduc	Toussaintius Chapleau/Ludovica Tessier
Bolduc	Georgium	22-FEB-1864	13-MAR-1864	Joannis Bolduc/Lucia Bolduc	F Meunier/S. Meunier
Bolduc	Josephinam	27-APR-1861	19-MAY-1861	Joannis Bolduc/Lucia Bolduc	A Blanc/L. Ledue
Bolduc*	John				
Bolduc*	Louis				
Bolduc*	Louise				
Bolen	Catherine	11-AUG-1850	14-OCT-1850	Peter Bolen/Alice Henne-y	P. McDonald/M. McDonald
Bolngan*	John	02-APR-1859	13-APR-1859	John Boligan/Bridget Hennoth--	P. Quin/C Quin
Bolngan*	John				
Bon-ha-d*	Josephina	04-SEP-1855	29-SEP-1855	Jeremias Bon-ha-d/Eliseph Petit	G. Olllet/C Cornet
Bondin	Emiliam	17-AUG-1868	21-AUG-1868	Caroli Bondin/Edessa Joubert	Julianus Beaudin/Ludovica Joubert
Bonin	Delphinam	19-APR-1868	19-APR-1868	Eduardi Bonin/Julia Louari	Pascal Létourneau/Thrissa Robert
Bonin	Eduardum Eugenium	05-SEP-1872	08-SEP-1872	Edmondi Bonin/Julia Bonin	Eugenius Bransheau/Aurelie Larivière
Bonin	Odilam Ludovicam	19-JUL-1864	21-JUL-1864	Edwardi Bonin/Julia Bonin	P. Émery/L Émery
Bonin*	Adeline	13-DEC-1858	22-DEC-1858	Edward Bonin/Julie Baetle	Octave Desroches/Adeline Dufraine
Bonin*	Adeline	13-DEC-1858	22-DEC-1858	Edward Bonin/Julie Buer--	Octave Desroches/Adeline Dufraine
Bonin*	Adeline				
Bonnel	Plunam Mariam Stellam		27-JUN-1897	Frederici Bonnel/Catharina Hoffmann	Alfredus Clish/Stella Atkinson
Bontour*	Sarah				
Boot*	Jacobum	03-JUL-1858	15-JUL-1858	Joannis Boot/Magdalena Zimmerman	J. Zimmerman/C. Cazvor

15

Surname	Given Name	Birth	Baptism	Parents	Godparents
Boraso	Corolum Franciscum	04-JUN-1876	11-JUN-1876	Caroli Boraso/Melina Marco	B. Baltazar/ wife
Borasseau	Elizabetham Barbaram	04-JUL-1870	18-AUG-1872	Petri Borasseau/Francisca Borasseau	Josephus-A. Stratz/Barbara Gibel
Borasseau	Mariam Adelaidam	07-JUN-1866	08-JUN-1866	Caroli Borasseau/Lina Borasseau	F. Marcou/E. Cyr
Borland*	Maria	21-DEC-1856	21-DEC-1856	Jojesh Borland/Delmera Baltazar	M. Baltazar/J. Desblane
Borossina	Elizabetham	08-DEC-1864	10-DEC-1864	Huberti Borosseau/Leocadia Lécuyer	T Deschênes/M. Gervais
Bossing*	Cornelius				
Bossiny*	Cornelium	02-FEB-1859	13-FEB-1859	Bartholomii Bossiny/Maria Lerry	E Gludan/A. Superant
Botdet	Esther Franciscum	25-SEP-1878	13-OCT-1878	Juli-Josephi Botdet/Lowesa Beauchard	C. Letourneau/M. Bodet
Bott	Mariam Magdalenam	03-DEC-1860	09-DEC-1860	Joannis Bott/Magdalena Bott	M. Sontag/L. Sontag
Botz	Albertum	04-JAN-1862	02-MAR-1862	Andrea Botz/Elizabetha Botz	J. Seing/A. Smith
Botz	Augustum	07-AUG-1859	02-MAR-1862	Andrea Botz/Elizabetha Botz	J. Seing/A. Smith
Bouchar	Marguaritam	01-JUL-1862	01-JUL-1862	German Bouchar/Emelina Bouchar	T Deschenes/L. Lescuyer
Bouchard	Franciscam	29-DEC-1853	29-JAN-1854	Jeremia Bouchard/--i-ca Petit	I. Munnsier/V. Petit
Bouchard*	Josephuam	04-SEP-1855	28-SEP-1855	Jeremie Bouchard/Elizabetha Petit	G Ollet/C. Cornet
Bouchard*	Marie Elizabeth				
Bouché	David	24-FEB-1875	28-FEB-1875	Francisci Bouché/Julie Bissett	Franciscus Bissept/Maria DeLajeunesse
Bouché	Henricum	21-JAN-1877	21-JAN-1877	Francois Bouché/Judet Beiset	T. Lajeunesse/ wife
Boucher	Belonsiam	02-MAY-1871	07-MAY-1871	Leonis Boucher/Tharsila Faneuf	Baptista Dupus/Clementia Faneuf
Boucher	Carolinam	18-APR-1866	22-APR-1866	Octavi Boucher/Rosalia Boucher	P Boucher/E. Marcou
Boucher	Franciscum Israelem	02-AUG-1879	03-AUG-1879	Francisco Boucher/Judith Bessette	G. Besset/P. Lajeunesse
Boucher	Georgiam Annam	07-JAN-1873	07-JAN-1873	Francisci Boucher/Judith Bessette	Theophilius Rieve/Bernardina Bessete
Boucher	Georgium Israelam		14-JAN-1884	Francisco Boucher/Judith Bessette	Israel Lemieux/Georgiana Boucher
Boucher	Josephum Albertum	17-MAY-1886	23-MAY-1886	Francisco Boucher/Judith Bessette	Franciscus Robert/Maria Beaudin
Boucher	Juliam Eleonoram	28-NOV-1881	04-DEC-1881	Francisco Boucher/Judith Bessette	Israel Bessette/Julia Chenart
Boucher	Leonem Eduardum Silvestr	19-MAY-1893	21-MAY-1893	Francisco Boucher/Judith Bessette	Franciscus Marcoux/Josephina Roy
Boucher	Ludovicum Carolum	17-APR-1888	22-APR-1888	Francisco Boucher/Judith Bassette	Michael Pommniville/Sophia Gratton
Boucher	Mariam Josephinam	08-MAY-1870	23-MAY-1870	Leonis-Josephi Boucher/Tharsila Fernet	Carolus Marcou/Josephina Marcou
Boucher	Mariam Ludovicam Victori	11-FEB-1872	13-FEB-1872	Francisci Boucher/Julia Bessete	Cyrilus Bessete/Delima Leduc
Boucher	Mary Louise	03-DEC-1851	19-DEC-1851	German Boucher/Louise Petit	J. Petit/T. Petit
Boucher	Virginam	07-APR-1865	09-APR-1865	Octavi Boucher/Rosalia Boucher	M Ebert/E. Marcou
Boulay	Emeritum Mauritium	31-MAR-1873	02-APR-1873	Ludovici Boulay/Adelina Boulay	Eduardus ------/Emilia Bernier
Boulay	Paulum Fredericum	18-SEP-1872	02-MAR-1873	Josephi Boulay/Rosa Linz	Ferdinandus Trout/Elizabeth Trout
Bourassa	Susannam	26-MAR-1851	03-SEP-1852	Stephani Bourassa/Maria Bourassa	L. Duranco/C. Beaupré
Bourrassas	Mariam Josephinam	20-DEC-1873	29-DEC-1873	Caroli Bourrassas/Me--ia Marcou	Franciscus Marcou/Josephina Marcou
Boutet	Ludovicum Paulum	09-MAY-1871	14-MAY-1871	Ludovici Boutet/Adelina Boutet	Paulus Gagnier/Clotilda Gagnier
Bowen	Leonem Jessum	23-SEP-1890	19-OCT-1890	Joanne Bowen/Elizabeth Canse	Alexander Durocher/Hilda Banneville
Boyé	Mariam Carolinam	08-NOV-1876	17-NOV-1876	Antoni Boyé/Maria-Louise Lemeux	P Lemieux/ wife
Boyea*	John Martin				
Boyer	Mariam Aguela	19-JUL-1874	25-JUL-1874	Antoni Boyer/Marla lemieux	Julianus Lemieux/E----- Lemieux
Boyle	Martinum	17-MAY-1853	19-JUN-1853	Michaelis Boyle/----- Boyle	F. O'Neil/M. O'Neil
Br-k-*	Josephum	15-JUL-1855	22-JUL-1855	Casper Br-k/Maria Lindus	J. L---/G. ----
Brackett	Jacobum	07-DEC-1862	07-DEC-1862	Nelson Brackett/Helena Brackett	D Trocquett/J Rondeau
Brady	Mariam Catharinam Blanch	31-OCT-1908	22-NOV-1908	Jacobo Brady/Catharina Sheehy	Carolus Matheu/Maria Sheey
Brady*	Jocobum	18-NOV-1856	19-NOV-1856	Joannis Brady/Maria Francis	M. Collan/M. Madden
Brake	Mariam Helenam	06-MAR-1874	22-MAR-1874	Lamb Brake/Isabella Gautier	Calixtus Perron/Agnes Gautier
Branan*	Catharine				
Branan*	Catherina	25-JUN-1854	06-APR-1859	Thimity Branan/Mary Cannaty	J Curans/M. Deris
Branan*	John	25-JUN-1854	06-APR-1859	Thimity Branan/Mary Cannaty	T Conners/M. Conners
Branan*	John Timothy				

Surname	Given Name	Birth	Baptism	Parents	.	Godparents
Branan*	Rosanna					
Branan*	Thimty	25-JUN-1854	06-APR-1859	Thimty Branan/Mary Cannaty		J ----/M. ----
Brands*	Marguaret					
Brandsfort*	Margerth	08-SEP-1859	04-OCT-1859	William Brandsfort/Maria Mellan		M Welshs/E He-
Brandt	Arnoldum	12-MAR-1863	23-MAY-1863	Frederici Brandt/Anna Brandt		A. Berge/E. Starver
Brandt	Idam Mariam	17-JAN-1865	07-MAY-1865	Frederici Brandt/Anna Brandt		G. Holl/M Jacobs
Brandt	Mariam Isabellam	23-AUG-1907	25-AUG-1907	Walter Brandt/Elmina Sauve		Eduardo Sauve/Elodia Venne-Sauve
Brandt	Mariam Luciam	09-JUN-1910	12-JUN-1910	Walter Brandt/Elmina Sauve		Eduardu Sauve/Melma Beauregard-Gervais
Branen*	Rosam	21-APR-1860	23-MAY-1860	Petri Branen/Elisabetha Martin		Patricus ----Inn/---- ----
Brannel	Mariam Elizabetham	22-MAR-1880	22-MAR-1880	Petro Brannel/Felicitate Allain		J Brannel/H. Lebeau
Bransheau	Mariam May	10-MAY-1873	11-MAY-1873	Norberti Bransheau/Honora-Ludovica Bransheau		Eugenius Bransheau/Maria Bransheau
Braquete	Helenam	06-JUN-1864	12-JUN-1864	Nelson Braquet/Helena Braquete		N. Boisvert/A. Faucher
Braquett	Adelam	14-JUL-1861	04-AUG-1861	Nelson Braquet/Helena Braquett		F. Pedlant/J Faucher
Braquette	Mariam Helenam	09-MAR-1866	11-MAR-1866	Nelson Braquette/Helena Braquette		F. Durocher/S. Pellant
Brasney	Joannam	29-OCT-1861	03-NOV-1861	Barthololei Brasney/Maria-Anna Brasney		S. Cane/M. Cane
Bratz	Clifford Franciscum	22-MAY-1908	14-NOV-1908	Francisco Bratz/Adelina Robidoux		Josephus Robidoux/Maria-Helena Boivin
Bray	Hubertum	01-MAR-1855	04-MAR-1855	Huberti Bray/Maria Mullen		L. Landerman/M. Mullen
Bray	Ludovicum	09-JAN-1858	25-JAN-1858	Philippi Bray/Maria Malheur		L. Belieu/---- Bellieu
Bray*	Ysidore	20-AUG-1857	23-AUG-1857	Philip Bray/Marie Malheur		---- Hubert/P. Malheur
Brazeau	Elizabetham Dolores	03-APR-1903	12-APR-1903	Alberto-Josepho Brazeau/Francesca Ackerman		Narcissus-Georgius Brazeau/Catharina Oaks
Brazeau	Francescam Ezildam	10-SEP-1904	25-SEP-1904	Alberto Brazeau/Francesca Ackerman		Georgius Ackerman/Theresia Buck
Bray*	Isedorum	20-AUG-1857	23-AUG-1857	Philippi Bray/Maria Malheur-Bray		I. Hubert/P. Malheur
Bré	Mariam	28-AUG-1853	28-AUG-1853	Huberti Bré/Maria Moller		L Moller/F Sir
Breadale	Paulum Eddie	01-JAN-1893	21-FEB-1893	Jacobi Breadale/Sophia Meunier		Arthurus Chenart/Ezilda Chenart
Brederle	Leonem Clarenttum	30-JUL-1890	20-AUG-1890	Jacobo Brederle/Sophia Meunier-Lapierre		Victorem Dupuy/Ezilda Tessier
Breister	Benjaminem Walter	02-SEP-1892	04-SEP-1892	Frederico-Carolo Breister/Elizabeth Charbonneau		Stephanus Dufresne/Helosa Lebeau
Breister	Carolum	30-MAR-1896	12-APR-1896	Frederico Breister/Elizabeth Charbonneau		Eusebius Charbonneau/Gertrude Comery
Breister	Joannem	20-NOV-1864	24-NOV-1864	Petri Breister/Anna-Marguarita Breister		J Schusseler/M. Gores
Brelan	Marguaritam	01-OCT-1861	20-OCT-1861	Josephi Brelan/Delonisa Brelan		J Balthazar/M. Gayet
Brelau	Rosalam	08-OCT-1863	25-OCT-1863	Josephi Brelau/Delmira Brelau		A. Ebert/J Lemaire
Brele	Carolum	24-JUN-1865	25-JUN-1865	Josephi Brele/----, Brele		J. Gervais/---- Gervais
Brelen	Joannem	16-JUL-1866	16-JUL-1866	Josephi Brelen/Delima Brelen		B. Lefort/J. Loiselle
Brenael	Danielem Franciscum Jose	29-JUL-1888	05-AUG-1888	Francisco-Josepho Brenael/Helena Keeney		Michael-Daniel Brenael/Francisca-Felicitas Allain
Brennan	Anna-Maria	16-DEC-1851	09-FEB-1852	Patrick Brennan/Elizabeth Martin		P. Martin/A. Martin
Brennan	Jacobum	03-MAY-1852	15-JUL-1852	Timothei Brennan/Maria Connaughty		T Connaughty/M. Realy
Bresse*	Rosalia		03-NOV-1850			Rev. Bonduel/Mgr. Joubert
Brewster	Albert	22-DEC-1850	16-FEB-1851	Albert Brewster/Harriette Prus--		T. Prus--/L. Prus--
Brewster	Celestia Lousa	16-SEP-1856	01-JAN-1857	Solemones Bricau/Maria Dourf		A Bricau/P Bricau
Bricau*	Adelinam	11-FEB-1865	26-FEB-1865	Solimi Brico/Sarah Brico		P. Dufresne/S. Dufresne
Brico	Agnetam Melindam	21-DEC-1860	29-DEC-1860	Solimi Brico/Sarah Brico		F. Lagnier/E. Brico
Brico	Guillelmum	21-APR-1867	12-MAY-1867	Salomonis Brico/Sarah Brico		C Tremblé/P Dodelin
Brico	Isidorum	08-JUL-1863	12-JUL-1863	Ludovici Brico/Philomena Brico		L. Brico/S. Dodelin
Brico	Joannem Baptistam	02-JAN-1866	15-JAN-1866	Ludovici Brico/Philomena Brico		H. Dodelin/C. Rothis
Brico	Josephinam	11-MAR-1868	13-MAR-1868	Ludovici Brico/Philomena Brico		Salomon Brico/Sarah Brico
Brico	Josephum	25-OCT-1864	30-OCT-1864	Ludovici Brico/Philomena Brico		I. Durocher/O. Brico
Brico	Marcelinam	07-FEB-1867	10-FEB-1867	Antoni Brico/Saloma Brico		L. Brico/G. Meuner
Brico	R Delima	12-SEP-1868	27-SEP-1868	Antoni Brico/Saloma Brico		Salomon Brico/Sarah Brico
Bricot	Sarahm Annam	03-JAN-1863	11-JAN-1863	Celini Bricot/Sarah Bricot		R. Murry/E. Pariso

17

Surname	Given Name	Birth	Baptism	Parents	Godparents
Brieau*	Saloman	15-SEP-1856	01-JAN-1857	Saloman Brieau/Maria Dory	A. Brieau/P Brieau
Bredale	John Patrick	13-MAR-1858	01-APR-1858	Deon Bredale/Mary Hagam	Mathew Hagen/Honora Hagen
Briens	Mariam Annam	22-OCT-1854	26-OCT-1854	Dyonisii Briens/Catherina Wells	J. Waters/S. Kelly
Brigittam	Franciscam	19-JUL-1852	19-JUL-1852	Jacobi Wells/Brigitta Weld	C Crory/C Smith
Brink	Petrum	04-OCT-1909	31-OCT-1909	Michaele Brink/Anna Shepard	Petrus Milleage/Carolina Spilla
Brion	Alexandrem Jocobum	05-AUG-1853	04-SEP-1853	Josephi Brion/Flora Brion	F. Mederique/M. McCarty
Brion*	Elisabeh	17-JUL-1855	09-AUG-1855	Joseph Brion/Gloria Tri-nt	W Flanigan/J. Whelen
Brion*	Elisabetham Maraim	15-JUL-1855	05-AUG-1855	Joseph Brion/Florentia Triant	G. Flannigan/J. Whelan
Brion**	Joseph Elias	10-SEP-1851	07-SEP-1851	Joseph Brion/Florence Brion	L Beaudreaux/R Brion
Briscoe	Corinnam Beatricam	13-OCT-1906	23-JUL-1907	Emos-Pollard Briscoe/Corinna Prefontain	Ludgerio Préfontaine/Blanche Prefontaine
Briscoe	Henricum Leonem Kotzka	24-MAR-1901	05-MAY-1901	Amos Briscoe/Corinna Préfontaine	Rev.C. Boucher/Julia Simonin
Briscoe	Raymundum Neal	21-JUL-1899	24-SEP-1899	Amos Briscoe/Corinna Prefontaine	Ludgerus Prefontaine/Julia Simonin
Brissette	Georgium	03-OCT-1897	24-OCT-1897	Arthuro Brissette/Maria Foster	Ludgerus No-pré/Elmira Lefort
Broadrick	Suzanne	09-MAR-1858	01-APR-1858	P'trick Broadrick/Bridget Martin	-----/Rozanne Broadrick
Brock*	Joseph	15-JUL-1855	22-JUL-1855	Casper Brock/Maria Stander	J Loider/G. Hall
Brockway	Andream	16-DEC-1879	28-JAN-1880	Benjamin Brockway/Ludovica Rouleau	A. Roy/C. Mcdonald
Brockway	Carolum	13-MAR-1873	29-APR-1873	Caroli Brockway/Ludovica Brockway	He----- Rulo/Maria Rulo
Brockway	Delphnam Myrtle	17-MAR-1887	06-NOV-1895	Samuele Brockway/----- Gates	Calixtus Evans/Delphina Leduc
Brockway	Eduardi	16-NOV-1877	18-FEB-1878	Benjamin Brockway/A---ise Roulou	A Roulou/D -----
Brockway	Elizabeth Lorettam	10-JUN-1907	07-JUL-1907	Andrea Brockway/Clara Bessey	Gulielmus Brockway/Melvina Marcoux-Brockway
Brockway	Fredericum Henricum	25-MAY-1883	10-JUN-1883	----- Brockway/Louisa Roleau	Joannes McGoven/Maria Coughlin
Brockway	Gulielmum Wilbert	09-MAR-1901	17-MAR-1901	Gulielmo Brockway/Melma Marcoux	Alexander Marcoux/Eleonora Lajeunesse
Brockway	Joannem Baptistam	30-DEC-1893	06-NOV-1895	Samuele Brockway/----- Gates	Israel Lemieux/Melina Larose
Brockway	Louisam	31-JUL-1871	06-NOV-1895	Samuele Brockway/----- Gates	Antonius Gilbert/Joanna Frederic
Brockway	Mariam Zoellam	17-JUL-1906	22-JUL-1906	Gulielmo Browkway/Alvina Marcoux	Franciscus Marcoux/Josephina Balthazar-Marcoux
Brockway	Zoahm Adelaidam	12-JAN-1870	16-FEB-1870	Benjamini Brockway/Edmila Rulo	Georgius Odete/Julia Odete
Broderic	Kiern	11-DEC-1851	14-JAN-1852	Patrick Broderic/Brigitte Martin	H. Martin/J. Martin
Broderick	Michaelem	20-FEB-1854	10-JUN-1854	Patritii Broderick/Bridgida Martin	T Vain/H. Welsh
Brodrich	Catherina	06-OCT-1850	10-NOV-1850	Patrick Brodrich/----- Broderich	----- Martin/R. Leon
Brody*	Jocobus	18-NOV-1856	19-NOV-1856	John Brody/Maria Francis	M. Callon/M Madden
Brosseny*	Margerctham	14-JUL-1856	26-JUL-1856	Bartholomei Brosseny/Maria Li---an	J Brasseny/J Lierny
Brossny*	Margret	14-JUL-1856	26-JUL-1856	Bartholemus Brossny/Marie Perran	J Brossny/J Lerry
Broullet	Mariam Claram	08-APR-1872	09-APR-1872	Hypoliti Brouillet/Adelina Bessetc	Zephirius Dumont/Maria Bessete
Brown	-----				
Brown	Annam Gertrudam	12-SEP-1865	23-SEP-1866	Francisci Brown/Anna Brown	B. Rost/G. Ka-te
Brown	Magdalenam	07-DEC-1863	22-MAY-1864	Nicholai Brown/Magdalena Brown	P. Shanel/M Wilcome
Brown	Maria	09-JAN-1852	25-JAN-1852	John Brown/Maria Zimmer	P. Linen/M. Cash
Brown	Mathcum	06-SEP-1860	18-SEP-1860	Josephi Brown/Walburta Brown	J. Wimer/-----
Brown	Mattheuem Guillelmum	24-JUL-1852	21-SEP-1852	Bernardi Brown/Maria Galaher	C. Carbory/R. Galaher
Brown*	Babera	10-DEC-1855	16-DEC-1855	Joannis Brown/Maria Chemmer	Niclus Devir/Babera Yeng
Brown*	Barbera	10-NOV-1855	16-NOV-1855	Joannis Brown/Maria Crammer	----- Devis/B. Yong
Brown*	Barberam	10-DEC-1855	16-DEC-1855	Joannis Brown/Maria Crammer	N Davis/B Young
Brown*	John	03-JUN-1858	07-OCT-1858	Nicholas Brown/Magdeleine Wilcome	Peter Shenea/Marguerite Wilcome
Brown*	John	05-APR-1860	13-MAY-1860	Nicolaus Brown/Madilina Wolcomc	Nicolaus Schannel/Anna Schannel
Brown*	Maria				
Brown*	Mariam	24-JUL-1858	06-SEP-1858	Joannis Brown/Maria Galliger	Joannes Carbory/Maria Carbory
Brown*	Mary				
Brucher	Eugeniam Louisam	04-JUL-1905	05-JUL-1905	Alberto Brucher/Maria-Anna Bastian	Jacobus Waltz/Eugenia Bastian

18

Surname	Given Name	Birth	Baptism	Parents	Godparents
Bruck*	Honoram	18-FEB-1857	01-MAR-1857	Joannis Bruck/Elena Rayan	J. Carný/E Carný
Bruck*	Maria Eugenia	27-AUG-1856	14-SEP-1856	William Bruck/Maria Dalton	J Harlon/----- Flag--y
Brucker	Eduardum Albertum Ludovi	25-AUG-1907	25-AUG-1907	Alberto Brucker/Maria-Anna Bastion	Albertus Dufraisne/Alexina Bastian-Dufraisne
Bruederle	Philippinam	31-MAR-1878	09-JUN-1900	Joannes Breuderle/Maria Thuervachter	-------/Olympia Brunet
Bruederle	Agai Margarittam	25-JUL-1894	04-SEP-1894	Jacobo Bruedrle/Sophia Meunier-Lapierre	Jacobus Phalen/Josephina Meunier
Bruer	Edwin	11-AUG-1879	10-SEP-1879	Edwin Bruer/Milia Cloutier	J. Lhussier/H. Cloutier
Bruer	Maria Philomenam	03-JAN-1881	15-APR-1881	Eduardo Bruer/Emelia Cloutier	M. Comeau/A. Pelland
Brugan	Julianam	15-JUL-1854	02-NOV-1854	Michaelis Brugan/Juliana -Iossy	G. Phelan/M Phelan
Bruker	Mariam Gertrudem Marcell	21-AUG-1901	25-AUG-1901	Alberto Bruker/Maria-Anna Bastien	Joannes-Baptista Bastien/Maria Bruker
Brunet	Franciscum Gedeonem	12-AUG-1897	12-AUG-1897	Avila Brunet/Delma Lebeau	Gedeon Brunet/Angela Mecier
Brunet	Franciscum Maglorium	20-JAN-1902	21-JAN-1902	Avila Brunet/Delma Lebeau	Michael Conaboy/Olivina Lebeau
Brunet	Josephum	08-JUL-1885	08-JUL-1885	Gedeone Brunet/Melina Bastien	Thomas Lepine/Josephina Brunet
Brunet	Josephum Armandum Leon	28-SEP-1900	30-SEP-1900	Ferdinando Brunet/Matilda Potvin	Josephus Brunet/Olympia Brunet
Brunet	Josephum Carolum Clarent	11-FEB-1904	11-FEB-1904	Josepho-Avila Brunet/Delina Lebeau	Ferdinandus Brunet/Mathilda Potvin
Brunet	Josephum Ferdinandum	21-NOV-1896	22-NOV-1896	Ferdinando Brunet/Mathilda Potvin	Gedeon Brunet/Georgina Gauthier
Brunet	Josephum Gedeonem Laur	06-SEP-1907	08-SEP-1907	Avila Brunet/Delma Lebeau	Lucas Brunet/Maria Brunet
Brunet	Josephum Moisem Gulielm	29-SEP-1899	01-OCT-1899	Avila Brunet/Delma Lebeau	Thomas Lepine/Josephina Brunet
Brunet	Luc Joseph	15-MAR-1880	16-MAR-1880	Luca Brunet/Eudoxia Jolie	C. Jolie/E. Brunet
Brunet	Magdelanam-Miriam-Nives	18-AUG-1907	25-AUG-1907	Joseph Brunet/Sarah Pratte	Felix Pratte/Sarah Duquette-Pratte
Brunet	Margarittam Mariam	01-APR-1890	02-APR-1890	Gedeone Brunet/Melina Bastien	Ovides Senecal/Maria-Rosa-Delima Venne
Brunet	Margerian Bernadettam	28-APR-1910	08-MAY-1910	Josepho Brunet/Estella Pratte	Paulus Gangner/Josephine Chaf
Brunet	Mariam Adelinam Luellam	25-JUN-1908	28-JUN-1908	Avila Brunet/Adelina LeBeau	J.J. Balthazar/Emilio LeBeau-Balthazar
Brunet	Mariam Annam Melvinam	24-MAR-1896	25-MAR-1896	Avila Brunet/Delma Lebeau	Moyses Lebeau/Melina Lebeau
Brunet	Mariam Emmam	11-JUN-1885	17-JUN-1885	Luca Brunet/Eudoxia Joly	David Carriere/Lea Theriault
Brunet	Mariam Ester Olepine	29-DEC-1877	30-DEC-1877	Julien Brunet/Melina Bastian	P Sauvé/ wife
Brunet	Mariam Honorinam Teresa	19-MAR-1882	20-MAR-1882	Gedeone Brunet/Rosa-Melina Venne	Evaristus Corbielle/Eudoxia Joly
Brunet	Mariam Mathildam	07-MAY-1898	08-MAY-1898	Ferdinando Brunet/Mathilda Potvin	Thomas Lepine/Josephina Brunet
Brunet	Mariam Rosam	26-APR-1882	27-APR-1882	Lu---co Brunet/Eudoxia Joly	----- Brunet/Teresa Joly
Brunet*	Josephum Napolemem Ed	04-JUN-1905	04-JUN-1905	Ferdinando Brunet/Mathilda Potvin	Avila Brunet/Delina LeBeau-Brunet
Brunet*	Josephum Napoleonem Ed	04-JUN-1905	04-JUN-1905	Ferdinandi Brunet/Mathilda Potvin	Avila Brunet/Delima LeBeau-Brunet
Brunete	Josephinam	04-DEC-1870	04-DEC-1870	Gedeonis Brunete/Melina Bastien	Lucas Brunet/Mathilda Venne
Brunete	Josephum Ferdinandum	23-JUN-1869	23-JUN-1869	Gedeonis Brunete/Melina Bastien	Joannes-Baptista Bastien/Rachel Venne
Brunete	Mariam Josephinam	11-MAY-1868	11-MAY-1868	Gedeoni Brunette/Helena Basquin	Ferdinandus Brunete/Adelma Paquette
Brunett	Mariam Clochildam	31-DEC-1875	02-JAN-1876	Jedien Brunett/Melina Bastian	E. Ninn/ wife
Brunette	Josephum	24-SEP-1873	24-SEP-1873	Cyrilus Brunette/Medina Bastien	Moyses P--qum/Adelaida P--qun
Brunette	Josephum Alphonsum	19-MAY-1880	19-MAY-1880	Gideoni Brunette/Melina Bastien	J. Brunette/C. Bastien
Brunkhorst	Magaratam Lorettam	06-MAR-1910	30-MAR-1910	Georgio Brunkhorst/Stella Atkinson	----- Perinzo-Newman
Brunnell*	Joannem	24-MAY-1858	04-JUL-1858	Joannis Brunnell/Maria Moran	J Brunnell/A Brunnell
Brussel	Mariam Elizabeth	21-JAN-1874	20-FEB-1874	La----L. Brussel/Elizabeth Gautier	----- Gautier/Maria Gautier
Bruwer	Mariam Henriettam	23-APR-1882	13-AUG-1882	Edwardo Brunner/Emelia Cloutier	Ludgerus Prefontaine/Catarina Cray
Bu-	Leonam Mariam	23-MAY-1897	30-MAY-1897	Josepho Buh/Georgina Roy	Liguarius Roy/Maria Faucher
Bubar*	Olivenam	12-SEP-1857	27-SEP-1857	Jeremia Bubar/Lousia Petit	P L'culier/M Chnard
Buch	Augustum Josephum	11-AUG-1866	06-OCT-1866	Augusti Buch/Christina Buch	J. Sheffer/E Wabush
Buch	Mariam Lousam Beatrice	20-JUN-1902	29-JUN-1902	Josepho Buch/Georgina Roy	Arsenus Roy/Emma Allard
Buch*	Gulielmus	26-MAY-1856	05-OCT-1856	Phiranus Buch/Maria Cambert	M. -ha--/M. Thib--t
Buck	Mariam Joannem	14-JAN-1859	23-JAN-1859	Joannis Buck/Ellena Ryan	D King/M Kelly
Buck	Stephen Joseph	24-FEB-1920	07-MAR-1920	Stephen-J Buck/Haninjau	Norbert Buck/Mrs-Martha Green
Buck*	Gulielmum	26-MAY-1856	05-OCT-1856	Christiani Buck/Maria Combert	M. Stras/M. Hibert
Buck*	Michaelem	26-JAN-1856	10-FEB-1856	Joannis Buck/Elena B--ch	T. Frimann/B. Diniger

19

Surname	Given Name	Birth	Baptism	Parents	Godparents
Buck*	Thamam Joannem			Joannis Buck/Ellena Lyon	Deglin King/Maria Kelly
Buckler	Guillelmum Henricum	31-OCT-1866	26-FEB-1867	Joannis Buckler/Joanna Buckler	J Perron/M Pellant
Buh	Josephum Leonem	25-SEP-1894	30-SEP-1894	Josepho Buh/Georgina Roy	Phlias Roy/Ludovica Roy
Buh-	Olivam Mariam	04-MAY-1900	06-MAY-1900	Josepho Buh-/Georgina Roy	Stephanus Buh-/Anna Roy
Bul-s*	Nelson Ludovicum	07-JUL-1860	12-JUL-1860	Nelson Bul-s/Edessa Jabert	S. Hubet/M. Sasoni
Buller*	James	17-SEP-1855	22-SEP-1855	William Buller/Maria-Anna Slon	J. Russel/M. Olery
Buller*	John	18-SEP-1855	22-SEP-1855	William Buller/Maria-Anna Slon	J Rosseter/A. Garper
Bullis	Albinam Appollonam	30-MAR-1863	05-APR-1863	Nwlson Bullis/Edessa Bullis	D Ebert/A Joubert
Bullis	Amatam	17-JUL-1871	23-JUL-1871	Nelsons Bullis/Edessa Bullis	Eugenius Bransheau/Elizabeth Gosselin
Bullis	Carolum	30-AUG-1876	03-SEP-1876	Nelson Bullis/Edis Jubert	J Bullis/H. Bullis
Bullis	Edessam Apollnam	25-DEC-1869	05-JAN-1870	Nelsons Bullis/Edessa Bullis	David Hebert/Clotilda Hebert
Bullis	Helenam Elenoram	13-NOV-1861	17-NOV-1861	Nelson Bullis/Clarissa Bullis	F. Lozon/E. Joubert
Bullis	Joannem Edwardum	07-AUG-1864	21-AUG-1864	Nelson Bullis/Edessa Bullis	C. Joubert/O. Joubert
Bullis	Mariam Adelnam	08-JAN-1828	21-MAR-1883	Joanne Bullis/Adelina Beaudet	Nelson-Ludovicus Bullis/Clarissa ---bert
Bullis	Stephanum Alfredum	04-MAR-1866	01-APR-1866	Nelsons Bullis/Edessa Bullis	N. Ebert/M. Kirk
Bullis*	Nelson				S----- Hubet/----- Hubet
Bullis*	Nelson Ludovicum	07-AUG-1860	12-AUG-1860	Nelson-Ludus Bullis/Edes Jubert	J Cerny/E. Cerny
Burck*	Henora	18-JAN-1857	01-MAR-1857	John Burck/Ellen Ragan	J. H--len/E. Flayerty
Burck*	Mariam Eugeniam	24-AUG-1856	14-SEP-1856	Gulielmi Burck/Maria H--len	Joannes Gray/Maria McCay
Burck*	Michaelem	21-MAR-1860	22-APR-1860	Petri Burck/Anna Garverty	T Freman/B D---
Burck*	Michaelis	26-JAN-1856	10-FEB-1856	John Burck/Ellen Burck	J. McMahan/E Malheur
Burd	John	18-NOV-1851	18-FEB-1852	Michael Burd/Mary Stanten	J Crauley/M. Harnet
Burk	Joannem D.	28-AUG-1863	12-SEP-1863	Matheu Burk/Maria Burk	Ignatius Clotz/Catherine Sneller
Burk	Mary	30-OCT-1858	12-JAN-1859	Michel Burk/Julie Murphy	Michel Burk/Julie Murphy
Burk*	Catherine	23-DEC-1858	12-JAN-1859	Thomas Burk/Hene Kervey	Michel Burk/Julie Murphy
Burk*	Catherine	23-DEC-1858	12-JAN-1859	Thomas Burk/Hene Vervey	J. Burk/M. McNamara
Burk*	Jas.	27-JAN-1859	05-FEB-1859	Mc. Burk/Bridget McNamara	B. Peti/J. Rily
Burk*	Jas. Ptrick	03-MAR-1859	17-MAR-1859	Mcl. Burk/Maria Nugent	D Ryan/A. Crooke
Burke	Guillelmum Telesphorum	21-MAY-1863	31-MAY-1863	Joannis Burke/Helena Burke	J. Roach/M. O'Brian
Burke	Guillelmum Telesphorum		19-MAR-1861	Guillelmi Burke/Maria Burke	T. Burke/M Ga-er
Burke	Hughium		23-FEB-1862	Petri Burke/Anna Burke	M. Burke/B. Burke
Burke	Joannem	09-MAR-1862	28-MAR-1862	Guillelmi Burke/Maria Burke	D. Ryan/B. Ryan
Burke	Mariam	06-FEB-1862	16-FEB-1862	Joannis Burke/Helena Burke	
Burke*	Catherine				
Burke*	Helenam		02-SEP-1860	Joannis Burke/Helena Burke	J Kerny/M Bolan
Burke*	Helenam		02-SEP-1860	Jaonnis Burke/Helena Burke	Jabobus Kerny/Maria Bolan
Burke*	Helenam		02-SEP-1860	Joannis Burke/Elena Burke	J Kerny/M Bolan
Burke*	James				
Burke*	Michel				
Burke*	Thomas John				
Burnal*	Honora				
Burnell	Mariam Arnam	27-MAR-1862	15-MAY-1862	Jacobi Burnell/Maria Burnell	M Flinn/H Flinn
Burnell*	Honora Felice	09-MAY-1860	27-MAY-1860	James Burnell/Maria Roghan	Thomas Whelan/Margeret -----
Burnell*	Joannem	02-MAY-1858	04-JUL-1858	Joannes Burnell/M-ron Rogan	John Burnell/Anna Burnell
Burnes	Mariam Eugeniam	01-FEB-1855	05-FEB-1855	Marci Burnes/Rosanna Oreilly	E. Burnes/R. Harmon
Burns	Franciscum	17-MAY-1852	03-DEC-1852	Francisci Burns/Maria Clary	T. Clary/M Clary
Burns	Joannem		22-MAY-1853	Dyonisius Burns/Catherina Waldo	P. Ladmer/A. Conroy
Burns	Joannem Henricum		19-SEP-1863	Thoma Burns/Bridgitta Burns	J. Griffin/M. Drum
Burns	John Edward	16-JAN-1851	26-JAN-1851	Maurice Burns/Susanna Riley	J. McCabe/-. S-s---

20

Surname	Given Name	Birth	Baptism	Parents	Godparents
Burns	Philippum Theobaldum	17-JAN-1861	16-FEB-1861	Dyonsii Burns/Catharina Burns	J Coughlin/J Coughlin
Burns	Richardum		08-AUG-1863	Dyonsii Burns/Catharina Burns	J Burns/C Fitzsimmons
Burns	Robert		25-DEC-1850	Dennis Burns/Catherine Welsh	W P---/C. Smith
Burns	William	02-FEB-1858	07-MAR-1858	Denis Burns/Jane Ross	Bartholomy T---gg/Mary D--k--
Burns*	Elenam		07-NOV-1858	Dennus Burns/Maria-Cathur Weels	Thamas Blai/Maria Blais
Burns*	Ellen				
Burns*	Gillielmum Josephum	05-MAY-1856	08-JUN-1856	Denisie Burns/Chaterna Welsch	P Nuttigans/M. Mcconnan
Burns*	Gulimus Joseph		08-JUN-1856	Denis Burns/Catherina Welchs	P. Nuttens/M. Mccannan
Burns*	Norbertum	13-JUL-1857	02-AUG-1857	Maurieu Burns/Rosana Rayly	J McGrath/M. McGrath
Buss	Reynaldum	11-JAN-1861	04-JUL-1861	Joannis-Georgus Buss/Christina Buss	J Bissens/M Stratz
Butler	Jacobum Edwardum	17-APR-1863	06-JUL-1863	Patricii Butler/Honora Butler	T Phalan/M. Doyle
Butler*	Charles	20-MAR-1859	13-APR-1859	McI Butler/Helen Brown	M. Reily/P. Reily
Butler*	Charles				
Butler*	Mary				
Butteler*	Gulielmi	18-SEP-1855	22-SEP-1855	Joannes Butteler/Anna Gasper	G. Russel/J. Russel
Butteler*	Joannem	22-JUN-1856	02-AUG-1856	Patricu Butteler/Honora Ragan	M Flind/H O'Bryan
Butteler*	Joannem	18-SEP-1855	22-SEP-1855	Joannes Butteler/Anna Gasper	G Russel/J Russel
Butteler*	Jocobi	18-SEP-1855	22-SEP-1855	Joannes Butteler/Anna Gasper	G Russel/J Russel
Butteler*	Mariam	22-DEC-1858	14-FEB-1859	Patricius Butteler/Honora Rayan	J. Galaur/M. Galaur
Butteler*	Mariam Annam		06-FEB-1853	Guillelmi Butler/Maria-Anna Shea	P. Mckesit-er/M. Oconnel
Butler	Brigitte	17-SEP-1851	25-SEP-1851	Anthony Byrnes/Mary Mellar	J McGown/E. Norton
Byrnes	Joannem		22-MAY-1853	Maurici Byrnes/Rosanna Reilly	P Ri--/---- Rt--
Byrnes	Agnes	23-FEB-1858	17-APR-1858	Wiliam C--ela/--isin Kenderen	James Meglog-pan/Marie -ray
C--elan*	Margeta	02-MAR-1858	04-APR-1858	Charles C-Ivan/Maria Kelly	William Weshs/Mariam Dayle
C-Ivan*	Juliamam	10-NOV-1858	28-NOV-1858	Denis C-nly/Jon--- Logelain	Robert Mullen/Anna Hughes
C-nly*	George Thomas			Pat Ca-rnet/Marg Matthew	R. Matthew M M----
Ca-riet-*	Clementiam	19-FEB-1856	24-AUG-1856	Joseph Cadert/Rosanna Broeker	M. Broeker/L. C--pper
Cadert*	Mariam	18-JAN-1861	27-JAN-1861	Cornelius Cahil/Maria Cahil	G Gallagher/B Gallagher
Cahil	A-a-iam	06-DEC-1858	19-DEC-1858	Cornelie Cahill/Maria McCarthy	Joannes Manly/Maria McGarry
Cahil*	Anasiam	06-DEC-1858	19-DEC-1858	Cornelii Cahil/Maaa Morrisy	Joannes Manly/Maaa Gerry
Cahil*	Anastasia				
Cahil	Helenam	19-AUG-1862	21-AUG-1862	Cornelii Cahil/Maria Cahil	T Gough/A. Molton
Cahil*	Jocabum	26-JUL-1857	02-AUG-1857	Cornelii Cahil/Maria Morris	D Gary/M. Gill
Caily*	Mariam	03-JUL-1858	03-JUL-1858	Petri Caily/Maria Lenschs	Jacobus Flind/Ellisu Flind
Casy*	Joannem Augustinum	20-MAY-1856	20-JUN-1856	Jocobi Caisy/Maria Riburan	J Riburan/M. Gr--n
Cal---	Mariam Annam	24-DEC-1859	28-DEC-1859	James Cal---/Joanna Conner	Michel Megar/Winne Gryffen
Calagan*	Patrick				
Calaghan	Jacobum Edwardum	06-SEP-1861	15-SEP-1861	Joannis Calaghan/Joanna Calaghan	J. Ritchcy/M. Ennis
Calahan	Elizabetham	10-NOV-1863		Joannis Calahan/Rosanna Calahan	M. Gorman/E Malone
Calahan*	Edward				
Call*	Patrick				
Callaghan	Helenam		17-MAY-1863	Joannis Callaghan/Joannah Callaghan	P. Nugent/A Duffy
Callaghan	Michaelem	07-JUN-1863	30-JUN-1863	Bernardi Callaghan/Catharina Callaghan	P. Martin/A. Collins
Calligan	Mary Ann				
Calligan*	Siciliam	14-JAN-1857	18-JAN-1857	Martini Calligan/Brigetha Nutgens	P. Murphy/M Harty
Calombe	Eugenium Josephum	06-JUL-1877	22-JUL-1877	John Calombe/Maria-Josephina Hennigan	----- Painge/ wife
Camasbor	Orlan Henry	29-NOV-1920	26-DEC-1920	Nick Camasbor/Helen Hopper	Henry Hopper/Louisa Gilnezy
Campbell	Isidorum	18-MAR-1855	25-MAR-1855	Josephi Campbell/Flagiola Campbell	I. Chenard/S. Sir
Cane	Brdgitam		14-OCT-1860	Diglani Cane/Anna Cane	P. Henchy/H. Lynch

21

Surname	Given Name	Birth	Baptism	Parents	Godparents
Cane	Guillelmum	09-APR-1861	24-APR-1861	Michaelis Cane/Maria Cane	F McDermott/R McDermott
Cane	Mariam Annam	07-NOV-1862	09-NOV-1862	Michaelis Cane/Catharina Glanon	P Flinn/M. Mangan
Camada	Joannem Maile	13-DEC-1857	22-JAN-1858	Thoma Cannada/Maile Jadener	J Daylic/M. Connor
Camoty*	Elisabeh	12-JUN-1856	02-AUG-1856	Thimthy Cannoty/Maria Currans	R. Cannoty/M. Cannoty
Canoboy	Franciscum Michaelem Er	09-AUG-1908	13-AUG-1908	Michaele Canoboy/Lovina LeBeau	Gulielmus McEasy/Bell Canoboy
Canon*	Mary	05-JAN-1859	05-FEB-1859	John Canon/Ellen Evritt	J Rooney/A. Rooney
Canon*	Mary				
Carbary*	Jocobum Ludovicum	09-JUL-1860	05-AUG-1860	Martini Carbary/Sera McMann	Thomas Kerrans/Margereth Corbet
Carbit*	Deonsium	22-AUG-1856	24-AUG-1856	Joannes Carbit/Julia Currans	M. Currans/J. Currans
Carbit*	Mia Maria	20-FEB-1858	19-MAR-1858	John Carbit/Julie Currans	Julu Naschs/Julie Naschs
Carboneau	Domtilliam	27-JUN-1869	28-JUN-1869	Franciscus Carboneau/Odila Carboneau	Josephus Préfontaine/Adelina Préfontaine
Carboneau	Elizabetham	18-JAN-1867	20-JAN-1867	Eusebii Carboneau/Gertrudis Carboneau	L. Beaudreau/S. Brion
Carboneau	Eulalam Amatam	16-JUL-1868	19-JUL-1868	Eusebii Carboneau/Gertrudia Carboneau	Franciscus-Xaverius Carboneau/Odilia Côté
Carboneau	Leonardum	17-AUG-1860	23-SEP-1860	Francisci Carboneau/Adela Carboneau	E Vadnay/A Dufresne
Carboneau	Ludovicam	31-OCT-1863	26-JAN-1864	Narcissi Carboneau/Odilla Carboneau	F. Carboneau/M. Carboneau
Carboneau	Mariam Melvinam	10-MAR-1867	30-MAR-1867	Francisci Carboneau/Odila Carboneau	A Carboneau/A. Carboneau
Carboneau	Richardum	03-JUN-1865	25-JUN-1865	Francisci Carboneau/Odila Carboneau	F. Dufrésne/---- Ste.-Marie
Carboneau	Rosaliam	30-DEC-1861	19-JAN-1862	Frncisci Carboneau/Odila Carboneau	A Gauther/F. Robert
Carboneau*	Celina				
Carboneau*	James Napolion	05-MAY-1856	08-JUN-1856	Francois Carboneau/Odilida Gilbert	J Duroché/S. Hi--anet
Carboneau*	Ludovicum Napolion	05-MAY-1856	08-JUN-1856	Francisci Carboneau/Odelda Gilbert	J. Duroché/J --ivernet
Carboneau*	Victor	03-AUG-1857	23-AUG-1857	Francois Carboneau/Odekia Gilbert	C. Miller/A. Brion
Carboneau*	Victorem	03-AUG-1857	23-AUG-1857	Francisci Carboneau/Adelina Gilbert	C. Miller/A. Brien
Carbono	Mariam	02-JAN-1876	02-JAN-1876	Francisci Carbono/Ellen White	F Carbono/ wife
Carbory	Carolum	08-NOV-1862	16-NOV-1862	Patricii Carbory/Helena Carbory	P Malone/M. Gough
Carbory	Mariam Helenam	21-SEP-1860	07-OCT-1860	Patricii Carbory/Helena Carbory	G. Dolan/M. Gough
Carbory	Mary Jane	15-AUG-1851	20-SEP-1851	Charles Carbory/Mary McDod	O. McGregor/J. Harkins
Carbory*	Elena	22-AUG-1855	30-SEP-1855	Charles Carbory/Maria McDevit	N Lum/S. Donelly
Carbory*	Elisabetham	19-JUN-1857	26-JUL-1857	Caroli Carbory/Maria McDavid	P Harkens/C. Harkens
Carbory*	James Louis	12-JUN-1857	19-NOV-1857	Patrick Carbory/Ellen Burns	F ----/M. Burns
Carbory*	Jocabum	12-JUN-1857	19-NOV-1857	Patric Carbory/Elena Burns	F. --gn/M. Burns
Carbory*	Patrick				
Carbory	Josephum	19-OCT-1853	29-NOV-1853	Caroli Carbory/Maria McDeed	J. McLevy/R. McGlogelan
Carbory*	Elizam	22-AUG-1855	30-SEP-1855	Caroli Carbory/Maria McDevid	N. Lam/R. Donelly
Carboy*	Patricum	05-MAR-1859	13-MAR-1859	Patrici Carboy/Ellena Burns	W. Rayan/B. Galvin
Cardert*	Clementa	19-FEB-1856	22-AUG-1856	Jossah Cardert/Rossina Brocker	---- Brocker/L --o---r
Cardon	Annonimus	30-JAN-1895	01-FEB-1895	Georgii Cardon/Sara Balthazar	
Carey	Thomam	13-DEC-1863		Michaelis Carey/Maria-Anna Carey	M. O'Brien/B. Nugent
Carley	Evam Bellam		12-SEP-1887		Maglorio Dumas/----- -----
Carment	Annam	20-FEB-1907	03-MAR-1907	Salamone Carment/Maria Kouber	Georgius-Ayaub Gastine/Maria Scaff
Carmody	Agnetam Rosaliam	01-SEP-1862	14-SEP-1862	Danielis Carmody/Maria Carmody	T Newcomb/M. Keerans
Carney	Jacobum	10-AUG-1863	11-AUG-1863	Jacobi Carney/Helena Carney	J Conner/M. Duffy
Carney	Michaelem	10-AUG-1863	11-AUG-1863	Jacobi Carney/Helena Carney	J Conner/M. Duffy
Carny*	Thomas				
Carny*	Maria	07-FEB-1858	20-MAR-1858	James Carny/Ellen Cloos	Thamas Gouf/Margeta Mollen
Carny*	Mariam	07-FEB-1858	20-MAR-1858	Jacobi Carny/Ellena Cloos	T Gery/M. Mallen
Carolin*	Thomam	27-MAR-1860	08-APR-1860	Jacobus Carny/Elena Clos	Patricus Hughs/Joanna Harimann
	Mary Jane				

22

Surname	Given Name	Birth	Baptism	Parents	Godparents
Caron	Albertum	31-MAY-1882	01-JUN-1882	Francisco Caron/Celina Grener	Calixtus Errard/Delphinna Leduc
Caron	Mariam Louisam Amanda	10-JAN-1884	13-JAN-1884	Francisco Caron/Celina Grener	Eduardus Venne/Dalila Beaupre
Caron	Melinam	07-OCT-1880	07-OCT-1880	Francisco Caron/Celina Grenier	D. Carière/L. Térier
Carpenter	Henriettam Mariam	03-JUL-1910	21-JUL-1910	Manly Carpenter/Zoa Surprenand	----- --/Adelina-Maria Moquin-Fox
Carpenter	Manley Arthurum		13-JUN-1903		Gilbertus Surprenant/Zoea Barbeau
Carpenter	Margartam Agnetem	12-OCT-1908	05-NOV-1908	Manly Carpenter/Zoa Surprenand	Gilvertus Suprenand/Zoa Barbeau-Surprenand
Carr*	Mary Jane	04-APR-1858	16-FEB-1859	Edw Carr/Catherine Loyed	J. Furgusson/C. McGinity
Carr*	Mary Jane				
Carrell	Harriettam	28-OCT-1852	28-OCT-1852	Joseph Carrell/Harrietta McDonald	D. Burns/E Ustin
Carrier	Josephum	19-MAY-1855	19-JUL-1855	Joannis-Baptista Carrier/Maria Peron	C Peron/P. Carrier
Carro-*	Jocabum Eduardum	15-JUL-1857	09-AUG-1857	Michaelis Carro-/Elisa Dennely	H Curly/W. Griffen
Carrol	Joannem Henricum	24-JUN-1854	11-JUL-1854	Michaelis Carrol/Margarita Doyle	----- --/M. Mullen
Carroll	Mariam	16-APR-1854	16-JUL-1854	Josephi Carrol/Harrietta McDonnell	J McCoy/A. Rojan
Carroll	Joannem	25-DEC-1863	03-JAN-1864	Danielis Carroll/Elizabetha Carroll	J. Haverty/M. Haverty
Carron*	Jocobus Edmundi	15-JUL-1857	09-AUG-1857	Michel Carron/Elisa Donnely	H Curly/W. Griffen
Cars	Mariam Pal-are	24-DEC-1875	27-DEC-1875	Clemens Cars/Adelle Louffe	J Cars/ A.Cars
Cartazan	Leandrum Theodorum	26-APR-1855	30-APR-1855	Michaelis Cartazan/Rosalia Phang	L. Landerman/J. Mer
Carticher	Esther Ludovicam	22-JAN-1875	24-JAN-1875	L-for Cartcher/Lucina Dufraine	Nazar Munier/Maria Dufraine
Carter	Arthurum	29-SEP-1886	26-APR-1889	Francisco Carter/Virginia Durocher	Alexander Durocher/Elizabeth Durocher
Carter	Claudium Michaelem		27-FEB-1910	Elmero Carter/Mable Porter	Adolphus DeVillers/Doria Perron
Carter	Franciscum Elmer	05-OCT-1884	26-APR-1889	Francisco Carter/Virginia Durocher	Adolphus Durocher/Sophia Pellant
Carter	Heleniam Elizabetham	01-AUG-1852	12-SEP-1852	Harvey Carter/Marguerita Mullen	J. Lawler/M. Mullen
Cartier	Henricum ------	21-JUL-1873	27-JUL-1873	Claford Carter/Damina Dufresne	Petrus Dufresne/Onesima Meunier
Cary	Catherine	18-SEP-1857	07-FEB-1858	Mcl. Cary/Ellen Slattery	Phlippe Massenth/Elizab Oberty
Cary	Mariam	15-FEB-1862	23-FEB-1862	Guillelmi Cary/Catharina Cary	J Cary/M. Murry
Cary*	Jeremiah				
Casey	Edwardum	31-OCT-1861	25-NOV-1861	Jacobi Casey/Maria Casey	P. Tierney/M. Liston
Cassidy*	Guillelmus	02-AUG-1856	10-AUG-1856	Petrus Cassidy/Joanna Mcman	----- --/----- Dogethy
Casten	Mariam Annam	24-JAN-1863	25-JAN-1863	Thoma Casten/Maria Casten	T Brown/B. Casten
Caufield	Mariam Annam	12-SEP-1852	26-SEP-1852	Patricii Caufield/Brigitta Kirshum	M. Mullen/M. Egan
Caufield	Thomas	12-DEC-1850	14-DEC-1850	Patrick Caufield/Brigitte Crushen	W. Welsh/M. July
Cavanagh*	Mariam Leocadie	16-MAY-1859	12-JUN-1859	Danielis Cavanagh/Cath. O'Donahoe	M. Manning/A. Fitzgerald
Cavanaugh	Marguaritam Annam	25-MAR-1862	30-MAR-1862	Joannis Cavanaugh/Marguarita Cavanaugh	G. Gibson/M. Gibson
Cavanaugh*	Mary				
Cavanaugh*	Mary Louisa				
Cavennish	Franciscum Eduardum	22-APR-1858	29-APR-1858	Joannis Cavennish/Margeretha Sh--son	T. Chousan/M. Egan
Cayer	Narcissum	25-JUL-1864	27-SEP-1864	----- -----/Sophia Cayer	P Cayer/C Cayer
Cayet	Mariam Leucadiam	02-OCT-1861	27-JUL-1862	----- -----/Maria Cayet	J. Dumas/M. Perron
Cayriet*	George Thomas				
Chagnon	Mariam Eugeniam	26-JUL-1872	26-JUL-1872	Eli Chagnon/Philomena Chagnon	Josephus Leduc/Marguarita Leduc
Chagnon	Mariam Josephinam	26-APR-1871	26-APR-1871	Elia Chagnon/Philomena Chagnon	Guillelmus Chagnon-Leduc/Delphina Leduc
Chagnon	Mariam Victoriam	03-AUG-1873	05-AUG-1873	Elias Chagnon/Philomena Leduc	Theodulus Millotte/Rosa Leduc
Chain*	Catherinam	22-MAR-1857	30-MAR-1857	Patricii Chain/Hanora Connar	J Honne-an/M Honne-an
Chall*	Catharina-				
Chall*	Catharina	04-AUG-1860	12-AUG-1860	Patrici- Chall/Maria Barole	Joannes Doley/Julie Dooley
Chambeau	Ludovicum Josephum	17-AUG-1876	27-AUG-1876	Ludovici Chambeau/Lucie Letournau	P. Leturn--/ wife
Channière	Josephum Eusebium	22-DEC-1867	01-JAN-1868	Joannis-Baptista Channière/Rosalia Ebert	E Laliberté/C. Roi
Chanty*	Joannem	24-MAR-1858	24-MAR-1858	Patrici Chanty/Elisabetha Casshely	J. Casshely/A. Birmingham
Chapeleau	Mariam Virginam	02-JAN-1869	03-JAN-1869	Toussaintis Chapeleau/Virgivia Chapeleau	Joannis Dero----/Celina Dero----

23

Surname	Given Name	Birth	Baptism	Parents	Godparents
Chapeleau	Toussaint Wilfredem	16-JUL-1870	17-JUL-1870	Toussanti Chapeleau/Virginia Chapcleau	Franciscus Marcou/Josephina Marcou
Chapeller	Davidem		22-SEP-1873	-----Chapeller/Zilta Ebert	Eugenii Brancheraud/Maria Brancheraud
Chaperon	Adelbertum Leonem	20-MAY-1901	26-MAY-1901	Davide Chaperon/Etta Lepine	Josephus Lepine/Sophia Beaudreault
Chaperon	Albertum Davidem		04-MAR-1888	Davido Chaperon/Delia Loiseau	Gulielmus Loiseau/Anna Trahan
Chaperon	Carolum Walter	14-JAN-1884	27-JAN-1884	David Chaperon/Delia Loiseau	Ferdinandus Bergemann/Josephina Timm
Chaperon	Claram Emma	09-NOV-1877	08-DEC-1877	Theophle Chaperon/Clara Wellard	----- rge/ wife
Chaperon	David Edmundem	05-OCT-1879	12-OCT-1879	Davidi Chaperon/Delia L'Oiseau	S Demers/E Loiseau
Chaperon	Doram Mariam	15-JUN-1890	15-JUL-1890	David Chaperon/Delia Loiseau	Henricus Schneider/Julia Loiseau
Chaperon	Eduardum Carlisle	15-MAR-1903	22-MAR-1903	Davide-Eduardo Chaperon/Etta Lepine	Davidus Chaperon/Delia Bird-Loiseau
Chaperon	Gulielmum Henricum	09-FEB-1886	28-FEB-1886	David Chaperon/Delia Loiseau	Carolus Loiseau/Martha Bisson
Chaperon	Idam Josephinam	24-OCT-1881	06-NOV-1881	David Chaperon/Rosa-Delima Loiseau	Alexander ---coup/Angelina Beaudreault
Chaperon	Joannem Donaldum	05-FEB-1910	13-FEB-1919	Eduardo Chaperon/Etta Lepine	-----/May LePine
Chaperon	Josephum Earl		20-NOV-1898	Davide Chaperon/Delia Loiseau	Ludgerius Dupuy/Juliano Lucier
Chaperon	Léon	26-SEP-1862	02-NOV-1863	Ludovici Chaperon/Adelina Chaperon	O. Dodelin/S. Dodelin
Chaperon	Mariam Ethel	18-FEB-1905	03-MAR-1905	Eduardi Chaperon/Esther Lepine	Alexander Marcoux/Orzelia Beaudreau
Chaperson	Gertrudam Leonam	31-JAN-1906	06-JAN-1907	Eduardo Chaperon/Etta LePine	Josephus Dubois/Cedulia Beaudrea-Dubois
Chaquette	George Edé	13-JUN-1875	04-JUL-1875	Joseph Chaquette/Hélène Jolin	Joseph Como/Flavie Robert
Charbonneau	Josephum	22-JUL-1867	04-AUG-1867	Francisci Charboneau/Eulalia-Cecilia Charboneau	E. Charboneau/G. Comrie
Charbonneau	Amatam Gladice	07-MAR-1902	09-MAR-1902	Eusebio Charbonneau/Delphina Pomminville	Josephus-Eusebus Charbonneau/Gertrudis Comeau
Charbonneau	Dyonisiam	20-AUG-1869	28-SEP-1869	Francisci-X Charbonneau/Emilia-C Charbonneau	Josephus Lemire/Dyonisia Lemre
Charbonneau	Errol Arthurum	30-APR-1905	02-MAY-1905	Eusebii Charbonneau/Delia Pominville	Fredericus Breister/Elizabeth Charbonneau
Charbonneau	Haroldum Arthurum	30-APR-1905	02-MAY-1905	Eusabis Charbonneau/Delia Pomainville	Fredericus Breister/Elizabeth Charbonneau
Charbonneau	Josephum Israelem	09-SEP-1908	13-SEP-1908	Eusebis Charbonneau/Delphna Pomainville	Michael Pomainville/Sopha Gratton-Pomainville
Charbonneau	Walter Clarence Paulum	29-DEC-1909	01-JAN-1910	Eusebis Charbonneau/Delphine Pomainville	Gulielmus Pomainville/Eleonora Marcoux
Charbono	Eda	15-OCT-1875	02-NOV-1875	Louis Charbono/Agnes Mody	W. Curry/ wife
Charbory*	Elisubcht	09-JUN-1857	26-JUL-1857	Charles Charory/Marie McDevid	P. Harkens/C Ceres
Charete	Joannem Baptistam	11-AUG-1872	08-SEP-1872	Joannis-Baptista Charete/Ludovica Charete	Eduardus Charete/Julia Lemre
Charky*	Jocobus	25-FEB-1858	27-FEB-1858	Michel Charky/Brigeta Dou-y	Michel C-rons/Brigeta Donnell
Charron	Margaritam Catharinam	16-MAY-1907	26-MAY-1907	Achilla Charron/Margarita Landolf	Theodorus Landolf/Mamie Landolf
Charron	Nicholaum Leonem	09-JAN-1909	24-JAN-1909	Achilla Charron/Margarita Laudolf	Nicholaus Landolf/Maria Laudolf
Chartrand	Delima		07-JUN-1868	Francisci Chartrand/Adelina Chartrand	Franciscus Chartrand/Henrieta Touchete
Chartrand	Emeritum	27-JUL-1862	30-AUG-1862	Francisci Chartrand/Vitalna Chartrand	S. Touchete/H. Leclerc
Chartrand	Eulaliam	08-FEB-1865	19-FEB-1865	Francisci Chartrand/Vitalna Chartrand	J Gauther/E. Dionne
Chartrand	Franciscum	03-JUL-1868	25-OCT-1868	Francisci Chartrand/Vitalna Touchete	Josephus Touchete/Henrica Tourchete
Chaumière	Mathildam	28-MAY-1861	30-MAY-1861	Baptista Chaumière/Rosala Chaumière	G Wo--et/V Wo--et
Chaumière	Domitillam	12-SEP-1867	13-OCT-1867	Moysis Chaumière/Philomena Chaunière	M Tremblé/M Tremblé
Chaunière	Josephinam	26-SEP-1864	18-DEC-1864	Baptista Chaumière/Rosala Chaunière	C Tremblé/C. Fernet
Chaunière	Mariam Josephinam	06-FEB-1866	13-FEB-1866	Moysis Chaunière/Philomena Chaunière	I. Chaunière/P. Létourneau
Chaunere*	Otto Petrus	05-JAN-1858	01-FEB-1858	Engelutrs Chauniere/Anna-Maria Bigeter	Welgelmus ----nn-/----- ----
Chef	Albertum	02-MAY-1866	13-MAY-1866	Petrus Chef/Christina Chef	J. Chef/F. Thibaudeau
Chef	Aliciam	30-APR-1867	12-JUL-1867	Petri Chef/Christina Chef	M. Montblot/M. Bastien
Chef	Amabilem	28-JUL-1872	28-JUL-1872	-----/Philomena Chef	Carolus Beauregard/ Salomé
Chef	Andream Henricum	10-MAR-1865	19-MAR-1865	Petri Chef/Christina Chef	P Chef Jr./J. Touchete
Chef	Julianam	23-JUL-1862	27-JUL-1862	Petri Chef/Christina Chef	A. G-zet/C Garro
Chef	Ludovicam Paulam	07-AUG-1873	10-AUG-1873	Petri Chef/Christina Trudeau	Theo---- Viene/Maria Des------
Chef	Marguaritam	08-OCT-1863	11-OCT-1863	Petrus Chef/Christina Chef	L. Samson/P. Rondeau
Chef	Mariam Leam	08-JUL-1874	08-JUL-1874	Petri Chef/Josephina Touchette	Eugenius Robert/Christna Duquette
Chef	Onesimum	20-MAR-1870	20-MAR-1870	Petri Chef/Christina Chef	Onesimus Kéné/Christina Rondeau
Chef	Petrum Josephum	26-MAY-1872	09-JUN-1872	Petri Chef/Josephina Chef	Josephus --quete/Virginia Touchete

24

Surname	Given Name	Birth	Baptism	Parents	Godparents
Chef*	Gulemus	23-APR-1857	26-APR-1857	Pierre Chef/Christine Randeau	F Pellant/C. Delap---
Chef*	Gulhelmum	23-APR-1857	26-APR-1857	Petri Chef/Christina Randeau	F. Pellant/C. Delarochette
Chef*	Henricum	17-DEC-1858	19-DEC-1858	Petri Chef/Christina Randeau	Ludovicus Randeau/Josephus Randeau
Chef*	Joannem	17-AUG-1860	19-AUG-1860	Petrus Chef/----- Rondeau	Juger Duquet/Josephina Pedelant
Chef*	Joannes	17-AUG-1860	19-AUG-1860	Petri Chef/T -andeau	J. Duquet/J Peldelant
Chef*	John				
Chef	Louis Henry				
Cheff	Franciscum	17-DEC-1875	20-DEC-1875	Francisci Cheff/Avelli Gray	J. Duquet/J. Cheff
Cheffer	Elizabetham	24-FEB-1855	21-APR-1855	Josephi Cheffer/Maria Meyers	J Wagoner/E. Everling
Cheffer	Michaelem	12-FEB-1857	15-FEB-1857	Davidus Cheffer/Margeretha Hurlings	M. Curlings/F. Curran
Cheffer	Annam Mariam	08-SEP-1855	16-SEP-1855	Danielis Cheffer/Margareta Hurlings	J Cheffer/A. But-
Cheffer*	Joannem	05-MAR-1859	19-APR-1867	Josephi Cheffer/Maria Landsmacher	J. Haas/M Curlings
Cheffer*	Josephum	05-MAR-1859	20-MAR-1859	Danielis Cheffer/Margetha Curlings	J. Chffa/A. -hu--bais
Chefs*	Ludovicum	17-DEC-1858	19-DEC-1858	Peter Chefs/Christna Randeau	Ludovicus-Josephus Randeau/Christina Chefs
Cheil*	Marguaritam	01-JUN-1858	01-JUL-1858	Patricii Cheil/Maria Bowlen	C. Donagh--/M Cox
Cheiland*	Marguerite	01-JUN-1858	01-JUL-1858	Patrick Cheiland/Mary Bowler	Cornelius Donahue/Mary Cox
Chenar	Arbelum Alexandrum	20-MAR-1865	18-APR-1865	Theophili Chenar/Maria Beaudin-Chenar	P. Odet/
Chenar	Emilam	15-NOV-1862	15-FEB-1863	Teophili Chenar/Maria Chenar	T Deschenes/C. Deschenes
Chenar*	Joseph				
Chenar*	Theophile				
Chenard*	Ludovicum	01-FEB-1858	02-FEB-1858	Isedori Chenard/Sophia Sir	T Chenard/- Chenard
Chenart	Carolum Albertum	03-AUG-1883	12-AUG-1883	Ludovico Chenart/Philumena Denault	Alphonsus Chenart/Ezilda Tessier
Chenart	Eugenium	30-DEC-1886	09-JAN-1887	Alphonso Chenart/Ezilda Tessier	Josephus Chenart/Maria-Joanna Staff
Chenart	Franciscum Oliverum	30-JUN-1881	24-JUL-1881	Alphonso Chenart/Ezilda Tessier	Franciscus Marcoux/Emelia St.-Germain
Chenart	Georgium Eduardum	06-OCT-1886	14-NOV-1886	Ludovico Chenart/Philumena Deneau	Georgius Chenart/Ezilda Chenart
Chenart	Ludovicum Moisen	16-SEP-1881	22-SEP-1881	Ludovico Chenart/Philamena Daneau	Moises Bissonnette/Adela Daneau
Chenart	Maram Angelam	12-APR-1884	27-APR-1884	Alphonso Chenart/Eszilda Tessier	Ludovicus Chenart/Philomene Denneau
Chenart	Rosam Ellam	27-OCT-1889	19-NOV-1889	Ludovico Chenart/Philumena Deneau	Petrus Deneau/Clementina Beaulieu
Cherben	Ema Mecede	24-MAR-1878	24-MAR-1878	Jorge Cherben/Lina Pangier	S. Dupuis/E. Pangier
Cherdan*	Brigetham	21-SEP-1855	15-OCT-1855	Philipi Cherdan/Elisabetha Ward	B Cherdan/S McGrath
Cherghenger	Jeremas	20-SEP-1857	20-SEP-1857	Jeremias Cherghenger/Lebadena Nubber	J. Heiss/C. Heiss
Chill--	Maria Desée	28-DEC-1879	07-MAY-1880	Roberto Chill--/Adele Belhumeur	A. Roi/----- ----
Chinard	Philomina	01-NOV-1855	16-NOV-1855	Issidore Chinard/Sophia Sir	V. Langlois/P Sir
Chinard*	Ludovicus	01-FEB-1858	02-FEB-1858	Isidore Chinard/Sophie -ee	Thophelus Chinard/Julie Chinard
Chinard*	Philomenam	10-DEC-1855	16-DEC-1855	Bedoni Chinard/Sophia Sir	V Langlois/P Sir
Chinard*	Philomina	10-DEC-1855	16-DEC-1855	Isidore Chinard/Sophie Sir	Vital Langlois/Phil---- Sir
Chinard*	Theophilem	08-NOV-1858	13-NOV-1858	Theophli Chinard/Sara Boraseau	Peter Leceulier/Margertha Goyet
Chiperon	Marion Ethel	18-FEB-1905	03-MAR-1905	Eduardo Chiperon/Otha Lepine	Alexander Marcoux/Orzelia Beaudreau-Marcoux
Chogeson	Marge				
Choieri*	Moises	22-SEP-1858	23-SEP-1858	Baptita Choieri/Rosalia Hubert	Antoine Demarai/Dclai Delu-
Choll*	Catharina	04-JUL-1860	12-JUL-1860	Patrici Choll/Maria Bor-le-	J. Dooley/J. Dooley
Chonière*	Agapita				
Chonière*	Loyes				
Choquet	Eusebium	03-AUG-1865	17-SEP-1865	Josephi Choquet/Helena-Marie Jolin	M Jolin/M Larie
Choquete	Josephum Franciscum Guil	09-JAN-1873	16-FEB-1873	Joseph Choquete/Helena ------	Frs Beauchemin/Celina Lucier
Choquette	Henricam	22-JUL-1869	25-JUL-1869	Josephi Choquete/Maria-Helena Choquete	Michael Jolin/Olivia Paulin
Chorets*	Mathias	28-DEC-1857	17-JAN-1858	Josechs Chorets/Margeta Ring	Mathias Miller/Regina Muller
Christ	Annam Catharinam Emilia	10-DEC-1863	08-MAY-1864	Nicholai Chrrst/Catharina Christ	C. Rohr/C. Paas
Chu----	Maria Ludovica	31-MAY-1879	01-JUN-1879	Eli--- Chu---/Philomena Leduc	S. Houdon/J. Leduc

25

Surname	Given Name	Birth	Baptism	Parents	Godparents
Chull*	Janna	03-JUL-1859	04-SEP-1859	Carlum Chull/Caterina Kelly	D Will/E Kelly
Cicar	Alfert	18-DEC-1875	26-DEC-1875	Desire Cicar/Inez Laplante	A. Randoux/M. Randeau
Cla-y*	Mariam	16-DEC-1859	04-FEB-1860	Thoma Cla-y/Maria Bays	Jacobus Nashs/Maria ---Ivy
Clack*	Elisabth	18-MAY-1858	29-MAY-1858	Carnelius Clack/Catherina Kelly	Francus Wall/Martha Wall
Clack*	Maria		03-JAN-1857	Thamas Clack/Maria Lensh	C. Donego/M -----
Clack*	Mariam	14-DEC-1856	03-JAN-1857	Thoma Clack/Maria Lienschs	C. Dunegan/B. Gillan
Clancy*	Bridget				
Clancy*	Brigitta	22-MAR-1860	24-MAR-1860	John Clancy/Margoretta White	Joannis Malone/Margaretta Miles
Clarck*	Elisabetham	14-MAY-1858	27-MAY-1858	Cornelii Clarck/Catherina Kelly	F. Wall/M Wall
Clarck*	James	31-JUL-1855	19-AUG-1855	Cornelius Clarck/Cath Kelly	T Stanton/M. Kelly
Clarck*	Maria Lisabeh	07-NOV-1856	14-DEC-1856	L--y Clarck/Ma-- Be--	J. Galliger/E. ----]
Clarck*	Mariam Elisabetham	17-NOV-1856	14-DEC-1856	L. Clarck/Maria Bie	J Galliger/M. Galliger
Clarek	Margeretham	07-FEB-1857	22-FEB-1857	Carnalius Clarek/Catherina Kelly	J Doyle/A Doyle
Clark	Jacobum Francisceum	12-JUN-1854	04-JUL-1854	Jacobi Clark/Rosa Neuken	P. Neuken/M. McCune
Clark	Margeta	07-FEB-1857	22-FEB-1857	Cornelius Clark/Cather Kelly	J Dug--/H Doyle
Clark	Mariam Annam	06-NOV-1852	11-DEC-1852	Jacobi Clark/Rosa Newcome	G Gipson/M. Mcenroe
Clark	Thomam	27-AUG-1852	03-SEP-1852	Thoma Clark/Maria Lynch	P. Geelan/B. Geelan
Clark*	John				
Clarke	Catharinam		02-DEC-1860	Guillelmi Clarke/Maria Clarke	J. Sicor/H. Murphy
Clarke	Emiliam	03-JUL-1863	06-JUL-1863	Cornelii Clarke/Catharina Clarke	M. Cane/M. Cane
Clarke	Helenum Joannam	20-AUG-1863	25-OCT-1863	Joannis Clarke/Elizabetha Clarke	R Flood/J. Mangel
Clarke	Marguaritam	18-FEB-1863	28-FEB-1863	Guillelmi Clarke/Maria Clarke	P. Farrell/M. Cavanaugh
Clary	Thomas	10-SEP-1851	15-NOV-1851	Maurice Clary/Johanna McDonald	J Corbet/M Burns
Clay*	Mary				
Clay	Annam	08-DEC-1854	16-DEC-1854	Joannis Clay/Maria Smet	P. Shoemaker/A Capserett
Cleffert*	Mary Ann	20-JAN-1859	15-FEB-1859	John Cleffert/Cath. Henson	E Maloy/M. Flint
Cleffert*	Mary Ann				
Clerck	Genevam	12-OCT-1853	23-OCT-1853	Thoma Clerck/Maria Lynch	J Poran/M Derrelhy
Clerek*	Jocobus	31-JUL-1855	19-AUG-1855	Cornelius Clerck/Catharina Kelly	T Stenten/M. Kelly
Cliche	Carolum Cyrlum	08-MAR-1869	27-MAR-1869	Ludovici Cliche/Delphina Dufresne	Cyricus Corbeil/Anastasia Dufort
Cliche	Elizabetham	16-AUG-1866	26-AUG-1866	Joannis Cliche/Delphina Dufresne-Cliche	F. Dufresne/E. Ste.-Marie
Cliche	Evaristam	24-OCT-1861	03-NOV-1861	Ludovici Cliche/Delphina Dufrain	E. Vadney/A Dufresne
Cliche	Joannem Baptistam	24-JUL-1879	03-AUG-1879	Ludovico Cliche/Delphina Dufresne	L. Cliche/E Dufresne
Cliche	Juliam Delphinam	19-DEC-1862	21-DEC-1862	Ludovici Cliche/Delphina Cliche	P. Dufresne/C Meunier
Cliche	Julianum	27-MAR-1868	27-MAR-1868	Ludovici Cliche/Dolphina Dufresne	Julianus Edoun/Elizabetha Malheur
Cliche*	Sarahm Ellam	12-FEB-1865	19-FEB-1865	Ludovici Cliche/Delphina Cliche	P. Dufresne/S. Ste.-Marie
Clm*	Louis				
Clis*	John				
Clish	Ludovicum	05-MAY-1860	05-MAY-1860	Ludovici Clis/Adeline Dufrain	Antonus DuFort/Justine Clis
Clish	Michaelem Josephum	14-JUL-1884	05-AUG-1884	Ludovico Clish/Delphne Dufresne	Petrus Lepne/Josephne Corbeille
Clish	Nazarum Alfredum	06-JUN-1882	25-JUN-1882	Ludovico Clish/Delphina Dufrain	-----Nazarus Dam/Catarina Andres
Cliss	Josephum	24-SEP-1875	26-SEP-1875	Ludovici Cliss/Adolphina Dufrain	P. Dufran/J ------
Clom	Marcellum Guillelmum	22-FEB-1869	04-APR-1869	Joannis Clom/Maria-Josephina Clom	Guillelmus Riche/Emilia Joli
Closset	Georgeum Thomam	03-APR-1854	08-MAY-1854	Thoma Closset/Maria Cay	J Regan/A Regan
Closy*	Thamas Hennery	26-NOV-1855	23-JAN-1856	Thamas Closy/Maria Bays	C. Gilan/E. Bays
Closy*	Thomam Henricum	26-NOV-1855	23-JAN-1856	Thoma Closy/Maria Bays	C. Gillan/E Bays
Clow-	Joannem	13-JUN-1864	03-JUL-1864	Joannis Clow-/Maria-Josephina Clow-	P. Breister/M. Brester
Clum	Ludovicum Ambrosium	25-MAR-1872	15-APR-1872	Joannis Clumi/Josephina Clum	Petrus Coté/Delma Colomb
Clumb	Eugerum Norbertum	27-JUL-1870	20-AUG-1870	Joannis Clumb/Maria-Josephna Clumb	Ludgerus Préfontaine/Cezarina Chaumière

Surname	Given Name	Birth	Baptism	Parents	Godparents
Clyche	Margaritam	18-OCT-1873	18-OCT-1873	Ludovicu Clyche/Delphina Dufresne	Noel Dufresne/Margarita Dufresne
Clynch	Tomam Henricum	14-JUN-1884	15-JUN-1884	Thom-Henry Clynch/Oliva Lussier	Moise Tremblay/Marie-Eugenie Lussier
Cobuss	Isabellam	29-JAN-1860	13-SEP-1860	Francisci-Josephi Cobuss/Maria-Catherine Cobuss	S. Dietzenbach/----- -----
Cod*	Joannem	19-APR-1857	20-APR-1857	Patricii Cod/Maria McCay	P. Mcnulty/M. ---va-
Cod*	John	09-APR-1857	20-APR-1857	Patrick Cod/Maria McCay	P. McNelly/M. ---van
Codd	Guillelmum	24-JUL-1852	25-JUL-1852	Patricii Codd/Maria McCoy	P. McNealy/R. McCoy
Coddi*	Marie	22-MAY-1857	07-JUN-1857	Kirian Coddi/Anna Phalan	D Phalan/A Mullon
Codi*	Mariam	22-MAY-1857	07-JUN-1857	Kirran Codi/Anna Phalan	D Phalan/A. Mullen
Cody	Keeranum	07-DEC-1861	13-JAN-1862	Keeram Cody/Anna Cody	J Fagan/H. Cody
Cody	Mariam	22-APR-1861	22-APR-1861	Patricii Cody/Maria Cody	P Cane/B. -ernan
Cody*	Martin Augustin				
Cody*	Martinum Augustin	20-SEP-1859	02-OCT-1859	Herron Cody/Aanna Phellon	P Phelan/C. Flannigan
Coens*	Jacob				
Coens*	Jocob	14-AUG-1858	23-SEP-1858	Jocob Coens/Katerina --ee	Hueh D--phy/---- --phy
Coff---*	Mariam Eugeniam	20-SEP-1856	20-DEC-1856	Petrus Coff---/Brigetha Ciressin	P. Kelly/ M
Coffield*	Bedelia				
Coffner	Barbaram	07-JUL-1862	11-SEP-1862	Joannis Coffner/Maria Coffner	J Coffner/B Goëther
Cogelan*	Agnes	23-FEB-1858	17-APR-1858	Wellhelm Cogelan/Theresa Kinderan	J McGlogelan/M. Craé
Cokeler	Joannem	10-JAN-1863	14-JAN-1863	Guillelmi Cokeler/Theresa Cokeler	E Cary/C. Leonard
Colagan*	Patrick	07-FEB-1859	13-MAR-1859	Mcl. Colagan/Margeret Honagham	E. O'Harden/C O'Harden
Colahan*	Eduardum	06-MAY-1859	07-MAY-1859	Patritii Colahan/Annam Hennesse	T Ready/H. Smith
Coleman	Catharinam	28-DEC-1854	01-JAN-1855	Patrick Coleman/Bridgidda O'Brien	P. O'Brien/M O'Brien
Coleman	Helenam Marguaritam		15-JAN-1861	Patrick Coleman/Bridgetta Coleman	J Brown/M Tracy
Coleman	Michaelm Jeremiam	26-APR-1863	11-MAY-1863	Patricii Coleman/Bridgetta Coleman	P Gillen/M Walsh
Coleman	Patrick Henry	17-OCT-1851	28-OCT-1851	Patrick Coleman/Brigitte Bryan	J. Obrian/S Coleman
Coleman*	Brigta	29-OCT-1856	02-NOV-1856	Patrick Coleman/Brigitta O'Bryan	T. Bassy/H. Legée
Colette	Michaelem		16-MAR-1908	Samuelo Colette/Anna Lambert	Paulus Lambert/Angela Robidoux
Colette	Paulum		16-MAR-1908	Samuelo Colette/Anna Lambert	Onesimus Robidoux/Marcelne Robidoux
Coll*	Patricum	27-DEC-1858	10-JAN-1859	Patricii Coll/Mara McCay	Philiphus Hagun/Dora Nicholus
Coll*	Patricum	27-DEC-1858	10-JAN-1859	Patricii Coll/Mara McCay	Philiphus Halpin/Sera Nicolus
Collin	Adelam	20-NOV-1865	21-NOV-1865	Octavi Collin/Julia Anna Collin	P. Garo/R. Garo
Collin	Amablem		25-AUG-1867	Octavi Collin/Julia Collin	G Collin/A Garo
Collin	Julian Annam	26-JAN-1870	27-JAN-1870	Octavi Collin/Julie-Anna Collin	Joannes Beaulieu/Maria Ducharme
Collin	Mariam Octaviam	30-MAR-1853	15-JUN-1853	Octavi Collin/Octavia Collin	G Ouellette/----- Ouellette
Collin*	Francis				
Collin*	Maria Arieta	24-APR-1857	29-APR-1857	---ovi Collin/Marie Beaulieu	L. Petit/F Maret
Collin*	Mariam	27-APR-1857	29-APR-1857	Antone Collin/Mara Beaulieu	L Petit/F Manet
Colman*	Brigetham	29-OCT-1856	02-NOV-1856	Patrici Colman/Brigetha O'Bryan	T Barry/H. Legee
Colombe	Georgium Israelem	19-DEC-1865	07-JAN-1866	Georgii Colombe/MariaColombe	I. Bassette/J. Bassette
Colombe	Mariam Margaritam	12-JUN-1873	22-JUN-1873	Joannis Colombe/Maria-Josephina ---nnicka	Joseph Moridz/Margarita Moridz
Colombe	Mariam Rosam Delma	08-AUG-1867	03-NOV-1867	Joannis Colombe/Maria-Josepha Colombe	J Aucher/M. Colombe
Colp	Mariam Annam Helenam	03-OCT-1861	13-OCT-1861	Bernardi Colp/Maria Elizabetha Colp	J Pomerich/H. Wirtzburger
Colp	Michaelem	02-MAR-1864	20-MAR-1864	Bernardi Colp/Elizabetha Colp	M. Giebel/M. Breister
Columbe	Franciscum	28-SEP-1874	11-OCT-1874	Joannis Columbe/Josephina Henniger	David Beaupré/--o- Durant
Comeau	Alfredum Davidem	10-JAN-1896	02-FEB-1896	Arthuro Comeau/Maria Vass	Medorus Comeau/Mathilda Diette
Comeau	Edgardum Arthurum		28-MAY-1899	Arthuro Comeau/Philumena Voss	Ludovicus Michotte/Ida Hilt
Comeau	Ellahue Josephum	31-AUG-1903	31-JUL-1906	Arthuro Comeau/Philumena Voss	Deusdotus Michotte/Julianna Lucier-Dupus
Comeau	Helenam Philumenam	20-MAR-1894	05-APR-1894	Arthuro Comeau/Philumena Voss	Josephus Comeau/Margarita Duffy
Comeau	Josephum Georgium	19-OCT-1889	27-OCT-1889	Josepho-Medardo Comeau/Mathilda Diette	Josephus Comeau/Ezilda Diette

Surname	Given Name	Birth	Baptism	Parents	Godparents
Comeau	Josephum Victorem	23-APR-1902	02-OCT-1902	Arthuro Comeau/Maria Vass	------/Celina Lucier
Comeau	Laurentium Ambrostum	08-AUG-1897	15-AUG-1897	Arthuro Comeau/Maria Bu-	Ludgerus Dupuy/Juliana Lussier
Comeau	Mariam Ednam	16-JUL-1897	25-JUL-1897	Medardo Comeau/Mathilda Diette	Joannes Mengel/Maria Qunn
Comeau	Mariam Majaram	02-SEP-1900	02-OCT-1902	Arthuro Comeau/Maria Voss	Gullelmus Durocher/Jessic Comeau
Comeau	Mariam Rosam Annam	03-MAR-1891	07-MAR-1891	Medardo Comeau/Mathilda Diette	Joseph Diette/Celina Lucier
Comeau	Maximan	05-FEB-1906	31-JUL-1906	Arthuro Comeau/Philomena Voss	Celonise Cerrard/------
Comeau	Alfredum Ernestum		16-APR-1871	Nelson Coming/Julia Bertrand	Nelson Strong/Maria Tete
Comung	Narsisium	30-OCT-1878	14-APR-1878	Josephi Commin/Josephna Gothier	C. Errard/ (wife)
Commin	Bernard Charles	22-JUL-1912	17-AUG-1918	Arthur Commo/Wilhelmina Voss	Charles Errard/Dorothy Commo
Commo	Franciscum Fabicn	03-MAR-1915	17-AUG-1918	Arthur Commo/Wilhelmina Voss	Charles Errard/Dorothy Commo
Commo	Georgum Victor	31-MAY-1875	05-JUN-1875	Josephi Commo/Selina Lucia	Essau Lucia/Magerth Lucia
Commo	Raymond George	08-FEB-1919	16-FEB-1919	George Commo/Etta-Marie DuBois	Geo. Dubois/Mathilda Commo
Commo	Josephum Arthurum Isaiam	30-NOV-1869	05-DEC-1869	Joseph Como/Maria-Celina Lucier	Eusebius Laliberté/Cleophia Roi
Como	Josephum Théodorum	11-APR-1868	19-APR-1868	Joseph Como/Celina Lucier	Josephus Choquette/Sophrinia Lucier
Como	Medarum	15-OCT-1865	22-OCT-1865	Joseph Como/Celina Lhuissier	L. L'huissier/P. Regnier
Como	Victoriam Celinam Josephi	29-MAY-1872	01-JUN-1872	Joseph Como/Celina Lucier	Camillus Lucier/Adelina Garo
Conaboy	Bellam Angelam	14-MAY-1892	15-MAY-1892	Michaeli Conaboy/Malvina Lebeau	Moses Lebeau/Angela Messier
Conerty*	Marguaret				
Cones*	------				
Conglan*	Margeretham	28-NOV-1856	30-NOV-1856	Patricius Conglan/Maria Butteler	A. Hammon/M. Kenny
Conklin	Catharnam	28-NOV-1852	20-FEB-1853	Timothei Conklin/Maria Calaghan	A. Kelly/A. Kelly
Conlen*	Gullelimus Edwardus	01-FEB-1860	29-FEB-1860	Joanni Conlen/Catherina Arkason	Jocobus Ford/Maria-Anna Ford
Conlen*	Margarete	15-MAR-1860	16-MAR-1860	Michaelis Conlen/Sara McLane	Francis Kinney/Hannah Nicklaus
Conlen*	Marguarite				
Conlon*	William Edward				----- Hannar/M. Kinny
Conly	Magrita	28-NOV-1856	30-NOV-1856	Rock Conlon/Marre Botteler	
Conly	Danielem	27-AUG-1861	27-AUG-1861	Joannis Conly/Maria Conly	M. Henneffy/B Carroll
Conly	Edwardum	29-JUN-1861	21-JUL-1861	Joannis Conly/Anna Conly	G Walsh/M. Corby
Conly	Georgium Henricum	24-JUN-1863	12-JUL-1863	Joannis Conly/Anna Conly	M Burke/J. Bott
Conly*	Marguaritam	09-FEB-1863	15-FEB-1863	Dyonisii Conly/Joanna Conly	T. Logelun/C. Logelun
Conly*	Dionisium	22-NOV-1856	23-NOV-1856	Densius Conly/Joanna Logelum	T. Logelan/C. Logelan
Conly*	Dionsius	22-NOV-1856	28-NOV-1856	Denis Conly/Jannis Logelan	
Conly*	Julianne				
Conly*	William				W Leger/M. ---niton
Conly*	Williamum Joannem	09-JUN-1859	20-JUN-1859	Joannis Conly/Anna Leger	J Connaughty/ C.Connaughty
Connaughty	Hellen	02-OCT-1851	09-NOV-1851	Timothy Connaughty/Mary Kierns	M. Connaughty/C. Eagan
Connaughty	Lauram Joannam	24-APR-1861	05-MAY-1861	Timothei Connaughty/Maria Connaughty	J Connaughty/ A.Connaughty
Connaughty	Sarahm	12-AUG-1863	25-OCT-1863	Timothei Connaughty/Maria Connaughty	J Flinn/M. Tomis
Connel	Mariam Helenam	15-JAN-1863	19-JAN-1863	Guillelmi Connel/Anna Connel	N Mckillen/M. Mckillen
Connelly	Mariane	14-OCT-1863	18-OCT-1863	Joannis Connelly/Maria Connelly	T Toomey/M. Toomey
Conner	Catharnam	18-JUL-1861	21-JUL-1861	Michaelis Conner/Rosa Conner	P Onell/A Brannan
Connerty*	Mageretham	17-JAN-1859	05-MAR-1859	Thimothie Connerty/Maria Cerran	P. Madden/M. Sheridan
Conngham	Mary-Ann	19-APR-1851	20-JUN-1851	Patrick Connigham/Ann Flannery	P. McCabe/M. Loughlin
Connolly	Jacobum	13-MAY-1858	14-MAY-1858	Petri Connolly/Catherina Grat-	Ptrick McCabe/Mary Coughlin
Connolly	James	03-MAY-1858	14-MAY-1858	Peter Connolly/Catherine Graham	T. Corkeran/B. Newton
Connolly	Jeremiam	06-NOV-1860	18-NOV-1860	Dyonisii Connolly/Joanna Connolly	Nicholas Clotz/Clarcy Clotz
Conolly	Jane	02-JAN-1858	03-APR-1858	P'trick Connolly/Cath Brennan	----- Conroy/M McTevy
Conroy	Franciscum	03-OCT-1850	05-OCT-1850	Patrcu Conroy/Elizabetha Conroy	
Conroy	Joannem	01-FEB-1855	10-FEB-1855	Dyonisii Conroy/Joanna Jeavy	G Loghlen/M. Loghlen

28

Surname	Given Name	Birth	Baptism	Parents	Godparents
Cooct	Petrus Joseph	03-JUN-1857	07-JUN-1857	---- Coon/Marie Lees	P. Miller/M Mengel
Coon	Ireneam Esther	23-MAR-1897	25-APR-1897	Carolo Coon/Mathilda Langlois	Cyprianus Langlois/Angelina Gauther
Coon	Ruth Mariam	28-FEB-1896	12-APR-1896	Carolo Coon/Mathilda Langlois	Pacificus Landeman/Maria DesCoubron
Coons	Josephum	15-MAY-1861	20-JUN-1861	Jacobi Coons/Catharina Coons	M. Loughlin/---- -----
Cooper	Henriettam Catarinam	28-SEP-1894	01-OCT-1894	Eduardo Cooper/Joanna Henzel	Nazarius Dame/Catarina Endres
Coque	Mergreth Melvina	06-NOV-1876	12-NOV-1876	Ludovi Coque/Lorensitia Lalet	E Fontane/M. Lalet
Corbeil	Josephinam	18-APR-1867	21-APR-1867	Cyrili Corbeil/Anastasia Dufort-Corbeil	A Dufort/J Cliche
Corbeil	Josephum	18-JUN-1869	20-JUN-1869	Cyrili Corbeil/Anastasia Dufort	Josephus Corbeil/Catharina Co-liar
Corbel	Josephum Napolionem	28-APR-1873	29-APR-1873	Napoleons Corbeil/Melinda Lebeau	Josephus/Angela Lebeau
Corbeil	Ludovicum Edwardum	27-MAR-1874	29-MAR-1874	Hormida Corbeil/Sarah Chef	Cyrillus Corbeil/Christina Duquette
Corbeil	Mariam Rosam	16-JUL-1874	17-JUL-1874	Cyrili Corbeil/Anastasia Dufrane	Hormidas Corbeil/Clara Corbeil
Corbeil	Mathildam Euphrosinam	27-JAN-1871	29-JAN-1871	Cyrili Corbeil/Anastasia Dufort	Josephus Corbeil/Mathilda Corbeil
Corbeil	Petrum Hormisdam Sigtfri	24-DEC-1872	26-DEC-1872	Hormisda Corbeil/Sarah Chef	Petrus Chef/Catharina Pouillar
Corbeil	Wilfredum	14-APR-1873	14-APR-1873	Cyrili Corbeil/Anastasia Dufort	Napoleo Corbeil/Melma Lebeau
Corbeile	Mariam Joannam	05-DEC-1876	06-DEC-1876	Sirile Corbeile/Estase Dufeaux	T. Corbeile/M. Dufort
Corbeille	Alexandrum Evaristum	04-APR-1883	04-APR-1883	Evaristo Corbeille/Mathilda Venne	Cyrillus Corbeille/Anasthasia Dufort
Corbeille	Augustinum Bartholemeum	22-OCT-1897	26-OCT-1897	Petro-Trefleo Corbeille/Ostia Maheu	Moises-Fredericus Corbeille/Malvina Corbeille
Corbeille	Ernestum Franciscum Xave	06-MAR-1891	08-MAR-1891	Napoleone-Zotico Corbeille/Melinda Lebeau	Franciscus Marcoux/Josephina Roy
Corbeille	Eugenium	03-JAN-1890	03-JAN-1890	Evaristo Corbeille/Mathilda Venne	Arthurus Venne/Rosa-Anna Corbeille
Corbeille	Evelinam Hortensiam	19-JUL-1894	20-JUL-1894	Petro-Trefleo Corbeille/Ostia Maheu	Josephus Corbeille/Rosana Corbeille
Corbeille	Franciscum Christinum	20-FEB-1905		Alexandro Corbeille/Anna Kraemer	Christianus Kraemer/Mathilda Vanne-Corbeille
Corbeille	Josephum A---am	21-APR-1881	24-APR-1881	Evarista Corbeille/Mathilda Venne	E Venne/S Bastien
Corbeille	Josephum Alfredum Napol	01-JUN-1884	01-JUN-1884	Evaristo Corbeille/Mathilda Venne	Napoleon Corbeille/Melinda Lebeau
Corbeille	Josephum Ferdinandum	16-APR-1888	22-APR-1888	Evaristo Corbeille/Mathilda Venne	Ferdinandus Brunet/Elodia Venne
Corbeille	Malvina	24-SEP-1880	26-SEP-1880	Cyril Corbeille/Anastasia Dufort	L. Clish/D. Dufrêsne
Corbeille	Marcum Stanislaum	07-MAY-1901	27-MAY-1901	Petro-Treffleo Corbeille/Ostia Maheu	Petrus Corbeille/Amanda Corbeille
Corbeille	Mariam	09-JUN-1887	11-JUN-1887	Treffeo Corbeille/Dorithea Mahen	Napoleo Corbeille/Melind Lebeau
Corbeille	Mariam Amandam	10-MAY-1885	10-MAY-1885	Cyrillo Corbeille/Anastasie Dufort	Petrus Lepine/Josephine Corbeille
Corbeille	Mariam Annam Catharinam	16-APR-1892	17-APR-1892	Petro-Traffleo Corbeille/Otia Maheu	Petrus Lepine/Josephina Corbeille
Corbeille	Mariam Ednam	14-OCT-1887	16-OCT-1887	Napoleone Corbeille/Melinda Lebeau	Michael Lajeunesse/Rosa-Anna Lebeau
Corbeille	Mariam Ezildam	10-FEB-1883	11-FEB-1883	Napoleone Corbeille/Melinda Lebeau	Cyrillus Corbeille/Anastasia Dufort
Corbeille	Mariam Florentiam Melindam		02-DEC-1902	Josepho Corbeille/Leoma Brunet	Napoleo-Zoticus Corbeille/Melinda Lebeau
Corbeille	Mariam Melinam Hildam	24-NOV-1900	27-NOV-1900	Josepho Corbeille/Leona-Clotilda Brunet	Moises Lebeau/Angela Messier
Corbeille	Moisem Fredericum	01-JUL-1875	04-JUL-1875	Napoleon Corbeille/Melandie Lebeau	Moise Lebeau/Catherine Couillard
Corbeille	Norbertum Alphonsium		28-SEP-1880	Napoleone Corbeille/Melanda Lebeau	E. Corbeille/M. Venne
Corbeille	Olivinam L.M.	05-MAR-1887	06-MAR-1887	Evaristo Corbeille/Mathilda Venne	Eldericus Venne/Olivina Venne
Corbeille	Petrum Arthuium	17-MAR-1891	18-MAR-1891	Evaristo Corbeille/Mathilda Venne	Petrus Lepine/Josephina Corbeille
Corbeille	Petrum Ernestum	16-SEP-1885	17-SEP-1885	Nepoleone Corbeille/Melinda Lebeau	Petrus-Trefflus Corbeille/Adelina Venne
Corbeille	Ursulam Emeliam	20-JUL-1890	20-JUL-1890	Petro-Treffleo Corbeille/Josephina-Ostia Maheu	Evaristus Corbeille/Mathilda Venne
Corbeille	Zephernium Evans	25-JUN-1888	28-JUN-1888	Petro-Treffleo Corbeille/Ostia Mahen	Felix Corbeille/Anastasia Dufort
Corbet*	Ludovicum	09-JUL-1860	12-JUL-1860	M. Corbet/S Mcmann	T. Herrans/M. Corbet
Corbett	Mauritium	29-NOV-1862	29-NOV-1900	Joannis Corbett/Julia Corbett	R. Gibbons/C. Gibbons
Corbin	Thomum Eduardum	25-APR-1884	06-JUL-1884	Joanne Corbin/Catharina Decez	Jacobus Langlois/Maria Decez
Corbit*	Genesius	22-AUG-1856		John Corbit/Julie Currans	M. Currans/J. Currans
Corbit*	Mariam	10-MAR-1858	19-MAR-1858	Joannis Corbit/Julia Currans	J Nash/J. Nash
Corbit*	Celinam	13-OCT-1858	22-OCT-1858	Franci Corboneau/Odella Gilbert	---li- Pariseau/Delna Gonselain
Corboneau*	Honoram	19-MAY-1852	03-JUL-1852	Edwardi Corey/Maria Donovan	L. Kief/M. Kief
Corey	Jeremiah	01-MAY-1860	06-MAY-1860	Joannis Corey/Brigetta Rine	Thomas Gylin/Hellena Keren
Corey**	M Annam	02-MAR-1860	12-MAR-1860	Thoma Corken/Brigeta Gorman	Martinus Flynn/Margeth Wells
Corken*					

Surname	Given Name	Birth	Baptism	Parents	Godparents
Corkeran	Thomam Franciscum	23-MAR-1863	26-APR-1863	Michaelis Corkeran/Rosa Corkeran	G Wells/M Wells
Corkeran	Thomam Petrum	17-FEB-1862	19-FEB-1862	Thoma Corkeran/Bridgitta Corkeran	G Walsh/H Flinn
Corkn*	John				
Cornerty*	Elisabetham	12-JUN-1856	02-AUG-1856	Thimotei Cornerty/Maria Curran	R Connerty/M Connerty
Corolyn	Maria Jana	07-JUL-1860	15-JUL-1860	Patricii Corolyn/Maria Boyle	Petri Hartgrove/L Hartgrove
Correr	Hubertum Fredericum	08-MAY-1865	21-MAY-1865	Edmundi Correr/Elizabetha Correr	H. Correr/M Flatten
Corrigan	Cesilia	12-JAN-1857	18-JAN-1857	M---- Corrigan/Brigeth -----	Patrick -----/Maria -----
Corrigan*	Anna				
Corrigan*	Annam	24-JUN-1859	24-JUL-1859	Antoni Corrigan/Maria Nicholas	M. -1gens/A. -1gens
Cosgriff*	Patrick	10-JAN-1859	06-FEB-1859	Ptnck Cosgriff/Bridget Glinn	M. Devine/A. Mangan
Cosgriff*	Patrick				
Costar	Jacobum	08-MAR-1862	08-MAR-1862	Joseph Costar/Dorothea Costar	H Borasseau/----- -----
Costas	Samuel	04-JUL-1889	24-NOV-1919	George Costas/Lula Manzy	Hermne Gash/Hermina LeSage
Costella*	Mary				
Costell*	Mariam	21-APR-1859	01-MAY-1859	Jacobi Costelli/Margetha Flannigan	D Stan---/S. Flannigan
Costello	Jacobum	22-MAY-1861	27-MAY-1861	Jacobi Costello/Marguarita Costello	P. Sho---ess/E. Sho--ess
Cezarium	20-JAN-1868	26-JAN-1868	Narcissi Cote/Elizabeth-A. Cote	Josephus Touchete/Onesima Touchete	
Coté	Joannem	08-SEP-1870	26-SEP-1870	Narcissi Coté/Elizabetha Coté	Thersilus Faneut/Franciscus Coté
Coté	Mariam Emliam	24-OCT-1872	24-OCT-1872	Narcissi Coté/Elizabetha Coté	Gilbertus Leclerc/Adelma Gagner
Côté	Mariam Jo----	09-NOV-1873	09-NOV-1873	----cisci Côté/Elizabeth Moran	Joseph Fielle/Sophia Fielle
Coté	Petrum	21-JUL-1877	22-JUL-1877	Narsis Coté/Else Meriam	A Plank/F Coté
Coté	Victorem	11-MAR-1865	26-MAR-1865	Narcissi Coté/Elizabetha Coté	N. Boisvert/E Robidou
Cote*	Carolum William	22-JUL-1859	29-APR-1860	Joseph Cote/Angelica LeDuc	Francois Bodrieux/Clemtta LaRose
Coughlin	Catharinam	26-OCT-1861	27-OCT-1861	Joannis Coughlin/Marguarita Coughlin	M Stack/A. Stack
Coughlin	Joannem Patricium	18-NOV-1862	30-NOV-1862	Joannis Coughlin/Marguarita Coughlin	J Rafferty/C. Flanegan
Coughlin	Mariam	26-OCT-1861	27-OCT-1861	Joannis Coughlin/Marguarita Coughlin	R. McGown/A. Coughlin
Counaty	Mariam	08-DEC-1853	11-FEB-1854	Timothei Counaty/Maria Curran	J. Curran/M Egan
Coutoure	Mariam Helenam	09-MAY-1870	11-MAY-1870	Eusebii Coutoure/Ludovica Coutoure	Felix Lozon/Eulalia Lozon
Couture	Baptistam	03-MAR-1864	06-MAR-1864	Huberti Couture/Maria Couture	F. Durocher/P. Durocher
Couture	Hubertum		06-MAR-1864	Huberti Couture/Maria Couture	N Braquette/H Pedlant
Covough*	Maria	30-JAN-1860	15-FEB-1860	Danielis Covough/Margaret Hordyen	Michaelis Scannel/Hellena Scannel
Coy	Jacobum	30-APR-1858	14-MAY-1858	Guillelmo Coy/Maria Mangan	E. Mangan/M. Ward
Coy	James	30-MAY-1857	14-MAY-1858	William Coy/Mary Mangan	Edmund Mangan/Mary-Anne Ward
Cr---son	Joannes	09-APR-1858	21-APR-1858	Thomas Cr---son/Anna Ho--igan	James Peters/Brigeta Melus
Crams	Francicus Henricus	16-MAR-1857	10-MAY-1857	Moris Crams/Francisca Dold	Augusti Do--ner/Rossa Gerdert
Craine*	M Ann	23-MAY-1858	26-JUN-1858	Mark Craine/-enne Lang	Patrick Farel/Ann Coulon
Cramer*	Petrum	10-MAR-1860	12-MAR-1860	Hebert Cramer/Agnes Werds	Petrus Prester/Fel--- Rogers
Cramme*r	Evam Catherinam	01-AUG-1856	01-AUG-1856	Josephi Crammer/Maria Stephani	P. Mayer/E. Stephani
Crammer	Eduardus	15-OCT-1855	01-JAN-1856		T. Peron/M Peron
Crammer	Matum	04-JUL-1859	29-JUL-1859	Joannis-Petrus Crammer/Catherina Peren	Andreas Duncan/Clementina -sson
Crammer*	Eduardum	15-DEC-1855	01-JAN-1856	Joannis Crammer/Sobria Toutsaint	P. Peron/M Peron
Crammer*	Eduardus	15-OCT-1855	01-JAN-1856	Jannis-Petri Crammer/Sobria Peron	T Peron/M Peron
Crammer*	Eva Catherina	01-AUG-1856	01-AUG-1856	Josephus Crammer/Maria Stphani	P Mayer/E. Stephanie
Crammer*	Felicem	24-NOV-1857	29-NOV-1857	Eriard Crammer/Anna-Agnes Werts	F. Rogers/M Rester
Crammer*	Felix	24-NOV-1857	29-NOV-1857	Eduard Crammer/Maria-Anna Werts	F. Rogers/M Ruster
Crammer*	Mat		29-JUL-1859		
Cranay	Catharinam Lucillam	20-SEP-1905	01-OCT-1905	Francisco Cranay/Spha Hanson	Gulielmus Desrochers/Rosa Desrochers
Crandle	Mariam Josephinam	21-APR-1861	14-JUL-1861	Joannis Crandle/Celina Crandle	L. Beaudreau/S. Bryant
Crane*	Annam	25-MAY-1858	26-JUN-1858	Marci- Crane/Wina Lang	P. Forel/A. Conlin

30

Surname	Given Name	Birth	Baptism	Parents	Godparents
Cranly*	Elenam	11-FEB-1858	23-FEB-1858	Patrici Cranly/Brigetha Cranly	P Huges/B Martin
Cranz	Josephum Donatum	15-JAN-1882	08-APR-1884	Guilelmo Crany/Adela Durocher	Adolphus Pellant/Alphonsine Loberge
Crauly*	Elisabeth	27-FEB-1860	18-APR-1860	Patric Crauly/Brigetha Crauly	James Connerty/Anna Welshs
Cremer	Bernardum	23-JAN-1854	23-APR-1854	Joanins-Petri Cremer/Sarah Perrin	B. Peron/M. Peron
Cremmer*	Jacobum	03-MAR-1859	05-MAR-1859	Josephi Cremmer/Maria Stephani	J Cremmer/G. Stephani
Crignan*	Mariam	02-SEP-1858	02-SEP-1858	Jacobi Crignan/Catherina Hacy	E Miles/A Miles
Crignon*	Mary	02-SEP-1858	07-SEP-1858	James Crignon/Cath Hoey	Ewd Miles/Alice Miles
Crimen*	Petri	02-JUL-1860	12-JUL-1860	Jacobi Crimen/Catherina Thery	M. Thery/J. Thery
Crimon*	Peter				
Crimon*	Petrus	08-JUL-1860	12-AUG-1860	Jacobi Crimon/Catharina Hery	Maria Hery/Jacobi Heri
Crinan*	Thoma	21-MAY-1855	28-JUN-1855	Jacobi Crinan/Catharina Gay	J Conely/R Gay
Crinon*	Thamas	21-MAY-1855	25-JUN-1855	Jacobus Crinon/Kathrina Guy	J Connly/R. Guy
Cristel*	Elenam	13-FEB-1859	27-FEB-1859	Patria Cristel/Maria Jory	M Gary/----- Gary
Cristel*	Ellen				
Cristel*	Thamam	02-JUN-1857	07-JUN-1857	Patrici Cristel/Maria Folli	J. Waters/S. Kelly
Critteler*	Joannes	22-JUN-1856	09-AUG-1856	----- Critteler/Henora Rogan	M. Flind/H O'Bryan
Cro-	Anna Jane	25-JUN-1851	18-JUL-1851	Michael Cro-/Eliza Donnely	F. Halpin/B. Halpin
Crofield*	Bedeliam	18-JUL-1859	25-JUL-1859	Patrici Crofield/Bridgetta Cricham	T. Reily/----- -----
Croghan*	C. Marguaret				
Croghan*	Catherine Margueret	01-JAN-1859	05-FEB-1859	Ptrick Croghan/Cath Ryan	J. Hughes/B. Cellers
Crolly	Patricum	31-AUG-1853	02-OCT-1853	Patrici Crolly/Maria Bleek	T Crolly/A. Crolly
Crossen	Bernardum	10-OCT-1854	23-DEC-1854	Bernardi Crossen/Elizabetha Mous	J. Galligar/M. Galligar
Crossen	Helenam	10-DEC-1854	23-DEC-1854	Bernardi Crossen/Elizabetha Mous	D Gallaher/R. Gallaher
Crouly	Joanem	18-JAN-1853	18-JAN-1853	Patrici Crouly/Brigita Crouly	M McGrcgor/M. M--ony
Crouly*	Annam	27-JAN-1860	15-FEB-1860	Patrici Crouly/Marie Bladle	Thamas Mruthet/Brigeth Crouly
Crouly*	Thamam	14-MAY-1857	10-JUL-1857	Patrici Crouly/Maria Brick	T Marten/B. Kelly
Crow	Helenam	14-MAR-1863	17-MAR-1863	Joanins Crow/Helena Crow	D. Ryan/M Hack
Crowley	David	15-APR-1858	05-MAY-1858	Joanins Crowley/Elizabetha Knutken	J Landry/M. -at-
Crowley	Mariam	17-MAR-1863	12-APR-1863	Patrici Crowley/Maria Crowley	C. Hughes/B Martin
Crowley	Mary Ann	16-APR-1858	05-MAY-1858	John Crowley/Cath.-Elizabeth Hickson	James Landry/Mary-Ann Hickson
Crowley	Michaelem	30-MAY-1862	27-JUN-1862	Patricii Crowley/Bridgitta Crowley	J. Rosseter/A. Rosseter
Crowley*	Anna				
Crowley*	Elizabeth				
Crowley*	Mariam	20-AUG-1857	28-AUG-1858	Danielis Crowley/Maria Rock	T. Curran/F. Guilbert
Crowly	Brigidam	05-JAN-1854	04-FEB-1854	Patritri Crowly/Brdgida Crowly	P. Whitty/B Crowly
Cramer*	Peter				
Crammer	Mariam	09-JUN-1865	11-JUN-1865	Henrci Crämmer/Barbara Crammer	H Holtzman/M Stephans
Crammer*	James				
Crammer*	Mat. Um				
Cullen	Fransiscum	17-MAR-1876	08-OCT-1876	Godfroy Cullen/Vergina Dubois	P Dubois/V Jasco
Cullen*	Franciscum	22-JUN-1860	01-JUL-1860	Octavi Cullen/Maria Boliar	Franciscus Belter/Savoi Dufrane
Cummings*	Patrick				
Cummins	Marguaritam		14-SEP-1862	Joanins Cummins/Aurelia Cummins	M. Krämmer/M. Shron
Cune	Michaelem	03-FEB-1861	25-FEB-1861	Laurentri Cune/Anna Cune	P. Ma-ken/A. Ma-ken
Cunngham*	Joannem	24-MAY-1858	13-JUN-1858	Joanins Cuningham/Brdgitta Kelly	M McGarry/R Dougherty
Cunngham*	Patricum		29-JUL-1858		
Curley	Joannes Pu--	19-NOV-1855	25-NOV-1855	Joanins Curley/Catherine Eurling	M Smet/----- -----
Curling*	Louisiam Josephinam	11-NOV-1858	23-MAR-1859	Michaelis Curling/Christina Curling	F. Curling/J Focht
Curran	Carolus Henricus	03-JUL-1860	29-JUL-1860	Patrici Curran/Catharina Mullan	Michaelis Mullain/Bridgetta Murry

Surname	Given Name	Birth	Baptism	Parents	Godparents
Curran	Joannem Martinum	08-APR-1878	08-MAY-1878	Mauritii-Eduardi Curran/Evelin-Gertrudi Berry	J. Flagerthy/M. Lauer
Curran	Mariam Elizabetham	12-MAY-1862	08-JUN-1862	Patricii Curran/CatharinaCurran	P Fitzpatri--/C. King
Curran	Thomas	02-APR-1858	18-APR-1858	Peter Curran/Cath Castgrove	P'trick Murphy/Mary Murray
Curran*	Charles Henry				
Curran*	Patricium	17-NOV-1855	20-NOV-1855	Patricii Curran/Maria McGrevy	J McCrory/M. ----
Curran*	Patrick	14-NOV-1855	20-NOV-1855	Patrick Curran/Marie Gillegrevy	J McCrory/M. Kirran
Curran*	Thomas Henry				
Currans	Joannem	13-JUL-1853	22-AUG-1853	Michaelis Currans/Elisa Donnaly	G Gall/T. Lionad
Curren*	Thomas Henricus	12-JAN-1860	19-FEB-1860	Micaelus Curren/Maria-Anna --------	Joseph-Janell Curren/Maria-Anna Curren
Cusee*	Patricius	01-MAR-1860	18-MAR-1860	Patricii Cusee/Johanna Cusee	Daniells Henry/Brigitta McMulen
Cushion	Sarah	13-MAY-1852	22-JUN-1852	Timothy Cushion/Brigtt Nollin	P Cushion/C. Leonard
Cusick	Mariam	18-JUN-1853	30-JUN-1853	Patricii Cusick/Joanna McMahan	G. Connol/J. Connol
Cusik*	Patrick				
Cussick*	Guilelmum	02-AUG-1856	10-AUG-1856	Patricii Cussick/Joanna McMan	M. Ne--/E. Dorgerty
Cuzick	Ellen Mary	04-MAY-1852	27-JUN-1852	Patrick Cuzick/Johanna McMillion	J. Corbert/M. Oconnell
D'Anneau*	Mariam Clementiam	06-AUG-1855	11-AUG-1855	Petri D'Anneau/Clementia Beaulieu	L Petit/F. -
D'Annan*	Maria Clementina	06-MAY-1855	11-AUG-1855	Perri- D'Annian/Clementina Beauquin	L. Petit/-. Murrais
D------*	Margaret Elled				
D------	Guilielmum Georgium Mic	24-JAN-1872	03-FEB-1872	Caroli D------/Maria -------	Vitalis Edouin/Melina Edouin
D------y	Jocabum	19-JUL-1860	29-JUL-1860	Bernardi D------y/Elena C------	Joannes Flynn/Sera Dogerty
D-e-enberg	Henricum		27-APR-1879	Petrus D-e-enberg/Anna-M---- V--ans	
D-t-----*	Mariam Celinam	12-JUN-1858	15-JUN-1858	Josephi D-t-----/--tr--a Verneuf	O. Dodelin/H. Verneuf
Dade	Mariam Ludovicam	19-SEP-1861	20-OCT-1861	Joannis Dade/Maria Dade	L. Beaudreau/C. Beaudrieau
Dadelain*	Olivier	10-MAR-1858	14-MAR-1858	Stanislaus Dadelain/Perpecula Pariso	Pollitu- Paris/Martina Lamere
Daily	Saram Mariam	05-MAR-1901	16-JUN-1901	Joanne Daly/Josephina Corbeille	Amabilis Gervais/Philumena Cheff
Daily*	Josephus	19-MAR-1858	20-NOV-1858	Jos Daly/Catherine Murry	Jas Murry/Elizabeth Dillen
Daiman	Mariam Adelam	05-MAR-1854	09-MAR-1854	Petri Daiman/Maria Denne	J. Sellet/V. Petit
Dan*	Mariam	18-OCT-1859	06-NOV-1859	Thoma Dan/Brigetha Ri-d-n	E Dan/M. B--dion
Dalen*	Margeritham	28-JAN-1858	07-FEB-1858	Petri Dalen/Catherinam Donnely	P. Doun/M. Higgens
Dallighan	Joannem	31-AUG-1863	06-SEP-1863	Patricii Dallighan/Maria Dallighan	G Lémori/H. Dollighan
Dalson	Jacobum Guilielmum Harry	23-NOV-1907	01-DEC-1907	Harry-J Dalson/Angela-Rose Desrochers	Guliel Desrochers/Maria Perron-Desrochers
Dalton	Joannem	04-AUG-1854	27-AUG-1854	Joannis Dalton/Catharina Flaherty	G Daly/A. Daly
Daly*	Gulumis Jocobus		23-AUG-1857	John Daly/Anna Leny	J. Mccauly/M. Mccauly
Daly*	Joseph				
Dam	Carolum	23-DEC-1871	03-MAR-1872	Eduardi Dam/Eulogia Dam	Carolus Thill/Catharina Thill
Dam	Mariam Lodovicam	29-FEB-1876		Najari Dam/Catherina Androus	B. Androus/M. Stollenbeck
Dam	Rosam Barbaram		13-MAY-1872	Nazarii Dam/Catharina Dam	Jacobus Berors/Barbara Handerson
Dame	Joannes-Baptistam	13-NOV-1873	21-NOV-1873	Nazarri Dame/Catharina Gudras	Petrum Dufresne/Sarah Dufresne
Dame	Josephum Ludovicum	12-SEP-1883	16-SEP-1883	Nazario Dame/Catarina Andres	Josephus Felker/Elizabeth Ste.-Marie
Dan	Wilfredum	22-JAN-1870	20-FEB-1870	Eduardi Dan/Philomena Dan	Josephus Tillete/Catharina Hansel
Dana*	Aloysium Michaelem	13-NOV-1864	13-NOV-1864	Joannis Dana/Ludovica Dana	P. Peck/B. R-ng
Dana*	Anna Carolina				
Dandelin	Carolum Oliverum	19-JUN-1884	15-JUL-1884	Stanislos Dandelin/Josephine Pariseau	Franciscus Dufrense/Elisa Ste.-Marie
Dandelin	Elizabeth	17-NOV-1889	26-NOV-1889	Stanislaus Dandelin/Josephina Pariseau	Eduardus Pariseau/Melanisa Dupuy
Dandelin	Georgium Fredericum	20-MAY-1883	04-JUN-1883	Stanislao Dandelin/Josephina Pariseault	Eduardus Gagnier/Edessa Pariseault
Dandelin	Guilielmum Henricum	08-FEB-1880	15-MAR-1880	Stanislas Dadelin/Josephina Pariseau	J Pariseau/E. Pariseau
Dandelin	Helenam Esther	02-OCT-1881	10-OCT-1881	Stanislao Dandelin/Josephina Pariseau	Vitalis Gratton/Esther Guenard
Dandelin	Ludovicum Franciscum	08-AUG-1885	04-OCT-1885	Stanislao Dandelin/Josephina Pariseau	Ludovicus Pariseau/Julia Dandelin
Dandelin	Oliverum Jeremiah	13-SEP-1887	19-SEP-1887	Stanislao Dandelin/Josephina Pariseau	Bruno Pariseau/Maria Dallaire

Surname	Given Name	Birth	Baptism	Parents	Godparents
Danceau	Emliam	28-APR-1864	12-JUN-1864	Petri Danceau/Martina Danceau	J. Petit/E. Bellmeur
Daniel	Almra Phlomena	03-FEB-1878	16-MAR-1878	Joseph Daniel/Alousa Porrier	J. Leduc/P Leduc
Daniel	Andream Carolum	14-SEP-1899	17-SEP-1899	Carolo Daniel/Josephma Johnson	Joannes McGowans/Elizabeth Daniel
Daniel	Annam Malvinam	06-AUG-1901	11-AUG-1901	Carolo Daniel/Josephma Johnson	Gulilmus Brockway/Malvina Marcoux
Daniel	Baptistam Ludovicum	10-SEP-1868	20-SEP-1868	Joseph Daniel/Ludovica Daniel	Petrus Burel/Maria G Daniel
Daniel	Federicum	01-SEP-1875	26-SEP-1875	Francissi Daniel/Catherena Mayou	A Leduc/M. Breau
Daniel	Guillelmum	29-DEC-1874	15-OCT-1871	Francisci Daniel/Adelaida Faneuf	Moyses Tremblé/Joanna Lucier
Daniel	Haretam	29-DEC-1874	10-JAN-1875	Josephi Daniel/Louisa Pane	Petrus Brurel/Maria Bur--l
Daniel	Jacobum	13-AUG-1853	16-AUG-1853	J Daniel/Maria-Anna Urlings	J Urlings/C Sphenum
Daniel	Josephnam	06-MAR-1873	02-APR-1873	Josephi Daniel/Ludovica Daniel	Petrus Dubois/Virginia Dubois
Daniel	Josephum Benjamnem	06-NOV-1897	12-NOV-1897	Carolo Daniel/Josephma Johnson	Josephus Daniel/Elizabeth Priorer
Daniel	Mariam Melvinam		04-NOV-1871	Francisci Daniel/Adelaída Faneuf	Carolus Tremblé/Clementia Fernet
Daniel	Rosaliam		15-OCT-1871	Francisci Daniel/Adel. Faneuf	J.-Ba-- Dupuis/Dyonisia Baillargeon
Dano	Mariam Rosalam	12-SEP-1865	26-NOV-1865	Petri Dano/Clementina Beaudreau	B Perron/-. Perron
Dany*	Guliemus Hennery	18-NOV-1857	29-NOV-1857	John Dany/Louisa Resseler	P Servatius/M. Servatius
Darel	Franciscum	14-JUL-1866	15-JUL-1866	Josephi Dariel/Ludovica Darel	F. Rondeau/E. Lepine
Dart*	Petrum Josephum	03-JUN-1857	07-JUN-1857	Michaelis Dart/Maria Rees	P Miller/M. Mangol
Dauché*	Octavium	08-AUG-1858	22-AUG-1858	Octavius Dauché/Delina Degrain	Pascal Dufrain/Sesar-- St -Ma---
Daugherty	Carolum Edwardum	03-FEB-1863	15-FEB-1863	Bernardi Daugherty/Carolina Daugherty	J. Loughlin/A. Loughlin
Daugherty	Danelem	09-NOV-1863	12-DEC-1863	Danelis Daugherty/Helena Daugherty	G. Murry/R Murry
Daugherty	Edmundum	06-JUN-1862	19-JUN-1862	Edmundi Daugherty/Anna Daugherty	P. Holoran/M. Liston
Daugherty	Michaelem Edwardum	01-JUL-1862	01-JUL-1862	Jacobi Daugherty/Bridgitta Daugherty	J Cane/J. Daugherty
Daulton	Ellen	10-NOV-1851	19-NOV-1851	John Daulton/Catherine Flaherty	E Flaherty/E. Flaherty
David	Richardum	13-JUL-1853	16-OCT-1853	Patricii David/Ester David	T Emmerson/E Derrelhy
Davis	Ema	17-JAN-1875	24-JAN-1875	Jeremi Davis/Mathilda Touchett	Charbius Bulgard/Ma Touchett
Davitt*	John				
Davy	Christinam	01-NOV-1860	14-MAR-1861	Patricii Davy/Esthera Davy	D. Davy/-----
Davy*	A Rosana	11-JUN-1855	19-AUG-1855	Patrucus Davy/Esther Davy	J Emmerson/H. Larry
Davy*	Rosamam	11-JUN-1855	19-AUG-1855	Patricii Davy/Esther Davy	J Emmerson/H. Jarry
Dayl--*	-l-na-	16-JUN-1858	27-JUN-1858	Petri Dayl--/Babera Moran	James Tirny/Caterina T--tows
De--meur*	Henricum	03-DEC-1858	14-JAN-1859	Joannis-Bat De--meur/Maria Peron	Josephus Pro/Catherina Peron
Dedde-	Marian Josepham	10-JUN-1876	20-JUN-1876	Philip Dedde-/Maria-Anna Trin----	C. Serve/M. Dedde-
Defraine	Georgium Pascalem	12-APR-1876	24-APR-1876	Francisci Defraine/Elisia St-Marie	D. Doudelan/E Dufraine
Defraine	Mariam	06-JUN-1854	11-JUN-1854	Petri Defraine/Lisa Muner	J Jubert/S. Brian
Defresne	Eugenium Andream	28-JUL-1905	30-JUL-1905	Alberto DeFresne/Alexma Bastien	Andreas Morris/Emma DuFriesne-Morris
Deitte	Mae			Alfred Deitte/Edesse Letourneau	John Mengel/Malinda Stearns
Delajeunesse*	Henricum	26-AUG-1855	27-AUG-1855	R---- Delajeunesse/Leonarda Gayet	J Gayet/M Lajullin
Delamontagne	Franciscum	11-JUL-1860	22-JUL-1860	----- Delamontagne/Elisabeta ----net	H---- ---ct/----- ----
Delamontagne*	Francis				
Delamontagne*	Guillelmum	17-JUN-1858	20-JUN-1858	Antoni Delamontagne/Isabella Rattia	J. Gosselin/L. Chretien
Delamontagne*	Gulielmum Joannem	17-JUN-1858	20-JUN-1858	Mone Delamontagne/Elisabha -othi--	Joannes Gosslan/Louisa Chretian
Delaurier	Mariam Josephinam	21-DEC-1902	18-JAN-1903	Georgio Delaurer/Adelma Dionne	Eduardus Ryaume/Evelna Ryaume
Delaville*	Petrus Josephus	10-JUL-1857	12-JUL-1857	Petrus-Josephus Delaville/Lisabeht Defarge	J. Hussois/A. Hussois
Deleers	Laurentium Napoleonem	29-APR-1907	05-MAY-1907	Alphonso-J. Deleers/Edna Corbeille	Alfredus Corbeille/Maria Kenney-Corbeille
Delfi	Catherinam	18-AUG-1852	09-SEP-1852	Huberti Delfi/Catherina Leonard	A. HouletL. Leonard
Delille	----	09-JAN-1860	11-JAN-1860	Clementus Delille/Marie Delille	M---- -----/Philome Deliss
Delisse*	Josephum Victorem	26-AUG-1858	29-AUG-1858	Petri Delisse/Francisca Lamblot	J. Delisse/P. Delisse
Delivers*	-----				
Dellis*	Josephum Victorem	26-AUG-1858	29-AUG-1858	Ptk. Dellis/Franca Lomblo-	Julium Josephus/

33

Surname	Given Name	Birth	Baptism	Parents	Godparents
Deltour	Rosalıam Jasephınam	17-NOV-1877	20-NOV-1877	Amandus Deltour/Delle Case	J Deltour/A. Detour
Demarch	Avila Constantia	13-SEP-1878	13-SEP-1878	Salemen Demarch/Marıa Pomenville	S. Demarch/S Dejardın
Demars	Alfredum	04-AUG-1867	01-SEP-1867	Narcıssı Demars/Estherıs Demars	J Lafontaıne/S. Dupus
Demars	Elızabetham	22-AUG-1866	22-AUG-1866	Julıana Demars/Lucıa Demars	G. Trudeau/A. Trudeau
Demars	Henrıcum	20-MAY-1870	12-JUN-1870	Julıanı Demars/Ludovıca Demars	Solomon Demars/Mathılda Letourneau
Demars	Josephum	06-MAR-1873	09-MAR-1873	Julıanı Demars/Lucıa Letourneau	Josephus Letourneau/Octavıa Dermars
Demars	Julıanum	11-AUG-1867	18-AUG-1867	Salomonıs Demars/Amelıa Demars	J. Demars/L. Demars
Demars	Julıanum	25-FEB-1863	22-MAR-1863	Julıanı Demars/Lucıa Demars	G Demars/M. Molheur
Demars	Leucadıam	23-MAY-1867	30-MAY-1867	Joseph Demars/Marguarıta Demars	E Lefeve/M. Ste.-Marıe
Demars	Lucıam	28-JAN-1862	16-FEB-1862	Julıanı Demars/Lucıa Demars	P. Letourneau/S Zerce
Demars	Marıam Martha	15-APR-1876	16-APR-1876	Julıen Demars/Lucıa Letourneau	C. Letourneau/M. Dufraine
Demars	Salomonem	11-MAY-1869	15-MAY-1869	Julıanı Demars/Lucıa Demars	Salomon Demars/Marıa Letourneau
Demars	Simeonem	10-APR-1869	11-APR-1869	Salomonıs Demars/Emilıa Lacosta	Narcıssus Gayete/Alexandra Demars
Demarse	Josephum	04-MAY-1875	09-MAY-1875	Julıen Demarse/Lucıa L'etourneau	Perre Dufraıne/Sophıa Bord-e-
Demarsh	Ludıvıa	10-AUG-1877	12-AUG-1877	Julıen Demarsh/Luce Letourneau	C. Zı-----t/L. Bodreaux
Demasse	Susannam	08-JUL-1852	11-JUL-1852	Michaelis Demasse/Marıe Demasse	G Raymond/F. L--den
Demer*	Goderfrıdum		02-SEP-1860	Goderfrıdi Demers/Sophıa Demers	Sımon Percıer/Sophıa Pera
Demers	Alarıam	14-JAN-1880	15-FEB-1880	Solamone Demers/Marıa Pomınville	J Demers/L. Letourneau
Demers	Celnam Demers	29-DEC-1871	30-DEC-1871	Julıanı Demers/Lucıa Letourneau	Narcıssus Gayet/Emerentıa Demers
Demers	Francıscam Marıam	09-FEB-1907	10-FEB-1907	Francısco Demers/Mathılda Clıohe	Ludovıcus Lepıne/Marıa Clıche-Lepıne
Demers*	Godefrıdum		02-SEP-1860	Godefrıde Demers/Sophıa Demers	S. Percıer/S Pera
Demers*	Godefrıdıum	01-SEP-1860	09-SEP-1860	Godefrıdı Demers/Sophıa Demers	S. Zercıer/S Pero
Denevan*	Jocabum	22-MAY-1858	29-MAY-1858	Wılh Denevan/Catherına Lıenshs	J Gıslon/B Oconnel
Denıen	Alfred	24-APR-1879	27-APR-1879	Antonıı Denıen/Marg Randant	J. Lıppıne/E. Randant
Denoyé	Alexander Raymond	01-APR-1877	08-APR-1877	Hubert Denoyé/Eursule Carrıere	E. Denoyé/M. Denoyé
Denoyé	Josephum	15-JUL-1860	16-JUL-1860	Huberti Denoyé/Delıa Bodrıcaux	Antonıus Duclos/Lousa Gautıer
Denoye*	Ludovıcum Norbertum	25-AUG-1875	29-AUG-1875	Hubertus Denoyé/--chel Carrıère	Noel Bissonnet/Agnes Papquet
Denoye*	Delıa	14-MAR-1858	04-APR-1858	Hubert Denoye/Delıa Bodrıaux	Joseph Bodrıaux/Elıza Jubert
Denoyé*	Delıcıam	17-MAR-1858	04-APR-1858	Hubertı Denoyé/Delıcıa Bodrıeau	J. Bodrıeau/A. Jubert
Denoyer*	Matıldam	13-JAN-1856	27-JAN-1856	Hubertı Denoyer/Delna Bodrıeaux	L. Bodreau/S. --nant
Deny*	Annam Carolınam	27-MAY-1860	01-JUL-1860	Joannes Deny/Louısa --asser	Nıcolus Cramner/Clementına Hoderder
Deny*	Gulıelmum	14-NOV-1857	29-NOV-1857	Joannı Deny/Lousa Rosseler	P. Servatıus/C. Serwe
DePetıt	Susanna	26-SEP-1851	28-SEP-1851	Wıllıam DePetıt/Ludovıca-Elızabeth Basslar	J. Bı--ar/S. Bı-ar
Der--sse*	M---ın	30-MAR-1858	04-APR-1858	---- Der--sse/Marıa Dufraın	Evarıst Vanıs/Angelıa Defraıne
Deroche*	Emelıam		06-AUG-1858	Elıa Deroche/Anna Belam----	L--n Deroche/Matılde Dufraıne
Deroché*	Joannem	30-OCT-1856	01-NOV-1856	Ludgerıi Deroché/Mathılda Dufraıne	A. Deroché/H. Rendeaux
Deroche*	Josephınam Delphınam		03-OCT-1858	Adolphus Deroche/--ıeta -andeau	Franceus Deroche/Dıphena Dufraıne
Deroche*	Marıa	11-AUG-1860	19-AUG-1860	Francoıs Deroche/M----- Pellant	A Duroche/R. P-----
Deroché*	Marıe-Mıal--	14-AUG-1860	19-AUG-1860	Francıs Deroche/---aph Pellant	Alexıs Derocher/Hubert Basset
Deroché*	Melnam	30-MAR-1858	04-APR-1858	Lucıanı Deroché/Matılda Dufraınc	L. Deroché/M. Dufraıne
Deroché*	Rosalıam	09-JUL-1860	12-JUL-1860	E. Deroché/C.---	P. Chef/R. Deroché
Deroché*	Rosalıam	09-AUG-1860	12-AUG-1860	Elı Deroché/Carolıne Deroché	Perre Chef/Rosalıa Deroché
Deroche*	Victoria	05-MAR-1910	16-MAY-1857	Antoıne Deroche/Delıma Defraın	A. Derıche/D. Defan
Deronın	Josephum Lester	05-MAR-1910	21-MAR-1910	Elıa Deronın/Flora Beaudın	Achılle Beaudın/Nellıe Beaudın
Derou	Lellles Gertrude	23-DEC-1875		Ed. Derou/Nansi Gell	P. Leduc/M Sham---
Deroun	Josephum Guy Clarentıum	02-SEP-1905	10-SEP-1905	Elıa Deroun/Flora Beaudın	Elızeus Beaudın/Exıdla Deroun
Deroun	Marıam Agnetıam Adelıam	09-MAY-1867	17-JUL-1867	Joannıs Deroun/Melna Derouın	T. Chapel--/C. Lapointe
Deruche*	Wıllıam	09-OCT-1859	09-OCT-1859	Luger Deruche/Matılda Dufraın	J. Deroche-/S. Dufraın
Desale*	Francıus Henrıcus	08-JUN-1858	09-JUN-1858	Clemens Desale/Marıan Durdu	Julıus DeLısse/Jellıete D'Or

34

Surname	Given Name	Birth	Baptism	Parents	Godparents
Desalle*	Franciscum Henricum	08-JUN-1858	09-JUN-1858	Clementis Desalle/Albina Dorder	J. Delisse/F D'or
Desautels	Joannam Linam		13-SEP-1865	Juliam Desautels/Joanna McGennis	A. Desautels/------
Desautels	Josephinam	23-MAY-1862	29-JUN-1862	Petri Desautels/Joanna Desautels	E. Bransheau/M. Desautels
Deschenes	Edmundum Josephum	31-AUG-1868	20-SEP-1868	Eugenii Deschenes/Josephina Deschenes	Eugenius Panuguère/Hortensia Lisseman
Deschenes	Francis Xavier	26-MAY-1852	07-JUN-1852	Teophile Deschenes/Charlotte Chenard	F. Laguisse/J. Deschenes
Deschênes	Moysen	06-FEB-1865	06-FEB-1865	------/Marguarita Deschènes	M. St.-Pierre/J. St -Pierre
Descoteaux	Lucina		01-DEC-1850	Peter Descoteaux/Mary Wheeler	L Beaudreaux/M Clavet
Descoteaux	M---y		04-DEC-1850	Peter Descoteaux/Mary Wheeler	J. Clavet/------
Deseers	Mariam Viviannam	30-JUN-1909	04-JUL-1909	Alphonso J. Desears/Edna Corbeille	Josephus DeLeers/Melnda LeBeau-Corbeille
Desjardins	Mariam Helenam	25-MAY-1902	30-MAY-1902	Alphonso Desjardins/Maria Tardif	Josephus Frecnar/Helena Fontaine
Deslauriers		12-JUN-1870	19-JUN-1870	Isidori Deslauriers/Alicia Carrière	Ludovicus Laplante/Mathilda Carrière
Deslauriers	Alicam Mariam	28-JAN-1906	18-FEB-1906	Georgio Deslauriers/Adelina Dionne	Abraham Dionne/Tillie Kilyke
Deslauriers	Georgium Israel	08-JAN-1904	24-JAN-1904	Georgio Deslauriers/Adelina Dion	Michael Ryaume/Marianna Parenteau
Deslauriers	Mariam Leam	01-MAR-1872	07-APR-1872	Isidori Deslauriers/Alicia Corrière	David Carrière/Lea Theriau
Deslisse	Carolum Josephum	20-MAR-1863	04-APR-1863	Julii Deslisse/Pppilippina Deslisse	J. LeBeau/------ -----
Desloriers	Viviannam Mariam	20-MAR-1907	24-MAR-1907	Georgio Desloriers/Adelina Dionne	Airla Lepne/Nancy-Maria McDonald
Desmarais	Josephinam	02-AUG-1860	11-AUG-1861	Antoni Desmarais/D. Desmarais	E. Vadney/E. Lamontagne
Desnoyer	Eduardum	17-JAN-1854	01-FEB-1854	Huberti Desnoyer/Delia Bodrieaux	H. Denoyer/S Poderet
Desnoyers	Abrahamum Israelem	24-APR-1863	17-MAY-1863	Abrahami Desnoyers/Delilah Desnoyers	I Beaudrieau/H. Lemaire
Desnoyers	Davidem	18-SEP-1870	02-OCT-1870	Huberti Desnoyers/Ursula Desnoyers	Franciscus Carrière/Josephina Duprat
Desnoyers	Eliam	12-FEB-1873	23-MAR-1873	Huberti Desnoyers/Ursula Desnoyers	David Carrière/Lea Theriau
Desnoyers	Exildam	02-MAR-1868	10-MAY-1868	Huberti Desnoyers/Ursula Desnoyers	Joannis Fernet/Exilda Fernet
Desnoyers	Juliam Adelinam	19-NOV-1865	07-DEC-1865	Huberti Desnoyers/Adelina Desnoyers	E Joubert/J Beaudrieau
Desnoyers*	Joseph				
Desnoyers*	Matilda	13-JAN-1856	27-JAN-1856	Hubert Desnoyers/Delia Bodriau	----- Bodriau/S. Brant
Despas	Alfredum	02-NOV-1864	02-NOV-1864	Alfredi Despas/Maria Despas	P Fontane/L. Fontaine
Despas	Florimondum	06-JAN-1863	07-JAN-1863	Florimondi Despas/Phlomena Despas	A Dedlisse/M. Fontaine
Despins	Mariam Ludovicam	25-FEB-1864	27-MAR-1864	Florinandi Despins/Philomena Despins	V Poingrère/M Desmarais
Desrochers	Aurelium Normam	08-AUG-1905	13-AUG-1905	Ledgero Desrochers/Maria Rheaume	Eduardus Desrochers/Evelina Rheaume
Desrochers	William Edwnum Stanisla	14-JUN-1905	18-JUN-1905	Eduardo Desrochers/Eva Rheaume	Ludgerus Desrochers/Marta Rheaume-Desrochers
Desvillers	Adolphum Alfredum	18-AUG-1896	21-AUG-1896	Adolpho Desvillers/Alphonsina Lanctot	Alfredus Pingais/Elsea Desvillers
Desvillers	Albertum	08-FEB-1894	11-FEB-1894	Emilio Desvillers/Marie Laberge	Alfred Pingais/Alphonsina Lanctot
Desvillers	Arthurum	12-FEB-1890	13-FEB-1890	Amato Desvillers/Maria Laberge	Arthurus Laberge/Apollina Sauvé
Desvillers	Ceciliam Helenam	02-FEB-1901	06-FEB-1901	Adolpho Desvillers/Alphonsina Lanctot	Eduardus Gervas/Helena Desvillers
Desvillers	Eduardum	27-JAN-1886	28-JAN-1886	Amato Desvillers/Maria Laberge	Theophilo Desvillers/Adela Lomblot
Desvillers	Helenam Josephinam	22-DEC-1883	23-DEC-1883	Amato Desvillers/Maria Laberge	Eugenius Pinguer/Hartencia Lismond
Desvillers	Joannem Leonem	04-JUL-1898	10-JUL-1898	Emilio Desvillers/Maria Laberge	Joannes Ziegler/Nelsea Desvillers
Desvillers	Mariam Nelseam	28-SEP-1894	30-SEP-1894	Adolpho Desvillers/Alphonsina Lanctot	Josephus Lomblot/Maria Laberge
Desvillers	Mariam Stellam	29-JAN-1888	30-JAN-1888	Amato Desvillers/Maria Labarge	Adolphus Desvillers/Rosa Lomblat
Desvillers	Rosaliam Mabel	04-MAR-1892	06-MAR-1892	Emilo Desvillers/Maria Laberge	Josephus Lomblot/Catherina Kramer
Deterville*	Petrum Josephum	10-JUL-1857	12-JUL-1857	Petri-J. Deterville/Elisatha Defarge	J Huss---t/D. Huss---t
Dethro	Edmondum Ludovicum	12-APR-1878	12-MAY-1878	Antonio Dethro/Sopha Allard	Sister-Maria Dale/ brother
Develiers*	Fredericum	01-DEC-1857	06-DEC-1857	Carolus Develiers/Derina L'anneau	J. Larouse/M. Osseu-
Develiers*	Mariam Lousam	30-NOV-1858	05-DEC-1858	Augusti Develirs/Virg--- D---	Felix-John Jesse--/Jaqolore Cyrs
Develue	Ralph Adolph	01-AUG-1919	03-AUG-1919	Adolph-Alfred Develue/Agnes Pauger	Elsworth Pauget/Louise Pauger
Devet*	Joannem	01-OCT-1858	17-OCT-1858	Nicolaus Devet/Cath Smet	Joannis Brown/Elsabt Mossel
Devey*	Catharine				
Devey*	Catherine	25-MAR-1857	04-JAN-1859	Patrick Devey/Esther Devey	Hugh Devey/Honora Corrigan
Devey*	Catherine	25-MAR-1857	04-JAN-1858	Patrck Devey/Esther Devey	Hugh Devey/Honora Corrighn

Surname	Given Name	Birth	Baptism	Parents	Godparents
Devilers*	Federik	01-DEC-1857	06-DEC-1857	Charles Devilers/Derina L'anneaux	J. Larouse/M. Osseau
Devilers*	Judocus	24-JAN-1860	31-JAN-1860	M---- Devilers/---- D'Or	Macus Amrau/Delna Dusain
Devilerse	Alexandrum	03-NOV-1862	23-NOV-1862	Augusti Devilersc/Felicitatis Devilerse	D Michel/O. Mocquin
Devilerse	Virginam	18-JUN-1867	18-JUN-1867	Augusti Devilerse/Felicitatis Devilerse	A Devilersse/A Devilersse
Devilerse*	Marie Louise				
Deviliir*	Mariam Lousam	30-NOV-1858	05-DEC-1858	Huberti Devilir/Virgi-ta D'Or	Jehn Lossan/----- Lossan
Devillers	Albertum Theophilum	21-FEB-1908	01-MAR-1908	Theophalo Devillers/Elizabeth Lanetot	Carolus Devillers/Louise Devillers
Devillers	Clarentium Julium	02-NOV-1905	12-NOV-1905	Carolo Devillers/Maria Garot	Julius Paingaire/Catherine Garot-Dugleman
Devillers	Ludovicam Annam	04-FEB-1896	15-FEB-1896	Emilto Desvillers/Maria Laberge	Edwardus Lucier/Anna Richter
Devillers	Mariam Alccam	02-FEB-1882	03-FEB-1882	Amato Dcvillers/Maria Laberge	Carolus Beauregard/Falomie Yelle
Devillerse	Carolum Josephum	06-MAR-1865	12-MAR-1865	Augusti Devillerse/Felicitatis Devillerse	E Painguère/H. Lismore
Devillerse	Delimam		25-OCT-1863	Augusti Devillerse/Felicitatis Devillerse	V P-inguère/D Touchete
Devillerse	Teophilum Josephum		12-MAY-1861	Augusti Devillerse/Felicitatis Devillerse	M. Devillerse/A. D---d
Devin	Cathernam	14-DEC-1859	24-DEC-1859	Joannis Devin/Anna Olgetlar	Michaelis Olgelar/Maria Sullivan
Devin*	Mariam Annam	12-AUG-1857	16-AUG-1857	Joannis Devin/T.-Elena Clagelen	D. Sullivan/E. Griffen
Devine*	Maria E--ira	12-AUG-1857	16-AUG-1857	John Devin/Elles-- Logeln	D Sullivan/-. Griffin
Devoe	Donnell Franciscum	17-FEB-1908	29-MAR-1908	Rolando Devoc/Eleonora Boucher	David Boucher/Elizabeth Boucher
Devoe	Philliseam Ceciliam	04-MAR-1903	05-APR-1903	Rollino Devoe/Eleonora Roucher	Franciscus Boucher/Judith Bessette
Devry	Fidelem Ludovicum	28-OCT-1863	28-OCT-1863	Joseph Devry/Coleta Devry	F. Devry/-------
Devry	Fredericum Theodorum	13-OCT-1861	13-OCT-1861	Joseph Devry/---tta. Devry	F. Devry/A. Dany
Devry	Josephum Henricum	31-MAY-1869	24-OCT-1869	Josephi Devry/Coleta Vandrissen	Joannes-V. Devry/Coleta Rondeau
Devry	Vitalem Alphonsum	17-FEB-1866	07-OCT-1866	Josephi Devry/Coleta Devry	J Devry/T Devry
Diaume	Mariam Adelam Annam	09-JAN-1872	10-JAN-1872	Michaelis Diaume/Philomina Beau	Alexander Faucher/Flavia Sylvester
Diette	Alfredum Wilbert	01-SEP-1894	02-SEP-1894	Alfredo Diette/Edessa Letourneau	Josephus Diette/Maria Boomhart
Diette	Ceciliam Ethel	09-DEC-1908	15-NOV-1908	Alfredo Diette/Edessa LeTourneau,	Josephus Balthazar/Flora LeTourneau
Diette	Elizabeth Violam	03-JUL-1897	11-JUL-1897	Josepho Diette/Elizabeth Letourneau	Josephus Letourneau/Catharina McCabe
Diette	Floram Idam	08-APR-1901	14-APR-1901	Josepho Diette/Elizabeth Letourneau	Gulielmus Balthazar/Ida Letourneau
Diette	Georgium	28-SEP-1895	30-SEP-1895	Josepho Diette/Elizabeth Letourneau	Pascals Letourneau/Mathilda Diette
Diette	Josephum Arthurum	01-JAN-1897	03-JAN-1897	Alfredo Diette/Edessa Letourneau	Josephus Diette/Elisa Letourneau
Diette	Josephum Peasley	06-JUL-1889	07-JUL-1889	Josepho Diette/Elizabeth Letourneau	Josephus Diette/Maria Boomhart
Diette	Ludovicum Da--	22-OCT-1873	02-NOV-1873	Josephi Diette/Philomena Lemome	Nazarus Dame/Ludovica Melousson
Diette	Mariam Edessam	09-APR-1902	13-APR-1902	Alfredo Diette/Edessa Letourneau	Isaac St--Antoine/Maria-Joanna Letourneau
Diette	Mariam Ednam	08-MAR-1891	12-MAR-1891	Josepho Diette/Elizabeth Letourneau	Joannes Mengel/Ezilda Diette
Diette	Mariam Gratiam Margarita	29-MAR-1893	02-APR-1893	Josepho Diette/Edessa Letourneau	Alfredus Diette/Edessa Letourneau
Diette	Mariam Hazel	03-DEC-1895	03-DEC-1895	Josepho Diette/Elisa Letourneau	Isaacus St -Antoine/Maria Letourneau
Diette	Philumenam Florence Edn	06-SEP-1898	11-SEP-1898	Alfredo Diette/Edessa Letourneau	Medardus Comeau/Mathilda Diette
Diette	Rosam Mariam	19-JUN-1905	25-JUN-1905	Alfredo Diette/Edessa LeTourneau,	Joannes Mengle/Melina LeTourneau
Dillon*	Davidem	20-JUN-1858	03-JUL-1858	Patrici Dillon/Maria Scanlin	J. O'Ncil/C. Jacob
Dilon*	David	20-JUN-1858	03-JUL-1858	Ptrick Dilon/Mary Scanlon	Jeremieh O'Neil/Catherine Jacob
Dmegan*	Joannem	20-JUN-1858	04-SEP-1858	Michaelis Dinegan/Marie Dennigan	John Keef/Marie Connell
Dinel	Elizabetham	10-JUL-1871	16-JUL-1871	Ludovici Dinel/Dyonsia Gervais	Gilbertus Bernard/Melvina Gervais
Dinel	Mariam Isabellam Rosam	13-FEB-1905	27-FEB-1905	Dominico Dinel/Maria-Anna Rose	Nelson Dinel/Rosa Meas
Dinell	Dominicum	19-FEB-1876	21-FEB-1876	Ludovici Dinell/Dionsia Barbo-Jarvis	G Surprenant/---- Barbo
Dinelle	Agnetem Sylvam	03-OCT-1896	11-OCT-1896	Ludovico Dinelle/Dyonsia Gervais	Josephus Pariseault/Melina Beauregard
Dinelle	Israelem	09-JUL-1883	11-JUL-1883	Israel Dinelle/Sophia Belanger	Narcissus Dinelle/Armina Belanger
Dinelle	Josephum Eliseum	29-DEC-1888	06-JAN-1889	Narcisso Dinelle/Hermalma Belanger	Petrus Barbeau/Philumena Charron
Dinelle	Laurentium Eduardum	26-JAN-1887	30-JAN-1887	Narcisso Dinelle/Harmmia Belanger	Eduardus Durecher/Maria Archangela
Dinelle	Ludovicum	07-JUL-1874	12-JUL-1874	Ludovici Dinelle/Denisa Gervais	Narcisus Dinelle/Adelaida Gervais
Dinelle	Mariam Clotildam Relinam	15-FEB-1884	29-MAR-1884	Ludovico Dinelle/Dionysia Gervais	Gedeon Brunet/Melina Venne

Surname	Given Name	Birth	Baptism	Parents	Godparents
Dinelle	Mariam Doretheam Margar	17-OCT-1909	24-OCT-1909	Nelson Dinelle/Ella Carlsted	Dominicus Dinelle/Maria-Anna-Rose Dinelle
Dinelle	Mariam Isabellam Rosam	03-FEB-1905	21-FEB-1905	Dominico Dinelle/Maria-Anna Rose	Narcissus Dinelle/Rosa Meas
Dinelle	Mariam Ludovicam	08-APR-1886	25-APR-1886	Ludovico Dinelle/Dionysia Gervais	Ludgerus Noupré/Elmira Lefort
Dinelle	Narcissum	03-OCT-1884	12-OCT-1884	Narcisso Dinelle/Harmelina Belanger	Ludovicus Dinelle/Sophia Belanger
Dinelle	Narcissum	15-APR-1881	24-APR-1881	Ludovico Dinelle/Denisa Gervais	O. Rabidoux/E. Lambert
Dinelle	Telesphorum	07-JAN-1883	14-JAN-1883	Ludovico Dinelle/Dyonisia Gervais	Telesphorus Gervais/Delia Moquin
Dinelle-Denell	Mariam Melvinam Agneta	21-JUN-1908	05-JUL-1908	Dominico Dinelle/Maria-Annam Rose	Antonius Shumaker/Melvina Gervais-Barbeau
Dion	Honore D--maelis	21-DEC-1874	26-DEC-1874	Mich-- Dion/Philalese Bibo	Israel Beaupré/Anna Bibo
Dion	Rosam Mariam	05-JAN-1880	05-FEB-1880	Michaell Dion/Celonse Bibeau	J Simonin/J. Simonin
Dion	William George	10-DEC-1876	20-DEC-1876	Michali Dion/Philunis Bibo	H. Bibo/J. Clif
Divine	Sarahm Joannem	30-SEP-1861	06-OCT-1861	Joannis Divine/Helena Divine	J. O'conner/C Eagan
Divine	Suzannam	05-JAN-1864	17-JAN-1864	Joannis Divine/Helena Divine	J. Walters/S. Walters
Dix	Antonium Alexandrum	06-APR-1865	07-MAY-1865	Antoni Dix/Josephina Krembs	E. Krembs/A. Hoeflinger
Dix	Richardum Paulum Antoni	25-DEC-1861	02-FEB-1862	Richardi Dix/J. Dix	P Hanse-/-------
Dixneuste	Diliam	24-APR-1878	25-APR-1878	Ludovici Dixneuste/Denina Dun--	M. Lambert/ wife
Do-en*-	Margerette E-na	10-JUL-1859	24-JUL-1859	P-t-- Do-en-/Elina Murphy	M. May----/Mrs May----
Dodelin	Georgum	21-SEP-1860	02-OCT-1860	Dyonsii Dodelin/Perpetua Dodelin	J Pariso/E. Letourneau
Dodelin	Homerum	31-AUG-1862	28-SEP-1862	Stanslai Dodelin/Perpetua Dodelin	H. Periso/O. Leonard
Dodelin	Josephum Olivierum	26-NOV-1862	26-NOV-1862	Oliverii Dodelin/Celina Dodelin	J. Dodelin/A. Brico
Dodelin	Petrum	27-NOV-1864	11-DEC-1864	Stanslai Dodelin/Perpetua Dodelin	J Tremblé/E. Dodelin
Dodin	Mariam		02-SEP-1852	Stanslai Dodin/Perpetua Pariseaux	M. Pariseaux/M. Delaire
Dogerthy*	Brigeta	04-DEC-1857	16-JAN-1858	Eduard Dogerthy/Marie Gellan	Patrick Ragan/Anna Gellan
Dogerthy*	Brigetham	04-DEC-1857	16-JAN-1858	Edw Dogerthy/Maria Gillan	P. Rayan/A Jella--
Doheny	Jacobum	10-NOV-1862	23-NOV-1862	Patricii Doheny/Helena Doheny	G Reilley/A. Pitt
Doheny*	Eduardus		24-AUG-1856	Patrick Doheny/Ellisa Quikely	P. Rayan/M. Rayan
Doherty*	James	08-JUN-1858	04-JUL-1858	Edmound Doherty/Ann Russell	Jeremieh O'Neil/Mary McCady
Dohiney*	Eduardum		24-AUG-1856	Patricii Dohiney/Elena G--k----	P. Rayan/M. Rayan
Dolan	Isidorem	13-AUG-1852	12-DEC-1852	Andrea Dolan/Rosa Martin	N. Martin/M. Vaughan
Dolan	Thomam Edwardum	10-JUN-1863	21-JUN-1863	Joannis Dolan/Marguarita Dolan	M. O'Brien/H. Bolan
Dolan	William	08-JUL-1851	14-JUL-1851	Andrew Dolan/Rose Martin	T. Flod/M. Green
Dolan*	Bridget	19-MAR-1858	27-JUN-1858	Mcl Dolon/Graesy Obrien	Richard Matthew/Bridget-Ann Haven
Dolan*	Brdgittam	17-MAR-1858	27-JUN-1858	Michaelis Dolan/Gr--- O'Brien	R. Matthew/B. Nav---
Dolten*	Edmondus	16-JUN-1858	10-JUL-1858	John Dolten/Catherina Flagerty	Edemond Flagerty/Julia Flagerty
Dolton*	Edmundum	15-JUN-1858	10-JUL-1858	Joannis Dalton/Catherina Flagherty	D Flagherty/J. Flagherty
Donaghoe	John	23-MAY-1852	30-MAY-1852	Timothy Donaghoe/Ellen Moore	J O'Neil/E. O'Neil
Donahoe*	Cornelius				
Donaus	Margaritam Willdam	05-JUN-1880	06-JUN-1880	Isidore Donaus/Rosalia Veine	L Veine/C. Veine
Donavan	Jacobum Danielem	07-JAN-1883	03-MAR-1883	Michael Donavan/Margarita Fuller	Gulielmus Laughlin/Clara Mullane
Dondelain*	Michaelem	29-MAY-1856	29-JUN-1856	Densii Dondelain/Perpetua Parriso	H. ParrisoC. Menard
Dondelan*	Michaelis	25-MAY-1856	29-JUN-1856	Denis Dondelain/Perpetula Pariso	H Pariso/C. Innard
Dondelan*	Olivier	10-MAR-1858	14-MAR-1858	Stanslasi Dondelain/Perpecula Parriso	----- Parisso/M. Lamire
Donegan*	Joannem	20-JUN-1858	04-SEP-1858	Michaelis Donegan/Mariam Donegan	J Keefe/M Cornell
Donelhy*	Martha	24-SEP-1856	12-OCT-1856	William Dorethy/Cath Dorethy	R McGart/M Fossen
Donelly	Adelam	02-JUN-1854	04-JUL-1854	Antonii Donnely/Perpetua Pariso	J Parizo/E. Parizo
Donet	Mariam Louisam Victoriam		30-OCT-1881	Isidoro Donet/Rosalia Venne	Edwardus Venne/Maria Beaupre
Donly*	Thomane Franciscum	11-JUL-1858	01-AUG-1858	Michaelis Donly/Marguerita Ragan	J Shea/-. Serwe
Donn	Petrum Wellielmum	06-APR-1878	21-APR-1878	Nazar Donn/Catherina Endress	P. McPell/J. Endress
Donnely*	John				
Donnet	Rginam	14-JUL-1877		Issidore Donnet/Rosalie Vaine	J. Donné/D. Vaine

37

Surname	Given Name	Birth	Baptism	Parents	Godparents
Donneyo*	John	31-JAN-1856	10-FEB-1856	Larentius Donneyo/Lisa Donneyo	P Denson/A. Conroy
Donohoe*	Cornelium	19-JAN-1860	15-FEB-1860	Cornelii Donohoe/Julie Certain	Patrcus Cahill/Maria Conner
Donovan	Helenam	28-MAY-1861	01-JUL-1861	Michaelis Donovan/Maria Donovan	D Madden/A. Keef
Donovan	Timotheum	17-FEB-1863	28-FEB-1863	Guillelmi Donovan/Catharina Donovan	T. Hallaghan/M. O'conner
Donovan*	Ellen				
Dooley	Elizabeth Ettam	25-SEP-1884	10-OCT-1902	Henrico Dooley/Ida Schafer	Josephus Landerman/Ophelia Dumas
Dooley	Elizabetham	29-AUG-1861	14-SEP-1861	Guillelmi Dooley/Anna Dooley	C Bolduc/L Bolduc
Dooly	Edwardum	01-NOV-1862	19-JAN-1863	Michaelis Dooly/Marguarita Dooly	J Killgallon/A Stanton
Dooly	Joannem Franciscum	09-OCT-1863	18-OCT-1863	Guillelmi Dooly/Anna Dooly	P. Boyle/M. Dolan
Dooly	Marguaritam	05-JUL-1861	16-SEP-1861	Michaelis Dooly/Marguarita Dooly	M. Corkery/A. Weis
Door*	Margaret				
Door*	Mary Louise				
Doore*	Mariam Lousiam	26-MAY-1860	27-MAY-1860	Michaelis Doore/Elena ------	Petrus A------/Mary-Anna Grimmer
Doore*	Mariam Margeth	26-MAY-1860	27-MAY-1860	Michaelis Doore/Elena ------	------ ------/Maria-Cath Petri
Dor*	Mary Magdalan				
Dor*	Mary Magdelem	12-SEP-1858	25-SEP-1858	Michel Dor/Maria Lisey	Chs Thill/Marie Kramer
Doran*	C. Elisa				
Doroghty	Julia	23-JAN-1851	26-JAN-1851	Edward Doroghty/Mary Guillen	---- McGrath/A. Malway
Doroghty	Mariam Ceciliam	20-MAR-1853		Jacobi Doroghty/Anna McDonald	J. Mclaughlin/C. H--k---
Doroghty	William	25-MAR-1852	07-JUN-1852	Willam Doroghty/Catherine Doroghty	J Galaher/B. Galaher
Doron*	Elisabeth	31-MAR-1860	02-APR-1860	Michaelis Doron/Grace Obryne	Jocobus Terches/Louisa John
Dorr	Joannem	27-APR-1866	13-MAY-1866	Michaelis Dorr/Maria Dorr	J Wirtz/R. Reichert
Dorr	Petrum	22-JUL-1862	11-AUG-1862	Michaelis Dorr/Maria Dorr	P Thill/M. Thill
Dorrethy	Margarctham	03-AUG-1853	21-AUG-1853	Lunardi Dorrethy/Maria Gillan	J Roschetter/A. Roschetter
Dorrethy*	Mariam	25-AUG-1855	26-AUG-1855	Eduardi Dorrethy/Maria Gillan	J Mangan/B. McDormit
Dorrethy*	Martham	24-SEP-1856	12-OCT-1856	Gulielmi Dorrethy/Catherina Dorrethy	R. Mcgant/M. Cussen
Dorrethy*	Maria	25-AUG-1855	26-AUG-1855	Eduard Dorretty/Maria Gillan	J. Mangan/B. McDormit
Dotton	Honoram	06-MAR-1862	10-MAY-1862	Joannis Dotton/Catharina Dotton	M Mcisaac/M Brasney
Dougherty	James				
Dougherty	Mariam	03-JUN-1861	23-JUN-1861	Danielis Dougherty/Helena Dougherty	J. Dougherty/H Dougherty
Dougherty*	Jacobum	08-JUN-1858		Edmundi Dougherty/Anna Russell	J. O'Neil/M. Mchessay
Dougherty*	James	28-OCT-1858	16-NOV-1858	Daniel Dougherty/Helene Doner	Alexand Gallaher/Mary Chevel---
Douly*	Thamas Franciscum	11-JUL-1858	01-AUG-1858	Michal Douly/Margertha Rayan	John Seha/Sebe Ser----
Doun-*	Eduardum	05-AUG-1858	22-AUG-1858	Thamas Doun--/Brigetha Readen	Martinus Curans/------ Curans
Down	Brigittam Mc ----		17-DEC-1859	Joannis Down/Anna Down	Denis Down/Briget Rogan
Down	Claram Josephnam	18-NOV-1859	23-DEC-1859	Joannes Down/Catherina Doyle	Jacobus Moore/Maria Da-s
Doyle	Jacobum	30-MAY-1862	01-JUN-1862	Jacobi Doyle/Maria Doyle	M Doyle/C Ganon
Doyle	Jacobus	21-JUL-1860	29-JUL-1860	Patrici Doyle/Maria Doyle	Gorgius Gibson/Elisabetha Cra---
Doyle	Michaelem Esterum	15-APR-1862	15-APR-1862	Maurtu Doyle/Maria Doyle	P Neary/M. Rafferty
Doyle	Petrum	22-AUG-1863	06-SEP-1863	Petri Doyle/Barbara Doyle	P Tierney/M Kenny
Doyle	Richardum	26-OCT-1861	10-NOV-1861	Petri Doyle/Barbara Doyle	M. Doyle/A. McCune
Doyle*	Annam Mariam	25-DEC-1856	18-JAN-1857	Petri Doyle/Margeretha Mooran	J. Flend/M Fitzsimmons
Doyle*	Helenam	16-JUN-1858	27-JUN-1858	Petri Doyle/Barbara Moran	J. Tirney/C. Turtown
Doyle*	James				
Doyle*	Maria-Anna	25-DEC-1856	18-JAN-1857	Peter Doyle/Margeretha Moran	J. Flind/M. Fitsimons
Doyle*	Mariam	14-MAY-1860	20-MAY-1860	Morris Doyle/Maria Norry	Thamas Gannon/Maria Katten
Doyle*	Mary				
Doyle*	Michael				
Doyle*	Michaelem	18-FEB-1860	04-MAR-1860	Petri Doyle/Babera Moren	Corolus Ha-y/Anna Farly

Surname	Given Name	Birth	Baptism	Parents	Godparents
Drummond	Claudium Eduardum	31-OCT-1851	14-DEC-1851	Jacobo-G Drummond/Paulina-I Joubert	Carolus Bullis/Helena Joubert
Drums	Rosa	20-AUG-1857	30-AUG-1857	Andrew Drums/Ann Smith	H. Molway/M. Vaughn
Du--ert*	Cleram			Antonii Du--ert/Catherina Clis	L. Duranseau/J M-bllon
Du--meur*	Henricum			Joannis Bat Du--meur/Maria Peron	Joschus Pro/Catherine Perin
Dubois	Alexandrum Arnold	31-OCT-1899	05-NOV-1899	Josepho Dubois/Cedulia Beaudreault	Alexander Marcoux/Arzelia Beaudreault
Dubois	Alfredum Theodorem	06-JUL-1888	08-JUL-1888	Josepho Dubois/Cedulia Beaudreault	--orma Lyonans/Ludovica Beaudreault
Dubois	Clarentum Georgium	28-JUL-1908	02-AUG-1908	Josepho Dubois/Cedulia Beaudreau	Gulielmus Rhoder/Carolina Dubois-Rhoder
Dubois	Coram Josephnam	13-FEB-1884	17-FEB-1884	Josepho Dubois/Cedulia Beaudrault	Petrus Dubois/Sophia Brillon
Dubois	Deliam Elisam	07-JAN-1889	22-JAN-1889	Georgius Dubois/Emelia Tremblay	Moyses Tremblay/Maria-Eugenia Lussier
Dubois	Felicem	24-JAN-1870	29-MAY-1870	Petri Dubois/Virginia Dubois	Daniel Daugherty/Maria Garo
Dubois	Georgium	08-MAY-1866	10-JUN-1866	Petri Dubois/Virginia Dubois	J. Demars/M Dany
Dubois	Guilelmum	02-FEB-1865	01-MAR-1865	Petri Dubois/Virginia Dubois	J Dougherty/A Dougherty
Dubois	Hazel Mariam	15-JUN-1909	15-JUN-1909	Frederico Dubois/Ida Brown	Gulielmus Rhoder/Cara Dubois-Rhoder
Dubois	Inez Ceciliam	09-JUN-1909	13-JUN-1909	Elmero Dubois/Purl-Inez Field	Josephus Dubois/Cedulia Beaudrea-Dubois
Dubois	Joannem	03-MAY-1892	26-MAY-1892	Petro Dubois/Julia Kopolaska	Petrus Dubois/Virginia Gascon
Dubois	Joannem Emericum	03-DEC-1896	10-DEC-1896	Josepho Dubois/Cedulia Beaudreault	Ireneus Beaudreault/E Frenette
Dubois	Joannem Raimondum	12-MAR-1893	17-MAR-1893	Josepho Dubois/Cedulia Beaudreault	Alexandrum Durocher/Francisca Kenney
Dubois	Josephum	03-MAR-1886	05-MAR-1886	Josepho Dubois/Cedulia Beaudreault	Laurentius Beaudrealt/Virginia Gascon
Dubois	Lorentum Henricum	12-NOV-1890	16-NOV-1890	Josepho Dubois/Cedulia Beaudrault	Josephus Lepne/Sophia Beaudreault
Dubois	Ludovicum	19-DEC-1862	20-JAN-1863	Petri Dubois/Virginia Dubois	J. Walsh/C Walsh
DuBois	Mariam	27-MAY-1860		Petri DuBois/--er-ina Ga-leau	Palase L'Turneu/Marie Baumare
Dubois	Mariam Ludovicam	02-JUN-1872	03-JUN-1872	Fr. Dubois/Maria Dubois	Eduardus Porchero/Maria Porchero
Dubois	Mariane	27-MAY-1860	20-MAY-1860	Petri Dubois/Vorgina Gaslean	P. Elumen/A Basneau
Dubois	Mary				
Dubois	Pierre				
Dubois*	Joseph				
Dubois*	Josephum	25-SEP-1858	17-OCT-1858	Befu Dubois/Vergina Glasclau	Michel McGr--y/Cat McCort
Dubreuil	Mariam Adelaidam		06-OCT-1867	Ludovici Dubreuil/Justina Ch---t-	P Dubois/V Dubois
Duchaine	Desiderus	21-AUG-1856	31-AUG-1856	Theophile Duchaine/Charlota Chenard	D. Chnat/D Duchaine
Duchaine*	Laurentiam	12-SEP-1856	12-OCT-1856	Caroli Duchain/Julia Christian-	F. Lasson/D. Jubert
Duchène	Alfredum	03-MAY-1867	26-MAY-1867	Eugenii Duchène/Josephina Duchène	J. Painguère/M. Gervais
Duchesne	Eugenium Baptistam	19-JUN-1865	25-MAY-1865	Eugenii Duchesne/Josephina Gervais	J Gervais/M. Leclar
Duchen*	Lorentia	26-SEP-1856	12-OCT-1856	Charles Duchien/Julie Chretienne	F. Losson/----- Jubert
Duford	Juliam Amablem	29-SEP-1893	08-OCT-1893	Cyrillo Duford/Salomea Boivin	Petrus Lepine/Josephina Corbeille
Duford	Lauram	02-OCT-1892	08-OCT-1892	Ludovico Duford/Laura Durocher	Nicolaus Lamanche/Marcellina Livermois
Dufort	Albertam Agnetem	28-FEB-1887	02-MAR-1887	Josepho Dufort/Elizabeth Rochell	Gulielmus Rochell/Agnes Rochell
Dufort	Carolum Cyrillum	27-JUN-1895	24-JUL-1895	Josepho Dufort/Elizabeth Rockel	Cyrillus Corbeille/Anastasia Dufort
Dufort	Celiam Franciscam	22-DEC-1898	22-JAN-1899	Cyrillo Duford/Josephina Dufort	Ludovicus Dufort/Adela Durocher
Dufort	Cyrilum	11-SEP-1867	20-SEP-1867	Antonii Dufort/Justina Clche.	J. Duquete/O. Tessier
Dufort	Josephinam	27-JUN-1865	09-JUL-1865	Antonii Dufort/Justina Dufort	G. -/A. Dufort
Dufort	Josephum	18-JAN-1863	01-FEB-1863	Antonii Dufort/Justina Dufort	J. Labonté/F. Tessier
Dufort	Mariam Mildred	29-AUG-1900	09-SEP-1900	Cyrillo Dufort/Salomea Boivin	Paulus Gagnier/Josephina Duquet
Dufort	Mariam Stellam	07-SEP-1890	14-SEP-1890	Ludovico Dufort/Adela Durocher	Alexander Durocher/Maria Lamanche
Dufort*	Melnam	11-MAR-1861	17-MAR-1861	Antonii Dufort/Josephina Dufort	E Vadney/A. Dufresne
Dufort*	Elisa		30-AUG-1857	Antonius Dufort/Christina Cli---	L. Duranseau/J. Molilim
Dufort*	Lous				
Dufort*	Ludovicum	17-JUN-1859	28-AUG-1859	Antonie Dufort/Justina Clef	L. Clef/D. Dufraine
Dufort**	Franciscum Xaverium Lau	20-FEB-1896	08-MAR-1896	Cyrille Dufort/Salomea Boivin	Franciscus-Xaverius Hurteau/Laura Durocher
Dufraine	Dulania	30-JAN-1854	30-JAN-1854	Petrus Dufraine/Anna Muner	L. Bodreaux/M. Brien

39

Surname	Given Name	Birth	Baptism	Parents	Godparents
Dufraine	Eduardum	07-AUG-1878	08-SEP-1878	Antoni Dufraine/Elisi-e St.-Marie	E Vernet/ (wife)
Dufraine	Josephnam	24-AUG-1877	09-SEP-1877	Noel Dufraine/Margerth Lepine	L Elis/J Lepine
Dufraine	Josephum	25-APR-1875	09-MAY-1875	Noel Dufraine/Margerth Lepine	Josephus Lepine/Emma Gothic
Dufraine*	Evaristum	20-FEB-1856	02-MAR-1856	Petri Dufraine/Olivine Manmer	E Vernais/A Dufraine
Dufraine*	Evaristus	20-FEB-1856	02-MAR-1856	Perlu Dufraine/Olivma Meunier	E -umus/D Dufraine
Dufraine*	Maria	04-JUL-1858	18-JUL-1858	Perre Dufraine/Oli--- M---it	Joseph Parris,/Delphina Dufrain
Dufraisne	Bernardum Romanum	02-JUL-1906	08-JUL-1906	Georgs DeFraisne/Anna Welling	Nicholas Welling/Louis Welling
Dufraisne	Elizabeth Adelem	22-APR-1908	27-APR-1908	Alberto Dufraisne/Alexina Bastien	Pacificus Bastien/Adelis Robidoux-Bastien
Dufraisne	Laurentium Eduardum	31-DEC-1907	05-JAN-1908	Georgio Dufraisne/Anna Wellin	Eduardus Dufraisne/Catharine Welling
Dufraisnc	Mariam Catharnam	26-OCT-1908	01-NOV-1908	Eduardo Dufraisne/Catharine Welling	Casparus Welling/Gratia Morris
Dufraisne	Rosam Mariam	31-MAR-1907	07-APR-1907	Alberto Dufraisne/Alexina Bastien	Arthurus Venne/Maria Defraisne
Dufresne	Agnetiam	04-FEB-1866	04-MAR-1866	Francisci Dufresne/Elizabetha Dufresne	E. Vadney/A. Dufresne
Dufresne	Agnetiam	04-FEB-1866	04-MAR-1866	Francisci Dufresne/Elizabetha Dufresne	E. Vadney/A. Dufresne
Dufresne	Albertum	24-OCT-1869	05-DEC-1869	Francisci Dufresne/Elizabetha Ste.-Marie	Octavus Durocher/Adelina Durocher
Dufresne	Alfredum	26-DEC-1862	11-JAN-1863	Petri Dufresne/Onesima Dufresne	P. Dufresne/C. St.-Marie
Dufresne	Alphonsam	27-MAR-1868	26-APR-1868	Petri Dufresne/Onesima Dufresne	Franciscus Dufraine/Elizabetha Ste -Marie
Dufresne	Ambrosium Rollins	27-AUG-1904	28-AUG-1904	Georgio Dufresne/Anna Welling	Gulelmus Balthazar/Eva Welling
Dufresne	Blancam Emeliam	12-MAR-1902	16-MAR-1902	Alberto Dufresne/Alexina Bastien	Eduardus Dufresne/Elizabeth Dufresne
Dufresne	Edwardum	24-OCT-1862	26-APR-1863	Pascalis Dufresne/Sarah Dufresne	F. Dufresne/E. St. Marie
Dufresne	Elizabetham Elodiam	25-NOV-1899	26-NOV-1899	Alberta Dufresne/Alexina Bastien	Eugenius Bastien/Agnes Dufresne
Dufresne	Estherem	12-SEP-1865	21-NOV-1865	Petri Dufresne/Onesima Dufresne	N Dufresne/O Dufresne
Dufresne	Evaristam Levi	25-FEB-1871	25-MAR-1871	Noelis Dufresne/Marguarita Lépine	Evaristus Vadney/Angelica Dufresne
Dufresne	Franciscum	19-SEP-1861	22-SEP-1861	Francisci Dufresne/Elizabetha Dufresne	P. Dufresne/S Dufresne
Dufresne	Franciscum	28-APR-1873	05-MAY-1873	Noélis Dufresne/Marguarita Dufresne	Pascal Dufresne/Sarah Ste.-Marie
Dufresne	Franciscum	01-MAR-1872	10-MAR-1872	Isidori Dufresne/Emila Dufresne	Isaacus St.-Antoine/Onesima Meunier
Dufresne	Franciscum Stephanum	01-JAN-1904	03-JAN-1904	Alberto Dufrésnc/Alexina Bastien	Stephan Dufrésne/Heloisa Lebeau
Dufresne	Isidorum	08-JUL-1867	14-JUL-1867	Isidori Dufresne/Emilia St.-Antoine	M. St -Antoine/D. Benet
Dufresne	Juliam Gratiam	27-OCT-1882	12-NOV-1882	Francisco Dufresne/Elisa Ste.-Marie	Stephanus Dufresne/Agnes Dufresne
Dufresne	Lauram	22-JUL-1869	01-AUG-1869	Isidori Dufresne/Emilia St-Antoine	Petrus Dufresne/Julia St Antoine
Dufresne	Margarttam Rachel	07-APR-1898	10-APR-1898	Alberto Dufresne/Alexina Bastien	Georgus Dufresne/Maria-Anna Bastien
Dufresne	Mariam	01-OCT-1866	14-OCT-1866	Noelis Dufresne/Marguarita LePine-Dufresne	J Lepine/E. Lepine
Dufresne	Mariam	22-JUL-1868	26-JUL-1868	Joseph Dufresne/Maria Dufresne	Franciscus Roneau/Eleonora Lepine
Dufresne	Mariam Franciscam Isabell	25-MAR-1902	30-MAR-1902	Georgio Dufresne/Anna Willing	Petrus Willing/Gratia Dufresne
Dufresne	Martinam	10-JUL-1871	13-AUG-1871	Francisci Dufresne/Elizabetha Ste.-Marie	Noel Dufresne/Marguarita Lépine
Dufresne	Noel	22-AUG-1868	13-SEP-1868	Noelis Dufresne/Marguarita Dufresne	Petrus Dufresne/Onesima Meunier
Dufresne	Secondam Elizabetham	24-JUL-1863	02-AUG-1863	Francisci Dufresne/Elizabetha Ste -Marie-Dufresne	P. Dufresne/----- Meunier
Dufresne	Sophroniam	25-OCT-1860	18-NOV-1860	Petri Dufresne/Olivma Dufresne	F. Belhumeur/Zoah Dufresne
Dufresne	Stephanum	07-DEC-1867	01-JAN-1868	Francisci Dufresne/Eliza Ste.-Marie	----- Cliche/D. Cliche
Dufresne	Stephanum Kenneth	21-JUL-1910	24-JUL-1910	Alberto Defresne/Alexium Bastian	Geraldus Finnegan/Sarah Dufresne-Finnegan
Dufrésne	Susana Angelicam	11-MAR-1881	27-MAR-1881	Francisco Dufrésne/Elisa St.-Marie	N. Da--/C. Andres
Dufresne*	Mariam	04-JUL-1858	18-JUL-1858	Petri Dufrésne/Olivma Meunier	J Pariso/D. Dufresne
Duke	Marguaritam	30-APR-1853	15-MAY-1853	Gilberti Duke/Maria Finney	C Clark/M Egan
Duke	Mary-Ann	18-OCT-1850	15-JUL-1851	Gilbert Duke/Mary Finney	J. Watters/M Oconnell
Duly	Catherina	15-NOV-1859	02-JAN-1860	Michaeli Duly/Margareta Ryan	Patricus McNeil/Maria McNeil
Dumas	Eduardum Wayne	17-AUG-1908	06-SEP-1908	Olivarius Dumas/Eleonora Martin	Emericus Martin/Iona Martin
Dumas	Josephum Edwardum	31-MAY-1864		Joannis-Baptista Dumas/Maria Dumas	J. Perron/M Thomas
Dumas	Josephum Franciscum	03-NOV-1866	11-JUN-1867	Joannis-Baptista Dumas/Maria Dumas	L. Paquete/A Dumas
Dumas	Josephum Moysem	07-AUG-1861	06-SEP-1861	Joannis-Baptista Dumas/Maria Dumas	J Houle/C. Lemaire
Dumas	Josephum Urbanum	09-NOV-1862	16-MAR-1863	Joannis-Baptista Dumas/Maria Dumas	J Perron/P. Perron

40

Surname	Given Name	Birth	Baptism	Parents	Godparents
Dumas	Mariam Emiliam	01-AUG-1851	03-SEP-1852	J Baptista Dumas/Maria Perant	B Perant/M. Lagrise
Dumas	Mariam Marguaritam	03-MAR-1869	10-JUL-1869	Joannis-Baptista Dumas/Maria Perron	Josephus Perron/Adelina Morris
Dumas	Myriam Annam Eleonoram	19-SEP-1906	30-SEP-1906	Oliverio Dumas/Eleonora Martin	Leo Martin/Eleonora Dumas-Martin
Dumas*	Henry				
Dumnise	Joannes	10-JAN-1860	15-JAN-1860	Joannis Dumnise/Catherina Dumnise	Joannes Junker/Maria Dumnise
Dun	Guillelmum Cornelium	26-AUG-1861	15-SEP-1861	Thoma Dun/Bridgitta Dun	J Leaghry/B. Reader
Dun*	Edwardum	05-AUG-1858	22-AUG-1858	Thoma Dun/Bridgitta Reardon	M Curran/----- Curran
Dun*	Mary				
Dunegan*	Joannem Gulielmum	31-JAN-1856	10-FEB-1856	Laurentu Dunnegan/Lisa Dunnegan	P Donnevan/A. Conroy
Dunvan*	Hellena	03-APR-1860	08-APR-1860	Timothias Dunivan/Hellena Moore	Thamas Fitzgiben/Catherina Ary
Dunn	Mary	01-MAR-1858	03-MAR-1858	John Dunn/Catherine Doyle	James Moore/Mary Horn
Dunphy*	Maria Anna	05-APR-1857	19-APR-1857	Niculus Dunphy/Maria Woods	J Dunphy/J. Woods
Dunphy*	Mariam	05-APR-1857	19-APR-1857	Nicolaum Dunphy/Maria Woods	J Dunphy/J. Woods
Dupuis	Eduard Joseph		18-DEC-1878	Stanislaus Dupuis/Eugenia Dupuis	O Robarge/B. Robarge
Dupuis	Eugene Stanislas Josephum	20-JUN-1875	26-JUN-1875	Stanislai Dupuis/Eugenie Paniere	Eugeni Paniere/Clottilda Gagé
Dupuis	Exilliam	14-MAY-1865	21-MAY-1865	Eusebii Dupuis/Zoah Mocquin	D. Mishote/M. Mocquin
Dupuis	Gulielium Arthurum	19-AUG-1885	20-AUG-1885	Ludgerio Dupuis/Julia Lucier	Joannis-Baptiste Dupuis/Pelagia Regnier
Dupuis	Ida Leonda	22-APR-1877	25-APR-1877	Deonis Dupuis/Eugema Pangiere	J. Sherblen/ wife
Dupuis	Joseph Jeremium -yl---	23-JUN-1884	25-JUN-1884	Onesime Dupus/Onesiphine Prefontaine	Ludger Dupuis/Julie Lussier
Dupuis	Josephum	01-SEP-1866	02-SEP-1866	Baptista Dupuis/Dyonisa Dupuis	J Parizo/B. Dupuis
Dupuis	Josephum Victorum	23-JUL-1879	27-JUL-1879	Eusebius Dupuis/Al--pho- Prefontaine	L Prefontaine/D. B-Itargeon
Dupuis	Liborium	01-AUG-1868	09-AUG-1868	Eugene Dupuis/Zoah Moquin	----- Langlois/Belonisia Dupuis
Dupuis	Mariam Delima	04-AUG-1869	15-AUG-1869	Baptista Dupuis/Dyonisia Dupuis	Josephus Maas/Eleonora Demars
Dupuis	Mariam Dyonisiam	02-FEB-1868	09-FEB-1868	Baptista Dupuis/Dionysia Baillargeon	Vitalis Edouin/Zoah Edoum
Dupuis	Mariam Virginiam	14-NOV-1872	24-NOV-1872	Stanislai Dupuis/Eugenia Dupuis	Baptista Dupuis/Hortensia Painguère
Dupuis	Octavum	11-FEB-1871	12-FEB-1871	Baptista Dupuis/Dyonisia Baillargeon	Petrus Bastien/Marc Mocquin
Dupuis	Simeonem	15-MAR-1867	17-MAR-1867	Eusebii Dupuis/Zoah Dupuis	E Ebert/S. Dupuis
Dupuis	Zoahm Alphonsinam		25-JAN-1863	Eusebii Dupuis/Zoah Dupuis	F Mocquin/Zoah Bourdeau
Dupuy	Alfredum	17-JUL-1882	20-JUL-1882	Francisco Dupuy/Rosana Clish	Hubertus Agagoines/Maria Moquin
Dupuy	Eduardum Fredericum	24-MAR-1901	20-APR-1901	Josepho Dupuy/Anna Walwitz	Theodorus Dupuy/Melanisa Dupuy
Dupuy	Josephum Franciscum	16-MAY-1881	21-MAY-1881	Stanislao Dupuy/Joanna Pe-----	J. Dupuy/D. Ballargeon
Dupuy	Josephum Gulielmum	13-MAR-1881	14-MAR-1881	Onesimo Dupuy/N--phara Préfontaine	M. Denault/M. Denault
Dupuy	Josephum Gulielmum	11-OCT-1880	13-OCT-1880	Amato Dupuy/Alphonsina Préfontaine	A Préfontaine/A. Maurice
Dupuy	Josephum Walace	21-MAY-1888	21-MAY-1888	Ludgerio Dupuy/Juliana Lucier	
Dupuy	Ludgerium Victorem	18-APR-1882	20-APR-1882	Ludgerio Dupuy/Julia Lucier	Ludovicus Lucier/Dyonisia Baillargeon
Dupuy	Mariam Helenam	22-MAY-1881	22-MAY-1881	Onesimo Dupuy/Albina Leberge	C. Beuregard/C. Aganer
Dupuy	Florentiam	16-AUG-1884	19-AUG-1885	Josepho Duquet/Julia Peterson	Josephus Duquet/Christina Cheff
Duquet	Petrum	24-NOV-1867	08-DEC-1867	Joseph Duquete/Christina Chef	M Montblot/S. Rondeau
Duquet	Sarahm Annam	02-MAR-1862	30-MAR-1862	Joseph Duquet/Christina Chef	A Dufort/J Cliche
Duqucte	Emeritum	30-DEC-1866	05-JAN-1867	Josephi Duquete/Olinda Duquete	E. Surprenant/E. Surprenant
Duquett	Flaviam Alphonsinam	19-MAY-1864	19-JUN-1864	Josephi Duquett/Olinda Duquett	L Cliche/E. Cliche
Duquett	Josephinam	25-DEC-1863	27-DEC-1863	Josephi Duquett/Christina Duquett	F Rondo/H Lépine
Duquett	Josephum	29-AUG-1860	16-SEP-1860	Josephi Duquett/Christina Duquett	P. Chef/C. Rondeau
Duquett	Mariam Virginiam	28-SEP-1862	29-SEP-1862	Josephi Duquett/Olympyada Duquett	J Gervais/M. Lecler-
Duquette	Franciscum	05-JUL-1868	05-JUL-1868	Josephi Duquette/Helena Tessier	Cyrilus Corbeil/Anastasia Dufort
Duquette	Josephum Aschley	02-MAR-1909	28-MAR-1909	Petro Duquette/Melina Barbeau-Gagner	Felix Pratte/Sarah Duquette-Pratte
Duquette	Stanley Alexandrum	18-MAY-1907	02-JUN-1907	Petro Duquette/Melina Barbeau-Gagner	Petrus Barbeau/Philomeme Charron-Barbeau
Duranceau	Ludovicum	13-MAY-1853	16-AUG-1853	Ludovici Duranceau/Josephina Momillion	S. Halle/J. Lamiere
Duranceau*	Francis				

Surname	Given Name	Birth	Baptism	Parents	Godparents
Duranceau*	Franciscum	02-MAY-1859	05-MAY-1859	Ludovici Duranceau/Josetha Amilon	M Monbalon/M. Pellant
Durango	Marie Olivie	03-SEP-1851	28-SEP-1851	Louis Durango/Josephine Monbillon	J Clavis/A. Malheur
Duranseau	Adelinam	09-NOV-1854	27-NOV-1854	Ludovici Duranseau/Josetta Maumillion	P. Har--/E. Moranson
Duranseau	M--na	16-JAN-1857	22-JAN-1857	Lewis Duranseau/Josephina -----ton	L. Mo---/M. -----
Duranseau	Marcellinam	06-FEB-1861	16-FEB-1861	Ludovici Duranseau/Josepha Duranseau	L Duranseau/M. Laplante
Durene	Mariam	14-JAN-1874	15-FEB-1874	Francisci Dufrene/Elizabeth Ste -Marie	Calixtus Errore/Maria Dufrène
Duroche*	Joannes	30-OCT-1856	01-NOV-1856	Joseph Duroche/M---- Dufraine	A. Duroché/----- -ndreau
Duroché*	Victoriam		16-MAY-1857	Octavii Duroch/Delina Defraine	A. Duchain/A. Defraine
Durocheche*	Maria Cilona	12-JUN-1858	13-JUN-1858	Joseph Durocheche/Euphosia Veruf	Olivier DoDelain/Selna Vernuf
Durocher	Adeladam	28-MAR-1863	05-APR-1863	Adolphi Durocher/Henrietta Durocher	P. Chef/C. Rondeau
Durocher	Adeladam	14-SEP-1862	14-SEP-1862	Francisci Durocher/Sophia Durocher	F. Pedlant/J. Chalifoux
Durocher	Adelam	22-NOV-1868	06-DEC-1868	Adolphi Durochi/Henrica Rondeau	Carolus Tremblé/Clementia Faneuf
Durocher	Alexium	25-MAY-1867	16-JUN-1866	Octavi Durocher/Adelina Durocher	N Lamouche/U. Lamouche
Durocher	Angelam Rosam	29-MAR-1887	29-MAR-1887	Gulielmo Durocher/Maria Perron	Carolus-Adolphus Durocher/Aurelia Durocher
Durocher	Carolum Adolphum	30-JUL-1861	04-AUG-1861	Francisci Durocher/Sophia Pellant	A. Durocher/H. Rondeau
Durocher	Carolum Adolphum Joseph	10-APR-1893	13-APR-1893	Carolo-Adolpho Durocher/Rosa-Celina Prefontaine	Rev.-Carlus Boucher/Maria-J Simonin-Prefontaine
Durocher	Edwardum	14-JUL-1867	28-JUL-1867	Edwardi Durocher/Maria Durocher	E. Beaumar/M. Burke
Durocher	Edwardum		16-SEP-1860	Adolphi Durocher/Henrica Durocher	L. Durocher/A. Brico
Durocher	Eliam	20-NOV-1862	23-NOV-1862	Ludgeri Durocher/Domitilla Durocher	E Durocher/C. Bellimeur
Durocher	Franciscum	10-MAR-1870	10-APR-1870	Octavi Durocher/Adelina Durocher	Franciscus Dufresne/Elizabetha Dufresne
Durocher	Genovefam Antoniam	03-JAN-1904	06-JAN-1904	Adolpho Durocher/Rosa-Delima Prefontaine	Guilielmus Durocher/Maria Perron
Durocher	Guillelmum	10-MAR-1866	25-MAR-1866	Francisci Durocher/Sophia Pellant-Durocher	E. Durocher/C. Durocher
Durocher	Guillelmum	17-JAN-1869	07-FEB-1869	Octavi Durocher/Adelina Dufresne	Petrus Dufresne/Onesime Meunier
Durocher	Gulielmum	14-MAR-1885	16-MAR-1885	Gulielmo Durocher/Maria Perron	Franciscus Durocher/Sophia Pellant
Durocher	Henricum	31-MAR-1872	14-APR-1872	Eduardi Durocher/Henrica Durocher	Josephus Lépine/Elizabetha Rondeau
Durocher	Henricum Bernardum	24-APR-1899	27-APR-1899	Carolo-Adolph Durocher/Rosa-Caluma Prefontaine	Patricius-Henricus Lyons/Alixia Prefontaine
Durocher	Isidorum	21-SEP-1865	15-OCT-1865	Octavi Durocher/Adelina Durocher	E Vadney/A. Dufresne
Durocher	Joannem Franciscum	28-AUG-1888	29-AUG-1888	Gulielmo Durocher/Maria Perron	Nicolaus Lamarche/Marcellima Livernois
Durocher	Josephnam	08-MAY-1866	13-MAY-1866	Adolphi Durocher/Henrica Durocher	M. Blondeau/J. Rondeau
Durocher	Josephnam	22-AUG-1860	16-SEP-1860	Octavi Durocher/Adelina Durocher	F. Durocher/S Pedlant
Durocher	Lauram	01-MAR-1865	19-MAR-1865	Francisci Durocher/Sophia Durocher	N. Braquette/H. Pedlant
Durocher	Lauram Mariam Florentiam	02-FEB-1901	10-FEB-1901	Carolo-A Durocher/Maria-Rosa-S. Prefontaine	Franciscus Hurteau/Laura Durocher
Durocher	Ludgerium Claudem	14-MAR-1902	16-MAR-1902	Ludgerio Durocher/Maria Ryaume	Jacobus Charron/Sophia Pellant
Durocher	Ludovicam Adeliam	29-APR-1863	03-MAY-1863	Leonis Durocher/Eulalia Durocher	J Joubert/C. Durocher
Durocher	M Vital				
Durocher	Marcellinam	02-JAN-1864	06-JAN-1864	Octavi Durocher/Adelina Durocher	F. Bellimeur/Zoah Dufresne
Durocher	Mariam Adelinam	12-DEC-1866	23-DEC-1866	Hyacinthi Durocher/Philomena Durocher	J Durocher/A. Faucher
Durocher	Mariam Elizabetham	09-AUG-1868	23-AUG-1868	Leonis Durocher/Rosalia Durocher	Josephus Faucher/Adelaida Faucher
Durocher	Mariam Joannam	02-FEB-1865	05-FEB-1865	Elia Durocher/Carolina Durocher	D Sicor/Zoah Sicor
Durocher	Mathildam	20-FEB-1862	02-MAR-1862	Octavi Durocher/Adelina Durocher	L. Durocher/M. Dufresne
Durocher	Mathildam	07-MAR-1861	10-MAR-1861	Ludgeri Durocher/Mathilda Dufresne	P. Dufresne/O. Meunier
Durocher	Napoleonem Victorem	22-JUN-1896	28-JUN-1896	Adolpho Durocher/Rosa Prefontaine	Alexander Durocher/Lucretia Prefontaine
Durocher	Sophiam	20-FEB-1864	28-FEB-1864	Francisci Durocher/Sophia Durocher	N Boisvert/M. Pedlant
Durocher	Sophiam Josephnam	04-FEB-1865	12-FEB-1865	Isaia Durocher/Maria Durocher	O Dodelin/S. Dodelin
Durocher	Vitalinam	08-JUL-1865	16-JUL-1865	Ludgerii Durocher/Mathilda Durocher	N Dufresne/C. Lefort
Durocher	Wallace Edwin Stanilas	14-MAY-1905	18-JUN-1905	Edmund Durocher/Eva Rhiaume	Ludger Durocher/Marie Rhiaume
Durocher*	Emliam	02-AUG-1858	06-AUG-1858	Elia Durocher/Carolina Bellimeur	P. Durocher/M. Deschênes
Durocher*	Josephine Delphine				
Durocher*	Octaviam	08-AUG-1858	22-AUG-1858	Octavi Durocher/Adelina Dufresne	P. Dufresne/S. St.-Marie

42

Surname	Given Name	Birth	Baptism	Parents	Godparents
Durocher*	Rosalia				
Durocher*	William				
Duroy	Mariam Olivam	24-MAR-1876	24-MAR-1876	Ligouri Duroy/Marie Fauché	F. Peddelant/M. Landurand
Eagan	Elizabeth	09-JUN-1852	27-JUN-1852	John Eagan/Susan Martin	T Stanton/A. M-l-ay
Eagers	Joanam Claram	13-APR-1853	03-MAY-1853	Caroli Eagers/Maria Walsh	G. Gipson/E. Ready
Earlng*	Louise Josephine				
Ebbert*	Isaac	30-MAY-1856	10-JUN-1856	Antoni Ebbert/Julia Elbert	I St.-Antoine/M Jubert
Ebbert*	Issaci	30-MAY-1856	01-JUN-1856	Antoine Ebbert/Julie Ebbert	I. St.-Antoine/M. Jubert
Ebert	Adam Adolph				
Ebert	Adolphum	24-FEB-1863	17-MAR-1863	Baptista Ebert/Rosalia Chaunière	H. Ebert/M. Beaumar
Ebert	Alexandrum	20-AUG-1865	22-OCT-1865	Antoni Ebert/Julia Anna Ebert	O. Boucher/E. Murry
Ebert	Antonum	01-MAY-1862	11-MAY-1862	Antoni Ebert/Julia Ebert	A Suspins/M. Ebert
Ebert	Carolum Augustum	21-JUL-1861	18-SEP-1861	Rudolphi Ebert/Ludovica Ebert	C. Ebert/G. Hankin
Ebert	Delphinam	19-NOV-1864	15-JAN-1865	Leonis Ebert/Scholastica Ebert	F. Blondin/E Blondin
Ebert	Eduardum Davidem	09-AUG-1872	31-DEC-1872	Moysis Ebert/Adelaïda Ebert	David Ebert/Tharsila Mckullen
Ebert	Josephinam	19-NOV-1864	15-JAN-1865	Leonis Ebert/Scholastica Ebert	F Gauthier/M. Gauthier
Ebert	Josephum	23-FEB-1864	06-MAR-1864	Antoni Ebert/Julia Ebert	J. Lebeau/R. Ebert
Ebert	Ludovicam Theresam	24-DEC-1863	17-MAY-1864	Rudolphi Ebert/Ludovica Ebert	L. Danis/
Ebert	Ludovicum Napoleonem	17-APR-1874	10-MAY-1874	Napolionis Ebert/Maria Ebert	Isidorus Hebert/Felicitatis Hebert
Ebert	Ludovicum Reinholdum	23-NOV-1865	26-DEC-1865	Rudolphi Ebert/Ludovica Ebert	P. Servatius/----- -----
Ebert	Mariam Albinam	13-FEB-1866	18-FEB-1866	Moysis Ebert/Ludovica Ebert	O. Boucher/J. Balthazar
Ebert	Mariam Liam	20-MAY-1864	22-MAY-1864	Eusebii Ebert/Rachelis Ebert	E. Dupuis/E. Dionne
Ebert	Moysem	23-DEC-1866	17-FEB-1867	Antoni Ebert/Julia Ebert	M. Ebert/E. Ebert
Ebert	Teophilum	03-AUG-1862	18-OCT-1862	Leonis Ebert/Callistina Ebert	H. Flemant/C. Ryan
Ebert*	Joseph				
Eblic	Adolphus	09-FEB-1856	18-FEB-1856	Perre Eblic/Locadie Chnard	----- Tibodeau/J. Gayet
Eculiere*	Melinam	10-JAN-1856	12-JAN-1856	Noelis Eculiere/Learda Parriso	R. Marrais/P. Parriso
Ecuyer	Carolnam	03-JAN-1867	15-JAN-1867	Petri Ecuyer/Carolina Ecuyer	C. Lafort/A. Miget
Eden	Joannem	10-APR-1863	26-APR-1863	Dyonisii Eden/Bridgitta Eden	J. Glannon/A. Burns
Edon	Alfredus	19-FEB-1882	19-FEB-1882	Severo Edoin/Adelina Maurice	Vatalis Edoin/Inelina Denault
Edon	Mariam Glaudissam	19-MAY-1895	26-MAY-1895	Telesphoro Edion/Adela Fontaine	Joannes Steinbarth/Marcellina Edom
Edon	Mariam Selinam			Vital Edoin/Melina Edom	Leon Edon/M. Democqun
Edon	Vitalem Rudolphum	22-APR-1891	26-APR-1891	Thelesphore Edoin/Della Fontane	Vital Edoin/Maria Sa--a-
Edoin	Vitalem Telesphorem	16-JAN-1864	18-JAN-1864	Vitalis Edoin/Melina Deneau	E. Lafève/A. Prefontaine
Edom	--nam Melinam	20-MAR-1879	24-MAR-1879	Vitalis Edoin/Helina Deneau	O Dupus/N. T-ousniere
Edouin	Emmam	05-AUG-1870	06-AUG-1870	Leonis Edouin/Flavia Mocqun	Camilus Lefève/Octavia Edoun
Edoun	Mariam Adelnam	28-FEB-1881	02-MAR-1881	Severo Edouin/Maria-Adelina Maurice	G Maurice/R. Maurice
Edoun	Melinam Adelnam	13-SEP-1872	14-SEP-1872	Vitalis Edouin/Melina Deno	Alphonsus Robidou/L Lefève
Edoun	Melnam Josephinam	27-APR-1867	27-APR-1867	Vitalis Edouin/Melina Edoun	J Edoun/S. Deno
Edoun	Vitalem Odilonum	05-MAR-1871	06-MAR-1871	Vitalis Edouin/Melina Dano	Amal----- Deshautels/Adelme Benoit
Eduoin	Alexandrum Vitalem	21-OCT-1868	25-OCT-1868	Vitalis Eduoin/Melina Eduoun	L----- Fournier/Eulalia Malheur
Eduoin	Delna	09-OCT-1868	17-OCT-1868	Leonis Eduoun/Flavia Eduoin	Franciscus Ronddeau/Mathilda Martin
Edwin	Emmam	16-DEC-1864	18-DEC-1864	Leonis Edwin/Flavie Edwin	J Dumas/Zoah Bourdeau
Edwin	Ludovicus	26-AUG-1866	02-SEP-1866	Leonis Edwin/Flavia Edwin	D. Mishote/E. Edwin
Effar	Dorothéam		03-MAY-1863	Joannis Effar/Christina Effar	A. Dolphe/M. Stephans
Egers	Catherine	13-JAN-1852	09-MAY-1852	Charles Egers/Mary Welsh	M McCarthy/B. Ward
Elliot	Carolum Dorotheum	31-JUL-1862	31-JUL-1862	Thoma Elliot/Maria Elliot	M. Roughen/A. Roughen
Emason*	Joannem	13-OCT-1859	30-OCT-1859	Jacobi Emason/Maia Nicolus	S. Nicolus/B. Nicolus
Emerson*	Maria	23-SEP-1856	05-OCT-1856	Thamas Emerson/Hnna Corrigon	J. Ro---er/A. ---per

43

Surname	Given Name	Birth	Baptism	Parents	Godparents
Emerson*	Mariam	23-SEP-1856	05-OCT-1856	Thoma Emerson/Honora Corrigan	J. Rossetha/A. Harper
Emersson*	Anne Adeline				
Emery*	Henricum Levensem	07-JUN-1856	08-JUN-1856	Petri Emery/Theresia Rivere	C. Boisledue/M. Deshotel
Emery*	Henricus L-enns	07-JUN-1856	08-JUN-1856	Peter Emery/Theresa Rivers	C. Bois--due/M Deshotel
Emmerson	Joannem	09-APR-1858	21-APR-1858	Thoma Emmerson/Anna Horrigan	J Nicolaus/B. Nicolaus
Erard	Andream Ludovicum	11-JUN-1862	10-JUL-1862	Caroli Phillipi Erard/Elizabetha Erard	A. Brown/M. Zimmer
Erhart	Emiliam Maguaritam	04-AUG-1865	14-NOV-1865	Philuppi Erhart/Elizabetha Erhart	M. Brown/-----
Errand	Carolus Fabianus	20-MAR-1882	25-MAR-1882	Calxto Errand/Delphina Leduc	Ludovicus-L. Mangin/Delia Leduc
Errarid	Georgium Theodorum	03-MAR-1885	05-MAR-1885	Calixto Errand/Delphina Leduc	Cosma Lyonais/Ludovica Beaudreault
Errard	Geraldine Mary	02-OCT-1920	10-OCT-1920	Charles Errard/Helen Como	Joseph Errard/Josephne Balthazar-Errard
Errard	Israelem	19-SEP-1889	22-SEP-1889	Calixto-Eduardo Errard/Delphina Leduc	Israel Lemeux/Malvina Larose
Errard	Josephum Ephraim	05-JAN-1878	05-JAN-1878	Calx Errard/Delphene Leduc	J. Leduc/ wife
Errard	Leonard Charles	28-JAN-1919	02-FEB-1919	Josph Errard/Josephune Balthazar	Charles-F. Errard/Helena Commo-Errard
Errard	Mariam Catharnam Isabellam	21-JUL-1892	27-JUL-1892	Calixto-Eduardo Errard/Delphina Leduc	Nazarius Dame/Maria-Catharina Endres
Errard	Mariam Dephnam Celanis	28-JAN-1887	30-JAN-1887	Calixto Errard/Delphina Leduc	Joseph Claremont/Celanisa Errard
Errard	Mariam Melanam	19-SEP-1876	22-SEP-1876	Calx Errard/Delphne Leduque	E Errard/J. Ledugue
Errard	Rosam de Lima	19-FEB-1894	25-FEB-1894	Calixto-E. Errard/Delphina Leduc	Petrus Dufresne/Onesima Meunier-Lapierre
Estreicher	Nicholaum	13-JUN-1864	17-JUL-1864	Petri Estreicher/Clara Estreicher	N. Loselion/C. Reichman
Etier	Mariam Delma	04-JUL-1865	09-JUL-1865	Petri Etier/Henrica Touchete	F. Bertrand/C. Bérubé
Evans	Guillemi L.	30-APR-1867	05-NOV-1890	Joanne Evens/Catharina Clase	Josephus Touchette/Maria-Louisa Choinnise
Evans	Joannem Baptistam	15-OCT-1895	27-OCT-1895	Guilelmo Evans/Maria Gratton	Josephus Gratton/Aurelia Lepine
Evans	Mariam Irenam	01-MAR-1894	27-MAR-1894	Gulielmo Evans/Maria Gratton	David Gratton/Malvina Michotte
Evans	Sophroniam	08-OCT-1891	07-NOV-1891	Gulielmo Evans/Maria Gratton	Vitalis Gratton/Maria-Louisa Choinnere
Everling	Josephum	29-SEP-1854	27-NOV-1854	Joannis Everling/Anna-Maria Johan---	J. Cheffer/M. Coffman
Evern	Joannem	14-MAY-1863	21-MAY-1863	Michaelis Evern/Maria Evern	J. Ryan/A. Ryan
Fachant	Jeannem Baptistam	19-JUN-1860	28-APR-1861	Alexandri Fachant/Bernardina Fachant	A Turchant/O. Hctoussois
Fachant	Mariam Victorram	08-JUL-1862	06-DEC-1863	Alexandrii Fachant/Bernardina Fachant	C Moritz/M. Mortz
Fachant*	Josephinam	18-OCT-1855	20-OCT-1855	Alexandrii Fachant/Maria-Bernardina Teri-n	J. Bernard/----- ----
Fachant*	Mariam Philomenam	20-APR-1858	16-MAY-1858	Alexandri Fachant/Bernardina Terion	A. Peron/M. Peron
Fagan*	John				
Faris	Annam	13-APR-1906	20-MAY-1906	Shaker Farris/Maria Cazal	George-Ayoub Gastine/Anna Assef-Faris
Faris	Bertham	27-APR-1903	10-MAY-1903	Shaker Faris/Maria Kalille	Azoub George/Anna Asseff
Faris	Lousam	22-SEP-1906	18-NOV-1906	Amico Faris/Maria Habib	Shaker Faris/Rosa Faris
Faris	Mariam S.			Shaker Faris/Maria Kalile	Ayoke-George Gastine/Anna Assaf
Faris	Mariam S	19-JAN-1905	19-JAN-1905	Shaker Faris/Maria Kalille	Ayoke George/Anna Assaf
Farrell	Bernardum Thomam	28-AUG-1852	12-SEP-1852	Brian Farrel/Anna Donnelly	T Ward/M Ward
Farrell	Jacobum Hubertum	13-JUL-1863	01-AUG-1863	Bryan Farrell/Anna Farrell	P Farrell/C Hughes
Fatterly	Marguerite Philomenam Ca	02-MAR-1868	15-MAR-1868	Hi-ron--i Fatterly/Marguerita-Philomena Ebert	-----Maria Ebert
Fauché	Alphonsum Mariam Nicola	14-MAR-1875	15-MAR-1875	Josephi Fauché/P. Collombier	Petrus Lamouche/Marcelina Lamouche
Fauché	Felix	01-JAN-1876	23-JAN-1876	Alexander Fauché/Marie Silvester	M. Dion/ wife
Fauché	Ludovicum Alexandrum	01-MAY-1874	16-MAY-1874	Alexandri Fauché/Maria Sylvester	Joseph Sylvestre/Melana Sylvestre
Faucher	Arthurum Davidem	15-APR-1887	17-APR-1887	Alexandro Faucher/Maria Sylvestre	Rev.N.A. Rivière/Ezella Faucher
Faucher	Camillum Zephirum Joe	27-SEP-1885	04-OCT-1885	Alexandro Faucher/Maria Sylvestre	C. Boucher/Sopha Faucher
Faucher	Helenam Annam	23-JUN-1908	05-JUL-1908	Arthuro Faucher/Mathilda Freenor	Josephus Freenor/Helena Fontaine-Freenor
Faucher	Josephinam Albinam	31-DEC-1872	05-JAN-1873	Alexandri Faucher/Maria Faucher	Isaacus St.-Antoine/Julia-Anna St.-Antoine
Faucher	Josephinam Leocadiam	18-FEB-1910	06-MAR-1910	Arthuro Faucher/Mathilda Frsenor	Adphonsus Gardner-Desjardins/Marie Tardif
Faucher	Josephum Leonem	27-DEC-1909	01-JAN-1910	Josepho Faucher/Mathilda Corbeille	Olivarius Faucher/Maria Koehn
Faucher	Maria Elodia	11-NOV-1879	16-NOV-1879	Alexandri Faucher/Maria Sylvestre	A. Pellande/A. Faucher
Faucher	Mariam Elizabetham	11-AUG-1871	13-AUG-1871	Alexandri Faucher/Maria Sylvestra	Franciscus Pellant/Josepha Faucher

Surname	Given Name	Birth	Baptism	Parents	Godparents
Faucher	Mariam Eulodiam	24-APR-1908	27-APR-1908	Josepho Faucher/Matilda Corbeille	Ferdinandus Corbeille/Amanda Corbeille
Faucher	Mariam Ledam	22-MAR-1883	25-MAR-1883	Alexandro Faucher/Maria Sylvestre	Franciscus Pellant/Philumena Letorneau
Fauches	Arsenum Antonium	11-JUN-1881	25-JUN-1881	Alexandro Fauches/Maria Syvestre	Isaac St.-Antone/Julianna Lebe
Fayen	Nicholaum		09-APR-1866	Henrici Fayen/Anna Fayen	N Shaffer/B. Wirtz
Fayen	Theresam	18-FEB-1864	11-APR-1864	Henrici Fayen/Anna Fayen	P Thill/T Thill
Feder	Helenam Dorotheam	20-JUL-1866	29-JUL-1866	Ferdinandi Feder/Maria Feder	R. Herder/M. Carr
Fee	Franciscum Josephum	07-DEC-1861	13-JAN-1862	Joannis Fee/Helena Fee	P. Mcnally/S. McCoy
Fee*	Alice				
Fee*	Patrick James				
Fcc*	Petrus Jocabus	14-JUN-1860	26-JUN-1860	Joannis Fee/Ellena Kanc	D---is Dunn/Elisabetha Mullen
Feegan*	Joannem	07-APR-1860	06-MAY-1860	Joannis Feegan/Maria Cody	Thamas Rayly/----- Rayly
Feleth	Helen	10-APR-1908	15-JUN-1919	Benjamin Falieth/Anna Borker	-----/Alexina Bastien-Dufrane
Fellar	Mariam Adelam	24-JUN-1891	20-SEP-1891	Victore Feller/Catharina-Alida Mangin	M.H. Mangin-Mosher/Maria-Elena Coffy
Feller	Carolum Clarence	07-FEB-1869	18-AUG-1872	Victoris Feller/Adelaida Mangin	Joannes-Carolus Pierron/Adela Pierron
Feller	Catharinam Cora		18-AUG-1872	Victoris Feller/Adelaida Mangin	Germanus Mangin/Rosa Feller
Feller	Dorotheam		18-AUG-1872	Victoris Feller/Adelaida Mangin	Augustus Pierron/Adela Pierron
Fellers	Alidam	26-FEB-1880	16-SEP-1883	Victore Fellers/Catarina Alida Mangin	Petrus Letourneau/Sophia Bissonnette
Fellers	Doram	26-JUN-1882	16-SEP-1883	Victore Fellers/Catarina Alida Mangin	Calixtus Errard/Delphina Leduc
Fellers	Franciscus	19-MAR-1875	16-SEP-1883	Victore Fellers/Catarina Alida Mangin	Ludovicus-Lafayette Mangin/Adela Leduc
Fellers	Lauram	05-AUG-1877	16-SEP-1883	Victore Fellers/Catarina Alida Mangin	Ludovicus Archambeault/Lucia Letoureau
Felrath	Ruth Josephine	21-FEB-1919	30-MAR-1919	Benjamen Felreth/Anna Perisha	Aaron Raymond/Zoe Balthazar-Raymond
Fendner	Gertrudam Barbaram Alsin	06-DEC-1887	11-DEC-1887	Phillipo Fendner/Malvina Dufort	Ludovicus Dufort/Ottilie Fendner
Fendner	Petrum G-e	17-DEC-1883	23-DEC-1883	Philippo Fendner/Malvina Dufort	Petrus Lepine/Josephina Dufort
Fenlon*	John Henry				
Fenlon*	Margarttam	10-JUL-1859	24-JUL-1859	Gulielem Fenlon/Catherina Fitzpatrick	M. Fenlon/M. Fenlon
Fenlon*	Marguaret				
Ferdinand	Mariam Annam	19-JAN-1865	05-MAR-1865	Simonis Ferdinand/Elizabetha Ferdinand	P. Sholl/M. Shaffer
Ferdinand	Mariam Catharinam	09-JUN-1860	09-MAR-1862	Simons Ferdinand/Elizabetha Ferdinand	J. Shoeffer/M Shower
Ferdinand*	Jacob		15-JUN-1860	S. Ferdinand/E. Scholl	
Ferdinand*	Jocob	04-JUN-1860	08-JUL-1860	Simon Ferdinand/Elisabeth Schueler	Jocob Schueler/Maria-Francisca Flatten
Ferget	Carolum	17-AUG-1866	24-JUL-1867	Joannis Ferget/Julia Ferget	C. Lefort/A. Lépine
Ferman	Deliam	14-MAY-1875	16-MAY-1875	Amable Ferman/Philome Cheff	Jeremie Gervais/Christina Cheff
Fernet	Joannem Fredericum	29-MAR-1873	31-MAR-1873	Joannes Fernet/Emilia Bolduc	Isaïas Fernet/Lucia Bolduc
Ferres	Antonium	22-SEP-1904	09-OCT-1904	Josepho Ferres/Anna Asseff	Habeeb Moosey/Maria Scaff
Ferres	Helenam	18-AUG-1903	30-AUG-1903	Josepho Ferres/Anna Hasseff	Abib Moses/Maria Skaff
Ferres	Josephum Carolum	18-FEB-1898	02-MAR-1898	Josepho Ferres/Anna Hastef	Moises Habbib/Maria Scaff
Ferres	Ludovicum	28-FEB-1896	19-MAR-1896	Josepho Ferres/Anna Hassef	Habbib Moosey/Maria Ferres
Ferres	Mariam Adelinam	16-JAN-1902	02-FEB-1902	Josepho Ferres/Anna Assef	Abibb Moses/Maria Skaff
Ferres	Mariam Carolinam	20-DEC-1894	06-JAN-1895	Josepho Ferres/Anna Assef	Abba Musey/Maria Ferres
Ferres	Michaelem	18-MAR-1900	16-APR-1900	Josepho Ferres/Anna Hassef	Habeb Moses/Maria Scaff
Ferry	Vernam Mariam	22-APR-1910	05-MAY-1910	Gulielmo Ferry/Arbella Marcoux	Alexander Marcoux/Eleonora LaJeunesne
Field-Dubois	Purl Inez		19-DEC-1909		Alexander-L. Marcoux/Orzelia Beaudreau-Marcoux
Fielle	Mariam Angelam	28-MAR-1874	28-MAR-1874	Joseph Fielle/Sophia Lefevre	Hubert Baillargeon/Odelia Baillargeon
Figgan*	Annam	23-AUG-1856	14-SEP-1856	Joannes Figgan/Maria-Anna Bogamy	P. Bogamy/M. Bogamy
Fink	Adelaidam	27-OCT-1861	01-AUG-1862	Georgii Fink/Maria Fink	F. Neal/M. Gorman
Fisher	Augustinum	17-JUN-1866	17-JUN-1866	Pauli Fisher/Sophia Fisher	J. Shaffer/M. Shaffer
Fisher	Carolum	15-DEC-1859	28-OCT-1860	Georgii Fisher/Barbara Fisher	G. Shertzinger/M. Leyman
Fisher	Joannem	17-JUN-1866	17-JUN-1866	Pauli Fisher/Sophia Fisher	J. Shaffer/M. Shaffer
Fisher	Ludovicam	19-SEP-1861	25-NOV-1861	Georgii Fisher/Barbara Fisher	G. Shertzinger/M. Straus

Surname	Given Name	Birth	Baptism	Parents	Godparents
Fisher	Mariam		17-JUN-1866	Pauli Fisher/Sophia Fisher	J. Shaffer/M. Shaffer
Fisher	Petrum		17-JUN-1866	Pauli Fisher/Sophia Fisher	J. Shaffer/M. Shaffer
Fisscher*	Gulielmum	15-MAY-1856	08-JUN-1856	Georgii Fisscher/Babera Warly	J Schergenger/F. Baker
Fitsgurrall*	Joannem Martinum	31-AUG-1856	14-SEP-1856	Jacobi Fitsgurrall/Anna Bary	J Russell/E Cain
Fitshennery*	Margeritam		28-AUG-1855	Thoma Fitshennery/Namcy Leran	P. Kieran/C Kelly
Fitsimmons	Michaelem Joannem	04-NOV-1862	08-NOV-1862	Michaelis Fitzsimmons/Catharina Fitzsimmons	E. Wall/M. Dewey
Fitsimmons*	Joanes	23-MAY-1857	31-MAY-1857	Christoph Fitsimmons/Anna Ludden	D. ----/M Clary
Fitssimens*	Joannem	10-FEB-1856	18-FEB-1856	Mauricie Fitssimens/Catherina Lo-er	G. Welschs/A. Legee
Fitz-gerald*	Catharine				
Fitz-gerald*	Thomas				
Fitzgenery*	Margerita	26-AUG-1855	26-AUG-1855	Thamas Fitzgenery/Nancy Lieran	P. Lieran/C Kelly
Fitzgerald	Catharnam	12-FEB-1863	05-APR-1863	Michaelis Fitzgerald/Anna Fitzgerald	J. Cane/A. Cane
Fitzgerald	Davidem	19-FEB-1863	01-MAR-1863	J---- Fitzgerald/Joanna Fitzgerald	D Ahern/A ----
Fitzgerald	Edmondum	13-JAN-1854	05-FEB-1854	Jannis Fitzgerald/Julia Fitzgerald	T Fitzgerald/J Colton
Fitzgerald	Guillelmum	19-JAN-1862	10-FEB-1862	Michaelis Fitzgerald/Abb-tis- Fitzgerald	P. Scannel/M Scannel
Fitzgerald	Hannam Joannam	17-AUG-1854	27-AUG-1854	Patricii Fitzgerald/Maria Ranehan	J Fitzgerald/H Leahey
Fitzgerald	Jacobum	06-NOV-1854	19-NOV-1854	Jacobi Fitzgerald/Anna Burry	J. Reilly/H. Reilly
Fitzgerald	Mariam	20-AUG-1860	09-SEP-1860	Michaelis Fitzgerald/Abatissa Fitzgerald	J. -a---/B. Harrigan
Fitzgerald*	Brgita	24-JUN-1855	09-JUL-1855	Thoma Fitzgerald/Brgita Dolton	D. Fitzgerald/B. Fitzgerald
Fitzgerald*	Brgita		07-JUL-1855	Thamas Fitzgerald/Brgitta Dalton	D. Fitzgerald/B. Fitzgerald
Fitzgerald*	Catharina	24-JAN-1860	14-FEB-1860	Guliellimus Fitzgerald/Ester McGulin	Joannes Moder/Anna Mortin
Fitzgerald* **	Catharina	17-MAR-1860	12-MAR-1860	Petrus Fitzgerald/Honora Scannel	Cornelus Scannel/Julie Fitzgerald
Fitzgerald**	Thomas		06-MAY-1860	Thama Fitzgerald/Dorothe Ly--	Petrus Flood/Ann McCann
Fitzgibbons*	Marguaret				
Fitzgibons*	Margeretham	10-OCT-1858	07-NOV-1858	Joannis Fitzgibons/Maria Herry	Patrick O'Bryan/Mauck Kenderik
Fitzhennery*	Thamam	01-OCT-1857	04-OCT-1857	Thoma Fitzhennery/Nanc-- Lierri	P. Mangan/C. Berry
Fitzjurral	Eduardum Patricum	23-NOV-1859	12-DEC-1859	Jocabi Fitzjurral/Joanna B-sy	John Martin/Marthe Wall
Fitzjurral*	Thamas	06-MAY-1855	23-MAY-1858	Jacobus Fitzjurral/Anna Burry	Morris Fitzjurral/Ellena Rayly
Fitzjurrall*	Thomam	01-MAY-1858	23-MAY-1858	Jocobi Fitzjurrall/A. Burry	M. Fitzsimmons/E. Rayly
Fitzpatrick	Mariam Annam	19-MAR-1862	29-MAR-1862	Patricu Fitzpatrick/Theresa Fitzpatrick	P. Curran/M B-rs-y
Fitzsimmins* **	Brgitta	09-MAY-1860	08-MAY-1860	Thoma Fitzsimmins/Anna Leary	John Rositer/Ann Rositer
Fitzsimmons	Mauritum	22-MAR-1863	29-MAR-1863	Mauritii Fitzsimmons/Catharina Fitsimmons	J. Rosseter/C Burns
Fitzsimmons	Nicholum		10-NOV-1860	Mauritii Fitzsimmons/Catharina Fitzsimmons	J Dun/M Vaughn
Fitzsimmons*	Bridgit				
Fitzsimmons*	Joannem	23-MAY-1857	31-MAY-1857	Christophi Fitzsimmons/Anna Hidden	D Hidden/M. Clary
Fitzsimmons*	Joannes	10-FEB-1856	18-FEB-1856	Mores Fitzsimmons/Catherina Loiseau	W. Welschs/A. Leger
Fitzsimmons*	Nicholaum		06-JUL-1858	Mauritii Fitzsimmons/Catherina Lawlor	M & H. Fitzsimmons
Fitzsimons*	Nicholaus	30-JUN-1858	06-JUL-1858	Morris Fitzsimmons/Cath L-ola	Mcl Fitzsimmons/Honore Fitzsimmons
Fl--ry*	Helenam Eugeniam	22-JUL-1855	05-DEC-1855	Thomas Fl--ry/Maria Murry	J Greny/E Mury
Flaffelan	Mariam Circeter		11-SEP-1876	Ed. Flaffelan/----- -----	M. Tessé
Flanagham	Martinum		01-JAN-1854	Gulielmi Flanagham/Julia Whillam	B. O'Glogelan/M Flot
Flanders	Carolum Ruel	25-JUL-1879	12-JUN-1902	Carolo Flanders/Alicea James	Ludovicus Turenne/Delia Juneau
Flanders	Mariam Elvam	16-JUN-1906	05-JUL-1906	Carolo Flanders/Delia Turenne	Albertus Turenne/Rosa Turenne
Flanders	Mariam Vernon	12-MAR-1903	22-MAR-1903	Caroli Flanders/Delia Turenne	Ludovicus Turenne/Delia Juneau
Flanders	Rosam Doram	29-APR-1909	09-MAY-1909	Carolo Flanders/Delia Turenne	Ferdinandus Brunet/Mathilda Potvin-Brunet
Flanegan	Ceciliam	11-FEB-1862	27-APR-1862	Guillelmi Flanegan/Josepha Flanegan	D Stanton/C. Flanegan
Flanigan*	Daniel				
Flannegan*	Julie	28-DEC-1857	29-DEC-1857	William Flannegan/Julie Phalan	J. Birmingham/M. Flannigan
Flannigan*	Danielam	31-MAR-1860	15-APR-1860	Welim Flannigan/Johanna Phalun	Keran Cady/Anna Cady

46

Surname	Given Name	Birth	Baptism	Parents	Godparents
Flannigan*	Julian	28-DEC-1857	29-DEC-1857	Willem Flannigan/Julia Phalan	J Bermingham/ M.Flannigan
Flannigan*	Margareta	21-FEB-1858	07-MAR-1858	Bernardus Flannigan/Maria --ain	Francicus McGinity/Brigita McGinty
Flannigan*	Margeretham	21-FEB-1858	07-MAR-1858	Bernardi Flannigan/Maria Pa'ian	F Mcginty/B. Mcginty
Flatten	Guillelmum Albertum	12-DEC-1860	29-DEC-1860	Jacobi Flatten/Maria Flatten	J. Flatten/A. ------
Flatten*	Annam Mariam	10-JAN-1857	15-JAN-1857	Jocobi Flatten/Maria-Francisca Kurri-	E. Kurri-/A Kull--
Flatten*	Joannem Hubertus	12-JAN-1859	08-FEB-1859	Jacob Flatten/Maria-Franca Currie	Joannis-Hubert Currie/Anna Catherina Flatten
Flatten*	John Hubert				
Flatten*	Maria Agnes	10-JAN-1857	17-JAN-1857	Jocob Flatten/Maria-Francisca Kurrir	E Kurrir/A Huller
Flind*	Caterina	17-JAN-1858	20-JAN-1858	John Flind/Maria Fitzsimmons	Thamas Murphy/Chaterina D-nsy
Flind*	Cathernam	17-JAN-1858	20-JAN-1858	Joannis Flind/Maria Fitzsimmons	T Murphy/C Dunsy
Flind*	Gulielmum	11-AUG-1857	16-AUG-1857	Edmundi Flind/Catherina Li---hs	M. Flind/H. Karrigan
Flind*	Gulemus	11-AUG-1857	16-AUG-1857	Edemund Flind/Caterina ------	M. Flind/E. -aisyan
Flind*	Joanem	25-JUN-1858	27-JUN-1858	Edemondi Flind/Catherina Lienchs	Jocabus Russell/Maia Lienchs
Flind*	Joannem	11-JUN-1856	20-JUN-1856	Joannis Flind/Maria Fetzsimmons	J Kenny/J. McCay
Flind*	John	11-JUN-1856	20-JUN-1856	Joannes Flind/Maria Fitzsimmons	J Kenny/J. McCay
Flinn	Guillelmum	12-AUG-1861	14-AUG-1861	Jacobi Flinn/Maria Flinn	G. Connell/M. Crane
Flinn	Helenam Elizabetham	21-JAN-1863	25-JAN-1863	Petri Flinn/Maria Flinn	J. Fitzgerald/M. Flinn
Flinn	Jacobum	08-NOV-1862	09-NOV-1862	Jacobi Flinn/Maria Flinn	J. Loughlin/J. Daugherty
Flinn	Julian	15-FEB-1862	16-FEB-1862	Edmundi Flinn/Catharina Flinn	P. Hurley/M. Flinn
Flint	Rasilimam	07-DEC-1853	02-APR-1854	Jacobi Flint/Catharina Conway	P. Fitzgerald/S. Parsons
Flood	Cathernam	14-OCT-1863		Thoma Flood/Marguarita Flood	C. Flood/C. King
Flood*	Jacobum	14-JUN-1858	20-JUN-1858	Thoma Flood/Marguarita Kelly	T. Donnell/M. Wane
Flood*	Jacobum Thomam	29-JUL-1859	02-AUG-1859	Cristof Flood/Catherina Linch	M. McEnrow/M. Martin
Flood*	James Thomas				
Flood*	Michaelem	25-APR-1859	01-MAY-1859	Joannis Flood/Maria Fitsimmons	J. M---y/M. M---y
Flood*	Patrick	04-JUN-1858	20-JUN-1858	Thos Flood/Marguerite Kelly	Thos Doonell/Mary Hanes
Flood*	Susanam Annam	20-OCT-1855	21-NOV-1855	Patricii Flood/Anna Conlon	J. Conlon/M. Conlon
Flood*	Wiliam G---	16-APR-1860	29-APR-1860	Joannes Flood/Elisabeth Fitzjurral	Michaelis Mengen/Catherena Melady
Flood*	William John				
Florence	Ludovicum	09-APR-1875	11-APR-1875	Albert Florence/Taxeit Bodriaux	Franciscus Rondeau/----- Rondeau
Florend	Josephinam Loretam	28-SEP-1873	26-OCT-1873	Alberti Florent/Roxela Bodriau	Franciscus Bodriau/Catharinam Maloney
Florent	Dorotheam Ludovicam	31-MAY-1871	02-JUL-1871	Alberti Florent/Roxla Robillet	Comas Lyonnais/Ludovica Lyonnais
Florent	Franciscum Medericum	06-JAN-1867	13-JAN-1867	Alberti Florent/Praxida Florent	F. Beaudrieau/A. Fernet
Florin	Guillelmum Albertum	09-FEB-1865	19-FEB-1865	Alberti Florin/Prunella Florin	L. Beaudrau/S. Brion
Flowy*	Selena Eugenia	22-JUL-1855		Thomas Flowy/Maria Murry	J G-eny/E Mury
Flyn*	Joannes	04-JAN-1860	19-FEB-1860	Michalus Flyn/Hellena O'Brien	Joannes Flyn/Honora ------
Flynn	Guillelmum Martinum	19-MAR-1861	20-MAR-1861	Martini Flynn/Honora Flynn	G Walsh/E Walsh
Flynn*	Honora				
Flynn*	Honoram	05-FEB-1860	12-FEB-1860	Edemondo Flynn/Catherine Lienshs	Bernardus McDormel/M. Flynn
Flynn*	Joannem	25-JUN-1858	29-JUN-1858	Edmundi Flynn/Catherina Lynch	J Russell/M Lynch
Flynn*	John				
Fo---*	John Martan	31-AUG-1856	14-SEP-1856	James Fo---/Anne --ey	J. Russell/E Cain
Foche	Olieve	25-AUG-1877	26-AUG-1877	Alexander Foche/MariaSilvester	O Fouché/C Parlso
Fontaine	Adeliam	07-AUG-1868	15-AUG-1868	Vincentu Fontane/Maria Fontane	Narcissus Fontane/Maria Fontane
Fontaine	Catharinam	22-MAY-1863	31-MAY-1863	Petri Fontane/Ludovica Fontane	P. Chef/A. Fontane
Fontaine	Gratiam	13-JAN-1873	18-MAR-1873	Vincentu Fontaine/Maria Sanctuaire	L. Marcou/Florentia Losele
Fontaine	Guillelmum Eduardum	05-AUG-1870	20-AUG-1870	Nelson Fontaine/Ludovica Fontaine	Guillelmus Gauther/Rosalie Fontaine
Fontaine	Josephum Eduardum	22-FEB-1878	24-FEB-1878	Josephi Fontaine/S---ine Dupuis	C. Hubert/A. Delepine
Fontaine	Narcissa Fontane	22-JUN-1867	30-JUN-1867	Narcissa Fontane/Ludovica Melon-on	N Fontaine/J. Bouchard

Surname	Given Name	Birth	Baptism	Parents	Godparents
Fontaine	Leonem	02-NOV-1870	20-NOV-1870	Vincentu Fontaine/Maria Fontaine	Carolus Lucier/Rosalia Lucier
Fontaine	Ludovic-- Eduadum	26-MAR-1877	04-APR-1877	Edmund Fontaine/ Margret -----	L Willat/R. Rasset
Fontaine	Mariam Elisabeth	24-FEB-1875	03-MAR-1875	Vincentus Fontaine/Maria Santuare	Octavus Santuare/---- Santuare
Fontaine	Mariam Juliam	16-JUL-1861	21-JUL-1861	Narcissi Fontaine/Julia Fontaine	J Gagnon/C. Guérin
Fontaine	Mariam Louisam	10-APR-1855	15-APR-1855	Petri Fontaine/Lousa Porrier	N Fontaine/M Lamer
Fontaine	Olivinam	31-JAN-1865	12-FEB-1865	Narcissi Fontaine/Julia Fontaine	I. St.-Antoine/J. Lebeau
Fontaine	Sarahm Alfredam	06-AUG-1866	02-SEP-1866	Vincenti Fontaine/Maria Fontaine	M Santuare/M Ebert
Fontaine	Vitalinam	05-MAR-1861	14-MAR-1861	Petri Fontaine/Ludovica Fontaine	N Fontaine/V. Gagnon
Fontaine*	Eugenia	11-SEP-1857	27-SEP-1857	Petrus Fontaine/Maria Porrier	A Grisé/J. Lamere
Fontaine*	Eugeniam	11-SEP-1857	27-SEP-1857	Petri Fontaine/Maria Poirrier	A Grisé/J Meir
Foote	Mariam	13-JUN-1865	02-JUL-1865	Joannis Foote/Magdalena Foote	N Davis/M. Davis
Ford	John	25-SEP-1851	23-MAR-1852	Patrick Ford/Ann Connelly	J. Connelly/B. Connelly
Ford*	Susanna Anna	20-OCT-1855	21-NOV-1855	Patrick Ford/Anna Conlan	J. Conlon/----- -----
Fourier	Isaacum Alfredum	15-DEC-1867	29-DEC-1867	Alexi Fournier/Edmra Ebert	E Ebert/S Dano
Fourmer	Mariam Olivinam	29-JUL-1868	29-JUL-1868	Henrci Fournier/Olivina Desautels	Eugenius Fournier/Thaissa Moquin
Fournier-Préfont	Amablem Wilfredum	10-MAY-1871	14-MAY-1871	Isaa Fournier-Préfontane/Sophia Dano	Amabili Desautels/Aurelia Rabidou
Fournier-Préfont	Eduardum Vitalem	02-JAN-1873	05-JAN-1873	Isaïa Fournier-Préfont/Sophia Deneau	Ludgerus Fournier/Melina Deneau
Fournier-Préfont	Emiliam	12-MAR-1871	12-MAR-1871	Magliori Fournier-Préfontaine/Olivieri Desautels	Isaias Fournier/Anastasia Desautels
Fournier-Préfont	Mariam Cornam	16-SEP-1871	28-SEP-1871	Ludgeri Préfontaine/Cezaria Préfontaine	Isaïa Préfontane/Ursalna Lamarche
Fournier-Prefont	Wilfredum Martinum	10-NOV-1873	15-NOV-1873	Andrea Fournier-Prefontaine/Ludovica Moquin	Isaïa Fournier-Prefontaine/Ludovica Moquin
Fox	Brigitte	02-FEB-1852	03-MAR-1852	Thoma Fox/Eliza Conroy	B. Gertland/C Smith
Fox	Eugeniam	06-JUN-1854	12-JUL-1854	Thoma Fox/Elizabetha Coury	E. Doherty/M. Murray
Fox	Guillelmum Patricum			Terenti Fox/Anastasia Fox	T -----/A -----
Fox	Helenam	16-APR-1861	05-MAY-1861	Laurenti Fox/Anastasia Fox	J Reiley/M Henery
Fox	Robertum Eduardum	23-MAY-1917	25-MAY-1919	Eduardo-F. Fox/Mabel-C Gilman	D.C.W Leonard/Gertruda Lewis-Leriard
Fox	Thomam	23-AUG-1860	08-OCT-1860	Thoma Fox/Elizabetha Fox	J Kenny/S Nutty
Fox*	Jane				
Fox*	Joannam	22-JUL-1859	15-AUG-1859	Terentu Fox/Stecia Phelam	M --ly/R. Hickey
Fox*	Maria	16-JUN-1855	24-JUL-1855	Thamas Fox/Anestatia Phelan	T Fox/M. Phalan
Fox*	Mariam	16-JUN-1855	24-JUL-1855	Thoma Fox/Margarita Phalan	T Fox/M. Phalan
Fox*	Richardum	07-MAR-1858	29-MAY-1858	Turns Fox/Annasthehia Phalan	W. Phalan/M Norton
Frame	Josephum Victor	16-MAR-1877	08-APR-1877	Josephus Frame/Catherine Hardel	J. Mocquin/V. Mocquin
Fraine	Ludovicum Winfield	09-JAN-1880	01-FEB-1880	Joseph Frame/Catharina Hartel	W Mongeau/L. Mongeau
Freanor	Mariam Hazel	26-JUL-1906	21-APR-1907	Georgio Freanor/Clara Kanuber	Joannes Freenor/Tillie Freenor
Frederik	Ludovicum Hermanum	12-MAY-1887	30-SEP-1902	Caroli Frederik/Anna Frederik	Stephanus Buk/Gertrudis Hanngan
Fredert	Agnes Elisabeth	11-MAR-1876	02-APR-1876	Olivie Fredet/Ellen D-ne-o	A Demars/ wife
Fredet	Mariam Therisam	09-NOV-1877	20-NOV-1877	P-li-- Fredet/Ellen Donaho	D Cicar/M. Donaho
Fredette	Francois Olivier	26-OCT-1879	02-NOV-1879	Olivaris Fredette/Helena Donahoe	W. Flood/E Flood
Fredette	Joannum	28-OCT-1881	01-NOV-1881	Olivero Fredette/Helena Donahue	Nathanael Flordy/Maria Spelling
Freney*	Patrick	07-MAR-1859	13-APR-1859	Thos Freney/Bridget Dunn	M. Brogan/B. O'Donnell
Freney*	Patrick				
Freso	Mariam Elenam		22-SEP-1878	Narsisi Freso/Delina Allen	F. Giller/G Grager
Fritz	Paulum Jacobum	11-JAN-1862	02-FEB-1862	Francisci Fritz/Dorothea Fritz	J. -----/M Flatten
Fronthouse	Mariam Elizabetham	02-JUN-1862	19-JUN-1862	Thoma Fronthouse/Dorothea Fronthouse	T Surprenant/E Mignault
Frost	Adelnam Hazel	23-AUG-1897	08-OCT-1899	Alberto-Walter Frost/Emma Edoin	------/Rosa Prefontaine-Durocher
Frost	Agnetem Annam	13-MAR-1904	27-MAR-1904	Alberto Frost/Emma Edoin	Alexander Corbeille/Anna Kreamer
Frost	Guillelmum		30-SEP-1869	Guillelmi Frost/Maria Frost	Josephus Rau/Maria Rau
Frost	Mariam Ceciliam	18-MAR-1902	25-MAR-1902	Alberto Frost/Emma Edoin	Gulielmus Durocher/Maria Perron
Frost	Robertum Walter	24-SEP-1899	08-OCT-1899	Alberto-Walter Frost/Emma Edoin	Joannes Steinbarth/Marcellina Edoin

48

Surname	Given Name	Birth	Baptism	Parents	Godparents
Fulhant*	Jas-hna	18-OCT-1855	21-OCT-1855	Alexnder Fulhant/Maria Tiron	J Bernand/----- -----
Funk	Alfredum Leonem	19-AUG-1907	27-OCT-1907	Julio Funk/Paulina Sauve	Petrus Weber/Maria-Anna Cardinal
Funk	Almam Carolinam	25-DEC-1900	13-JAN-1901	Julio Funk/Theresia Russ	Hermanus Funk/Theresia Russ
Funk	Donald Albert	10-JUL-1918	04-AUG-1918	Edward Funk/Laura Balthazar	Albert Balthazar/Agnes Wendels
Funk	Ethel Lucillam Mariam	23-OCT-1908	20-DEC-1908	Julio Funk/Paulina Sauve	Pacificus Bastian/Rosa Brunet-Westphal
Funk	Florentiam Margatam	08-JUL-1899	30-JUL-1899	Julio Funk/Apolina Sauvé	David Senecal/Mariana Bastien
Funk	Irenam Josephinam	16-NOV-1897	19-DEC-1897	Julu Funk/Paulina Sauvé	Andreas Bastien/Corinna Sauvé
Funk	Josephum Georgium	05-FEB-1904	20-MAR-1904	Julio Funk/Paulina Sauvé	Georgius Dion/Maria Powers
Funk	Maglorium Laurentium	22-SEP-1905	29-OCT-1905	Julio Funk/Paulina Sauve	Josephus Sauve/Eulodia Venne-Sauve
Funk	Paulum Arthurum	11-AUG-1896	28-AUG-1896	Julio Funk/Paulina Sauve	Paulus Sauvé/Adela Robidoux
Funk**	Carolum Lester	28-JUL-1902	13-JUL-1902	Juln Funk/Paulina Sauvé	Albertus Dufresne/Alexina Bastien
Furman	Fredericum Guilelmum	06-JUN-1895	13-AUG-1895	Francisco Furman/Elisa Gilman	Guilelmus Roman/Lucia Gilman
Furman	Georgium Ludovicum	23-FEB-1890	01-JUN-1890	Francisco Furman/Elizabeth Gilman	Jacobus Fischer/Emma Gilman
Furman	Josephum Wallace	01-AUG-1888	30-SEP-1888	Francisco-M---am Furman/Elizabeth Gilman	Vitalie Edom/Mathilda Gilman
Fyc*	Thamas	01-AUG-1857	09-AUG-1857	John Fyc/Elina Kain	J. Duphy/A. Duphy
Fye*	Thomam	01-AUG-1857	09-AUG-1857	Joannis Fye/Elena Kain	J. Dufphy/A. Dufphy
G-ff-y	John Baptist				
Ga–en*	Anne				
Gafey	Hubert		07-SEP-1851	Thomas Gafey/Julia -----	J ---enar/E. Toner
Gafey	Michael		07-SEP-1851	Michael Gafey/Ellen Gafey	D. Galahar/M. Galahar
Gaffeny	Joannem	13-DEC-1859	28-DEC-1859	Patricus Gaffeny/Anna Flanigan	Patrick Kelly/Maria Duff
Gaffeny	Terrentius	04-NOV-1859	15-JAN-1860	Joannes Gaffeny/Alicia Gaffeny	Walter Stanton/Catherina Gaffeny
Gaffeny*	Anna	24-OCT-1855	28-OCT-1855	Patrick Gaffeny/Anna Flannegan	P Flannagan/M. -----
Gaffeny*	Catherina	20-OCT-1855	28-OCT-1855	Patrick Gaffeny/Anna Flannegan	J. Mallen/M. Flannegan
Gaffeny*	Ellena	01-OCT-1857	04-OCT-1857	Patrick Gaffeny/Anna Flannegan	J. Mullen/M. Flannegan
Gaffeny*	Thamas	19-AUG-1857	05-OCT-1857	Patrck Gaffeny/Anna Flannigan	D. Beaudon/C. Gaffeny
Gaffeny*	Thomam	19-AUG-1857	05-OCT-1857	Thamas Gaffeny/Julie Duffy	C. Tonner/M. Flannigan
Gaffeny*	Annam	20-OCT-1855	28-OCT-1855	Patricu Gaffeny/Anna Flanegan	C. Tonner/M. Flennigam
Gaffeny*	Elenam	01-OCT-1857	04-OCT-1857	Patrici Gaffeny/Anna Flannigan	P. Flannegan/M. Cogelan
Gaffey	Helenam	20-JUN-1862	06-JUL-1862	Michaclis Gaffey/Helena Gaffey	D Reardon/C. Gaffeny
Gaffney	Guilelmum	04-APR-1862	04-MAY-1863	Thoma Gaffney/Julia Duffy-Gaffney	P. Gaffey/A. Flanegan
Gaffney	Guilelmum	04-APR-1862	13-APR-1862	Patrcu Gaffney/Anna Flanagan	E. Magher/M. Magher-Duffy
Gaffy*	Joannem	07-MAY-1860	29-MAY-1860	Thoma Gaffy/Julie Duphy	J. O'Neil/M. Moor
Gaffy*	Joannes	07-MAY-1860	29-MAY-1860	Thoma Gaffy/Julia Duphy	Patricii Gaffy/Anna Flanigan
Gafney	Alice	09-MAR-1858	01-APR-1858	John Gafney/Alice Reily	----- Gaffy/A. Flanigan
Gafney	Ann	23-SEP-1851	23-OCT-1851	John Gafney/Christian Melady	Nicholas Gafney/Allen Gafney
Gafney	Margarttam Gladys	17-JUN-1902	29-JUN-1902	Jacobo-A. Gafney/Margaritta Resch	J Brig/C. Smith
Gagne	Genovefa		03-AUG-1873	Francisci Gagne/Emilia Lepine	Albertus Resch/Stella Resch
Gagné	Honoratum	10-FEB-1870	13-FEB-1870	Francisci Gagné/Emilia Lépine	Isaac Gagne/Rosalia Jeanotte
Gagnier	Carolum Ludovicum	16-APR-1883	22-APR-1883	Eduardo Gagnier/Edessa Pariseault	Moyses Montblot/Josephina Rondeau
Gagnier	Catharina Lauretta	08-FEB-1879	17-FEB-1879	Francisco Gagnier/Catharina Doherty	Guilelmus Blas/Isabelle Sutton
Gagnier	Florentiam Adelnam	15-NOV-1885	29-NOV-1885	Francisco Gagnier/Catharina Daugherty	J Mcdermott/H. Mcdermott
Gagnier	Franciscum Herbertum	17-SEP-1883	06-OCT-1883	Francisci Gagnier/Catarina Daugherty	Paulus Gagnier/Emelia Gagnier
Gagnier	Georgium Franciscum	01-OCT-1880	17-OCT-1880	Eduardo Gagnier/Edessa Pariseau	Joannes-Baptista Lefort/Anna Dixon
Gagnier	Gertrudam Annam	20-JAN-1890	26-JAN-1890	Eduardo Gagnier/Edessa Pariseau	F Gagnier/C. Daugharty
Gagnier	Guilelmum Mauritium	07-MAR-1868	14-JUN-1868	Pauli Gagnier/Clotilda Gagnier	Paulus Gagnier/Josephina Duquet
Gagnier	Guilelmum	07-MAY-1892	15-MAY-1892	Guilelmo Gagnier/Lea Moquin	Eduardus Bernier/Adelia Gagnier
Gagnier	Josephum	05-MAR-1887	10-MAR-1887	Francisco Gagnier/Emelia Lepine	Josephus Moquin/Mathilda Barbeau
					Francisus Lepine/Philumena Landerman

49

Surname	Given Name	Birth	Baptism	Parents	Godparents
Gagnier	Josephum Walter	15-NOV-1887	20-NOV-1887	Eduardo Gagnier/Edessa Parseau	Joseph Parseau/Melansa Dupuy
Gagnier	Julianum Norberum Albert	01-OCT-1881	09-OCT-1881	Francisco Gagnier/Emelia Lepine	Moises Gratton/Eliza Lépine
Gagnier	Mariam	26-MAY-1888	31-MAY-1888	Francisco Gagnier/Emelia Lepine	-------/Malina Gagnier
Gagnier	Mariam Esther	31-DEC-1884	04-JAN-1885	Eduardo Gagnier/Edessa Parseau	Gulielmus Gagnier/Edessa Bernier
Gagnier	Mariam Franciscam	07-FEB-1885	15-FEB-1885	Francisco Gagnier/Emelia Lepine	Franciscus Rondeau/Flavia Edoin
Gagnier	Mariam Joannam	18-APR-1881	09-MAY-1881	Francisco Gagnier/Catharina Dougherty	E. Gagnier/E. Pariseau
Gagnier	Mariam Josephnnam	11-NOV-1883	04-DEC-1883	Francisci Gagnier/Emelia Lepine	Alexander Edoin/------ -----
Gagnier	Mariam Mabel	28-SEP-1887	02-OCT-1887	Paulo Gagnier/Josephina Duquet	Felix Pratte/Sara Duquet
Gagnier	Paulum Laurentium	05-AUG-1885	30-AUG-1885	Paulo Gagnier/Josephina Duquet	Paulus Gagnier/Chrstine Cheff
Gagnier-Gardner	Joannem Baptistam Elmer	10-OCT-1893	15-OCT-1893	Gulielmo Gagnier-Gardner/Lea Moquin	Joannes-Baptista Lefort/Emelia Gagnier
Gagnon	Franciscum Adamum	18-APR-1868	19-APR-1868	Francisci Gagnon/Emilie Lépine	Franciscus Lépine/Elizabetham Roneau
Gagnon	Napoleonem		31-MAY-1863	Jacobi Gagnon/Marguarita Gagnon	I. St-Antoine/M. Houle
Gagnon	Rosaliam	07-MAY-1872	18-MAY-1872	Francisci Gagnon/Emilia Lépine	Petrus Chef/Chrstina Chef
Gagnon*	John				
Gagnon	Guillelmum	11-FEB-1866	18-FEB-1866	Jacobi Gagnon/Marguarita Gagnon	I. Marcou/V. Gagnon
Gagon	Ludovicum	27-FEB-1877	27-FEB-1877	Francisci Gaié/Maria Lepin	E. Allard/ wife
Gaié	Josephum Eduardum	26-FEB-1875	07-MAR-1875	Francis Gaigné/Melia Lepine	Joseph Lepine/Sophia Bodriceaux
Gaigné	Carolum	18-MAR-1858	23-MAY-1858	Petri-Jocabi Gaion/Margeretha Lemr	F. Marca-/P. Lebeau
Garon*	Marguariam	06-SEP-1861	16-SEP-1861	Jerema Galavan/Joanna Galavan	D Laughlin/M. Harican
Galavan	Elena	19-AUG-1856	14-SEP-1856	Janus Galigan/Margret ---ior	J. Faygon/E. Gory
Galigan*	Mariam	27-OCT-1862	27-OCT-1862	Jocabi Galigan/Margeretha O'Conner	J Figgon/E. Gory
Galigan*	Guillelmum Joannem		07-OCT-1861	Guillelmi Gallaghar/Bridgitta Gallaghar	T. Gibson/B. Gibson
Gallaghar	Joannem	13-JUN-1863	06-JUL-1863	Martini Gallagher/Anna Gallgher	J Eagan/J. Henessy
Gallagher	Joannem	23-NOV-1861	24-NOV-1861	Patricii Gallagher/Alicia Gallagher	P Muty/H Muty
Gallagher	Mariam	19-OCT-1863	19-OCT-1863	Guillelmi Gallagher/Bridgitta Gallagher	T Gough/E. G----gher
Gallagher	Anne	16-NOV-1858	21-NOV-1858	Martini Gallagher/Anna Gallagher	P. Macken/B. Cane
Gallagher*	James Francis			Will Gallagher/Bridget McGinn	Russell Gallagher/Marguerite Gallagher
Gallagher*	Jocobum Franciscum	03-FEB-1860	19-MAY-1860	Jerema Galligan/Brigeth Igan	Genina Lamb/----- -----
Galligan*	Jocuburn	16-FEB-1858	07-MAR-1858	Jocab Galligar/Rosanna Donelhy	J McGlogelon/M. Murry
Galligar	Jacobus	04-MAR-1857	08-MAR-1857	William Galligar/Brigta McGann	J. Galligar/E Galligar
Galligar*	Jocabum	12-MAY-1860	09-JUN-1860	Patricii Galligar/Ellis Fitzsimmons	Joannes Cann/Brigeth Fallon
Galligarv	James	16-FEB-1858	07-MAR-1858	James Galligar/Rosana Dorrelhe	John McGlogelan/Margerta Murry
Galliger	Josephum	07-DEC-1855	28-DEC-1855	Jocobi Galliger/Rosa Dougerty	A McMannikel/C. -----
Galliger	Mariam Eugenıam	25-JUL-1860	05-AUG-1860	Barry Galliger/-----abth Galliger	Michel Leitan/Maria Vain
Galliger*	James				
Galliger*	James Patrick				
Galliger*	Jocobum	04-MAR-1857	08-MAR-1857	Wilhelmi Galliger/Brigetha Megann	J. Galliger/E. Galliger
Galliger*	Jocobus Patricius	25-FEB-1860	29-FEB-1860	Joannes Galliger/Rosanna Daugherty	Danielus Ueling/Catherina Flavin
Galliger*	Mariam Eugeniam	25-JUN-1860	05-AUG-1860	Barry Galliger/Elzabeth Galeger	Michel Certan/Maria Voes
Galliger*	Patrick		13-FEB-1860	Jorgii Galliger/Maria Hartenet	Thamas McMan/Margetha Nash
Galliger*	Patricum	18-MAR-1863	22-MAR-1863	Jacobi Galloway/Joanna Galloway	J Mishott/M Medrich
Galloway	Joannem Bernardum	02-APR-1858	04-APR-1858	Coroli Galvan/Maria Kelly	W. Welshs/M. Doyle
Galvan*	Margarctham	22-OCT-1858	07-NOV-1858	Prrick Ganen/Ann Melia	Daniel Heraty/Hel. Roden
Ganen*	Ann	19-JUL-1859	24-JUL-1859	Thoma Gannon/Catherina Norry	M. Mogan/C. Herman
Gannon*	Margueret				
Gannon*	Jacobum	31-MAY-1861	02-JUN-1861	Thoma Ganon/Catharina Ganon	M. Doyle/M. Lomery
Ganon					

50

Surname	Given Name	Birth	Baptism	Parents	Godparents
Ganon	Joannem	09-JUL-1863	09-JUL-1863	Thoma Ganon/Catharina Ganon	P. Neary/C. Meyer
Ganon*	John				
Ganzan*	Joannem	22-APR-1859	20-JUN-1859	Joanni Ganzan/Susana Hokers	J. Dutter/M Michel
Ganzen*	Mariam	01-JUL-1857	02-JUL-1857	Joannis Ganzen/Maria Kinderek	-----/N Kinderek
Garber*	Elizabelte	05-JUL-1858	11-JUL-1858	Nicholas Garber/Mary Miller	Peter Servatus/Marguerite Phelan
Garden	Georgium Henricum	13-MAY-1880	18-MAY-1880	Georgio Garden/Barbara Baltazar	C. Garden/S. Moqui
Gardener	Margaritam	25-OCT-1854	05-DEC-1854	Joannis-Ferdinandi Gardener/Ellena Sweet	J Gardener/M Gardener
Gardon	Josephum Archibaldum	18-OCT-1896	07-NOV-1896	Georgio Gardon/Sara Balthazar	Georgius-Henricus Gardon/Lucia Gardon
Garni-	Thomam	24-MAY-1853	01-NOV-1853	Josephi Garni-/Maria Gorn	-----/C. McLaudy
Garo	Adolphum	13-MAY-1872	15-MAY-1872	Petri Garo/Rosalia Lecuyer	Joannes-Maria Marcou/Mathilda Marcou
Garo	Albinam	27-JAN-1873	02-FEB-1873	Davidis Garo/Maria Garo	Petrus Barbeau/Philomena Barbeau
Garo	Alfredum	02-JUL-1867	14-JUL-1867	Petri Garo/Rosalia Garo	J Gayet/M Gayet
Garo	Carolum	15-MAY-1861	20-JUL-1861	Pdtri Garo/Maria Garo	H. Borasseau/E. Bergnier
Garo	Eugenum	17-JAN-1869	24-JAN-1869	Petri Garo/Rosalia Lecuyer	Camillus Lucier/Clementia Garo
Garo	Georgium Henricum	04-FEB-1872	10-MAR-1872	Eduardi Garo/Anna Garo	Josephus Pommainville/Julia Bessete
Garo	Helenam Emiliam	01-DEC-1870	01-JAN-1871	Davidis Garo/Maria Garo	Ludovicus Marcote/Henrica Garo
Garo	Iodnam	30-JUL-1865	21-OCT-1865	-----/M. Garo	J. Garo/A. Garo
Garo	Josephnam	22-JUN-1863	23-JUN-1863	Petri Garo/Rosalia Garo	H. Borasseau/L. Lécuyer
Garo	Josephum	15-JAN-1871	22-FEB-1871	Petri Garo/Rosalia Garo	Josephus Masse/Zoah Langlois
Garo	Virginam	01-OCT-1865	08-OCT-1865	Pdetri Garo/Rosalia Lécuyer	T Deschênes/C. Deschênes
Garraty	Narsissus	02-MAY-1852	10-SEP-1853	Thoma Garraty/Julia Gafferson	P. Flannigan/A. Tonnon
Garreau*	Alexam	17-JUN-1857	03-JAN-1858	Petri Garreau/Maria Hussoi	P. Garreau/C. B----
Garret	Joannem	18-JUN-1858	23-JUN-1858	Joannis Garret/Maria Garret	J. Rosseter/M Rossiter
Garro	Virgniam	30-JUN-1862	01-JUL-1862	Petri Garro/Rosalia Garro	G. Woltet/V. Woltet
Garry	Thomam Jacobum	23-MAR-1861	28-APR-1861	Davidis Garry/Maria Garry	M. McHessy/M Garry
Garry*	Mariam	04-OCT-1858	10-OCT-1858	David Garry/Maria Garry	Cornilus C-hi--/Marger--- Kelly
Garry*	Mary				
Gary	Catharnam Annam	04-AUG-1863	09-AUG-1863	Davidii Gary/Maria Gary	J. Lyons/A Gary
Gasteen	Josephum Victorem	12-JUN-1901	09-JUL-1901	Georgio Gasteen/Maria Ferres	Carolus Ferres/Maria Shaff
Gastin	Petrum Ayoub	22-SEP-1905	08-OCT-1905	Georgio-Ayoub Gastine/Esther Faris	Shaker Faris/Maria Skaf
Gauf*	Abraham	17-NOV-1856	23-NOV-1856	Bernardi Gauf/Elisabetha Crummer	E. Crummer/S. Shoemacker
Gauthier	Adelaidam	20-DEC-1870	28-JAN-1871	Antonii Gauthier/Anna Gauthier	Michael Pomainville/Sophia Desjardins
Gauthier	Angelinam	05-NOV-1860	11-NOV-1860	Antonii Gauthier/Julia Gauthier	H. Laduc/R. Courcier
Gauthier	Carolum Albertum		05-OCT-1862	Francisci Gauthier/Anastasia Gauthier	J Serwe/M. Borasseau
Gauthier	Emiliam	22-NOV-1866	28-NOV-1866	Antonii Gauthier/Flavia Gauthier	P Trudel/M. Grizet
Gauthier	Flaviam Rosaliam	10-SEP-1865	01-OCT-1865	Ruperti Gauthier/Maria Gauthier	M. Larose/M. Ebert
Gauthier	Georgium Mariam		19-OCT-1862	Francisci Gauthier/Anastasia Gauthier	G Occottet/V. Occottet
Gauthier	Homerum		19-OCT-1862	Francisci Gauthier/Anastasia Gauthier	H Borasseau/A. Gauthier
Gauthier	Jeremiam Jerry	04-MAR-1869	10-MAR-1869	Antonii Gauthier/Clarisa Gauthier	Octavius T-----/Clarisa Gauther
Gauthier	Josephinam Eulaliam	21-JUL-1861	18-NOV-1861	Josephi Gauthier/Angelica Gauthier	I. Gauthier/A. Bourasseau
Gauthier	Josephum Carolem	07-OCT-1862	30-NOV-1862	Ruperti Gauthier/Maria Gauthier	J. Leduc/A. Gauthier
Gauthier	Josephum Henricum	30-OCT-1865	10-DEC-1865	Josephi Gauthier/Angelica Gauthier	A. Gauthier/F. Robert
Gauthier	Lucie Anne	29-JAN-1859	06-APR-1859	Antone Gauthier/Flavie Robert	C. Moiller/J Boudrieau-
Gauthier	Lucie Anne				
Gauthier	Ludgcrum	04-OCT-1864	30-OCT-1864	Antonii Gauthier/Flavia Gauthier	F. Dufresne/L Gosselin
Gauthier*	Charles Willm				
Gauthier*	Eugenic				
Gauthier*	Franciscum Josephum	25-FEB-1858	04-JUL-1858	Josephi Gauthier/Angelica Leduc	F. Durocher/D Dufresne
Gauthier*	Henricum	01-SEP-1856	14-SEP-1856	Henrci Gauthier/Maria Gauther	A Gauthier/M Bohemer

Surname	Given Name	Birth	Baptism	Parents	Godparents
Gauthier**	Georgium Franciscum	26-MAR-1868	01-MAR-1868	Ruperti Gauthier/Maria Gauthier	Guillelmus Gauthier/Elizabeth-A. Gauthier
Gautier	Franciscum Lafayette	25-FEB-1853	26-JUN-1853	Francisci Gautier/Anastasia Bourrassa	M. Bourassa/M Delare
Gautier	Séline		16-JUN-1852	Francis Gautier/Angelina Dresy	J. Réaume/C Tipchaux
Gautier*	Marelan		21-JUL-1855	Francois Gautier/Stusi- Boraseau	S Duranseau/J Mabillion
Gautier*	Mariam	20-APR-1857	16-MAY-1857	Antoni Gautier/Flavia Robbert	I Jubert/A. Bricau
Gautier*	Marie	20-APR-1857	16-MAY-1857	---- Gautier/Phivia Robbert	I Jubert/A Bricau
Gautier*	Marlinam	20-MAY-1855	21-JUL-1855	Francisci Gautier/Stascii Borusean	L Duranseau/J. Mobillion
Gavigan	Eduardum Eugenium	21-FEB-1905	26-MAR-1905	Eugenii Gavigan/Anna Rondeau	Petrus Rondeau/Eleonora Lepine-Paradis
Gavigan	Jacobum Arthurum	18-AUG-1903	22-AUG-1903	Jacobo-Eugenio Gavigan/Anna Rondeau	Michael Wickert/Maria-Vitalina Durocher
Gay*	Bernardum	24-FEB-1859	27-FEB-1859	Caroli Gay/Anna Farly	M. Dumpsey/M Murry
Gaye	Annam	02-AUG-1876	05-AUG-1876	Francois Gaye/Catherina Dogherty	J. Lefort/ wife
Gayé	Henricum Eduardum	23-OCT-1876	19-NOV-1876	Eduardi Gayé/Edith Pariso	P. Gayé/C. Pariso
Gayen*	Antoine				
Gayet	Aureliam	08-NOV-1862	23-NOV-1862	Josephi Gayet/Francisca Gayet	L. M-lheur/C. Bonse-
Gayet	Eleonoram	27-APR-1873	04-MAY-1873	Francisci Gayet/Celina Beaudin	Alexander Gayet/Eleonora Lajeunesse
Gayet	Eliam	11-APR-1863	12-APR-1863	Josephi Gayet/Marguarita Gayet	J. Gayet/M. Gayet
Gayet	Eulaliam	09-MAR-1865	12-MAR-1865	Josephi Gayet/Philomena Gayet	T Thibodeau/R. Gayet
Gayet	Jusephnam	06-SEP-1877	30-SEP-1877	Ludovici Gayet/Rasset Baltazar	A. Gayet/M Lajeunesse
Gayet	Linam	21-JUN-1865	22-JUN-1865	Francisci Gayet/Lina Beaudin	J Gayet/M. Gayet
Gayet	Ludovicam	21-MAY-1872	22-MAY-1872	Francisci Gayet/----	---- ----/Lina Beaudrieau
Gayet	Philomenam	17-JAN-1861	20-JAN-1861	Josephi Gayet/Philomena Gayet	I. Surprenant/J Gayet
Gayet*	M---anus	11-SEP-1856	12-SEP-1856	Joseph Gayet/Madeline Delavaline	J Pepit/E. Belhumeur
Gayete	Cordeliam	17-MAR-1871	18-MAR-1871	Narcissi Gayete/Merentia Gayete	Solomon Demars/Maria Gayet
Gayete	Ludovicum	04-FEB-1873	09-MAR-1873	Josephi Gayete/Philomena Thibodeau	Ludovicus Gayete/Rosalia Balthazar
Gayon*	Antonium		05-SEP-1858	Francis Gayon/Lu-- Buco----	Antonius ---etha/Lrn-- Laplante
Gazm*	William Henry	12-FEB-1859	16-FEB-1859	Francis Gazin/Mary-Augustine Violet	J. Furgusson/M Gazin
Gazm*	William Henry				
Gayet*	Alexandrum	11-SEP-1856	12-SEP-1856	Josephi Gayet/Magdalena Pelavaline	J Pepil/E Belhumeur
Gayon*	Rosaline	26-JAN-1856	27-JAN-1856	Jacobus Gayon/Margerita Lamer	J. Marcou/J Lamer
Ge-l-n	Mariam		23-MAR-1862	Patricii Ge-l-n/Maria Ge-l-n	J Liston/C. Casey
Gean* **	Alexander	27-JUL-1860	01-JUL-1860	Jocobi Gean/Margeth Lamer	Emery Surprenant/----- P-----
Geblmater*	Hueh	13-SEP-1858	17-OCT-1858	Hueh Geblimater/Maria Galliger	Mark Brossing/Margeta --ollen
Geelan	Annam	04-JUL-1863	22-AUG-1863	Patricii Geelan/Julia Geelan	P. Mcdonald/M. Geelan
Geelan	Mariam	26-AUG-1852	03-SEP-1852	Normandi Geelan/Elizabetha Geelan	D. Doroghty/M. Charette
Gegen	Henricum	16-OCT-1863	22-MAY-1864	Nicholai Gegen/Anna Gegen	J Leib/R. Leib
Georgium	Josephum	15-APR-1880	18-APR-1880	Stanislis Dupuis/Eugenia Pinguère	O. Dupus/A. Laberge
Gerber	Ludovicum	10-OCT-1860	11-NOV-1860	Nicholai Gerber/Maria-Anna Gerber	J Serwe/C Serwe
Gerber*	Elizabetham	05-JUL-1858	11-JUL-1858	Nicholai Gerber/Maria Miller	P. Servatus/M Phalan
Gerbil*	Elisabetha	06-OCT-1856	12-OCT-1856	Wendel Gerbil/Babera Yong	M. Gerben/E. Brown
Germann*	Jocobus Francis	17-JUL-1857	26-JUL-1857	John Germann/Catherina Nulty	T. N--um/E. Smit
Gerty*	Elisabath	04-APR-1857	06-APR-1857	Thamas Gerty/Margeta Gibilles	J. Mckey/A. Garrly
Gerty*	Elisabetham	04-APR-1857	06-APR-1857	Thoma Gerty/Margeretha Melles	J McKeep/A. Gerty
Gervais	Belonisiam	08-SEP-1871	17-SEP-1871	Narcissi Gervais/Adela Barbeau	Ludovicus Gi----/Dyonisia Gervais
Gervais	Clotildam	22-DEC-1867	29-DEC-1867	Isaaci Gervais/Virginia Grizet	P. Gervais/M Granville
Gervais	Emery Harnais	06-DEC-1876	10-DEC-1876	Aman---- Gervais/Philome Lecheff	A. Corbeille/M Cheff
Gervais	Evam Jocobam	09-JUL-1878	13-JUL-1878	Narsisi Gervais/Adelde Barbou	C. Bourgau/ wife
Gervais	Florentiam	26-MAR-1865	11-APR-1865	Isaaci Gervais/Virginia Gervais	S. Houle/M. Houle
Gervais	Florentiam Gertrudem	22-MAY-1904	27-MAY-1904	Telesphoro Gervais/Melina Beauregard	Gilbertus Marlow/Rosana Dinelle
Gervais	Genovefam Adelam	05-DEC-1901	08-DEC-1901	Telespharo Gervais/Melina Beauregard	Alfredo-Eugenio Beauregard/Olivina Gervais

52

Surname	Given Name	Birth	Baptism	Parents	Godparents
Gervais	Georgium Em	14-APR-1887	17-APR-1887	Emerici-T. Gervais/Olivina Charron	Jacobus Charron/Ada Barbeau
Gervais	Georgium Henricum	21-JUL-1869	10-AUG-1869	Alexandri Gervais/Elizabetha Gervais	Paulus Gagner/Clotilda Gagner
Gervais	Hermnnam	20-OCT-1866	04-NOV-1866	Ludovici Gervais/Josephina Gervais	N Lécuyer/E Lécuyer
Gervais	Isaacum	26-DEC-1871	06-JAN-1872	Isaaci Gervais/Virginia Grizet	Ludgerius Préfontaine/Cezarina Larochelière
Gervais	Jeremiam Alexandrum Jose	08-JUL-1883	22-JUL-1883	Jeremia Gervais/Mathilda Touchette	Josepho Aucher/Sophronia Lucier
Gervais	Josephnam	24-JUN-1861	07-JUL-1861	Isaaci Gervais/Virginia Gervais	A Grizet/C. Guérin
Gervais	Josephinam Leonam	22-APR-1878	26-APR-1878	Jeremia Gervais/Mr---das Tochet	P Cheff/ wife
Gervais	Josephum	03-AUG-1869	15-AUG-1869	Isaaci Gervais/Virginia Gervais	Josephus Faneuf/Clotilda Bissonet
Gervais	Josephum	06-MAY-1874	06-MAY-1874	Emery Gervais/Philomena Touchette	Carolus Beauregard/Onesima Touchette
Gervais	Josephum Jermiam Albert	27-AUG-1872	01-SEP-1872	Jeremia Gervais/Matilda Gervais	Josephus Touchete/Salomé Ruelle
Gervais	Lorettam Isabellam Winifr	08-FEB-1894	26-FEB-1894	Jeremii Gervais/Mathilda Touchette	Eugenius Robert/Josephina Touchette
Gervais	Ludovicum Claudium Eme	28-JUN-1875	04-JUL-1875	Emerie Gervais/Philomena Touchette	Joseph Touchette/Salomée Guellé
Gervais	Mariam	27-JUL-1868	04-AUG-1868	Narcissi Gervais/Adeela Barbeau	Ludovicus Barbeau/Catherina Boyce
Gervais	Mariam Claram	25-AUG-1891	30-AUG-1891	Emerico Gervais/Olivina Charron	Michael Dion/Delima Laquerre
Gervais	Mariam Doram	27-JUL-1895	01-AUG-1895	Emerio Gervais/Olivina Charson	Achilles Charson/Eva Gervais
Gervais	Mariam Elizabetham			Alexandri Gervais/Elizabetha Gervais	P. Letourneau/L. Letourneau
Gervais	Marie Emma Jenny	14-AUG-1879	19-AUG-1879	Isaac Gervais/Virginia Griset	J. Touchette/O. Veins
Gervais	Paulinam		05-SEP-1869	Narcissi Gervais/Adela Barbeau	Marcellus Picard/Paulina Will--que
Gesseher*	Gulimus	15-MAY-1856	08-JUN-1856	Jorge Gesseher/P--rly Everly	J Ju---er/F. Baker
Getrauter	Leonardum Matham	28-JUL-1908	02-AUG-1908	Henrico Gutrauter/Della Marecoux	Mathias Gutrauter/Anne-Maria Hurter
Gevigan	Eduardum Eugenium	21-FEB-1905	26-MAR-1905	Eugeno Gevigan/Anna Rondeau	Petrus Rondeau/Eleonora Lepine-Paradis
Ghus*	Margeretham	06-MAR-1859	07-MAR-1859	Joani Ghus/Theresia Kain	P. Ghus/B. Kelly
Gibbons	Jacobum	23-FEB-1862	23-MAR-1862	Roberti Gibbons/Marguarita Gibbons	J O'connor/J. O'conner
Gibeau	Adeliam	01-FEB-1867	03-FEB-1867	Alexi-Theophili Gibeau/Theresa Gibeau	H Robidou/A. Fontaine
Gibeau	Ophiliam	01-FEB-1867	03-FEB-1867	Alexi-Theophili Gibeau/Theresa Gibeau	J. Dumas/D Dumas
Gibel*	Anna	28-MAR-1858	04-APR-1858	Wendel Gibel/Bab--a Yong	Ch--- Thon-n--/Anna Rosseher
Gibel*	Annam	28-MAR-1858	04-APR-1858	Windel Gibel/Barbera Young	T Toourny/A. Rosschater
Gibel*	Catherina	23-NOV-1855	24-NOV-1855	Michael Gibel/Chaterna Yong	N Stevins/B Yong
Gibel*	Catherinam	23-NOV-1855	24-NOV-1855	Michaelis Gibel/Catherina Young	N Shivers/B. Young
Gibel*	Joannem	07-NOV-1858	28-NOV-1858	Th-h-e-l Gibel/Caterina Young	Joannis Zorris/Eva Mosé
Giblan*	John				
Giblan*	Margrita	11-APR-1857	20-APR-1857	Christopher Giblan/Ell---es	F -u-on/---- Giblan
Gibon*	Bridgit Ellen				
Gibon*	Joannem	02-AUG-1856	22-MAY-1857	Joannis Chappentia-Gibon/Maria Grogan	T Rayly/C Jocabs
Gibson	Georgum	27-APR-1867	06-OCT-1862	Joannis Gibson/Maria Gibson	R Mcgennis/---- -----
Gibson*	Thomas Henry				
Gibson*	Thomasu Henricum	03-JUL-1859	07-AUG-1859	Thomas Gibson/B---th Martin	J McIntoch/M. Wall
Giebel	Antoniam	25-JUN-1865	02-JUL-1865	Wendelini Giebel/Theresa Ackerman	F Simon/A. Comn
Giebel	Barbaram	12-MAY-1861	27-MAY-1861	Wendelis Giebel/Barbara Giebel	J. Schalle/B Giebel
Giebel	Mariam	16-JAN-1865	02-FEB-1865	Michaelis Giebel/Catharina Giebel	N Schouer/M. Kaufman
Gicbel	Petrum		26-APR-1863	Michaelis Giebel/Catharina Giebel	P. Kaufman/M. Lohmuller
Giebel*	Thamas	02-JUN-1857	07-JUN-1857	Patrck Giebel/Marie Jolly	J Water/S Kelly
Gieble**	Franciscum	29-JUL-1861	03-JUL-1861	Michaelis Gicble/Catharina Gieble	W. Gieble/---- ------
Gilbert	Adolphinam Elizabetham	27-APR-1867	28-APR-1867	Antonii Gilbert/Joanna Gilbert	C. Lyonnais/L. Lyonnais
Gilbert	Eleonoram Elizam	16-NOV-1881	16-NOV-1881	Antonio Comtois-Gilbert/Joanna Frederic	Petrus Dufresne/Onesima Meunier

53

Surname	Given Name	Birth	Baptism	Parents	Godparents
Gilbert	Estellam Dulainam	12-JAN-1904	14-FEB-1904	Jacobo Gilbert/Esther-Etta Cartier	Napoleo Marcoux/Sophrona Dufresne
Gilbert	Ettam Florentiam	21-JAN-1888	22-FEB-1888	Carolo-Frederico Gilbert/Florentia Mireau	Georgus Moquin/Ludovica Gilbert
Gilbert	Evelinam Lorettam	26-SEP-1909	10-OCT-1909	Jacobo Gilbert/Etta Cartier	Eduardus Desnoyers/Ida Desnoyers-Shelley
Gilbert	Florentiam Genovefam	24-MAY-1906	08-JUL-1906	Jacobo Gilbert/Esther Cartier	Raymundus Shelly/Daisy Marcoux
Gilbert	Luciam Mariam	18-AUG-1865	27-AUG-1865	Antoni Gilbert/Joanna-Elizabetha Gilbert	F. Dufresne/E. Ste.-Marie
Gilbert	Mariam Lucillam	11-FEB-1902	16-MAY-1902	Jacobo Gilbert/Esther Cartier	Cleophas Cartier/Dulcina Dufresne
Gilbert	Mariam Maiam		03-MAY-1874	Antoni Gilbert/Joanna Frédérik	Laurent Bodrio/Sophia Bodrio
Gilbert	Samuelem	11-AUG-1869	15-AUG-1869	Antoni Gilbert/Joanna Gilbert	Maglorius Préfontaine/Olivia Desautels
Gilbert*	William				
Gilert*	Willielmum	06-MAR-1859	13-MAR-1859	Antoni Gilert/Eugenia Lus--t	D. Sicor/J. Plante
Gill	Georgum	30-JAN-1861	20-FEB-1861	Christophori Gill/Elizabetha. Gill	J. Dyer/C. Gill
Gill	Marguaritam Elizabetham	16-MAY-1861	16-JUN-1861	Michaelis Gill/Maria Gill	J Hallaghan/B. Hallaghan
Gill	Martinum	21-APR-1853	24-APR-1853	Matini Gill/Brigitta Stanton	J Kenny/B. Reilly
Gill*	Joseph	16-FEB-1859	13-MAR-1859	Thos Gill/Julia Mangan	T Mcbride/E Cleffert
Gill*	Joseph				
Gillan	Bregitham	11-OCT-1853	24-OCT-1853	Barnÿ Gillan/Elisa-h-a Gilly	P. Halpan/M. D-yer
Gillan	Christophorum	12-FEB-1861	13-MAR-1861	Patricii Gillan/Julia Gillan	P. O'conner/E. Brenan
Gillan	Eugeniam	26-MAR-1855	05-APR-1855	Bernardi Gillan/Elizabetha Garry	C. Gillan/M. Dorrethy
Gillan	Joannem		25-JAN-1863	Thoma Gillan/Maria Gillan	G Brown/J. Powers
Gillan	Juliam	04-AUG-1861	04-AUG-1861	Joannis Gillan/Maria Gillan	P. Molone/M. Gough
Gillan	Thomam	26-MAR-1863	05-APR-1863	Christophori Gillan/Elizabetha Gillan	T Boyce/J. Boyce
Gillan*	Francens	01-OCT-1855	07-OCT-1855	Patrick Gillan/Julie Marten	P. Mangan/A. Marten
Gillan*	Franciscum	01-OCT-1855		Patricii Gillan/Julia Marten	P. Mangan/A. Marten
Gillan*	Honora				
Gillan*	Joannem	19-APR-1858	19-APR-1858	Patricii Gillan/Julia Marten	M. McGrath/E. Baÿs
Gillan*	Margeretham	17-APR-1857	20-APR-1857	Christophi Gillan/Elisabetha Bas	F Halpen/E. Gillan
Gille	Ludovicum	02-JUN-1877	03-JUN-1877	Josephi Gille/Sophia Lefeve	I Langlois/ wife
Gillen	Annam	18-MAY-1858	25-JUN-1858	Francisci Gillen/Sarah Coleman	T Reiley/C Mogan
Gillen	Brigittam	01-DEC-1852	05-DEC-1852	Francisci Gillen/Sara Gillen	C. Gillen/C. Coleman
Gillet	Emmam Joannam	04-SEP-1872	08-SEP-1872	Antoni Gillet/Joanna-Elizabetha Gillet	Narcissus Marion/Suzanne Marion
Gilliam*	Honnoram	15-FEB-1859	07-MAR-1859	Christophe Gilliam/Elisabth Cayes	C. Berrigan/H. Bays
Gillian*	Joannes	19-APR-1858	19-APR-1858	Patrick Gillian/Julu- Marten	Matth--- Megratt/Ellsabet Cays
Gillin	Christophorum	07-MAY-1854	21-MAY-1854	Francisci Gillin/Sarah Coleman	P. Mangan/B. Coleman
Gillis*	Joannes	09-AUG-1858	18-NOV-1858	Mcl Gillia/Mary Seullen	Antoine Zearoye/---alie Miller
Gillis*	John				
Gillman	Albertum	09-JAN-1872	14-JAN-1872	Petri Gillman/Maria Balthazar	Josephus Loisèle/Julia Balthazar
Gillman	Alfredum	25-JAN-1871	04-FEB-1871	Petri Gillman/Maria Balthazar	Alfredus B----/Salomé Loiselle
Gillman	Georgum		28-MAR-1869	Petri Gillman/Maria Gillman	Martinus Balthazar/Julia Lonsele
Gillman	Josephum	31-MAY-1868	02-JUN-1868	Joannis Gillman/Edmira Marcou	Jeremias Marcou/Josephina Boucher
Gillmartin*	Hugh				
Gillmartin	Elizabetham		22-MAY-1853	Hugh Gillmartin/Maria Goldon	M. Byrnes/C. Welch
Gillmartin	James	05-JUL-1851	22-MAR-1852	Mark Gillmartin/Catherine Cole	H Gillmartin/C. Harkns
Gillmartin	Joannam	06-DEC-1861	25-DEC-1862	Hughn Gillmartin/Maria Gillmartin	D Vaughn/B. McClean
Gillmartin	William Thomas	09-OCT-1851	23-NOV-1851	Hugh Gillmartin/Maria Golebare	M Duly/M. Sullivan
Gillon	Anna	18-MAY-1858	25-JUN-1858	Francis Gillon/Sara Coalin--	This R---y/Catherina Hagan
Gilman	Bertham Elizabeth	06-JAN-1883	20-JAN-1883	Josepho Gilman/Barbara Fox	Thomas Gilman/Elizabeth Gilman
Gilman	Jessé	25-NOV-1876	03-DEC-1876	Petri Gilman/Maria Baltazar	W. L'oissel/C. Gilman
Gilman	Joannem	13-MAR-1870	26-JUN-1870	Joannis Gilman/Emma Marcou	Zephirus Marcou/Rosalta Fontaine
Gilmarten*	Daniel	03-JUN-1857	07-JUN-1857	Hueh Gillmarten/Maria Galligar	T Brown/A. Cenray

54

Surname	Given Name	Birth	Baptism	Parents	Godparents
Gilmarten*	Danielem	03-JUN-1857	07-JUN-1857	Hugonis Gilmarten/Maria Gallegar	T. Brown/A. Conray
Ginel	Mariam Dyonisiam	24-JAN-1873	26-JAN-1873	Ludovici Ginel/Dyonisii Ginel	Josephus Mocqun/Maria-Archangela Dinel
Ginnan*	Mariam	27-MAR-1857	27-MAR-1857	Thoma Ginnan/Catherina Nerry	M. Doyle/M. Perry
Girben*	Elisabetham	06-OCT-1856	12-OCT-1856	Wendel Girben/Barbara Jon-	T. Rag-/---- -----
Gisbon*	Joannes	02-JUL-1856	22-MAY-1857	John Gibson/Marie Grogan	P. Servatius/A. Servatus
Glaeser	Mariam Ludovicum	16-MAY-1878	11-JUN-1878	----- -----/Maria Glaeser	
Glaser*	Eugene				
Glassy	Joannem Jacobum	22-DEC-1852	19-FEB-1853	Thoma Glassy/Maria Boice	G. Well/E. Boice
Glaven	Eugenium	10-JUL-1860	20-JUL-1860	Eugeni Glaven/Margeretha ----ina	Joannis Dalton/Caterina Flagerty
Glénat	Mariam Dianam	17-AUG-1868	17-AUG-1868	Eduardi Glénat/Marguarita Glénat	Carolus Alar/Emilia Sonet
Gloo-	J-	17-OCT-1856	19-OCT-1856	Eugene Gloo-/Margerit Ninan	B. Flagerty/E. Flagerty
Goan	Mariam Annam	15-JUL-1854	16-JUL-1854	Joannis Goan/Catharina Goan	J. McNulty/A. McNulty
Godet	Benjamin	01-OCT-1876	08-OCT-1876	Josephi-Evaristi Godet/Elnia Corbond	D. Godet/----- Gilbert
Godin	Julian	02-FEB-1869	10-FEB-1869	Ludovici Godin/Rosalia Godin	Michael Jolin/Mathilda Tremblé
Godin	Mariam Gertrudam	10-FEB-1881	13-MAR-1881	Calixto Godin/Emma Dupuy	I. St. Antoine/J. Lebeau
Golam*	Margaretham	05-DEC-1855	16-DEC-1855	Patrcus Golam/Elena Christel	P. Christel/S. Forland
Golan*	Margareta	09-DEC-1855	16-DEC-1855	Patrick Gola/Elina Christel	Patrick Chrstel/Wmne Ferland
Golan*	Margerita	05-NOV-1855	16-NOV-1855	Patrck Golan/Elena Chrstal	P. Christal/W. Forland
Gonier	Thomom	20-JAN-1879	30-JAN-1880	Francisco Gonier/Maria L'epine	T Rondeau/J. Pelland
Good*	Mariam Annam	19-JUL-1858	08-AUG-1858	Bodrieu Good/Carolina Cramer	Thamas --as/Maria-Eva Annan
Good*	Mariam Annam	19-JUL-1858	08-AUG-1858	----- Good/Carolina Cramer	T Paas/M. Annan
Gordin	Luciam	03-DEC-1868	26-APR-1869	Josephi Gordin/Aurelia Gordin	Alfredus Gordin/Elizabetha Gilbert
Gordon	Carolum Alexandrum	12-SEP-1870	25-SEP-1870	Josephi Gordon/Aurelia Gordon	Josephus Baillargeon/Emilia Belonis
Gordon	Eduardum	11-JUN-1868	02-AUG-1868	Josephi Gordon/Lucia Gordon	Carolus Gordon/Lucia Gordon
Gordon	Joannem Baptistam Adonis	22-MAY-1883	23-MAY-1883	Georgio Gordon/Barbara Balthazar	Alexandem Edoin/Sophia Balthazar
Gordon	Josephum Eduardum	22-JAN-1890	26-JAN-1890	Georgio Gordon/Sara Balthazar	Julianus Balthazar/Margarita Lajeunesse
Gordon	Josephus	05-AUG-1885	16-AUG-1885	Georgia Gordon/Sara Balthazar	Franciscus Boucher/Julia Bissette
Gordon	Mariam Alicem Falvey	17-JUN-1908	27-JUN-1908	Georgio Gordon-Jr-/Alices-Elizabeth Kelley	----- -----/Barbara Balthazar-Gordon
Gorès	Josephum Hubertum	24-NOV-1866	27-NOV-1866	Joannis-Hubert Gorès/Marguarita Gorès	J. German/A. Shuemacker
Gorès	Mariam Catharinam	21-JUL-1864	25-JUL-1864	Joannis-H. Gorès/Marguarita Gorès	J Krämmer/C Krämmer
Gorés	Mariam Marguaritam	03-OCT-1865	08-OCT-1865	Joannis-H. Gorés/Marguarita Gorés	J. Krämmer/M. H-s
Gorman*	Joannem	27-JAN-1859	28-JAN-1859	Joannes Gorman/Catherine Multy	J. Multy/M. C-nnely
Gorman*	Jocobum Franciscum	17-JUL-1857	26-JUL-1857	Joannis Gorman/Catherina Nulty	T. Reum/C. Smet
Goselain*	Abraham	23-NOV-1856	23-NOV-1856	John Goselain/Lenore Chetienne	D. Hubert/-. Lanevn
Gosselain	Corneliam Joannam	20-FEB-1869	04-JUL-1869	Joannis Gosselain/Elizabetha Gosselain	Cornelius Bransheau/Maria Branscheau
Gosselain*	Abraham David	10-NOV-1856	23-NOV-1856	Joannis Gosselain/Louisa Chretienne	D. Hubert/A. LaRiviere
Gosselin	Antonum	02-OCT-1862	12-OCT-1862	Joannis Gosselin/Elizabetha Gosselin	A. Joubert/E. Joubert
Gosselin	Antonium Edwardum	11-DEC-1884	08-FEB-1885	Carolo-Antonio Gosselin/Emma Harmon	Cosmo-E. Lyonais/Francisca-Elz Gosselin
Gosselin	Coram Ludovicam	15-JUN-1872	16-JUN-1872	Georgi Gosselin/Ludovica Leduc	Joannes Gosselin/Ludovica Gosselin
Gosselin	Edessam Eleonoram	20-DEC-1864	27-FEB-1865	Joannis Gosselin/Elizabetha Gosselin	N. Bullis/E. Bullis
Gosselin	Franciscam Elizabetham	01-AUG-1867	18-AUG-1867	Joannis Gosselin/Elizabetha Gosselin	H. Leduc/J. Beaudrieau
Gosselin	Ivan Linem	28-JUL-1883	20-DEC-1883	Antonio Gosselin/Emma Harman	----- -----/Edessa Gosselin
Gosselin	Joannem Henricum	15-AUG-1868	24-NOV-1868	Joannis-Henrici Gosselin/Ludovica Montgomery	Joannes Gosselin/----- Gosselin
Gosselin	Joannem Henricum	19-SEP-1872	01-OCT-1872	Johannis-Henrici Gosselin/Maria - Gosselin	Augustus L---/Lucinia Leduc
Gosselin	Ludovicam Georginam	22-APR-1871	07-MAY-1871	Joannis-Henrci Gosselin/Maria Gosselin	Georgius Gosselin/Ludovica Leduc
Gosselin	Rosam Helenam	06-MAR-1861	17-MAR-1861	Joannis Gosselin/Ludovica Christina Gosselin	F. Lozon/M. Joubert
Gosselin*	Emlie				
Gosslain	Emeliam	22-JAN-1859	06-FEB-1859	Joannes Gosslain/Lousia Chretien	C. Letourneau/M. Gosslian
Gother*	Eugeniam	06-MAR-1860	15-APR-1860	Huberti Gother/Maria Turquot	Israel Bodrieu/Maria Gother

55

Surname	Given Name	Birth	Baptism	Parents	Godparents
Goulé	Mariam Oliviam	28-APR-1876	30-APR-1876	Ludovici Goulé/Edelin Gaygné	J. Mcdormett/A Goulé
Goulet*	Josephum Augustinum	28-FEB-1882	02-APR-1882	Ludovico Goulet/Pamela Landermann	Augustinus Landermann/Teresa Joli
Goulet	Ludovicum Franciscum	19-APR-1886	19-APR-1886	Ludivoco Goulet/Pamela Landerman	Franciscus Lepine/Philumena Landerman
Goulet	Mariam Agnes	15-OCT-1874	18-OCT-1874	Ludovici Goulet/Adelna Gaygné	Franciscus Gaygné/Elena Gaigne
Goutier	Noe	31-MAR-1857	16-MAY-1857	Per Goutier/Marie Guillot	M. -----/M Hibert
Goutier*	Franciscum Josephm	25-FEB-1858	04-JUL-1858	Josephu Goutrier/M------ Leduc	Francicus Deroche/Delpha Dufraine
Govenach	Francus Edu-d	22-APR-1858	29-APR-1858	John Govenach/Margeta Chonson	Thamas Chonson/Maria-Anna Egan
Goyet	Diliam Laurentiam	25-MAR-1876	26-MAR-1876	Fransci Goyet/Lina-G. Bodin	L. Coq/R. Coq
Goyet	Josephum	10-MAY-1877	13-MAY-1877	Francisci Goyet/Lina Bodam	A. Goyet/M. Lajeunesse
Goyette	Albertum Ricardum	09-MAR-1898	13-MAR-1898	Alexandro Goyette/Maria Lajeunesse	Michael Pommnville/Sophia Gratton
Goyette	Alexandrum Leonem	12-JUL-1902	13-JUL-1902	Alexandro Goyette/Hermina Balthazar	Alexander Goyette/Maria Lajeunesse
Goyette	Eduardum Noe	02-OCT-1889	06-OCT-1889	Alexandro Goyette/Maria Lajeunesse	Franciscus Boucher/Judith Bessette
Goyette	Henricum	05-SEP-1884	07-SEP-1884	Alexandro Goyette/Hermlinda Lajeunesse	Henricus Lajeunesse/Eleonora Goyette
Goyette	Josephum Treffleum Clare	25-NOV-1903	28-NOV-1903	Alexandro Goyette/Merina Balthazar	Alexander Goyette/Hermina Balthazar
Goyette	Juliam Josephinam	22-MAY-1886	23-MAY-1886	Alexandro Goyette/Ermelinda Lajeunesse	Jacobus McGray/Philumena Lajeunesse
Goyette	Leonem	10-AUG-1892	14-AUG-1892	Alexandro Goyette/Maria Lajeunesse	Josephus Touchette/Onesima Viens
Goyette	Ludovicum	02-JAN-1874	11-JAN-1874	Ludovici Goyette/Rosa Baltazar	Josephi Goyette/Madelena Lavallee
Goyette	Mariam	19-MAY-1874	21-MAY-1874	Francisci Goyette/Adelna Bodin	Henricus Lageneste/Eleonora Lageneste
Goyette	Mariam Arminiam	30-MAR-1882	09-JUL-1882	Carolo Goyette/Maria Plante	Josephus Goyette/Magdalena Lavallee
Goyette	Mariam Magdalena	09-APR-1880	11-APR-1880	Francisco Goyette/Lina Beaudin	J Baltazare/M. Marcou
Goyette	Michaelem	17-APR-1883	22-APR-1883	Francisco Goyette/Lina Beaudin	Alexander Marcoux/Eleonora Lajeunesse
Goyon*	Rosalinam	26-JAN-1856	26-JAN-1856	Jocobi Goyon/Margeretha Lemer	J Marcou/J. Lemer
Graham	Edwardum	19-NOV-1849	06-JUL-1852	Allen Graham/Brigitta O'Connor	T. Moran/C Mcgravy
Graham	Mariam	25-MAR-1852	06-JUL-1852	Allen Graham/Brigitta O'Connor	J Connor/E Connor
Graham	Thomam	13-MAR-1863	22-MAR-1863	Edwardi Graham/Bridgitta Graham	F. Rodgers/C. Rodgers
Graham*	Allen	24-NOV-1858	29-NOV-1858	Allen Graham/Bridget O'Connor	Thimoty Linch/Catherine Graham
Graham*	Allen	24-NOV-1858	29-NOV-1858	Alen Graham/Bridget O'Connor	Thimothy Linch/Catherina Graham
Graham*	Ellen				
Graham***	Maria Anna				
Graham***	Maria Anna	18-MAR-1860	12-MAR-1860	Eduardus Graham/Brdigetta Durken	Walter Stanton/Maria Kelly
Gramm	Mattham	21-DEC-1860	24-DEC-1860	Josephi Gramm/Maria Gramm	M. Verner/A. Stephan
Grand-bois	Georgium	18-JAN-1867	20-JAN-1867	Davidia Grand-bois/Zoah Grand-bois	T. Tessier/M. Tessier
Grandbois	Josephum Eusebium	17-AUG-1872	22-AUG-1872	Davidis Grandbois/Zoah Tessier	Jos.-Eus. Trotier/Leucadia Suprenant
Graton	Davidem	07-MAR-1867	21-APR-1867	Vitalis Graton/Phoebea Graton	H. Parizo/C. Mérard
Graton	Mariam Philomenam	31-JAN-1873	01-FEB-1873	Vitalis Graton/Phébe Graton	Andreas Rondeau/Alicia Graton
Gratton	Alfredum Eduardum	14-DEC-1892	17-DEC-1892	Ludgerio Gratton/Maria-Lousa Michotte	Deodatus Michotte/Oliva Moquin
Gratton	Alsam Phoebeam	14-JAN-1892	17-JAN-1892	Moise Gratton/Elizabeth Lepine	Josephus Lepine/Sophia Beaudreau
Gratton	Arthurum Walter	20-MAY-1896	04-JUN-1896	Josepho Gratton/Aurelia Michotte	Gulielmus Evans/Maria Gratton
Gratton	Avilam Zepherinum	18-FEB-1892	20-FEB-1892	Davide Gratton/Malvina Michotte	Deodatus Michotte/Maria-Ludovica Choiniere
Gratton	Blancham Mariam Lucreti	19-AUG-1908	23-AUG-1908	David Gratton/Melvina Michotte	Franciscus Gratton-Jr-/Lucretia Robidoux-Maurice
Gratton	Davidum Eduardum	02-AUG-1895	10-AUG-1895	Davide Gratton/Maloina Michotte	Josephus Gratton/Aurelia Lepine
Gratton	Elizabeth Irenam	21-DEC-1896	23-DEC-1896	Moise Gratton/Elizabeth Lepine	Josephus Gratton/Aurelia Lepine
Gratton	Elizabeth Oliviam	18-AUG-1898	08-SEP-1898	Davide Gratton/Malvina Michotte	Ludgerus Gratton/Marie-Lousa Michotte
Gratton	Fidelem Remundam	08-MAR-1899	12-MAR-1899	Moise Gratton/Elizabeth Lepine	Petrus Lepine/Josephina Corbeille
Gratton	Franciscum	07-MAR-1894	31-MAR-1894	Josepho Gratton/Aurelia Lepine	Moises Gratton/Elizabeth Lepine
Gratton	Franciscum Georgium	21-JAN-1889	22-JAN-1889	Moyse Gratton/Elizabeth Lepine	Franciscus Lepine/Philumena Landerman
Gratton	Gulielmum	17-FEB-1895	24-FEB-1895	Ludgerri Gratton/Maria-Lousa Michotte	Vital Gratton/Maria Gratton
Gratton	Henricum	18-FEB-1886	22-FEB-1886	Moyse Gratton/Elizabeth Lepine	Vitalis Gratton/Maria-Ludovica Choi--iere
Gratton	Josephinam	12-FEB-1897	04-MAR-1897	Ludgerio Gratton/Maria Michotte	Desdatus Michotte/Oliva Moquin

56

Surname	Given Name	Birth	Baptism	Parents	Godparents
Gratton	Josephum Vitalem	05-JAN-1888	10-JAN-1888	Jospho Gratton/Aurelia Lepinc	Vital Gratton/Maria-Lousa Choinierc
Gratton	Laurentium		20-MAY-1900	Davide Gratton/Malvina Michotte	Georgius Langlois/Marra Moqun
Gratton	Mariam Cornnam	14-MAR-1903	29-MAR-1903	Davdc Gratton/Malvina Michotte	Franciscus Maurice/Josephina Michotte
Gratton	Mariam Delphinam	25-DEC-1883	30-DEC-1883	Moise Gratton/Elizabeth Lepine	------ ------/Melina Gagnier
Gratton	Mariam Josephinam		07-APR-1882	Moise Gratton/Elizabeth Lepine	Ludovicus Lepine/Emelia Rondeau
Gratton	Moisem Ernestum	10-MAR-1894	04-APR-1894	Moise Gratton/Elizabeth Lepine	Franciscus Gagner/Emelia Lepine
Gratton	Narcissum Nelson	13-JUL-1899	30-JUL-1899	Ludgerio Gratton/Maria-Lousa Michotte	Davidus Gratton/Malvina Michotte
Graus*	Maria Francisca				
Graus*	Mariam Franciscam	23-SEP-1859	24-OCT-1859	Henrici Graus/Maria Addelmann	F Adelmann/A Adelmann
Gray	Jacobum Thomam	19-MAY-1862	22-JUN-1862	Joannis Gray/Bridgitta Gray	H. Gaffney/A Gaffney
Gray*	Barnard				
Green	Guilielmum	06-JAN-1862	08-JAN-1862	Guillelmi Green/Helena Green	J Gill/B. Gill
Green	James	11-MAY-1852	15-JUN-1852	Patrick Green/Marguerite Roy	J. Kelly/J. Mitchel
Green	Joannam	25-APR-1863	26-APR-1863	Guillelmi Green/Helena Green	B Kenn/------
Green	Sarahm Annam	11-MAY-1863	08-JUN-1863	Michaelis Green/Sarah Green	M Kelly/M. Green
Green	Thomas	13-MAR-1852	24-JUN-1852	Daniel Green/Elizabeth Kerry	P. Kennedy/B. Farley
Green	Thomas	06-APR-1851	13-APR-1851	Patrick Green/Marguerite Roy	J. Ferguson/E Fox
Green*	Catharnam	11-JUN-1858	20-JUN-1858	Patrcii Green/Chriatna Lovely	P. Maloy/M. Mulvy
Green*	Catherina	11-JUN-1858	20-JUN-1858	Patrck Green/Christine Lovely	Patrck M--oes/Mary Mulvey
Green*	Catherina	05-OCT-1858	21-NOV-1858	Mcl Green/Sara Lane	Thos Green/Marguerite Doyle
Green*	Catherine				
Greffen	Christinam	03-FEB-1856	19-MAR-1856	Michaelis Greffen/Honnora Connell	J. Connell/M Welschs
Gregoire	Adelnam	04-APR-1868	05-APR-1868	Isaaci Gregoire/Maria Gregoire	Baptista Gayet/Flavia Gayet
Grégoire	Josephinam	04-APR-1869	09-MAY-1869	Joannis-Baptista Grégoire/Vitalina Gayet	Narcissus Gayet/Terentia Demars
Grenier	Mariam Emeliam	16-JUL-1883	30-SEP-1883	Olivero Grenier/Olivina Marcoux	Franciscus Marcoux/Josephina Roy
Grenier	Paulum Olivarium	28-JUN-1873	30-JUN-1873	Olivarii Grenier/Olivina Marcou	Franciscus Marcou/Amelia Marcou
Grey*	Jacobum	18-JUN-1858	25-JUL-1858	Joannis Grey/Bridgitta Gaffny	P. Burke/S. Brion
Grey*	Jocabum	18-JUN-1858	25-JUL-1858	Joannis Grey/Brigetha Gaffeny	Petrus Burck/Sophia Brion
Griggan	Jacobum	18-APR-1854	19-APR-1854	Michaelis Griggan/Anna Colholl	J King/A. Dorothy
Grisé	Esther Ruth	10-AUG-1896	16-AUG-1896	Carolo Grisé/Esther Dufresne	Napoleo Marcoux/Sophrona Dufresne
Grise	Franciscum Earl	27-JUL-1890	29-JUL-1890	Carolo Grisé/Esther Dufresne	Isaac Gervais/Virginia Grise
Grisé	Josephum Antonium	21-NOV-1897	28-NOV-1897	Carolo Grisé/Esther Dufresne	Josephus Lamblot/Catharine Kremer
Grisé	Laurentium Alfredum	14-MAY-1895	15-MAY-1895	Carolo Grise/Esther Dufresne	Pascalis Dufresne/Sarah Ste.-Marie
Grisé*	Petrum	05-JUN-1856	19-OCT-1856	Antone Grisé/Clothida H--rain	N. Fontane/J Lamir
Grisé*	Petrus	09-JUN-1856	19-OCT-1856	Antone Grisé/Clothida H--rain	N Fontane/J. McCay
Grissé*	Josephnam	08-JAN-1859	16-JAN-1859	Antonii Grissé/Clothida Hiera	Politus Hebbert/Vigena Grissé
Grizet	Carolum	16-MAR-1863	29-MAR-1863	Antonii Grizet/Clotilda Grizet	----- Gervais/M Grizet
Grizet*	Virginiam	27-FEB-1863	29-MAR-1863	Isaaci Grizet/Virginia Grizet	G Pariso/M Grizet
Grizet*	Josephine				
Gromme	Joannem Justitum	15-JAN-1860	29-NOV-1891	C S. Gromme/Frederica Ruechentahl	Rev C. Boucher/Catharina McGregor
Groton	Ludgerum	16-FEB-1865	18-FEB-1865	Vitalis Groton/Phoeba Groton	P. Letourneau/L. Letourneau
Grular	Christopher	26-NOV-1850		S---- Grular/Elizabeth Garret	---- Ant/M. Harkin
Gruin*	James	23-SEP-1855	11-NOV-1855	Donnel Grunn/Marrian Crammel	W Flannigan/S. Crammel
Guay*	M----		23-NOV-1856	Bernad Guay/Elesabeh Crammer	E Cremmer/S Shoemaker
Gue-*	Petrus Sebastiona	01-MAR-1860	18-MAR-1860	Joannis Guc-/Madaline Beck	Petrus Beck/Maria Spinhal
Gueppe	Joannem	13-MAY-1858	14-MAY-1858	Joanne Gueppe/Mgdalena Bach	N Gueppe/E Hayes
Gueppe	John	03-MAY-1858	14-MAY-1858	John Gueppe/Magdelaine Bach	Nicholas Gueppe/Elz Hayes
Guemon	Alfredum Elmer	20-APR-1897	25-APR-1897	Eduardo Guernon/Elizabetha Stada	Fredericus Stada/Rosana Corbeille
Guernon	Eduardum Nicolaum	06-JAN-1890	07-APR-1895	Eduardo Guernon/Lilia Stada	Nicolaus Roth/Margaritta Scholl

57

Surname	Given Name	Birth	Baptism	Parents	Godparents
Guernon	Mariam Idam	01-MAR-1871	05-MAR-1871	Eduardi Guernon/Marguarita Guernon	Isidorus Donat/Delima Veine
Guernon	Suzannam Annam	13-MAR-1895	07-APR-1895	Eduardo Guernon/Lilia Stada	Nicolaus Ra--lse/Suzanna Marte
Gur--*	Carolum	24-JUN-1858	25-JUL-1858	Danelis Gur--/Maria-Anna Cambell	Patrcus Rady/Julia Whelan
Guilleman	Elizabeth	11-MAR-1874	23-MAR-1874	Pet-- Guilleman/Maria Balthazar	Ludovicus Balthazar/--rb----- Balthazar
Guilleman	Georgiam Mariam	18-MAR-1874	25-MAR-1874	Narcisci Guilleman/Marguerita Robert	Franciscus Robert/Maria Robert
Guillen	Ann	11-SEP-1850	15-SEP-1850	Martin Guillen/Brigitte Stanten	M. Guillen
Guon*	Carolus	18-MAR-1858	23-MAY-1858	Jocabus Guon/Margereta LeMer	Franciscus McGinity/Philomena LeBeau
Gunder	Carolum Robertum	27-FEB-1864	17-APR-1864	Henrici Gunder/Maria Gunder	C. Anderson/M. Shu-tzer
Gunther*	Henricus	01-SEP-1856	14-SEP-1856	----- ----/Maria Gunther	A. Gunther/M. --thin
Gurno	Dorothy Lousa	22-DEC-1919	25-APR-1920	Edward Gurno/Frances Gilgenback	Emery Barbeau/Mathilda Burg
Gutrauter	Carolum Henricum Francis	04-OCT-1906	14-OCT-1906	Henrico Gutrauter/Julia-Odella Marcoux	Augustus Marcoux/Julia Leduc-Marcoux
Guyette	Donald Francis	26-JUL-1920	01-AUG-1920	Henry-C Guyette/Eva-Delpine Marcoe	Edward Marcoe/Christina Marcoe
Gypson	James	08-JAN-1851	12-JAN-1851	George Gypson/Mary Groger	C. Smith/------ ----
Gärtner	Annam	04-MAY-1863	16-MAY-1863	Ferdinandi Gärtner/Catherina Gärtner	A. Keller/A. Trier
H-	Mariam	08-JAN-1863	18-JAN-1863	L H----/F H-----	----- ----/----- ----
H---n*	Joannes	02-MAR-1857	19-MAR-1857	Charles H----n/Anna J---	T Rayly/A Noss
H--ssekiger	Franciscam Jenny Cathernnam		31-OCT-1874		----- ----/----- ----
Ha-e--y*	John	24-MAR-1858	24-MAR-1858	Patrick Ha-e--y/Ellisaht --don	Jo-- Cussehely/Anna Bun-yhan
Haal	Alfred	18-JUN-1877	22-JUN-1877	Alfred Haal/Ludociva Develers	A. Develers/ wife
Habib	Barbaram	02-DEC-1907	08-DEC-1907	Georgio Habib/Martha Faris	Ayoub-Georgius Gastine/Rosa Faris
Habib	Sarah	19-DEC-1905	18-FEB-1906	Georgio Habib/Martha Faris	Ayoub-George Gastine/Rose Faris
Hall	Mariam Stellam	14-JUN-1881	06-JUN-1882	Alberto Hall/Louisa Devillers	----- ----/Carlotta Chenard
Hallaghan	Ludovicam Mariam	14-JUN-1862	21-JUL-1862	Jeremia Hallaghan/Brdgtta Hallaghan	G Donovan/C. Donovan
Halligan*	Thamam	11-JUN-1857	28-JUN-1857	Michaeli Halligan/Maria Galvem	T Egan/M. Lemere
Halligan*	Thomas	11-JUN-1857	28-JUN-1857	Michel Halligan/Marie Galvian	T Egan/M. Lemery
Hallows	Haroldum Emerum	20-APR-1904	01-MAY-1904	Hugone Hallows/Rosala Martin	Emerus Martin/Iona Martin
Hallows	Hugonem Bernardum		28-SEP-1900	Francisci-D Hallows/Linssee Gilson	Leo Martin/Eleonora Dumas
Hallows	Hugonem Bernardum Leon	20-SEP-1902	21-SEP-1902	Hugone Hallows/Rosalia Martin	Leo Martin/Eleonara Dumas
Hallows	Leonem Dana	29-MAY-1908	05-JUL-1908	Hugh Hallows/Lilian-Rosa Martin	Laurentius Martin/Oneta Piehl-Martin
Halpen	Joannem	24-JUN-1855	01-JUL-1855	Patricu Halpen/Maria Melon	P Halpen/B. Gillon
Halpen	Patrick		22-JUL-1855	Patrick Halpen/Maria Melon	P --tpen/B. Gillan
Halpen	Usenum		29-DEC-1854	Francisi Halpen/Brigetta Gillan	J Linchs/L. -a--s
Halpen*	Brigctham	19-APR-1860	04-MAY-1860	Francis Halpen/Brigetha Gellan	Jocabus -elly/Elisa Carr--
Halpen*	Margeretham	04-MAR-1858	23-MAR-1858	Francisci Halpen/Brigetha Gellan	P. Halpen/J. Gellan
Halpin	Mary-Ann	24-MAY-1851	06-JUN-1851	Francis Halpin/Brigitte Guillen	M. Carrel/M. Charlotte
Halpn*	Bridget				
Halpon*	Margeteta	04-MAR-1858	23-MAR-1858	Franciscum Halpon/Brigeta Gellun	Philip Halpen/Jerima Gellun
Haly*	John				
Haly*	Lhu	29-NOV-1858	18-APR-1859	Ptrick. Haly/Helen Hennis	T Gough/W. Henis
Hambetzer*	Joscphus		29-DEC-1856	Gillimus Hambetzer/Anna-Maria Fort	J Serwe/S. Abeler
Hambiter	Welhielmam		13-MAY-1858	Welh. Hambiter/Anna-Maria Voght	P Ottenbrett/G Cheffer
Hambitzer*	Josephum		29-DEC-1856	Wilhem Hambitzer/Anna-Maria Fort	J Serwe/S Mela
Hamelton*	Mariam	30-MAR-1857	09-APR-1857	Michaelis Hamelton/Ellena Revy	T. Nutgens/E. Conn-r
Hamilton	Annam		07-JUL-1861	Michaelis Hamilton/Helena Hamilton	T Reiley/H Reiley
Hamilton*	James				
Hamilton*	Joannem	30-JUL-1858	01-AUG-1858	Michaelis Hamilton/Helena Kelly	E Coffee/B. O'connor
Hamilton*	Maria	30-MAR-1857		Michel Hamilton/Ellena Kery	T Muttins/J. Oconner
Hammon*	Maria	04-SEP-1856	14-SEP-1856	----- Hammon/---1s Rogers	P. Connol/M. Mcintigath
Hammon*	Mariam	07-SEP-1856	14-SEP-1856	Arthor Hammon/Elisa Rogers	P. Annol/M. Mcentyre

58

Surname	Given Name	Birth	Baptism	Parents	Godparents
Haney*	Elisabetha		07-APR-1860	Jacobi Hovey/Maria Short	Michaelis Hovey/Elisabetha Shephard
Hannigan*	Mariam Annam	14-FEB-1858	18-FEB-1858	Josephi Hannigan/Brigetha Harlan	J Baken/M. Schea
Hanniker*	Josephum Antonium	28-JUN-1857	30-JUN-1857	Joseph Hanniker/Catherina Lins-hs	J. Pergrig/M. Claÿ
Hannitler*	Josephus Antonius	28-JUN-1857	30-JUN-1857	Joseph Hannitler/Cath Luchs	J. Pongrig/M. Clay
Hansel	Christinam	05-MAY-1861	09-MAY-1861	Joannis Hansel/Catharina Hansel	G Ha-de-/C. Abler
Hansel	Mariam Reginam	05-JUL-1863	13-JUL-1863	Joannis Hansel/Maria-Catherina Hansel	G Stolenwerk/M Henderson
Hansel**	Joannem Petrum	26-SEP-1865	24-SEP-1865	Joannis Hansel/Catharina Hansel	P Estreicher/B. Hartseim
Hanson	Catharinam	04-MAR-1861	09-MAY-1861	Joannis Hanson/Susanna Hanson	J. Pomerich/C. Pomerich
Hanson	Mariam	15-NOV-1862	16-NOV-1862	Joannis Hanson/Susanna Hanson	P Willart/M. Pomery
Hardgrove*	Richard				
Hardgrove*	Richardum	16-MAY-1859	12-JUN-1859	Henrici Hardgrove/Maria Hennesse	J. Cavanaugh/B. Connor
Harey	Malachiam	30-SEP-1863		Michaelis Harey/Maria Harey	P. Madian/M. Madian
Haring	Cecilia Gail		20-OCT-1918	Oscar-Marlatt Haring/Olive-Eva Morris	Clarence Morris/Kathleen Culliane
Haring	Lucile Marie	15-JAN-1920	21-MAR-1920	Oscar Haring/Eva Maurice	Fred Maurice/Mary Banks
Harlan	Guillelmum	04-MAY-1858	16-MAY-1858	Thoma Harlen/Rosa-Anna Martin	P. Flood/R Cahill
Harlan*	James				
Harlan*	Mariam Annam	26-JUN-1858	04-JUL-1858	Joannis Harlan/Joanna Roach	J. Dalton/M. Brown
Harlan***	Thomas				
Harlan***	Thomam	17-FEB-1859	06-FEB-1859	Williami Harlan/Maria Harlan	J Harlan/R. --m-n
Harlen	William	04-MAY-1858	16-MAY-1858	Thomas Harlen/Rose-Anna Martin	Peter Flood/Rose Cahill
Harlen*	Jocobus Edurdus	25-MAY-1857	26-MAY-1857	John Harlen/Francia White	J Harlen/M. O'Bryan
Harlon*	Annam	26-JUN-1858	04-JUL-1858	Joannis Harlon/--nna White	Joannes Dollon/Margeta Brown
Harlon*	Jocobum Eduradum	25-MAY-1857	26-MAY-1857	Joannis Harlon/Maria White	J Harlon/M O'Bryan
Harmen	Eugenum	12-APR-1878	14-APR-1878	Eugene Robert/Virgine T-sset	J. Gervais/P. Gervais
Harnois	Edwardum			Philippi Harnois/Elizabetha Harnois	F. Moriss--/
Harnois	Estheram	02-MAR-1863	03-MAR-1863	Olivieri Harnois/Marguarita Harnois	G Wottet/V Wottet
Harnois	Ethelbertum		02-NOV-1863	Philippi Harnois/Elizabetha Harnois	C. Bransheau/----- -----
Harnois	Ludovicum	03-SEP-1853	10-APR-1854	Stephani Harnois/Elizabetha Marian	G Durando/L. Monett
Harnois	Marguaritam	10-FEB-1862	11-FEB-1862	Olivieri Harnois/Marguarita Harnois	J Petit/E. Bellimeur
Harnois	Mariam	08-APR-1866	15-JUL-1866	Olivieri Harnois/Marguarita Harnois	M. Marcote/T Gerard
Harnois	Mariam Ludovicam	03-SEP-1864	14-SEP-1864	Olivieri Harnois/Marguarita Harnois	S. Thibodeau/L. Thibodeau
Harnois*	George				
Harnois*	Jorgeum	13-NOV-1858	24-NOV-1858	Olivier Harnois/Margeritha Monet	Jorge Ollet/----- Ollet
Harnts*	Josephna				
Harrington*	Jhon	09-NOV-1857	29-NOV-1858	Cornelius Harrington/Johanna Keefe	Michel Keefe/Mary Harrington
Harry*	Mathias		22-AUG-1856	James Harry/Elen Lohmiller	J Mangen/A. Burningham
Hart	Jacobum		18-NOV-1860	Nicholai Hart/Bridgetta Hart	P. Darrigan/C. Pelletier
Hart	Margaritam	21-AUG-1853	04-SEP-1853	Nicolai Hart/Brigitte Smit	J Smit/M. Mollen
Hartnet*	William				
Hartzain	Joannem	08-AUG-1866	27-AUG-1866	Francisci Hartzain/Barbara Hartzain	J Hansel/M Abel
Hartzheim	Antonium	30-JAN-1865	01-FEB-1865	Francisci Hartzheim/Barbara Hartzheim	A Reichling/C. Hansel
Harz	Elizabeth Julianam	07-JAN-1882	29-JAN-1882	Frederico Hary/Catherina Snider	Joannes -----/Elizabeth Crudwig
Hassenfuss	Dionysiam Sarahm	07-JAN-1873	25-JAN-1873	Jacobi Hassenfuss/Aurelia Boivin	Oliverus Hurto/Adelina Hurto
Hauser	Franciscum	24-MAR-1860	09-DEC-1860	Georgii Hauser/Sarah Hauser	P. Pelletier/M. Christophel
Haverty*	Martin	13-MAR-1859	13-APR-1859	Martin Haverty/Mary Katen	P Reily/M. Reily
Haverty*	Martin				
Haus	Joannem Georgium		25-DEC-1864	Joannis Georgii Haus/Christina Haus	N. Schnür/M. Geifeld
Haze	Honoram		04-OCT-1861	Guillelmi Haze/Anna Haze	J. Hallaghar/B. Hallagher
Heart	Josephum	16-FEB-1858	24-FEB-1858	Nicolai Heart/Bigetha Smith	M. Smith/----- -----

Surname	Given Name	Birth	Baptism	Parents	Godparents
Heart*	Joannem	24-OCT-1855	04-NOV-1855	Nicolaus Heart/Brigetha Smet	F. McDormt/M. Smet
Heart*	Joannes	24-OCT-1855	04-NOV-1855	Theoulus Heart/Brigta Smet	F. McDormt/M. Smet
Hebart*	Helene	23-AUG-1857		Philpp Hebart/Elisabht -enkins	John Doeney/Helen Quilcy
Hebert	Félicité	26-OCT-1850	29-OCT-1850	Isdore Hebert/Florence Cyr	L. Malheur/F Cyr
Hebert	Florentiam Clotildam	28-JAN-1883	07-FEB-1883	Napoleone Hebert/Maria Hebert	Isadorus Hebert/Emelia Hebert
Hebert	Franciscum Nazarium	03-JUL-1884	06-JUL-1884	Isadoro Hebert/------ ------	Nazarius Lapme/Felicttas Hebert
Hebert	Fredericum Isidorum	18-SEP-1881	24-SEP-1881	Isdore Hebert/Julia Caron	Generatus Landermann/Henretta-Eugenie Barrette
Hebert	Ludovicum	28-SEP-1873	28-SEP-1873	Francisci Hebert/Mariam Baudru	Franciscus Boucher/Julia Faucher
Heden*	Mariam Annam	22-AUG-1858	29-AUG-1858	Denin--- Heden/Birgetha Claury	Fran--- McDermt/Clara Lensch
Hedfreed*	Theresiam	12-JAN-1857	12-JAN-1857	Andrei Hedfreed/Anna-Maria Lourens	---- -----/M. Sceport
Hegelon*	Jermeas	20-JAN-1857	01-MAR-1857	Thamas Hegelon/Ellen Flood	J. Logelin/J Hegelon
Hekart*	Caroline Ellen				
Hekison	Robertum Henricum	22-NOV-1874	22-JAN-1875	Caroly-Henrici Herktison/Catherna Bekket	Michael Mangan/------ Mangan
Heneffy	Catharnam	21-MAR-1861	28-APR-1861	Michaelis Heneffy/Maria Heneffy	D Stanton/C. Flanegan
Henker	Violam Ethelam	31-MAR-1903	05-APR-1903	Hermano Henker/Josephina Pratte	Gulielmus Henker/Estella Pratte
Hennason*	Brigetham Magetam	20-FEB-1860	12-MAR-1860	Thama Hemmason/Anna Corrigan	Michael Douly/Anna Rosseheter
Henneffy	Mariam Annam	06-JUL-1862	13-JUL-1862	Michaelis Henneffy/Maria Henneffy	T. Lamb/B. Lamb
Hennegan*	Hugh				
Hennegan*	Hugo	28-OCT-1859	30-OCT-1859	Hueh Hennegan/Brigt Haly	P. Turner/----- Turner
Hennery	Elizabetham	30-JUL-1852	17-AUG-1852	Richardi Hennery/Julia Hennery	M. Bergan/J. Bergan
Hennery	Willielmum	09-DEC-1859	12-DEC-1859	Michaelis Hennery/Mariam Carrall	Patricus Chasesy/Brgeth Carral
Hennigan	Patricum	27-JUL-1859	29-JUL-1859	Joannes Hennigan/Catherna Maguis	Mauricus Maguis/Margereth Hennigan
Henricum	Leo	21-APR-1879	04-MAY-1879	Caroli Henrcim/M-- La-eun	L Lebeau/E. Rou
Henry	Abigalam	12-JAN-1867	12-JAN-1867	Benjamini Henry/Maria-Anna Henry	M. Santuaire/M. Santuairc
Hensmann*	Anna Chaterna	28-AUG-1856	07-SEP-1856	Joannes Hensmann/Lisabeham Crochet	J S--/C. Herl
Hensmann*	Annam Catharnam	28-AUG-1856	07-SEP-1856	Joannis Hensmann/Elisabeth Roehts	J. Serwe/C. Le-b
Henson*	Mathias	09-OCT-1858	21-NOV-1858	Jhn Henson/Catherine Smith	Thos Relly/Mary Bennett
Heny	Martinum	16-DEC-1865	07-JAN-1866	Jacobi Heny/Marguarita Heny	M. Löhmüller/C Krämmer
Herald*	Josephum	19-MAR-1860	12-AUG-1860	Carolus-Philipi Herald/Elisabeth Jenkin	Francisca Huck
Herbert	Mary Louise	31-OCT-1850	04-JAN-1852	Sebastien Herbert/Elizabeth Thrang	J. Denny/L. Denny
Herbert**	John Lawrence	12-NOV-1851	04-JAN-1852	Michael Herbert/Elizabeth Thrang	M. Ina/E. Thrangh
Herman	Annam Mariam	04-MAR-1863	05-MAR-1863	Josephi Herman/Catharina Herman	H. Krämmer/A. Mertes
Herman	Mariam Franciscum	28-JAN-1866	04-FEB-1866	Josephi Herman/Catharina Herman	J. Gorès/F Krämmer
Herschleb	Josephum Clayton Carolum	04-MAR-1909	10-JUL-1909	Roy C Herschleb/Olympia Brunet	Ferdinandus Brunet/Mathilda Potvin-Brunet
Herschleb	Josephum Roy Carolum	02-NOV-1881	18-MAR-1906	Carolo-Henrio Herschleb/Sphia Withrock	Thomas Lepine/Delna LeBeau-Brunet
Herschleb	Mariam Nellie	18-MAY-1905	16-JUL-1905	Roy-C- Herschleb/Olympia Brunet	Gedeon Brunet/Delna LeBeau-Brunet
Herschleb	Talmam Esther	05-MAR-1903	31-MAY-1903	Roy Herschleb/Olympia Brunet	Thomas Lepine/Josephina Brunet
Hess	Joannem Eduardum	23-JUL-1906	29-JUL-1906	Joanne-P. Hess/Josephna Gardner	Henrico-B. Schertzinger/Paulins Schertzinger-Jonke
Hess	Mariam Josephinam	15-SEP-1902	21-SEP-1902	Joanne-Petro Hess/Josephina-Helena Gagnier	Eduardus Gagnier/Edessa Parnseau
Hetwer	Albertum	04-AUG-1866	12-AUG-1866	Andrea Hetwer/Maria-Anna Hetwer	J. Shottenborg/C. Servatus
Hetwer	Edwardum	14-AUG-1865	20-AUG-1865	Josephi Hetwer/Theresia Hetwer	A. Rothgery/M. Hetwer
Hetwer	Franciscum	27-MAR-1861	27-MAY-1861	Andrea Hetwer/Maria-Anna Hetwer	P Wilbert/M. Weikert
Hetwer	Helenam	03-DEC-1863	06-DEC-1863	Andrea Hetwer/Maria-Anna Hetwer	P Servatus/G. Servatius
Hibach	Adam Adolfu-	02-JAN-1858	26-NOV-1859	B -Del Hibach/Louisa Ank-fl	A Grames/Joseph Ebert
Hibach	Josephus Franciscus	13-SEP-1855	23-MAR-1856	Franclus Hibach/Madalan Urling	M Smet/M -thinds
Hibach*	Joannem Cornelium		03-NOV-1857	Francisci Hibach/Lerusa Nimberling	J. Cofmann/M. Striehts
Hibach*	John Carolus	04-OCT-1857	30-NOV-1857	Francis Hibach/Lousie ---baling	J. Caufmann/M. Shueths
Hibath*	Amaliam	23-MAR-1859	12-FEB-1860	Francis Hbath/Madelina Hibba---	Mathias Shieht/Maria-Anna Cabbert
Hibbach*	Anna				

60

Surname	Given Name	Birth	Baptism	Parents	Godparents
Hick	Joannem	24-APR-1862	27-APR-1862	Jacobi Hick/Catharina Hick	T Ganon/E. Murry
Hicken	Ludovicum Garrett Elmer	11-JAN-1892	31-JAN-1892	Henrico Hicken/Melina Rondeau	Eduardus Smith/Emma Hicken
Hickey	Rosam Annam	13-FEB-1861	25-FEB-1861	Jacobi Hickey/Rosa Hickey	P Mcmullen/A. Fox
Hicts*	Carolum	13-APR-1860	11-MAY-1860	Henrici Hicts/Maria Nutten	Robertus Quinn/Maria McTevy
Hidden*	Petrum		19-JUL-1857	Dionsii Hidden/Brigetha Crouly	J. Schelby/M. Mullen
Hiden*	Mariam Annam	22-AUG-1858	29-AUG-1858	Dyonisii Hiden/Bridgitta O'leary	F. McDermet/H. Lynch
Hiers*	Jannes	04-SEP-1857	27-SEP-1857	Jouim Hiers/Maia Tesely	A Annan/E Hiers
Hiers*	Joannem	04-SEP-1857	27-SEP-1857	Joannis Hiers/Maria Sesely	A Annan/E. Hiers
Higgans*	Anne	23-AUG-1856	14-SEP-1856	Joannes Higgans/Maria Cody	P Boganny/M. Boganny
Higgens*	Joannem	02-MAR-1857	15-MAR-1857	Coruli Higgens/Anna Farly	T Rayly/A. Narch
Higgins	Margaritam Bellam	14-FEB-1890	16-FEB-1890	Henrico Higgins/Adelna Gagnier	Arthurus Steen/Margarita Ryan
Hlaire	Baptustam	22-SEP-1860	23-SEP-1860	Caroli Hilaire/Rosalie Hilaire	D. Beaudrieau/F. Robert
Hill	Carolina Victoriam	10-MAR-1872	12-MAR-1872	Joannis Hill/Adelina Pallant	Damasius Trotter/Philomena Trotier
Hill	Carolum	12-JUN-1891	15-JUL-1891	Carolo Hill/Thilly Aderhold	Franciscus Boucher/Julia Bessette
Hill	Franciscum Josephum	29-AUG-1868	27-JUN-1869	Joannis Hill/Adelna Pellant	Moyses Thibodeau/Herminia Pellant
Hill	Mariam Edessam	04-MAR-1871	05-MAR-1871	Jacobi Hill/Adelia Pellant	Franciscus Pellant/Josepha Pellant
Hills	Sarahm Annam	17-MAR-1862	01-APR-1862	Joannis-Stephani Hills/Adelina Hills	T Rondeau/H. Rondeau
Hin	Josephinam	18-JUL-1879	27-JUL-1879	Francis Hin/Josephne Bouchard	C Hin/-. Rondeau
Hin--y	Mariam Annam	04-JUN-1863	04-JUN-1863	Patricii Hin--y/Helena Hin--y	T. Corkaran/B. Corkaran
Hinmason*	Bridgit				
Hippach	Victorem	19-FEB-1861	27-OCT-1861	Francisci Hippach/Magdalena Hippach	E Everling/-------
Hirlm-*	Catrina	08-SEP-1856	19-OCT-1856	Michel Hirling/Clementia Clisch	D Cheffer/C -inh-g
Ho-h-	Leonem Maximilianum	06-MAR-1865	23-MAR-1865	Nicholai Ho-h-/Maria-Elizabetha Ho-h-	B. Ho-h-/S Ho-h-
Hoakley	Helena		15-MAY-1850	Richard Hoakley/---- Hoakley	F. Gauther/A. Bourassa
Hobitzer	Theresa	21-DEC-1850	29-DEC-1850	Joseph Hobitzer/Elizabeth Housson	A Annen/---- H-man
Hockey	Franciscum Xaverum		13-JAN-1861	Caroli Hockey/Anna Hockey	J. McCoury/M. Kessan
Hodfdeu	Herbert Harry		11-NOV-1919	Faugm Hodfdeu/Elizabeth Blaue	Frank C. Zarne/----- ----
Hodgden	Leroy Gilbert	16-AUG-1920	08-SEP-1920	Herbert Hodgden/Charlotte O'Malley	Gilbert O'Malley/Rosella O'Malley
Hoeflinger*	Fredericam Helenam	19-APR-1860	02-SEP-1860	Caroli Hoëflinger/Antonia Hoëflinger	H. --essils/-------
Hoffman	Marjoram Henriettam	28-AUG-1906	28-OCT-1906	Roberto Hoffmann/Georgina Boucher	Franciscus Boucher/Julia Bassette-Boucher
Hoffman*	John				
Hoffshani	Joannem	23-FEB-1861	03-MAR-1861	Laurenti Hoffshani/Francina Hoffshani	R. Wolcot/S. Lavandoski
Hoffshani**	Julium	17-JUN-1866	03-JUN-1866	Laurentii Hoffshani/Franciscus Hoffshani	J Rathman/R. Vaughn
Hofmann*	Joannem	24-JUL-1859	28-AUG-1859	Joannis Hofman/Maria Scheffer	J Cheffer/M. Sneyder
Hofshani	Patricius	03-MAY-1864	15-MAY-1864	Laurentii Hofshani/Francisca Hofshani	A Landroski/R. Volgemuth
Hofshani*	Joseph				
Hoge	Mariam Eleonoram	16-APR-1904	22-APR-1904	Gustavo Hoge/Maria Balthazar	Joannes-Baptista Balthazar/Maria Marcoux
Hoile*	Georgium	29-SEP-1857	04-OCT-1857	Stephani Hoile/Maria L'Anglois	V L'Anglois/F Sir
Holloran	Mariam Helenam	22-APR-1863	03-MAY-1863	Jacobi Holloran/Marguarita Holloran	T. Burke/M. Flynn
Holmes	Oliverum Eugenum	11-NOV-1900	05-MAY-1901	Olivero-Eugeno Holmes/Sophia Beaudin	Carolus Beaudin/Sophia Nantelle
Holoter	Emilam Evam	16-SEP-1864	18-SEP-1864	Georgii Holoter/Sarah Holoter	A. Mertes/E. Gra-s
Holt	Franciscum Xaverum		03-FEB-1866	Joannis Holt/Isabella Bisson	F. Bisson/J. Bisson
Holtz	Annam Albertam	01-DEC-1881	17-JUL-1910	Carolo Holtz/Carolina Blankenhous	Leo Martin/Eleonora Dumas-Martin
Hopy	Emma Marguarittam		17-JUN-1864	Henrici Hopy/Catharina Hopy	M. Merges/----- ----
Hopy	Mariam Carolam		17-JUN-1864	Henrici Hopy/Catharina Hopy	M. Serwe/-----
Horder	Josephus Anselmus	02-APR-1857	17-APR-1858	Jacob Horder/Marguerite Halblip	Chrstophe Back/Rosalie Bugnon
Horlon*	Jocobus	06-MAR-1860	13-MAY-1860	Thoma Horlon/Anna M------	Joannis Ward/Ellen ------
Hortenett*	Guliellimi	20-SEP-1859	17-JAN-1860	Guliellmi Hortenett/Jane Meyer	Jacobus Crowley/--ata ---------
Hory	Jacobum		26-SEP-1852	M.ichaelis Hory/Maria McDonald	F. Mcjuty/B. McDonald

61

Surname	Given Name	Birth	Baptism	Parents	Godparents
Houle	Mariam Genovafavam	03-JAN-1864	06-JAN-1864	Stephan Houle/Maria Houle	J Moss/Zoah Langlois
Houle	Stephanum Severum	12-APR-1862	20-APR-1862	Stephan Houle/Maria Houle	T -----/M Lemaire
Houle*	Marie Elise				
Houssois	Henricum Josephum	24-MAR-1866	20-MAY-1866	Josephi Houssois/Maria-Theresa Houssois	F. Lorge/L. Houssois
Houssois	Josephinam	20-SEP-1860	23-SEP-1860	Josephi Houssois/Maria-Theresa Houssois	F. Wayne/A. Houssois
Houssois	Mariam Theresiam	29-JUN-1863	05-JUL-1863	Josephi Houssois/Maria-Theresa Houssois	J. Mahné/M. Suizence
Houssois*	Jacobum	26-JUN-1858	04-JUL-1858	Josephi Houssois/Maria-Theresa Tordeur	J Larose/M Houssois
Houssois*	Louisa	30-AUG-1856	01-SEP-1856	Joseh Houssois/Maria-Thursa Tibodeau	J. D'ellise/M. Houssois
Hovey*	Elizabeth				
Howlan	Bernardum	25-JUL-1861	14-OCT-1861	Jacobi Howlan/Marguartta Howlan	T Roughan/M. Flinn
Hubert	Mariam Julian	14-MAY-1868	18-MAY-1868	Eusebi Hubert/Rachelie Baillergeon	Hubertus Baillergeon/Marguarita Dupus
Hubert	Stephanum Eduardum	10-JUN-1875	27-JUN-1875	Caroli-Eduard Hubert/Sophia Shoulé	Louis Bulss/----- Bulss
Hubert*	Joseph	01-JUL-1860	01-JUL-1860	Ch---em Hubert/Julia Ebert	An---- Dupree/Delima Dumas
Hubert*	Madalnam	29-JUN-1858	04-JUL-1858	----- Hubert/Co---nna Marret	Joannes Gisselain/Maria Desautels
Hubert*	Magdalenam	29-JUN-1858	04-JUL-1858	Davidii Hubert/Catharia Marret	J. Gosselin/M. Deshotels
Hubert*	Rosalam	18-JUL-1858	20-AUG-1858	Joseph Hubert/Del-- Bryen	Petrus Dufrane/Philivia Robert
Hubert*	Rosalam	18-JUL-1858	21-AUG-1858	Joseph Hubert/-----ina F--	P. Dufresne/F. Robert
Hughes	Annam Theresam	12-JUN-1862	28-JUN-1862	Joannis Hughes/Theresa Hughes	P.Crowley/M. Doyle
Hughes	Petrum	14-JAN-1855	16-JAN-1855	Joannis Hughes/Anna Curran	J. Mc-wn/S. Coleman
Hughes*	Marguaret				
Huile*	Mariam Eliam	18-SEP-1859	21-SEP-1859	--hy-- Huile/Maria-A. Langlois	B. Huile/J Dufarge
Huit*	Esther Josephine	26-MAR-1844	21-DEC-1858	Edward Huit/Clarey McDonald	
Huit*	Esther Josephine				
Huit*	John	29-SEP-1846	21-DEC-1858	Edward Huit/Clarey McDonald	
Huit*	John				
Huit*	Joseph	19-APR-1842	21-DEC-1858	Edward Huit/Clarey McDonald	
Huit*	Joseph				
Huit*	Maria Julia				
Huit*	Mary Julia	27-JAN-1838	21-DEC-1858	Edward Huit/Clarey McDonald	
Huit*	Robert	14-AUG-1845	21-DEC-1858	Edward Huit/Clarey McDonald	
Huit*	Robert				
Hulzer	Georgium	13-JUL-1862	13-JUL-1862	Georgii Hulzer/Clara Martin	J Trier/A. Taney
Hurling	Annam Marguarittam	13-APR-1864	16-MAY-1864	Michaelis Hurling/Clementina Hurling	G. Jackfeld/A. Hurling
Hurlings*	Cathernam	08-SEP-1856	19-OCT-1856	Michaelis Hurlings/Clementia Choch	D. Cheffer/C. Hurlings
Hurteau	Annam Adelnam	01-OCT-1901	05-OCT-1901	Joanne Hurteau/Maria Turcot	Gulielmus Feeney/Anna Hurteau
Hurteau	Joannem Eduardum	01-JUL-1898	21-JUL-1898	Joanne Hurteau/Maria Turcot	Eduardus Turcot/Julia Turcot
Hurteau	Lauram Margarittam	30-JUL-1900	12-AUG-1900	Joanne Hurteau/Maria Turcot	Franciscus Hurteau/Laura Durocher
Hurteau	Mariam Florentam	30-MAY-1896	03-JUN-1896	Joanne Hurteau/Maria Turcot	Eduardus Turcot/Philumena Coté
Hurto	Ludovicum	03-JUN-1873	15-JUN-1873	Oliveri Hurto/Adelna Dag-t	Petrum Corbeille/Justina Hurto
Hurtot	Annam Evam	07-MAR-1867	09-MAR-1867	Oliveri Hurtot/Adelna Hurtot	F Hurtot/A Odete
Hurtot	Carolna Victoram	05-FEB-1869	28-FEB-1869	Oliveri Hurtot/Adelna Hurtot	Antonus Lemontagne/Adelna Hurtot
Hurtot	Chrstophum		04-MAY-1869	Oliveri Hurtot/Elizabetha Dugas	Josephus Rabidou/Adelna Rabidou
Hurtot	Elizabetham		24-SEP-1871	Oliveri Hurtot/Adelna Hurtot	Antonius Lefort/Justina Cliché
Hurtot	Mariam	15-JAN-1865	15-JAN-1865	Oliveri Hurtot/Olivna Hurtot	N Hurtot/M. Odet
Hurtot	Olivicrum		24-FEB-1867	Oliveri Hurtot/Elizabetha Hurtot	O Hurtot/A Hurtot
Huss	Annam		04-JUL-1866	Joannis-Georgi Huss/Christna Huss	G. Jackfeld/A Kaufman
Hussour*	Louisam	30-AUG-1856	01-SEP-1856	Joseph Hussoir/Mara-Thersa Thurdeur	J. D'elise/M. Hussoir
Hussois	Joannam	29-JUL-1869	12-SEP-1869	Joseph Hussois/Maria-Josepha Tordeur	Joannis Lei--/----- Lei--
Hussois*	Jocabus	26-JUN-1858	04-JUL-1858	Joseph Hussois/Marie Th---urde--	Jocyu Larorige/Marie-Louise Gus---is

62

Surname	Given Name	Birth	Baptism	Parents	Godparents
Hustin	Carolum Ottonem		03-JAN-1865	Joannis-Petri Hustin/Maria Hustin	C. Lamers/S. Krämmer
Husting	Albertum ------	23-JUN-1874	12-JAN-1874	Franciscus-Petri Husting/Mariam Juneau	Robert-E. Miller/Philomena Lan------
Husting	Paulium Cornelium Franci	23-JUL-1872	04-AUG-1872	Joannis-P. Husting/Maria-Magdalena J------	Petrus-Cornelius Bransheau/Paulina Demars
Hutchions	Esteram W.		21-SEP-1852		Rev. Godfert/C. Smith
Hürlings	Annam Mariam	18-JUN-1862	06-JUL-1862	Michaelis Hürlings/Clementina Hürlings	J. P----/A. Roselion
Höfflinger	Richardum Carolum	06-MAY-1863	07-JUN-1863	Caroli Höfflinger/Antoinette Höfflinger	M. Hofflinger/L. Krembs
Höflinger*	Fredericam Helenam	19-APR-1860	02-SEP-1860	Caroli Hoflinger/Antona Hoflinger	H Krenbo/------ ------
Iager	Josephum Fredericum	15-OCT-1865	31-MAY-1866	Nicholai Iager/Anna Iager	N. Brown/T. Wisinger
Illo*	Cathernam	19-OCT-1857	20-OCT-1857	Thoma Illo/Catherina Carbit	J Welsh/M. Harnet
Inard	Ida Avelina	30-DEC-1876	31-DEC-1876	Josephi Inard/Leomina Feffe	A. Deshotel/ wife
Jackfeld	-		29-JUL-1866		
Jacktfeldt	Gasparum Henricum	24-SEP-1863	25-OCT-1863	Godfredus Jacktfeldt/Marguarita Jacktfeldt	G Shlerdem/M. Shaefter
Jacobson	Odeliam Sopham Amoure	08-JUN-1903	14-JUN-1903	Josepho Jacobson/Eva-Maria Allard	Josephus Donet/Odelia Lepine
Jameau	Jose--	19-MAY-1855	18-JUL-1855	Joan.-Bapt Jameau/Maria Peron	----- Corriere/-. Peron
Janard	Ludovicum	03-JUL-1882	09-JUL-1882	Ludovico Janard/Emma Blanchet	Franciscus Rondeau/Eleonora Bérard
Janssen	Jacobum Clayton Christman	11-APR-1903	26-APR-1903	Jacobo-Gulielmo-C. Janssen/Florentia Létourneau	Christophorum Letourneau/Anna Janssen
Januard	Mariam	04-JAN-1881	04-JAN-1881	Ludovico Januard/Emma Blanchet	L. Lépine/E. Rondeau
Jenelon*	Joannes Henricus	30-MAR-1860	02-APR-1860	Michaeli Jenelon/Maria Duffy	Danielis Jenelon/Anna Mc---
Jensehs*	Chaternam	12-OCT-1856	26-OCT-1856	Jocobi Jensehs/Anna Curran	P. Mangan/A. Bent----
Jibob*	David	25-APR-1857	02-JUL-1857	David Jibob/Josette Guga--	M. Duquet/J. Bodin
Jicart*	Josephi	12-MAR-1859	16-MAR-1859	Josephi Jiscart/Gertrude Knipp	J. Goler/C Clotz
Jobod*	David	25-APR-1857	02-JUL-1857	David Jobod/Jubeth Juga-t	M. Duquet/J. Rodin
John	Edess Tessie Mariam	18-JUL-1903	27-MAY-1905	Michaelis John/Della Letourneau	Isaac St -Antoine/Joanna Letourneau-St.-Antone
Johnson	Annam Margarita	17-FEB-1916	04-JAN-1920	John Johnson/Amelia Birch	Wm. Cranney/Margarite Birch
Johnson	Catherine	24-DEC-1851	09-MAY-1852	Peter Johnson/Alice Kelly	T Ward/R. Clark
Johnson	William	10-NOV-1850	13-APR-1851	Peter Johnson/Alice Kelly	W. --ld/M. Keating
Johnson*	Alice	14-MAY-1860			Michaelus McLure/Mary Moiry
Johnson*	Alicia	30-DEC-1879	04-JAN-1880	Petri Johnson/Alicia Kelly	J Jolie/A. Laberge
Joli	Fredericum Josephum	24-APR-1878	24-APR-1878	Corolo Joli/Georgina Laberge	F. Laberge/T. Jolie
Jolie	Mariam Josephinam	15-JAN-1876	16-JAN-1876	Caroli Jolie/Jasena Laberge	C Jolie/M. G-el
Jolie	Mariam Rosanam	19-MAR-1868	22-MAR-1868	Charles Jolie/Maria-Jorsina Laverge	Eusebius Jolin/Julia Jolin
Jolin	Carolum	18-JUL-1903	27-MAY-1905	Michaelis-Napoleonis Jolin/Margueria Laroque	Isaac St.-Antoine/Joanna LeTourneau
Jolin	Edessam Jessia Mariam	14-APR-1870	01-MAY-1870	Michaele Jolin/Della Letourneau	Michael Joln/Emerantta Demars
Jolin	Eduardum	27-JUN-1869	27-JUN-1869	Michaelis-Napoleonis Jolin/Marguarita Joln	Jacobus Joln/Maria Letourneau
Jolin	Eusebium Henricum	20-FEB-1866	01-APR-1866	Eusebii Joln/Julia Beaumar	J Choquete/H. Jolin
Jolin	Helenam Hermazinam	16-NOV-1904	27-MAY-1905	Michaelis Jolin/Marguarta Jolin	Michael Pominville/Sophia Graton-Pominville
Jolin	Howard Joannem	16-NOV-1904	27-MAY-1905	Michaelis Jolin/Della Letourneau	Michael Pominville/Sophia Gratton-Pomainville
Jolin	Howard Johnson	19-JUN-1866	15-JUL-1866	Michaele Jolin/Della Letourneau	M. Joln/R. Jolin
Jolin	Juliam	30-NOV-1867	01-DEC-1867	Eusebii Joln/Julia Joln	A. Beaumar/O Beaumar
Jolin	Mariam	03-APR-1854	11-NOV-1854	Daneils Jones/Maria Kimberly	T. Gaffy/J. Gaffern
Jones	Gulielmum	17-AUG-1898	27-AUG-1901		Gulielmus Durocher/Maria Perron
Jones Johns	Carolum	16-JAN-1900	28-AUG-1898	Petro Josef/Maria Shaff	Josephus Ferres/Anna Assef
Josef	Ludovicum Elīha	08-JUN-1871	04-FEB-1900	Petro Joseph/Mara Eshaff	Shakur Ferres/Anna Isseff
Joseph	Martham	10-MAR-1904	08-JUN-1871	Josephi Joubert/Anna Bessete	----- Joubert/Mevinam Joubert
Joubert	Alexandrum	27-FEB-1903	03-NOV-1907	Stephano Joubert/Estella Casper	----- /Edessa Joubert-Bullis
Joubert	Alicem Orvam	04-JAN-1852	03-NOV-1907	Stephano Joubert/Estella Casper	----- /Edessa Joubert-Bullis
Joubert	Blanchan Irenam	02-OCT-1862	04-JAN-1852	Eusebii Joubert/Adelina Brian	S Joubert/S. Paudrat
Joubert	Edward Eusebius		26-OCT-1862	Eusebii Joubert/Adelina Joubert	H. Desnoyers/L. Beaudrnau
Joubert	Emmam Ludovicam				

63

Surname	Given Name	Birth	Baptism	Parents	Godparents
Joubert	Ferdinandum	27-FEB-1867	03-MAR-1867	Xaverii Joubert/Sophia Joubert	J Beaudin/E. Beaudin
Joubert	Georgium Franciscum	23-APR-1863	26-APR-1863	Antonii Joubert/Joanna-Eliza Joubert	F Mocquin/H. Mocqun
Joubert	Joannem Carolum	07-JUL-1874	06-SEP-1874	Josephi Joubert/Anna Bessete	Julianus Bodin/Ludovica Bodin
Joubert	Josephinam	06-FEB-1854	24-FEB-1854	Julien Joubert/Aloisa Jillien	J. Jubert/M. Ste-art
Joubert	Josephinam	03-AUG-1865	20-AUG-1865	Eusebii Joubert/Adelina Joubert	J. Joubert/L. Joubert
Joubert	Josephum	11-MAR-1870	22-MAR-1868	Josephi Joubert/Anna Bessete	Julianus Joubert/Ludovica Joubert
Joubert	Julianem	21-JAN-1870	30-JAN-1870	Xaverii Joubert/Sophia Chaunière	Julianus Joubert/Ludovica Joubert
Joubert	Mariam Melvinam	09-APR-1871	22-APR-1871	Antonii Joubert/Maria-Melvina Joubert	Julianus Joubert/Marguarita Maillete
Joubert	Michaelem	26-JUL-1867	16-AUG-1867	Eusebii Joubert/Adelina Joubert	J Joubert/E. Carrière
Joubert	Noahm	23-NOV-1860	02-DEC-1860	Eusebii Joubert/Carolina Joubert	J. Zerci/H. Desnoyers
Joubert	Xaverium	25-MAR-1866	01-APR-1866	Xaverii Joubert/Sophia Joubert	M Chaumère/L. Filion
Juber	Mariam Josepham	15-NOV-1876	15-NOV-1876	Antoine Jubert/Jenne Elazar	C. Errard/ wfe
Jubert	Charles	21-AUG-1857	23-AUG-1857	Antoine Jubert/Jan---Elissa Ferdnes	J. St. Jean/J. Moÿin
Jubert	Flamerentam	01-AUG-1855	28-DEC-1855	Isaac Jubert/Flamerantia Sir	E. Baret/M. -----
Jubert	Leli Elisaeth	15-NOV-1875	12-DEC-1875	Josephi Jubert/Anna Bisset	S. Marten/F. Jubert
Jubert	Mariam Delanam	01-MAR-1854	05-MAR-1854	Lubestuius Jubert/Adeline Regne	L. Boudrieaux/O. Munier
Jubert	Mariam Louisam	23-DEC-1854	24-DEC-1854	Julien Jubert/Maria Sto-gle	J. Jubert/L. Jillien
Jubert	Mariam Rasaliam	31-JUL-1877	01-AUG-1877	Francisci Jubert/Rosalie Baltazar	J. Baltazar/ wfe
Jubert*	Elisabeh		06-JUL-1856	Julien Jubert/Adelina Jubert	Eduard Jubert/Adelina Jubert
Jubert*	Elisabetham	17-APR-1856	06-JUL-1856	Julii Jubert/Mara Sling-	E Jubert/A. Jubert
Jubert*	Esther Maria	05-AUG-1856	10-AUG-1856	----- Jubert/Delma Brion	H Denoyé/A. Denoyé
Jubert*	Esther Mariam	05-AUG-1856	10-AUG-1856	Josephi Jubert/Adelina Brian	H. Denoyé/ D.Denoye
Jubert*	Jocabus	26-JUL-1857	02-AUG-1857	Camiles Jubert/Maria Moirris	D Gary/M Gill
Jubert*	L---	29-AUG-1857	27-SEP-1857	Jo---- Jubert/Lucia Fillion	D Hubert/A. Bron
Jubert*	Ludovicum	23-SEP-1857	27-SEP-1857	Julia-- Jubert/Lousia A----- Fellion	D Hubert/A. Bran
Jubyant*	Anna	04-JUL-1856	05-JUL-1856	Antonus Jubyant/Anna-Maria Hofman	N. Jubyjant/A. Get
Julette	Mathildam	27-MAR-1871	02-APR-1871	Josephi-D. Jurlette/Femi-a Mame	Nazarius Langlois/Mathilda Langlois
Julgaert*	Annam	04-JUL-1856	05-JUL-1856	Antoni Julgaert/Anna-Maria Hofmann	B. Juligaert/A. Net
Julius	Joannam	02-DEC-1905	17-DEC-1905	Abraham Julius/Halia Assef	Ayoub-George Gastine/Maria Skaf
Julius	Josephum	09-APR-1903	03-MAY-1903	Abraham Julius/Allia Assef	Azub George/Maria Skaff
Julius	Ludovicum Michaelem	26-OCT-1901	17-NOV-1901	Abrahami Julius/Alice Assef	J---- Julius/Maria Skaff
Julius	Mariam	04-SEP-1904	02-OCT-1904	Abrahamo Julius/Allia Hasseff	Jacobus George/Maria Scaff
Julius	Petrum Danielem	14-JAN-1908	16-FEB-1908	Abraham Julius/Alia Aseff	Georgius-Ayoub Gastine/Maria Aseff
Juneau	Harietta Ursula	29-DEC-1851	15-JAN-1852	Narcisse Juneau/Magdelen Yatt	E. Jud/M. Juneau
Justen*	Joannem Ignatium	26-MAR-1857	05-APR-1857	Joannes-Pet-- Justen/Victoria-Catherina Sal	J. Prees/C. Justen
Justin	Joannem Henricum		09-DEC-1861	Josephi Justin/Francisca Justin	H. Kraus/M. Kraus
Justin	Paulum Adolphum Oscarem	27-APR-1866	03-JUN-1866	J.oannis-Petri Justin/Maria-Magdalena Justin	A Bishof/M Justin
Justin	Petrum Maximiilianum Rol	17-APR-1868	10-MAY-1868	Joannie-Petri Justin/Maria-Magdalena Juneau	Joannes-Petrus Justin/Maria Justin
Justis*	James Ignatius	26-MAR-1857	05-APR-1857	Joannes-Petrus Justis/Victoria-Catherina Soli	J. P---s/C. Justi
K--ets*	Albertus	28-DEC-1857	03-MAR-1858	Hennery K--ets/Marie Nuttan	James McLevy/Maria-Ann Guen
K-rry*	Mathiam		24-AUG-1856	Jocobi K-rry/Elena -----	J Mengan/A. Bermingham
Kann	John	13-MAY-1857	13-MAY-1857	-----/Catherina Kain	Richard McKeep/Brigita Kelly
Kann*	Anne		24-APR-1859	Thomas Kann/Joanna Cronnan	I. Meunier/S. M------
Kann*	Anne				
Kaiser	Henrietam	24-AUG-1866	16-SEP-1866	Josephi Kaiser/Marguarita Kaiser	M. Reichert/H. Reichert
Kalb*	John				
Kalen	Rogers	18-APR-1858	16-MAY-1858	Mcl Kalen/Catherina Madden	Mcl M-ulen/Mary Kalen
Kane	Catharinam	13-SEP-1863	13-SEP-1863	Jacobi Kane/Anna Kane	J. Daugherty/C. Monaghan
Kane	Laurentium	29-OCT-1852	03-JAN-1853	Michaelis Kane/Maria Smith	N. Harf/R. Smith

64

Surname	Given Name	Birth	Baptism	Parents	Godparents
Karrel	Elizabeth	10-APR-1852	15-MAY-1852	John Karel/Catherine Reines	M. Reines/M. Reines
Kary	Annam	25-NOV-1854	01-JAN-1855	Joannis Kary/Maria Kelly	P. Kelly/H Kary
Kasset	Margaritam	20-JUN-1854	24-JUN-1854	Julien Kasset/Margarita Sir	P. C-ullier/S. Shenard
Katan	Annam Mariam	29-MAR-1854	22-APR-1854	Patritii Katan/Maria Mol---	------/M. Egan
Katen	Rodgerium	18-APR-1858	16-MAY-1858	Michaeli Katen/Catherina Madden	M. Mullen/M. Katen
Kaufman	Catharinam Elizabetham		24-SEP-1865	Caroli Kaufman/Elizabetha Kaufman	J Kaufman/C. Fitzsimmons
Kaufman	Elizabetham	12-JUL-1864	05-NOV-1864	Joannis Kaufman/Marguarita Kaufman	M Kersh/E. Kaufman
Kaufman	Joannem	25-OCT-1862	28-NOV-1862	Joannis Kaufman/Marguarita Kaufman	J. Kaufman/M. Kaufman
Kaufman	Joannem	03-MAR-1861	31-MAR-1861	Joannis Kaufman/Elizabetha Kaufman	J. Brown/M. Kaufman
Kaufman	Mariam Elizabetham	05-MAY-1863	04-JUN-1863	Caroli Kaufman/Elizabetha Kaufman	J. Kaufman/M. Brown
Kaufman	Mariam Marguaritam	13-MAR-1861	29-APR-1861	Joannis Kaufman/Maria Kaufman	P. Kaufman/M. Shieffer
Kaufman	Michaelem	18-OCT-1864	11-NOV-1864	Joannis Kaufman/Maria Kaufman	M. Kaufman/M. -elli-
Keating	Thomas	02-MAY-1852	13-JUN-1852	Michael Keating/Catherine Madden	M Ward/M. Gazin
Keating	William Henry	09-DEC-1851	12-JAN-1852	Patrick Keatng/Mary Mullen	T Mullen/M. Curran
Keely*	Catherine	31-JAN-1859	15-FEB-1859	Jas. Keely/Julia Murray	P. Mulvey/J. Doyle
Keenan	Guillelmum Christianum	25-DEC-1860	06-JAN-1861	Joannis Keenan/Joanna Keenan	G. Donovan/A. Nash
Keenan	Jacobum	28-FEB-1863	01-MAR-1863	Joannis Keenan/Joanna Keenan	J. Mack/C. Donaghar
Kegel	Raymondum Lester	13-JUL-1888	22-AUG-1888	Joanne Kegel/Elizabeth Pinnon	Nicolaus Sherea/Mary Pinnon
Keho	William Josepheum	20-MAR-1877	03-MAY-1877	William Keho/Sera-Jane Roberson	J. Robensen/ wife
Ken	Thomam	19-JUN-1852	07-JUL-1852	Joannus Kein/Brigitta F-an	T. Ken /B. Reilly
Ken	Thomas	16-SEP-1850	16-SEP-1850	John Kein/Brigitte Foran	R Tenessee/J. McGrath
Kelday*	Brigeta	23-NOV-1856	02-FEB-1857	Michel Kelday/Honnore Ratten	P. Kelday/B. Kelday
Kelely	Martin	17-DEC-1851	12-JAN-1852	Thomas Kelely/Ann Madden	M. Keating/B Fergusson
Kelley*	Catharine				
Kelligan*	Joannes	01-AUG-1857	04-OCT-1857	Michel Kelligan/Brigita Do-nly	J. Calligan/ M Belty
Kelly	Anthony	03-FEB-1851	18-FEB-1851	Patrick Kelly/Catherine Egan	J Kelly/E. Fitzgerald
Kelly	Ellenam	05-SEP-1852	24-SEP-1852	Jeremias Kelly/Julia Murphy	J. Norton/E Conroy
Kelly	Francis	18-JUN-1851	04-JUL-1851	William Kelly/Ann Sidar	T. Kelly/J Sidar
Kelly	Guillelmum	15-SEP-1852	23-JAN-1853	Guillelmi Kelly/Anna Kelly	P. Fitzgerald/E. Dalton
Kelly	Guillelmum Jacobum		23-SEP-1861	Guillelmi Kelly/Esthera Kelly	A Quakenbush/----- -----
Kelly	Jacobum	22-JAN-1862	25-JAN-1862	Petri Kelly/Barbara Kelly	J. Mullen/M. Cushion
Kelly	James John	02-FEB-1858	03-APR-1858	Mcl Kelly/Mary Connolly	John Connolly/Mary Brennan
Kelly	Joannem	02-SEP-1857	24-SEP-1857	----- -----/K Kelly	D Oconner/B. Barret
Kelly	Joannem	17-JUN-1852	29-JUN-1852	Thoma Kelly/Rosa Kelly	G Kelly/J. Rider
Kelly	Joannem	05-DEC-1852	18-JAN-1853	Joannis Kelly/Joanna Kane	R. McCabe/C Fin---
Kelly	Joannem	06-JAN-1855	18-FEB-1855	Michaelis Kelly/Margarita Quinn	J Kelly/S. Martin
Kelly	John	12-MAY-1852	30-MAY-1852	Patrick Kelly/Marguerite Smith	C. Clark/C Kelly
Kelly	Margaretham		22-MAY-1858	Guillemus Kelly/A. R----	M. R----/C. Garet
Kelly	Margaritam Joannam	16-AUG-1854	05-NOV-1854	Patrcu Kelly/Catharina Egan	G Kelly/R. Ryder
Kelly	Marguerite		23-SEP-1861	Guillelmi Kelly/Esthera Kelly	A. Quakenbush/----- -----
Kelly	Mariam	02-MAR-1858	22-MAY-1858	Will Kelly/Ann Rider	Thos Rider/Catherine Jacob
Kelly	Mariam	10-JUL-1862	13-JUL-1862	Guillelmi Kelly/Esthera Kelly	M Sullivan/A. McGown
Kelly	Michaelus	21-AUG-1859	09-JAN-1860	Patricius Kelly/Margareta Kelly	Eduardi-Cuthbert Jocab/Catharina Jocabi
Kelly	Peter	30-AUG-1850	15-SEP-1850	Patrick Kelly/Marguerite Kelly	J. ----/J. Marten
Kelly*	Caternam	06-JAN-1859	09-JAN-1859	Petri Kelly/Margeretha Flannigan	Patusse Gaffen/Anna Flannigan
Kelly*	Caternam	06-JAN-1859	09-JAN-1859	Petri Kelly/Margeritha Flannigan	Pat--- Gaffeny/Anna Flannigan
Kelly*	Catharine				
Kelly*	Catharine Anne				
Kelly*	Guillelmum	29-MAY-1859	25-DEC-1859	Antonii Kelly/Nzppiar Maley	D Burnset/J. Ross

65

Surname	Given Name	Birth	Baptism	Parents	Godparents
Kelly*	Joannes	12-APR-1859	24-APR-1859	Jacobus Kelly/Maria Conley	M. Mahony/C. Dwyer
Kelly*	Jocabum	11-SEP-1857	13-SEP-1857	Michaelis Kelly/Margeretha Kaury	J Burns/B. Murphy
Kelly*	Jocabus	12-SEP-1857	13-SEP-1857	Michael Kelly/Margerta Kerry	J. Basset/B. Murphy
Kelly*	John				
Kelly*	Katerna Anne	31-AUG-1859	04-SEP-1859	Patrc Kelly/Margareth Linchs	M. O--y-la--/E. Linchs
Kelly*	Maria	10-DEC-1855	16-DEC-1855	Michaelis Kelly/Maria Dan-	Patrick --t--ns/Brigita Murphy
Kelly*	Maria	10-NOV-1855	16-NOV-1855	Michaelis Kelly/Maria Adams	P. N----/B Murphy
Kelly*	Mariam	10-DEC-1855	16-DEC-1855	Michaelis Kelly/Maria Danis	P Nutgens/B. Murphy
Kelly*	Mariam	12-AUG-1860	19-AUG-1860	P. Kelly/M. Flannigan	M. Mol---gan/M Garathy
Kelly*	Mariam	30-JUN-1858	03-JUL-1858	Petr Kelly/Maria Lynch	J. Flynn/H. Flynn
Kelly*	Patrick				
Kelly*	Petricum	12-MAY-1859	26-JUN-1859	Joannis Kelly/Joanna Cane	P. Crowly/T. Hughes
Kelly*	Rabertin Linni--n	06-APR-1860	15-APR-1860	Michel Kelly/Mag---- Curry	Thamas Morris/Margaretha Ragan
Kelly*	William				
Kelly	Annam Mariam	08-SEP-1853	18-SEP-1853	Michaelis Kelly/Margarita Gruin	J Kelly/S. Kelly
Kennan*	Densius	30-MAY-1858	07-JUN-1858	John Kennan/Joanna Nas-h	Jeremas Burk/Magereta Lean
Kennan*	Dyonsium	30-MAY-1858	17-JUN-1858	Joannis Kennan/Joanna Nash	J Burke/M. Lean
Kennedy	Brigetta	16-JUL-1860	29-JUL-1860	Patrci Kennedy/Maria Clowery	Joannis Kennedy/Brigetta Kennedy
Kennedy	Cathernam	13-JUN-1858	27-JUN-1858	Mathew Kennedy/Joanna Roach	T. Kennedy/B Petit
Kennedy	Catherine	13-JUN-1858	27-JUN-1858	Mathew Kennedy/Jane Roche	Thos Kennedy/Bridget Petit
Kennedy	Joannem	30-MAY-1854	08-JUL-1854	Joannis Kennedy/Anna McArdle	P McKan/R. Mullen
Kennedy	Mary-Ann	29-FEB-1852	23-MAR-1852	John Kennedy/Ann McCarrell	P. Kennedy/H. Gypson
Kennedy*	Bridgit				
Kennedy*	Margaretta	31-MAR-1860	02-APR-1860	Martin Kennedy/Jena Roche	G Mathews/Julia Ricly
Kennedy*	Marguaret				
Kenni	Marguariiam Annam	24-FEB-1862	22-MAR-1862	Joannis Kenni/Joanna Kenni	C. Walsh/M. Walsh
Kenni	Sarahm Annam	15-MAR-1863	12-APR-1863	Joannis Kenni/Julia Kenni	J Dolan/H. Murphy
Kenni*	Catharine				
Kenni*	Margueret				
Kenni*	Thomas				
Kenno	Jacobum	27-JUL-1853	04-AUG-1853	Jacobi Kenno/Brigitta Gill	P. Rigny/M. Gill
Kenny	Andream	02-MAY-1853	03-MAY-1853	Joannis Kenny/Juditha Kenny	A. Kenny/M. Gill
Kenny	Honoram	16-JAN-1864	30-JAN-1864	Andrea Kenny/Marguarita Kenny	P Connell/J. Kenny
Kenny	Jacobum	11-DEC-1854	14-DEC-1854	Andrea Kenny/Margarita Terry	J. Kenny/C. Garrigan
Kenny	Joannem	11-JAN-1853	20-JAN-1853	Andrea Kenny/Marguerita McTevy	J Kenny/M Gill
Kenny	Mariam	03-MAY-1860	28-MAY-1860	Patricus Kenny/Maria Liger	---- ----/Maria Cennel
Kenny	Mariam	19-SEP-1860	30-SEP-1860	Andrea Kenny/Marguarita Kenny	J Mcdav--/M. McDavitt
Kenny	Michaelem	01-JAN-1855	17-JAN-1855	Joannis Kenny/Julia Cain	J. Kenny/M Mctery
Kenny*	Andream	10-NOV-1856	16-NOV-1856	Andrea Kenny/Margeretha MeTevy	M. Kenny/C. Mogon
Kenny*	Catharnam	27-JUL-1859	07-AUG-1859	Michaelis Kenny/Celia Harnam	McKellan/C. Egan
Kenny*	Elisam Eugenam	13-AUG-1857	16-AUG-1857	Joannis Kenny/Marra -arhy	J. Gillan/M. G--f
Kenny*	Joanna	10-FEB-1857	15-FEB-1857	Michel Kenny/Ellen Nelligan	E Kinny/M. O'conner
Kenny*	Joannem	02-JAN-1856	15-JUN-1856	Gulielm Kenny/Anna Rdon	---- ----/E. O'Neil
Kenny*	Joannes	02-JAN-1856	15-JUN-1856	William Kenny/Anne Rydan	E. O'Neil/---- ----
Kenny*	John				
Kenny*	Sarah G				
Kenny*	Thaman	06-JAN-1859	16-JAN-1859	Joannis Kenny/Judtha Con	Jocabus Nichelson/Maria McTevy
Kenny*	Joannam	10-JAN-1857	15-FEB-1857	Michaelis Kenny/Ellis Kelligen	E. Kenny/M Oconner
Kenny*	Mariam	17-SEP-1855	23-SEP-1855	Jacobi Kenny/Brigeta Gill	J Gill/B. Stantan

Surname	Given Name	Birth	Baptism	Parents	Godparents
Kenseler	Luciam Phelonisam	25-APR-1900	20-MAY-1900	Henrico Kenseler/Rosa-Maria Dion	Michael Lambert/Maria Dion
Kepper	Catherinam	19-DEC-1855	28-DEC-1855	German Kepper/Sophia H-rens	M H-rens/C Keper
Kerry	Marguaritam	11-MAY-1863	14-MAY-1863	Guilelmi Kerry/Catharina Kerry	D O'Neil/M. Clarke
Kerry	Patricum	04-FEB-1864	05-FEB-1864	Petri Kerry/Marguarita Kerry	T Toomy/M. Toomy
Kerry*	Margeretham	10-SEP-1858	10-OCT-1858	Andrea Kelly/Margeretha McLevy	Francius Wall/Elisabeth McTyvy
Kesh	Elizabetham Annam	01-MAR-1862	30-APR-1862	Henrci Kesh/Maria-Anna Kesh	J. Coleman/B Coleman
Kesselar*	Mariam Catherinam	24-MAY-1858	24-MAY-1858	Christopheli Kesselar/Anna-Maria Asmam	B Hammer/- Hammer
Kesseler*	Christophum Edmundum	18-SEP-1860	30-SEP-1860	Christoph Kesseler/Anna-Maria Kesseler	E Kerrer/A. Kerrer
Kesseler*	Gulielmum	18-SEP-1855	23-SEP-1855	Christophi Kesseler/Emelia Esmann	N Crammer/T. Esmann
Kesseler*	Gulielmus	18-SEP-1855	23-SEP-1855	Christopher Kesseler/Emelia Admann	N. Hammon/T. Admann
Kesselere*	Maria Catherina	24-MAY-1858	24-MAY-1858	Chrstole Kesselere/Anna-Maria Assman	Col- Bernad/Maria-Chaterna Hama--
Kessler	Joannem Clementem	20-JUL-1863	26-JUL-1863	Christophori Kessler/Anna-Maria Kessler	J. Paas/B. Trimboer
Kessy*	Joannes Augustinus	20-MAY-1856	20-JUN-1856	James Kessy/Maria Reburan	J. Reburan/M. Gruien
Keyley	Michaelem	13-AUG-1862	13-AUG-1862	Patricii Keyley/Marguarita Keyley	T Roach/M Brown
Keyley	Thomam	13-AUG-1862	13-AUG-1862	Patricii Keyley/Marguarita Keyley	T Roach/M. Brown
Kiby	Catharnam	08-OCT-1853	16-OCT-1853	Joannis Kiby/Maria Kellgan	-----/C McMann
Kider*	Martinus	27-FEB-1860	15-APR-1860	Thoma Kider/Catherine O'donel	Antonus Rilley/Brigetta Kider
Kiernan*	Mary Ann	30-SEP-1858	22-FEB-1859	Daniel Kiernan/Joanna Burk	J. Lucier/E. Brunelle
Kiernan*	Mary Ann				
Kilday*	Brigetham	23-NOV-1856	02-FEB-1857	Michaelis Kilday/Honnora Sutton	P. Kilday/B. Kilday
Killane	Annam	06-SEP-1863	26-SEP-1863	Patrcii Killane/Serah Killane	P. Nugent/M. Daugherty
Killgallan	Marguaritam	15-OCT-1862	30-OCT-1862	Joannis Killgallan/Catharina Killgallan	M. McNeil/M. Mccarthy
Killigan*	Joannem	01-OCT-1857	04-OCT-1857	Michaelis Killigan/Brigetha Downnely	J Calligan/M Belty
Kilmer	Florentiam Lauretta	24-NOV-1900	13-DEC-1900	Gilielmo Kilner/Eva-Jacqualina Gervais	Telesphorus Gervais/Melina Beauregard
Kilmer	Laurentium	16-JAN-1905	29-JAN-1905	Gilielmo Kilmer/Eva Gervais-Kilmer	Nohemas Moquin/Maria-Ferdinand Moqun
Kilmer	Laurentium	10-JAN-1905	29-JAN-1905	Guilelmo Kilmer/Eva Gervais-Kilmer	Nomas Moquin/Maria Ferdinand-Moqun
Kilmer	Norbert Clarence	29-JUN-1920	15-AUG-1920	William Kilmer/Ivy Jarvis	Clarence-Martin Fitzgerald/Dora Jarvis
Kilner	Gulielmum Narcissum Geo	09-JAN-1902	21-JAN-1902	Gulielmo-C Kilner/Eva Gervais	Emericus Gervais/Olivina Charron
Kilner	Josephum	19-MAR-1903	23-APR-1903	Guilelmo Kilner/Eva Gervais	Georgius Dion/Maria Powers
Kind	Mariam Rosalaam	25-JAN-1866	11-FEB-1866	Andrea Kind/Elizabetha Kind	M. Burchardt/M. Picor
Kind*	Patrick				
Kind*	Patricum	24-OCT-1858	07-NOV-1858	Chegland Kind/Anna Ninan	Gulim Brown/Maria Mo--
King	Lucina Blondine	28-SEP-1919	07-OCT-1919	John King/Mary LePine	Jos. Diette/Mary Hetzel
King	Mariam Narcissam	15-MAY-1853	16-MAY-1853	Francisci King/Julia Lemire	S Houl/G -----
King*	Catherinam	15-NOV-1855	02-DEC-1855	Michaelis King/Catherina Mooran	J. King/M. Nicolus
King*	Catherine	15-NOV-1855	02-DEC-1855	Michael King/Cather Morin	J. King/M. Nicolus
King*	Joannem	25-JAN-1860	06-MAY-1860	Patrci King/Maria Bayly	Thomas Rayly/Susana -----
King*	Martinum	13-JUN-1856	14-JUN-1856	Patrci King/Maria Carroll	T. King/J. Cranly
King*	Martinus	13-APR-1856	14-JUN-1856	Patrk King/Maria Kassell	T. King/J. Croning
King*	Thomanc		03-APR-1858	Patricii King/Maria Kelly	T Kelly/C. Mulkegy
King*	Thomas	09-FEB-1858	03-APR-1858	Patrck King/Maria Kayly	Thomas Keyly/Anna Mulkay
Kingsly*	Maria-Anna	18-FEB-1856	16-MAR-1856	Daniel Kingsly/Margertt Au--t	G Phelan/L Kennedy
Kingsly*	Mariam Annam	18-FEB-1856	16-MAR-1856	Danielis Kingsly/Margereta Niephel	G Phalan/L Kennedy
Kinny*	Andrew	16-NOV-1856	16-NOV-1856	Andrew Kinny/Margeta McTevy	M. Kinny/C Mogan
Kinny*	Maria	17-SEP-1855	23-SEP-1855	James Kinny/Porigal Gill	J Gill/B. Stanten
Kinsley	Elizabeth Alois	12-JAN-1920	03-AUG-1920	Alfred Kinsley/Elizabeth-Charlotte Bloechel	-----/Marguerrte Bloechel
Kinstler	Henricum Leeland	25-SEP-1901	13-OCT-1901	Henrico Kinstler/Maria Dion	Felix Roy/Anna Gentz
Kint	Antonum	22-JAN-1864	07-FEB-1864	Andrea Kint/Elizabetha Kint	M. Stephans/----- -----
Kinter*	Mariam Elsam		04-SEP-1859	Henry Knter/Marie Schetser	J Bagly/M. Mcg-r---

67

Surname	Given Name	Birth	Baptism	Parents	Godparents
Kintzler	Ethel Mariam	16-NOV-1903	24-NOV-1903	Henrico-Y. Kintzler/Maria Dion	Georgius Dion/Martha Powers
Kintzler	Josephum Clayton	06-NOV-1907	13-NOV-1907	Henrico Kintzler/Maria Dion	Hugh Hallows/Lalan Martin-Hallows
Kintzler	Lilliam Elizabeth	01-JAN-1910	09-JAN-1910	Henrico Kintzler/Maria Dion	Josephus Dion/Vivanna Lee
Kintzler-Dion	Henricum	13-DEC-1905	28-DEC-1905	Henrico-D. Kintzler/Maria Dion	Michael Dion/Philomena Charron-Barbeau
Kippoch	Ludovicum Albertum	20-APR-1864	15-MAY-1864	Francisci Kippoch/Magdalena Kippoch	M Heberly/M. Davis
Kiston	Mariam	09-OCT-1854	11-JAN-1855	Samuelis Kiston/Maria Nygan	J McCarty/M. Kiston
Klaus	Annam Mariam	11-JUL-1835	08-APR-1861		J Pomerich/C Pomerich
Klaus	Catharinam Emiliam	21-OCT-1860	08-APR-1861	------/Anna-Maria Klaus	J. Pomerich/C. Pomerich
Klay	Anthonium	08-FEB-1853	15-FEB-1853	Joannis Klay/Maria-Anna Smith	C Ca--ler/C. Klay
Kloct	Mariam Elisabeth	26-OCT-1853	06-NOV-1853	Ignatus Kloct/Sousana Sneeller	F Kern/C. Sneller
Ko-rer	Helenam Catharinam	28-NOV-1866	09-DEC-1866	Edmundi Ko-rer/Elizabetha Ko-rer	J Flaten/-----------
Kocle*	Georgius	29-SEP-1857	04-OCT-1857	S--- Kocle/Maria Langlois	V. Langlois/F. Slr
Koeng	Carolum	05-DEC-1863	05-DEC-1863	Frederici Koenig/Francisca Koenig	C Hamelonge/C. Shema
Koeng	Mariam Ludovicam	27-MAR-1862	27-APR-1862	Joannis Koenig/Ludovica Koenig	G. Zacher/M. Olinger
Koeng	Petrum Ludovicum	20-JUL-1860	28-OCT-1860	Frederici Koenig/Francisca Koenig	E Horn/A. Hoyt
Koepfer*	Carolnam	10-SEP-1858	19-SEP-1858	Permnii Koepfer/Sophia ------	Philppe Odenhuett/Aña-Maria Hamb-zer
Koepfer*	Caroline				
Koffman	Joannem		06-JAN-1858	Joannes Koffman/Maria Cheffer	T Rayly/M. Ollenbreth
Koggler	Mariam Annam	19-MAR-1855	24-MAR-1855	Permani Koggler/Sophia Var--ts	M. Baker/M. Smets
Kolp	Carolum Josephum	10-JUN-1866	15-JUL-1866	Bernardi Kolp/Elizabetha Kolp	J Wertzbuger/M. Ann--
Kraemmer	Jacobum	03-MAY-1865	14-MAY-1865	Nicholai Kraemmer/Catharina Kraemmer	J Heug/M. Lohmüller
Kramer	Gulielmum Edwinum Jose	29-MAY-1905	09-APR-1905	Betholdo-J. Kramer/Esther Gardner	Edwardus Gardner/Susanna Kramer
Kramer	Mariam Clementinam	19-SEP-1852	24-OCT-1852	Joannis-Petri Kramer/Cosaria-Catt--- Perant	A. Perant/C Perant
Krammer	Mariam Mathildam		10-JAN-1869	Francisci-P. Krammer/Cezaria Perron	Georgrus Raymond/Anna Dumas
Krembs	Aloysiam Antoniatam	05-NOV-1864	25-DEC-1864	Maurtii Krembs/Joanna Krembs	A. Krembs/L. Krembs
Krembs	Elizabetham Ludovicam	21-JUL-1861	28-JUL-1861	Caroli-Frederici Krembs/Eva Krembs	L Sontag/E. Mosel
Krembs	Helenam Mariam	09-MAR-1863	07-JUN-1863	Maurtii Krembs/Geneta Krembs	C Hofflinger/C Hass
Krembs	Magdalenam Josephinam	25-JUN-1863	06-JUL-1863	Caroli Krembs/Eva Krembs	J. Mengel/M Sontag
Kremer	Gulielmum Edwinum Jose	29-MAR-1905	09-APR-1905	Bertholdi-J. Kremer/Esther Gagne-Gardner	Eduardus Gagne/Susanna Kremer
Kremer	Helenam Edith	11-FEB-1910	20-FEB-1910	Bertholdo-Jacobo Kremer/Esterh-M Gardner	Arthurus-J Kremer/Josephina Gardner-Hess
Kremer	Jacobum Henricum	11-JUN-1888	18-JUN-1888	Joanne Kremer/Gertrude Kermer	Jacobus Martes/Anna-Maria Kremer
Kremer	Susannam Mariam	06-JUN-1907	06-JUN-1907	Bertholdo-J. Kremer/Esteher Gardner	Eduardus Kremer/Edessa Parriseau-Gardner
Krolly	Joannem	02-FEB-1855	02-MAR-1855	Patritu Krolly/Maria Black	D. Dorrethy/A. Dorrethy
Krümmer	Bernardum	17-MAR-1863	22-MAR-1863	Eberhardi Krümmer/Augustina Krümmer	B. Colp/E Colp
Krä------	Robertum	28-JUL-1862	30-JUL-1862	Nicholai Krä------/Clementina Krä------	J Her-d/J. Weber
Krämer	Petrum Josephum	30-MAY-1862	07-JUN-1862	Josephi Kramer/Maria Krämer	J. Stephani/M. Rothgeri
Krämmer	Annam	15-DEC-1864	16-DEC-1864	Josephi Krämmer/Maria Krammer	J Stephan/A. Cole
Krämmer	Annam Catharinam		15-MAR-1863	Joannis Krämmer/Cesaria Krämmer	J ------/C. Tenissen
Krämmer	Augustam	08-JAN-1864	30-JAN-1864	Mathei Krämmer/Maria-Anna Krämmer	P Muller/L. Thorp
Krämmer	Joannem Petrum	22-SEP-1866	29-SEP-1866	Josephi Krämmer/Maria Krämmer	J Stephani/A. Stephani
Krämmer	Joannem Petrum	14-JUL-1872	20-JUL-1872	Joannis-Petri Krämmer/Cezarina Perron	Josephus Morris/Adelina Morris
Kueller*	Chrstophele	06-AUG-1859	07-AUG-1859	Michaelis Kueller/Rosa Kelly	T Ro---/M. Wagner
Kunnagan*	John	24-MAY-1858	13-JUN-1858	John Kunnagan/Brigeta Kelly	Michel McGory/Ro---a Dogerty
Kwezs	Mertum	28-DEC-1857	03-DEC-1858	Henrici Kwezs/Maria Nuttens	J McTevy/M Gruen
Künderer	Hubertum Henricum	03-MAY-1861	18-AUG-1861	Henrici Künderer/Maria Künderer	J. Cramer/S. Hetzor
Köpfer	Hermanum	23-OCT-1861	01-NOV-1861	Peremini Kopfer/Sophia Köpfer	G Shertzinger/A. Stephan
L'Eargent	Josephina	05-DEC-1879	06-DEC-1879	Petro L'Eargent/Carolina Lefaure	J Lefaure/J. Lefaure
L'Anblot	Josephinam	13-MAR-1877	18-MAR-1877	Constant L'Anblot/Rosalia Devilers	J. Lamblat/A. Lamblat
L'Anglois	Adolphum Amandum	07-MAY-1878	07-MAY-1878	Edmundi L'Anglois/Margereth Rasett	M. Anglois/L. Rasett

68

Surname	Given Name	Birth	Baptism	Parents	Godparents
L'Anglois	Josephnam	22-FEB-1875	26-FEB-1875	Vitalis L'Anglois/Sophia Sir	Josephus Langlois/Josephina Mocquin
L'Anglois	Mariam	24-MAR-1855	25-MAR-1855	Vitalis L'Anglois/Juliette Sir	J. Rasset/M. Sir
L'Anglois*	Antonum	17-MAY-1855	22-JUL-1855	Angeli L'Anglos/Matilda Beaulieu	J. Venne/E. Veinne
L'anglot	Julianum Raymondum	24-OCT-1874	25-OCT-1874	Edmunc L'anglot/Margeth Brusett	Jocobus L'anglois/Margereth Sir
L'anné*	Louis	15-MAY-1856	25-MAY-1856	Francois L'anné/---ina Boriceau	L ----/P. -----
L'Anné*	Ludovicum	18-MAY-1856	29-MAY-1856	Francisci L'Annié/Elena Lucan	L. Bricou/P. Bricou
L'Anto	Flaves Eduardum	09-JAN-1877	14-JAN-1877	Hudané L'anto/Marie Dufraine	P Dufrane/ wife
L'Antoine	Isaacum		18-JUN-1855	Isaaci L'Antome/Julianna Lebeau	J. ----/D. Dessept
L'e--blon*	Joannes Jerephus		30-NOV-1857	Constam L'e--blon/Rosalie Develiers	A. Devilers/J Delveau
L'Eclaire	Mariam Alphusam	10-AUG-1877	12-AUG-1877	Julie L'Eclaire/Dina Langlois	I. Langlois/D. G---é
L'Eculé	Carolinam	12-AUG-1877	13-AUG-1877	Petri L'Eculé/Carolina Lefort	B. Lefort/M. Fort
L'Eculier	Adolphum	09-FEB-1856	18-FEB-1856	Petri L'Eculier/Licada Chinard	J Tibodeaux/J. Gayet
L'Eculier	Angelicam	09-DEC-1875	10-DEC-1875	Petri L'Eculier/Carolina Lefort	N. Lefort/P. Demarch
L'eculier*	Gorgium	30-APR-1858	02-MAY-1858	Petri- L'eculier/Licade Chunard	G. Ollet/V. Pettit
L'eculier*	Ludovicum	10-DEC-1857	03-JAN-1858	P----L'eculier/Lucarda Parriso	D. Dindelain/M. L'eculier
L'eculier*	Ludovicus	10-DEC-1857	03-JAN-1858	Perre L'Eculier/Lecarda Parriso	D. O'hair/M. L'eculier
L'Eculier*	Mariam Celestinam	14-DEC-1856	11-JAN-1857	C. L'Eculier/R. Rosscheler	L Bodrieaux/M Bodrieaux
L'Ecullier*	Jorge	30-APR-1858	02-MAY-1858	Petrus L'Ecullier/Leocadie Shinard	Jo---- Ollet/Vergina Pettit
L'emblin*	Joannem Josephum	30-OCT-1857	03-NOV-1857	Anstanti L'emblin/Rosala Develiers	A. Develiers/J. Delveau
L'éter	Carolum	31-DEC-1862	03-JAN-1863	Petri L'éter/Henrica L'éter	J. Duquette/O. Tessier
L'Etourneau	Ede Agnes	16-JAN-1878	03-FEB-1878	Pascal L'Etourneau/Marie Beangart	M. Tremblé/ wife
L'Oiseau	Georgium Reynolds	04-NOV-1907	10-NOV-1907	Leone L'Oiseau/Gratie Towns	David Chaperon/Delia-Louisa L'Oiseau
L'Oiseau	Gulielmum Leonardum	20-APR-1880	09-MAY-1880	Gulielmo L'Oiseau/Sophronia McDonald	O. Bisson/E. Loiseau
L'Osseel*	Guliemus	20-JUN-1857	05-JUL-1857	Josep L'Osseel/Iulia Baltazar	M. Baltazar/A. Desautel
Labarge	Josephum Alfred	10-JUL-1874	12-JUL-1874	Francisci Labarge/Maria Yelle	Caroli Jolly/Georgina Labarge
Labonté	Josephum	29-SEP-1862	19-OCT-1862	Joseph Labonté/Flavie Labonté	P. Lemaire/H. Desnoyers
Labonté	Virginiam	03-SEP-1865	01-OCT-1865	Joseph Labonté/Flavia Labonté	A. Dufort/J. Cliche.
Lacause*	Joseph Ferdinand				
Lacause*	Josephum Ferdinatum	19-AUG-1859	18-SEP-1859	Ferdinand Lacause/Mathilda Leduc	E. Robert/F. Robert
Lacause*	Nasaliam	07-JAN-1858	31-JAN-1858	Fernandi Lacause/Matilda Leduc	J. Bodreaux/J. Bodrieaux
Lacause*	Natalia	07-JAN-1858	31-JAN-1858	Ferdinadus Lacause/Isabella Leduc	Joseph Bodrieau/Judeth Bodrieaux
Laduc*	Alfredum	18-MAY-1859	29-MAY-1859	Alfredum Laduc/Lynlia Bodreau	F. Laduc/F Robert
Laduc*	Lilan Elenam	15-MAY-1859	29-MAY-1859	Alarie Laduc/Julia Bodrieau	F. Lank/S. Robert
Ladue*	Franciscum	30-MAY-1857	15-JUN-1857	Hilarie Ladue/Julia Dufraine	F. Dufraine/L. Ladue
Lafame	Generosum Vitalem	28-MAR-1891	29-MAR-1891	Generoso Lafame/Olivina Balthazar	Francisci Poquette/Medalina Lavalle
Laffey	Georgium Henricum	03-AUG-1862	08-DEC-1862	Joannis Laffey/Anna Laffey	P. Holoran/B. Mccartney
Lafontaine	Delima	22-MAR-1869	28-MAR-1869	Josephi Lafontaine/Sophronia Dupuis	Baptista Dupuis/Eleonora Demars
Lafontaine	Josephum Amitum	17-MAY-1866	29-MAY-1866	Josephi Lafontaine/Sophronia Lafontainc	H Baillargeon/Zoah Mocquin
Lafontaine	Mariam Delvnam	22-MAR-1869	28-MAR-1869	Josephi Lafontaine/Sophronia Dupus	B. Lego/Eulalilia Yelle
Lafontainc	Mariam Lucretam	14-MAY-1876	16-MAY-1876	-uget Lafontaine/Frederinne Leshulere	J Bourgon/-----Prefontaine
Lafontaine	Mariam	16-JAN-1877	28-JAN-1877	Joseph Lafontone/Sophria Dupus	O. Roberge/M. Dale
Lafontone	Mariam Cordiliam		28-JAN-1877	Joseph Lafontone/Sophria Dupus	F Lafontaine/ wife
Lafortane*	Alexandrnam		24-JUN-1855	Benjamin Lafortane/Sopha LaMennette	E Martel/C. Ver--it
Lafortane*	Mariam	27-NOV-1854	24-JUN-1855	Benjamin Lafortane/Sopha LaMennette	F Mennett/M Remeaux
Lafortune*	Alexandrino		24-JUN-1855	Benjamin Lafortune/Sophia Lamonnette	E. Martel/C. Vernait
Lafortune*	Maria		24-JUN-1855	Benjamin Lafortune/Sophia Lamonnette	F. Mennette/M. Remeau
Lagnier	Edwardum	24-MAR-1861	24-MAR-1861	Francisci Lagnier/Onesima Lagnier	L. Durocher/A. Brico
Lagner	Henricum	21-MAY-1864	22-MAY-1864	Francisci Lagner/Lucina Lagnier	J. Dodelin/P. Dodelin
Lagner	Josephum	01-MAY-1862	04-MAY-1862	Francisci Lagnier/Oliva Lagnier	O. Dodlin/S Doff

69

Surname	Given Name	Birth	Baptism	Parents	Godparents
Lagnier	Rosam Delima	14-JAN-1867	20-JAN-1867	Francisci Lagnier/Onesima Lagnier	S. Brico/S. Léonctin
Lahy	Honora	23-FEB-1858	07-MAR-1858	Cornelus Lahy/Mary Connell	Mcl Scanlon/Bridget Connors
Lang	Helenam Emmam	01-JAN-1870	09-JAN-1870	Alexandri Laing/Sophronia Lucier	Baptista Dupuis/Clotilda Agagnier
Lajeunesse*	Henry	26-AUG-1855	27-AUG-1855	Henrry Lajeunesse/----- Gayet	J. Gayet/M. La-alli-a
Lajeunesse	Alfredum Dostheum	19-NOV-1882	03-DEC-1882	Henrico Lajeunesse/Lucia Leduc	Josephus Lajeunesse/Julia Gratton
Lajeunesse	Antoniam	14-MAR-1861	17-MAR-1861	Henrici Lajeunesse/Eleonora Lajeunesse	A. Lajeunesse/M. Gayet
Lajeunesse	Belle Annie	08-SEP-1875	12-SEP-1875	Henrici Lajeunesse/L.-Honnore G-yet	A. Marcou/E. --dan
Lajeunesse	Eleonoram	21-DEC-1867	29-DEC-1867	Petri Lajeunesse/Eleonora Surprenant	H.Lajeaunesse/ J Surprenant
Lajeunesse	Emiliam	14-NOV-1866	06-DEC-1866	Henrici Lajeunesse/Eleonora Lajeunesse	C. Gayet/E. Surprenant
Lajeunesse	Ezildam Eleonoram	07-APR-1887	10-APR-1887	Michaele Lajeunesse/Rosana Lebeau	Moyses Lebeau/Angela Mecier
Lajeunesse	Franciscum Generosum M	03-JUL-1906	05-JUL-1906	Generoso Lefeunesse/Olivina Balthazar	Fransico Marcoux/Josephine Roy
Lajeunesse	Franciscum Xaverium	17-DEC-1873	01-JAN-1873	Tréfla Lajeunesse/Philomena Bessete	Theodolphus Rieve/Rosada Bessete
Lajeunesse	Generosum	28-FEB-1864	06-MAR-1864	Henrici Lajeunesse/Eleonora Lajeunesse	F. Gayet/E Malheur
Lajeunesse	Georgius Ludovicus	17-JUN-1875	20-JUN-1875	Treffli Lajeunesse/Philamine Bisset	Seril Bissept/Philome Robert
Lajeunesse	Hubertum	05-JAN-1880	11-JAN-1880	Henrico Lajeunesse/Lucia Leduc	H. Lajeunesse/W. Goyet
Lajeunesse	Josephum	09-JUN-1871	12-SEP-1871	Petri Lajeunesse/Elenora Lajeunesse	Josephus Gayet/Eleonora Lajeunesse
Lajeunesse	Josephum Alexandrum Purl	03-JUL-1906	05-JUL-1906	Generoso Lefeunesse/Olivina Balthazar	Axel Larson/Julia Bathazar-Larson
Lajeunesse	Josephum Georgium	23-FEB-1904	28-FEB-1904	Generoso Lajeunesse/Olivina Balthazar	Joannes-Baptista Balthazar/Maria Marcoux
Lajeunesse	Josephum Walter	17-FEB-1898	20-FEB-1898	Generoso Lajeunnesse/Olivina Balthazar	Josephus Lajeunesse/Julia Gratton
Lajeunesse	Julian Theophili	20-APR-1880		Theophili Lajeunesse/Philomena Besset-Lajeunesse-----	Guillet/M. Lajeunesse
Lajeunesse	Leonam Eleonoram	02-MAR-1902	09-MAR-1902	Generoso Lajeunesse/Olivina Balthazar	Alexander Marcoux/Eleonora Lajeunesse
Lajeunesse	Ludovicum	21-JUN-1869	17-JUL-1869	Henrici Lajeunesse/Eleonora Gayet	Ludovicus Gayet/Olivina Marcou
Lajeunesse	Ludovicum	13-AUG-1892	15-AUG-1892	Generoso Lajeunesse/Olivina Balthazar	Joannes-Baptiste Balthazar/Maria Marcoux
Lajeunesse	Ludovicum Josephum	08-JUL-1878	10-JUL-1878	Henricum Lajeunesse/Lucia Leduc	H. Leduc/ wife
Lajeunesse	Margarittam Mariam	11-MAR-1900	13-MAR-1900	Generosa Lajeunesse/Olivina Balthazar	Julianus Balthazar/Margaritta Lajeunesse
Lajeunesse	Marguaritam	17-JAN-1868	19-JAN-1868	Henrici Lajeunesse/Eleonora Lajeunesse	Josephus Balthazar/Marguarita Gayet
Lajeunesse	Mariam Alidam	06-MAR-1882	12-MAR-1882	Trefflio Lajeunesse/Philamena Bessette	Jacobus Lyonais/Philamena Lajeunesse
Lajeunesse	Mariam Ednam	05-FEB-1892	07-FEB-1892	Michaele Lajeunesse/Rosa Lebeau	Napoleo-Zoticus Corbielle/Melinda Lebeau
Lajeunesse	Mariam Evam Herminam	24-MAR-1894	31-MAR-1894	Generoso Lajeunesse/Olivina Balthazar	Gulielmus Balthazar/Hermina Balthazar
Lajeunesse	Mariam Olivinam		05-JAN-1890	Generoso Lajeunesse/Olivina Balthazar	Henricus Lajeunesse/Eleonora Goyette
Lajeunesse	Mariam Rosam Annam	28-DEC-1884	31-DEC-1884	Michaele Lajeunesse/Rosa-Anna Lebeau	Henricus Lajeunesse/Eleanora Goyette
Lajeunesse	Mariam Stellam	21-APR-1896	26-APR-1896	Generoso Lajeunesse/Ludivina Balthazar	Vitalis Langlois/Emelia Balthazar
Lajeunesse	Michaelem	28-APR-1862	25-MAY-1862	Henrici Lajeunesse/Eleonora Lajeunesse	J. Gayet/P. Thbodeau
Lajeunesse	Petrum	21-MAY-1865	10-JUN-1865	Henri Lajeunesse/Eleonora Gayet	P. Lajeunesse/R. Gayet
Lajeunesse*	Bernardum	09-MAY-1857	16-MAY-1857	Henrici Lajeunesse/Susanna Gayet	I Surprenant/M Gayet
Lajeunesse*	Bernardus	09-MAY-1857	16-MAY-1857	Henry Lajeunesse/Anna Gayet	I Surprenat/M. Gayet
Lajeunesse*	Joseph				
Lajeunesse*	Josephum	19-MAY-1859	19-MAY-1859	Henrici Lajeunesse/Leocadie Gayet	A Bissept/J Gayet
Laliberté	Josephum	19-SEP-1868	25-SEP-1868	Eusebii Laliberté/Cleopha Laliberté	Narcissus Beaudon/Emerentia Demars
Laliberté	Mariam Ludovicam	31-MAR-1874	17-APR-1874	Eusebii Laliberté/Chopha Roi	Caroli Tremblé/Clementia Fanofe
Lallier	Carlotta Julia	22-NOV-1873	30-APR-1874	Leonis Lallier/Charlotta-Julia Chollet	Narcissus-L. Bullis/Edena-E. Bullis
Lallier	Franciscum Eugenum	15-OCT-1851	05-SEP-1865	Leonis Lallier/Carolina Lallier	J. Pierron/M. Lallier
Lallier	Josephum	09-MAR-1869	13-AUG-1871	Leonis Lallier/Carola Lallier	Josephus Boutet/Adela Pierron
Lallier	Julian Mariam Carolam		23-JUN-1872	Leonis Lallier/Julia-Carola Lallier	Josephus Simonin/Julia Simonin
Lallier	Leonem Ludovicum	15-OCT-1864	05-SEP-1865	Leonis Lallier/Carolina Lallier	L. Lallier/M. Peirron
Lallier	Leoniam Rosaliam	09-SEP-1866	13-AUG-1871	Leonis Lallier/Carola Lallier	Augustus Pierron/Adela Pierron
Lalonde	Josephum Leonem	11-MAR-1884	12-MAR-1884	Leone Lalonde/Eulodia Landerman	Josephus Landerman/Ophilia Dumas
Lamb	Jacobum	07-DEC-1862	07-DEC-1862	Nicholai Lamb/Anna Lamb	F. McDermott/A. McDermott
Lamb	Mariam Annam	17-JUL-1863	19-JUL-1863	Thoma Lamb/Maria Lamb	M. Henneffy/M. Henneffy

70

Surname	Given Name	Birth	Baptism	Parents	Godparents
Lambelot	Mariam Georginam	12-NOV-1873	13-NOV-1873	Constantio Lambelot/Rosalia Devilerse	Antoivius Bastien/Margarita R-----
Lambert	Annam	01-MAY-1881	04-MAY-1881	Michael Lambert/Sophrona -----	E Hubert/R Baillargeon
Lambert	Benjaminem	15-MAY-1903	17-MAY-1903	Michaele Lambert/Maria Dion	Paulus Lambert/Corrina Barbeau
Lambert	Chrıstophorum	16-OCT-1892	26-OCT-1892	Michael Lambert/Maria Dion	Gilbertus Surprenant/Zoea Barbeau
Lambert	DEliam	02-OCT-1874	11-OCT-1874	Michael Lambert/Sophrona Barbeau	Petrus Barbeau/Mariam Serret
Lambert	Delphinam	01-MAY-1881	04-MAY-1881	Michael Lambert/Sophrona -----	O. Dupuis/S Dupuis
Lambert	Eliseam	08-AUG-1883	12-AUG-1883	Michael Lambert/Sophronia Barbeau	Gilbertus Surprenant/Zoe Barbeau
Lambert	Felonisam Lucıllam	10-MAY-1906	13-MAY-1906	Michaele Lambert-Jr./Maria-Lalie Dion	Christophorum Lambert/Estella Lambert
Lambert	Franciscum	04-MAY-1895	06-MAY-1895	Michaele Lambert/Maria Dion	Michael Lambert/Sophronia Barbeau
Lambert	Josephum	29-JUN-1870	02-JUL-1871	Michaelis Lambert/Sophronia Barbeau	Josephus Mocqun/Mathilda Lebeau
Lambert	Josephum Albertum	15-MAY-1894	19-MAY-1894	Michaele Lambert/Sophrone Barbeau	Michael Lambert/Maria Dion
Lambert	Josephum Aurelum	01-APR-1897	04-APR-1897	Michael Lambert/Sophrona -----	Gulıelmus Dion/----- Dion
Lambert	Lucianum Gilbertum	30-SEP-1872	30-SEP-1872	Caroli Lambert/Sophronia Lambert	Gilbertus Surprenant/Adela Barbeau
Lambert	Ludovicus	18-APR-1879	04-MAY-1879	Michaelis Lambert/Sop-- D-be--	L. Gi--el/D Gervais
Lambert	Mariam Esmerellam	02-JUN-1900	10-JUN-1900	Paulo Lambert/Corrina Barbeau	Ludovicus Barbeau/Malvina Gervais
Lambert	Mariam Evelnam	16-AUG-1904	27-AUG-1904	Paulo Lambert/Carınna Barbeau	Michael Lambert/Saphrona Barbeau
Lambert	Mariam Stellam	15-OCT-1892	21-OCT-1892	Michaele Lambert/Sophronia Barbeau	Gulielmus Gagnier/Lea Moquin
Lambert	Michaelem	01-MAR-1870	18-JUL-1870	Michaelis Lambert/Sophronia Barbeau	Petrus Barbeau/Philomena Cheauvin
Lambert	Paulum	30-OCT-1877	03-NOV-1877	Michiales Lambert/Soperhi Lambert	A. Rabdo/ wife
Lambert	Rignam	31-DEC-1875	01-JAN-1876	Michales Lambert/Sophorina Barbo	L. Barbo/V. Langlois
Lambert	Zephirnum	14-MAY-1880	30-MAY-1880	Michaelo Lambert/Sophorna Barbeau	A Barbeau/C. Dupus
Lamblo	Rosolam	07-APR-1875	25-APR-1875	Constinus Lamblo/Rosalia Devilers	Augustinus Beltour/Emelia Lamblo
Lamblot	Adelinam	17-MAR-1866	13-APR-1866	Constant Lamblot/Rosalia Lamblot	N1-her/A. Dvıllerse
Lamblot	Alfredum Josephum	31-MAR-1868	13-APR-1868	Constant Lamblot/Rosalia Devillerse	Eugenus Painguère/Hortensıa Lisman
Lamblot	Aurelıam	30-OCT-1861	10-NOV-1861	Constanti Lamblot/Rosalia Lamblot	J Mossart/A. Létourneay
Lamblot	Carolum Josephum	19-APR-1870	15-MAY-1870	Constantin Lamblot/Rosalia Devlerse	Carolus Vanderthot/Florentia Lamblot
Lamblot	Constatium Josephum	16-JAN-1872	19-JAN-1872	Constantii Lamblot/Rosalia Devillerse	Hector Lamblot/Emilia Lamblot
Lamblot	Edouardum Victorem	07-MAR-1891	22-MAR-1891	Josepho Lamblot/Catharına Furman	Victor Lamblot/Elizabeth Hannon
Lamblot	Eugenium Josephum	16-DEC-1864	25-DEC-1864	Constanti Lamblot/Rosalia Lamblot	E. Painguère/F. Dorr
Lamblot	Josephum	26-FEB-1863	01-MAR-1863	Constantii Lamblot/Rosalia Lamblot	J. Espuate/A. Devillerse
Lamblot	Walter Josephum	23-APR-1888	29-APR-1888	Josepho Lamblot/Catharina Kremer	Alfredus Lamblot/Adela Lamblot
Lamblot*	Emlie				
Lamblot*	Nestor				
Lamblot*	Victor	02-DEC-1858	06-DEC-1858	Constant Lamblot/Rosalie Devilerss	Jacques LeRouse/Philomne Delliste
Lamblot*	Victor	02-DEC-1858	06-DEC-1858	Constant Lamblot/Rosalai Devilerse	Jacques LeRousse/Philomina Delliste
Lamontagne	Josephum Dannelem	25-APR-1868	10-MAY-1868	Antonii Lamontagne/Isabella Lamontagne	Josephus-Daniel Tessier/Ludovica Tessier
Lamontagne	Mariam Annam	03-APR-1862	06-APR-1862	Antonii Lamontagne/Elızabetha Lamontagne	O. Dodeln/C. Vadney
Lancteau	Josephum Zephyrum	11-JUL-1873	13-JUL-1873	Josephi Lancteau/Anna Parent	Theophılius Fontaine/Emilia Parent
Lanctot	Alfredum	14-JAN-1889	15-JAN-1889	Deusdata Lanctot/Maria Dufresne	Napoleo Marcoux/Sophrona Dufresne
Lanctot	Josephum Pal--mum	04-MAR-1880	14-MAR-1880	Francisco Lanctot/Anastasia Desautels	D. Lanctot/E. Lef---
Lanctot	Mariam Emmam	01-APR-1881	10-APR-1881	Deodata Lanctot/Maria Dufresne	T. Lanctot/A. Desautel
Lanctot	Mariam Violam Maud	29-OCT-1883	01-NOV-1883	Deodato Lanctot/Marıa Dusfresne	Cleophas Cartier/Dulcınea -----
Landergan*	Eduardus	24-SEP-1855	15-OCT-1855	Gulıemus Landergan/Ellen Brıtan	J. Carbret/M. --hannel
Landerman	Albertum	31-MAY-1885	01-JUN-1885	Josepho Landerman/Ophlia Dumas	Augustinus Landerman/Aurelia Molleus
Landerman	Franciscum Hilarium	04-OCT-1876	09-OCT-1876	Hilari Landerman/Dilima Moquin	L Landerman/ wife
Landerman	Franciscum Pacıficum	10-JUL-1886	11-JUL-1886	Josepho Landerman/Ophilia Dumas	Pacifius Landerman/Maria DesCoirbron
Landerman	Isidorum Generosum	29-AUG-1854	10-SEP-1854	Leandrı Landerman/Crellly Muller	I. Schenard/S. Sear
Landerman	Joseph	03-MAR-1879	05-MAR-1879	Joseph Landerman/-Olphilia D---	F. Lan--/-----
Landerman	Josephum Iseder	19-MAY-1877	20-MAY-1877	Josephi Landerman/--lie Dumer	J. Malheur/ wife

71

Surname	Given Name	Birth	Baptism	Parents	Godparents
Landerman	Josephum Magloire	19-MAR-1876	20-MAR-1876	Josephi Landerman/Ophilia Duma	M. Duma/P. Landerman
Landerman	Josephum Narcissum Victo	26-JUL-1874	27-JUL-1874	Ludovici Landerman/Margarita Mocquin	Filias Landerman/Rosalia Veine
Landerman	Josephum Noc Irving	23-JUL-1896	24-JUL-1896	Josepho Landerman/Ophilia Dumas	Isidorus Landerman/Rosa-Delima Martin
Landerman	Lelam Mariam Violam	19-JUL-1906	18-AUG-1906	Ludovico Lauderman/Elizabeth Duley	Hugh Hallows/Lilian Martin-Hallows
Landerman	Mariam Josephinam	01-JAN-1877	02-JAN-1877	Ludovici Landerman/Margareth Moquin	J B--rjon/P. Landerman
Landerman	Mariam Teresiam Eleonor	19-AUG-1894	19-AUG-1894	Josepho Landerman/Ophilia Dumas	Lucas Brunet/Eudoxia Joly
Landerman*	Eduardum	27-SEP-1855	15-OCT-1855	Gulielmi Landerman/Elena Bretant	J Carboret/M Schaniel
Landerman*	Isedori----Pascalum	27-AUG-1857	06-SEP-1857	Leandris Landerman/--ilia Malheur	I. Hubert/M. Hubert
Landerman*	Isedorius Pacificus	27-AUG-1857	06-SEP-1857	Leander Landerman/Orilha Malheur	I. Hubert/M Hubert
Landerman*	Philipum	16-JUN-1859	28-JUN-1859	Alexandri Landerman/Orelia Malheur	P. Brag/A. Peltier
Landermann	Amelia Martha	24-NOV-1851	06-DEC-1851	Leander Landermann/Aurelia Malheur	L. Pelletier/M. Malheur
Landermann	Joseph Augustumum Israel	30-MAY-1874	31-MAY-1874	Joseph Landermann/Ophilia Dumas	Augustnius Landerman/Desais Dumas
Landermann	Leander Abraham	27-APR-1879	04-MAY-1879	Hilari Landermann/Rosina Dillman	F. Matheu/H. Mathieu
Landermann	Leonem	24-JAN-1882	24-JAN-1882	Josepho Landermann/Ophilia Dumas	Josephus Moquin/Eleanore Martin
Lando	Mariam	28-JAN-1875	29-JAN-1875	Alex Lando/Levina Allard	Franciscus Laberge/Carolina Ba-et
Landregan	Helenam	19-APR-1858	16-MAY-1858	Gulielmo Landregan/Helena Britan	T Burke/H Farley
Landregan	Joannem	19-APR-1858	16-MAY-1858	Guilelmo Landregan/Helena Brian	P. Vaughn/M. Griffin
Landregan	Marguerit	08-NOV-1851	16-NOV-1851	William Landregan/Ellen Landregan	W. Nash/E. Dalton
Landreman	Elizabetham	25-JAN-1866	28-JAN-1866	Ludovivi Landreman/Marguarita Landreman	L. Landreman/T. Mocquin
Landreman	Felicitatam Aureliam	31-JUL-1861	04-AUG-1861	Leander Landreman/Aurelia Landreman	A. Landreman/T. Landreman
Landreman	Josephum Richardum	20-AUG-1864	28-AUG-1864	Leandri Landreman/Aurelia Landreman	J. Landreman/U Matthew
Landreman	Ludovicum Josephum	22-JUL-1872	24-JUL-1872	Ludovici Landreman/Marguarita Mocquin	Theophilus Langto/Zoah Mocquin
Landreman	Ludovicum Leonem	02-MAY-1903	17-MAY-1903	Ludovico Landreman/Etta-Elizabeth Dooley	Josephus Landreman/Ophilia Dumas
Landreman	Mariam	09-NOV-1867	10-NOV-1867	Leandri Landreman/Aurelia Landreman	F. Veine/M. Landreman
Landreman	Mariam Ludovicam	02-JUN-1867	10-JUN-1867	Ludovici Landreman/Marguarita Landreman	D. Toville/M. Landreman
Landreman	Mariam Ludovicam	14-JUN-1869	15-JUN-1869	Ludovici Landreman/Marguarita Mocquin	Josephus Landreman/Anastasia Landreman
Landreman	Mariam Marguaritam	12-JUL-1864	17-JUL-1864	Ludovici Landreman/Marguarita Landreman	I. Landreman/Zoah Bourdeau
Landreman	Moysem Elizeum	03-OCT-1862	05-OCT-1862	Augustina Landreman/Theresa Landreman	L Landreman/A. Molheur
Landreman*	Philippe				
Landremann	Ernestum Ricardum	05-APR-1881	10-APR-1881	Hilaro Landremann/Delima Moquin	S. Landremann/E Moquin
Landri	Amatam Ludovicam	28-APR-1868	24-JUL-1868	Josephi Landri/Suzanna Landri	Michael Landri/Maria Garo
Landrigan	Ellen	19-APR-1858	16-MAY-1858	William Landrigan/Ellen Britan	Thomas Burk/Ellen Farley
Landrigan	John	19-APR-1858	16-MAY-1858	William Landrigan/Ellen Britan	Phill Vaughan/Mary Griffin
Lang	Ludovicam		10-MAR-1872	Alexandri Lang/Sophronia Lang	Camilus Lucier/Adelina Gordon
Lang--	Mariam Theodulam	05-JUL-1870	10-JUL-1870	Theophili Lang--/Anastasia Lang---	Amabilis Desautels/Magdalena Desautels
Langlois	Adam Mariam Emmam	03-MAR-1894	13-MAR-1894	Cypriano Langlois/Angelna Gauthier	Franciscus Demers/Ida Audet-Lapointe
Langlois	Alfredum	09-JAN-1868	25-JAN-1868	Vitalis Langlois/Flavia Langlois	Isias Langlois/Emelia Barbeau
Langlois	Cezarium	29-DEC-1865	14-JAN-1866	Vitalis Langlois/Flavia Langlois	J Langlois/Zoah Langlois
Langlois	Edmundum Amatum	22-APR-1883	22-APR-1883	Edmundo Langlois/Margarita Racette	Maglorius Prefontaine/Olivine Desautels
Langlois	Elmiram Zoeam	07-AUG-1884	10-AUG-1884	Edmundo Langlois/Marguarittam Racette	Ludgerius Nospre/Elmira Lefort
Langlois	Ernestum Vital	18-JAN-1891	19-JAN-1891	Georgio Langlois/Marie Moquin	Vital Langlois/Vitalna Audet
Langlois	Florentiam Vitalinam	20-OCT-1898	30-OCT-1898	Georgio Langlois/Maria Moquin	Noe Moquin/Vitalna Moquin
Langlois	Generosum Isidorum	07-JUN-1902	08-JUN-1902	Vitali Langlois/Emelia Balthazar	Generosus Lajeunesse/Olivine Balthazar
Langlois	Georgium	18-JUL-1870	07-AUG-1870	Vitalis Langlois/Flavia Langlois	Joannes Fernet/Zoah Langlois
Langlois	Henricum Vitalem	01-DEC-1880	11-JAN-1881	Isaac Langlois/Regina Elsburg	V. Langlois/P. Langlois
Langlois	Herminiam Esther		17-JUL-1881	Edmundo Langlois/Margaritta Racette	Narcissus Duprez/Herminia Racette
Langlois	Joannam Ettam	12-FEB-1899	18-FEB-1899	Cypriano Langlois/Angelna Gauthier	Adolphum Durocher/Emma Gauthier
Langlois	Joseph	25-DEC-1850	01-JAN-1851	Vital Langlois/Flavia Cyr	I.----/S. Cyr
Langlois	Josephum	04-APR-1870	05-APR-1870	Josephi Langlois/Martha Landreman	N---- Langlois/Mathilda Langlois

72

Surname	Given Name	Birth	Baptism	Parents	Godparents
Langlois	Josephum Arthurum	25-JUL-1891	28-JUL-1891	Edmundo Langlois/Margaritta Racette	Noe Langlois/Zoe Racette
Langlois	Josephum Georgium	28-JUN-1892	03-JUL-1892	Georgio Langlois/Maria Moquin	Josephus Moquin/Flavia Cyr
Langlois	Leonem Alexandrum	14-APR-1895	21-APR-1895	Georgio Langlois/Maria Moquin	Alexander Moquin/Eva Moquin
Langlois	Leonem Ludovicum	10-JUN-1892	12-JUN-1892	Cyprano Langlois/Angelina Gauthier	Josephus Diette/Elizabeth Letourneau
Langlois	Margaritam Lilian	14-MAR-1910	20-MAR-1910	Vitele Davida Langlois/Emilia Balthazar	Alexander Goyette/Emma Balthazar
Langlois	Mariam Beloniam	10-APR-1870	15-MAY-1870	Isaia Langlois/Eulalia Langlois	Stephanus Houle/Flavia Langlois
Langlois	Mariam Gertrudem	23-DEC-1882	25-DEC-1882	Cyprano Langlois/Angelina Gauthier	Antonius Gauther/Flavia Robert
Langlois	Mariam Josephinam	11-SEP-1886	19-SEP-1886	Edmundo Langlois/Margaritta Racette	Franciscus Marcoux/Josephina Roy
Langlois	Mariam Martham	06-MAY-1874	07-MAY-1874	Joseph Langlois/Martha Landerman	Leander Landerman/Aurelia Landerman
Langlois	Mariam Vivianam	26-JAN-1897	06-FEB-1897	Georgio Langlois/Maria Moquin	Israel Lefebvre/Zoe Langlois
Langlois	Martham Alseam	25-NOV-1884	30-NOV-1884	Cyprano Langlois/Angelina Auger	Josephus Langlois/Martha Landermann
Langlois	Matilda	14-JUN-1875	20-JUN-1875	Joseph Langlois/Matilda Landerman	Josephus B-relais/Filicite Maleur
Langlois	Norbertum Cesarum	25-JUN-1890	29-JUN-1890	Cesario Langlois/Francisca Gosselin	Joannes Gosselin/Flavia Cyr
Langlois	Olivinam	12-AUG-1863	15-SEP-1863	Vitalis Langlois/Phoebe Langlois	F ----/---- ---
Langlois	Orvillum Ludovicum	31-JAN-1889	03-FEB-1889	Cesario Langlois/Francisca Gosselin	Vitalis Langlois/Ludovica Chretian
Langlois	Sulpitium		07-JUN-1861	Nazare Langlois/Mathilda Langlois	A. Boulai-/Zoah Langlois
Langlois	Vitalem	12-APR-1861	01-MAY-1861	Vitalis Langlois/Flavia Langlois	W Wottet/F. Cyr
Langlois	Zoam Olivuam	19-MAR-1853	07-APR-1853	Vitalis Langlois/Flavia Cyr	L. Mallem/C Syr
Langlois*	Antoine		22-JUL-1855	---- Langlois/Mathilda Conlais	J Touchet/O. Vienne
Langlois*	Vital	11-NOV-1858	21-NOV-1858	Vitale Langlois/Flavie Scyr	Theidore Baudoin/Philomene Muller
Langlois*	Vital				
Langto	Mariam Albinam	10-MAR-1868	29-MAR-1868	Theophili Langto/Anastasia Desautels	Henricus Fournier/Olivinam Desautels
Languedoc	Mariam Juliam	04-JUN-1863	07-JUN-1863	Mederici Languedoc/Philomena Languedoc	F. Roi/J. Roi
Lanser*	Joannem	11-JAN-1856	17-JAN-1856	Matthcw Lanser/Gertruda Rida	J Pulvermaker/M Rida
Lanto	-hioph--	11-JUN-1876	18-JUN-1876	Chiopha Lanto/Annastasia Deshottel	A Hotel/A. Parent
Lanto	Arsinam	26-FEB-1878	28-FEB-1878	Josephi Lanto/Anna Parent	J. Lanto/A. Desparents
Lanto	Cordiliam	22-MAR-1876	25-MAR-1876	Joseph Lanto/Anne Parent	J. Poppino/A. L'autet
Lanto	Mariam Ludovicam	10-FEB-1877	11-FEB-1877	Alexsi Lanto/Olivina Laberge	T Lanto/G Laberge
Lanville*	Archy			Martin Lanville/J---- Burns	----- ----/---- ----
Lapierre	Nazarium Arthurum	12-FEB-1883	18-FEB-1883	Nazaro Lapierre-Meunier/Felecitate Hebert	Isadorus Hebert/Julia Caron
Lapine	Josephum Franciscum Leo	11-DEC-1894	15-DEC-1894	Thoma Lapine/Josephina Bennet	Scila Brunet/Delma Lebeau
LaPlante	Davidem	23-OCT-1869	24-OCT-1869	Ludovici Laplante/Emilia Carrière	David Carré/Lea Therieau
LaPlante	Ludovicum Simonem Ligo	24-NOV-1870	27-NOV-1870	Ludovci Laplante/Febronia Faucher	Ligorius Roi/Maria Faucher
Laplante	Mariam Magdunimam	15-JUL-1873	20-JUL-1873	Henrici Laplante/Eleonora Saquette	Alexander Saquette/Margarita O'Conell
Lapointe	Josephum Leonem Arthur	01-MAR-1871	01-MAR-1871	Zotci Lapointe/Ludovica Lapointe	Leo Laporte/Zoah Brouillete
Lapointe	Josephum Ludgerium Corn	16-DEC-1872	16-DEC-1872	Hormida Lapointe/Maria-Angelica Lapointe	Isaacus Gervais/Cezarina Larochelière
Laporte	Hectorem Zotique	29-OCT-1869	31-OCT-1869	Zotique Laporte/Ludovica Veine	Agapitus Veine/Domitilla Venne
Laporte	Isedore	23-JAN-1877	28-JAN-1877	Jodik Laporte/Leopolda Pratt	J Pratt/O. Larock
Laporte	Issedore Arthor	22-AUG-1878	01-SEP-1878	Setick Laporte/Leopode-Polidene Prette	T Prette/E. Gosselan
Laporte	Josephum Bala--- Adelar	05-MAY-1880	07-MAY-1880	Adelar Laporte/Delima Veine	N Laporte/M. Laporte
Laporte	Josephum Gustavum	25-SEP-1873	28-SEP-1873	Zotuque Laporte/Ludovica Venne	Franciscus Carboneau/Rosalia Veine
Laporte	Ludovicum Josephum	09-MAY-1878	12-MAY-1878	Adelar Laporte/Delina Vaine	L Vaine/ wife
Laporte	Mariam Ludovicam Alexa	22-APR-1872	28-APR-1872	Zotci Laporte/Ludovica Venne	Ludovicus Venne/Christina Venne
Laporte	Ovilam		10-FEB-1880	Zotco Laporte/Leopoldina Pratt	A Roi/M. Laporte
Laporte	Zoticum Edwin	12-FEB-1884	13-FEB-1884	Zotci Laporte/Leopoldina Pratte	Hector Laporte/Josephina Pratte
Larbontie	Ludovicum Alphunsum	22-OCT-1875	24-OCT-1875	Louis Larbontié/Jorsina Tasse	C. Carr/A -----
Laro	Claram Emmam	20-OCT-1873	25-DEC-1873	Eduardi Laro/P---- Hill	Zephirius Dumont/Sophia Bessete
LaRoque	Edessam Emmam	15-JUN-1869	21-JUN-1869	Josephi Laroque/Emma Lemaire	Nelson Bullis/Edessa Bullis
Larose	Alfredum	17-FEB-1868	24-MAY-1868	Jacobi Larose/Ludovica Larose	Josephus Regner/Joanna Marissy

73

Surname	Given Name	Birth	Baptism	Parents	Godparents
Larose	Carolum	17-FEB-1870	24-MAR-1870	Jacobi Larose/Ludovica Hussois	Carolus Vandersteen/Adela Devilerse
Larose	Henricum		30-JUN-1872	Jacobi Larose/Ludovica Hussois	Victor Lamblot/Maria Larose
Larose	Josephum	20-JUL-1883	06-AUG-1883	Jacobo Larose/Lousa Han----	Josephus Lomblot/Philumena Larose
LaRose	Josephum Royal	29-MAR-1905	14-MAY-1905	Ludovici-Josephi Larose/Laura Dix	Josephus Brunet/Honorina Brunet
LaRose	Josephum Rozalem	29-MAR-1095	14-MAY-1905	Ludovico-Josepho LaRose/Laura Oix	Jospehus Brunet/Honorina Brunet
Larose	Lousam	08-DEC-1874	12-DEC-1874	Caroli Larose/Louisa Osso-t	Amadus Dellour/Maria Larouche
Larose	Ludovicum Josephum	16-AUG-1881	26-AUG-1881	Jacobo Larose/Lousa Housay	Alfredus Larose/Veronca Larose
Larose	Ludovicum Normanum	29-NOV-1907	22-MAR-1908	Ludovico LaRose/Laura Dix	Petrus Baumna/Clara Bauman
Larose	Mariam Josephinam	30-DEC-1876	14-JAN-1877	Jocob Larose/Lousa Orse-1	J. Rabido/A. Rabido
Larose	Philomenam	17-DEC-1865	01-APR-1866	Jacob Larose/Ludovica Larose	F. Lorge/A. Houssois
Larose	Philomenam	27-FEB-1862	25-MAR-1862	Jacobi Larose/Ludovica Larose	F. Despas/P. Detdrich
Larose	Veroncam	05-FEB-1864	27-MAR-1864	Jacobi Larose/Ludovica Larose	J Méme/M --icen--
Larose*	Mariam Theresam	21-AUG-1860	02-SEP-1860	Jacobi Larose/Maria Larose	J Hautbois/M.--eur
Larose*	Mariam Theresam	24-AUG-1860	02-SEP-1860	Jacobi Larose/Maria-Ludovica Larose	J. Houssous/M Tordeur
Larson	Josephum Axel		16-DEC-1902		Ludovicus Balthazar/Luvina Balthazar
Lassel*	Gulielmum	26-JUN-1857	05-JUL-1857	Joseph Lassel/Julia Baltazar	M. Baltazar/A. Deschatel
Lat---	Dominique	25-MAR-1858	01-APR-1858	Joseph Lat--/Elizabeth Shoemaker	Nicholas Henry/Mary Lossillion
Latran*	Peter				
Latran*	Petrus		25-DEC-1859	Joseph Latran/Elizabetha Shoemaker	J. Henry/C. Matthew
Lau--t-	Mariam		15-AUG-1857		D. Hubert/C. Maurin
Lauderman	Earl Franciscum	15-DEC-1907	23-AUG-1908	Ludovico Lauderman/Elizabeth Duley	-----------/Theresa Landderman
Laughlin*	Thomas				
Lauler*	Annam	13-DEC-1858	06-FEB-1859	Mathia Lauler/Maria McCabe	T. McCabe/E. Bary
Laulor*	Richard				
Laundermann	Mariam Rosam	11-OCT-1883	14-OCT-1883	Josepho Laundermann/Ophilia Dumas	Leo Martin/Mathilde Barbeau
Laurin	Emmam Virginiam	26-FEB-1870	27-FEB-1870	Vitalis Laurin/Ph------ Robert	Felix Tetro/Marcila Laurin
Lavandoski	Joannem	03-MAY-1861	12-MAY-1861	Andrea Lavandoski/Sophia Lavandoski	C. Wildner/F. Hofsh---
Lavandoski	Juliam	11-FEB-1863	22-FEB-1863	Andrea Lavandoski/Sophia Lavandoski	A. Hetwer/B. Trimboer
Lavaty*	Luciam Catherinam	04-MAR-1859	22-APR-1859	Joannis Lavaty/Maire --getan	M. Kelly/M. Migan
Lavelle	Martinum		18-NOV-1860	Martini Lavelle/Joanna Lavelle	J Bacon/H Kelly
Lavergne	Franciscum Joannem	31-DEC-1904	08-JAN-1905	Georgio Robert/Josephina Rondeau	Joannes Maccay/Josephine Robert-Maccay
Laverty*	Lucie Catharine				
Laville*	Anthey	05-JAN-1859	10-JAN-1859	Martin Lanville/J Burns	
Lawler	Mariam	14-JUL-1853	14-AUG-1853	Josephi Lawler/Maria Burns	M. McGraw/E. Ba--en
Lawlor	Joannem	07-JUN-1862	29-JUN-1862	Mathei Lawlor/Maria Lawlor	P. Lamb/C. Lamb
Lawlor*	Anne		04-APR-1861		
Lawry	Gulielmum Franciscum	14-DEC-1898	15-JAN-1901	Gulielmo Lawry/Corinna-Lousa Fleurent	Placidus Beaudreault/Arzelia Beaudreault
Laymun	Anna Agnes	03-NOV-1874	07-MAY-1879	Jacobi Laymun/Anna-Agnetis Laymun	-----------/M. V-uem---
Leager	Laurentius		17-AUG-1873	Joannis Leager/Elizabeth Hartin	Antonus Gautier/Emilia Trahant
Leaghry	Annam		04-APR-1861	Joannis Leaghry/Anna Learghy	P. Blut/M. Blut
Leaghry	Petrum	28-MAY-1863	04-JUL-1863	Joannis Leaghry/Anna Learghy	J. Reilley/A. Reilley
Leaghy	Claram	22-APR-1861	30-JUN-1861	Joannis Leaghry/Barbara Leaghy	T Dun/B. R--rdan
Leaghy*	Annam	23-JUL-1858	01-AUG-1858	Willihmi Leaghy/Anna Galliger	Thamas Galliger/Maria Dayle
Leaghy*	Annam	23-JUL-1858	01-AUG-1858	Guilelm Leaghy/Anna Galligher	T. Galligher/M. Doyle
Least	Josephus	16-FEB-1858		P-lan- Least/Brigeta Smet	----/-Margereta Smet
Lebeau	Hermnam	02-OCT-1868	04-OCT-1868	Josephi Lebeau/Hermina Lebeau	Moysis Lebeau/Maria Faucher
Lebeau	Hermnam	07-MAY-1866	13-MAY-1866	Josephi Lebeau/Hermina Lebeau	F. Marcou/A. Faucher
Lebeau	Hyacinthum	15-JUN-1870	26-JUN-1870	Josephi Lebeau/Hermina Faucher	Franciscus Marcou/Emilia Marcou
Lebeau	Josephum Franciscum Moysem		03-APR-1870	Moysis Lebeau/Angela Meunier	Flavia Marcou/Josephina Marcou

74

Surname	Given Name	Birth	Baptism	Parents	Godparents
Lebeau	Marguaritam	20-APR-1861	21-APR-1861	Joseph Labeau/Adelina Labeau	M. St.-Antoine/D St.-Antonie
Lebeau	Mariam Emiliam	19-MAR-1874	29-MAR-1874	-----si Lebeau/Angela Mercier	Napolio Corbeil/Melinda Lebeau
Lebeau	Mariam Josephinam Liciam	29-SEP-1874	11-OCT-1874	Joseph Lebeau/Ermma Fosché	Francois Pellant/------ Pellant
Lebeau	Melvinam	10-JUN-1872	14-JUN-1872	Mauritii Lebeau/Angea Lebeau	Belonis Marcou/Mathilda Marcou
Lebeau	Narcissum	16-SEP-1870	21-SEP-1870	Ludovici Lebeau/Emilia Roi	Franciscus Marcou/Josephina Marcou
Lebeau	Olivinam	25-MAR-1868	05-APR-1868	Moysis Lebeau/Angela Lebeau	Isaacus St.-Antone/Julia-Anna St.-Antone
Lebeau*	Lousa	19-JUL-1857	19-JUL-1857	Joseph Lebeau/Adelina Morrissept	C. Morrissept/P. Bricau
Lebeau*	Luisam	19-JUL-1857	19-JUL-1857	Joseph Lebeau/Adelina Morrissept	C Morrissept/P. Bricau
Lebeau*	Margaretam	12-APR-1859	17-APR-1859	Joseph Lebeau/Delima Morris	J. Marcoux/M. Benoit
Lebeau*	Marguarite				
Lebeau*	Mariam	18-JUL-1855	05-AUG-1855	Josephi Lebeau/Adelina Morissette	I. St.-Antoine/J. Lebeau
Lebeaux	Isaac	05-JUN-1876	18-JUN-1876	Josephi Lebeaux/Arme Fauché	A. Fauché/J. Rando
Lebel	Eliam Josephum	06-SEP-1867	15-SEP-1867	Roderici Lebel/Henrica Lebel	E. Real/H. Rulo
Lebel	Emiliam ALiciam	14-AUG-1868	26-NOV-1868	Josephi Lebel/Marguarita Gervais	Guilbertus Leclaire/Adalna Gagner
Lebel	Ludovicum	31-JAN-1866	03-FEB-1866	Josephi Lebel/Marguarita Lebel	L. Gervais/J. Gervais
Lebel	Noa--	06-AUG-1865	05-NOV-1865	Rodrique Lebel/Henrica Lebel	J. Lebel/M. Lebel
Lebel	Petrum Samuelem	14-JAN-1870	03-DEC-1870	Uldrici Lebel/Henrica Rulo	Petrus Rulo/Ludovica Rulo
Leblanc	Georgium	17-DEC-1866	17-DEC-1866	Augusti Leblanc/Lucia Leblanc	N. Lyonnais/M. Leduc
LeBlanc	Mariam	11-FEB-1869	27-FEB-1869	Augustini Leblanc/Lucinda Leblanc	Antonius Lemontagne/Maria Carboneau
Leblanc	Rosam Annam	06-NOV-1862	16-NOV-1862	Augustini Leblanc/Lucia Leblanc	A. Papineau/M. Leduc
Leblanc*	Guillmum Gilbertum	12-JUL-1859	14-AUG-1859	Auguste Leblanc/Rosania Leduc	H Leduc/C Beaudrieaux
Leblanc*	Wm. Gilbert				
Lebois	Josephinam Delphinam	09-AUG-1875	15-AUG-1875		Edmondus Mocquin/Elida Roy
Lecler	Albinam	15-APR-1869	18-APR-1869	Gilberti Lecler/Adelina Gagner	Georgius Odete/Henrica Touchete
Leclère	Carolum Eusebium	10-JAN-1865	15-JAN-1865	Eusebii Leclère/Clarissa Leclère	S. Houle/A Desmarais
Leclche	Mathildam	21-DEC-1871	24-DEC-1871	Ludovici Lecliche/Delphinaa Dufresne	Isidorus Dufresne/Emilia St.-Antone
Lecoq	Cesarium Vitalem	08-NOV-1884	01-JAN-1885	Ludovico Lecoq/Larentia Racette	Vitalis Langlois/Flavie Cyr
Lecoq	Julien	08-APR-1875	15-MAY-1875	Ludovici Lecoq/Laurencica Rasset	Marsel Picard/Paulina Lecoq
Leculier*	Leonadam	04-MAR-1860	14-APR-1860	Petrus Léculier/Locadie Shenard	Noel Leculier/Leonada Parizo
Lécuyer	Carolum	23-FEB-1870	06-MAR-1870	Petri Lécuyer/Carolina Lafort	Carolus Lefort/Adea Lépine
Lécuyer	Franciscum	03-FEB-1884	09-FEB-1884	Carolo Lecuyer/Carolina Lefort	Franciscus Gagner/Catharina Daugherty
Lécuyer	Georgium	24-NOV-1860	25-NOV-1860	Noelis Lécuyer/Eleonora Lécuyer	J. Pariso/H Lécuyer
Lecuyer	Henricum	06-JAN-1873	19-JAN-1873	Petri Lecuyer/Carolina Lefort	Noel Lecuyer/Eleonora Lefort
Lecuyer	Josephinam	29-JUN-1865	30-JUL-1865	Noelis Lecuyer/Eleonora Lecuyer	M. Pariso/U. Pariso
Lecuyer	Lous Henry	18-JAN-1851	02-FEB-1851	Noel Lecuyer/Lenore Pariseaux	M. St.-Antoine/M. Petit
Lecuyer	Mariam Delphinam	22-NOV-1872	25-DEC-1872	Noelis Leduc/Ludovica Bertrand	Nicholaus Lamarche/Marcelna Lamarche
Lecuyer	Melnam	15-JUN-1863	21-JUN-1863	Noelis Lecuyer/Maria Lecuyer	J Pariso/E. Pariso
Lécuyer	Petrum	16-MAY-1868	17-MAY-1868	Petri Lécuyer/Carolina Lafort	Eugenius Nombri/Edmira Lefort
Ledoski*	Michael				
Ledreau	Mariam Joannam	18-AUG-1866	09-SEP-1866	Pascalis Ledreau/Maria Ledreau	J. Demars/L. Demars
Leduc	Franciscum Exsaverie	30-AUG-1876	03-SEP-1876	Olivier Leduc/Sophe Bissept	F. Bouché/ wife
Leduc	George				
Leduc	Henry Urban	25-SEP-1862	05-OCT-1862	Hilarii Leduc/Eulalia Leduc	J. Leduc/M. Borasseau
Leduc	Honoram Virginiam	27-JUL-1872	31-JUL-1872	Bemigii Leduc/Sophia Leduc	Josephus Leduc/Marguarita Leduc
Leduc	Josephum Olivarium	17-AUG-1874	23-AUG-1874	Olivarii Leduc/Sophia Bessette	Cyrilli Bessette/Delphina Leduc
Leduc	Marguaritam Josephinam	07-JUN-1868	14-JUN-1868	Petri Leduc/Ludovica Bertrand	Ludovicus Bertrand/Eulalia Beaudrieau
Leduc	Mariam Josephinam	20-JUN-1869	20-JUN-1869	Petri Leduc/Ludovica Leduc	Josephus Leduc/Philomena Garo
Leduc	Mariam Ludovicam	22-OCT-1860	11-NOV-1860	Josephi Leduc/Marguarita Leduc	J. Leduc/L. Beaudreau
Leduc	Mariam Mageretham	03-MAR-1878	25-APR-1878	Saloman Leduc/Philmi Leduc	C. Erard/M. Leduc

75

Surname	Given Name	Birth	Baptism	Parents	Godparents
Leduc	Mariam Rosam Delima	04-APR-1871	04-APR-1871	Remigii Leduc/Sophia Leduc	Franciscus Bessete/Delima Leduc
Leduc	Moysem	08-DEC-1864	02-JUL-1865	Petri Leduc/Mathilda Duquette	G. Beaudin/J Beaudin
Leduc	Petrum Paulum	29-JUN-1879	06-JUL-1879	Calx Leduc/Daphna Leduc	C Bessette/D Bessette
Leduc	Rosam De Lima	21-NOV-1862	07-DEC-1862	Petri Leduc/Mathilda Leduc	J. Leduc/M. Leduc
Leduc*	Franciscus	30-MAY-1857	19-JUN-1857	Hilarus Leduc/Julie Bodreau	F. Dufran/L. Leduc
LeDuc*	Georgium	05-MAY-1860	19-AUG-1860	Petri Leduc/Mathilda DuQuet	Ebert LeDuc/John Bodeau
Leduc*	Joannem	21-DEC-1858	26-DEC-1858	Joannis Leduc/Sophie Chenard	Cho--bus Chenard/Sopha Pellant
Leduc*	Joseph--	09-MAY-1860	19-AUG-1860	P. Leduc/M Duquet	----- Leduc/-.Bodeau
Leduc*	Julia	28-FEB-1856	28-FEB-1856	----- Leduc/Julie Bodrieau	H. Denoyé/S. Poderet
Leduc*	Julian	28-FEB-1856	28-FEB-1856	Laurentus Leduc/Julia Bodrieaux	H Denoyé/S. Podret
Leduc*	Louise Helène				
Leduc*	Wilfred				
Lee*	Patrick				
Lee*	Ptrick	05-MAR-1859	17-MAR-1859	Cornelus Lee/Cath. Colahan	J. O'Connor/C. O'Connor
Lefaure	Guillelmum	29-MAY-1874	31-MAY-1874	Joseph Lefaure/Zoa Dorothy	Carolus Lefaure/Angelica Lefaure
Lefaure	Mariam Emilam Alphonsi	07-MAY-1874	10-MAY-1874	Caroli Lefaure/Adelaïda Lepine	Narcisse Lefaure/Selna Lefaure
Lefève	Alphonsinam	19-MAY-1870	22-MAY-1870	Camili Lefève/Mathilda Lefève	Camillus Lefève/Leonia Lefève
Lefève	Delman Alphonsinam	25-MAY-1871	27-MAY-1871	Camilis Lefève/Delma Lefève	Camilis Lefève/Flavia Mocquin
Lefève	Franciscum	27-JUN-1867	07-JUL-1867	Camilis Lefève/Domitilla Martin	P Roi/M. Lesage
Lefève	Josephinam	11-DEC-1874	13-DEC-1874	Aussemin Lefève/Celima Edewin	Leo Edewin/Maria Gyl
Lefève	Mathildam Adelaïdam	15-JUL-1872	10-AUG-1872	Camilli Lefève/Celima Lefève	Vitalis Edouin/Delima Edouin
Lefevere	Carolum Ludovicum	17-FEB-1877	20-FEB-1877	Casseimre Lefevere/Dilmore Ede-in	F. Rando/F. Edoin
Lefevere	Franciscum	26-MAY-1877	27-MAY-1877	Elsian Lefevre/Elisabeth Jubert	J. Marten/J. Jubert
LeFevre	Ludovicum Israelem	07-SEP-1873	14-SEP-1873	Israelis Lefevre/Zoa Langlois	Vital Langlois/Flavia Langlois
Leffer*	Sopham	02-FEB-1859	05-FEB-1859	Eduardi Leffer/Joset Deneveau	G. DuMers/S. Sersine
Lefontaine	Mariam F-vi--iam	30-OCT-1877	02-NOV-1877	Frederick Lefontaine/Josephine Belargent	J Lefontaine/V. Belargent
Lefor*	Sophie				
Lefort	Adelam	20-FEB-1871	12-MAR-1871	Caroli Lefort/Adelaïda Lépine	Eugerus Al---/Edmira Lefort
Lefort	Angelam		15-FEB-1869	Petri Lefort/Lucia Johnson	Carolus Lefort/Angela Millete
Lefort	Baptistam	22-MAY-1868	27-MAY-1868	Baptista Lefort/Edmira Rondeau	Franciscus Rondeau/Flavia Rondeau
Lefort	Carolinam	02-MAR-1865	05-MAR-1865	Caroli Lefort/Adelaïda Lefort	J. Lepine/J. Rondeau
Lefort	Carolum	07-MAY-1869	09-MAY-1869	Caroli Lefort/Adelaïda Lépine	Baptista Rondeau/Carolina Lefort
Lefort	Elmiram	15-JAN-1865	14-JAN-1866	B. Lefort/E. Lefort	C Lefort/E Lépine
Lefort	Emelinam Paulinam	15-JUN-1878	16-JUN-1878	Baptis Lefort/Melie Gaigner	E. Gaigner/ wife
Lefort	Helenam	03-JUL-1875	04-JUL-1875	Jean-Baptuste Lefort/Amelie Gagné	Ludger Nonpré/Elmire Lefort
Lefort	Joannam Mabel	19-JUN-1889	04-AUG-1889	Georgio Parkinson/Malvina Lefort	Joannes-Baptista Lefort/Emelia Gagnier
Lefort	Joannem Bablas Amatum	21-FEB-1876	01-MAR-1876	Charles Lefort/Delaide Lepine	F Gayé/M Lepine
Lefort	Joannem Basptirtam	09-JUN-1877	10-JUN-1877	Narcisi Lefort/Elima Demars	J. Lefort/E Lefort
Lefort	Josephinam Loretam		12-JAN-1873	Caroli Lefort/Adelaïda Lépine	Josephus Lefort/Josephina Lefort
Lefort	Josephinam Mariam	27-MAR-1895	02-JUL-1895	Gulielmo Lefort/Edith Raler	Raymond-Franciscus Lefort/Josephine Dougherty
Lefort	Josephum Raymondum	30-JUL-1872	06-AUG-1872	Josephi Lefort/Zoah Daugherty	Guillelmus Daugherty/Anna Daugherty
Lefort	Julian	10-FEB-1867	12-FEB-1867	Caroli Lefort/Adelaïda Lefort	J. Ferget/J. Lépine
Lefort	Narcissum	25-DEC-1873	25-DEC-1873	Narcissi Lefort/Celina Demars	Petrus Lefort/Elmira Effort
Lefort	Petrum	27-SEP-1872	27-OCT-1872	Petri Lefort/Maria Lefort	Eugerus Nompléa/Edwina Lefort
Lefort	R Delima	18-DEC-1870	25-DEC-1870	Narcissi Lefort/R.-Delima Lefort	Carolus Lefort/Angela Lefort
Lefort	Raymondum	25-MAR-1876	26-MAR-1876	Joseph Lefort/Joel Dogherty	F. Gage/C. Gage
Lefort	Raymondum Franciscum	30-JUN-1878	04-JUL-1878	Josephi Lefort/Joanna Dogherty	Rev. Dogherty/M. Dogherty
Leforte	Jocobum Edmundum	19-SEP-1874	08-NOV-1874	Petri Leforte/Melissa Janson	Josephus Lefort/Jos Daephie
Legar	Georgium Arthur	22-MAY-1874	31-MAY-1874	Georgii Legar/Helena Bird	Julius Demars/Leucadia Demars

76

Surname	Given Name	Birth	Baptism	Parents	Godparents
Legeau	Mariam Georgiam	06-MAY-1868	10-MAY-1868	Ludovici Lebeau/Emilia Lebeau	Liguorius Roi/Maria Faucher
Legee*	Maria Ellena	03-AUG-1855	05-AUG-1855	Guillemus Legee/Margerita Given	R. King/E. Legee
Legee*	Mariam Elenam	03-AUG-1855	05-AUG-1855	Gulielmi Legee/Margerita Given	R. Ring/E. Legee
Léger	Luciam	17-OCT-1865	29-OCT-1865	Francisci Leger/Emilia Leger	L. Leger/M. Leger
Legion	Michaelis	12-JAN-1857	15-FEB-1857	Daniel Legion/Margerita Herlings	M. Herlings/F. Curran
Legions*	Jannes	01-SEP-1856	02-NOV-1856	Patrick Legions/Maria Clians	J Jommery/C. Jommery
Lego	Georgium	22-MAR-1869	29-MAR-1869	Balonsii Lego/Eliza Patenode	Josephus Lafontaine/Maria Mocquin
Lego	Mariam Adeliam	05-FEB-1873	09-MAR-1873	Belonsii Lego/Adelia Padenode	Hubertus Agagnier/Aldelaïda Agagnier
Lego	Petrum Jeremiahm	02-MAR-1871	05-MAR-1871	Belonsii Lego/Elizabetha Padenode	Baptista Dupuis/Clotilda Agagnier
LeJeunesse	Elmer Joannem	08-MAY-1909	16-MAY-1909	Jeremia LaJeunesse/Olivina Balthazar	Joannes-M. Balthazar/Olivina LaJeuensse
Lemaire	Emmam	19-SEP-1863	24-SEP-1863	Joseph Lemaire/Eleonora Lemaire	S Lemaire/E. Lécuyer
Lemaire	Mariam Sopham	22-JUL-1865	28-JUL-1865	Petri Lemaire/Herminia Lemaire	S Lemaire/S Pinard
Lemaire	Stephanum	02-MAR-1864	26-MAR-1864	Petri Lemaire/Herminia Lemaire	H. Desnoyers/S. Poudrete
Lemi	Guillelmum	26-JUL-1869		Joseph Lemi/Olivia Bergeron	Joanis-Baptista Bergeron/Maria Lefort
Lemieux	Agnete Melandy	08-APR-1906	15-APR-1906	Antonio LeMieux/Mable Benedict	Alfredus Auchen/Della LeMieux
Lemieux	Antonium	19-SEP-1879	21-SEP-1879	Israel Lemieux/Melina Larose	A Boyer/M. Boyer
LeMieux	Bernardum Franciscum	11-APR-1910	17-APR-1910	Jeremiah LeMieux/Julia Parc	Jacobus-Joannes Bowen/Emma Beaudreau
Lemieux	Emma Ida	29-AUG-1886	29-AUG-1886	Israele Lemieux/Melina Larose	Achilles Charron/Ezilda Lemieux
Lemieux	Exildam	04-SEP-1871	15-OCT-1871	Israelis Lemieux/Delima Larose	Josephus Maassi/Zoah Langlois
LeMieux	Frument Antoninam	05-SEP-1908	13-SEP-1908	Antonio LeMieux/Mable Benedict	Achilla Charron/Margarite Landolf-Charron
Lemieux	Gedeonem	03-FEB-1868	09-FEB-1868	Gedeonis Lemieux/Elmira Lemieux	Israel Lemieux/Malina Larose
Lemieux	Israelem Francis	15-NOV-1869	29-NOV-1869	Israelis Lemieux/Melina Larose	Alexius Préfontaine/Flavia Bessete
Lemieux	Josephum	12-OCT-1884	14-OCT-1884	Israel Lemieux/Melina Larose	Calixtus Errard/Delphina Leduc
Lemieux	Josephum Amandum	11-MAR-1876	12-MAR-1876	Israel Lemieux/Mmie Larose	H Denoyé/ wife
Lemieux	liam	17-MAR-1869	21-MAR-1869	Adolphi Lemieux/Flavia Bessete	Gedeo Lemieux/Edmira Patenode
Lemieux	Mariam Delphnam	09-JUL-1882	09-JUL-1882	Israele Lemieux/Melina Larose	Michael Pommnville/Sophia Gratton
Lemieux	Mariam Rosam	18-NOV-1877	22-NOV-1877	Israel Lemieux/Melina Larosse	F. Bouché/J. Bessept
Lemieux	Mauam Zoam		28-FEB-1874	Israel Lemieux/Melina Larose	David Carriétr/Della Carrière
Lemieux	Melinam	06-DEC-1867	08-DEC-1867	Israelis Lemieux/Melina Larose	X. Lemieux/M. Mortin
Lemieux	Moysem Flliam	06-MAY-1870	08-MAY-1870	Gedeonis Lemieux/Elmira Pad-----	Gilbertus Leclerc/Adelina Gagné
Lemieux	Narcissum		15-JUL-1881	Israel Lesteux/Melissa Larose	Jacobus Charron/Rosa-Delima Leguere
Lemieux	Narcissum	08-APR-1869	11-APR-1869	Geodeonis Lemieux/Edmira Pellant	Rudophus Lemieux/Flavia Bessete
LeMieux	Sylvam Dulcinam	17-FEB-1908	23-FEB-1908	Iereinia LeMieux/Julia Para-Perry	Isreal LeMieux/----- LeMieux-Bellmar
Lemire	Mariam Joannam	11-JUL-1869	17-JUL-1869	Joseph Lemire/Dyonsia-Joanna Dumas	Josephus Dumas/Dyonsia Duquette
Lemontagne	Adeladam	09-FEB-1866	18-FEB-1866	Antonii Lemontagne/Elizabeth Lemontagne	A Odet/M Odet
Lenard*	Jocobus	01-OCT-1856	29-JAN-1857	Michaelis Lenard/Catherina Conroy	T Rayly/C. Jocobus
Lenney*	Thamas	01-OCT-1857	04-OCT-1857	Thamas Lenney/Ancy Lierry	P. Mogan/C Berry
Lensch*	Joannes	11-JAN-1856	17-JAN-1856	Mathias Lensch/Gertruda Reda	J. -----/M. Reda
Lenschs*	Mariam Annam	20-AUG-1857	11-SEP-1858	Jocab- Lenschs/Anna Cirran	L/ Dael
Lenschs*	Margeretham	23-JAN-1857	11-FEB-1857	Thimotei Lenschs/Brigetha Timety	M. Burck/B. Durkan
Lenver	Margaritam Theresam	09-MAR-1855	11-MAR-1855	Josephi Lenver/Maria Ca--	P Coleman/M Burns
Leona	Mariam Angelicam	06-APR-1878	24-APR-1878	Eduard Leona/Sophia Besset	J Tremblé/J Leduc
Léonard	Georgium Guillelmum	03-MAY-1862	16-NOV-1862	Joannis Léonard/Ludovica Léonard	G. Léonard/C. Léonard
Leonard	Josephum Vitalem	15-FEB-1875	20-FEB-1875	Josephi Leonard/Maria Lefeve	Ludovicus Leonard/Angelica Cumnin
Lépage	Hubertum	12-OCT-1863	10-NOV-1863	Moysis Lépage/Clementina Lépage	F. Surprenant/----- -----
Lepage	Ignatium	13-FEB-1870	13-FEB-1870	Ignatii Lepage/Maria Chef	Adolphus Durocher/Henrica Rondeau
Lepage	Napoleonam	26-OCT-1861	03-NOV-1861	Moysis Lepage/Clotilda Lepage	P. Chef/C Rondeau
Lepage	Paulinam	26-OCT-1861	03-NOV-1861	Moysis Lepage/Clotilda Lepage	C. Lhuissier/R. Larochelle
Lepein	Genevivam	31-MAY-1877	17-JUN-1877	Francisci Lepein/Lucia Gothier	A. Gothier/ wife

77

Surname	Given Name	Birth	Baptism	Parents	Godparents
Lepeine	Joannem Viola	28-JUL-1878	28-JUL-1878	Josephi Lepeine/Sophia Bodriau	L Lepeine/M. Randeau
Lepeine	Mariam Cesiliam	17-JUN-1878	18-JUN-1878	Caroli Lefort/Adelade Lepeine	N Branchaud/M. Deshotel
Lepine	Adam Etam	11-AUG-1882	12-AUG-1882	Josepho Lepine/Sophia Beaudnault	Alexandar Marcoux/Arzilia Beaudrnault
Lepine	Aureliam	06-OCT-1865	08-OCT-1865	Francisci Lepine/Isabella Lepine	F. Abler/E. Lepine
Lépine	Baptistam	10-JUL-1866	15-JUL-1866	Josephi Lépine/Josephina Lépine	B Rondeau/M. -
Lepine	Carolinam Emeliam	02-AUG-1894	05-AUG-1894	Josephi Lépine/Sophronia Beaudreault	Franciscus Gagnier/Emelia Lepine
Lepine	Ceciliam Elodiam Gladys	19-MAR-1902	28-MAR-1902	Josepho Lepine/Sophia Beaudreault	Eduardus Lepine/Maria Reinmand
Lepine	Coram Paulinam	07-DEC-1880	12-DEC-1880	Josepho Lepine/Sophia Beaudriau	C. Lionnais/L. Beaudriau
Lepine	Eduardum Theodore	23-OCT-1876	29-OCT-1876	Josephi Lepine/Sophia Bodreau	L Bodriau/ wife
Lépine	Eleonoram	01-JUL-1868	19-JUL-1868	Josephi Lépine/Elizabetha Rondeau	Baptista Rondeau/Julia-Anna Chef
LePine	Ema Elida	08-APR-1878	21-APR-1878	Joseph Lepine/Ema Gothe	A Gothe/ wife
LePine	Francis Arlan	05-DEC-1920	26-DEC-1920	Lawrence LePine/Lorrane --Rey	John-J. King/Carrie LePine
Lepine	Franciscum	10-FEB-1876	13-FEB-1876	Josephi Lepine/Ema Gothier	J. Lepiene/ wife
Lepine	Genovefam	06-APR-1874	12-APR-1874	Josephi Lepine/Josephina B---do	Franciscus Gagné/Maria Lepine
Lepine	Gratiam Emmam	22-OCT-1891	25-OCT-1891	Josepho Lepine/Sophia Beaudreau	Placidus Beaudreau/Elphea Frenet
Lepine	Henricum Eduardum	31-MAR-1886	04-APR-1886	Josepho Lepine/Sophia Beaudreault	Moyses Gratton/Elizabeth Lepine
Lepine	Henricum Franciscum	31-MAR-1875	18-APR-1875	Josephi Lepine/Josephina Randeau	Joseph Lepine/Ersete Randeux
LePine	James Edward	03-OCT-1920	19-DEC-1920	Harry LePine/Ethel Bott	Lawrence LePine/Carrie LePine
Lépine	Joannem Baptistam	23-MAR-1865	02-APR-1865	Joannis-Baptista Lépine/Maria Lépine	J. Lépine/E. Rondeau
Lepine	Joannem Baptistam Amatu	26-AUG-1882	26-NOV-1882	Joanne-Baptista-Amato Lepine/Louisa Bergeron	Josephus Lepine/Louisa Rondeau
Lepine	Josephuram	20-FEB-1887	20-FEB-1887	Petro Lepine/Josephina Corbeille	Josephus Lepine/Elizabeth Rondeau
Lépine	Josephinam	11-MAR-1868	15-MAR-1868	Francisci Lépine/Elizabetha Lépine	Josephus Lépine/Josephina Rondeau
Lepine	Josephinam Hildam	21-NOV-1892	21-NOV-1892	Thoma Lepine/Josephina Brunet	Petrus Lepine/Josephina Corbeille
Lépine	Josephum	23-MAR-1865	02-APR-1865	Joannis-Baptista Lépine/Maria Lépine	C ----/----- -----
Lépine	Josephum	05-JUN-1864	12-JUL-1864	Josephi Lépine/Josephina Lépine	F. Rondeau/A. Lemarre
Lépine	Josephum	16-APR-1872	05-MAY-1872	Josephi Lépine/Josephina Lépine	Carolus Lefort/Adelaïda Lépine
Lépine	Josephum Davidem Lauren	26-AUG-1901	26-AUG-1901	Thoma Lepine/Josephina Brunet	David Paradis/Eleonora Lepine
Lepine	Josephum Ferdinandum	18-JAN-1904	19-JAN-1904	Thoma Lepine/Josephina Brunet	Ferdinandus Brunet/Mathilda Potvin
Lépine	Josephum Loudovicum Alb	01-JAN-1899	01-JAN-1899	Thoma Lepine/Josephina Brunet	Adelbertus Brunet/Marianna Bastien
Lepine	Josephinam Thomam	20-DEC-1886	20-DEC-1886	Thoma Lepine/Josephina Brunet	Joseph Lepine/Elizabeth Rondeau
Lepine	Josephum Thomam Axilam	28-AUG-1885	28-AUG-1885	Thoma Lepine/Josephina Brunet	Gedeon Brunet/Melina Bastien
Lepine	Lauram	21-JUN-1866	24-JUN-1866	Josephi Lepine/Elizabetha Lepine	N Dufresne/M Dufresne
Lépine	Laurentium Leonardum	17-FEB-1898	20-FEB-1898	Josepho Lepine/Sophia Beaudreault	Laurentius-D. Beaudreault/Maria-Eleonora Burges
Lepine	Luciam Mariam	15-JAN-1904	31-JAN-1904	Eduardo Lepine/Eleonora Reinwand	Leonardus Reinwand/Maria Gunton
Lepine	Lucinam Delphinam	20-MAY-1910	22-MAY-1910	Ludovico Lepine/Maria Cliché	Petrus LePine/Josephina Corbeille
Lepine	Ludovicum	03-SEP-1870	10-SEP-1870	Josephi Lépine/Elizabetha Rondeau	Ludovicus Lépine/Emilia Rondeau
Lepine	Mariam Adelam	11-OCT-1888	14-OCT-1888	Josepho Lepine/Sophia Beaudreault	Josephus Dubois/Cedulia Beaudreault
Lepine	Mariam Blancam Leoniam	22-AUG-1890	24-AUG-1890	Thoma Lepine/Josephina Brunet	Ludovicus Lepine/Leonia Brunet
Lepine	Mariam Coralia	02-FEB-1897	02-FEB-1897	Thoma Lepine/Josephina Brunet	Alphonsus Brunet/Honora Brunet
Lepine	Mariam Coram	27-MAR-1883	28-MAR-1883	Francisco Lepine/Philumena Landerman	Augustinus Lauderman/Teresa Joly
Lepine	Mariam Corinam Florentia	27-MAR-1906	01-APR-1906	Thoma Lepin-Sr/Josephina Brunet	Avila LePine/Leonia LePine
Lepine	Mariam Corneliam	01-FEB-1897	02-FEB-1897	Thoma Lepine/Josephina Brunet	Josephus Corbeille/Olympia Brunet
Lépine	Mariam Edmiram	18-AUG-1868	23-AUG-1868	Josephi Lépine/Winifrida Rondeau	Josephus Rondeau/Maria Rondeau
Lepine	Mariam Emmam	10-APR-1880	24-OCT-1880	Josepho Lepine/Josephina Randeau	F Rondeau/F. -édoin
LePine	Mariam Josephinam Anast	20-FEB-1907	24-FEB-1907	Thoma Lepine-Sr/Amanda Corbeille	Thomas LePine-Sr/Josephina Brunet-LePine
Lépine	Melnam	22-JUL-1866	29-JUL-1866	Ludovici Lépine/Emilia Rondeau-Lépine	F. Gagnier/E. Lépine
Lépine	Melindam	17-APR-1870	01-MAY-1870	Josephi Lépine/Josephina Lépine	Franciscus Lepine/Isabella Brodeur
Lépine	Melvinam	03-APR-1870	10-APR-1870	Francisci Lépine/Elizabetha Lépine	Baptista Rondeau/Julianna Chef
Lépine	Odelia	18-FEB-1872	23-FEB-1872	Francisci Lépine/Isabella Brodeur	Josephus Lépine/Adelia Leclerc

Surname	Given Name	Birth	Baptism	Parents	Godparents
Lepine	Petrum	06-NOV-1884	07-NOV-1884	Petro Lepine/Josephina Corbeille	Cyrillus Corbeille/Anastasia Dufort
Lepine	Petrum Roy Emeraldum	07-JAN-1905	15-JAN-1905	Emerico Lepine/Cecilia Watkins-LePine	Petrus Hauf/Elizabeth Schneider-Hauf
Lepine	Petrum Roy Emeraldum	04-DEC-1901	15-JAN-1905	Emerico Lepine/Cecilia Watkins-Lcpine	Petrus Hauf/Elizabeth Schneider-Hauf
Lepine	Prosperum Eduardum	04-DEC-1901	15-DEC-1901	Eduardo Lepine/Maria Reinwand	Matheus Franey/Henrica Reinwand
Lepine	Rosam Annam Genofesam	07-AUG-1895	07-AUG-1895	Petro Lepine/Josephina Corbeille	Arthurus Pratte/Rosa-Anna Corbeille
Lepine	Salomonum	22-JUN-1864	26-JUN-1864	Josephi Lepine/Elizabetha Lepine	T. Rondeau/J. Pedlant
Lepinen	Henricum	28-MAR-1876	12-APR-1876	Josephi Lepinen/Josephena Rando	M. Lepinen
Leppard	Carolum Gulielmum	31-JUL-1891	09-AUG-1891	Georgio Leppard/Virgina Turcot	Josephus Robidoux/Philumena Coté
Leppard Leppe	Georgium Antoncium	10-AUG-1892	14-AUG-1892	Georgio Leppard/Virginia Turcot	Antonius Nichels/Maria-Rosalia Turcot
Lepper	Davidem Eduardum	01-MAY-1901	14-SEP-1901	Georgio Lepper/Virginia Turcot	Thomas Lepine/Julia Turcot
Lepperd	Georgium	21-JUL-1867	23-NOV-1890	----- ---/---- ----	C. Boucher/Phlamena Coté
Leroi	Josep-p---e	08-DEC-1873	10-DEC-1873	Ligorii Leroi/Mana Fauché	Damas Trottier/Philomena Trottier
Lerry	Joannem	05-MAY-1853	05-JUL-1853	Joannis Lerry/Ellena Shea	M. Gallaghar/Rev Godfert
Lery*	Patrick	24-APR-1857	29-APR-1857	John Lery/Anna Oconnel	D. Oconnel/E. Kelly
Letournau	Ferdinand	02-SEP-1876	01-OCT-1876	Petri Létournau/Sophina Bissonnet	J. Jubert/ wife
Letourneau	Josephum	17-OCT-1873	17-OCT-1873	Petri Letournau/Sophina Bussonette	Petrus Letourneau/Phoeba Bussonette
Letourneau	Adela Josephina	21-AUG-1874	30-AUG-1874	Paralis Letourneau/Maria Bonnhaur	Augustus Marcou/Mathilda Letourneau
Letourneau	Adelam	15-OCT-1870	30-OCT-1870	Christophi Letourneau/Maria Bré	Harius Fernet/Felicitas Molheur
Letourneau	Edessam	12-AUG-1872	18-AUG-1872	Pascalis Létourneau/Maria Létourneau	Carolus Wolete/Mathilda Beaumar
Letourneau	Edwardum Victorem	15-MAY-1882	21-MAY-1882	Josepho Letourneau/Mathilda Letourneau	Baschalis Letourneau/Marta Boomhauer
Letourneau	Elizabetham	07-FEB-1863	22-MAR-1863	Christophi Letourneau/Maria Létourneau	J. Demars/L. Demars
Létourneau	Elizabetham	07-FEB-1864	14-FEB-1864	Pascalis Letourneau/Maria Letourneau	C. Beaumar/J. Beaumar
Letourneau	Emeliam Grattam	25-APR-1901	01-JUN-1901	Pachali Letourneau/Mathilda Wilke	Paschalis Letourneau/Maria Baumhars
Létourneau	Emmam	10-APR-1867	28-APR-1867	Chrstophi Létourneau/Maria Létourneau	J. E----/E. E----
Letourneau	Emmam Grattam	18-OCT-1883	28-OCT-1883	Pascali Letourneau/Maria Boomhaur	Josephus Diette/Elsa Letourneau
Létourneau	Eulaliam	16-MAY-1872	09-JUN-1872	Christophon Létourneau/Maria Létourneau	Chrrs. Létourneau/Nathalia Landri
Letourneau	Georgium	21-JUL-1879	03-AUG-1879	Pascali Létourneau/Marna Bo-hwarhn	J. Demers/E. Gosselin
Letourneau	Georgium Henricum	09-AUG-1874	23-AUG-1874	--rytonliori Letourneau/Maria Moleure	Germanus Moleure/Maria Landerman
Letourneau	Idam Agnetem	03-APR-1903	12-APR-1903	Paschale Letourneau/Mathilda Milquet	Josephus Balthazar/Flora Letourneau
Letourneau	Josephum	19-AUG-1868	23-AUG-1868	Pascalis Létourneau/Adelada Létourneau	Josephus Létourneau/Carolina Beaumar
Létourneau	Josephum Christophum	23-NOV-1868	29-NOV-1868	Petri Letourneau/Sophia Letourneau	Josephus Létourneau/Maria Bré
Létourneau	Josephum Henricum	06-JAN-1871	18-JAN-1871	Christophi Létourneau/Maria Létourneau	Petrus Letourneau/Sophia Bissonet
Letourneau	Luciam Jasse	06-JAN-1882	15-JAN-1882	Pascalio Letourneau/Luarca Boomhan	Isace St.-Antoine/Lucia-Joanna Letourneau
Letourneau	Mariam Coram Stellam	04-MAY-1886	07-MAY-1886	Pascali Letourneau/Maria Baumhauer	Alexander Marcoux/Arzelia Beaudreault
Létourneau	Mariam Emmam	31-OCT-1883	11-DEC-1883	Josepho Letourneau/Mathilda Letourneau	Josephus Diette/Eliza Letourneau
Létourneau	Mariam Herminiam	15-AUG-1868	23-AUG-1868	Josephi Létourneau/Adelada Létourneau	Petrus Létourneau/Sophia Beaulieu
Létourneau	Mariam MarCelinam	25-MAY-1871	28-MAY-1871	Petri Letourneau/Sophia Letourneau	Narcissuc Letourneau/Lucia Letourneau
Letourneau	Mariam-Mina	23-MAR-1865	02-APR-1865	Chrstophi Létourneau/Maria Létourneau	Zoah Trudot/A. Trudot
Letourneau	Marie Edessa Demars	03-JUN-1879	08-JUN-1879	Julien Latourneau/Lucie Letourneau	E. Latourneau/---- D--
Letourneau	Noahm	26-JUN-1872	15-AUG-1872	Josephi Letourneau/Adelina Letourneau	Franciscus Bessete/Julia Bessete
Létourneau	Pascalem	15-FEB-1862	02-MAR-1862	Pascalis Létourneau/Marna Létourneau	C. Létourneau/J. Beaumar
Letourneau	Philomenam	22-OCT-1876	05-NOV-1876	Chrstoph Letourneau/Maria Malheur	P. L'Etourneau/ wife
Letourneau	Philoméne Agnes	03-JUN-1879	22-JUN-1879	Petro Letourneau/Sophia Bissonnette	F. Pellanet/P. Letourneau
Létourneau	Rosam Delma	27-AUG-1870	04-SEP-1870	Pascalis Létourneau/Mana Létourneau	Zacharius Trudeau/Alida Trudeau
Letourneau	Zoe Paulinum	20-JUL-1883	29-JUL-1883	Petro Letourneau/Sophia Bissonnette	Josephus Venne/Maria Letourneau
Levain*	Louis				
Levendosky*	Antonus	06-JAN-1858	17-JAN-1858	Andreas Levendosky/B--dia Oska	Masson Hevists/Rossalia Levandosky
Levensdosky*	Antonium	06-JAN-1858	17-JAN-1858	Andre Levensdosky/Bordia Oska	M. Kevists/R. Levensdosky
Leverin	Petrum Amatum	10-JAN-1874	05-MAR-1874	Francisci-Petri Levern/Virginia R----	Joannis-Petrus Husting/Maria Deshotels

79

Surname	Given Name	Birth	Baptism	Parents	Godparents
Ley	Franciscum	28-JUN-1875		Leonis-D Ley/Justina Hyurto	Olin Hurto/Adline Dugas
Lhussier	Josephum	03-JAN-1864	06-JAN-1864	Caroli Lhussier/Rosalia Lhuissier	E. Surprenant/C Durocher
Lhussier	Julam		17-MAR-1861	Caroli Lhussier/Rosalie Lhuissier	E Durocher/J. Ebert
Liam	Mariam	06-MAR-1883	07-MAR-1883		Ludovicus Lepine/Emelia Rondeau
Liensh*	Caterina	13-OCT-1856	26-OCT-1856	James Liensh/Catherina Curran	P. Mangan/M. Click
Lierry*	Patricum	27-APR-1857	29-APR-1857	Joannis Lierry/Anna O'Connel	D O'Connel/E. Kelly
Ligons*	Joannem	10-SEP-1856	04-NOV-1856	Patrcii Ligons/Maria Ligons	J Emmery/C. Gommery?
Limhower*	Mathidam	12-NOV-1857	19-NOV-1857	Tholas Limhower/Lousa Taga	D. Delam--/----- ------
Lin*	Margereta	23-JAN-1857	11-FEB-1857	Thmity Lrn/Briitia Timily	M. Buck/B. Durkan
Linard*	Jocobum	02-DEC-1856	29-JAN-1857	Michaelis Linard/Catherina C-nroy	T. Rayly/C. Jocabs
Linden	Antonium	03-MAY-1865	21-MAY-1865	Mathia-Josephi Linden/Maria-Anna Linden	A. Rothgary/A. Linden
Linscot	Georgium Guillelmum		16-MAY-1869	Guillelmi Lnscot/Philomena Odete	Toussaintus Chapeleau/Virginia Odete
Lionais	Claudum Alvinum	28-MAR-1880	11-APR-1880	Cosmo Lionais/Ludovica Baudreaux	I. Beaudiaux/C Beaudiaux
Lionais	Ludovicus Augustinus	19-MAY-1880	23-MAY-1880	Eduard Lionais/Sopha Bassette	C. Lionais/L. Beaudieau
Lionay	Jeogium Isedorem	04-AUG-1876	06-AUG-1876	Hom-l- Lionay/Louise Bodriaux	J. Lepin/ wife
Liong	Josephum Eduardum	24-MAR-1876	26-MAR-1876	Eduardi Long/Sopha Bisset	J Lionay/P. Lefeve
Lions*	Henry	16-JAN-1859	15-FEB-1859	Patrick Lions/Maria Crignon	H. Crignon/B. Crignon
Lions*	Henry				---- -/---- ---
Lisson	Joanam Rachel	17-JUL-1870	29-JUL-1870	Jacobi Lisson/Virginia Lemaire	A. Lemaire/E. Robidou
Lisson	Oviliam	10-JUL-1867	14-JUL-1867	Jacobi Lisson/Virginia Lemaire	
Litten	Joannem		08-FEB-1859		
Lo*	Norbertus	13-JUL-1857	02-AUG-1857	Morris Lo/Rosan Kaly	J. Nugrat/Mrs. Nugrat
Lo----wer*	Matilda		15-NOV-1857	Hrunz Lo----wer/Hosita Toga	J Gayet/A. Delavaly
Logelan*	Jeremiam	20-FEB-1857	10-MAR-1857	Thoma Logelan/Elina Flood	J. Logelan/ J.-----
Logelon	Jemiras	20-FEB-1857	01-MAR-1857	Thamas Logelon/Ellen Flood	Jeremias Logelon/Joanna Logelon
Logelon	Maria Anna	17-APR-1857	10-MAY-1857	William Logelon/Cathera Gui--k	Denis Ronon/Brigita Scannon
Logelon*	Thomam	01-OCT-1859	09-OCT-1859	Willielmi Logelon/Catrina Cusik	J. Mangan/E. Flood
Lohman	Aureliam	27-FEB-1853	26-JUN-1853	Martini Lohman/Theresa Siebert	N. Winkel/A Winkel
Lohmiller*	Francis Simon				
Loiseau	Bertham Lousam	15-JAN-1885	29-APR-1885	Gulielmo Loiseau/Sophronia McDonald	Carolus Loiseau/Martha Bisson
Loiseau	Emeliam Josephinam	25-OCT-1881	06-NOV-1881	Carolo Loiseau/Martha Bisson	David Chaperon/Emelia Trahon
Loiseau	Franciscum	12-MAR-1888	18-MAR-1888	Carolo Loiseau/Martha Bisson	Gulielmus Loiseau/Josephina Levac
Loiseau	Gulielmum	05-JAN-1855	25-FEB-1855	Petri Loiseau/Amelia Triant	O. Br--/D. Brian
Loiseau	Gulielmum Leonardum	02-JUL-1891	09-AUG-1891	Gulielmo Loiseau/Sophronia McDonald	Calixtus-E. Errard/Emelia Trahan
Loiseau	Guy Arthurum	03-NOV-1887	08-NOV-1887	Gulielmo Loiseau/Sophronia McDonald	Georgius Strong/Margaritta Cramer
Loiseau	Helenam		01-MAR-1863	Petri Loiseau/Emilia Loiseau	J. ----/M. Baudriau
Loiseau	Josephum Carolum	14-AUG-1884	14-SEP-1884	Carolo Loiseau/Martha Bisson	Bernardus Perron/Catharina Lemieux
Loiseau	Ludovicum	13-OCT-1890	23-NOV-1890	Carolo Loiseau/Martha Bissan	Josephus Brunet/Christina Chef
Loiseau	Mariam	25-MAR-1853	26-JUN-1853	Petri Loiseau/---- Loiseau	P. -an--/---- -an--
Loiseau	Mariam Violam	18-MAR-1883	01-APR-1883	Gulielmo Loiseau/Sophronia McDonald	David Chaperon/Delia Loiseau
Loiseau	Odilam		01-MAR-1863	Patri Loiseau/Emilia Loiseau	F. Beaudriau/M. Rondeau
Loiseau (Bird)	Martham Josephinam	21-NOV-1902	30-NOV-1902	Leone Loiseau (Bird)/Gatia Towne	Carolus Loiseau (Bird)/Josephina Loiseau (Bird)
Loisel*	Joannem	02-JUN-1859	03-JUL-1859	Josephi Loisel/Julia Baltazair	B. Baltazar/M. Goyet
Loisèle	Cyrilum	11-APR-1867	28-APR-1867	Josephi Loisèle/Julia Loisèle	C. Bessèle/J. Loisèle
Loisele	Franciscum Israclem	29-DEC-1870	01-JAN-1871	Josephi Loisele/Julia Balthazar	Martinus Loisele/Saloma Loisele
Loisele	Medarum	06-MAY-1869	16-MAY-1869	Joseph Loisele/Julia Balthazar	Baptista Balthazar/Maria Gillman
Loiselle	Hermniam	05-FEB-1865	12-FEB-1865	Josephi Loiselle/Julia Loiselle	M. Balthazar/S. Balthazar
Loiselle	Mariam Rosam Annam	.11-DEC-1867	15-DEC-1867	Antoni Loiselle/Edmira M-riel	N. Langlois/M. Langlois
Loiselle	Mathidam	17-JUN-1862	29-JUN-1862	Josephi Loiselle/Julia Loiselle	J. Gayet/M. Marcou

80

Surname	Given Name	Birth	Baptism	Parents	Godparents
Loiselle*	John				
Lomblat	Franciscum Eugenum	19-JUN-1900	01-JUL-1900	Josepho Lomblat/Catarina Kreamer	Josephus-Walter Lomblot/Mathilda Kreamer
Lomblat	Josephum Alfredum	07-MAR-1893	05-APR-1893	Carolo Lomblat/Martha Lousa Hoper	Alfredus Lomblat/Rosila Desvillers
Lomblat	Catharnam Rutham	28-MAR-1893	02-APR-1893	Josepho Lomblat/Catharina Kremer	Paulus Gagner/Josephna Duquet
Lomblot	Olivam Edessam	06-SEP-1904	25-SEP-1904	Joseph Lomblot/Catharina Kremer	Albertus Kremer/Edessa Trotter
Lomiller	Jocobum	03-FEB-1860	09-FEB-1860	Michelis Lomiller/Ellen Kerry	Joannes Waters/M--- Oconner
Lomiller*	Elsabeth	01-APR-1855	04-JUL-1855	Mateu Lomiller/Theresa Seber	W Clich/E Bibbeler
Lomiller*	Elsabetham	10-APR-1855	04-JUL-1855	Ma-n Lomiller/Cheriscia Leber	U Neboch/E. Bisseler
Lomiller*	Semonen	14-AUG-1857	22-OCT-1858	Ma--- Lomiller/Theresa Siber	Francus-Simon Ferdinand/Chsalt Slorin
Looycr*	Leanard				
Lor---*	Richardum Paul--	31-MAY-1860	01-JUL-1860	Mathew Lor---/Maria McCabe	Curan McCabe/Margeth Cafield
Lord	Olivam	01-MAY-1885	31-AUG-1885	Elias Lord/Eliza Malone	Telesphorus Edoin/Elizabeth Whalen
Lorge	Elmram	24-MAY-1867	14-JUL-1867	Francisci Lorge/Adelaida Houssois	J. Houssois/M. Tordeur
Lorge	Eugenuam	24-FEB-1863	29-MAR-1863	Francisci Lorge/Adelada Lorge	J Houssois/M. Tordeus
Lorge	Franciscum	07-NOV-1870	18-NOV-1870	Francisci Lorge/Adela Lorge	Paulus Vilain/Anna Morris
Lorge	Mariam	20-NOV-1865	01-APR-1866	Francisci Lorge/Adelauda Lorge	J Larose/L Houssois
Lorge	Victoriam Angelicam	21-MAR-1869	17-JUN-1869	Francisci Lorge/Adelaida Houssois	Lo-- Morris/Maria Morris
Lorrain	Vitalinam	09-JUL-1872	10-JUL-1872	Vitalis Lorrain/Philomena Robert	Ludovicus Lucier/Pélagia Regnier
Loshinski	Dorothy	03-DEC-1918	15-DEC-1918	Thomas Loshinski/Lucia Pepo-ski	Frank Loshnski/Helen Toba-Loshnski
Losilion	Evam	28-DEC-1863	14-JUN-1864	Ludovici Losilion/Lucinda Losilion	N. Marita/A. Shoemacher
Losselion	Theresam Franciscam	19-JUN-1858	01-JUL-1858	Nicolai Losselion/Maria Cook	J Losselion/F. Cook
Lossilion*	Theresa Francisca	17-JUN-1858	01-JUL-1858	Nicholas Lossillion/Mary Cook	John Lossillion/Francisca Cook
Loughlin	Joannem		29-SEP-1861	Gullelmi Loughlin/Catharina Loughlin	M. Loughlin/M. Doyle
Loughlin	Mariam Annam	08-MAY-1863	14-MAY-1863	Michaelis Loughlin/Maria Loughlin	J Loughlin/B. Burke
Loughlin*	Elizabeth				
Louise*	Maria				
Louseau	Christine	10-OCT-1851	22-FEB-1852	Pierre Louiseau/Amelie Strong	L. Beaudraux/S. Poudret
Louler*	Joseph Augustinus		05-MAY-1856	Joseph Louler/Maria Bone	J McKeep/A. Baken
Lower	John	14-APR-1851	15-APR-1851	Martin Lower/Eliza Landis	P. Vaughan/C. Mclady
Lower*	Anna Maria	01-JUL-1857	10-JUL-1857	Joepg Lower/Mari Bony	J Lower/M. --g---
Lower*	Annastatiam	01-JUL-1857	10-JUL-1857	Josephi Lower/Marna Bo-y	J. Lower/M. Rattigrath
Lower*	Josephum Augustum			Joseph Lower/Marna B-r---	J. McKeep/A. Baker
Lower*	Maria Calista	14-DEC-1855	11-JAN-1857	Charles Lower/Rossali Rosseheller	L. Bodreau/M. Bodricau
Loyd	George	03-FEB-1851	09-MAR-1851	George Loyd/Anna Carson	T Ward/M. Lawler
Loyd*	John				
Loyd*	John				
Loyd* **	Joannes	18-JAN-1860	22-JAN-1860	Joannis Loyd/Maria Colman	Joseph-Patricus McG---/Catharina Loyd
Loyed*	John	13-SEP-1858	07-OCT-1858	Thos Loyed/Ann McNan--	John Loyed/Mary Colmann
Loyel*	Elisabetham	08-JAN-1859	27-FEB-1859	Thoma Loyel/Ellis Flood	W. Loyel/B Henderphan
Lozon	Carolum	07-AUG-1863	11-OCT-1863	Francisci Lozon/Maria Lozon	M. Willmet/----- ----
Lucia	Emma Luarentia	25-DEC-1877	26-DEC-1877	Bapt Lucia/Odilea Lepage	V Fontaine/ wife
Lucia	Ludovicum	13-FEB-1875		Ludovicus Lucia/Plagia René	Camil Lucia/-----\-----
Lucia	Thomam Henney	18-MAR-1876	26-MAR-1876	Joseht Lucia/Marian Du--hy	J. Du--hy/P. Baié
Lucia	Annam Margaritam	22-NOV-1905	10-DEC-1905	Isaac Lucier/Della Zinke	Josephus Lucier/Lulu Kelly
Lucier	Caroline Angèle	03-MAR-1847	22-FEB-1859	Joseph Lucier/Emelie Brunelle	
Lucier	Carolus	18-MAR-1858	24-MAR-1858	Charles Lucier/-- Ruschel	Franc-Pellant/Josephus Fouché
Lucier	Clarey Adeline	03-MAR-1845	22-FEB-1859	Joseph Lucier/Emelie Brunelle	
Lucier	Fidèle	26-AUG-1854	22-FEB-1859	Joseph Lucier/Emelie Brunelle	
Lucier	Floridam Luciam	06-JAN-1877	14-JAN-1877	Bapts Lucier/Odilla Payé	M. Santuare/ wife

81

Surname	Given Name	Bnth	Baptism	Parents	Godparents
Lucier	Guillelmum	09-OCT-1866	14-OCT-1866	Caroli Lucier/Rosa Lucier	J Cotton/M. Liston
Lucier	Guillelmum Edwardum	07-MAR-1872	11-MAR-1872	Baptista Lucier/Adelia Lucier	Ignatius Lepage/Maria Lepage
Lucier	Helenam	25-AUG-1881	26-AUG-1881	Jospho Lucier/Maria Duby	Eugenius Dupuy/Julia Dupuy
Lucier	Jacobum Edmundum	30-MAR-1881	03-APR-1881	Isaia Lucier/Margarita Duffy	L Lucier/P Regnier
Lucier	Joseph	28-JUL-1852	22-FEB-1859	Joseph Lucier/Emelie Brunelle	
Lucier	Ludovicum Arthurum	18-MAY-1874	02-JUN-1874	J.-Baptista Lucier/Delia Page	Carolus Lucier/Rosalia-Lucier Larochelle
Lucier	Mariam Emelinam	01-FEB-1908	20-APR-1908	Isaia-Francesco Lucier/Della Zinke	Fred-Josephus Lucier/Nellie-Maria White-Lucier
Lucier	Mary Albine	25-MAR-1843	22-FEB-1859	Joseph Lucier/Emelie Brunelle	
Lucier	Mary Ann	30-OCT-1844	22-FEB-1859	Joseph Lucier/Emelie Brunelle	
Lucier	Mary Olive	20-OCT-1840	22-FEB-1859	Joseph Lucier/Emelie Brunelle	
Lucier	Ovide	09-JAN-1850	22-FEB-1859	Joseph Lucier/Emelie Brunelle	
Ludoskey*	Michael	01-SEP-1859	18-SEP-1859	Abdrus Ludoskey/Badana Husk-y	A E-a-us/-. LensMayer
Luny	Mariam	04-AUG-1861	01-SEP-1861	Timothei Luny/Joanna Luny	M. Shirk/M. Mahony
Lussier	Georgium Ludovicum	17-AUG-1873	17-AUG-1873	Joseph Lussier/Maria Duffy	Ludovicus Lussier/Anna White
Luto*	John	13-JAN-1856	02-MAR-1856	Niclu Luto/Jeane Kerran	M. Rissos/J. Rossile
Lynch	Alisam		09-SEP-1860	Jacobi Lynch/Anna Lynch	J Se-ly/M. Kern
Lynch	Cornelium Augustinum	14-SEP-1863		Joannis Lynch/Marguarita Lynch	J. Mangan/A. O'Conner
Lynch	Franciscum	23-MAY-1863	24-MAY-1863	Joannis Lynch/Catharina Lynch	F. Lynch/M. Nealan
Lynch	Frederick				
Lynch	Jacobum	17-JUL-1863	15-AUG-1863	Jacobi Lynch/Anna Lynch	P. Coffee/M. Clarke
Lynch	Marguaritam		09-JUN-1861	Joannis Lynch/Catharina Lynch	P. Gano-/J. Gano-
Lynch*	Joannem Cornelium	10-SEP-1859	02-OCT-1859	Joannis Lynch/Maria Mangan	C. Flood/T. Mangan
Lynch*	John Cornelius				
Lynch*	Mary Ann				
Lyneis-Lyonnais	Claudum Albinum	08-JUN-1910	17-JUN-1910	Claudio Lyneis/Francisca Dreis	Georgius Lyneis/Catharine Dreis
Lynis	Annam Mariam	19-AUG-1853	28-AUG-1853	Petri Lynis/Thresia Ganjan	L Ganjan/A. Ganjan
Lyonnais	Arthurum Haroldum	22-MAY-1902	01-JUN-1902	Claudio Lyonais/Georgina Cartier	Cosma Lyonais/Louisa Beaudreault
Lyonnais	Carolum Franciscum	03-OCT-1883	07-OCT-1883	Cosmo Lyonais/Ludovica Beaudriault	Gulielmus Lyonais/Joanna Lyonais
Lyonnais	Georgium Loyd	02-JUN-1904	19-JUN-1904	Georgio Lyonais/Hilda Reinmand	Cosma Lyonais/Ludovica Beaudreau
Lyonnais	Joannem Edwinum	30-OCT-1885	08-NOV-1885	Cosmo-Edwino Lyonais/Edessa-Eleonora Gosselin	Cosma Lyonais/Lousia Beaudreault
Lyonnais	Julian	24-FEB-1874	01-MAR-1874	Eduard Lyonais/Sophronia Bessette	Petrus Bessette/Rosalia Tibado
Lyonnais	Louisam Thelmam	01-APR-1900	06-MAY-1900	Claudio Lyonais/Georgina Cartier	Cleophas Cartier/Dulcineam Dufresne
Lyonnais	U Augustum	10-NOV-1886	21-NOV-1886	Edwino-Cosmo Lyonais/Edessa Gosselin	Jacobus-Augustus Tones/Maria-Lina Gosselin
Lyonet	Adolum Léo	30-JUL-1874	02-AUG-1874	Cosma Lyonet/Ludovica Baudrio	Joseph Lyonet/ -o-mia
Lyonnais	Adelaidam Ludovicam	07-JUL-1870	31-JUL-1870	Coma Lyonnais/Ludovica Lyonnais	Franciscus Beaudreau/Alphia Beaudreau
Lyonnais	Carolina	19-APR-1872	21-APR-1872	Eduardi Lyonnais/Sophia Lyonnais	Perus Bessete/Sophia Bessete
Lyonnais	Christinam	26-JAN-1869	07-FEB-1869	Josephi Lyonnais/Lucia Bessette	Petrus Bessete/Sophia Bessete
Lyonnais	Cosmam Edwinam	06-JUL-1863	19-JUL-1863	Cosma Lyonnais/Ludovica Lyonnais	L Beaudricau/S Brico
Lyonnais	Guillelmum	26-JUN-1870	03-JUL-1870	Eduardi Lyonnais/Sophia Bessete	Ludovicus Lyonnais/Angela Lyonnais
Lyonnais	Joannam Adelam	23-APR-1868	17-MAY-1868	Come Lyonnais/Ludovica Lyonnais	Narcissus Lyonnais/Maria Leduc
Lyonnais	Josephum Alexandrum	09-OCT-1867	20-OCT-1867	Joseph Lyonnais/Lucia Lyonnais	L Lyonnais/M. Lyonnais
Lyonnais	Josephum Guillelmum	23-AUG-1872	14-OCT-1872	Coma Lyonnais/Ludovica Lyonnais	Albertus Florent/F---- Florent
Lyonnais	Luciam Amatam	15-MAY-1869	16-MAY-1869	Eduardi Lyonnais/Sophia Bessete	Hubertus Leduc/Merentia Beaulieu
Lyonnais	Luciam R Delinam		02-AUG-1868	Narcissi Lyonnais/Maria Leduc	Ludovicus Lyonnais/Angela Lyonnais
Lyonnais	Ludovicam Georgiam	27-AUG-1866	23-SEP-1866	Narcissi Lyonnais/Maria Lyonnais	F. Leduc/J. Beaudin
Lyonnais	Ludovicum Albertum	15-SEP-1865	24-SEP-1865	Coma Lyonnais/Ludovica Lyonnais	L. Lyonnais/A. Lyonnais
Lyonnais	Margeriam Francescam	03-JUN-1906	17-JUN-1906	Claudio Lyonnais/Francesca Dreis	Jacobus Dreis/Julia Baker-Dreis
Lyonnais	Moysem Fredericum	17-AUG-1870	11-SEP-1870	Josephi Lyonnais/Lucia-Victorina Lyonnais	Baptista Rondeau/Julia-Anna Chef
Lyonnais-Lynais	Eduardum Romanum		23-SEP-1906	Georgio Lyonnais-Lynais/Hilda Reinwand	Eduardus LePine/Mamie Reinwand

82

Surname	Given Name	Birth	Baptism	Parents	Godparents
Lyonnais-Lyneis	Josephum Claudium	18-NOV-1906	18-NOV-1906	Claudio Lyonnais-Lyneis/Francesca Dreis	
Lyons	Jacobum	24-JUN-1854	27-NOV-1854	Patricii Lyons/Maria Kr-ka-	B. Brethny/E. Mckillit
Lyons	James	27-MAR-1852	13-APR-1852	John Lyons/Catherine Nash	J Fergusson/A. Sheridan
Lyons	Thomam Christophorum	08-JUN-1861	08-JUN-1861	Joannis Lyons/Helena Lyons	G. Lémery/C. Kelly
Lyons*	Jacobum	07-SEP-1859	09-SEP-1859	Joannis Lyons/Catherina Lymery	H Dougherty
Lyons*	James				
Lÿan	Mariam Annam	30-SEP-1853	22-OCT-1853	Joannis Lÿan/Anna Flot	P. McGlogelin/A. Moffet
M-lony*	James Edward				
Ma---a*	Michales	13-AUG-1855	25-AUG-1855	Patrick Ma---a/Brigita Croly	J We--hs/M. Ble-
Maas	Carolina	23-AUG-1872	25-AUG-1872	Gilberti Maas/F -Lucia Maas	Josephus Maas/Zoah Langlois
Maas	Guillelmum	11-DEC-1866	16-DEC-1866	Josephi Maas/Zoah Maas	S. Houle/M. Houle
Mack	Ignatum Edwardum	15-JUN-1866	29-JUL-1866	Martini Mack/Anna Mack	I Reichert/A Reichert
Mack	Martinum		25-MAY-1862	Joannis Mack/Catharina Mack	F. Sergler/---- -----
Macks	Mariam Violam	13-AUG-1904	31-AUG-1904	Frederici Wacks/Maria-Elsea Desvillers	
Macou*	Augustus	09-FEB-1857	22-FEB-1857	Jean-Marie Macou/Melinda Hemble	I. St-Antoine/G. Bean
Madden	Catherine	28-NOV-1850	09-DEC-1850	Patrick Madden/Mary Sheridan	G Fitzgerald/M Green
Madden	Hudson	24-MAR-1852	13-APR-1852	Patrick Madden/Mary Sheridan	P. Mlly/B. Martin
Madden*	D. Anne				
Madden*	Daly Ann	01-MAR-1859	13-MAR-1859	John Madden/Mary Rooney	T. Rooney/E. Jordan
Mageny*	William	19-AUG-1857	23-AUG-1857	John Mageny/Brgita Kief	P. Sullivan/E. Megeny
Magenÿ**	Wilhelmum	19-AUG-1857	23-AUG-1857	Joannis Magenÿ/Brigetha Kief	P. Sullivan/E. Magenÿ
Mahiné	Mariam Theresam	03-APR-1863	05-JUL-1863	Joannis-Josephi Mahiné/Maria-Theresa Mahné	J Houssois/M. Tordeur
Mahony	Jacobum	02-SEP-1852	12-SEP-1852	Michaelis Mahony/Catherina Mahony	P. Mahony/M. Carvey
Mahony	Joannem	15-APR-1855	21-APR-1855	Michaelis Mahony/Catharina Curley	J. Mckcen/A. -arsh
Maid*	Francis	23-JAN-1859	06-FEB-1859	Thos Maid/Bridget McGinity	P. Maid/C. Kernan
Maid*	Francis				
Maillon	Wilfredum Eduardum	23-MAY-1858	27-JUN-1858	Eduardi Maillon/Rosalia Dumas	V. Graton/P. ------
Maillou	Wilfred Edward	23-MAR-1858	27-JUN-1858	Edward Maillou/Rosalie Duma	Vitale Gratton/Phébée ------
Main	Franc--is	11-JUN-1856	24-AUG-1856	Francois Main/---olina Loinlain	P. Morris/M. Gage
Maissé	Sophiam	25-OCT-1861	10-NOV-1861	Joannis-Josephi Maissé/Maria-Theresa Maissé	J Larose/M Houssois
Malbo	Franciscus Patricus	06-JAN-1860	09-JAN-1860	Patricii Malbo/Maria-Anna Malbo	Patricus Oconnor/Margarata Oconnor
Males*	Cathernam	18-JUL-1856	21-MAY-1857	Roberti Males/Anna-Maria Swartz	J. Weber/C. Jocabs
Malheur	Félicité		06-JUN-1851	Louis Malheur/Felicite Malheur	J Sire/G. Sire
Malheur	Maram Theresiam	13-SEP-1877	16-SEP-1877	Jermann Malheur/Maria Landerman	L Maleur/T. Jolie
Malheur*	Joseph	28-JUN-1855	01-JUL-1855	Josus Malheur/Inesi Sir	G Ollet/S. Sir
Malheur*	Josephus	28-JUN-1855	01-JUL-1855	Ludovici Malheur/Inesi Sir	G Ollet/S. Sir
Malis*	Catherina	18-JUL-1856	21-MAY-1857	Rabat Malis/Anna-Maria Swartz	J Weber/C Jocobus
Malleur	Leonardam	04-JUN-1853	05-JUN-1853	Ludovici Malleur/Felicitatis Cyr	P. Bray/M Malheur
Mallon*	Maria Anna	25-JUN-1857	28-JUN-1857	John Mallon/Ann Melle	P Savers/M. Cussin
Malo	Ema Josephenam		07-APR-1878	Juberti Malo/Josephina Leclare	J. Pengaure/ wife
Malone	Annam Joannam	13-APR-1861	12-MAY-1861	Andrea Malone/Honora Malone	E Cary/C. Ca--
Malone	Josephum	28-NOV-1874	07-JAN-1875	Joannes Malone/Brigetht-E. Whelan	Jocobus Cullan/Ellisabeth Marten
Malone	Petrum	20-JUL-1862	25-JUL-1862	Johannis Malone/Elizabetha Malone	J. Gillen/A. Gillen
Malone*	Elsetha	01-MAR-1860		Joannis Malone/Elseltha Whalin	Ricardus Malone/Margaretta Flanigan
Malone*	Elizabeth				
Malory**	Joseph	22-APR-1851	20-APR-1851	Perre Malory/----- Malory	J -ounaugh---/A. -ounaugh---
Manahan	Joseph	18-AUG-1851	26-OCT-1851	Joseph Manahan/Marguerite Lain	R. Kan/M Connel
Manahan	Marguerit	06-JUL-1851	07-JUL-1851	John Manahan/Mary Hammond	J. McGrath/R. Hammond
Mangan	Bridgittam	29-AUG-1863	31-AUG-1863	Jacobi Mangan/Marguarita Mangan	C. Daugherty/M. McGrath

Surname	Given Name	Birth	Baptism	Parents	Godparents
Mangan	George Francis		06-JAN-1861	Michaelis Mangan/Joanna Mangan	J. Rafferty/M. McLeavy
Mangan	Joannem Elizabetham	13-APR-1857	20-APR-1857	Michaelis Mangan/Joanna Cay	J McLevy/M. Mangan
Mangan*	Annam Mariam		05-SEP-1859	Stephani Mangan/Cath Moran	E. Mangan/M. G-----
Mangan*	Joannus				
Mangan*	John Henry				
Mangan*	Julia	05-MAY-1859	12-JUN-1859	Jacobi Mangan/Helena Cane	J Connell/H Cane
Mangan*	Juliam	31-MAY-1857	31-MAY-1857	Sephani Mangan/Catherina Moran	C. Gay/M. Dayer
Mangan*	Petrum	12-MAR-1859	13-MAR-1859	John Mangan/Ann Rooney	J. Mangan/M. Rooney
Mangan*	Thomas				
Mangan*	Thomas				
Mangel	Ludovicum	22-FEB-1863	08-MAR-1863	Valentini Mangel/Marguarita Mangel	L. Sontag/M. Fisher
Mangel	Rosa				
Mangel	Valentinum	13-OCT-1864	13-NOV-1864	Valentini Mangel/Marguarita Mangel	D Thill/C. Vonreik
Mangin	Catarnam Alidam	29-JUN-1849	16-SEP-1883		Josephus Lepine/Lousa Rondeau
Mangin	Mariam Adelem	12-DEC-1867	25-MAR-1884	Jeremia Mangin/Maria-Anna Anderson	Calixtus Errard/Delphina Leduc
Mangin	Susannam	07-SEP-1852	12-SEP-1852	Cornelii Mangin/Maria Lawler	J. Flood/R. Flood
Mangin-Masher	Mariam M. Corneliam	26-APR-1886	02-MAY-1886	Ludovico-L. Mangin-Masher/Ludovica-Delia Leduc	Calixtus Errard/Delphina Leduc
Mangin-Mosher	Agnetam	02-MAY-1895	19-MAY-1895	Jeremia Mangin-Mosher/Maria Anderson	Martinus Mosher/Maria Coffy
Mangan*	Moris	08-APR-1857	19-APR-1857	Patrick Manigan/Caterina Curran	B. Seggens/J. Curran
Mannegan	Henricum Bernardum	08-JUL-1853	08-JUL-1855	Joannii Mannegan/Maria Hammon	T. Komeset/J. Hammon
Mannegan*	Joannem	10-JUN-1857	28-JUN-1857	Joannis Mannegan/Maria Hammon	R. Harlon/B. Manly
Manneyham	Elisaltham	14-OCT-1853	23-DEC-1853	Joseph Manneyham/Margerieta Lynon	P. McGiveran/C Agan
Mannigan*	John	19-JUN-1857	28-JUN-1857	John Mannigan/Mary Hammen	J Harlon/B. Manly
Mannigan	Jorgium Franciscum		15-JUL-1860	Jan--- Mannigan/Maria Hammon	Thamas Grift/Anna H-----
Mannigan*	Hennery	02-JUL-1855	08-JUL-1855	John Mannigan/Maria Hammon	T. Lovi-/J. Hammon
Mannigan*	Maursium	08-APR-1857	19-APR-1857	Patrici Mannigan/Catherina Curran	B. Siggens/J. Currans
Manning	Helena	11-FEB-1858	07-MAR-1858	Mcl Manning/Catherine Morarty	Thos Connor/Catherine Donnally
Manning	Mariam Alixiam	16-DEC-1895	20-DEC-1895	Joanne Manning/Catharina O'Brien	Patricia Scannell/Margaritta O'Brien
Mannon	Felix	13-JUN-1853	16-AUG-1853	Joannis Mannon/Maria Hamm--	O Rogers/C. Harlin
Mantha*	Bernardus	29-SEP-1857	20-OCT-1857	John Mantha/Brigita Kelligan	J. O'Bryan/S. Mangan
Maran	Rachel		20-SEP-1863	Thoma Maran/Rachael Maran	T. Roch/B. Dirkin
Marceau*	Augustinum		22-FEB-1857	Joannis Marceau/Matilda Ramblé	I. St.-Antoine/J. Lebeau
Marceau	Alexdrum	21-FEB-1855	25-FEB-1855	Jeremia Marceau/Josephina Borchard	L. Surprenat/J. Lerner
Marceau	Mariam Oliviam	22-DEC-1854	25-DEC-1854	Francisci Marceau/Emilie Sir	J. Marceau/F. Sir
Marcell	Mariam Franciscam	26-NOV-1850	30-JUL-1854	Luca Marcell/Maria Loos	I Snow/S. Snow
Marcelle	Joannem H-ericum	11-APR-1858	23-JUN-1858	Lou-- Marcelle/Maria Fitzjurrals	Thanos Rochs/M Rochs
Marcelle	Joannem Henricum	11-APR-1858	23-JUN-1858	Luc Marcelle/Maria Fitzgerral	T Roach/M. Roach
Marcks*	Elisam	07-MAR-1857	07-JUN-1857	Joannes Marcks/Eva Susser	G Rayhart/M Rayhart
Marco	Alexander	05-MAR-1877	07-MAR-1877	Alexander Marcou/Lanore Lajeunesse	H. Lajeunesse/M. Lavallé
Marco	Malvinam	02-NOV-1878	03-NOV-1878	Alexandri Marco/Laura Young	J Guyet/L. Guyet
Marcoe	Elenore	02-SEP-1880	08-SEP-1880	---ler Marcoe/----- Lajeunesse	
Marcoe	Laurentium Franciscium	08-JUL-1900	08-JUL-1900	Francisco Marcoe/Leona Burnham	Franciscus Hurteau/Laura Durocher
Marcoe-Marcoux	Dorotheam Mariam	07-FEB-1910	06-MAR-1919	Samuele Marcoe/Maria Schreiner	Alex-L. Marcoe/Orzelia Beaudreau
Marcot*	Damas				
Marcot*	Jocobum Leandrem	25-MAR-1857	05-APR-1857	Mat. Marcot/Theresia Bru-t	L. Landerman/V. Mulhern
Marcot*	Jocobus Leander	25-MAR-1857	05-APR-1857	Mattias Marcot/Tersila Bruet	L. Landerman/O. Malheur
Marcote	Anastasiam	05-MAR-1863	08-MAR-1863	Mathias Marcote/Thersila Marcote	O. Beaulieu/M. Ebert
Marcote	Josephinam	09-APR-1869	11-APR-1869	Mathia Marcote/Thessila Marcote	Pascalis Letourneau/Maria Letourneau
Marcote	Olivierum	18-APR-1861	21-APR-1861	Mathia Marcote/Thercilla Marcote	I. Fernet/J. Lemaire

84

Surname	Given Name	Birth	Baptism	Parents	Godparents
Marcote	Victorem	05-APR-1865	09-APR-1865	Mathia Marcote/Thersilla Marcote	F. Beaudrieau/A Fernet
Marcott*	Damascum	18-APR-1859	10-JUN-1859	Mathea Marcott/Tarsilia Bruet	J. Marcoe/D. Tramble
Marcou	Amatum	20-NOV-1867	01-DEC-1867	Joannis-Maria Marcou/Helena Marcou	F Miller/S. Miller
Marcou	Eduardum	13-FEB-1875	07-MAR-1875	Joseph Marcou/Elisabeth Peddeland	Samuel Marcou/Malin-S Marcou
Marcou	Eduardum Alexandrum	18-MAY-1872	02-JUN-1872	Isidori Marcou/Maria-Anna Marcou	Franciscus Marcou/Josephina Marcou
Marcou	Franciscum Eduardum	19-JUL-1874	26-JUL-1874	Francisci Marcou/Josephina Tooy	Is---- St.-Antoine/Julienne St.--us--in
Marcou	Franciscum Jacobum	20-JAN-1870	01-MAY-1870	Isidori Marcou/Mana-Anna Marcou	Franciscuc Marcou/Emilia Marcou
Marcou	Francium Alexandrum	10-SEP-1875	19-SEP-1875	Alexander Marcou/Leonara Lajeunesse	F. Marcou/ wife
Marcou	Helenam		26-JUN-1864	Joannis-Marie Marcou/Helena Marcou	J. Marcou/D. Tremblé
Marcou	Isidorum	16-NOV-1870	20-NOV-1870	Joannis-Marna Marcou/Helena Snow	Isidorus Snow/Emilia Snow
Marcou	Joannam Mariam	01-MAR-1866	04-MAR-1866	Joannis-Marie Marcou/Helena Marcou	I. St.-Antoine/S. Snow
Marcou	Joannem	18-JUN-1858	23-JUN-1858	Joannis Marcou/Janet --	Joannis Rosseth--/M Rosseth--
Marcou	Joannem Baptistam	08-MAR-1870	20-AUG-1870	Josephi Marcou/Elizabetha Pallant	Damasius Trotier/Philomena Trotier
Marcou	Joannem Ludovicum	30-OCT-1873	07-MAR-1875	Samuel Marcou/Levena-A. Duranton	Ludovicus Goodin/Rosalia Goddin
Marcou	Jorge Hennery	05-SEP-1877	16-SEP-1877	Josephus Marcou/-li- Pedelant	J. Marcou/ wife
Marcou	Josephum Athur	30-MAR-1880	04-APR-1880	Francisco Marcou/Josephina Roi	H Labossière/E. Roi
Marcou	Josephum Isedore	23-AUG-1875	09-SEP-1875	Samuel Marcou/Livina Duranseau	I. Pratt/P. Marcou
Marcou	Ludovicum	01-FEB-1877	02-FEB-1877	Joannis Marcou/Elina Snow-Chnard	Siste- M. Dale/Rev. Dale
Marcou	Mariam Claram	07-SEP-1876	24-OCT-1876	Josephi Marcou/Elise Peddelant	J Rabidou/A. Peddelant
Marcou	Mariam Josepham	17-MAR-1870	20-MAR-1870	Josephi Marcou/Elizabetha Pellant	Franciscus Pellant/Mathilda Tremblé
Marcou	Mariam Melvnam	03-JUL-1871	05-JUL-1871	Francisci-E Marcou/Josephina Roi	Franciscus Marcou/Julia Anna Roi
Marcou	Mariam Olivnam	17-AUG-1875	05-SEP-1875	Joannis-Marna Marcou/Elena Sinard	Samuel Marcou/----- Marcou
Marcou	Mariam Sophiam	25-DEC-1873	06-JAN-1874	Joannis Marcou/Helena Chenard	Petrus Bisonette/---ena Chenard
Marcou	Napoleonem	27-MAY-1861	16-JUN-1861	Joannis-Maria Marcou/Domitilla Marcou	J. Marcou/E. Chenard
Marcou	Noahm		03-JAN-1869	Joannis-Maria Marcou/Helena Snow	Ludovicus Godin/Philomena Marcou
Marcou	Rosalam		04-AUG-1872	Samuelis Marcou/Olivina Duranseau	Ludovicus Duranseau/Josepha Duranseau
Marcou	Samuelem Henricum	16-NOV-1869	09-JUL-1870	Salomonis Marcou/Olivina Duranceau	Joannes-Maria Marcou/Domitilla Marcou
Marcou*	Aelxander	26-JUN-1859	24-JUL-1859	Joannis Marcou/Matilda Tromblé	J Lebeau/M Fée
Marcou*	Alexandre				
Marcoux	Adelam Mariam	21-DEC-1887	25-DEC-1887	Napoleone Marcoux/Sophronia Dufresne	Alexander Marcoux/Azelia Beaudreault
Marcoux	Alexim	28-FEB-1853	13-MAR-1853	Francisci Marcoulx/----- Marcoulx	J. R---t/M. Benoit
Marcoux	Alfredum G	23-DEC-1885	06-JAN-1886	Napoleone Marcoux/Sophronia Dufresne	Petrus Dufresne/Onesima Meunier-Lapierre
Marcoux	Augustnum Napoleonem	04-SEP-1882	05-SEP-1882	Augusto Marcoux/Julia Leduc	Calixtus Errard/Mathilda Tremblay
Marcoux	Bernicem Catharinam	11-MAY-1907	26-MAY-1907	Joanne Marcoux/Josephina Lebeau	Laurentus Gardner/Catharine Dobrindt
Marcoux	Clarentum Leonem	15-JUL-1909	25-JUL-1909	Francisco Marcoux/Josephina Balthazar	Michael Wattstern/Josephina Marcoux-Wettstein
Marcoux	Franciscam Hazel	15-SEP-1903	20-SEP-1903	Alexandro Marcoux/Eleonora Lajeunesse	Alexandro Marcoux/Eleonora Lajeunesse
Marcoux	Franciscum	17-JUL-1898	08-SEP-1898	Samuele-Henrico Marcoux/Anna Elsner	Samuel Marcoux/Maria Elsner
Marcoux	Franciscum Leonem Wilbe	14-JUN-1896	28-JUN-1896	Eduardo Marcoux/Christina Zebel	Franciscus Marcoux/Theresia Ackerman
Marcoux	Georgum Leonem	09-OCT-1891	15-OCT-1891	Francisco Marcoux/Josephina Roy	Eduardus Marcoux/Malvina Marcoux
Marcoux	Gulielmum	08-DEC-1897	12-DEC-1897	Alexandro Marcoux/Eleonora Lajeunesse	Josephus Lajeunesse/Julia Gratton
Marcoux	Harry	20-SEP-1905	20-DEC-1906	Josepho Marcoux/Lousa Duranseau	
Marcoux	Henricum	13-JUN-1885	14-JUN-1885	Alexandro Marcoux/Eleanora Lajeuness	Michael Lajeunesse/Rosa Lebeau
Marcoux	Isabellam	24-SEP-1899	08-OCT-1899	Francisco Marcoux/Josephina Balthazar	Guilielmus Brockway/Malvina Marcoux
Marcoux	Jeremam	13-JUN-1885	14-JUN-1885	Alexandro Marcoux/Eleanora Lajeuness	Jamus-Baptista Balthazar/Maria Marcoux
Marcoux	Josephinam	02-JUN-1887	12-JUN-1887	Alexandro Marcoux/Eleonora Lajeunesse	Joannes Balthazar/Emelia Lajeunesse
Marcoux	Josephum	24-JUL-1907	04-AUG-1907	Francisco Marcoux/Josephina Balthazar	Josephina LaJennesse/Julia Gratton
Marcoux	Josephum Albnum	07-JAN-1905		Francisco Marcoux/Josephina Balthazar	Gulielmus Pomainville/Eleonora Marcoux-P.
Marcoux	Josephum Albnum	07-JAN-1905	22-JAN-1905	Francisci Marcoux/Josephina Balthazar	Gulielmus Pommville/Eleonora Marcoux-P.
Marcoux	Josephum Napoleonem Al	10-JUN-1889	16-JUN-1889	Francisco Marcoux/Josephina Roy	Napoleo Corbeille/Melinda Lebeau

85

Surname	Given Name	Birth	Baptism	Parents	Godparents
Marcoux	Josephum Narcissum	30-DEC-1881	02-JAN-1882	Francisco Marcoux/Josephina Roy	Joannus-Baptista Balthalzar/Ar--ina Marcoux
Marcoux	Josephum Oliverum	09-APR-1881	10-APR-1881	Augusto Marcoux/Julia Leduc	J. Marcoux/M Bondy
Marcoux	Josephum Wilfridum	21-JUL-1886	23-JUL-1886	Francisco Marcoux/Josephina Roy	Alexander Marcoux/Eleonora Lajeunesse
Marcoux	Julianum	28-FEB-1853	02-MAR-1853	Francisci Marcoux/----- Marcoux	I. Marcous/S. Snow
Marcoux	Laurentium	19-OCT-1899	22-OCT-1899	Alexandro Marcoux/Eleonora Lajeunesse	Gulielmus Brockway/Malvina Marcoux
Marcoux	Laurent:um Walter	09-JUL-1901	14-JUL-1901	Francisco Marcoux/Josephina Balthazar	Michael Balthazar/Philumena Robert
Marcoux	Lucnam Leam	25-AUG-1902	31-AUG-1902	Joanne Marcoux/Josephina Lebeau	Georgius Marcoux/----- -----
Marcoux	Marcellinam Olivnam	09-SEP-1882	10-SEP-1882	Samuele Marcoux/Olivina Duranceau	Alexander Marcoux/Arzilia Beaudriault
Marcoux	Maria Irene	22-AUG-1892	27-AUG-1892	Napoleone Marcoux/Sophronia Dufresne	Carolus Grise/Esther Dufresne
Marcoux	Maram	14-AUG-1879	15-AUG-1879	Joanna-Maria Marcaux/Hellena Chenard	J. Marcaux/H. Marcaux
Marcoux	Mariam Arabellam	28-SEP-1889	29-SEP-1889	Alexandro Marcoux/Eleanora Lajeunesse	Jeremias Marcoux/Sophia Miner
Marcoux	Mariam Dephnam Evam	06-NOV-1884	16-NOV-1884	Francisco Marcus/Josephina Roy	Ludovicus Beauregard/Delphina Plante
Marcoux	Mariam Emeliam	04-NOV-1882	05-NOV-1882	Alexandro Marcoux/Eleanora Lajeunesse	Henricus Lajeuness/Lucia Leduc
Marcoux	Mariam Josephinam	11-MAR-1894	18-MAR-1894	Alexandro Marcoux/Eleonora Lajeunesse	Josephus Corbeille/Maria Lajeunesse
Marcoux	Mariam Mabel		08-DEC-1891	Alexandro Marcoux/Eleonora Lajeunesse	Ludovicus Balthazar/Margaretta Lajeunesse
Marcoux	Mariam Stellam	02-DEC-1895	08-DEC-1895	Alexandro Marcoux/Eleonora Lajeunesse	Generosus Lajeunesse/Olivina Balthazar
Marcoux	Mariam Stellam Esmam	18-JUN-1897	26-JUN-1897	Napoleone Marcoux/Sophronia Dufresne	Pascalis Dufresne/Sarah Ste.-Maria
Marcoux	Philomenam Daisie	11-MAY-1890	18-MAY-1890	Napoleone Marcoux/Sophronia Dufresne	Felix Pratte/Philumena Marcoux
Marcoux	Reg--lam Napoleonem	05-DEC-1894	16-DEC-1894	Napoleone Marcoux/Sophronia Dufresne	Felix Pratte/Sara Duquette
Marcoux	Ruba--Jacobum	10-APR-1897	10-FEB-1907	Noe Marcoux/Anna Lariviere	Earl Paingaree/----- -----
Marcoux	Ruth Mariam	15-JUL-1896	08-SEP-1898	Samuele-Henrico Marcoux/Anna Elsner	Gulielmus Durocher/Maria Perron
Maret*	Urselinam		03-MAY-1857	Roberti Maret/Elmra Parriseau	D. Doubelain/P Pariso
Maret*	Urselisch	03-APR-1857	03-MAY-1857	Robat Maret/Edema Pariseau	D Dodelain/P Pariseau
Marets*	Matham	28-DEC-1857	17-JAN-1858	Josephi Marets/Margeretha Reny	M. Miller/R Miller
Margent*	Peter		31-MAY-1857	Steven Margen/Chartina Mogan	C. G-----/M. Dongar
Maricl	Josephinam	30-JUL-1853	22-AUG-1853	Petri Marel/Amelia Mason	P Maison/M. Delai
Marigay	Eduadum	23-APR-1860	13-MAY-1860	Michaelis Marigay/Elisath Quinn	Jocobus Scannel/Maria --elum
Marigay*	Gulielmum	27-NOV-1857	20-DEC-1857	Michaelis Marigay/Elisabetha Grueun	E. Dero--/S. Rogers
Marigay*	Gulemus	21-NOV-1857	20-DEC-1857	Michel Marigay/Ellisath Gruin	E. Derine/S. Rogers
Marion	Edmundum	23-APR-1872	24-APR-1872	Seraphim Marion/Delima Marion	Franciscus Marcou/Maria-Anna Brouillet
Marion	Narcissum Seraphinum	05-SEP-1870	05-SEP-1870	Seraphini Marion/Emma Marion	Narcissus Marion/Suzanna Marion
Marion	Philomenam Mariam		02-SEP-1872	Joannis Marion/Eleonora Char	Narcissus Bissonet/ Desanges
Markow	Emmam Ludovicam	21-APR-1873	26-JUL-1894	Ernesto Markow/Emelia Honey	Gilbertus Surprenant/Zoe Barbeau
Markow*	Eduardum Leonem Toussa	01-NOV-1904	06-NOV-1904	Frank Markow/Leona Markow	Eduardus Durocher/Evelyn Durocher
Markow*	Eduardum Leonum Touiss	01-NOV-1904	06-NOV-1904	Francisco Markow/Leona Burnham	Eduardus Durocher/Evelma Rheaume
Marks*	Allisa	07-MAR-1857	07-JUN-1857	John Marks/Eva Suster	J. Ragnat/M. Heis
Marleau	Mariam Bermicam	20-JAN-1907	27-JAN-1907	Gilberto-Jospeho Marleau/Rosam-Annam Dinelle	Ludovicus Dinelle/Josephina Marleau
Marleau	Mariam Sedatam	01-MAY-1910	04-MAY-1910	Gilberto Marleau-Jr /Rosalia Dinelle	-----/Philomene Charron-Barbeau
Marlo	Jubertum	08-JUN-1876	09-JUN-1876	Jubert Marlo-Marlou/Josephina Duclaire	J. Duclaire/D. Gaigné
Marrais*	Mariam Elioam	29-SEP-1857	13-OCT-1857	Olivier Marrais/Margeretha Morris	D Petit/F. Morris
Marreher	Mariam	19-OCT-1853	28-OCT-1853	Michaelis Marreher/Elisa Quinn	M. Belam/E. Onill
Marsden	Jacobum Edwardum	21-JUL-1861	10-AUG-1861	Edwardi Marsden/Cathanna Marsden	T. Isaacs/M. Marsden
Martan	Juliam	20-DEC-1852	04-SEP-1853	Nicolai Martan/Maria-Anna Dens	J. Dens/J. Martan
Martel	Eugenum	19-NOV-1854	19-NOV-1854	Eduardi Martel/Elizabetha Jornert	P. Martel/H. Remond
Martel	Henricum	17-AUG-1860	14-OCT-1860	Ewardi Martel/Elizabetha Martel	I. Fernet/M. Ebert
Martel	Lo---d--		19-NOV-1854	Eduardi Martel/Elizabetha Jornert	J Trimble/G. Gerard
Martel	Marcellina		24-JUN-1855	Eduaradus Martel/Elissa Vernet	F. Mari-a/M Beseau
Martel*	Marcillinam	15-MAY-1855	24-JUN-1855	Eduardi Martel/Elisa Vernet	F. Marene/M. Remeaux
Marten	Franciscum	03-JAN-1877	07-JAN-1877	Ferry Marten/Flavia Jubert	A. Lefevi-/E. Le-ebve

86

Surname	Given Name	Birth	Baptism	Parents	Godparents
Marten*	Elenam	01-JAN-1857	18-JAN-1857	Joannis Marten/Sara Chats	H McDevid/M. McNulty
Marten*	James	26-SEP-1857	15-NOV-1857	Thomas Marten/Margeta Braydy	C. Cubory/J Ke-y
Marten*	Jocobum	26-SEP-1857	19-NOV-1857	Thomas Marten/Margeretha Braydy	C. Corbery/J Kenny
Marten*	Luci	17-JUN-1856	26-JUL-1856	----- Marten/Elisabh Rother	N. Dufrain/A. Dufrain
Marten*	Sera Ellena	01-JAN-1857	18-JAN-1857	John Marten/Sera -----	Hueh McDovit/Maria -----
Martes	Malvinam Elizabeth	24-JAN-1888	27-JAN-1888	Antonio Martes/Julia Fontaine	Aldericus Venne/Olivina Fontaine
Martha*	Michaelem	13-AUG-1855	25-AUG-1855	Patrcu Martha/Bregetha Crouly	J Welschs/M. Polek
Martin	Arthurum Carolum	10-AUG-1890	13-AUG-1890	Leone Martin/Eleonora Dumas	Ne---ias Moquin/Eleonora Martin
Martin	Catharnam	02-FEB-1855	27-APR-1855	Nicolai Martin/Maria-Anna Lynch	G. Martin/C. Lynch
Martin	Eleonoram Wilhelmnam	21-MAY-1908	21-JUN-1908	Laurentio-J Martin/Oneta Piehl	Arthurus Martin/Ione Martin
Martin	Emericum	14-MAR-1881	20-MAR-1881	Leono Martin/Eleonora Dumas	E. Dumas/M. Dupuy
Martin	Emery Wm	03-SEP-1919	21-SEP-1919	Emery Martin/Agnes Feadner	Charles Leonard/Gertrude Lewis-Leonard
Martin	Evelnam Naemam	26-SEP-1897	30-SEP-1897	Leone Martin/Eleonara Dumas	Laurentius Martin/Lilia-Rosa Martin
Martin	Franciscum Joannem	29-AUG-1854	10-SEP-1854	Francisci Martin/Maria Gallaher	N Tinte/E. Gallaher
Martin	Genofevam Leam	10-NOV-1892	20-NOV-1892	Laurentio Martin/Eleonora Dumas	David Carrere/Lea Theriault
Martin	James	11-NOV-1850	07-DEC-1850	Nicholas Martin/Mary-Ann Lynch	-----
Martin	James Richard	13-JUL-1851	30-NOV-1851	Patrick Martin/Marguerit Hammon	R. Ardell/M. Donnevan
Martin	Josephnam	05-DEC-1868	17-JAN-1869	Emertii, Martin/Josephina Martin	Julianus Joubert/Ludovica Joubert
Martin	Josephum	20-FEB-1875	21-FEB-1875	Leonard Martin/Leonard Dumond	Joseph Landerman/----hilin Dumond
Martin	Josephum Carolum	17-OCT-1862	30-NOV-1862	M. Martin/Elizabetha Martin	J. Sigler/E. Sigler
Martin	Laurantium Merlino	09-AUG-1906	19-AUG-1906	Laurantio-J. Martin/Oneda Piehl	Leo Martin/----- -----
Martin	Laurenam Vivianam	29-JUL-1904	07-AUG-1904	Laurentio Martin/Josephia Piehl	Leo Martin/Gulielmina Paran
Martin	Mariam Annam	04-JUN-1883	07-JUN-1883	Leones Martin/Eleonora Dumas	Leo Lucas Brunet/Eudoxa Joly
Martin	Mariam Fellicitas Eleonor	06-JUL-1873	07-JUL-1873	Leonts Martin/Honora Dumas	Israël Dumas/Felicitas Hebert
Martin	Mariam Flaviam	25-DEC-1871	31-DEC-1871	Emertii Martin/Josephna Martin	Aurelus Martin/Flavia Martin
Martin	Mariam Helenam		13-JAN-1861	Joannis Martin/Sarah Martin	J. Harican/M. -ogan
Martin	Mariam Zoe	13-JUN-1888	15-JUN-1888	Leone Martin/Eleonora Dumas	Paulus Sauvé/----- Jakobs
Martin	Markum Mariam	21-DEC-1875	16-JAN-1876	Emeri Martin/Josepha Jubert	L Maten/S Lefeve
Martin	Martinum Izar	24-JUL-1874	26-JUL-1874	Izarcia Martin/Maria Joubert	Emery Martin/Josephina Joubert
Martin	Matildam Ludovicam	06-OCT-1850	12-JAN-1853	Patrcii Martin/Margarita Hammon	H Cook/M. Cook
Martin	Napoleonem	03-SEP-1885	05-SEP-1885	Leone Martin/Eleonora Dumas	Gilbertus Surprenant/Zoca Barbeau
Martin	Nicholas	11-NOV-1850	07-DEC-1850	Nicholas Martin/Mary-Ann Lynch	J. -----/E. -----
Martin	Owenium Phillipum	08-JUN-1863	26-JUN-1863	Thoma Martin/Marguarita Martin	J. Kenn/M. Crowley
Martin	Philippum	03-APR-1854	06-APR-1854	Thoma Martin/Margarita Bradley	P. Crowly/M. Click
Martin	Rosalia	21-APR-1878	27-APR-1879	Johannis Martin/Leonora Martin	M Martin/J. Martin
Martin	Thomas	19-DEC-1851	23-FEB-1852	Thomas Martin/Marguerite Bradley	J Welsh/C. Mccourt
Martin	William	22-JUL-1877	19-AUG-1877	Jocobi Martin/Ellis Corran	-----/E Corkeran
Martin*	Eugene Edward				
Martin*	Hugh	01-DEC-1858	25-JAN-1859	Nicolas Martin/Mary-Ann Linch	P. -uilan/M. Linch
Martin*	Hugh				
Masech	Joseph George	14-JUL-1918	18-AUG-1918	Joanne Masech/Anna Tomasich	Peter Milosevich/Soka Gugol
Masse	Guilbertum Albertum	08-JUL-1874	12-JUL-1874	Gilberti Masse/----ana Catherine ----	Julius Leclerc/Exilda Masse
Massenthi	Mary	06-MAY-1855	07-FEB-1858	Philippe Massenthi/Elisabeth Oberty	Mcl Cary/Ellen Slattery
Massete	Joannem Baptistam	06-MAY-1864	15-MAY-1864	Edward Massete/Adelina Massete	B. Gervais/M Gervais
Mathew*	Joannes Sebastiona	12-FEB-1860	18-MAR-1860	Sebastiana Mathew/Emelie Widhalf	Joannes Rodin/----- -----
Matthew	Michel	20-SEP-1851	17-NOV-1851	Francis-C. Matthew/Barttie-V Matthew	M. Barttel/D Fryer
Matthew*	John S				
Matthey	Gilbertum Norman	16-JUL-1908	05-APR-1909	P.-Francisco Mathey/May DuFort	-----/Lizzie DuFort
Mauer	Federicum	21-JUN-1860	05-AUG-1860	Petri Mauer/Clotilde Perin	

87

Surname	Given Name	Birth	Baptism	Parents	Godparents
Maures	Frerericum			Petri Maures/Clotilda Peren	---- Peren/Julie -----
Maurice	Adelnam Gratiam	02-NOV-1888	06-NOV-1888	Andrea Maurice/Emma Dufresne	Franciscus Dufresne/Domitilde Perron
Maurice	Andream	22-JUN-1890	24-JUN-1890	Andrea Maurice/Emma Dufresne	Eduardus Durocher/Sara Dufresne
Maurice	Bereniciam Mariam	02-MAY-1895	15-MAY-1895	Josepho Maruce/Agnete Fontaine	David Normile/Maria Fontaine
Maurice	Catherine		09-DEC-1850	Francis Maurice/Christine Leontine	L. Maurice/C. Perin
Maurice	Clarentium Leonem	28-JAN-1904	31-JAN-1904	Andrea Maurice/Emma Dufresne	Georgius Dufresne/Anna Melling
Maurice	Eduardum Alfredum	18-MAY-1886	27-MAY-1886	Francisco Maurice/Josephna Michalte	Paulus Vilasis/Anna Maurice
Maurice	Francescam Elizabeth	03-JUL-1897	05-JUL-1897	Andrea Maurice/Emma Dufresne	Wilfridus Bastien/Martha Dufresne
Maurice	Franciscum Josephum	05-JUL-1884	06-JUL-1884	Francisco Maurice/Josephna Michotte	Deodatus Michotte/Clotilda Lanctot
Maurice	Georgium Henricum	06-JUL-1888	15-JUL-1888	Francisco Maurice/Josephna Michatte	Franciscus Maurice/Oliva Moquin
Maurice	Hermine Adelade	03-JUL-1919	13-JUL-1919	Frank-J. Maurice/Lucrece-Grace-Marie Robidoux	Joseph Bastien/Esther Robidoux
Maurice	Hubertum Franciscum Jose	24-DEC-1909	28-DEC-1909	Francisco Maurice/Lucretta Robidoux	Joannes Robidoux/Catharina Leon
Maurice	Josephnam	29-SEP-1852	17-OCT-1852	Petri Maurice/Clotilda Peront	G. Maurice/M. Peront
Maurice	Josephum Andream	20-MAR-1893	26-MAR-1893	Andrea Maurice/Emma Dufresne	Stephan Dufresne/Heloisa Lebeau
Maurice	Leonardum Josephum	08-AUG-1884	11-AUG-1884	Josepho Maurice/Agnete Fontaine	Vence Fontaine/Maria Santueres
Maurice	Lousa M.		29-SEP-1907	Frank Maurice/Grace Robideau	
Maurice	Ludovicum Andream	29-MAR-1852	13-MAY-1853	Ludovici Maurice/Domitila Perrant	A. Perrant/M. Maurice
Maurice	Ludovicum Eugenum	21-MAY-1895	25-MAY-1895	Andrea Maurice/Emma Dufresne	Eugenus Bastien/Agnes Dufresne
Maurice	Mariam Appollinam	05-DEC-1852	06-JAN-1853	Francisci Maurice/Clotilda Maurice	G Maurice/A. Perant
Maurice	Olivam Evam	06-APR-1891	19-APR-1891	Francisci Maurice/Josephina Michotte	Alexander Moquin/Lousa Michotte
Maurice	Paschalem	03-DEC-1898	11-DEC-1898	Andrea Maurice/Emma Dufresne	Paschalis Dufresne/Sara Ste.-Marie
Maurice	Paulum	01-MAR-1864	02-MAR-1864	Francisci Maurice/Clotilda Maurice	P. Vilain/A. Maurice
Maurice*	Georgium		02-SEP-1860	Francisci Maurice/Adelna Maurice	G. Maurice/C. Reaume
Maurice*	Georgium		02-SEP-1860	Francisci Maurice/Delina Maurice	G. Maurice/C. Riaume
May	Franciscum		25-DEC-1863	Henrici May/Suzanna May	N Sho----/A. Sho----
May	Josephum Henricum		25-DEC-1863	Henrici May/Suzanna May	J. May/E. Hirch
Mayan*	Thomam	19-FEB-1859	20-FEB-1859	Michaeli Mayan/Catherina Harlen	P Murphy/C. --urry
Mayer	Isidorus	20-JUL-1856	17-AUG-1856	Francus Mayer/Franca P---ens	---- Gibel/-----bucke
Mayer*	Maria Annam Cathoriam	25-APR-1878	05-MAY-1878	Joseph Mayer/Anna Laus	C. Pess/A. Mikels
Mayer*	Anne K--				
Mayon	Josephum		16-JUN-1866	Pauli Mayon/Sophia Mayon	P. Rulo/L. Ster
Mayou	Josephinam	02-MAY-1870	17-MAY-1870	---- -----/Catherine Mayou	Josephus Choquete/Helena Choquete
Mayou	Noam	12-MAR-1868	17-MAY-1868	Hypoltus Mayou/Sophia Rulo	Herminia Rulo/Ludovica Rulo
Mayou	Rosaliam	15-APR-1870	28-NOV-1870	Hypolita Mayou/Sophia Mayou	Antonus Mayou/Angelca Mayou
Mayrand	Mariam Virginam Isabella	09-JUL-1902	20-JUL-1902	Gulielmo Mayrand/Winnfreda Leet	Henricus Tessier/Maria-Virginia Coté
Mayrand	Winnefredam Evelnam	09-OCT-1908	25-OCT-1908	Gulielmo Mayrand/Winnefreda Leath	Gulielmus Teahen/Anna Hughes
Mayer	Mariam	19-DEC-1855	28-DEC-1855	Nicolai Mayer/Babera Snyder	M. Kerke/M. Snyder
Mayer*	Joannem	17-MAR-1854	02-DEC-1855	Nicolai Mayer/Babera Snyder	J Hofmann/M. Snyder
Mc-----	William	15-NOV-1859	28-NOV-1859	John Mc----/Anna Dains	Patrick McNeil/Anna McEnly
Mc---*	Caterna	14-OCT-1857	20-OCT-1857	Thamas Mc----/Katerina Carbit	J Welsh/M. Harnet
Mc--nnan*	Jocobus	10-SEP-1857	20-SEP-1857	John Mc---nnan/-----B---dely	M. D--ly/-------
Mc--n-*	Patricium	02-MAR-1856	02-MAR-1856	B Mc--n-/Brigetha Rayse	T Gar-/M. Gar-
Mc--y*	Catharnam	03-MAY-1860	05-MAY-1860	Joannes Mc---y/Margeret Clair	Carolus Mullen/Ellen Dufphy
Mc-lay*	Robert Henry				
McCa-*	Brigetham	12-JUN-1859	02-JUL-1859	Richardi McCa-/Rosana Erling	F. Grogan/ M.Lagelan
Mcca--et	Bridget				
McCab*	Martinum	12-OCT-1857	25-OCT-1857	Joannis McCab/Catherina Damres	C. Ohary/A. Finlay
McCabe	Catharnam	12-MAR-1863	31-MAR-1863	Richardi McCabe/Rosa-Anna McCabe	J McCabe/C Connaughty
McCabe	Catharnam	05-JUN-1863	26-JUL-1863	Terentii McCabe/Anna McCabe	F. Callaghan/C. Rodgers

88

Surname	Given Name	Birth	Baptism	Parents	Godparents
McCabe	Franciscum Andream	17-JAN-1863	17-JAN-1863	Petri McCabe/Anna McCabe	J Nary/M. Cane
McCabe	Mariam Annam	17-JAN-1863	17-JAN-1863	Petri McCabe/Anna McCabe	M. Daugherty/M. Cane
McCabe	Petrum	18-JUL-1861	04-AUG-1861	Terentu McCabe/Honora McCabe	J Duffy/A. Cashman
McCabe	Richardum	12-MAR-1861	01-APR-1861	Richardi McCabe/Rosa Anna McCabe	J ----/J Nash
McCabe	Rosam Annam	29-NOV-1861	19-JAN-1862	Michaelis McCabe/Helena McCabe	J Callaghan/J. Connor
McCabe	Saram	08-NOV-1852	21-NOV-1852	Jacobi McCabe/Elizabetha McCabe	T McCabe/A. Collaghan
McCabe*	Bridget				
McCabe*	Mariam Joannam		02-SEP-1860	Michaelis McCabe/Helena McCabe	P. Davis/H Mallen
McCabe*	Mariam Joannem		02-SEP-1860	Michaelis McCabe/Helena McCabe	P. Davis/H Mullan
McCannan*	John				
McCannon*	Jorgium	29-APR-1859	02-JUN-1859	Patrci McCannon/Anna Derrelhy	J. McCullin/E. MCcullin
McCardle	Marguartam	17-DEC-1860	29-DEC-1860	Jacobi McCardle/Maria McCardle	P. Loughlin/M. Loughln
McCart*	Danelis	03-JUN-1860	25-JUN-1860	Patrcu McCarty/Maria Roche	Petrus McCarty/Brgitta Clark
McCarthy	Charles				
McCarthy	Georgium Danielem	18-SEP-1868	04-OCT-1868	Georgii McCarthy/Rosa-Anna McCarthy	Joannes Norton/Marguarita Norton
McCarthy	Johanna	24-FEB-1852	06-APR-1852	Davd McCarthy/Mary Kingston	F. McCarthy/M Fistgerald
McCarthy*	Marcum Henricum	21-AUG-1884	12-OCT-1884	Michaele McCarthy/Elizabeth Lu---z	----/Louisa Mullis
McCarthy*	Charles	01-MAR-1859	17-APR-1859	Daniel McCarthy/Mary Kington	S. Kingston/M. Kinsgton
McCarthy*	John				
McCarthy*	Maria Anna	11-AUG-1855	09-SEP-1855	Jeremias McCarthy/Nanci Kingston	J. Murphy/M. Dayer
Mccarthy	Narsisum	26-OCT-1853	12-NOV-1853	Danelis McCarthy/Maria Kiston	J McCarthy/M Kelby
McCarty	Florentium	09-JUN-1854	10-JUL-1854	Joannis McCarty/Anna Kingston	H. McCarty/M. Kelly
McCarty	Joannes	08-JUL-1860	29-JUL-1860	Mathas McCarty/Catherina Harlen	Joannis Laffis/Elisabetha Boyle
McCarty*	Mariam Annam	11-AUG-1855	09-SEP-1855	Jeremii McCarty/Nanci Kingstone	J. Murphy/M. Dayel
McCay	Josephum	09-DEC-1859	27-DEC-1859	Joannis McCay/Marie Powers	Patricus McCay/Joanna Powers
McCay*	Anna	20-OCT-1856	26-OCT-1856	Joannes McCay/Maria Powers	P. McCay/J McCay
McCay*	Martin	11-OCT-1857	25-OCT-1857	John McCay/Catherina Demsis	C. May/A Farly
McCay*	Sera	22-OCT-1855	31-OCT-1855	John McCay/Margreta --ar-	P Cork/S. Donly
McCay*	Seram	22-OCT-1855	31-OCT-1855	Joannis McCay/Margerietha Clair	P. Corek/S. Denby
McCay*	Annam	20-OCT-1856	26-OCT-1856	Joannes McCay/Maria Pa--ers	P. McCay/E. McCaÿ
McClain	Danielem	11-APR-1860	25-APR-1860	Jacobi McClain/Bergetta -aulsen	Edwind Nicolise-/Sara Nicolse-
McClain	Thoma	09-APR-1859	09-APR-1859	Charles McClann/Mina Bebury	Patrcus Gillan/An---- Ch---ay
McClan*	Martha				
McClallan	Mariam	31-JUL-1861	12-AUG-1861	Jacobi McClallan/Bridgitta McClallan	H. Gillmartin/S. Nicholson
Mcclane	Danel				
McClean	Sarahm	04-MAY-1863	31-MAY-1863	Jacobi McClean/Bridgitta McClean	J. Nicholson/M. Nicholson
McClean	Theresam	02-NOV-1861	10-NOV-1861	Caroli McClean/Anna McClean	E Wall/J. Toomy
McClone*	Maria	27-JAN-1860	29-JAN-1860	Charles McClone/Anna Raburn	Thomas Truman/Maria ----onne
McCoen*	Maria Rosa	20-MAY-1858	23-MAY-1858	Joannes McCoen/Maria-Anna McIntyre	L Dael/Rossa McGinnis
McCoil	James	27-SEP-1851	05-SEP-1851	John McCoil/Marguerite Clear	E Dunn/C McCoil
McCollen*	Mariam	15-APR-1860	29-APR-1860	John McCollen/Catherina McCay	Patricus McCollen/Ellen McGaly
McCollough*	Elizabeth	27-OCT-1858	12-JAN-1859	Michel McCollough/Ann Terey	Owen Bannen/Rose Bannen
McCollough* **	Elizabeth	27-OCT-1859	12-JAN-1859	Michel McCollough/Ann Jerey	Oroen Bannin/Rose Bannin
McColough*	Jacobus	08-APR-1859	24-APR-1859	Joannes McColough/Rosa Noulty	J Miles/C Loyed
McCormick	Annam	01-SEP-1861	15-SEP-1861	Thoma McCormick/Anna McCormick	E. Dun/A. White
McCormick	Joannam	20-DEC-1862	29-DEC-1862	Joannis McCormick/Anna McCormick	G. Dun/E Malachy
McCormick	Mary Ann	20-APR-1852	25-APR-1852	John McCormick/Ann Dunn	J. McCullogh/R. McCoy
Mccormick	William J.			J. Mccormick/A. Dunn	P. McNely
McCormk	Thomam	14-DEC-1853	01-JAN-1854	Joannis McCormik/Anna Donne	D Donne/S. McCullun

89

Surname	Given Name	Birth	Baptism	Parents	Godparents
McCowan	Guillelmum Henricum		29-DEC-1861	Guillelmi McCowan/Lucretia Tra---t	T Deschõuxs/C. Deschõuxs
McCowan	Lucretia		29-DEC-1861	Guillelmi McCowan/Lucretia Tra---t	G -----/L. -----
McCoy	Bridget An--	27-MAY-1858	27-MAY-1858	John McCoy/Margueret Clear	Thos Oreily/Sara McCoy
McCoy	Brigettam A.	27-MAY-1858	27-MAY-1858	Joanne McCoy/Marguarita Clear	T. O'reiley/S. McCoy
McCoy	Carolum Clifford	09-MAY-1905	06-AUG-1905	Carolo McCoy/Maria Bisson	-----/Ermina Bisson-Trilbey
McCoy	Joanna Agnes	13-DEC-1874	21-JAN-1875	Bernardi McCoy/Elisabeth Welshs	Daniel Mcclain/Maria Flino
McCoy	Joannem	08-AUG-1862	22-AUG-1862	Joannis McCoy/Marguarita McCoy	J Scanlin/----- Cahill
McCoy	Michaelem	11-MAR-1863	12-MAR-1863	Patrici McCoy/Maria McCoy	S McCoy/----- -----
McCoy*	Catharina				
Mccrathy*	James				
McCrauly*	Elisam Eugeniam	27-JUL-1857	12-SEP-1857	Caroli McCrauly/Maria Lavarty	J. Laverty/E. Mccay
McCree*	Jocobus	03-FEB-1857	19-MAR-1857	Patrick McCree/Anna Gibbens	R. Gillan/M. Gillans
McCroly*	Elisa Eugenia	27-JUL-1857	12-SEP-1857	Charles McCroly/Mai Laferty	J Laferty/E. McCay
McCrory	Bernardum	05-OCT-1854	28-OCT-1854	Joannis McCrory/Maria Kerrins	M Kerrins/A. Reilly
McCrory	Carolum	02-JUL-1852	19-SEP-1852	Caroli McCrory/Maria Laferty	B. Gafney/M. Kerns
McCrory	Joannem	17-AUG-1852	19-SEP-1852	Joannis McCrory/Maria Kerns	C. McCrory/M. McCrory
McCroury	Margareta	03-APR-1857	10-MAY-1857	John McCroury/Maria Kiernans	John Rayly/Chatari ------
McCuen*	Jocobum	23-MAR-1856	25-MAR-1856	Joannis McCuen/Maria McEntyer	J. Lensehs/T. McEntyer
McCullagh	Mariam Annam	17-DEC-1852	13-MAR-1853	M,ichaels McCullagh/Anna Clark	J Clark/M. Anna
McCullan**	Ann	31-DEC-1850	09-JAN-1851	Michael McCullan/Ann Carry	F. Mcginty/C. Griffin
McCullen	Ceciliam	20-FEB-1863	09-MAR-1863	Patricii McCullen/Anna McCullen	J McCullen/H. McCullen
McCullen	Georgium	17-APR-1862	27-APR-1862	Joannis McCullen/Catharina McCullen	P. McCullen/M. McCoy
McCullen	Helenam	02-APR-1861	02-APR-1861	Patrici McCullen/Anna McCullen	J McCullen/H McCullen
McCullen*	Margereetham	04-MAY-1857	16-MAY-1857	Niel McCullen/Matilda McCormick	J McCullen/M. McCormik
McCullen*	Maria				
McCullen*	Mariam	14-FEB-1856	26-FEB-1856	----- McCullen/Matilda McCormick	L Welschs/B. Donelhy
McCullen*	Petrus		13-JUL-1856	John McCullen/Catherina McCay	D Donne/E. McCullen
McCullen*	Petrus		18-JUL-1856	Joannis McCullen/Catherina McCay	D McCay/E. McCullen
McCullogh	Rosa	04-MAR-1852	11-APR-1852	John McCullogh/Rosa Nalty	T Carey/C. Gypson
Mccullogh*	Elizabeth				
McCullum*	Maria	14-FEB-1856	26-FEB-1856	-oly McCullum/Matilda McCormick	L. Welschs/B. Dorrethy
McCullum*	Martham	18-AUG-1859	04-SEP-1859	Penly McCullan/Mathilda McConnll	T Ca-ty/M. Mccormik
McCulough*	James				
McCune	Joannem Jacobum	03-APR-1862	03-APR-1862	Joannis McCune/Maria-Anna McCune	T. Gough/M. Fitzgerald
McCune	Mariam Annam	08-SEP-1853	09-SEP-1853	Joannis McCune/Margareta Clair	J McCune/S. Donoly
McCune	Rosam	08-DEC-1853	22-DEC-1853	Joannis McCune/Anna-Maria Mclyron	P. Gillan/S. Gillan
McCusin*	Mariam Rosa	20-MAY-1858	23-MAY-1858	Joannis McCusin/Maria-Anna McIntyre	L. Dael/R. Megens
McCuun*	Jacobus	23-MAR-1856	25-MAR-1856	John McCuun/Marian McIntyre	J Lun-ths/U. McIntyre
McDarmit	Carolum	27-MAY-1859	05-JUN-1859	Bernardi McDarmit/Anna Lany	J. Cennel/M. O'Connel
McDarmit*	Seram	10-MAY-1857	16-MAY-1857	Bernardi McDarmit/Anna Delanÿ	P R---/B. R----
McDavitt	Franciscam	09-AUG-1861	14-AUG-1861	Hughii McDavitt/Maria McDavitt	J. Dougherty/A Dougherty
McDermit*	Jacabus	28-APR-1858	02-MAY-1858	B--net McDermit/Anna Delany	Patrick Mannigan/Elisabeth --ray
McDermit*	Michael	04-SEP-1857	06-SEP-1857	Bernardus McDermit/Margeta Smit	J Smit/M. Smit
McDermitt	Maria Joona	03-DEC-1879	08-DEC-1879	Joone McDermitt/Helena Gardner	F. Gardner/C Gardner
McDermot	Joannem	30-DEC-1854	07-JAN-1855	Bernardi McDermot/Margarita Smith	L Belliet/C. Smith
McDermot*	Charles				
McDermott	Catharnam	02-MAY-1862	11-MAY-1862	Francisci McDermott/Alica McDermott	N Lamb/A. McDermott
McDermott	Guillelmum		12-MAY-1861	Bernardi McDermott/Marguarita McDermott	F. McDermott/A. McDermott
McDermott	Jacobum Edwardum	25-FEB-1861	10-MAR-1861	Timothei McDermott/Catharina McDermott	P. Halligan/M. McDermott

90

Surname	Given Name	Birth	Baptism	Parents	Godparents
McDermott	Joannem Josephum	09-DEC-1862	21-DEC-1862	Timothei McDermott/Catharina McDermott	J. ----/M. McDermott
McDermott	Mariam Annam		09-SEP-1860	Francisci McDermott/Alicia McDermott	B Shepard/M. Smith
McDermott*	Louis				
McDonald **	Maria Elisabatha	08-MAY-1860	29-JAN-1860	Patricii McDonald/Catharina McDonald	Patricius Vaughn/Maria McDonald
McDonald*	Julia	10-JAN-1859	12-JAN-1859	Esward McDonald/Mary Murphy	Patrick Cusick/Joanna Cusick
McDonald*	Julia				
McDonald*	Julie	10-JAN-1859	12-JAN-1859	Edward McDonald/Marg Murphy	Patrtick Cusick/Joanne Cusick
McDonald*	Martin	31-OCT-1858	05-FEB-1859	Jas. McDonald/Mary Joice	M. McDonald/B. Furgus
McDonald*	Martin				
McDonnell	Sophronam		13-DEC-1875	Caroli McDonnell/Catherina Coal	C. -1-seau/M. Bisson
McDonold*	Mary Elizabeth				
McDormit	Ludovicum	16-JUL-1860	19-JUL-1860	William McDormit/Anna Rayly	Joannes Godfert/Julia Ocenner
McDormit*	Jocabum	25-APR-1858	02-MAY-1858	Bernardi McDormit/Anna Delainy	P Mannegan/E. Conroy
McDormit*	Michaelem	03-SEP-1857	13-SEP-1857	Guilelmi McDormit/Anna Ra\'y`ly	M. Levy/-----
McDormit*	Michaelem	04-SEP-1857	06-SEP-1857	Bernardi McDormit/Margeretha Smith	J. Smith/M. Smith
McDormit*	Michaelis	03-SEP-1857	13-SEP-1857	Gulielmus McDormit/Anna Raily	----- Lıvly/-----
McDormit*	Serra	10-MAY-1857	16-MAY-1857	Bernardus McDormit/Anna Delany	P. Roger/B. Roger
McDuffit*	Chaterna	15-JUL-1855	15-JUL-1855	Hugh McDuffit/Maria Mckenny	J. Hartan/M. Dorrethy
McDuffy*	Catharinam	21-JUN-1855	19-JUL-1855	Hughii McDuffy/Maria McKenney	J Nortan/M. Daugherty
McElder*	William				
McElder*	Willielmum	22-MAR-1859	14-MAY-1859	Jocabi McElder/Maria Martin	J. Kennada/B. Fallin
Mcenrow*	Catherinam	31-JUL-1855	02-OCT-1855	Eduardi McEnrow/Elisatha Lawler	P. Cussick/J. McMann
McG----*	Joannam	02-JUN-1860	11-JUN-1860	Roberti McG-----/Margeth Cayan	Joannis Cagelan/Joanna Cagelan
Mcga--n*	Maria	01-JUL-1857	02-JUL-1857	John Mcga--n/Marie Kendrik	A. Kendrick/----- -----
McGarry	Brigittam	17-AUG-1857	27-AUG-1854	Michaelis McGarry/Catharina Harrigan	D. Co--ly/M. Clifford
Mcgary*	Elisam	17-AUG-1857	23-AUG-1857	Michaelis Mcgary/Maria Rochs	J Rochs/M. Rochs
McGibon* **	Bridget Ellen	29-DEC-1858	05-FEB-1859	Mc McGibon/Margueret Shean	W Murray/E. Murry
McGillan	Annam	21-MAY-1863	07-JUN-1863	Thoma McGillan/Bridgitta McGillan	J McGillan/J Cummins
McGilney	Mariam Margaritam	19-SEP-1889	23-DEC-1889	Gilberto McGilney/Hermina Racette	-----/Margarita Racette
McGiveran	William	28-JAN-1858	13-FEB-1858	Hugh McGiveran/Cath Curran	Patrick McGiveran/Lucie Kennedy
McGiveren*	Joannem	16-APR-1857	20-APR-1857	Patrici McGiveren/Lucia Cannada	H. McGiveren/C Curran
McGivern*	John	16-APR-1857	20-APR-1857	Patrick McGivern/Luci Cannada	H. McGivern/C Curran
McGlaughlin*	Jacobus	15-APR-1860	29-APR-1860	Petri McGlaughln/Margareta Heff---	Danelis Kennedy/Maria ------
McGory	Peter	15-SEP-1851	28-SEP-1851	Michael McGory/Catherine Yaeger	J. Manahan/----- Manahan
McGovern	Marguerite	19-JUN-1852	24-JUN-1852	John McGovern/Anna Carbory	J McDonald/E. Reif
McGown	Bridgittam Elizabetham	16-MAR-1862	Roberti McGown/Marguarita McGown	B. Daugherty/A. McGown
McGragor	Guilelmum	22-OCT-1882	08-NOV-1882	Michaele McGragor/Anna Walsh	Jacobus-H. Walsh/Helena Walsh
McGrat*	Thamas	26-MAR-1857	29-MAR-1857	Mathi McGrat/M--ina Gellan	J Rosseher/M. Gibben
McGrath	Anna	28-JUN-1860	15-JUL-1860	Thoma McGrath/Maria Danehar	A---tus Moriarty/Brigetta Glynn
McGrath	Catherine	28-OCT-1851	04-NOV-1851	Matthew McGrath/Ann Gillan	E Doughty/A. Medway
McGrath	Guillelmum	02-MAR-1862	24-APR-1862	Jacobi McGrath/Maria McGrath	J. Doyle/A. Rosseter
McGrath	Hugh Timothy	22-JAN-1852	08-JUN-1852	Thomas McGrath/Mary Donogher	M. McGrath/M. McGrath
McGrath	Jacobum Thadum Finely		06-FEB-1853	Joannis McGrath/Maria-Anna Burns	P Coleman/R. Burns
McGrath*	Mary -a-d--	12-OCT-1850	18-OCT-1850	Matthew McGrath/Anne Guiilly	J McKeon/M. Fitsgerald
McGrath*	Nicholaum	08-APR-1863	14-MAY-1863	Jacobi McGrath/Maria McGrath	J. Rosseter/M. Mcteavy
McGrath*	Anne				
McGrath*	Hugo	08-APR-1856	19-APR-1856	Joannis McGrath/Nanci Mckeen	J Serwe/A. Ragan
McGrath*	Hugo Gosselaum	08-APR-1856	20-APR-1856	Joannes McGrath/Nassy McKeep	J. Lower/A Rogan
McGrath*	Joannem	04-SEP-1857	03-NOV-1857	Jocabi McGrath/B. L--	J. Lierry/E. Cau--y

Surname	Given Name	Birth	Baptism	Parents	Godparents
McGrath*	John	04-SEP-1857	30-NOV-1857	James McGrath/Brigeta Lau	J. Lierry/E. Kausy
McGrath*	John				
McGrath*	Thomam	26-MAR-1857	29-MAR-1857	Matheu McGrath/Anna Gillan	J Rosseheter/M Gibbens
McGraw	Annam Jocobam	15-JAN-1854	25-JAN-1854	Mathia McGraw/Anna Gillan	P. Reys/B. McDormit
McGray	Martham Joannam	23-JUL-1860	10-SEP-1860	Patricu McGray/Anna McGray	J. Rosseter/J. Lamb
McGray*	Anna Eugenia				
McGreg	Matunum	17-AUG-1862	14-SEP-1862	Patricii McGreg/Anna McGreg	M. Lawless/A. Rosseter
McGreger*	Henricum	25-NOV-1855	27-NOV-1855	Eduardi McGreger/Sara Hemerson	H. McGreger/E. McGreger
McGreger*	Jocabum	03-FEB-1857	17-MAR-1857	Petrum McGreger/Anna Gibbens	R. Gibbens/M. Gibbens
McGregor	Catharnam	17-APR-1862	04-MAY-1862	Owenus McGregor/Maria-Anna McGregor	E. Mulony/M. Dogherty
Mcgregory	Margereth Emma	19-AUG-1876	12-OCT-1876	Petri Mcgregory/Anna Pryal	H. McGregory/K. McGregory
McGry*	Annam Geniam	24-MAY-1860	29-JUN-1860	Joannis McGry/Brigeth Gaffeny	Michael Douly/Catherine Welshs
McHenry*	John				
McHessy	Edwardum Patricium	16-MAR-1862	06-APR-1862	Joannis McHessy/Maria Kenrick	E McHessy/C Cosgrove
McHessy	Mariam Annam	01-JUN-1862	15-JUN-1862	Thoma McHessy/Catharina McHessy	D. O'conner/E. Nash
McHessy	Mauritium	11-DEC-1861	15-DEC-1861	Maurtu McHessy/Catharina McHessy	D Garry/M. Garry
McHessy*	Thomas				
McHesy*	Joannum	18-SEP-1859	18-SEP-1859	Joannes McHesy/Maria Kinevill	J. B--tten/M. --guthy
McIntosch*	Mariam	14-MAY-1856	18-MAY-1856	Jocobi McIntosch/Margeretha Galliger	J. Galliger/E. Rey
McIntosh	Margeretham Brignam	07-SEP-1857	13-SEP-1857	Jocabi McIntosh/Margeretha Galliger	J. Galliger/B. M----
McIntosh	Mariam Joannam	14-FEB-1863	15-FEB-1863	Jacobi McIntosh/Maria McIntosh	F. Halpin/M. McCune
McIntosh	Mariam Johannam	26-APR-1852	25-JUL-1852	Laughlin McIntosh/Maria Brophy	D. Conroy/A. Conroy
McIntosh*	Maria	14-MAY-1856	18-MAY-1856	James McIntosh/Margerth Galligar	----- Galligar/E. Okey
McIntyre	Joannam	21-NOV-1880	25-NOV-1880	Joanne McIntyre/Elizabeth Sheridan	B. Sheridan/A McIntyre
McKeek*	John Eduard	01-OCT-1856	19-OCT-1856	Barney McKeek/Maria McCay	J. Gruen/S. Gruen
McKeep*	Bernardum Joannem	10-OCT-1856	19-OCT-1856	Bernardi McKeep/Maria McCay	J Gren/S. Grien
McKellen	Danielem	20-MAY-1863	07-JUN-1863	Danielis McKellen/Mathilda McKellen	J Conolly/B. O'Harn
McKenrow*	Catherina	31-JUL-1855	02-OCT-1855	Edward McKenrow/Elisabeth Lo----	P. Crussick/J. Mcmann
McKeon	Catherine	04-NOV-1851	30-NOV-1851	John McKeon/Mary-Ann Mcjute-g---	J. Kennedy/C. Holleghan
McKessey*	Thomam	02-OCT-1859	09-OCT-1859	Thoma McKessey/Catherina Corbet	E McKessey/M. -tme---
McKesy	Jacobum	05-NOV-1854	08-NOV-1854	Thoma McKesy/Catherina Balweths	P. Oconner/M. Cook
McKin	Nicolaum	11-SEP-1852	21-SEP-1852	Patricii McKin/Anna Byrne	J. Kennedy/M. Byrne
McKisen*	Honnora	03-OCT-1857		Moses McKisen/Catherina Donnel	J. Hateny/C. Hateny
McKison*	Honoram	03-NOV-1857	08-NOV-1857	Moris-- McKison/Catherina Donnel	J. Hurteny/C. Hurteny
McLair	Danelim	11-APR-1860	29-APR-1860	J McLair/J. ------	
Mclaughlin*	James				
McLone*	Charles John				
McLonin*	Carolum Joannem	15-FEB-1860	26-FEB-1860	Joannes McLonin/Maria Bradcly	------ /Susanna Dorrethy
McMahan	Mary Jane	20-MAY-1851	12-OCT-1851	John McMahan/Mary Griffin	P. Manahan/N. Boh-
McMahon	Annam	15-APR-1855	17-APR-1855	Patritu McMahon/Maria-Anna ---ck-	------ -----/C. ---ck-
McMahon*	Catharine				
McMahon*	Maria Anna				
McMahone* **	Maria Anna	25-MAR-1860	12-MAR-1860	Patricii McMahone/Catherine Beck	Patricus Corlan/Maria McGons
McManhan*	Catharina	17-JAN-1860	29-JAN-1860	Thoma McManhan/Margareta Hend---in	Joannis Dunvan/Margaret O Connor
McMancal*	Catharinam Elisabeth	21-AUG-1859	01-SEP-1859	Niel McManical/Chaterina --ar--ens	P. McManikel/M. Larkins
McMarthy*	Daniel				
McMongle	Nealum	07-JAN-1863	28-JAN-1863	Neali McMongle/Catharina McMongle	H. Mctegert/M. Daugherty
McMongle*	Catharine Eliz.				
McNagle	Joannem Patricum	16-FEB-1861	25-FEB-1861	Cornelii McNagle/Catharina McNagle	P. Harican/M. Harican

Surname	Given Name	Birth	Baptism	Parents	Godparents
McNally*	James	16-SEP-1858	28-NOV-1858	James McNally/Bridget Whitten	John Jordan/Bridget Burns
McNamee	Joannem Thomam		31-MAR-1861	Michaelis McNamee/Bridgitta McNamee	M. O'Bren/M Mcgarry
McNamee	Laurentium Michaelem	10-AUG-1863	14-AUG-1863	Michaelis McNamee/Bridgitta Rice	C. Kelly/------
McNeal	Amilıam	20-OCT-1864	13-NOV-1864	Thoma McNeal/Lucretia McNeal	R. Gauther/M Strong
Mcneal*	Ellen				
McNealy	Joannem	25-JUN-1853	04-JUL-1853	Patricii McNealy/Susanna McCoy	T Durin/C. McCoy
McNee	Elizabeth	06-MAR-1858	07-MAR-1858	Michel McBuomla/Rice-McNee, Bridget	George Goff/Letitta Greenan
McNeel	Edu--- Henn--		02-MAY-1858	Michel McNeel/Sara Corny	Michel Carter/Margeta Karry
McNeel*	Elenam Mageretam	20-JUL-1860	19-AUG-1860	B--her McNeel/Elisa --held	Thomas Emerson/Sara McNeel
McNeil	Mariam	01-NOV-1862	03-NOV-1862	Patricii McNeil/Suzanna McNeil	P. McCormick/M. Call
McNeil*	Ele-ram	20-OCT-1860		B---- McNeil/Elisa --lk--	T. Emerson/S. McNeil
McNeil*	Saram	14-APR-1860	19-MAY-1860	Michelis McNeil/Sara Carly	Hueh Harrigan/Anna Mullen
McNeil*	Seena				
McNemy	Patrick	01-MAR-1856	02-MAR-1856	----- McNemy/Brigita Ryx	C. Corey/M Corey
McNennon*	Jocobum	10-SEP-1857	20-SEP-1857	Joannis McNennon/Nancy Bradely	M Dorgethy/----- -----
McNiel	Eduardum Henricum	21-APR-1858	02-MAY-1858	Mich. McNiel/Sara Corny	M. Carter/M. Carter
McNuÿt	Joannem Florian	14-OCT-1866	11-NOV-1866	Georgii McNuÿt/Cunigunda McNuÿt	J. Shleicr/E Shleier
Mctagert*	Hugh				
McTapart	Catherna	01-JAN-1860	01-JAN-1860	Eugenii McTapart/Margareta Daughterty	Daniel Daugherty/Helena Dunner
McTerger*	John				
McTigeret*	Hugo	24-OCT-1858	12-DEC-1858	Julum-Huck McTigeret/Margartha Dogety	Bernardus Nuhsis/Mary Kespertz
McTigeret*	Hugo	24-OCT-1858	12-DEC-1858	Hueh McTigeret/Margertha Dogerty	Barnadus He-fisis/Mary Herferty
McVeely	Rosam Annam	08-AUG-1854	13-AUG-1854	Patritii McVeely/Susanna Mccoy	----- Ladd/M. Ladd
McVoy	Richard Henry	28-NOV-1850	12-JAN-1851	Matthew McVoy/Catherine Welsh	----- Johnson/E. Clark
McYntyre	Helenam Odilıam	15-JAN-1861	27-JAN-1861	Patricii McYntyre/Theresa McYntyre	J. Ryan/A. McCune
Mead	Gertrudem	07-AUG-1888	28-AUG-1888	Joanne Mcad/Anna Smith	-----/Catharina Smith
Meade	Mariam		24-APR-1864	Israelis Meade/Maria Meade	A Strong/J. Parri---
Mee*	Bridget				
Mee*	Thomas				
Meer*	Brigtham		24-SEP-1859	Franciscus Meer/Margeretha Kelly	T. --annan/M Mega------
Meer*	Thomam	23-SEP-1859	24-SEP-1859	Franciscus Meer/Margeretha Kelly	J. Cokely/M. Gerrithy
Megary*	Ellisla	17-AUG-1857	23-AUG-1857	Michel Megary/Chatena Harkens	J Rochs/M. Rochs
Megun*	Henricus	25-NOV-1855	27-NOV-1855	Eduard Megun/Sera Hemerson	H. McGrevy/E. McGrevy
Mela*	Margerith		27-JUN-1857	Andrew Mela/Honorra Stenten	W. Bryon/M. Duphÿ
Melay	Andracum	05-OCT-1863	11-OCT-1863	Andraci Melay/Hanora Melay	M. Doyle/M. Doyle
Melay*	Elisabeth	12-SEP-1855	28-SEP-1855	Andreas Melay/Anne Stanton	M. Gill/A. Gill
Melaỳ*	Elisabetham	14-SEP-1855	28-SEP-1855	Andrea Melay/Anna Stantan	M. Gill/A. Gill
Melay*	Margeretham		27-JUN-1857	Andrcii Melaý/Honura Stentan	G Brown/M. Duffehy
Meleny*	Jacobum Eduardum	31-OCT-1859	12-NOV-1859	Patrıc-- Meleny/Anna Duclaır	C. McGregry/M. Melony
Meller	Flora Elisa	13-APR-1877	06-MAY-1877	Francii Meller/Sophia Shnnard-Snow	E. Tremble/A. Shinard
Meller*	Maria	09-APR-1856	09-APR-1856	Chales Meller/Rose Gosselain	C. Duchane/J. Chrıstınn
Melly*	Annatattam	01-SEP-1857	03-NOV-1857	Corali Melly/Brigetha Lenshs	J. Melly/A. Melly
Melly*	Augusta	01-SEP-1857	30-NOV-1857	Charles Melly/Brigıta Llenchs	J Molly/A. Melly
Melon*	Marie		27-SEP-1857	John Melon/Elsabt Whelan	M. Melon/A Garety
Melon*	Martham	18-SEP-0185	27-SEP-1857	Joannis Melon/Elizabeth Whelan	M. Melon/A. Garrety
Melonn*	Maria-Anna	01-JUL-1857	12-JUL-1857	Patrick Melonn/Anna Dollan	J. Harlon/M. Dollon
Melony	Patrick Charles	17-SEP-1850	22-SEP-1850	Michael Melony/Catherine Melony	J. Mel---/C. Kelly
Melony*	Mariam Annam		12-JUL-1857	Patricii Melony/Anna Dollon	J. Harlon/M Dollon
Melony*	Mary Ann	29-MAY-1858	20-JUN-1858	James Melony/Mary Kelly	Florence McCarthy/Elızabeth Kelly

93

Surname	Given Name	Birth	Baptism	Parents	Godparents
Menck	Jane Melice	14-JUN-1854	09-MAY-1858	William Menck/Ellen Mitchell	Peter Bohen/Emelia Kelly
Mené*	Henricu Georgeus	24-APR-1858	16-MAY-1858	Joannes-Josephus Mené/Maria-Theresia Snesens	Jocanbus Larose/Maria Morris
Mengel	Joannem Rudolphum	04-APR-1894	08-APR-1894	Joanne Mengel/Azilda Diette	Josephus Diette/Maria Mengel
Mengel	Mariam Mabel	16-JUL-1896	19-JUL-1896	Joanne Mengel/Ovila Diette	Medardus Comeau/Mathilda Diette
Mengle	Josephum Fredericum	17-SEP-1886	26-SEP-1886	Joanne Mengle/Azilda Diette	Josephus Diette/Margaritta Justin
Mengtel*	------		21-NOV-1858	Valentine Mengtel/Marguerite Mengtel	----- Joans Heilt/----- Mosel
Menzel*	Polum	21-APR-1860	25-APR-1860	Valentim Menzel/Margeret Josten	Charles Tell/Jane- Plai-
Mere	Martam	06-AUG-1878		Elderick Mere/Lucie Mere	
Mernardy	Mariam Annam	02-OCT-1854	29-OCT-1854	Michaelis Mernardy/Joanna Colter	M. Stuk/H. Harman
Metivier	Josephinam	11-FEB-1869	21-MAR-1869	Narcissi Metivier/Zephirina Metivier	Mathildus Derouin/Celina Derouin
Meunich*	Emmam Estellam	08-APR-1859	07-MAY-1859	Guillielmi Meunich/Maria-Anna Mitchell	J. Furgusson/M. Furgusson
Meunier	Mariam Ludovicam	01-JUN-1864	04-JUL-1864	Joannis-Joseph Meunier/Maria-Theresa Meunier	J Houssos/M. Tordeur
Meunier	Nazare Olivarium	13-SEP-1879	14-SEP-1879	Nazare Meunier/Felicitata Hébert	O Comtas/F. Hebert
Meunier	Paulinam Victoriam	12-OCT-1865	22-JAN-1866	Joannis-Josephi Meunier/Maria-Theresa Meunier	P. Velam/A. Morris
Meunier-Lapierre	Albertum	25-MAY-1881	29-MAY-1881	Nazario Meunier-Lapierre/Felicita Hébert	Cyriacus Meunier-Lapierre/Emelia Hébert
Meunier-Lapierre	Leonem Vitalem	25-APR-1885	05-MAY-1885	Nazario Meunier-Lapierre/Felicitate Hebert	Vitalis Langlois-Fontaine/Flavia Cyr
Meyer	Catharinam	16-JUL-1860	19-SEP-1860	Nicholai Meyer/Barbara Meyer	W. Giebel/C. Yo-k
Meyer	Hazel Ethel	10-MAR-1908	10-MAY-1908	Joanne Meyer/Ina Beaudry	Antonius-Carl Meyer/Ursula Charron-Beaudry
Meyer	Herbertus Ovid	28-SEP-1904	10-MAY-1908	Martino Tates/Lavina Marcoux	Antonius-Carl Meyer/Ursula Charron-Beaudry
Michel	Edward	16-MAY-1852	15-JUN-1852	Patrick Michel/Jane Carr	J. McCullogh/M. Ma--en
Michote	Mariam Ludovicam	24-JAN-1869	31-JAN-1869	Deodati Michote/Olivina Mocquin	Julianus Mocquin/Mathilda Mocquin
Michote	Melvinam	21-MAR-1871	26-MAR-1871	Deodati Michote/Olivina Mocquin	Leo Edouin/Zoah Mocquin
Miller	Carolum	28-MAR-1868	12-APR-1868	Francisci Miller/Sophia Snow	Baptista Cyr/Emilia Chenar
Miller	Eduardum	25-DEC-1869	09-JAN-1870	Francisci Miller/Sophia Miller	Nicholaus Lamouche/Marcellina Lamouche
Miller	Franciscum	08-NOV-1861	01-DEC-1861	Francisci Miller/Sophia Miller	J. Marcou/H. Snow
Miller	Henricum	12-JAN-1869	09-MAY-1869	Isaaci Miller/Agnetia Fontaine	Petrus Dufresne/Onesima Miller
Miller	Isidorum	25-JAN-1871	12-FEB-1871	Francisci Miller/Sophia Miller	Isidorus Ebert/Maria Ebert
Miller	Josephinam	25-JUL-1866	18-AUG-1866	Francisci Miller/Sophia Miller	A Chenar/L. Tessier
Miller	Petrum Isaacum	16-FEB-1873	02-MAR-1873	Francisci Miller/Sophia Snow	Israel Bessete/Julia Bessete
Miller	Sophiam	26-FEB-1865	12-MAR-1865	Francisci Miller/Sophia Miller	F. Robort/M. Robert
Miller*	Mariam Juliam		04-APR-1856	Charoli Miller/Rosa Gosselain	C. Duchane/J ------
Miné	Franciscam Adelaidam	16-JUN-1870	03-JUL-1870	Joannis-Joseph Miné/Maria Miné	Xaverius Hurtot/Maria Juliana Miné
Miné	Mariam Clarissam		20-OCT-1867	Josephi Miné/Maria-Theresa Miné	A. Lafontaine/E. Lafontaine
Miné*	Henricum Georgium	24-APR-1858	16-MAY-1858	Joannis Miné/Maria-Theresa S-----	J. Raise/M. M-ire
Mishot	Josephinam	22-MAY-1863	23-MAY-1863	Deodati Mishot/Olivia Mishot	F. Mocquin/Zoah Bourdeau
Mishote	Franciscum Josephum	18-MAY-1867	19-MAY-1867	Deodati Mishote/Olivia Mishote	E. Dupuis/T Mocquin
Mishote	Olivinam	10-MAR-1865	19-MAR-1865	Desidati Mishote/Olivina Mishote	J Mocquin/F. Mocquin
Mitchell	Eduardum Melvil	27-FEB-1894	11-MAR-1894	Josepho Mitchell/Maria Smith	Eduardus Smith/Anna Smith
Mitchell	Florentiam Annam	13-SEP-1887	23-OCT-1887	Josepho Mitchell/Maria-Lousia Smith	Joannes-C Smith/Anna Smith
Mitchell	Franciscum Josephum	21-NOV-1897	28-NOV-1897	Josepho Mitchell/Maria Smith	Felicianus-J Hannon/Eduardum Smith
Mitchell	Jerome Edward	21-OCT-1920	07-NOV-1920	Francis-Joseph Mitchell/Adella Reichelt	Melville-Ed Mitchell/Angeline Graltor-Mitchell
Mitchell	Mabel Mariam	14-NOV-1885	06-DEC-1885	Josephi Mitchell/Maria Smith	Franciscus Smith/Maria Brosnahan
Mitchell	Maud Genefvam	15-AUG-1890	24-AUG-1890	Josepho Mitchell/Maria Smith	Joannem-C. Smith/Margaritta O'Connel
Mitten*	Joannem	30-JUL-1858	01-AUG-1858	Michelis Mitten/Ellen Kelly	Ed---dus Coffy/Brigetha O'Connor
Mo-r*	Antonius	12-JUL-1855	09-AUG-1855	Joannes Mo-r/Anna-Chateria -itten	A. Llen/C. -ndmiller
Mocquin	Alfredum	23-FEB-1872	03-MAR-1872	Alphonsi Mocquin/Adelina Mocquin	Ludovicus Lyonars/Henrica Mocquin
Mocquin	Alphonsum Franciscum	01-JUN-1865	10-JUN-1865	Alphonsi Mocquin/Ludovica Mocquin	Vitalis Edouin/Mathilda Mocquin
Mocquin	Franciscum Alexandrum	14-DEC-1869	16-JAN-1870	Francisci Mocquin/Henrica Porcheron	L. Mocquin/L. Mocquin
Mocquin	Josephum			Josephi Mocquin/Adelina Mocquin	Antonius Boivin/Olivia Mocquin

94

Surname	Given Name	Birth	Baptism	Parents	Godparents
Mocqun	Josephum Georgium	08-JAN-1869	17-JAN-1869	Joseph Mocqun/Vitalina Mocqun	Franciscus Mocqun/Zoah Moqun
Mocqun	Liam	24-NOV-1868	06-DEC-1868	Joseph Mocqun/Mathilda Barbeau	Noah Riendeau/Ophilia Dumas
Mocqun	M. Dorotheam	02-AUG-1867	18-AUG-1867	Joseph Moqun/Vitalina Mocqun	J Mocqun/J. Odet
Mocqun	Magdalenam	04-DEC-1870	04-DEC-1870	Joseph Mocqun/Mathilda Mocqun	Josephus Dumas/Ludovica Duquete
Mocqun	Napoleons	11-AUG-1873	11-AUG-1873	Joseph Mocqun/Mathla Desbarbaux	Leo Martin/Eleonora Martin
Mocqun	Petrum Georgium	20-OCT-1867	20-OCT-1867	Francisci Mocqun/Henrietta Mocqun	A. Gilbert/A. Mocqun
Mocqun	Zephirmum	05-SEP-1871	10-SEP-1871	Joseph Mocqun/Vitalina Mocqun	Alexius Mocqun/Anastasia Mocqun
Mocqun*	Francis Xavier				
Mogan	Joannem	14-JUL-1863	16-JUL-1863	Michaelis Mogan/Catharina Mogan	T Netlan/J. Daugherty
Mogan	Mariam		14-JUL-1861	Michaelis Mogan/Catharina Mogan	T St--yn/M. Costello
Mogan	Sibi Lucy		16-NOV-1856	Michel Mogan/Cath Harman	M. ----ull/M. Flagerty
Mogan*	Thomas				
Moin	Franciscum Exs.	19-JUN-1856	24-AUG-1856	Francisci Moin/Clothilda Lontain	P. Morris/M Cahier
Moqun	Narssisum	19-NOV-1876	19-NOV-1876	Josephus Moiqun/Phitaline Nodet	L Edon/M Moiquin
Moleton	Mary	28-MAR-1858	01-APR-1858	Nicholas Moleton/Hélene Lossillion	Richard Lossillion/Mary Lossillion
Molle--	Bridgidam	31-JAN-1854	02-FEB-1854	Michaelis Molle--/Maria Krissane	J O'Bren/A. Kilroy
Molleur	Delphine	02-SEP-1879	14-SEP-1879	Germano Molleur/Maria Landerman	A Lardermann/M. Cyr
Molleus	Mariam Rosam	06-MAY-1886	06-MAY-1886	Germano Molleus/Maria Landerman	---- ----/Pomela Landerman
Montier	Josephum	02-OCT-1871	03-OCT-1871	Joannis Moniter/Maria Hubert	Olivierus Hurtot/Julia Ebert
Montblot	Franciscum Alvidam	23-DEC-1866	06-JAN-1867	Moysis Montblot/Josephina Montblot	T Rondeau/J. Pedlant
Montn	Franciscum	30-AUG-1868	05-SEP-1868	Michaelis Montn/Mathilda Montn	Franciscus Beauchemin/Olivia Beauchemin
Monts	Amedum	24-APR-1868	26-APR-1868	Amédéi Monts/Julie Monts	Josephus Gayet/Magdalena Gayet
Moor	Ann Maria	04-AUG-1850	15-SEP-1850	John Moor/Catherine Tailor	P Nott/A. Julshi
Moor*	Antonium	12-JUL-1855	05-AUG-1855	Joannis Moor/Anna-Catherina Tellen	A Tellen/C. Redmuller
Moor*	Edmundum	24-JUL-1858	01-AUG-1858	Thoma Moor/Brdgitta Branan	M. McCabe/A. Leaghry
Moor*	Edumund	24-JUL-1858	01-AUG-1858	Thoma Moor/Brigetha Bro----	Michel McCabe/Anna Lierry
Moor*	Jane				
Moor*	Margeretham	15-NOV-1856	23-NOV-1856	Thoma Moor/Brgetha Bremin	P Fitzpatrick/E. Baken
Moor*	Margerita	19-NOV-1856	23-NOV-1856	Thamas Moor/Brigita Brannan	P. Fits---uck/E. -a-e-
Moore	Anna Catherna	11-DEC-1851	22-FEB-1852	John Moore/Anna-Catherina Feelan	H Julich/A. Ruthaus
Moore	Georgium Evert	26-MAR-1902	10-APR-1902	David Moore/Joanna Lepine	Josephus Lepine/Sophia Beaudreault
Moore	Gulielmum	17-FEB-1855	19-FEB-1855	H--- Moore/Brigidda Brennan	J Duly/M. Lewer
Moore	Ieronimum Laurentum	04-APR-1908	14-APR-1908	David Moore/Eugenia-Viola LePne	---- ----/May Lepine
Moore	Joannem	10-DEC-1860	29-DEC-1860	Thoma Moore/Bridgetta Moore	J Bacon/H Kelly
Moore	John	02-MAR-1858	03-MAR-1858	James Moore/Mary Dunn	John Dunn/Catherine Dunn
Moore	Josephum Walter Haroldem	04-AUG-1903	12-OCT-1903	Davide Moore/Genefeva Lepine	Carolum Marcoux/Arzela Beaudreau
Moore	Juliam Elizabetham		21-DEC-1862	Thola Moore/Bridgitta Moore	G Rochel/A. Rosseter
Moore	Lauram Gabellam Corinam	24-MAY-1910	31-AUG-1910	David Moore/Eugenia LePine	---- ----/Grace LePine
Moore	Maria	13-JUL-1860	15-JUL-1860	Joannis Moore/Maria Dunn	Michael Gaffney/Catherine Doyle
Moore	Stellam Etha Mariam	21-AUG-1905	14-SEP-1905	David Moore/Eugenia LePine	---- ----/Cedulia Beaudreau-Dubois
Moore*	Johanna	23-NOV-1858	29-NOV-1858	Patrick Moore/Rosanna Twig	David Twigg/Mary Twig
Moore*	Mary				
Moqun	Annam Emeraldam	29-APR-1906	13-MAY-1906	Alexandro Moqun/Anna Moqun	Edmundus Moqun/Addie Moqun
Moqun	Cordeliam	11-FEB-1885	18-FEB-1885	Josepho Moqun/Vitalina Audette	Joannes Rondeau/Julia Cheffe
Moqun	Elizabetham		24-AUG-1862	Francisci Moqun/Henrica Moqun	M. Dieudonné/Zoah Moqun
Moqun	Ernestum Hilarium	07-JUL-1883	22-JUL-1883	Josepho Moqun/Vitalus Beaudette	Hilarius Landermann/Delima Moqun
Moqun	Joannem Baptistam	13-OCT-1879	26-OCT-1879	Josepho Moqun/Vitalina Rudet	T Chapleau/E. Hollegen
Moqun	Josephum Franciscum	22-APR-1909	05-MAY-1909	Alexandro Moqun/Anna Moqun	Elmerus Gagnier/Stella Moqun
Moqun	Juliam Josephinam	26-SEP-1886	10-OCT-1886	Josepho Moqun/Vitalina Audet	Franciscus Maurice/Josephina Michatte

95

Surname	Given Name	Birth	Baptism	Parents	Godparents
Moqun	Ludovicam Emmam	17-JUN-1893	25-JUN-1893	Josepho Moqun/Vitalina Audet	Georgius Audet/Ludovica Lavigne
Moqun	Mariam			Joseph Mocqun/Methda Marbo	E. Dumand/A. Servait
Moqun	Mariam Alphosmam	11-APR-1881	12-APR-1881	Francisco Moqun/Maria Asselin	O Papineau/A Agagner
Moqun	Mariam Josephinam	27-DEC-1905	31-DEC-1905	Nahemias Moqun/Maria Ferndinand	Alexander Moquin/Isabella Ferdinand-Moqun
Moqun	Mariam Zoam	07-AUG-1906	12-AUG-1906	Georgio Moqun/Philomena Tromblay	Alphonsus Snow/Exilda Tesser-Snow
Moqun	Noel	08-AUG-1881	11-SEP-1881	Josepho Moqun/Vitalina Audet	Ludovicus Landerman/Flora Loiselle
Moqun	Omnium Santorun	14-JAN-1878	24-JAN-1878	Josephi Mocquin/Etalie Odet	J. Fraine/V. Odet
Moqun	Vitalinam	04-JUN-1864	05-JUN-1864	Josephi Moqun/Vitalina Mocquin	D. Mishote/Zoah Riendeau
Moqun	Zoeam Apollinam	14-FEB-1890	02-MAR-1890	Josepho Moqun/Vitalina Audet	Georgius Langlois/Mare Moqun
Moqun*	Franciscum	05-JUL-1860	15-JUL-1860	Francisci Moqun/A.--- Ducomb	Vital Langlois/Julia Mangan
Moqun**	Andrium	23-DEC-1874	07-DEC-1874	Josephi Moqun/Vitalina Odet	Andreas Prefontaine/Matilda Moqun
Moran	Mary Francis	09-MAY-1852	08-JUN-1852	Thomas Moran/Marguerite McGrath	J. McGrath/A. McGrath
Moran*	John Patrick	27-OCT-1858	12-JAN-1859	Michel Moran/Cath Kelly	Thos Hoeg/Julie Ho--d
Moran*	John Patrick	18-APR-1858	12-JAN-1859	Michel Moran/Cath Kelly	Thos Hoey/Julie Hoyer
Moran*	John Patrick				
Moran*	Laurence				
Moran*	Laurentius	20-FEB-1860	22-APR-1860	Michaeli Moran/Catherina Kelly	Thomas McCarty/Margareta Kily
Morgan	Hélenam Adeliam	08-DEC-1868	15-JUN-1872	Archer Morgan/Martina Burrel	Petrus Burrel/Maria Burrel
Morgan	Mariam Josepham	31-MAR-1876	02-APR-1876	Francisci Morgan/Josephina Roy	L Leroy/M. Roy
Morgan*	John				
Morgan*	Maria	13-APR-1857	20-APR-1857	Michel Morgan/Jane Cay	J. McTevy/M Mangan
Moriarty*	Catherine	28-NOV-1858	29-NOV-1858	Morris Moriarty/Ann Fitzgerald	Thos McGrath/Mary O'Sullivan
Moriarty*	Catherine				
Moriaty	Thomam	24-APR-1853	05-JUL-1853	Michaelis Moriaty/Maria Connor	J. Connor/B McGovern
Moris*	Jean Baptista	27-JUL-1856	22-AUG-1856	Louis Morris/Sa--- Peren	J. Biron/M. Peren
Morris	Adelnam	28-OCT-1854	06-NOV-1854	Petri Morris/D. Peron	F. Morris/M. Peron
Morris	Adelinam	11-DEC-1854	20-FEB-1855	Francisci Morris/Carolina Lantin	C. Bresseaux/M. Morris
Morris	Frederic				
Morris	Guillelmum	10-JUN-1864	12-JUN-1864	Guillelmi Morris/Delima Morris	A Grizet/C. Deschènes
Morris	Marguaritam Annam	13-FEB-1863	22-FEB-1863	Francisci Morris/Suzanna Morris	T Dufresne/C. Dufresne
Morris	Mariam Rosaliam		07-APR-1870	Angeli Morris/Maria Morris	Paulus Vilain/Anna Morris
Morris	Mary Victoria	01-MAR-1851	09-MAR-1851	Pierre Morris/Clotilde Peron	J. Dumas/M. Peron
Morris	Victoriam	07-JUN-1862	29-JUN-1862	Guillelmi Morris/DeLima Morris	T. Das/-. Morris
Morris*	Elisa-Nanci	09-DEC-1855	06-JAN-1856	Perre Morris/Clotuna Peron	F. Morris/C. Peron
Morris*	Elisam	05-JAN-1856	06-JAN-1856	Petri Morris/Cealina Peren	F. Morris/C Peren
Morris*	Joannem Baptistam	27-JUL-1856	24-AUG-1856	Ludovici Morris/Sophia Peron	J. Peron/M. Peron
Morris*	Maria E--a	29-SEP-1857	13-OCT-1857	Olivier Morris/Margeta Morris	D Petit/F. Morris
Morris*	Rasaliam	08-JUL-1858	16-SEP-1858	Petri-Francis Morris/Clemtina Lantin	Paulus Cochi/Anna Rahier
Morris*	Rosalie				
Morrison	Edwardum		19-OCT-1869	Jacobi Morrison/Lucretia Morrison	Joannes Morrison/Emilia Bird
Morrison	Elizabetham		18-JUL-1852		P Harnois/E. Joubert
Morrisson	Joannem	22-FEB-1854	21-APR-1854	Richardi Morrisson/Maria Bruderell	J Molylou/M. Mullen
Morrisy	Terence	06-OCT-1850	28-OCT-1850	Terence Morrissy/Catherine Kelly	M. Smith/M. Horn
Mortin*	Eugenius Eduardus	11-MAR-1860	19-MAY-1860	Thoma Mortin/Margaret Beasly	Thomas Craly/Maria Connaghty
Moses	Mariam	08-OCT-1899	28-OCT-1899	Habib Moses/Amina Fatouche	Josephus Ferres/Anna Hassef
Moses	Mariam Anastasiam	16-JUN-1903	19-JUL-1903	Abib Moses/Amina Factous	Josephus Ferris/Warde Anton
Moses	Michaelem	12-MAY-1905	27-MAY-1905	Habeb Moses/Amena Platurok	Josephus Faris/Anna Asef
Moses	Michaelem	12-MAY-1905	21-MAY-1905	Habeeb Moses/Amena Platurch	Josephus Faris/Anna Aseff
Mosher	Ednam Elizabeth	15-MAY-1890	18-MAY-1890	Lafayette Mosher-Mangin/Delia Leduc	Mirton Mosher/Maria Cuffey

96

Surname	Given Name	Birth	Baptism	Parents	Godparents
Mosher	Ludovicum Lafayette		24-DEC-1880		-----/M. Doire-Bondy
Motesdorf	Catharinam	11-MAY-1861	05-JAN-1861	Petri Motesdorf/Maria Motesdorf	J Hansen/C. Totz--
Moulvey	Catherine	14-APR-1858	25-APR-1858	Prrick Moulvey/Mary-Ann Daly	Thos Ready/Helena Ready
Mourris	Theodorum	27-JUN-1854	16-JUL-1854	Petri Mourris/Coletta Peron	P Callier/M. Delan
Moyese*	Annam Mariam	22-MAR-1860	02-APR-1860	Own Moyese/Maria-Anne Melone	Patricus Melone/Cathera Melone
Mucker*	Christoph				
Mulady	Marguaritam Juliam	13-FEB-1864	14-FEB-1864	Roberti Mulady/Maria Mulady	M. Mulady/A. Aslon
Mullen	Bridgittam	25-JAN-1862	26-JAN-1862	Joannis Mullen/Anna Mullen	C. Ma-ly/B. Maley
Mullen	James	18-APR-1852	21-APR-1852	Hugh Mullen/Mary McCoil	M. Cam/----- Cam
Mullen	Josephum		03-FEB-1861	-----/Maria-Anna Mullen	G. Dooley/A Dooley
Mullen	Rosannem	18-JUL-1863	19-JUL-1863	Patricii Mullen/Maria Mullen	J Murry/B. Murry
Mullen	Saram	07-MAY-1853	03-JUL-1853	Hughes Mullen/Maria McCoy	P. Makin/B. Kain
Mullen*	Juliam	20-JUN-1856	22-JUN-1856	Michaelis Mullen/Maria Chrismen	J. Mullen/C. Gargan
Mullen*	Julie	20-JUN-1856	22-JUN-1856	Michel Mullen/Marie Chrman	J Mullen/C Gargan
Mullen*	Mariam	04-SEP-1856	13-SEP-1856	Hugo Mullen/Maria McCay	-----/R. Mullen
Mullen*	Mariam Annam	25-JUN-1857	28-JUN-1857	Joannes Mullen/Anna Miller	P. Tavas/M Cussen
Mullen*	Michael				
Muller	Franciscum	27-AUG-1863	06-SEP-1863	Francisci Muller/Sophia Muller	J. Boldin/L. Boldin
Mulligan	Thomam		07-SEP-1863	Thoma Mulligan/Maria Mulligan	P. Mcnally/C Haze
Mullon*	Maria	04-SEP-1856	13-SEP-1856	Hueh Mullon/Maria McCay	R. Mullon/----- -----
Mulony	Georgum Patricium	07-FEB-1863	22-FEB-1863	Patrici Mulony/Anna Mulony	G Kelly/M. Dolan
Mulony*	Mariam Annam	29-MAY-1858	20-JUN-1858	Jacobi Mulony/Maria Kelly	F. McCarthy/E Kelly
Mulum*	Michaelem	08-JUL-1859	10-JUL-1859	John Mulum/Anna Melan	M. Mul--/M. Chrisson
Mulunsens*	Mariam	03-AUG-1856	07-SEP-1856	Petri Mulunsens/Susana Bodricau	A Declou/R. Gautier
Munch*	Emma Estella				
Muné	Ludovicum	08-OCT-1874	25-OCT-1874	Francisci Muné/Sophia Shnard	George Bodum-/Sophia Shnard
Munier	-olinham	18-DEC-1877	01-JAN-1888	Naser Munier/Filiceti Hubert	P. Fernet/ wife
Munier	Elizabetham	27-JUN-1854	09-JUL-1854	Isaac Munier/Susanna Hadden	F Munier/C. Muner
Munier	Fredricum	05-JAN-1878	27-JAN-1878	-ia- Munier/Agnes Fontaine	F. Lafoi/D. Defraine
Munier**	Josephum Alphonsum	23-DEC-1878	01-DEC-1878	Franc-- Munier/Sophia Chinard	J. Robert/S Munier
Muphy*	Honoram		02-JAN-1858	Thoma Muphy/Helena Dam	M. Dolon/J. Boni
Murhy*	Janne	02-JAN-1857	09-JAN-1857	Patrick Murhy/Alicia Murphy	J McCarty/M. Word
Murph-*	Gulielmus Petrus	03-MAY-1857	07-JUN-1857	John-W. Murph-/Ellis Lasy	G. -----/E. M-----
Murph--*	Mariam Eugeniam	02-AUG-1859	14-AUG-1859	Joannes-Wil Murph--/Helena Casy	J. Martin/----- Martin
Murphy	Catharnam	14-JUL-1862	21-JUL-1862	Michaelis Murphy/Maria Murphy	J Kelly/M Callaghan
Murphy	Catharnam	18-DEC-1860	23-DEC-1860	Patricii Murphy/Joanna Murphy	J. Vaughn/C. Walsh
Murphy	Helenam	24-AUG-1862	24-AUG-1862	Thoma Murphy/Henrica Murphy	G Clarke/M. McDermott
Murphy	Joannem	11-JAN-1862	12-JAN-1862	Joannis Murphy/Alicia Murphy	J. Rosseter/A. Mckee
Murphy	Marguerit Ann	03-NOV-1851	23-NOV-1851	William Murphy/Eliza O'Neal	M. Linam/E. McGown
Murphy	Sarahm Ann		11-JUN-1863	Joannis-W. Murphy/Bridgitta Murphy	F. Clarke/A. Rosseter
Murphy	Thomam Jacobum	18-MAY-1863	04-JUL-1863	Timothei Murphy/Anna Murphy	M. Burke/J. Murphy
Murphy	Veronicam	26-NOV-1863	10-JAN-1864	Bernardi Murphy/Anna Murphy	J Murphy/A. Emerson
Murphy*	Daniel				
Murphy*	Danelis	31-MAY-1860	03-JUN-1860	Michaeli Murphy/Maria-Anna Ker--on	Joanna Manly/Maria Lienshes
Murphy*	Elenam	29-OCT-1858	07-NOV-1858	Patrick Murphy/Joanna Daly	Joannes Rayan/Lorta Wall
Murphy*	Ellen				
Murphy*	Gulielmum Patricium	31-MAY-1857	07-JUN-1857	Joannes-W. Murphy/Elles Casy	W. Phalan/E McGrath
Murphy	Honnora	08-APR-1857	14-APR-1857	Patrick Murphy/Jonanna Daly	J. Gille/R. Kelly
Murphy	Honnoram	08-APR-1857	14-APR-1857	Patrici Murphy/Joanna Daly	J. Gill/T. Kelly

97

Surname	Given Name	Birth	Baptism	Parents	Godparents
Murphy*	Honora	07-JAN-1858		Thos Murphy/Helen Murphy	Mcl Desoln/Julia Coonc
Murphy*	Jeremiam	30-MAY-1858	07-JUN-1858	Jeremia Murphy/Anna Wall	E Wall/M Rıng
Murphy*	Jerımas	30-MAY-1858	07-JUN-1858	Jeremas Murphy/Anna Wall	Eduard Wall/Margerta Ring
Murphy*	Joannes	02-JAN-1857	09-JAN-1857	Patrcii Murphy/Anna Ward	F. McCarty/M. Ward
Murphy*	Joseph				
Murphy*	Josephum		04-SEP-1859	Jeremi Murphy/Anna Wall	C McCla--/Mrs Brassehcter
Murphy*	Maria	02-JAN-1856	06-JAN-1856	Jeremas Murphy/Anne Wall	H Bellar/M Kelly
Murphy*	Mariam	02-JAN-1856	06-JAN-1856	Jeremei Murphy/Anna Wall	H Benner/M. Kelly
Murphy*	Mary Eugena				
Murphy*	Thamas	19-DEC-1857	20-DEC-1857	Michel Murphy/Mıs-- Kendell	T Kiggan/M. Harkins
Murphy*	Thomam	19-DEC-1857	20-DEC-1857	Michaelıs Murphy/Maria Kevel	T Kiggen/M. Harken
Murphy*	Thomam	19-JUL-1859	24-JUL-1859	Thomas Murphy/Elena Murphy	P Doyle/M. Fitssimmens
Murphy*	Thomas				
Murras*	Lisabetham	04-MAR-1859	11-APR-1859	Norberti Murras/Edem--- Pariso	M. Deroché
Murray	Guielmum	21-MAR-1854	23-APR-1854	Thoma Murray/Catherına Cramen	J. Bary.M. Murray
Murray	Gullelmı	17-DEC-1859	18-DEC-1859	Marck Murray/Cath--a David	Joannis McEssy/Marie Fitsimmons
Murray	Henry	05-SEP-1851	25-DEC-1851	Robert Murray/Elmre Pariscau	L. Landermann/A. Malheur
Murray	Jacobum	19-AUG-1852	03-SEP-1852	Gillelmı Murray/Marguerita Murray	P Servatius/G. Servatius
Murray	James	07-JAN-1852	20-JAN-1852	Thomas Murray/Catherine Brennan	P. -----/M. O'Bren
Murray	Joannem	08-MAY-1854	23-JUN-1854	Matthei Murray/Maria Levin	------ -----/M. Gallien
Murray	Marguerite Ann	19-JUL-1851	24-FEB-1852	Thomas Murray/Marguerite Clements	J. Murray/C Murray
Murray	Roseanna	05-AUG-1850	22-SEP-1850	William Murray/Marguerite Murray	J. Harkins/C Harkins
Murry	Catharnam	15-JUL-1862	04-AUG-1862	Thoma Murry/Maria Murry	P. Mo-ken/A. Mo-ken
Murry*	Elizabeth				
Murry*	Matıldam	08-JUN-1855	27-JUN-1855	Roberti Murry/Matilda Panso	E Rochet/M Defrane
Murry*	Matilde	08-JUN-1855	27-JUN-1855	Robert Murry/Matilde Pariso	E. Robert/M Dufrainc
Murry	Franciscus	27-JUL-1853	04-SEP-1853	Joannis Murry/Chaterına Garrety	J. Connoty/E. Mollon
Murtha*	Bernardum	29-SEP-1857	20-OCT-1857	Joannis Murtha/Brıgetha Kelligan	J O'Brayan/S Mangan
Mury	Mariam	14-JUL-1853	14-AUG-1853	Joannis Murý/Maria Pouwer	T. Hanson/M. Col-on
Myer*	James	14-MAR-1854	02-DEC-1855	Nicolus Myer/Babera Snyder	J. Kofman/M. Snyder
Nary	Mariam	07-OCT-1863	07-OCT-1863	Jacobi Nary/Marguarita Nary	J Nary/J. Nary
Naset	Margartam	20-APR-1854	14-MAY-1854	Jacobi Naset/Margarita Colbat	P Mc-a--/M. Jenks
Nash	Guillelmum	06-OCT-1861	07-OCT-1861	Jacobi Nash/Marguerita Nash	D. Macken/M. Macken
Nash*	Jocabum	19-MAY-1857	23-MAY-1857	G---- Nash/Maria Harrat	J. Connor/J. Nash
Nash*	Jocobus	19-MAY-1857	23-MAY-1857	William Nash/Marie Harret	J Canal/J Nash
Nash*	John	24-AUG-1858	25-SEP-1858	James Nash/Marguerite Corbet	John Kennan/Julia Curran
Nash*	John				
Nast-Abel	Mariam Ellam		19-DEC-1909	Eduardo Nast-Abel/Ida Abel-Nast	Arthurus Jarvis/Gratta Jarvis
Naughlin*	-				
Naughtn*	Cath	02-APR-1859	13-APR-1859	Anthony Naughtin/Mary Jordan	H. Jordan/B Jordan
NcNealy	Pat---um	10-MAR-1861	14-MAR-1861	Patrcıı NcNealy/Susanna NcNealy	J. McCullen/S. Douly
Neary	Joannem Thomam	13-JUL-1863	14-JUL-1863	Patrcıı Neary/E lzabetha Neary	T Ganon/E. Eagan
Nehlburg*	Elızabetham	01-JUL-1855	01-JUL-1855	Josephı Nelhburg/Helena Ineglagen	M. Smetz/E. Hendun
Neilen	Catharnam	13-JUL-1862	13-JUL-1862	---- Neilen/Maria Neilen	M Maghan/C Litch
Neilen	Joannem	10-AUG-1863	15-AUG-1863	Thoma Neilen/Maria Neilen	D Stanton/S. Flanegan
Neis	Irwin Eduardum	24-JUL-1906	23-SEP-1906	Eduardo Neis/Laura Donet	Josephus Gratton/Aurolia LePıne-Gratton
Neiss	Josephum Ralph	28-AUG-1904	11-SEP-1904	Eduardo Neiss/Laura Daunais	Josephus Daunais/Odelia Lepıne
Neitman	Joannem	24-SEP-1860	21-JUN-1863	Georgıı Neitman/Alicia Neitman	P. Cronan/M. Drıscoll
Nelburg*	Joannes	28-JUL-1851	01-JUL-1855	Josephı Wethburgburg/Elızabetha Ineglanger	M. Smetz/E. Kendun

98

Surname	Given Name	Birth	Baptism	Parents	Godparents
Nelly	Huye		18-DEC-1859	Jacobi Nelly/Julia Smet	William Brennan/Joanna Herman
Nelson	Henricam Gladys	01-SEP-1895	01-OCT-1904	Gulielmo Nelson/Helena Gaffney	Thomas Lucier/Maria Kelly
Nelson	Oliverum	16-OCT-1879	19-OCT-1879	Henrici Nelson/Henrietta Beaulieu	H Lajeunesse/L Leduc
Nemer	Joannem Josephum Wade	07-DEC-1907	19-JAN-1908	Farıs Nemmer/Sopha Nemmer	Josephus Farrs/Rosa Farrs
Nepoch	Gulielmum Carolum	09-OCT-1861	13-OCT-1861	Guillelmı Nepoch/Elizabetha Nepoch	G Rochet/C. Rogers
Neppach	Franciscam	11-APR-1861	21-MAR-1862	Guillelmı Neppach/Elizabetha Neppach	M. Hanson/----- -----
Neppach	Vincentium	27-SEP-1865	19-NOV-1865	Guillelmı Neppach/Elizabetha Neppach	V Hırsh/M Annen
Nerat*	Josephınam	19-MAR-1860	12-JUL-1860	----- Nerat/E Sın---	F. H---
Nettleson	Carolınam Florentıam	03-APR-1877	15-JUN-1877	Caroli-Henrıe Nettleson/Catherıa-Elısabet Bekket	W Welshs/N. Welshs
Nettleson	Carolum Shath	03-APR-1877	15-JUN-1877	Caroli-Henrıe Nettleson/Catherıa-Elısabet Bekket	T Flud/J. Mcmullen
Newell	Petrum	17-AUG-1854	27-AUG-1854	Theophılı Newell/Charlotta Snow	P Legne/M. Snow
Newmann	Marıam Loıs Laurram	30-MAR-1919	13-APR-1919	Francı-Arthur Newmann/Mary-Maud Perrızo	Hubert Perrızo/Leona-Anna Perrızo
Nibach	Josephum Francıscum	13-SEP-1855	23-MAR-1856	Francıcı Nıbach/Magdalena Ebberlıng	M. Strats/M. Gı-ınd
Nibach*	Antonum	02-MAR-1856	09-MAR-1856	Gulielmı Nıbach/Elısabetha Passeler	A Servatus/C. -ttmiller
Nicholes	Marıam	17-JUL-1862	02-AUG-1862	Joannıs Nıcholes/Marıa Nicholes	M. Nicholes/S. Nicholes
Nicholes	Sarahm	14-JUL-1862	05-AUG-1862	Nicholaı Nicholes/Helena Nicholes	P. Nicholes/H. Nicholes
Nicholeson	Jacobum	02-NOV-1862	21-NOV-1862	Patrıcı Nıcholeson/Odılıa Nıcholeson	J Nıcholeson/B. Nicholson
Nicholson	Edwardum	18-FEB-1863	01-MAR-1863	Jacobı Nıcholson/Sarah Nicholson	J. Kelly/S. Nicholson
Nicholson	Joannem	16-SEP-1863	06-OCT-1863	Edwardı Nıcholson/Helena Nicholson	J. Nicholson/M. Nicholson
Nicholson	Joannem	13-APR-1861	05-MAY-1861	----- Nıcholson/----- -----	J. Emerson/B. Nicholson
Nicholson	Marıam	23-OCT-1863		Stephanı Nıcholson/Helena Nicholson	P. Nicholson/M. King
Nicholson	Sarahm	16-SEP-1861	05-OCT-1861	Patrıcıı Nıcholson/Odelıa Nicholson	S. Nicholson/S. Nicholson
Nicholson	Sarahm	13-FEB-1861	17-FEB-1861	Jacobı Nıcholson/Marıa Nicholson	J. Nicholson/M Nicholson
Nichtmans*	Jorge	30-SEP-1857	25-OCT-1857	Jorge Nichtmans/Ellıs Mangan	M. Common/E Nıchtmans
Nicolaus*	Chatırına	10-JUN-1858	13-JUN-1858	Stephanus Nicolaus/Brıdatet Morgan	Antonus Servatus/Cath---- Prusser
Nicolson*	Edward				
Nicolus*	Catharınam	10-JUN-1858	13-JUN-1858	Stephanı Nicolaus/Elızabetha Morgan	A. Servatus/C. Prusser
Nicolus*	Marıa Anna	27-MAY-1858	30-MAY-1858	John Nicolus/Anna Gill	James Kenny/Bergeta Gill
Nicolus*	Marıam Annam	27-MAY-1858	30-MAY-1858	Joannıs Nicolus/Anna Gill	J. Kenny/B Gill
Niehlman*	Gorgum	30-SEP-1857	25-OCT-1857	Georgus Niehlman/Elisa Mangan	M. Common/E. Niehlman
Nieleson*	Edwardum	05-MAY-1859	22-MAY-1859	Joannes Nieleson/Marie Lacet	P. Nieleson/M Wall
Nielman*	Nelson	04-MAR-1859	08-MAY-1859	Georgı Nielman/Ellen Commers	T. Gibben/----- -----
Nielman*	Nelson				
Nımar	Marıam	08-OCT-1903	06-DEC-1903	Farrıs Nımar/Sopha Harris	Josephus Ferrıs/Warna-Rosa Anton
Noeflinger*	Fredericam Helenam	19-APR-1860	01-SEP-1860	Caroli Noeflinger/Antona Noeflinger	Helena Krısseks/----- -----
Nolin	Alexıam Leonıam	15-SEP-1866	03-DEC-1866	Cezarıı Nolın/Sophia Nolin	M. Pıcard/P. Lecoque
Nolin	Franciscum Wallacium	16-APR-1863	04-APR-1863	Joannıs Nicolus/Anna Gill	M. Santuaıre/M Ebert
Nolin	Ludovicum Napoleonem	27-OCT-1861	03-NOV-1861	Cezarıı Nolın/Sophia Nolin	A Ebert/G. Hebert
Nolin	Narcissum	25-DEC-1864	08-JAN-1865	Cezarıı Nolın/Sophia Nolin	J. Real/C Nolin
Normeyer	Marıam	01-AUG-1879	06-AUG-1879	Davidı Normeyer/Emma Smith	J. Normeyer/M. Colmn
Novak	Marıam Vırgınıa	01-APR-1920	25-JUN-1920	Anton Novak/Katherıne Gonrıng	Alen Gonrıng/Mrs -Jos. Cyarnezki
Nugent*	James Patrick				
Nulty	Joannem		13-MAY-1855	Joannıs Nulty/Julia Smet	J Devet/C Nulty
Nulty	Marıam Annam	07-MAY-1855	09-FEB-1862	Jocobı Nulty/Julia Nulty	J Mıles/A. Nulty
Nulty*	Jacobum	15-FEB-1857	22-FEB-1857	Jocobı Nulty/Julie Smet	M. Hay/R. Schelly
Nulty*	James	19-FEB-1857	22-FEB-1857	James Nulty/Julie Smet	M Hay/R. Nulty
O'Brayan*	Brıgetham Sicilıam	24-SEP-1857	27-SEP-1857	Jacobı O'Brayan/Anna Kelroy	P -ılray/M. Kelligan
O'Brayan*	Joannem		16-DEC-1858	William O'Brayan/Anna Curry	Jocabus Mangan/Mary McGrath
O'Brayan*	Robertum Henricum	08-FEB-1857	08-MAR-1857	Joannıs O'Brayan/Chaterına Cannon	E. Curran/C Kelly

99

Surname	Given Name	Birth	Baptism	Parents	Godparents
O'Brayan*	Nicolasem	02-MAR-1857	15-MAR-1857	Nicolaius O'Brayan/Margeretha McGillan	J Gillan/M. Cork
O'Brian	Jacobum Edwardum	12-APR-1861	28-APR-1861	Joannis O'Brian/Anna McGown	R. McGown/M. McGown
O'Brian*	Joanna				
O'Brian**	Catharinam	25-APR-1861	24-MAR-1861	Patrici O'Brian/Maria O'Brian	D. Normal/H McCawly
O'Bren	Annam	25-JAN-1880	04-FEB-1880	Nicolas O'Brien/Anna Fox	J. Ha--ky/A. Mc----
O'Brien	Annam Joannam	04-NOV-1861	17-NOV-1861	Jacobi O'Brien/Anna O'Brien	J Fry/M. Burke
O'Brien	Catharinam Bridgittam	05-JUN-1863	15-JUN-1863	Joannis O'Brien/Anna O'Brien	M Co--/C. Co--
O'Brien	Dionisum	10-JUN-1854	02-JUL-1854	Nicolai O'Brien/Margarita Mcgill	J McGovern/R. Reilly
O'Brien	Elizabetham	26-AUG-1863	09-SEP-1863	Thoma O'Brien/Helena O'Brien	M. Mullen/M. Linsmith
O'Brien	Franciscum Edwardum		19-NOV-1864	Thoma O'Brien/Ellena-Marguarita Ge----- O'Brien	F. Ladysmith/M. McDermott
O'Brien	Guillelmum Joannem	12-APR-1863	19-APR-1863	Patricii O'Brien/Anna O'Brien	G Brennan/M O'Brien
O'Bren	Guillelmum Patricium	05-SEP-1862	14-SEP-1862	Nicholai O'Brien/Marguarita O'Brien	T Boyce/A. Rosseter
O'Brien	Joannem	21-JUN-1862	13-JUL-1862	Patricii O'Brien/Maria O'Brien	J. Fitzgibbons/E. Fitzgibbons
O'Brien	Joannem	03-OCT-1863	18-OCT-1863	Joannis O'Brien/Maria O'Brien	T Hanton/B. Shea
O'Brien	Luciam Annam	15-AUG-1861	16-AUG-1861	Gullelmi O'Brien/Anna O'Brien	H. Bennet/A. Fl-t
O'Brien	Michaelem Jacobum	10-JUL-1863	02-AUG-1863	Michaelis O'Brien/Joanna O'Brien	P. O'haloran/A. O'haloran
O'Brien*	Catharina	06-JUN-1862	16-JUN-1862	Joannis O'Brien/Honora McGowan	M. McGowan/C. Harges--
O'Brien*	Catharinam	06-JUN-1862	16-JUN-1862	Joannis O'Brien/Hannora McGowan	Mich. McGowan/Cath Kru-ge
O'Brien*	Ellen				
O'Brien*	Helene	23-NOV-1858	29-NOV-1858	John O'Brien/Mary Linch	James O'Brien/Mary Hardgrove
O'Brien*	Helene	23-NOV-1858	29-NOV-1858	John O'Brien/Mary Linch	Jas O'Brien/Mary Hardgrove
O'Brien*	Jane				
O'Brien*	John				
O'Bren*	John				
O'Brien*	Marguaret				
O'Brien*	Mary				
O'Brine*	Hellena Marie Margareta	25-DEC-1859	09-JAN-1860	Thoma O'Brine/Hellena-Margaret Phillips	S--- Mathews/Mary McDurmot
O'Bryan*	Brigita			William O'Bryan/Anna Curry	M. Oharan/A. Oharan
O'Bryan*	Brigita Scelia	24-SEP-1857	27-SEP-1857	James O'Bryan/Anna ---ay	P. -----/M. Kelligan
O'Bryan*	Joannam	20-SEP-1859	20-NOV-1859	Michaelis O'Bryan/Joanna Fin	M. Ha---n/A. Willhs
O'Bryan*	Joannam	05-FEB-1860	12-FEB-1860	Jocab O'Bryan/Anna Kelroy	Michel Kelroy/Maria O'Bryan
O'Bryan*	Joannem	11-MAR-1859	28-MAR-1859	Joannis O'Bryan/Ellena McGouvan	W. Mcnelly/E. Kasy
O'Bryan*	Joannem	01-DEC-1858	16-DEC-1858	Willem-A O'Bryan/Anna Carry	Jocabus Mangan/Ana-M--he- McGrath
O'Bryan*	Maria Anna	24-AUG-1856	14-SEP-1856	John O'Bryan/Elli- Welsh	P King/M. Smit
O'Bryan*	Mariam	24-JUN-1860	08-JUL-1860	Nicolus O'Bryan/Margereth McGill	Eduardus Wall/Maria Marten
O'Bryan*	Mariam Annam	24-AUG-1856	14-SEP-1856	Joannis O'Bryan/Elisa Welschs	P. King/M. Smet
O'Bryan*	Nicolus	02-MAR-1857	19-MAR-1857	Nicolus O'Bryan/Margereta Mcgillan	J Gillan/M. Cox
O'Bryan*	Robert Huberti	08-FEB-1857	08-MAR-1857	John O'Bryan/Chatera Gannen	E Curran/C ----
O'Bryn*	Margarethum	13-FEB-1859	07-MAR-1859	Johani-Patric O'Bryin/Maria Fitzgibbins	T Fitzgibbins/E. Fitzgibbins
O'Bryan*	Brigetham	17-MAR-1857	17-MAR-1857	Wilhem O'Bryan/Amma Carry	M O'Haran/A. O'Haran
O'Connel*	Andrew				
O'Connel*	Danlus	22-JAN-1860	15-FEB-1860	Jeremiah O'Connel/Elisabeth Lorey	----- -----/Anna Lorey
O'Connell*	Andream	24-OCT-1858	26-OCT-1858	Patric O'Connell/Maria Bullet	Martin -ell/Caterina Calten
O'Connel*	John				
O'Connor*	Mary				
O'Connor	Patricum	14-MAY-1854		Patricii O'Connor/Joanna Cobbat	M. Naset/G. Naset
O'Connor*	Margarittam	20-JUN-1859	07-AUG-1859	Patritu O'Connor/Margaritta Mcdermott	P. Mulvey/M. Mulvey
O'Connor*	Marguaret				
O'Connor*	Mariam	04-JUN-1859	12-JUN-1859	Jacobi O'Connor/Maria Cox	T. C---r/M. Connell

100

Surname	Given Name	Birth	Baptism	Parents	Godparents
O'Hara	Emondum	05-MAR-1854	16-FEB-1855	Samuelis O'Hara/Lousa McCann	J. McGally/----- -----
O'Hara	Mariam Annam	12-FEB-1860	19-FEB-1860	Michaelis Ohara/Anna Cabbory	Jocobus Shelly/Joanna Oconner
O'Hara*	Charlotam		12-FEB-1857	Samuelis O'Hara/Elisa Meam	Josephus Leduc/----- -----
O'Hara*	Li-ia				
O'Harn	Marguaritam	11-SEP-1862	01-DEC-1862	Patrcu O'Harn/Mana O'Harn	R. Henessy/B. Crowly
O'Harra	Carolum Henricum	15-AUG-1862	12-JAN-1863	Samuelis O'Harra/Ludovica O'Harra	M Mcgoley/M. O'Harra
O'Harra	Franciscum	26-MAR-1860	02-FEB-1861	Samuelis O'Harra/Ludovica O'Harra	M Mcauley/----- -----
O'Harra*	Mary Anne				
O'Hern*	Thomas	22-MAR-1860	24-MAR-1860	Patrci O'Hern/Mana Haley	Joannes Mory/Brigetta Mory
O'Hern*	Thomas				
O'Loughlin	Jacobum	31-JAN-1862	10-MAR-1862	Andrea O'Loughlin/Helena O'Loughlin	J. McCoy/M Bellamy
O'Loughlin	Terencium	21-AUG-1862	13-OCT-1862	Petri O'Loughlin/Bridgitta O'Loughlin	M. Bellamy/C. Bellamy
O'Neal	Mary	22-FEB-1852	22-FEB-1852	James O'Neal/Elizabeth Bellarmi	P. Codd/----- Codd
O'Neal	Thomam	16-FEB-1853	19-FEB-1853	Jacobi O'Neal/Elizabetha Bergen	M Belaui-/A. Cashman
O'Neel*	Edemundum	17-JUN-1857	27-JUN-1857	Jocobi O'Neel/Elisabeth Belami	M. Margan/E. Margon
O'Neil	Honoram	27-FEB-1854	05-MAR-1854	Joannis O'Neil/Elizabetha Bellarmign	J McCayn/J. McVelly
O'Neil	Joannem	01-MAR-1855	04-MAR-1855	Jacobi O'Neil/Elizabetha Behami	T. Dem--/H. O'Neil
O'Neil	Marguaritam	03-NOV-1862	04-NOV-1862	Joannis O'Neil/Marguarita O'Neil	R. O'Neil/M. -----
O'Neii	Michaelem	29-JUN-1856	05-JUL-1856	Jocobi O'Neil/Elisabetha Belami	M. Belami/A. Chasmon
O'Neil	Philipp	02-JAN-1851	05-JAN-1851	James O'Neil/Elizabeth Belmay	T. Murphy/C. McCarthy
O'Neil*	Elizabeth				
O'Niel*	Elisabetha	31-DEC-1858	15-JAN-1859	Jocabis O'Neil/Elisabeh Belarmi	Michel Berarmi/----- Belarmi
O'Rayly	Juliam	15-APR-1856	24-AUG-1856	M. O'Rayly/Maria Meglogetun	-----/C. Huipen
O'Roarck*	Patrick	29-MAR-1859	13-APR-1859	Denis O'Roarck/Bridget	P. O'Roarck/E O'Roarck
O'Roarke*	Patrick				
Oclare	Theresam Rosam	02-MAR-1873		Frederci Oclare/Joanna Oclare	Isaacus Oclare/Theresa Seibel
Oconnor*	Joannes	27-NOV-1859	15-JAN-1860	Cornelius Oconnor/Catherina Le-ie	Joannes Cavanugh/Maria O'Connor
Odell	Eduardum	23-OCT-1875	23-NOV-1875	Joannis Odell/Matilda Roulo-	S Roulo-/A Roulo-
Odet	Adelnam		24-SEP-1865	Georgii Odet/Vitalina Odet	J. Moquin/V. Moqun
Odet	Mariam Magdalenam	01-MAR-1868	07-MAR-1868	Ludovici Odet/Rosa Dugas	Georgius Odete/Adelina Dugas
Odete	Emiliam	24-JUN-1860	15-AUG-1868	Baptista Odete/Mathilda Odete	Georgius Odete/Julia Odete
Odete	Franciscum Xaverium		26-JAN-1873	Baptista Odete/Mathilda Rulo	Franciscus-Xaverius Hurto/Emilia Odete
Odete	Virginiam	01-AUG-1870	07-AUG-1870	Joannis-Baptista Odete/Mathilda Odcte	Toussant Chapeleau/Maria Porrer
Oellet*	Alexia	03-FEB-1858	07-FEB-1858	--ttymon Oellet/Delna Sir	Isedore Hebert/Florence Sir
Oestreicher	Joannem	20-MAR-1863	13-APR-1863	Petri Oestreicher/Aanna Oestreicher	J. Hansel/C Loselion
Ofcha--*	Josephum		11-SEP-1859	Laurentii Ofcha--/Francisca Pretz	J.-uffe-/R. Volchess-----
Oh-ra*	Liliam	12-JUN-1859	09-JUL-1859	Samueli Oh-ra/Louisa Mer	Persall/E. Ohoria
Ohary*	Migam	07-MAY-1857	05-OCT-1857	Samuelis Ohary/Moni-a Meam	C. Ohary/E. Ohary
Ohay*	Anngas	07-MAY-1857	09-OCT-1857	Samuel Ohay/Mouse M-am	C. Ohary/E. Ohary
Oillet	Mariam Delenam	23-JAN-1876	24-JAN-1876	Hubert Oillet/Maria Lebeau	M. Lebeou/ wife
Olet	Mariam Rosannam	06-NOV-1874	28-NOV-1874	Hubert Ollet/Maria Boe-edne	Josephus Lebeau/Irma Lebeau
Ollaugh-	Patricum Germanum	08-MAR-1861	19-MAY-1861	Petri Ollaugh-/Bridgitta Ollaugh-	A O'Laughlin/H Ollaugh-
Ollenbreth*	Anna Maria	27-SEP-1856	05-OCT-1856	Philipus Ollenbreth/Sophia Abbeler	J. Abbeler/A. Fogt
Ollet	Eduardum	29-MAR-1876	02-APR-1876	Francos Ollet/Rosa Dupies	H. Ollet/ wife
Ollet	Josephum	21-JUL-1878	04-AUG-1878	Charles Ollet/Louise Chaperon	B. Peron/ wife
Ollet	Mariam	08-APR-1876	16-APR-1876	----- Ollet/Louise -----	L. Ollette/L. Ollet
Ollet	Mariam Elizam Gratiam	31-AUG-1874	27-DEC-1874	Eegidii Ollet/Lousia Bon-hart	Leander --gee/Ester Ollet
Ollet	Mariam Florida	20-SEP-1874	11-OCT-1874	Petrus Ollet/Carolini Siroi	Josephus Deiet/Julie Lemere
Ollet	Ovilem Franciscum	05-AUG-1864	28-AUG-1864	Ovils Ollet/Celina Ollet	F. Marcou/M. Cyr

Surname	Given Name	Birth	Baptism	Parents	Godparents
Ollet*	Alexiam	03-FEB-1858	07-FEB-1858	Wilhelmi Ollet/Silena Sir	I Hubert/F. Sir
Ollet*	Ludovicum	06-FEB-1856	10-FEB-1856	Humar- Ollet/Selina Sir	I. Chenard/S Sir
Ollet*	Ludovicus	06-FEB-1856	10-FEB-1856	Lamar Ollet/Selina Sir	I Chnard/S. Sir
Ollet*	Mariam	02-APR-1860	08-APR-1860	Wilman Ollet/S-l--- Sir	Vital Langlois/Flavia Sir
Ollet*	Mary				
Onel*	Edemundus	14-JUN-1857	27-JUN-1857	James Onel/Elisabt Belami	M. Margan/E. Marigon
Oreilly	Malachy	31-DEC-1851	15-JAN-1852	Malachy O'Reilly/Elizabeth Donnelly	P. McDonald/----- McDonald
Osko	Sebastianum Ervin Kenneth	20-FEB-1903	17-MAY-1903		Martinus Bisson/Julia Loiseau
Othro	Ludovicum	03-AUG-1887	15-SEP-1887	Ludovico Othro/Maria Gilligan	Josephus Pariseau/Maria Dallaire
Othrom	Cathernam	07-FEB-1881	22-MAR-1881	Ludovico Othrom/Maria Gilligen	P. Derhe--/E. -is-br--
Ottenbirtt*	Elisabetham	23-MAY-1858	30-MAY-1858	----- Ottenbrtt/Sophia Abeler	G Barchel/E. Shaler
Ottenbrett*	Elisabeth	23-MAY-1858	30-MAY-1858	Pliphus Ottenbret/Sophia Abeler	Gulimun Barchel/Eliseh Abeler
Ottenbrett*	Annam Mariam	27-SEP-1856	05-OCT-1856	Philipi Ottenbrett/Sophia Abbeler	J Abeler/A Vought
Ouelette	Celina	29-FEB-1852	03-MAR-1852	Uillemer Ouelette/Celina Cyr	L Petr/L. Cyr
Ouellet	Hubert	18-DEC-1850	02-JAN-1851	Vilmer Ouellet/Celina Cyr	H. Oulette/M. Cyr
Ouellete	Ludovicum Ferdinandum	15-NOV-1873	23-NOV-1873	Francisci Ouellette/Sophia Dupuy	Ludovicus Ouellette/Laura Ouellette
Ouellette	Marian.	09-JAN-1852	29-AUG-1852	--berti Ouellette/Clarissa Coté	L. Chaperon/M. B-ller
Oulet-Wolete	Alfredum	15-JAN-1867	30-JAN-1867	Huberti Oulet-Wolete/Celesta Oulet-Wolete	H. Wolet/C. Wolet
P---rd	Julian Sophiam	16-APR-1874	19-APR-1874	Marelli P---rd/Paulna Willcox	Ludovicus Willkoxe/Laurenta Bessette
Pa--i--amer	Eliza	18-NOV-1857	15-FEB-1858	Ian Pa--i--amer/C---ria Peron	Isreal resmond/Philom---- ---my
Paas	Reginam	02-JUN-1860	16-SEP-1860	Joannis Paas/Catherina Paas	M. Uhrling/----- -----
Paddan	Rosam Annam		12-SEP-1860	Francisci-Joseph Paddan/Bridgitta Paddan	J. Paddan/S. Lavalla--
Padley	Mariam Marguaritam	01-JUN-1866	15-JUL-1866	Abrahami Padley/Philomena Ebert	N Eberd/D Ebert
Pado-kc	Rosaliam		12-SEP-1852		J. Lynam/M. Mullen
Page	Timotheum	13-JUN-1867	13-JUN-1867	Eunici Page/Maria Page	P. Chef/C. Page
Pagel	Marvin Francis	20-SEP-1919	05-OCT-1919	Frank Pagel/Theresa Schmidt	Wm Kinstey/Odelia Zuchts
Paié	Eddie	20-SEP-1878	22-SEP-1878	Joseph Paié/Adeline Duclaire	J. Robert/ wife
Painguère	Adolphum Josephum	25-JUN-1867	24-JUL-1867	Eugenii Painguère/Hortensia Lismont	A. Devilersse/D Painguère
Painguère	Alphonsinam	18-NOV-1864	18-DEC-1864	Eugenii Painguère/Hortensia Painguère	B. Gervais/M. Gervais
Painguère	Josephum		30-JUL-1866	Eugenii Painguère/Hortensia Painguère	J Painguère/M Gervais
Painguère	Josephum Victorem	05-JAN-1872	07-JAN-1872	Josephi Painguère/Adelina Lectari	Theophilus Langto/Anastasia Desautels
Painguère	Mariam Josephnam	04-MAY-1870	15-MAY-1870	Eugenii Painguère/Hortentia Lisman	Isaias Lucier/Virginia Painguère
Painguère	Mariam Octaviam	12-NOV-1861	26-OCT-1862	Eugenii Painguère/Hortensia Painguère	C. Lacouque/O Beauchère
Painter	Gulielmus		19-JUL-1905		Michael Lambert/----- -----
Painter	Thomam Gulielmum	13-NOV-1897	18-AUG-1906	Gulielmo Painter/Ada Dolan	Leono Martin/Eleonora Dumas-Martin
Pale	Cathernam	23-JUN-1856	16-APR-1865	Petri Pale/Ludovica Pale	J. Thalan/C Servatius
Panlily*	Jannem		20-OCT-1856	----- Panlily/Anna Cambell	M Sneller/M. Mullen
Papineau	----Iliam Mariam	06-JAN-1874	11-JAN-1874	Joseph Papineau/Eulalia Parent	Joseph Poirier/Anna Fontaine
Papineau	Henricam Eulaliam		26-OCT-1862	Adolphi Papineau/Henrica Papineau	A. Leblanc/L. Leduc
Papineau	Josephum Henricum		04-AUG-1872	Oliveri Papineau/Alphonsina Agagner	Hubertus Agagner/Maria Mocquin
Papineau	Ludovicum	06-DEC-1874	12-DEC-1874	Olivie Papineau/F.-Alphonsa Ngany	Joseph Pariseau/Emelie Parant
Papineau	Ludovicum Edwardum		16-SEP-1860	Adolphi Papineau/Henrica Papineau	E Branshaw/M. Deshotels
Papineau	Mariam Angelicam	29-JUN-1872	07-JUL-1872	Josephi Papineau/Emilia Parent	Olivierus Papineau/Delma Edouin
Paquete	Israelem	12-JAN-1867	30-JAN-1867	Israelis Paquete/Josephina Paquete	H Wolete/P. Paquete
Paquetc	Mariam Ludovicamm Melo	19-SEP-1870	25-SEP-1870	Felcis Paquete/Emma Paquete	Petrus Paquete/Cornelia Beadricau
Paqun	Alfredum Joannem	20-MAR-1863	03-MAY-1863	Eugenii Paquin/Hortensia Paqun	S. Serwe/J. G---
Paqun	Georgiam Annam	22-MAY-1869	30-MAY-1869	Theophili Paqun/Mathilda Leféve	Josephus Boyer/Nina Paqun
Paqun	Hermesium	24-JUN-1867	30-JUN-1867	Onesimi Paquin/Mathilda Paqun	J. Paquin/A. Dubord
Paradis	Davidem Henricum	09-MAR-1889	10-MAR-1889	Davide Paradis/Eleonora Lepine	Josephus Lepne/Elizabeth Rondeau

102

Surname	Given Name	Birth	Baptism	Parents	Godparents
Paradis	Josephum	02-MAR-1866	04-MAR-1866	Leons Paradis/Carolna Paradis	J. Gayet/M. Gayet
Paradis	Mariam Evaristam	16-JUN-1902	16-JUN-1902	Davide Paradis/Eleonara Lepine	Thomas Lepine/Josephina Brunet
Pariseau	Edwinum Franciscum	16-JUL-1899	25-JUL-1899	Eduardo Pariseau/Malvina Marcoux	Eduardus Marcoux/Christina Giebel
Pariseau	Genofevam Edessam	16-JUL-1899	25-JUL-1899	Eduardo Pariseau/Malvina Marcoux	Eduardus Gagnier/Edessa Pariseault
Pariseau	Helenam Leoniam	23-MAR-1897	28-MAR-1897	Josepho Pariseau/Melinda Dupuis	Henricus Schank/Anna Dupuis
Pariseau	Hubertum Dewey	09-SEP-1898	18-SEP-1898	Josepho Priseau/Melinda Dupuy	Eduardus Priseau/Malvina Marcoux
Pariseau	Hypollite	21-FEB-1851	21-MAY-1851	Hubert Pariseau/Catherine Louard	M. Pariseau/P. Briant
Pariseau	Idam Malvinam	20-FEB-1902	23-FEB-1902	Eduardo Pariseau/Malvina Marcoux	Alexander Marcoux/Eleonara Lajeunesse
Pariseau	Josephinam Evam	03-AUG-1897	08-AUG-1897	Eduardi Pariseau/Malvina Marcoux	Franciscus Marcoux/Josephina Roy
Pariseau	Leonem Wilfredum	20-JUL-1903	26-JUL-1903	Eduardo Pariseau/Malvina Marcoux	Wilfredus Marcoux/Emelia Marcoux
Pariseau	Marceline	25-JAN-1858	25-JAN-1858	Michel Panseau/Marceline Hebert	Hubert Panseau/Cath Leonard
Pariseau	Mariam Irenam	17-MAY-1892	22-MAY-1892	Josepho Pariseau/Melanisa Dupuy	Ludgerus Dupuy/Edessa Pariseau
Pariseau	Mariam Maud	07-JAN-1888	10-JAN-1888	Josepho Pariseau/Melanisa Dupuy	Hubertus Pariseau/Catharina Guinard
Pariseau	Mariam Violam	10-APR-1889	16-APR-1889	Josepho Pariseau/Melanisa Dupuy	Joannes-Baptista Dupuy/Dyonisia Baillargeon
Pariseau*	Joseph	24-JAN-1858	24-JAN-1858	Hubert Pariseau/Cath Leonard	Jos Pariseau/Delphine Dufrane
Pariseau*	Norbert				
Pariseault*	Olivine Or-elie	25-JUN-1858	11-JUL-1858	Homer Pariseau/Olivino Leonard	Hypolite Pariseau/Martine Hebert
Pariseault	Josephum Clarentium	31-MAY-1895	09-JUN-1895	Josepho Pariseault/Melinda Duprey	Felix Pratte/Josephina Pariseault
Pariseault	Mariam Isabellam	15-APR-1894	28-APR-1894	Josepho Pariseau/Melanisa Dupuy	Eduardus Gagnier/Juliana Lucier
Pariseaux	Henricum	04-MAY-1854	09-JUL-1854	Huberti Pariseaux/Catharina Inard	H. Parizo/M. ----
Pariso	Adelam	30-MAY-1862	22-JUN-1862	Brunonis Pariso/Maria Pariso	H Pariso/O. Léonard
Pariso	Edessam	04-APR-1862	13-APR-1862	Hypolthi Pariso/Oliva Bellimeur	H Pariso/O. Léonard
Pariso	Estherem	01-NOV-1862	23-NOV-1862	Huberti Pariso/Catharina Pariso	S. Dodelin/P Pariso
Pariso	Felicem	20-NOV-1860	23-DEC-1860	Brunonis Pariso/Maria Pariso	J. Pariso/J. Bissonet
Pariso	H--mire	21-DEC-1859	09-JAN-1860	--mire Pariso/Livina Geneys	Epatius Geneys/Livina Bilman
Pariso	Hypolitum	05-JUL-1862	03-AUG-1862	Michaelis Pariso/Marcellina Pariso	B. Pariso/M. Dellair
Pariso	Hypolitum	26-JAN-1865	01-MAY-1865	Hypolity Pariso/Olivina Bellimeur	F. Bellimeur/Zoah Dufresne
Pariso	Josephinam	04-JUL-1863	05-JUL-1863	Joannis Pariso/Maria Pariso	A Grizet/C. Guerin
Pariso	Josephinam	27-APR-1864	05-JUN-1864	Michaelis Pariso/Marcellina Pariso	J. Rondeau/E. Dodelin
Pariso	Josephum	22-OCT-1862	23-NOV-1862	Josepho Pariso/Sophronia Pariso	H. Pariso/C. Leonard
Pariso	Juliam	20-DEC-1859	15-JAN-1860	Hubert Pariso/Catherina Inard	Bruno Pariso/---- Pariso his wife
Pariso	Ludovicum	19-DEC-1864	15-JAN-1865	Huberti Pariso/Catharina Pariso	L. Lécuyer/E. Lécuyer
Pariso	Ludovicum	26-APR-1864	08-MAY-1864	Josephi Pariso/Sophronia Pariso	H Pariso/O. Pariso
Pariso	Mariam	16-MAR-1866	01-APR-1866	Michaelis Pariso/Marcellina Pariso	H Pariso/O. Pariso
Pariso	Mariam	20-SEP-1864	02-OCT-1864	Georgii Pariso/Maria Pariso	H. Pariso/C. Pariso
Pariso	Mariam Emmam	09-AUG-1861	11-SEP-1864	Brunonis Pariso/Maria Pariso	D. Dodelin/P. Tremblé
Pariso	Melinam	30-AUG-1861	29-SEP-1861	Homeri Pariso/Olivina Pariso	S. Dodelin/P Pariso
Pariso	Michaelem	05-NOV-1860	16-DEC-1860	Michaelis Pariso/Marcellina Pariso	B. Chenar/R. Ebert
Pariso*	-ephina	28-JAN-1856	03-FEB-1856	Hubert Pariso/Catherina Inard	M. Pariso/S. Prlant
Pariso*	Eduardum	11-MAR-1859	11-APR-1859	Michelet Pariso/Marcelina Ebert	Pariso/O. Enard
Pariso*	Edward				
Pariso*	Georgum	18-JUL-1855	05-AUG-1855	Brunonis Pariso/Maria Delare	M. Pariso/M Deframe
Pariso*	Joannem	10-OCT-1856	16-NOV-1856	Brunonis Pariso/Maria Delare	J. Delare/L. Borascau
Pariso*	Norbertum	29-JAN-1859	27-FEB-1859	Brunonei Pariso/Maria Delare	H. Parrnseau/C ----
Pariso*	Olivinam	25-JUN-1858	11-JUL-1858	Homeri Pariso/Olivina Leonard	H. Pariso/M. Ebert
Pariso*	Epotelum	02-MAR-1856	09-MAR-1856	Omer Parisso/Olivina Innard	H Pariso/C. Innard
Parisso*	Josephinam	28-JAN-1856	03-FEB-1856	Huberti Parisso/Catherina Innard	M. Parrnso/S. Pellant
Parisso*	Josephum	24-DEC-1857	02-JAN-1858	Huberti Parisso/Cath. Leward	J. Pariso/D. Dufren-
Parizeau	Eduardum Ernestum Katzka	19-OCT-1900	04-NOV-1900	Josepho Parizeau/Melinda Dupuis	Josephus Dupuis/Anna-Catharina Walwitz

Surname	Given Name	Birth	Baptism	Parents	Godparents
Parizo	Delimam	31-MAY-1867	23-JUN-1867	Michaelis Parizo/Marcelna Parizo	T Boisvert/L. Boisvert
Parizo	Delphinam	05-MAY-1867	05-MAY-1867	Georgii Parizo/Maria Grizet	I Gervais/V. Guzet
Parizo	Donotum	14-AUG-1870	04-SEP-1870	Joseph Parizo/Octavia Aganier	Josephus Poirier/Maria Agagnier
Parizo	Edessam	20-JUL-1866	07-SEP-1866	Brunonis Parizo/Maria Parizo	N Lécuyer/E Parizo
Parizo	Edessam		04-OCT-1868	Josephi Parizo/Octavia Agagnier	Huberti Agagnier/Maria Moquin
Parizo	Edwardum	01-JUN-1867	03-AUG-1867	Huberti Parizo/Catharina Parizo	E. Bernier/E Gagnier
Parizo	Franciscum	18-AUG-1870	29-AUG-1870	Hubert Parizo/Catharina Parizo	Dyonisius Dodelin/Edessa Parizo
Parizo	Mariam	09-MAR-1867	19-APR-1867	Hypoliti Parizo/Olivia Parizo	B. Parizo/M. Parizo
Parkeson	Joseph	08-OCT-1851	02-JAN-1852	Charles Parkeson/Catharine Curly	------/M Siddler
Parrizeau	------	14-FEB-1908	14-FEB-1908	Edwardo Parrizeau/Melina Marcoux	
Parrizeau-Perrizo	Catherinam Bernadettam	11-FEB-1908	16-FEB-1908	Eduardo Perrizo/Melina Marcoux	Albertus-W. Secor/Eva Marcoux
Pass	Catherinam	15-NOV-1855	25-NOV-1855	Joannis Pass/Chaterina Eurling	J. Eurling/M. Smet
Patrick	Joannes	02-FEB-1858	15-JUL-1860	Joannis Patrick/Catherine Morgan	Octavius Morgan/Corina Morgan
Patrick	Mary Jane	03-NOV-1857	07-MAR-1858	John Patrick/Catherine Morgan	Edward Morgan/Mary Margan
Patriso*	Joducus	18-JUL-1855	09-AUG-1855	Bruno Patriso/Maria Delaur	M. Pariso/M. Dufraine
Patt	Ferdinandum		05-JUN-1892	Hermani Patt/Maria Creift	Paschalis Letourneau/Maria Boomhauer
Patten	Marguaritam	28-FEB-1862	01-MAR-1862	Michaelis Patten/Bridgitta Patten	T. Patten/B Gill
Peacor	Mariam Agnetiam	28-AUG-1866	28-AUG-1866	Guillelmi Peacor/Lucia Létourneau	P Letourneau/L. Letourneau
Peck	Arthurum Clarentium	04-MAR-1896	04-MAR-1896	Martoni Peck/Maria-Ludovica Venne	Ovidius Senecal/Rosa-Delima Venne
Peck	Mariam Eucldem Edmundum	08-DEC-1894	08-DEC-1894	Murton Peck/Maria-Lousa Venne	Eucldes Venne/Sophia Bastian
Pedeland	Josephum Am-ry	27-JUL-1876	30-JUL-1876	Francisci-Exaver Pedeland/Philome Letournau	J Letournau/A Bis
Pedlant	Adelam	28-SEP-1861	06-OCT-1861	Francisci Pedelant/Josepha Faucher	F Durocher/J. Pedlant
Pesker	Marjery Alerina	27-MAR-1919	06-APR-1919	Eric Pensker/Suzie-Anne Freenor	Francis Freenor/Albina Hawkin
Pellan	Franciscum Xaverum	16-SEP-1874	17-SEP-1874	Francisci-Xaveri Pellan/Philomena Letourno	Petrus Letourneau/Josetta Pellan
Pelland	Maria Josephina	07-OCT-1879	09-NOV-1879	F.X. Pelland/Philomène L'Etourneauu	T Rondeau/J. Pelland
Pellant	Adelaidam Mariam	25-DEC-1872	26-DEC-1872	Francisci----verni Pellant/Philomena Letourncau	Franciscus Pellant/Lucia Letourneau
Pellant	Adolphum Napoleonem	05-DEC-1881	06-DEC-1881	Francisco Pellant/Philomena Letourneau	Adolpheus-Napolea Pellant/Alphonsina Laberge
Pellant	Mariam Josephum Arthur	02-OCT-1905	08-OCT-1905	Josepho Pellant/Josephina Robidoux	Adolphus Pellant/Erminia Robidoux
Pellant	Mariam Philomiam	20-MAR-1878	20-MAR-1878	Francis-X. Pedelant/Philome Letournau	J. Rabidieu/ wife
Pellant*	Adesse	05-SEP-1859	25-SEP-1859	Francois Pellant/Josephte Fouché	T. Randeaux/P. Pellant
Pellant*	Adolphum Napolion	10-DEC-1856	04-JAN-1857	Francisci Pellant/Josephina Lasché	A Pepineau/S. Pellant
Pellant*	Adolphus	20-DEC-1856		Francois Pellant/Jossette Lossehe	A. Pannen/S. Pellant
Pellant*	Edesse				
Pelleter	Georgium	26-MAR-1862	30-MAR-1862	Ludovici Pelleter/Catharina Pelleter	N Hart/B. Hart
Peltier*	Rossa	27-FEB-1857	08-MAR-1857	Fons Peltier/Catherina Smit	P Smet/A. Smet
Peltier*	Mariam Elisabeth	27-APR-1853	16-AUG-1853	Ludovici Peltier/Catherina Smet	L. Landerman/A. Mouler
Peltier*	Margeretham	21-MAR-1859	26-MAR-1859	Ludovici Peltier/Catherina Smit	B. McDormet/M McDormet
Peltier*	Margueret				
Peltier*	Rosam	27-FEB-1857	08-MAR-1857	Ludovici Pelter/Cathernam Smit	P. Smet/A. Smet
Penneau*	Jorgeum	08-MAR-1859	21-AUG-1859	Dolphis Penneau/-riete Landreux	P Bray/------ Bray
Pentely*	Joannes	27-JUN-1856	20-OCT-1856	------ Pentely/Anna Cambell	M. Snebler/M. Maclan
Penter*	Joannem	02-SEP-1860		Joannis Penter/Elizabetha Penter	F Maurice/C Raume
Pepi--o	William Thomam	01-FEB-1876	12-APR-1876	Aldolphus Pepi--o/Alexandria Landry	------ Tessié/L -i--s
Pepinau	Olivinam	18-AUG-1878	29-AUG-1878	Olivri Pepinau/Alflossa Ajaaé	A Peldelant/A. Olle--
Pepino	Mariam Emma	29-NOV-1876	03-DEC-1876	Olivie Pepino/Alphonsa Agaé	J. Porrier/S Pepino
Pepinou	J-essi Flore Mariam	06-MAR-1876	12-MAR-1876	Josephi Pepinou/Marie Parent	I. Raymont/ wife
Peren*	Emiliam	27-JUN-1858	27-JUL-1858	Baptista Peren/Sophia Rayon	Andreas Perin/------ Peren
Perin*	Joannem Baptistam			------ ------/Margereth Perin	Joannes-Bapt Perin/Catherina Perin
Perin-*-	George		10-JUN-1860		

Surname	Given Name	Birth	Baptism	Parents	Godparents
Peron	Josephum	24-AUG-1878	26-AUG-1878	Josephi Peron/Maria Rayaum	J Rayaume/M. Dumar
Peron*	Emliam	27-JUN-1858	29-JUL-1858	Baptista Peron/Sophia Royon	A. Peron/W. Peron
Perriso*	Joannes	10-OCT-1856	16-NOV-1856	Brino Perriso/Maria Delaine	J. Delane/L. Br--seau
Perron	Clifford Louis	05-JUL-1920	18-JUL-1920	Edward Perron/Irene Whelan	Pat.-Henry Whelan/Effie Haskin
Perron	Coram Angelinam	16-MAY-1883	19-NOV-1883	Josepho Perron/Maria Ryaume	Bernard Perron/Catarina Lemieux
Perron	Francescam Margaritam	01-SEP-1907	01-SEP-1907	Joanne-Baptiste Perron/Cecilia Hautain	Guilielmus Destrochers/Maria Perron
Perron	Joannem Baptistam	02-JUL-1870	15-OCT-1870	Joannis-Baptista Perron/Maria Pellant	Joannes-Baptista Dumont/Philomena Trotter
Perron	Joseph Martin	18-SEP-1920	26-SEP-1920	Joseph-H. Perron/Onay-Saturnus Clancy	John Flynn/Alice Perron-Flynn
Perron	Ludovicum Eduardum	05-JUN-1888	22-JUN-1888	Josepho Perron/Maria Ryaume	Raymundus Beaudom/Sophia Ryaume
Perron	Mariam	29-JUN-1868	05-JUL-1868	Joannis-Baptista Perron/Maria Pellant	Andreas Perron/Josepha Pellant
Perron	Mariam Alixam	25-MAR-1885	18-OCT-1885	Josepho Perron/Maria Ryaume	Josephus Rinerhart/Anna Dumas
Perron*	Jean Baptiste				
Perssa	Matheas	19-OCT-1855	21-OCT-1855	Joannes Perssa/Maria-Francisca Bourgois	M. Bourgois/M. Serwé
Peter*	Theresia	08-SEP-1855	09-SEP-1855	Mathias Peter/Catherna Peterin	J Lehy/T. Lehy
Peter*	Theresiam	08-SEP-1855	09-SEP-1855	Matteu Peter/Catherina Peterin	F. Joannes/T. Lery
Peters	Josephum		27-MAR-1864	------/Helena Peters	A. Perron/D. Perron
Peters	Mariam Josephinam	04-SEP-1872	15-SEP-1872	Henrici Peters/Marguarita Peters	Henricus Thill/Maria Noy
Petit	Auriliam		09-OCT-1853	Joannis Petit/Nanci Shivans	------/L. Jubert
Petit	Cecilia	27-FEB-1851	27-FEB-1851	John Petit/Nancy Petit	I. Hebert/----- Hebert
Petit	Celeta	27-FEB-1851	27-FEB-1851	John Petit/----- Petit	----- Thibodeau/L. Cyr
Petit	Edessam	16-NOV-1868	22-NOV-1868	Josephi Petit/Elmira Bellimeur	Carolus Gayet/Adela Wolet
Petit	Henricum	21-JAN-1871	24-JAN-1871	Josephi Petit/Edmira Petit	Hubertus Parizo/Catharina Parizo
Petit	Laurianam		09-OCT-1853	Joannis Petit/Nanci Shivans	------/J. Demier
Petit	Marguaritam	27-JUN-1866	01-JUL-1866	Josephi Petit/Edmira Petit	J Gayet/M. Gayet
Petit	Mariam Victorram	24-MAY-1853	04-JUN-1853	Francisci Petit/Emilia Pony	L Petit/F. Petit
Petit*	Emeliam	24-MAR-1857	29-MAR-1857	Josephi Petit/Emilia Belhumeur	F. Belhumeur/M Petit
Petit*	Eumire	24-MAR-1857	25-MAR-1857	Joseph Petit/Eumier Bellhumeur	F. Bellheu/M. Petit
Petit*	Joseph George				
Petit*	Josephum Georgium	10-JUL-1859	07-AUG-1859	Josephi Petit/Edinam-Bel Dushene	G. -llet/-----.-llet
Petit*	Thomam Christophorum	17-JUL-1859	24-JUL-1859	Garret Petit/Brigitta Kennady	J. Kennady/C. Fenlon
Petit*	Thomas Christoph				
Petri	Angelica	10-DEC-1878		Claudus Petri/Caroline Petri	E Fort/P. Mar-----
Petri	Carolum Guillelmum	27-JUL-1860	21-OCT-1860	Martini Petri/Marguarita Petri	J. Da--/----- -----
Petri	Edmundum Jacobum	19-MAR-1865	09-APR-1865	Martini Petri/Martha Petri	J Petri/E. Jenner
Petri	Mariam Clementinam	06-OCT-1875	17-OCT-1875	Hennerie Petri/Margeth Hannard	H Ditter/Sister-Maria Dale
Petri	Mariam Elisabethasm Bijou	02-SEP-1853	09-SEP-1853	Joannis Bijou/Josephina Tillman	A. Bijou/E. Tillmann
Petters	Albertum Emelium		14-OCT-1880		
Peuter*	Joanem	01-SEP-1860	02-SEP-1860	Joann Peuter/Elizabetha Peuter	Franciscus Maurice/Clementia Riaume
Peuter*	Joanem		02-SEP-1860	Joannis Peuter/Elizabetha Peuter	F. Maurice/C. Riaume
Pfeitner	Carolum Henricum Thoma	19-MAR-1882	02-APR-1882	Philippo Pfeitner/Malvina Dufort	Cyrillus Corbeille/Anastaa Dufort
Pfeitner	Leonardum Cyrillum	03-JUN-1894	27-JUN-1894	Philippo Pfeitner/Malvina Duford	Cyrillus Duford/Salomea Boivin
Pfeitner	Philippum Alfredum Franc	03-FEB-1891	14-FEB-1891	Philippus Pfeitner/Malvina Dufort	Alfredus Balthazar/Delima Pratte
Phalan	Catharnam Mathildam	02-NOV-1863		Guillelm Phalan/Marguarita Phalan	M Barrigan/J. Barrigan
Phalan	Danielem	15-FEB-1862	10-MAR-1862	Danelis Phalan/Maria Phalan	M Barngan/S. C-ddy
Phalan	Franciscum	17-MAY-1861	19-MAY-1861	Guillelmi Phalan/Marguarita Norton	J. Waters/S. Waters
Phalan	Helenam	04-APR-1861	22-APR-1861	Patricii Phalan/Helena Phalan	J Dohany/A. Phalan
Phalan	Honoram	16-OCT-1863		Danelis Phalan/Maria Phalan	K Cody/R. Cody
Phalan	Jacobum Patricium	08-MAR-1863	12-APR-1863	Patricii Phalan/Helena Phalan	M. Berrigan/C. Flanigan
Phalan*	Cornelius				

105

Surname	Given Name	Birth	Baptism	Parents	Godparents
Phalan*	Gulielmum	11-JAN-1856	12-JAN-1856	Gulielmi Phalan/Margeretha Norton	J Rapy/M. Whelon
Phalan*	Guliames	10-JAN-1856	12-JAN-1856	Gullimus Phalan/Margerta Norton	J Rayly/M -----
Phalan*	James				
Phalen*	Jacobum	09-NOV-1859	12-NOV-1859	Willaim Phalen/Margetha Nat-n	T. Fox/M. Phala-
Pheffer	Michel	29-JAN-1859	09-FEB-1859	Joseph Pheffer/Mary-Agnes Henmichel	Mark Schnur/Agnes Schnur
Phelan	Ethelam Margaritam	11-JUL-1888	17-JAN-1889	Jacobo-R. Phelan/Josephina Miller-Meunier	Alexandreum Durocher/Maria Thorton
Phelan	Michaelem	10-NOV-1854	13-NOV-1854	Gulielmi Phelan/Margarita Norton	M Reilly/H Reilly
Phogeson	Margeham	19-APR-1860	20-APR-1860	Patrick Phogeson/Elizabeth Madan	M. Kelly/M. Kerry
Picar	Marcellum	09-MAY-1867	09-MAY-1867	Marceli Picar/Paulina Wilcoque	L Wilcoque/S. Wilcoque
Pickan	Carolum Henricum	06-APR-1854	07-APR-1854	Milelii Pickan/Maria Hynes	J. Hynes/A. Pel-e-
Picktho--	Elizabetham Mariam	10-AUG-1862	06-SEP-1862	Caroli Picktho--/Catharina Picktho--	Q. Foxheim/E. Foxheim
Picor	Mariam Victoriam		19-DEC-1871	Marceli Picor/Paula Wilcox	Desideratus Sicor/Zoah Sicor
Piehl	Netam Josephinam	13-NOV-1881	14-OCT-1902	Francisco Piehl/Guilelmina Parnan	Leo Martin/Yona Martin
Pierron	Carolum		13-AUG-1871	Joannis-Caroli Pierron/Adela Pierron	Augustus Pierron/Adela Pierron
Pierron	Florentiam Adnam Rosam	04-JUL-1864	05-SEP-1865	Joannis Pierron/Marguarita-Adelina Pierron	L. Lallier/P. Beaumill
Pierson	Claram Emmam	03-NOV-1886	14-NOV-1886	Josepho Pierson/Adela Pellant	Franciscus-Xavier Pellant/Hermina Pellant
Pierson	Mariam Rosam de Lima	10-MAR-1888	11-MAR-1888	Josepho Pierson/Adela Pellant	Adolphus Durocher/Adelaida Faucher
Pill*	Annam Catherina	16-FEB-1859	20-FEB-1859	Caroli Pill/Catherina Mo--rer	D Pill/C. Schoemaker
Pingé	Henricum Julium	30-JUL-1876	30-JUL-1876	Josephe Pingé/Adelina LeClair	U. Pingé/ wife
Pinguere	Albertum	06-JAN-1874	07-JAN-1874	Joseph Pinguere/----a Leclerc	Gilbertus Leclerc/Adelina -----
Pinguere	Marcelnam	10-NOV-1873	13-NOV-1873	Eugenii Pinguiere/Hortensia Nismont	Emilus-P. ---mont/Celina Pinguere
Pixlar	Laurentiam	02-DEC-1875	05-DEC-1875	Mersell Pixlar/Paulina Wilcoxs	S. Nolen/S. Wilcoxs
Plaatz*	Nicholas M.				
Plaets*	Niellium Mathew	22-FEB-1859	05-JUN-1859	Laurentii Plaets/Regina -itter	N Haas/F. Justen
Plante	Alexises	29-JAN-1876	03-FEB-1876	Moise Plante/Marie Eveque	J Gaiyet/ wife
Plante	Moises	15-NOV-1880	16-DEC-1880	Moises Plante/Maria Leveque	J. Balthazar/S. Tessier
Platz	Agnetiam Josephinam		10-APR-1865	Lauretu Platz/Regina Platz	B. Adleman/A. Ditter
Platz	Franciscum		02-NOV-1861	Laurentu Platz/Eva-Regina Platz	G. Ditter/A. Ditter
Plouff	Mary Dorothy Jeanne	02-MAR-1918	20-OCT-1918	Geo.-Elme Plouff/Edith Bennett	Solomon Lepine/Hedwig Plouff-Hyer
Po-ett*	Jcobus	08-JUL-1858	15-JUL-1858	John Po-ett/Madalina Simmermann	Joco Simmermann/Caterina Casper
Poch*	Albertum	23-MAR-1858	11-JUL-1858	Chrstiani Poch/Maria-Anna Gambet	M. Stratz/B. Walri-
Poch*	Albertus	23-MAY-1858	11-JUL-1858	Christian Poch/Maria-Anna Gambet	Martine Stratz/Barbara Wehrie
Poirier	Adelaïdam	17-JUL-1870	24-JUL-1870	Josephi Poirier/Maria Agagner	Baptista Dupus/Christna Agagner
Poirier	Carolum Guilielmum	18-OCT-1870	01-NOV-1870	Josephi-Daniel Poirier/Ludovica Poirier	Carolus Tremblé/Clementia Porrier
Poirier	Magdalenam	26-APR-1869	09-MAY-1869	Josephi Porrer/Maria Agagner	Oliverus Papineau/Alphonsina Agagner
Poirier	Mariam	22-NOV-1872	22-NOV-1872	Josephi Porrer/Maria Poirier	Josephus Parizo/Elizabetha Padenode
Poirier	Mariam Annam	04-DEC-1866	08-DEC-1866	Josephi Porriet/Maria Porrer	E Dupus/V. Verse
Poirier	Mariam Josephinam	14-MAY-1874	24-MAY-1874	Josephi Poirier/Maria Agagnée	Bernardum Perron/Catharina Perron
Pomainville	Mariam Myrtle	15-FEB-1906	18-FEB-1906	Gulielmo Pomainville/Eleonora Marcoux	Franciscus Marcoux/Josephina Balthazar-Marcoux
Pomainville	Paulum Alexandrum	27-SEP-1908	04-OCT-1908	Gulielmo Pomainville/Eleonora Marcoux	Eusebius Charbonneau/Delphina Pomainville
Pomeroy	Joseph	04-MAY-1850	19-APR-1851	John Pomeroy/Mary Stellay	J. Perrodn/----- ---
Pomerville	Genevieve	23-JUN-1904	29-JUN-1904	William Pomerville/Eleanor Marcoe	Purle Marcoe/----- Marcoe
Pominville	Eugère Andréas	25-JAN-1880	26-JAN-1880	Michaeli Pominville/Sophia Graton	A. Rondeau/A. Rondeau
Pommenville	William	30-MAR-1875	30-MAR-1875	Michaelis Pommenville/Sophia Graton	Michel Pommenville/Sophia Duyardin
Pommnville	Mariam Luellam	25-NOV-1901	01-DEC-1901	Gulielmo Pommnville/Eleanora Marcoux	Alexander Marcoux/Eleanora Lajeunnesse
Popion	Augusti Josephi	05-FEB-1878	10-FEB-1878	Josephi Popion/Mila Parent	----- Servais/A. --d-
Popion*	Adolphus	20-DEC-1857	17-JAN-1858	Adolphus Popion/Ar-ette Landré	David L'Oison/Marie Jubert
Poppion*	Adolphum Nopolonum	12-JAN-1858	17-JAN-1858	Adolphi Poppion/Arrieta L'andré	D. L'oison/M. Jubert
Porcheron	Arthurem	29-MAY-1870	29-MAY-1870	Eduardi Porcheron/Ludovica Bransheau	Franciscus Mocquin/Henrica Mocquin

Surname	Given Name	Birth	Baptism	Parents	Godparents
Porseau*	Hipolite	02-MAR-1856	09-MAR-1856	Omer Poriseau/Olivine -enoid	H. Pariso/C Inaerd
Porlier	Oliverum	17-NOV-1852	26-JUN-1853	Ludovici Porlier/Genovafa Ardut	V. Langlois/D Peront
Porrier	Emma Merriam	08-JUL-1878	13-JUL-1878	Joseph Porrier/Maria Agarue	O. Laroberger/ wife
Potter	Franciscum A	12-AUG-1882	04-JAN-1886	Benjamin Potter/Catharina Mullen	Rogerus Raten/Anna Mitchell
Pouglois	Margaritam Loisam	26-JUN-1880	27-JUN-1880	Edmundi Pouglois/Margareta Racette	E Moquin/Z. Racette
Pouruer	David Alexim Wilfridem	07-JUN-1874	13-JUN-1874	Vitalis Pouruer/Helena Lemieux	Georgius Raymond/Anna Lemieux
Power	Catharinam	10-JUL-1858	03-SEP-1865	Joannis-Baptista Power/Ludovica Power	B. Colp/C Tautges
Power	Joannem Petrum	22-AUG-1865	03-SEP-1865	Joannis-Baptista Power/Ludovica Power	P. Sholl/E Colp
Power	Marguaritam	19-FEB-1860	03-SEP-1865	Joannis-Baptista Power/Ludovica Power	J. Pomerich/M Schoffer
Power	Michaelem Rufum	06-MAY-1906	19-SEP-1906	Arthuro Power/Dina Lambert	-----/Sophronia Barbeau-Lambert
Prat	Ludovicem Arthurem	26-MAY-1874	31-MAY-1874	Isidori Prat/Philomena Ma-----	Joseph Pratte/Henrietta Pratte
Pratt	Mariam Philomenam	03-JAN-1877		Ersedori Pratt/Philome Marcou	I. St.-Antoine/ wife
Pratt	Melvinam	27-JAN-1871	29-JAN-1871	Isidori Prat/Philomena Pratt	Joannis-Marie Marcou/Mathilda Marcou
Pratt*	Clara Jane	27-FEB-1860	15-APR-1860	Lou Pratt/Marg. Pratt	Joannes Furlong/Carolina Furlong
Pratt*	Clara Jane				
Pratte	Birkus Alfred Ralph	19-MAY-1884	27-JUN-1884	Alfred Pratte/Octave Prefontaine	Ludger Prefontaine/Julie Simonin
Pratte	Josephum Clarentium	15-APR-1884	16-APR-1884	Felice Pratte/Sarah Duquet	Isidorus Pratte/----- -----
Pratte	Josephum Guilelmum	18-OCT-1885	20-OCT-1885	Alfredo Pratte/Octavia Prefontaine	Zoticus Laparte/Onesiphora Prefontaine
Pratte	Mariam Stellam	06-NOV-1882	12-NOV-1882	Felice Pratte/Sara Duquet	Josephus Duquet/Christine Chaffe
Pratte	Nathaliam Emmam	09-FEB-1881	13-FEB-1881	Theodoro Pratte/Emma Desautels	T. Lanctot/A. Moquin
Pre----tt	Jacobum	27-FEB-1856	17-MAY-1856	Jacobis Pre----tté-/----- -----	
Prefontaine	Alexum Honoratum Carolum	05-MAY-1885	10-MAY-1885	Ludgerio Prefontaine/Julia Simonin	Eduardus Turcot/Phlamena Coté
Prefontaine	Andream Vitalem	20-JUL-1889	21-JUL-1889	Alexo Prefontaine/Elmira Hubert	Edmundus Allard/Adelina Maurice
Prefontaine	Aurelium Carinnam	23-MAR-1893	14-MAY-1893	Andreo Prefontaine/Adeline Maurice	Alexus Prefontaine/Domitilda Perron
Prefontaine	Desideratum Oust-----	27-JUN-1874	28-JUN-1874	Ludgeri Préfontaine/Cesara Lamheliere	Maglorius Prefontaine/Sophia Lefevre
Prefontainc	Henricum Maglorre	28-AUG-1875	29-AUG-1875	Maglore Prefontaine/Olivine Deshotel	Bersis Fontaine/Ema Deshotel
Prefontaine	Honoratum Christianum	08-JUN-1869	19-JUN-1869	Alexii Préfontaine/Edmira Hubert	Honoratus Fournier/Olivina Deshautels
Préfontaine	Isadore	13-FEB-1876	17-FEB-1876	Armidas Prefontaine/Edelene Lemieux	A Prefontaine/H. Lemieux
Préfontaine	Josephum	21-APR-1871	29-APR-1871	Joseph Prefontaine/Sophronia Dupuis	Hubertus Agagnier/Elizabetha Billete
Préfontaine	Julian	09-FEB-1872	18-FEB-1872	Alexis Préfontaine/Edmira Hubert	Andreas Préfontaine/Belonisa Dupuis
Prefontaine	Mariam Alisam	01-SEP-1878	02-SEP-1878	Luci Prefontaine/Sessara-Lorisis Sh----	B. Prefontaine/O. Prefontaine
Prefontaine	Mariam Philomenam Rosa	29-MAY-1870	01-JUN-1870	Ludgeri Préfontaine/Cezarina Préfontaine	Josephus Ochne/Aurelia Robidou
Prefontaine	Mariam Rosam Blancam	20-MAR-1887	21-MAR-1887	Ludgerio Prefontaine/Julia Limonin	Alfredus Pratte/Octavia Prefontaine
Prefontaine	Mariam Theresam Lousam	15-DEC-1882	17-DEC-1882	Ludgerio Prefontaine/Julia Simonin	Josephus-Albertus Simonin/Augustina Simonin
Prefontaine	Mariam Virginiam Celinam	26-JUL-1873	27-JUL-1873	Ludger Prefontaine/Cezarina Larichelière	Isaac Gervas/Virgina Grisey
Prefontaine	Mariam Vitalinam	18-MAR-1883	19-MAR-1883	Vitale Préfontaine/Maria-Octavia Pinguer	Georgius Sherburn/Celina Pinguer
Prefontaine	Nataliam Lisam	18-APR-1877	19-APR-1877	Maglore Préfontaine/Olivina Deshotels	A Deshostel/Sister-M. Dale
Préfontaine	Oliverum	25-NOV-1870	04-DEC-1870	L----rii Préfontainc/Eulalia Veine	Alexus Préfontaine/Edmira Hebert
Préfontaine*	Josephinam	28-AUG-1875	07-SEP-1875	Alexis Préfontaine/Edmira Hubert	Antonius Demalade/Delié Delamontaigne
Préfontaine*	Josephinam	28-AUG-1875	07-SEP-1875	Alexi Prefontainc/Edmire Hubert	A. Demalade/D Montagne
Preis	Ludovicam Elizabetham	30-SEP-1861	06-OCT-1861	Joannis Preis/Catharina Preis	J. Wagner/E. Me-lerq
Preis	Mathiam Guillelmum	18-MAY-1864	29-MAY-1864	Joannis Preis/Catharina Preis	M. Hoffman/M Wyler
Preister	Nicholaum	31-MAY-1862	01-JUN-1862	Petri Preister/Anna Marguarita Prester	N Krämer/M. Poeley
Preister*	Rose				
Prester*	Rosam	21-MAR-1859	22-MAR-1859	Petri Prester/Anna-Maria Wertz	E. Crammer/R Denni
Priss	Mariam		06-JUL-1901		Rev.C. Boucher/----- -----
Prister*	Anna Maria		08-FEB-1857	Peter Prister/Margerita Werts	J Slink/A. Lemans
Pro--don	Josephum	06-JAN-1875	07-JAN-1875	Josephi Pro--don/Armina Pedland	Franciscus Berland/Adelina Pedland
Prosse-*	Rosaliam	30-AUG-1859	04-SEP-1859	Joannes Prosse/Catherine Jirter	A. Mayer/M. Jost--

Surname	Given Name	Birth	Baptism	Parents	Godparents
Prosseur	Edessam Josephinam		16-JUL-1865	Jacobi Prosseur/Lucia Prosseur	F. Leger/E. Nicholas
Provencher	Isabellam	12-JUL-1901	14-JUL-1901	Georgio Provencher/Josephna Lafontaine	Georgius Dion/Maria Powers
Purner	Mariam Agnetem Gratiam	22-DEC-1903	03-JAN-1904	Arthuro Purner/Rosa-Delima Diotte	Eugenius Pingar/Marie-Esther Diotte
Queen*	Carolum	24-JUN-1858	25-JUL-1858	Danelis Queen/Maria-Anna Campbel	P. Ready/J. Phalan
Quenkenbush	Eugeniam	12-JAN-1857	25-MAR-1859	Michaelis Quenkenbush/Nanci Meling	J. C---ly/----- C----ly
Quné	Franciscum	09-OCT-1874	11-OCT-1874	Franciscus Quné/Margret Randeau	Joannes-Baptista Randeau/Juliam Chef
Qunlan	Jeremiahm	23-APR-1863	19-MAY-1863	Jeremiah Qunlan/Sarah Qunlan	P. McCabe/M. McCabe
Qündle*	Adelaida				
R---p*	Antonius	02-MAR-1856	09-MAR-1856	Gulimius R---p/Elisath Passilar	A. Servatius/C. -t-mill--
R-tt---	Ludovicam	16-APR-1866	22-APR-1866	Francisci R-tt---/Lina Dodelin	A. Lo---/E. R-tt---
Rabadou	Josephum	26-SEP-1876	16-OCT-1876	Joseph Rabadou/Maria Boisvin	A. Boisvin/A. Boisvin
Rabido	Mariam Adelenam	03-DEC-1875	05-DEC-1875	Joseph Rabido/Admelia Peddelant	E. Peddelant/A. Peddelant
Rabido	Mariam Victorian	01-JUL-1876	05-JUL-1876	Alphonse Rabido/Louise Moiquin	H. Landerman/ wife
Rabidou	Elizabetham	03-NOV-1870	04-NOV-1870	Moysis Rabidou/Emilia Fernet	Isaias Fernet/Mathilda Fernet
Rabidou	Guillelmum	07-DEC-1869	08-DEC-1869	Alpho--- Rabidou/Ludovica Rabidou	Moyses Rabidou/Henrieta Mocqun
Rabidou	Mariam Claram	12-SEP-1870	12-SEP-1870	Josephi Rabidou/Hermina Pellant	----- Pellant/Aurélia Préfontaine
Rabidou	Mariam Emiliam	06-AUG-1872	09-AUG-1872	Moysis Rabidou/Emilia Rabidou	Leo Eduom/Phébe Eduoin
Rabidou-	Ludovicum Alexander	18-APR-1874	26-APR-1874	Alphonsi Rabidou-/Ludovica Mocqun	Da---ed Michotte/Oliva Michotte
Rabodou	Joannem	21-APR-1877	22-APR-1877	Josephi Rabodou/Armena Pedelant	P. Beaupre/E. Pedelant
Racet	Adolphe	21-APR-1851	15-JUN-1851	Julien Racet/Marguerite Sire	J. Sire/G. Sire
Racet	Susannam Laurentiam	11-AUG-1852	17-AUG-1852	Juliani Racet/Marguerita Racet	Rev. Godfert/M. Cyre
Raché	Eduardum	19-JUN-1876	26-JUN-1878	Maxim Raché/M---nda Fervert	M. Balta-a-/C. Vernet
Rademacher	Henricum	04-MAR-1864	27-MAR-1864	Petri Rademacher/Theresa Rademacher	J. Boss/B. Trimboer
Rafferty	Margueritam	17-FEB-1861	19-FEB-1861	Joannis Rafferty/Maria Rafferty	M. Curran/C. Curran
Ragan*	Catherinam	02-DEC-1858	19-DEC-1858	Joannes Ragan/Anna Fox	Patricus Murphy/Elena Jerbeth
Ragan*	Julia	08-JAN-1857	11-JAN-1857	John Ragan/Anna Fox	T. Fox/T. McIntyre
Ragan*	Mariam Annam	07-JUN-1855	15-JUN-1855	Patricii Ragan/Brigetha ---t	J. Cogelon/E. Cogelon
Ragan*	Silvester	06-APR-1856	04-MAY-1856	Michaelis Ragan/Elena Meginis	M. Jay/E. M---h
Ragan*	Thamas	22-SEP-1857	27-SEP-1857	Patrick Ragan/Thersa McIntyre	F. McIntyre/M. Re---ons
Rally	Mariam Annam	23-JUN-1854	17-FEB-1855	Joannis Rally/Anna Jumi	P. Currans/M. Mcgivery
Randant	Maria	05-JAN-1879		Anfrea Randant/Albin Graton	M. Trembley/M. Trembley
Randeau	Emma	08-AUG-1875	22-AUG-1875	Francici Randeau/Octavie Edewin	Cassemre Lefeve/Ema Edwin
Randeau	Josephnam	11-APR-1875	09-MAY-1875	Franciscus Randeau/Maria Demarai	David Sicar/Josepham Demarai
Randeau	Melvina	19-DEC-1874	20-DEC-1874	Andria Randeau/Albina Graton	Michael Pomenville/Sophia Graton
Randeau*	Exilda	06-NOV-1858	21-NOV-1858	Thos Randeau/Josephine Touché	Pierre Sherff/Jose---- Touché
Randeau*	Franciscum		03-JUN-1860	Thama Randeau/Josephna Pedelant	Stephani Hoile/----- -----
Randeau*	Michaelem	14-APR-1858	22-OCT-1858	Joseph Randeau/Margeritha Bodain	Mack Dupat/Matilda Duquet
Rando	Jorgium Ludovicum	19-OCT-1876	22-OCT-1876	Thoma Rando/Josephna Pedelant	Rev.-L Dale/Sister-M. Dale
Rando	Josephum	28-NOV-1877	16-DEC-1877	Francois Rando/Fa-ie Eddom	J Lepenne/L. Rando
Rando	Vital	24-MAR-1877	25-MAR-1877	Francois-André Rando/Albina Gratham	B. Rando/E. Grathand
Raney	Ren-----um Petrum	08-AUG-1864	21-AUG-1864	Christophi Ranson/Regina Raney	R. Muller/A. Sh-----er
Ransom	Henricum Emmet	10-MAR-1888	11-JUN-1888	Emmet Ransom/Mathilda Gilman	Franciscus Marcoux/Josephina Roy
Ransom	Josephum Howard Mitton	11-DEC-1890	29-NOV-1891	Arthuro Ransom/Mathilda Gilman	Telespharus Edoin/Maria-Emma Gilman
Ransom	Leonem Earl	18-NOV-1889	23-DEC-1889	Arthuro Ransom/Mathilda Gilman	Alexander Edoin/Lucia Gilman
Rante	Anna		10-MAY-1896		Evaristus Beaudet/Elma Carbonneau
Rasset*	Margarita	03-MAR-1856	15-APR-1856	Julius Rasset/Margirit Sir	V. Langlois/P. Sir
Rasset*	Margetetham	03-MAR-1856	15-APR-1856	Juln Rasset/Margetetha Sir	V. Anglois/P. Sir
Rathé	Joannem	16-DEC-1863	19-JUN-1864	Maxmi Rathé/Emitilla Rathé	J. Fernet/J. Fernet
Rathé	Juliam Annam	06-JAN-1867	26-JAN-1867	Maxmi Rathé/Mathilda Rathé	F. Beaudreau/A. Fernet

108

Surname	Given Name	Birth	Baptism	Parents	Godparents
Rathé*	Josephum	15-JAN-1859	05-FEB-1859	Maximi Rathé/Matilda Vernet	H Gautie/M. Turgnot
Ratry	Benjamin Franklin	18-OCT-1889	20-OCT-1889	Gulielmo Ratry/Philumena Talbot	Franciscus Boucher/Judith Bessette
Rauly*	Mariam	20-AUG-1857	28-AUG-1858	Danielis Rauly/Marie Rock	Thamas Curran/Fanny Gulb---
Raush	Josephum Guillelmum	21-OCT-1866	21-OCT-1866	Nicholai Raush/Catherina Raush	A Drek/M. Sheaffer
Raute	Gulielmum Augustum Fran	29-APR-1910	22-MAY-1910	Theodoro Raute/Ella Beudette	Gulielmus Utecht/Genovefa Othrow-Raute
Rayan*	Catherenam	02-DEC-1858	19-DEC-1858	Joannis Rayan/Anna Fox	Patricus Murphy/Elena -erbeth
Rayan*	Petrum	08-OCT-1858	09-OCT-1858	Michel Rayan/Hellena Megenis	--this Lemmery/----- -----
Rayheart	Louisam	22-FEB-1857	07-JUN-1857	Georgius Rayheart/Elisubeth Suster	J. Marks/S Suster
Rayly	Joannum	27-NOV-1859	28-NOV-1859	Michel Rayly/Margetha Phalan	Thamas Rayly/Ellira ------
Rayly	Mariam	15-DEC-1859	15-DEC-1859	Patrick Rayly/Maria Hagan	Th--- Mur---/Marie Day
Rayly	Rosam Elisatham	21-DEC-1859	08-JAN-1860	Joannis Rayly/Anna Fenny	Carolus McCrony/ ----McCrony
Rayly*	Ma--	20-OCT-1858	22-OCT-1858	Thoma Rayly/Illena--- Nash	Caroly H---/--ia Farly
Rayly*	Thomas	14-MAY-1857	10-JUL-1857	Patrck Rayly/Maria ------	T Marten/B. Kelly
Rayly*	Thamas Gulemus	28-OCT-1856	02-NOV-1856	Michel Rayly/M--hi Phalan	G Phalan/M Plan--
Rayly*	Thomam Guillelmus	28-OCT-1856	02-NOV-1856	Michaelis Rayly/Matilda Phalan	G Phalan/M. Plan--
Rayly*	Sectliam	03-FEB-1858	07-FEB-1858	Patric Rayly/Maria Rayan	P. Coffy/A Flannigan
Raym--	Georgi		05-MAR-1879		
Raymond	Celinam Mariam	29-SEP-1876	01-OCT-1876	Israel Raymond/Salone Popino	J. Popino/ wife
Raymond	Dolores Agnes	21-JUL-1918	21-JUL-1918	Aaron Raymond/Zoe Balthazar	Albert Guillette/Frances Balthazar
Raymond	Franciscum	12-JUN-1880	13-JUN-1880	Israel Raymond/Salamo-- Popineau	G. Raymond/E. Raymond
Raymond	Frenam	17-AUG-1881	11-SEP-1881	Israel Raymond/Salome Papineau	Franciscus Dupuy/Catarina Cramer
Raymond	Georgius	07-FEB-1879	10-FEB-1879	Israel Raymond/Salomé Raymond	B. Perron/C. Perron
Raymond	Isaiam	06-DEC-1882	08-DEC-1882	Israel Raymond/Salomea Papineau	Narcas Maqun/Azilina Gervais
Raymond	Jacobum Eduardum	08-MAR-1884	01-APR-1884	Isracle Raymond/Salomia Papineau	Jacobus Connaughty/Catharina Perron
Raymond	Josephum Israel	19-NOV-1877	20-NOV-1877	Israel Raymond/Salome Pepineau	O. Pepineau/M. Bayé
Raymond	Mariam Salomeam	30-JUN-1885	12-JUL-1885	Israel Raymond/Salomea Papineau	Cornelia Moison/Telesphorus Edoin
Rayan*	Julian	08-JAN-1857	11-JAN-1857	Joannis Rayan/Anna Fox	T Fox/T. McIntyre
Rayan*	Maria	13-JUN-1855	19-AUG-1855	Patrick Rayan/Brigta Rcht	J Cogelan/E. Cogelan
Rayan*	Selvester	06-APR-1856	04-MAY-1856	Michel Rayan/Ellen McGenis	M Gaÿ/E -tich
Rayan*	Thamam	22-SEP-1857	27-SEP-1857	Patrici Rayan/Theresa McIntyre	F. McIntyre/M. Raburans
Rayly*	Wilhelmum Jocabum	08-AUG-1857	23-AUG-1857	Joannis Rayly/Anna Feny	J. McCrauly/M. Mccraly
Ready	Joannem	03-MAR-1855	13-APR-1863	Thoma Ready/Maria Ready	A. Conolly/M. King
Ready	Marguaritam	01-DEC-1861	23-FEB-1862	Thoma Ready/Maria Ready	J Phalan/B. Nugent
Real	Eliam Josephum	02-JUN-1870	16-JUL-1870	Elizeé Real/Parisa Tetro	Josephus Lafontaine/Odilia Leclerc
Réaume	Mary Rose Delma	26-MAY-1852	16-JUN-1852	Joseph Réaume/Sophia Provot	P. Nolty/E. Charon
Reed	Alexander	18-SEP-1875	19-SEP-1875	Alexandri Reed/Sophrina Lucia	J.--mmo/J Lucia
Reeves	Mariam Bellam	12-JUL-1882	06-OCT-1882	Selah Reeves/Maria-Anna Butler	Thomas Finegan/Anna Rossiter
Regan	Edmundum	11-FEB-1855	21-FEB-1855	Michaelis Regan/Helena Magennis	----- -----/C. Dallen
Regan	Helenam	03-MAR-1855	15-APR-1855	Joannis Regan/Anna Fox	P. Regan/C Fox
Regan	Marguaritam	01-DEC-1861	15-DEC-1861	Timothei Regan/Julia Regan	A Flood/---- ----
Rehl	Bernardum	29-JAN-1896	31-JAN-1896	Ricardo Rehl/Mathilda Corbeille	Cyrillus Corbeille/Anastasia Dufort
Rehl	Cyrillum Clarentium	20-MAR-1905	20-MAR-1905	Ricardo Rehl/Maria-Joanna Corbeille	Thomas Lepine-Jr /Amanda Corbeille
Rehl	Cyrilium Clarentium	20-MAR-1905	20-MAR-1905	Richardi Rehl/Maria-Joanna Corbeille	Thomas Lepine-Jr /Amanda Corbeille
Rehl	Josephum	14-AUG-1888	15-AUG-1888	Petro Rehl/Alphonsina Corbeille	Felix Corbeille/Anastasia Dufort
Reich	Sigismondum	10-FEB-1861	18-MAR-1861	Josephi Reich/Theresa Reich	G. Shertzinger/----- -----
Reichart	Joannem Georgium	21-MAY-1864	17-JUL-1864	Ignatii Reichart/ReginaReichart	G. Vekert/A. G--z
Reichelt	Guillelmum Henricum	20-JUN-1862	22-JUN-1862	Benedicti Reichelt/Augusta Reichelt	G. Rost/E. Lang
Reichelt	Wolfangum Guillelmum	20-JUN-1862	22-JUN-1862	Benedicti Reichelt/Augusta Reichelt	W. Lang/M. Cron
Reichert	Catharnam	23-SEP-1858	21-JUL-1861	Joannis Reichert/Clementina Reichert	G Shertzinger/ C Shertzinger

109

Surname	Given Name	Birth	Baptism	Parents	Godparents
Reichert	Emmam	23-APR-1860	11-SEP-1864	Joannis Reichert/Leopoldina Reichert	G Shertzinger/ C.Shertzinger
Reichert	Guillelmum Fredericum	08-DEC-1861	21-JUL-1861	Joannis Reichert/Clementina Reichert	G Shertzinger/ C.Shertzinger
Reichet	Annam		16-NOV-1862	Joannis Reichet/Leopoldina Reichet	G Shertzinger/C. Shertzinger
Reichling	Elizabetham	03-DEC-1863	06-DEC-1865	Antonii Reichling/Christina Reichling	F. Hartzheim/E Bügel
Reichling	Joannem	20-FEB-1864	02-MAR-1864	Antonii Reichling/Christina Reichling	J. Hansel/E. Abler
Reichling	Nicholaum	15-JUN-1862	18-JUN-1862	Antonii Reichling/Christina Reichling	N. Abler/C Hansel
Reider*	Ellen				
Reider*	Helenam	12-NOV-1858	12-JAN-1859	Thoma Reider/Catharina Odonel	Cath Keley/----- -----
Reider*	Helenam	12-NOV-1858	12-JAN-1859	Thoma Reider/Catharina OèDonel	----- -----/Cath Keley
Reider*	Martin				
Reiley	Jacobum		20-SEP-1863	Michaelis Reiley/Marguarita Reiley	J Fagan/M Fagan
Reiley	John				
Reiley	Martham	10-NOV-1861	17-NOV-1861	Michaelis Reiley/Marguarita Reiley	J. Russel/M. Co-fi-n
Reily	Joannem -----	08-JUN-1884	25-JUN-1884	John Reily/Martha Rely	Richard Rely/Mary Rely
Reily*	Helen Amelia	27-JUL-1858	07-SEP-1858	Malachin Reily/Elisabeth Donelly	Patrick McCarthy/Mary McDonald
Reily*	Helenam	27-JUL-1858	07-SEP-1858	Ma----- Reily/----- -----	P McCarthy/M. McDonald
Reschke	Carolum Orvilem	05-JUL-1908	20-JUL-1908	Carolo Reschke/Melvna Dinelle	Gedeo Brunet/Melvina Gervais-Barbeau
Reschke	Leonem Josephum Normad	19-FEB-1907	03-MAR-1907	Carolo Reschke/Minne Denelle	Ermicus Gervais/Olivina Charron-Gervais
Reske	Ludovicum Laurentuum Fre	25-JUL-1904	03-AUG-1904	Carolo Reske/Maria Dinelle	Ludovicus Dinelle/Delina Beauregard
Reyley*	M.				
Rheinhardt	Mary Merna	06-AUG-1918	18-AUG-1918	Charles Rheinhardt/Ione Martin	L J Martin/Lillian Martin-Hallows
Ri--y	Jacobum	01-AUG-1859	07-AUG-1859	Joannis Ri--y/Anna Welsh	Wilhelmus Logelan/Ellina Flind
Richard	Albiam Reginam	27-OCT-1880	27-OCT-1880	Emundo Richard/Anna McDonald	F. Marcoux/J. Roy
Richer	Eulaliam	13-AUG-1870	15-AUG-1870	Guillelmi Richer/Eulalia Joli	Carolus Joli/Leucadie Jolie
Richer	Mariam Elizabetham	21-MAR-1873	30-MAR-1873	Guillelmi Richer/Eulalia Joli	Carolus Joli/Maria Lafontanne
Richer	Thomas	31-JUL-1869	02-AUG-1869	Guillelmi Richer/Eulalia Joli	Stanslaus -----/Emlia Joli
Richy	Mariam Ludovicam	22-MAR-1874	22-MAR-1874	Guillelmi Richy/Eulalia Jolly	Thomas Jolly/Emilia L----- Richy
Riendeau	Baptistam		14-MAR-1861	Noëls Riendeau/Marguarita Riendeau	P. Leduc/V. Duquett
Riendeau	Josephinam	10-OCT-1862	30-NOV-1862	Noëls Riendeau/Marguarita Riendeau	J. Mocquin/M. Riendeau
Riendeau*	Cyrianum	17-JUN-1856	10-AUG-1856	Noel Riendeau/Margeretha Budin	P L'Etourneaux/M. Juet
Ries	Ferdnandum Meinradum	11-NOV-1861	14-NOV-1861	Constantini Ries/Maria Ries	M. Ries/B. Trmboer
Rieve	Josephnam Mariam Ludov	24-MAR-1868	29-MAR-1868	Theodulph Rieve/Pr---da Rieve	Cyrilus Bessette/Maria Robert
Rieve	Sophiam Veronicam	08-FEB-1871	12-FEB-1871	Theodolphi Rieve/Rachelis Bessete	Israel Bessete/Julia Bessete
Ring	Josephum	10-SEP-1852	26-SEP-1852	Guillelmus Ring/Marguerita Ring	P. Fistgerald/S. Snow
Ring	Marguaritam	27-JUN-1863	23-JUL-1863	Richardi Ring/Anna Ring	G Walsh/J. Flinn
Ring*	Eugenia	06-SEP-1856	13-SEP-1856	Richardus Ring/Joanna Welsh	G. Welsh/C Kelly
Ring*	Eugenam	06-SEP-1856	13-SEP-1856	Richardi Ring/Joanna Welschs	Q Welschs/C. Kelly
Ring*	Maria	20-JUN-1858	13-JUL-1858	Richardus Ring/Joanna Welsh	Richard King/Elisabeht Welshs
Ring*	Mariam	20-JUN-1858	13-JUL-1858	Richardi Ring/Joanna Walsh	R. Ring/E. Walsh
Rinhard	Annaman Louisam	29-APR-1876	15-JUN-1876	Joseph Rinhard/Annam Dumund	J. Dumund/M. Morris
Rister*	Annam Mariam	08-FEB-1857	08-FEB-1857	Petri Rister/Margeretha Wertz	J King/A. Lemarr
Ritchey	Guillelmum Edwardum	01-JUL-1862	06-JUL-1862	Joannis Ritchey/Winifrida Ritchey	R. Mollety/M. Fitzgerald
Ritssiert	David	30-JAN-1876	30-JAN-1876	William Ritssiert/Dellie Julie	D. Currer/ wife
Ritt--	Louis				
Rive	Mariam Melvinam	15-JUL-1873	27-SEP-1873	Theodulum Rive/Praxidam Bessette	Jeremas Rive/Zelaidas Rive
Rivor	Adelaidam	22-AUG-1870	24-NOV-1870	Basili Rivor/Merenta Rivor	Petrus Houle/Ada Hurteau
Rivor	Henricum		24-NOV-1870	Basili Rivor/Merentia Rivor	Antonius Borvin/Adelia Dugas
Ro-sach	Petrum Henricum		08-AUG-1861	Henrici Ro-sach/Catharina Ro-sach	G. Roghel/A. Sneder
Roach	Marguaritam Joannam	28-FEB-1862	02-MAR-1862	Joannis Roach/Bridgitta Roach	P. Mccarthy/M. Connell

110

Surname	Given Name	Birth	Baptism	Parents	Godparents
Roach	Thomam Franciscum	30-MAR-1862	06-APR-1862	Thoma Roach/Maria Roach	J. Roach/M. Ryan
Roach*	David Michel				
Roach*	M. Ellen				
Roach*	Margetham Elenora	17-FEB-1860	26-FEB-1860	Thama Roach/Maria ------	Joannes Waters/Margetha Conner
Roachs*	David Michaelem	05-MAY-1859	08-MAY-1859	Joannes Roachs/Brigetha Cou-t--	P. Kelly/M. ---ushs
Robage	Mariam Exeda Livinia	27-SEP-1873	30-NOV-1873	Octavii Robage/Belansia Dupuy	Baptista Dupuy/Mathilda Mocqin
Robage	Octavium Arthurem	20-MAY-1872	26-MAY-1872	Octavii Robage/Belonisia Dupus	Hubertus Baillargeon/Clotilda Dupus
Robarge	Josephum ----bertum	26-APR-1880	27-APR-1880	Octavii Roberge/Melani-e Dupus	S. Dupuis/D Bayageon
Robat*	Soseptina	24-APR-1857	03-MAY-1857	Francois Robat/Marie Bod--tau	G. Ollet/V. -----
Robedeu	Wilfred	10-JAN-1879		Moses Robedeu/Minnie Robedeu	M. Balthasar/----- Balthasar
Rober	Josephum Ignatium	20-JUN-1876	25-JUN-1876	Ugem Rober/Virgené Touschet	H. Lalajeunesse/M Touschet
Roberge	Josephum	11-DEC-1875	12-DEC-1875	Octavi Roberge/Bellanisia Laberge	J. Lafontaine/S. Dupus
Roberge	Mariam Cordeliam Leonis	15-DEC-1881	17-DEC-1881	Octavo Roberge/Melanisa Duputy	Onesamus Dupuy/Eugenia Pinger
Roberge	Mariam Helenam	29-APR-1876	30-APR-1876	Francois Roberge/Marie Ruell	J Jolie/O. Roberge
Roberge	Octavi	11-DEC-1875	12-DEC-1875	Octavi Roberge/Bellanisia Laberge	J. Lafontaine/S. Dupus
Robert	Alfredum	08-SEP-1893	10-SEP-1893	Francisco Robert/Marcellina Balthazar	Michael Balthazar/Philomena Robert
Robert	Alvam Olivinam	08-APR-1897	18-APR-1897	Josepho Robert/Rosalia Marcoux	Alexander Marcoux/Arzelia Beaudreault
Robert	Arthur Leonem	20-FEB-1880	29-FEB-1880	Eugenii Robert/Virginie Touchette-Robert	A. Touchette/E. Gauthier
Robert	Arthurum Georgium	03-MAY-1895	10-MAY-1895	Georgio Robert/Josephina Rondeau	Franciscus Rondeau/Octavia Edoin
Robert	Davidem	02-JUN-1865	04-JUN-1865	Davidis Robert/Julia Surprenant	I. Surprenant/J. Gayete
Robert	Emiliam	19-AUG-1865	10-SEP-1865	Francisci Robert/Maria Robert	F. Meunier/D. Cayen
Robert	Florentiam Mable	01-MAY-1907	19-MAY-1907	Georgio Robert/Josephina Rondeau	Severus Rondeau/Irenea Robert
Robert	Franciscum	05-OCT-1860	07-OCT-1860	Francisci Robert/Maria Beaudoin	I. Rassett/S Beaudoin
Robert	Franciscum Joannem Lave	31-DEC-1904	08-JAN-1905	Georgie Robert/Josephina Rondeau	Joannes-P. McCasy/Josephna-Robert McCasy
Robert	Georgium	29-MAY-1863	15-JUN-1863	Francisci Robert/Maria Robert	T Beaudin/L. Ebert
Robert	Georgium Guillelmum	10-JUL-1874	10-JUL-1874	Eugenii Robert/Virginia Touchette	Petrus Chef/Mathildis Gervais
Robert	Guillelmum	08-NOV-1867	10-NOV-1867	Davidis Robert/Julia Surprenant	P. Lajeunesse/E Surprenant
Robert	Harold Giorgium	12-SEP-1900	07-OCT-1900	Josepho Robert/Josephia Rondeau	Georgius Robert/Josephia Rondeau
Robert	Isadorum	05-APR-1887	07-APR-1887	Francisco Robert/Marcelina Balthazar	Francisco Robert/Maria Beaudoin
Robert	Josephnam	21-MAY-1868	06-JUN-1868	Francisci Robert/Julia Robert	Cyrilus Barete/Maria Barete
Robert	Josephum	18-OCT-1866	21-OCT-1866	Davidia Robert/Julia Robert	J Gayet/M. Gayet
Robert	Josephum	06-APR-1870	20-APR-1870	Francisci Robert/Maria Robert	Franciscus Bessete/Marguarita Lemieux
Robert	Josephum Clarentium	11-MAY-1898	15-MAY-1898	Josepho Robert/Rosalia Marcoux	Michael Balthazar/Philumena Robert
Robert	Josephum Franciscum Alb	29-FEB-1892	06-MAR-1892	Francisco Robert/Marcellina Marcoux	Joannes-Baptista Balthazar/Maria Marcoux
Robert	Josephum Laurentium	11-NOV-1898	13-NOV-1898	Francisco Robert/Marcellina Balthazar	Ludovicus Balthazar/Emelina Robert
Robert	Josephum Regium	25-JUL-1907	04-AUG-1907	Francisco Robert/Marcelina Balthazar	Isidorus Robert/Josephina Balthazar
Robert	Mariam Ceciliam	24-FEB-1906	04-MAR-1906	Francisco Robert/Marcelina Balthazar	J.J. Balthazar/Emilio LeBeau-Balthazar
Robert	Mariam Edessam	04-JUL-1895	09-JUL-1895	Josepho Robert/Rosa Marcoux	Franciscus Robert/Marcellma Balthazar
Robert	Mariam Esther	03-DEC-1893	09-DEC-1893	Josepho Robert/Maria-Rosa Marcoux	Franciscus Robert/Maria Beaudoin
Robert	Mariam Irenam	05-APR-1890	07-APR-1890	Georgio Robert/Josephina Rondeau	Franciscus Robert/Maria Beaudoin
Robert	Norbertum Amatum	04-MAY-1882	07-MAY-1882	Eugenio Robert/Virginia Fouchette	Edmundus Langlois/Margarita Racette
Robert	Wilfredum Fredericum Jose	15-FEB-1872	03-MAR-1872	Eugenii Robert/Virginia Touchete	Josephus Touchette/Flavia Bastien
Robert*	Josephinam	24-MAR-1857	03-MAY-1857	Francisci Robert/Maria Bodain	J. Ollet/V. Petet
Robert*	Philomena				
Robert*	Philomenam	16-DEC-1858		Francisci Robert/Maria Boduen	Theodorius Bodeun/Philomena Mathews
Robert*	Philomenam	16-DEC-1858	10-JAN-1859	Francisci Robert/Maria Bod-en	Theodorius Bod-en/Philomena Mathew
Robido	Moises	15-FEB-1875		Moises Robido/Milie Vernet	Franciscus Bodrieaux/Alphie Bodrieaux
Robidou	Alexium Joannem	05-NOV-1871	05-NOV-1871	Josephi Robidou/Herminia Pallant	Josephus Ste.-Marie/Josepha Pallant
Robidoux	Angelam	21-SEP-1882	24-SEP-1882	Onesimo Robidoux/Esther Lambert	Michael Lambert/Sophronia Barbeau

111

Surname	Given Name	Birth	Baptism	Parents	Godparents
Robidoux	Annam Joannam	09-MAY-1881	27-MAY-1881	Josepho Robidoux/Maria Boivin	Oliverus Husteau/Anna Supple
Robidoux	Carolum Arthur	01-SEP-1878	01-SEP-1878	Arthurum Robidoux/Ludovica Moquin	M Préfontaine/O. Desautel
Robidoux	Honoratum Maglorium	24-SEP-1883	30-SEP-1883	Josepho Robidoux/Hermina Pellant	Maglorius Préfontaine/Olivina Desautels
Robidoux	Josephum Ludgerium	21-JUL-1886	21-JUL-1886	Josepho Robidoux/Hermina Pellant	Ludgerius Durocher/Maria-Clara Robidoux
Robidoux	Mariam Annam	18-APR-1885	19-APR-1885	Josepho Robidoux/Hermina Pellant	Franciscus Durocher/Sophia Pellant
Robidoux	Mariam Elizabeth	29-SEP-1888	30-SEP-1888	Josepho Robidoux/Hermnia Pellant	Alexius Prefontaine/Elmra Hubert
Robidoux	Mariam Helenam	07-AUG-1882	25-AUG-1882	Josepho Robidoux/Maria Boivin	Petrus Barbeau/Phlumene Boivin
Robidoux	Mariam Helenam	28-MAR-1881	03-APR-1881	Moise Robidoux/Emelia Moquin	A. Robidoux/L. Moquin
Robidoux	Mariam Jasephinam	25-MAY-1881	26-MAY-1881	Josepho Robidoux/Armina Pellant	T Rondeau/J. Pellant
Robidoux	Mariam Lucretiam	21-JUN-1882	22-JUN-1882	Josepho Robidoux/Hermina Pellant	Vitulis Prefontaine/Azilda Rondeau
Robin	Ann	20-OCT-1851	17-DEC-1851	Peter Robin/Alice Hennery	M. Robin/B. Ferguson
Robinson	George Anne	22-JAN-1877	28-JAN-1877	James Robinson/Maria Lions	R. Dillon/M. Brown
Robinson	John	05-OCT-1851	24-FEB-1852	Michael Robinson/Mary Judge	H. Mullen/M. McCoy
Robinson*	Maria	07-DEC-1856	14-DEC-1856	P.--- Robinson/Maria Gage	P. ---/M. -----
Robinson*	Mariam	07-DEC-1856	14-DEC-1856	Michaelis Robinson/Maria Guge	P. Guge/M. Curran
Roble	Giorgium	15-SEP-1900	27-OCT-1900	Victore Roble/Maria Ledo	Georgius Langlois/Maria Moquin
Roche	Michael	13-JUL-1860	15-JUL-1860	Joannis Roche/Maria Corey	Joannis Maeth/Maria Mangan
Roche*	Joannem Eduardum	23-JUL-1857	26-JUL-1857	---- Roche/Maria --n--	M. Megsu----/E Lancort
Roche*	Michael				
Rochel	Annam Margueritam	05-APR-1864	10-APR-1864	Guillelmi Rochel/Agnetta Rochel	P Léon/M. G-res
Rochel	Josephum	24-JUL-1862	27-JUL-1862	Guillelmi Rochel/Agnetia Rochel	J Trner/H. Leinen
Rochel	Ursulam	12-DEC-1865	17-DEC-1865	Guillelmi Rochel/Agnetia Rochel	P Leinen/U Hersh
Rochell	Annam	16-MAR-1889	25-APR-1889	Josepho Dufort/Elizabeth Rochell	----- -----/Iona Rochell
Rochs*	Joannes	15-FEB-1856	10-MAY-1856	Niculus Rochs/Margith Kagelan	N. Pierre/M. Mc-evit
Rochs*	Joannes Eduardus	23-JUL-1857	26-JUL-1857	Thamas Rochs/Mara Own	M. Migary/E. Liensch
Rochts*	Mariam Annam	23-MAY-1857	24-MAY-1857	Joannes Rochts/Brigetha Casten	G. Brown/B. Brown
Rockaway	Joannem		21-OCT-1865	Benjamin Rockaway/Ludovica Rockaway	P. Ruls/L. Eter
Rodier*	Maria	12-FEB-1858	17-FEB-1858	Antonius Rodier/Margereta Sneyder	Chisr---ts Aldmann/Maria Crammer
Rodrier*	Mariam	13-FEB-1858	17-FEB-1858	Antonius Rodrier/Margeretha Snyder	C. Atemann/M. Cramer
Roeht*	Marie Anna	23-MAY-1857	24-MAY-1857	John Roeht/Brigita Conlon	W. Brown/M. -----
Roehts*	Joannem	15-FEB-1856	10-MAY-1856	Nicholaii Roehts/Margeretha Kagelun	N. Perr--/M. McLevy
Rogan	Joannam	29-APR-1858	16-MAY-1858	Joanne Rogan/Maria Slattery	T, Vaughn/M. Walsh
Rogan	Johanna Jane	29-APR-1858	16-MAY-1858	John Rogan/Mary Slatterey	Thimoty Vaughan/Marguertte Walsh
Rogers*	Anna Maria	02-MAR-1858	04-APR-1858	Felix Rogers/Caterina D--kon	Walters Shantun/Mona D--urgan
Rogers*	Annam Mariam	02-APR-1858	04-APR-1858	Filici Rogers/Catherina Durkin	W Stantan/A. Durkan
Rogery*	Gertruda	02-JAN-1856	12-JAN-1856	Antoine Rogery/Margeta Snyder	J. Simmons/G. Servatus
Rogery*	Gertrudam		12-JAN-1856	Antoni Rogery/Margeretta Snÿder	F. Simmons/G. Servatius
Roi	Ludovicum Philippum	19-JUL-1872	04-AUG-1872	Liguorii Roi/Maria Faucher	Franciscus Mocquin/Josepha Pellant
Roi	Mariam Emiliam	03-JAN-1873	05-JAN-1873	Isaia Roi/Josephina Roi	Franciscus Marcou/Emilia Marcou
Roi	Mariam Julianam	08-JUN-1854	10-JUN-1854	Francisci Roi/Julia La---r	L Landerman/A. Mcriles
Roi	Mariam Reginam	22-APR-1871	23-APR-1871	Leguorii Roi/Maria Faucher	Ludovicus Laplante/F------ Laplante
Roi	Mariam Victoriam Ludovi	22-DEC-1867	25-DEC-1867	Ligourii Roi/Maria Faucher	F. Pellant/F Faucher
Roi	Narcissum Olivierum	04-DEC-1869	05-DEC-1869	Ligourii Roi/Maria Foucher	Ludovicus Lebeau/Emilia Roi
Roi*	Maria Eugenie		20-APR-1857	Francois Roi/----- L--mer	J. Losson/----- Jubert
Roi*	Mariam Eugeniam	24-MAR-1857	20-APR-1857	Francisi Roi/Julia LeMeir	F. Lasson/E. Hubert
Roi* **	Mariam Eugeniam	17-APR-1856	15-APR-1856	Francici Roi/Julia Lemer	I. Chenard/S. Sir
Roiseau-Labonté	Petrum Augustinum	16-AUG-1870	03-SEP-1870	Eusebil Roiseau-Labonté/Sophia Roi	Josephus Choquéte/Helena Choquéte
Roman	Henricum	26-APR-1858	28-MAY-1858	Maurtio Roman/Emilia Rose	T. Reiley/A. Duffy
Roman	Henry	26-APR-1858	28-MAY-1858	Maurice Roman/Emelia Rose	Thos Reily/Ann Duffy

112

Surname	Given Name	Birth	Baptism	Parents	Godparents
Ronan	Helenam	26-APR-1863	23-MAY-1863	Dyonisii Ronan/Bridgitta Ronan	T Loughlin/C. Loughlin
Rondeau	Alexandrum Frederic	14-APR-1887	17-APR-1887	Francisco Rondeau/Flavia Edoin	Alexius Tremblay/Melania Edoin
Rondeau	Carolum	21-MAY-1868	14-JUN-1868	Alvida Rondeau/Maria Rondeau	Antonus Bastien/Marguarita Bastien
Rondeau	Eleonoram	13-JUN-1871	18-JUN-1871	Francisci Rondeau/Flavia Rondeau	Leo Edoun/Flavia Mocquin
Rondeau	Emmam	12-JAN-1871	29-JAN-1871	Josephi Rondeau/Maria Rondeau	Petrus Dufresne/Onesima Dufresne
Rondeau	Franciscum Alexandrum	01-MAR-1866	04-MAR-1866	Thoma Rondeau/Josephina Rondeau	F. Rondeau/J. De---
Rondeau	Fredericum	08-SEP-1869	12-SEP-1869	Thoma Rondeau/Josephina Pelland	Modestus Montblot/---- -----
Rondeau	Georgiam Annam	06-NOV-1866	18-NOV-1866	Alvida Rondeau/Maria Rondeau	A Desmarais/A Desmarais
Rondeau	Georgium Arthurum	14-OCT-1889	20-OCT-1889	Francisco Rondeau/Flavia Edoin	Georgius Robert/Josephina Rondeau
Rondeau	Georgium Henricum	14-DEC-1881	25-DEC-1881	Francisco-Alfred Rondeau/Maria Demers	Josephus Duquet/Christina Cheffe
Rondeau	Guillelmum	26-SEP-1873	11-OCT-1873	Isidori Rondeau/Maria Lem-ra	Desideratus Picore/Zoa -----
Rondeau	Henricum Felander	03-NOV-1887	20-NOV-1887		Franciscus Rondeau/Eleonora Lepine
Rondeau	Henriettam Theresam	30-DEC-1905	26-SEP-1906	Henrico Rondeau/Maria Sullivan	----- ----/Nora Sullivan
Rondeau	Joannem Baptistam	15-JUL-1884	20-JUL-1884	Francisco Rondeau/Felavia Edoin	Franciscus Moquin/Henrietta Percheron
Rondeau	Josephinam	05-DEC-1868	27-DEC-1868	Francisci Rondeau/Flavia Rondeau	Franciscus Rondeau/Eleonora Lépine
Rondeau	Maria Josephinam	27-MAY-1875	09-MAY-1875	Thomas Rondeau/Sophena Peddeland	Ligory Roi/Chrstina Randeaux
Rondeau	Mariam Adelaidam	27-SEP-1871	08-OCT-1871	Thoma Rondeau/Josephina Rondeau	Franciscus Pallant/Flavia Faucher
Rondeau	Mariam Elizabetham	10-OCT-1861	03-NOV-1861	Thoma Rondeau/Josephina Rondeau	J. Lemaire/M. Pedlant
Rondeau	Mariam Floram	11-DEC-1867	15-DEC-1867	Thoma Rondeau/Josephina Rondeau	J Durocher/A. Fourcher
Rondeau	Mariam Olivam	15-AUG-1882	20-AUG-1882	Francisco Rondeau/Octavia Edoin	Ludgerius Noupré/Elmire Lefort
Rondeau	Melaniam	17-AUG-1866	24-JUL-1867	Baptista Rondeau/Melania Rondeau	F. Rondeau/E. Lépine
Rondeau	Melindam	14-APR-1870	17-APR-1870	Joannis-Baptista Rondeau/Ada Rondeau	Franciscus Rondeau/Eleonora Rondeau
Rondeau	Severum	22-MAR-1880	28-MAR-1880	Francisco Rondeau/Flavia Edoun	S. Edoun/A Morris
Rondeau	Thomam Josephum	26-MAR-1864	27-MAR-1864	Thoma Rondeau/Josephina Rondeau	S. Houle/C. Joubertville
Rondeau*	Exilda				
Rondeau*	Francis				
Rondeau*	Michael				
Rony	Jacobum	02-JAN-1861	20-JAN-1861	Dyonisii Rony/Bridgitta Rony	T Nugent/A. Flood
Rony*	Jacobum	01-AUG-1859	07-AUG-1859		
Rony*	James				
Roque	Josephum	26-NOV-1871	26-NOV-1871	Josephi Roque/Anna Roque	Nazarius Meunier/Joanna Lemaire
Rori	Josephum Petrum	01-AUG-1879	02-AUG-1879	Lagori Rori/Maria Faucher	O. Comtas/A Faucher
Ross*	Carolum	09-NOV-1857	11-JUL-1858	Joannis Ross/Chrstina Yong	J Teng/M Leiman
Ross*	Carolus	09-NOV-1857	11-JUL-1858	John Ross/Christine Young	John Leing/Maria Layman
Rosseheter*	Annam Mariam	24-MAR-1857	27-MAR-1857	Jocabi Rosseheter/Elena Furlong	J Brown/A Rosseheter
Rosset	Mariam Zoé	15-JUL-1860	05-AUG-1860	Julien Rosset/May Sir	Joannes-Maria Marceau/Maria Marceau
Rossete	Mariam Hermiruiam	08-JUN-1863	28-JUN-1863	Juliani Rossete/Marguarita Rossete	F. Marcou/E. Marcou
Rossete*	Mary Zoeh				
Rosseter*	Maria Anna	24-MAR-1857	24-MAR-1857	James Rosseter/Ellen Furlong	J Brown/A Rosshetter
Rost	Evam Dorotheam	12-APR-1865	23-APR-1865	Guillelmi Rost/Anna Crö-s	W. Gra-s/E. Gra-s
Rost	Henricum	13-MAY-1863	23-MAY-1863	Petri Rost/Anna-Marguarita Kr--s	B. Reichelt/A. Cröers
Rothe	Isaium	16-OCT-1870	06-JUL-1872	Maxmi Rothe/Mathilda Rothe	Moyses Robidou/Emilia Robidou
Rothé	Ludovicum	16-MAY-1860	02-JUN-1860	Maxim Rothé/Matilda Fanet	Mathilda Hubert/Lusie Fanet
Rothgery	Elizabetham	01-JAN-1864	17-JAN-1864	Antonii Rothgery/Marguaritha Rothgery	A. Hanan/E. Hirsh
Rothgery	Josephum	26-AUG-1861	26-AUG-1861	Antonii Rothgery/Anna-Marguaritha Rothgery	J Crämmet/M. Reeis
Rouchar	Mariam Emiliam	04-MAY-1867	05-MAY-1867	Octavii Rouchar/Rosalia Ebert	L. Petit/E. Cyr
Roulo	Mariam Ludovicam	13-AUG-1877	26-AUG-1877	Armeni Roulo/Rosalia Jubert	M. Roulo/M. Roulo
Rouny*	Anna	13-APR-1857	13-APR-1857	John Rouny/Anna Woods	J. Nulty/E. Flood
Rouny*	Annam	12-APR-1857	13-APR-1857	Joannes Rouny/Anna Woods	J. Nulty/E. Flood

113

Surname	Given Name	Birth	Baptism	Parents	Godparents
Rousson	Alexandrum	02-AUG-1853	20-AUG-1853	Bernardi Rousson/Maria Galligan	J Galligan/M. Galligan
Roy	Annam Luciliam	27-JUL-1900	29-JUL-1900	Phili-- Roy/Anna-Catharina Jentz	Petrus Roy/Emelia Jentz
Roy	Arthurum Glen	01-MAR-1905	12-MAR-1905	Arthuro Roy/Elizabeth Williams	Petrus Roy/Agnes Gratzka
Roy	Artor Ludovicum	11-JAN-1875	12-JAN-1875	Liogora Roy/Maria Foché	Franciscus Marcou/Amenia Lebeau
Roy	Florentiam Myrtle	14-MAR-1898	20-MAR-1898	Olivero Roy/Melvina Pratte	Arthurus Pratte/Albertina Pratte
Roy	Georgium Elmo	14-DEC-1909	25-DEC-1909	Petro Roy/Agnes Gratzhe	Eduardus Touchette/Anna Roy-Touchette
Roy	Helenam	18-MAR-1902	30-MAR-1902	Arthuro Roy/Elizabetha Williams-Braun	Phileas Roy/Irenea Braun
Roy	Josephum		21-JUN-1903	Petro Roy/Agnete Gratzke	Ligarius Roy/Maria Faucher
Roy	Josephum Warren Arnold	17-FEB-1898	23-MAY-1898	Philippo Roy/Edith-Adela Coon	Josephus Buh/Georgina Roy
Roy	Ludovicam Mariam	05-JAN-1902	12-JAN-1902	Philo Roy/Anna Jentz	Arsenus-Josephus-L. Roy/Emma Allard
Roy	Ludovicum Josephum Mar	01-MAY-1878	02-MAY-1878	Ligore Roy/Maria Fouché	L. Dale/M Dale
Roy	Mariam	03-OCT-1908	11-OCT-1908	Olivario Roy/Malvina Pratte	Arsenus-L.-J. Roy/Emma Allard-Roy
Roy	Mariam Annam Alicem	13-FEB-1884	17-FEB-1884	Ligouriem Roy/Maria Faucher	Oliverus Roy/Ludovica Roy
Roy	Mariam Estellam	22-JUN-1901	30-JUN-1901	Olivero Roy/Malvina Pratte	Felix Pratte/Sara Duquet
Roy	Mary July	19-AUG-1850	19-AUG-1850	Francis Roy/July Lemre	S. Hoakley/G. Leclerc
Roy	Robert Victoriam	26-AUG-1905	27-AUG-1905	Oliverio Roy/Malvina Pratte	Victor Lonblot/Josephine Hanker-Pratte
Roy*	Maria Eugenia		19-APR-1856	Francois Roy/Julien Lemare	I. Chenard/S. Sir
Ruh	Martham Ruth	03-JUL-1906	05-JUL-1906	Hermano Ruh/Melina Errard	Augustus Marcoux/Julia Leduc-Marcoux
Rulo	Guillelmum	03-JUL-1870	22-MAR-1871	Benjamins Rulo/Ludovica Rulo	Joannes Rosseter/Anna Rosseter
Rulo	Henrietam	07-SEP-1868	17-SEP-1868	Hermani Rulo/Merentia Rulo	Cyrilus Rulo/Maria Mayou
Rulo	Ludovicum	27-JAN-1868	19-FEB-1868	Cyril Rulo/Maria Rulo	Hermina Rulo/Sophia Rulo
Rulo	Marguaritam Helenam	18-JUN-1865	06-DEC-1865	Cyril Rulo/Maria Rulo	J. Coughlin/M. Coughlin
Rulo	Mattheum	21-JUN-1872	23-JUN-1872	Hermni Rulo/Emerantia Rulo	Josephus Lépine/Elizabetha Rondeau
Rulo	Rosaliam		13-JAN-1867	Armini Rulo/Merentia Rulo	P Rulo/L. Etier
Rummle*	Rosa Francisca Maria	28-SEP-1858	18-NOV-1858	Ferdnand Rummle/Mary Forster	Jacab Flatten/Mary-Francis Flatten
Russ	Petrum Paulum	04-MAY-1863	04-JUL-1863	Joannis-Georgii Russ/Christina Russ	A. Pomerick/R. Voll-emuth
Russell	Marguaritam Elizabetham	21-OCT-1863	01-NOV-1863	Jacobi Russell/Rosa Russell	J. Fitzgerald/M. Tracy
Russell	Mariam Helenam	25-DEC-1861	29-DEC-1861	Jacobi Russell/Rosa Russell	M Reily/M Curran
Russell*	Thomas	31-DEC-1858	10-JAN-1859	MichelRussell/Helene Mahaney	Thos Roche/Helene Carney
Russell* **	Thomas				
Russell* **	Thomas	10-JAN-1859	31-DEC-1858	Michel Russell/Helene Mahaney	Thomas Roche/Helene Carney
Ryan	Annam	10-JAN-1863	11-JAN-1863	Patrici Ryan/Theresa Ryan	T. Holoran/C Mee
Ryan	Franciscum Michaelem	10-JAN-1883	20-FEB-1883	Edmundo Ryan/Maria-Anna Corcoran	Peter Ryan/Margarita Ryan
Ryan	Georgium		26-MAY-1868	Joannis Ryan/Anna Ryan	Michael Ryan/Suzanna Howorth
Ryan	Guillelmum		13-FEB-1853	Martin Ryan/Ellena McMahan	T Vaughn/M. McMahan
Ryan	James	31-MAR-1851	19-JUN-1851	Martin Ryan/Ellen McMahan	C. Morgan/M M-lo-y
Ryan	Joannem	18-AUG-1863	30-AUG-1863	Joanns Ryan/Anna Ryan	J O'connor/J. Haze
Ryan	Marguaritam	07-JAN-1862	26-JAN-1862	Joanns Ryan/----- Ryan	N O'Brien/A. O'Brien
Ryan	Mariam	11-SEP-1863	11-SEP-1863	Danieli Ryan/Bridgitta Ryan	G Ryan/M Ryan
Ryan	Mariam Annam Theresam	04-NOV-1862	04-DEC-1862	Michaelis Ryan/Helena Ryan	R. Kennedy/M. Burke
Ryan	Michael	08-NOV-1850	10-NOV-1850	Patrick Ryan/Anna Calvi	J Lawler/M. ------
Ryan	Patricum	15-APR-1861	21-APR-1861	Michaelis Ryan/Helena Ryan	G Burke/C Dolton
Ryan	Richardum	06-JUL-1863	12-SEP-1863	Timother Ryan/Julia Ryan	E. Pitt/J Annis
Ryan	Thomam	22-JUN-1852	20-JUL-1852	Patrici Ryan/Brigitta Ryan	P. Mccray/M. Mcclone
Ryan	Thomam	01-DEC-1852	12-DEC-1852	Patrici Ryan/Rosa Cahill	C Mangan/M. Mangan
Ryan*	Catharine				
Ryan*	Francis				
Ryan*	Mary				
Ryan*	Peter				

114

Surname	Given Name	Birth	Baptism	Parents	Godparents
Ryans*	Mariam	28-MAY-1860	25-JUN-1860	Patricii Ryans/Rosa Cahil	Joannes Newman/Rosa Flood
Sago	Jacobum Henricum		18-DEC-1862	Joannis Sago/Julia Sago	M. Clarke/------ ------
Saligan	Joannem	21-JAN-1865	13-MAR-1865	Michaelis Saligan/Anna Saligan	J. Haas/B. -ickel
Salmond	Mariam Ludovicam Rosali	14-JUN-1872	16-JUN-1872	Raphaelis Salmond/Elizabetha Salmond	Michaei Balthazar/Rosalie Balthazar
Salter	Cora Mariam	04-JAN-1887	26-OCT-1906	Roberto Salter/Maria Botzam	Joannes Fitzpatrick/Rose Botza-Fitzpatrick
Samuell	John	07-DEC-1851	12-DEC-1851	Michael Samuell/Ellen Fistgerald	T ------/B. Fistgerald
Sanctuare	Adelaïdam Elizabetham	23-AUG-1871	24-SEP-1871	Michaelis Sanctuare/Mathilda Sanctuaire	Josephus Oreal/Amati Préfontane
Sanctuere	Eduardum	01-OCT-1873	13-MAR-1876	Octavii Sanctuere/Abigan Hennery	------ ------/M. Lemieux
Sanctuere	William Henricum	03-MAR-1876	13-MAR-1876	Octavii Sanctuere/Abigan Hennery	------ ------/M. Lemieux
Sandal*	Jocabus		29-AUG-1857		T Rayly/C. Jocobus
Sandal*	Jocobum		29-AUG-1857		T. Raÿly/C. Jacobs
Santuare	Abrahamum	16-JUN-1865	02-JUL-1865	Michaelis Santuaire/Mathilda Ebert	E. St.-Réal/M. Santuaire
Santuare	Alfredum	11-OCT-1864	12-JAN-1867	Octavi Santuaire/Abigaïla Santuaire	C. Nolin/M. Santuaire
Santuare	Amatam Helenam	10-AUG-1869	15-AUG-1869	Octavii Santuaire/Abigaelis Santuaire	Napoleo Martin/Eleonora Dumas
Santuaire	Guillelmum Josephum	10-SEP-1869	26-SEP-1869	Guilelmi-Josephi Santuaire/Mathilda Santuaire	Josephus Rial/Clotilda Rial
Santuare	Mariam	19-JUL-1867	11-AUG-1867	Michaelis Santuaire/Mathilda Santuaire	F. Landreman/R Veine
Santuare	Mariam Elizabetham	23-AUG-1866	12-JAN-1867	Octavi Santuaire/Abigaïla Santuaire	M. Santuaire/M Fontaine
Santuare	Narcissum Napoleonem		04-JUN-1863	Michaelis Santuaire/Mathilda Santuaire	J. Ebert/O. Nolin
Santuare	Ophiliam	24-JUL-1868	23-AUG-1868	Octavi Santuaire/Abigaïla Santuaire	Marcellus Picor/Paulina Picor
Sauvé	Josephum Arthurum Zenon	05-APR-1871	09-APR-1871	Philomonis Sauvé/Christina Bastien	Moyses Bastien/Delima Rocage
Sauvé	Josephum Clavet Delude	07-MAR-1875	07-MAR-1875	Philemond Sauvé/Christian Derancaut	Eluda Vaine/Sophia Deranceau
Sauvé	Josephum Stanislaum	18-JAN-1872	20-JAN-1872	Stanislai Sauvé/Emilia Sch.	Augustus Landreman/Leucadia ------
Sauvé	Maglorum	03-JUN-1869	03-JUN-1869	Philomonis Sauvé/Christina Sauvé	Maglorius Sauvé/Maria Landreman
Sauvé	Mariam Emmam	07-OCT-1870	09-OCT-1870	Stanislai Sauvé/Emilia Joli	Maglorius Sauvé/Euphrasia Joli
Sauvé	Mariam Herminiam	25-JAN-1873	25-JAN-1873	Philomonis Sauvé/Christna Bastien	Paulus Sauvé/Marguarita Vaine
Sauvé	Mariam Ludovicam	19-JUN-1876	20-JUN-1876	Stanislas Sauvé/Emilia Joly	L. Brunet/E. Joly
Sauvé	Marian Corenth	16-APR-1875	16-APR-1875	Pauli Sauvé/Margertha Vaine	Magloire Sauvée/Rosalna Vaine
Sauvé	Philomenam	26-MAY-1868	27-MAY-1868	Philomonis Sauvé/Christina Bastien	Baptista Bastien/Marcila Veine
Sauvey	Mariam E. P		01-NOV-1873	Pauli Sauvey/Margarita Venne	Francisci Venne/Marcelina Venne
Savéz	Joannem Mariam Victor	27-SEP-1876	27-SEP-1876	Pauli Savéz/Margeret Vane	S. Vaine/E. Jolie
Sawyer	Aliciam	13-APR-1863	26-APR-1863	Joannis Sawyer/Anna Sawyer	J Han-l--/M. Han-l--
Scannel	Catherine	04-JUL-1851	11-JUL-1851	Cornelus Scannel/Mary Clary	M. Scannel/C. Hogan
Scannel*	Bridget				
Scannel*	Donelius				
Scannell*	Bridget	10-DEC-1858	19-DEC-1858	Mc-- Scannell/Helene Fitzgerald	Dennis Fitzgerald/Cecilia McCalan
Scannell*	Bridget	10-DEC-1858	19-DEC-1858	Mcl Scannell/Helene Fitzgerald	Denis Fitzgerald/Cecilia McCalan
Scaul	Mathias	02-MAR-1855	03-OCT-1858	Jacob Scaul/Gertruda Handschomaker	Marie Ver--s/Mathas ------
Scaul	Stbelom		03-OCT-1858	Jacob Scaul/Gertruda Handschomaker	Antom Dek/Sebela Curlings
Scaul	Simeonem	02-NOV-1856	03-OCT-1858	Jacob Scaul/Gertruda Handschomaker	Simien Vadinand/Els-- Scaul
Sch--l*	Michelem	29-OCT-1859	30-OCT-1859	Jacb. Sch--l/Cathar Hen--master	D. -ithel/A. Sch--l
Schaman	Carolus	01-APR-1858	21-APR-1858	Pel-- Schaman/Cata--a Michel	C-rel Hi--ert/Margeth Olinger
Schanck	Henriettam	24-JUL-1898	07-AUG-1898	Henrico-Henry Schanck/Maria Duprez	Ludgerius Dupuy/Juliana Lucier
Schank	Leonem Earl	15-JAN-1897	15-JAN-1897	Henrico Schank/Anna Dupuy	
Scharky*	Jocobum	25-FEB-1858	27-FEB-1858	Michaelis Scharky/Brigetha Do--sy	M Currans/B. Donnell
Scheffer*	Anna Maria	08-SEP-1855	16-SEP-1855	Daniel Scheffer/Anna-Margereta Hurlings	J Cheffer/A. Puts
Schermann*	Niculus	10-DEC-1855	16-DEC-1855	Philus Schermann/Catherna Michel	N. Stivens/E. B---in-
Schermer*	Otto-Petrum		01-FEB-1858	Englcb-- Schermer/Anna-Maria Bigeler	W. Wenner/----- ------
Schermam*	Nicolaum	10-DEC-1855	16-DEC-1855	Philipi Schernam/Maria Michel	N. Stivens/E. -----m
Schleier	Joannem Florianum	23-FEB-1864	19-MAR-1864	Joannis Schleier/Catharina Schleier	W. Giebel/A. Romach

115

Surname	Given Name	Birth	Baptism	Parents	Godparents
Schneider	Andream Elmer	04-JUL-1891	01-AUG-1891	Henrico Schneider/Josephina Fritz	Josephus Daniel/Ludovica Poirier
Schneider	Ida Mariam Ruth	18-APR-1896	10-MAY-1896	Henrico Schneider/Josephina Fritz	Georgius Lyonais/Ida Lyonais
Schneider	Otto		28-JUN-1871	Joanns Schneider/Rosa Dana	Guillelmus Dana/Ludovica Dana
Schoemaker*	Elisabeth	11-OCT-1855	12-OCT-1855	Petrus Schoemaker/Margerita Ogan	M.Schoemaker/ E.Schoemaker
Schoemaker*	Joannem	04-MAR-1858	07-MAR-1858	Petri Schoemaker/Margeretha Scher	J Schoemaker/B. Osha
Schoeve	Victor Henry	04-JUL-1920	11-JUL-1920	Louis-C. Schoeve/Clara Huhn	Harry Huhn/Mrs.-J. Ziegler
Schoners	Eminam	05-DEC-1859	07-DEC-1859	Bapt Schoners/Rosalia Verre	Thamas Bodin/Charistia Flora
Schossel*	Anna Maria				
Schrzinger	Germanum Christophe	14-JUL-1859	29-JUL-1859	Germann Schrzinger/Catherina Ges	Christopher Serwe/Maria Hes
Schummer*	Annam	27-JAN-1859	09-OCT-1859	Engelberti Schummer/Anna-Maria B-gel	W. ---eiman-/A. Ch-rbeno
Schummer*	Anne				
Schummer*	William		09-OCT-1859	Engelberti Schummer/Anna-Maria B-gel	W. ---eman-/M. Mossel
Schummer*	William				
Scooley	Sophiam	17-AUG-1866	05-APR-1869	Stephani-D. Scooley/Isabella Scooley	Edessa Bullis/Maria Vancoeur
Scott	Delphinam	09-OCT-1863	05-MAR-1867	Francisci Scott/Josephina Scott	J. Réal/L. Nolin
Scott	Guillelmum Wallace	25-SEP-1860	10-JAN-1864	Francisci Scott/Josepha Scott	M. Straiz/J. Leco-q
Scott	Mariam Angelam	03-FEB-1858	06-JAN-1861	Francisci Scott/Josepha Scott	M. St.-Pierre/C. Deschenes
Se-ar*	Mary Agnes	28-JAN-1888	02-APR-1858	Nicol Se-ar/Anna Chausman	James Erberling/Anna Cheffer
Seager	Dasiam Mariam	18-JUL-1880	12-FEB-1888	Georgio Seager/Helena Loiseau	Evaristo Beaudette/Emma Carbonneau
Seager	Harold Alexandrum	03-FEB-1858	03-OCT-1880	Georgius Seager/Helena L'Oiseau	D. Chaperon/D. Chaperon
Sebar*	Mariam Agnes	02-DEC-1876	01-APR-1858	Nicolaio Sebar/Anna Chausman	J. Ebberling/A. Cheffer
Sebastian	Andriam		03-DEC-1876	John Sebastian/Roshel Vin	G. Brunet/M. Sebastian
Secor	Guillelmum S	02-JUN-1868	16-JUN-1868	Joannis Secor/Julia Secor	-------/Helena Conway
Secla*	Maria	19-SEP-1856	05-OCT-1856	Ferdus Seela/Maria Caufman	J. Caufman/M. Snyder
Seela*	Mariam	19-SEP-1856	05-OCT-1856	Frederici Seela/Maria Cofman	J Cofman/M. Snyder
Seing	Petrum	22-FEB-1859	02-MAR-1862	------/Theresa Seing	J. Seing/T. Waerly
Seligan	Nicholaum	06-FEB-1862	10-MAR-1862	Michaelis Seligan/Anna Seligan	N. Justin/G. Petri
Selliger	Catharinam	18-JAN-1861	29-JAN-1861	Michaelis Selliger/Anna Selliger	C. Crämmer/------ ----
Sellivam*	Jan--	18-JUL-1858	22-AUG-1858	Joannes Sellivam/Catherina Dour--	Jocobus Lenschs/Ellena McGlogelan
Senecal	Henrette ---ssé	18-MAY-1875	04-JUL-1875	Théophile Senecal/Adelme Gilman	Pierre Gilman/Melnie Edouam
Senecal	Josephum Alexandrum	03-SEP-1883	04-SEP-1883	Ovido Senecal/Melina Tessier	Moises Bastien/Sophia Bastien
Senecal	Josephum Carolum Maxim	23-MAR-1891	23-MAR-1891	Ovide Senecal/Rosa-Delima Venne	Joannes-B Bastien/Rochelle Venne
Senecal	Josephum Ernestum	21-OCT-1896	25-OCT-1896	Ovide Senecal/Maria-Rosa-Delima Venne	Ovidus Senecal/Marianna Bastien
Senecal	Josephum Ludovicum Alde	29-JAN-1899	29-JAN-1899	Ovide Senecal/Maria-Rosa-Delima Venne	Aldericus Venne/Melina Fontaine
Senecal	Josephum Ovidum	15-OCT-1881	16-OCT-1881	Ovide Senecal/Rosa-Delima Venne	Euclidus Venne/Adelma Bosage
Senecal	Mariam Elmam	07-NOV-1889	07-NOV-1889	Davide Senecal/Maria-Rosa-Delima Venne	Aldericus Venne/Malvina Fontane
Senecal	Mariam Ludovicum Angeli	20-JUN-1894	20-JUN-1894	Ovide Senecal/Maria-Melina Venne	Paulus Sauvé/Maria-Louisa Venne
Senecal	Mariam Mercedem	18-JUL-1892	19-JUL-1892	Ovide Senecal/Maria-Louisa-Melima Venne	Gedeon Brunet/Melina Bastien
Senecal	Mariam Rosam Bernicem	18-JUN-1910	03-JUL-1910	Alexandro Senecal/Martha Holz	Ovid Senecal/Rosa Delima Venne
Senecal	Mariam Rosam de Lima	19-DEC-1884	21-DEC-1884	Ovide Senecal/Mara-Rosana-Delima Venne	Euclides Venne/Agnes Brazcau
Servatius	Catherine	10-MAY-1851	24-MAY-1851	Peter Servatius/Catherine Holt	B. Stephani/A. Holt
Servatius	Evam Catharinam	24-SEP-1860	24-SEP-1860	Petri Servatius/Gertruda Servatius	D Knittal/C. Halligan
Servatius	Guillelmum	29-OCT-1852	07-NOV-1852	Petri Servatius/Gertruda Servatius	J. Stephany/E. Stephany
Servatius	Helenam Catharinam	04-APR-1866	08-APR-1866	Antoni Servatius/MariaServatius	P. Stephan/C. Servatius
Servatius	Leonem Alexandrum	28-FEB-1864	03-MAR-1864	Andrea Servatius/Maria Servatius	P. Servatius/G. Servatius
Servatius	Mariam	21-DEC-1855	28-DEC-1855	Petri Servatius/Maria Gedrant	F. S-mmai-/M. Sphopani
Servatius	Michaelem Franciscum		15-FEB-1863	Petri Servatius/Gertruda Servatius	M. Holl/M. Jacob
Servatius	Petrum	06-SEP-1865	01-OCT-1865	Petri Servatius/------ Servatius	P. Stephani/A. Stephani
Servatius*	Rosa	04-NOV-1858	09-NOV-1858	Peter Servatius/Gertrude Hall	John Gores/Rosa Deny

116

Surname	Given Name	Birth	Baptism	Parents	Godparents
Servatus	Margaritam	25-AUG-1854	27-AUG-1854	Petri Servatus/Gertruda Hall	P. Stephanus/ M.Dreikhausen
Serwe	Albertum Cornelium	01-OCT-1862	01-OCT-1862	Christophori Serwe/Maria-Francisca Serwe	A. Becker/C. Serwe
Serwe	Annam Isabellam	12-DEC-1865	24-DEC-1865	Joanns-Christophori Serwe/Maria-Francisca Serwe	G Shertzinger/A Serwe
Serwe	Crescentiam Cathernam	26-FEB-1862	04-MAR-1862	Josephi Serwe/Crescentia Serwe	B. Serwe/C Serwe
Serwe	Elizabetham	05-APR-1864	17-APR-1864	Josephi Serwe/Crescentia Serwe	N. Clotz/E. Serwe
Serwe	Elizabetham	08-MAY-1861	12-MAY-1861	Christophori Serwe/Maria-Francisca Serwe	M. Serwe/E. Serwe
Serwe	Joannam	12-FEB-1861	17-FEB-1861	Josephi Serwe/Crescentia Serwe	C. Serwe/J. Clotz
Serwe	Joannem		11-MAY-1864	Christophori Serwe/Francisca Serwe	J H-Izknecht/M. Trimb----
Serwe	Mariam	20-JUL-1854	30-JUL-1854	Christophori Serwe/Francisca Bourgeois	M. Serwe/M. Bourgeois
Serwe	Mariam Josephnam	04-NOV-1866	09-NOV-1866	Josephi Serwe/Cresentia Serwe	M. Serwe/C Cloutz
Serwe*	Matheas	19-OCT-1855	20-OCT-1855	Joannes Serwe/Maria-Francisca Bourgois	M. Bourgois/M. Serwe
Serwe*	Francis				
Serwe*	Franciscum	26-FEB-1859	01-MAY-1859	Michaelem Serwe/Anna-Sibela Seller	F Seller/F. Bourgois
Serwe*	Joseh-	06-JUL-1857	09-JUL-1857	Cheris Serwe/Maria-Francisca Bourjoise	J Serwe/B. Bourjois
Serwe*	Josephum	06-JUL-1857	09-JUL-1857	Christophi Serwe/Francisca Burgois	J. Serwe/B. Bourgois
Serwe*	Maria Elisabeth	12-APR-1856	08-JUN-1856	Michaelis Serwe/Dibila Tellen	M Tellen/L De-e
Serwe*	Mariam Elisabetham	12-APR-1856	08-JUN-1856	Michaelis Serwe/Sebela Tellin	-----/L. Deny
Serwe*	Mariam Rosam	26-AUG-1859	05-SEP-1859	Christophon Serwe/Maria-Francisca Bourgeois	Serwe/-. Bourgeois
Serwe*	Mary Rose				
Sevain*	Moisium	12-JAN-1859	16-JAN-1859	Martinus Sevain/Joanna Burns	Antonius Berret/Sicelia Berret
Severin	Carolus Richard	13-MAY-1919	15-JUN-1919	Maximiliano/C. Severin	Emile Severin/Mira Harme-Severin
Severine	Lucia Annette	23-MAY-1920	20-JUN-1920	Emile Severin/Myra Harmes	D C E. Geiss/Mrs. Geiss
Sh-ffer	Mariam Agnettam	22-FEB-1861	30-JUN-1861	Josephi Sh-ffer/Maria-Agnetia Sh-ffer	J Tautges/F. Mensch
Shaeffer	Franciscum	09-FEB-1862	23-FEB-1862	Danielis Shaeffer/Marguarita Shaeffer	F. Hurling/M. Davis
Shaeffer	Matham Josephum	06-DEC-1863	29-DEC-1863	Josephi Shaeffer/Maria-Anna Shaeffer	M. Shaeffer/M. Jackfeld
Shambeau	Esias	30-SEP-1874	09-OCT-1874	Emgel Shambeau/Julia Vernet	Naviere Delaporte/Thardie Vernet
Shanahan	Michaelem	26-SEP-1852	16-OCT-1852	Cornelii Shanahan/Ellena Fitspatrick	C. O'Brien/C Sullivan
Shaneal*	Anna Maria	04-JAN-1860	19-FEB-1860	Nicolas Shaneal/Maria Sha----	Petrus O'Neal-Shaneal/Catharina -------
Shaon	Mariam Agnes	06-JUN-1875	06-JUN-1875	Elias Shaon/Philomene Leduc	Josephus Leduc/-----Leduc
Shaw	Isabellam		01-DEC-1861	Joannis Shaw/Anna Shaw	A Mcdonald/H. Mcdonald
Shawner	Suzannam	13-NOV-1862	28-JUN-1863	Petri Shawer/Anna Shawer	G. Botch/M. Brown
Shawneel	Mary	13-NOV-1850	12-JAN-1851	Peter Shwneel/Ann Wilcome	P. Welcome/M. Reif
Shea*	Guillelmam	15-JUN-1858	01-JUL-1858	Guillelmmi Shea/-----Legheay	D Cavanaugh/M. Dumphy
Shea*	Lawrence				
Shea*	Mary				
Sheaffer	Annam Maguaritam	12-MAY-1866	23-JUN-1866	Matthei-Josephi Sheaffer/Catharina Sheaffer	J Sheaffer/M. Sheaffer
Sheaffer	Annam Mariam	04-NOV-1865	12-NOV-1865	Danielis Sheaffer/Anna-Marguarita Sheaffer	M. Sheaffer/A Urling
Shée*	Mariam	16-AUG-1859	25-SEP-1859	Joannes Shée/Brigett O'Brayan	J. O'Brayan/A Shée
Sheffer	Josephum	02-DEC-1852	29-MAY-1853	Joseph Sheffer/Maria-Anna Eushmacher	J. Serwe/A. Carr
Sheffer*	Joanns	05-JAN-1857	19-APR-1857	Joseph Sheffer/Maria Handema-er	J. --aes/M. Curling
Sheffer*	Michaelem		07-FEB-1859		
Shepro	Charles Bernard	16-FEB-1919	16-MAR-1919	Edward Shepko/Ettie Lepine	Leon Bird/Grace Thomas-Bird
Sherben	Georgium	01-OCT-1875			J Delton/Sister-Maria Dale
Sherburn	Gorgium	24-JUN-1876	25-JUN-1876	Gorgem Sherburn/Philome Pengier	E Paingir/O. Lismond
Sherburn	Henricum Josephum	27-JUL-1884	28-JUL-1884	Gulielmo Sherburn/Alphonsina Pinguer	----- Pingue/Hortentia Lismond
Sherburne	Mariam Agnetem	10-NOV-1880	10-NOV-1880	Georgius Sherburne/Celina Pinger	L. Clich/A. Pinger
Sheridan	Eliza Jane	25-SEP-1851	12-OCT-1851	Barney Sheridan/Elizabeth Morgan	G. Gipson/M. Gipson
Sheridan	Franciscum	19-JUN-1888	09-SEP-1888	Mathio Sheridan/Maria Carr	Thomas Carr/Carolna Carr
Sheridan	Joannem		15-JAN-1861	Patricii Sheridan/Sarah Sheridan	J. Sealy/J. Serwe

Surname	Given Name	Birth	Baptism	Parents	Godparents
Sheridan	Matthias	20-FEB-1851	09-MAR-1851	Philipe Sheridan/Eliza Ho-d	P. ---ony/C -----
Sherky*	Catharina	25-FEB-1860	29-FEB-1860	Michaeli Sherky/Brigetta Dorcy	Michaelis Gormand/Maria Dorcy
Sherky*	Catharine				
Sherman	Catherinam	16-FEB-1866	28-FEB-1866	Philippi Sherman/Catharina Sherman	C. Shaeffer/C. O'linger
Sherman	Rosam		20-OCT-1861	Philippi Sherman/Catherina Sherman	P. Pehl/R. Denis
Shertzinger	Carolum	03-NOV-1863	15-NOV-1863	Germani Shertzinger/Catharina Shertzinger	P Köpfer/E Serwe
Shertzinger	Claram	11-AUG-1861	26-AUG-1861	Germani Shertzinger/Catharina Shertzinger	D Kuittle/M. Hess
Shertzinger	Franciscam	26-DEC-1865	30-DEC-1865	Germani Shertzinger/CatharinaShertzinger	J Shertzinger/F Flash
Shertzinger*	German Christoph				
Shey*	William	15-JUN-1858	01-JUL-1858	William Shey/- Geehy	Daniel Cavanagh/Mary Dumphy
Shields	Jesse Emmam	11-JAN-1886	23-JUN-1886	Roberto Shields/Adela Belhumeur	-----/Maria Moquin
Shirtzinger*	Germanum Christoph.		29-JUL-1859	Germani Schirtzinger/Catherina Ges	C. Ser--/M Hes
Shisler	Andream	05-JAN-1862	15-JAN-1862	Andrea Shisler/Catharina Shisler	J. Klee/M Stephan
Shleiden	Gasparum	24-MAR-1865	07-APR-1865	Gaspari Shleiden/Suzanna Shleiden	J Pomerich/M Linz
Shoeffer*	Joseph				
Shoeffer*	Michel				
Shoemaker*	Elisabetham	11-OCT-1855	14-OCT-1855	Petri Shoemaker/Elisabeth Ogan	M Shoemaker/E Shoemaker
Shoemaker*	Joannes	04-MAR-1858	07-MAR-1858	Peter Shoemaker/Margeta Oker	Joannes Shoemaker/Babera Oker
Shoemaker*	Maria Anna				
Shoemaker*	Maria-Anna	01-MAR-1860	12-MAR-1860	Petrus Shoemaker/Maria Losslyng	Pet-- Losslyng/Maria Losslyng
Shol*	Michae[				
Shoneal	Catharina				
Shorky	Joannem	05-MAR-1863	08-MAR-1863	Michaelis Shorky/Brigtta Shorky	M. Mullen/M. Krishan
Shorll	Jacobum	18-AUG-1852	05-SEP-1852	Jacobi Schorll/Catherina H---ach	J Flatten/F. Kaurrer
Shoufs	Mariam Annam	19-SEP-1853	02-OCT-1853	Joannis-Francisci-Y. Shoufs/Joanna-Cath Grimmer	-----/M. Nallan
Shroyer	Ludovicum Sullivan	04-JAN-1898	09-DEC-1906	Danele Shroyer/Bessie Lewis	Ludgerus Desrochers/Maria Rheaume-Desrochers
Shumacher	Nicholaum	25-SEP-1860	27-SEP-1860	Petri Shumacher/Marguarita Shumacher	N. Hacker/M. Shuhmacher
Shussler	Mariam Annam	02-JAN-1866	04-FEB-1866	Frederici Shussler/Anna Shussler	J Kaufman/M. Brill
Shwartz	Josephum Guillelmum	21-OCT-1866	21-OCT-1866	Josephi Shwartz/Maria-Anna Shwartz	G. Hall/M. Colin
Shäffer	Franciscum	07-FEB-1866	27-MAY-1866	Josephi Shäffer/Maria-Agnetta Shäffer	F. Hurling/M. Hall
Shöpher	Catherine	15-AUG-1850	15-SEP-1850	Joseph Shophcr/Agnes Shöpher	J. Smith/C. Prieng
Sicar	Salemon Simon		10-MAR-1878	Jorge Sicar/Elena Oesseau	S. Demarsh/A. Triant
Sicard	David	04-DEC-1859	12-DEC-1859	Desere Sicard/Zoe LaPlante	Francois Deroche/Sophie Pellant
Sicard	Georgium Davidem	17-SEP-1884	05-OCT-1884	Davide Sicard/Margaritta Kinney	Joannes-Franciscus Kinney/Virginia Sicard
Sicheler	Fredaricum	13-OCT-1864	13-NOV-1864	Frederici Sicheler/Anna Sicheler	J Sicheler/E. Sicheler
Sicor	Annam Elizabetham	26-SEP-1860	26-SEP-1860	Joannis Sicor/Julia Sicor	G. Clarke/M. Moronye
Sicor	Josephinam	12-JAN-1862	19-JAN-1862	Desiderati Sicor/Zoah Sicor	A Desmarais/A Lamontagne
Sicor	Marcelinam	19-JUL-1868	21-JUL-1868	Desiderati Sicor/Zoah Sicor	Nicholaus Lamarche/Marcelina Lamarche
Sicor	Virginiam	17-DEC-1863	20-DEC-1863	Desidern Sicor/Zoah Sicor	E. Durocher/C. Durocher
Sicor*	Elenam	01-JAN-1859	17-JAN-1859	Joannis Sicor/Julie De--nis	-----/Brigetha Kinnigan
Sicor*	Joannem Josephum	10-MAR-1857	06-MAY-1857	Joannis Sicor/Maria Devenes	B. McCay/E. McCay
Sicor*	John				
Sicor*	Mariam Elenam	01-JAN-1859	17-JAN-1859	Joannis Sicor/Julia De---is	B. Kinnigan/----- -----
Sicor*	Mary Ellen				
Sicord	Helenam	02-MAY-1888	25-MAY-1888	Davide Sicord/Margarita Kenney	Desideratus Sicord/Helena Kenney
Sicorn*	Joannes Josephus	10-MAR-1857	06-MAY-1857	John Sicorn/Julie Devenis	J McCay/----- -----
Sieger	Franciscum	03-FEB-1890	29-SEP-1890	Georgio Sieger/Ellena Loiseau	Albertus Brunet/Odila Jalbert
Sieger	Gulielmum Alfredum Geor	26-NOV-1885	29-NOV-1885	Georgio Sieger/Helena Loiseau	Carolus Loiseau/Martha Bisson
Sieger	Josephum	08-NOV-1882	10-JUN-1883	Leonis Sieger/Helena Loiseau	-----/Lucia Louffe

118

Surname	Given Name	Birth	Baptism	Parents	Godparents
Sieger	Josephum Wilfredum	26-NOV-1885	29-NOV-1885	Georgio Sieger/Helena Loiseau	Thomas Plouffe/Georgina Ouellette
Sieman	Corolum	07-APR-1858	21-APR-1858	Philipu Sieman/Catherina Michel	P. Hiena-t/M. O'Hara
Sigar	Margerith Gertrudum	26-JAN-1876	14-MAY-1876	Josephi Sigar/Ellen Oiseau	W. L'oiseau/M. L'oiseau
Silian	Josephinam	27-AUG-1866	21-SEP-1866	Michaelis Silian/Anna Sillian	F. Hartzein/A. Thornton
Sillian	Reginam		18-MAY-1863	Michaelis Sillian/Anna Sillian	J. Longabach/R. Miller
Simons	Petrum	18-AUG-1854	27-AUG-1854	Francisci Simons/Margarita Stephani	P. Stephani/M. Stephani
Sinard-Snow	Carolum Isedore	23-JAN-1877	28-JAN-1877	Alph--- Sinard-Snow/Isde Tessé	J. Marcou/M. Miller
Sinard-Snow	Israel Aartor	29-AUG-1875	05-SEP-1875	Alphonsu Sinard-Snow/Maria-Louisa Isselda	I. Bissept/J. Chinard
Sinard-Snow	Israel Sartor	24-AUG-1875	05-SEP-1875	Alphossi Sinard-Snow/Maria-Louisa Isselda	Israel Bissept/Julia Chnard
Singleton	Derrill John	16-MAR-1919	23-MAR-1919	John-A. Sngleton/Marie Brunette	Leo Brunette/Edna Corbeille
Sisell*	Chaterinam	23-APR-1856	20-MAY-1856	Andrew Sisell/Chaterina Chommer	--- ----/C. Chemmer
Sissel*	Chaterina Constantina	23-APR-1856	20-MAY-1856	Andreas Sissel/Chateria Chimmer	C. ----/---- ----
Sizer	Georga	16-JUN-1883	09-SEP-1906	Jobez-Willaim Sizer/Emma Coverman	Jolen Gathazar/Josephine Bathazar
Skaf*	Antonum	24-NOV-1904	06-DEC-1904	Assed Skaf/Sophia Salem	Habeb-Moyses Farhate/Amena Salem-Bouhater
Skaf*	Antonius	24-NOV-1904	06-DEC-1904	Assed Skaf/Sophia Salem-Bouhater	Habeb-Moses Farhate/Amena Salem-Bouhater
Skaff	Helenam Nazliam	03-FEB-1897	21-FEB-1897	Assado Skaff/Sophia Cather	Abbeb Moses/Amina Cather
Skaff	Mariam Carolinam Eva	16-MAY-1901	22-JUN-1901	Assed Skaff/Sophia Bokat	Habeb Moses/Maria Skaff
Slattery*	Wenifred				
Slattery*	Wennifridum	14-APR-1859	10-JUL-1859	Joannes Slattery/Wennefra Hayan	C. Hayan/E. Kelly
Smet	Dorothy Elizabeth	04-APR-1920	14-APR-1920	August Smet/Catherine Corijano	Wm. Corijans/Elizabeth Hoffman
Smet	Harry Franci	17-NOV-1919	23-NOV-1919	Joseph Smet/Katharine Vine	August Smet/Irene Jackson
Smet*	Joannem Mariam	30-NOV-1858	03-DEC-1858	Guilimi Smet/Marie Kelly	Maria Gay/----- -----
Smet*	Joannem Thamam	30-NOV-1858	03-DEC-1858	Guilimi Smet/Mara Kelly	-----/Maria Gayl
Smet*	Madalinam	23-MAY-1859	29-MAY-1859	Jacobi Smet/Christina Radmiller	J Pacs/M. Gardener
Smet*	Magdalen				
Smt*	Elanam Mariam	20-MAR-1859	27-MAR-1859	Willielmi Smt/Anna-Maria Lisoway	P. Prester/A. Sl---
Smit*	John Thomas				
Smith	Annam	15-MAY-1866	31-MAY-1866	Patricii Smith/Anna Smith	T. Smith/M. Smith
Smith	Carolum	25-AUG-1893	06-SEP-1893	Georgio Smith/Lyema Suprenant	Gilbertus Surprenant/Zoea Barbeau
Smith	Joannem Nicholaum	17-JAN-1866	13-MAY-1866	Jacobi Smith/Christina Smith	N Shnur/L. Gartner
Smith	Josephum	28-DEC-1862	15-MAR-1863	Pauli Smith/Marguarita Smith	J. Perron/M. Paquette
Smith	Josephum	24-JUL-1864	02-OCT-1864	Joannis Smith/Maria-Anna Smith	J. Serwe/M. S-----
Smith	Mariam	04-JUL-1861	11-AUG-1861	Jacobi Smith/Christina Smith	M. Smith/M. Smith
Smith	Mariam Melvinam	25-JUL-1868	26-JUL-1868	Moysis Smith/Aloisia Roi	Zar Roi/Julianna Ebert
Smith	Morris	06-FEB-1851	09-FEB-1851	Patrick Smith/Charlotte Smith	C. Flood/C. Smith
Smith	Patricum Georgium	11-SEP-1868	29-SEP-1868	Patricii Smith/Anna Smith	Ludovicus Pelletier/Bridgita Heurt
Smith	Paulum	28-FEB-1866	20-MAR-1866	Pauli Smith/Marguarttha Smith	J Smith/M. Bern
Smith*	Eduardus	09-APR-1860	09-MAY-1860	Joannis Smith/Maria McInrow	Petri Smith/Ann McInrow
Smith*	Edward				
Smith*	James	21-SEP-1858	11-NOV-1858	John Smith/Mary McEnrow	Jeremiah Murphy/Ann Ward
Smith*	James				
Smith*	Mary				
Smitt	Joannem	23-SEP-1864		Pauli Smitt/Marguerita Smitt	J. Abel/M. Abel
Snared	Petrum Josephum	17-AUG-1862	19-SEP-1862	Henrici Snared/Anna-Sybilla Snared	P Shneider/E. Shneider
Sno	Aemilianum Ludovicum			Alfred Sno/Ester Sno	E Trimle/A. Trimle
Snow	Mariam Emiliam	21-JAN-1853	30-JAN-1853	Isidori Snow/Sophia Cyr	J R--st/M. R--st
Snow	Mariam Exildam	07-MAR-1872	10-MAR-1872	Alphonsi Snow/Exilda Snow	Franciscus Miller/Zoah Tessier
Snow	Mary Olivia	19-JUN-1851	22-JUN-1851	Isidore Snow/Sophia Sire	J. Sire/C. Snow
Snow*	Charlota		12-FEB-1857	--nne- Snow/Elisa Meam	J Serwe/----- -----

119

Surname	Given Name	Birth	Baptism	Parents	Godparents
Snow-Chenar	Mathildam	14-NOV-1867	17-NOV-1867	Isidori Snow-Chenar/Domitilla Campbell	I. Bessete/J. Bessete
Snow-Chenar*	Josephum	28-APR-1860	29-APR-1860	Isodon Snow/Sophia Sir	----/Madam Lameer
Snow-Chenar*	Josephnam Deltam	26-SEP-1886	24-OCT-1886	Henrica Snyder/Josephina Fritz	David Chaperon/Delia Loiseau
Snyder		12-JUN-1853	26-JUN-1853	Philippi So-er-nam/Catherina Michel	M. Loh-eler/M. Brown
So-er-nam	Mariam	31-AUG-1865	10-SEP-1865	Ludovici Sontag/Magdalena Sontag	A. Breis-ich/M. Crembs
Sontag	Annam Emilam	24-MAR-1861	31-MAR-1861	Ludovici Sontag/Magdalena Sontag	V Mangel/M. Mangel
Sontag	Elizabetham Marguaritam	06-MAY-1863	17-MAY-1863	Ludovici Sontag/Magdalena Sontag	F. Kunde/C. Zimmerman
Sontag	Fredericum Carolum	19-SEP-1920	03-OCT-1920	Verne-Ellis Spence/Elizabeth-Catherine Roble	Arthur-R. Sullivan/Marguerite-M Roble-Sullivan
Spence	Geraldus Franciscus	26-OCT-1896	05-NOV-1919	George Spence/Kate Grecis	Hubert Perrizo/Isabelle Perrizo
Spence	Joseph Verne Ellis	12-JUN-1864	13-JUN-1864	Petri Spry/Eda Spry	J. Bodo/L. La---te
Spry	Josephnam	17-APR-1855	21-APR-1855	Josephi Sruprenant/Julia Gaget	A. Gaget/M. Delevale
Sruprenant	Elizabetham	26-AUG-1861	27-AUG-1861	Josephi St -Jean/Julia-Anna St -Jean	J St Jean/H. Boucher
St Jean	Vitalnam				
St Pierre*	Marie Rose Delima				
St.-Antoine	Adelaidam		02-SEP-1852	Isaaci St.-Antoine/Juliana Lebeau	M St.-Antoine/M. Benoit
St.-Antoine	Alfredum Loyd	16-AUG-1898	10-SEP-1898	Isaaci St.-Antoine/Maria-Joanna Letourneau	Edouardus St.-Antoine/Julia-Stella St -Antoine
St.-Antoine	Eduardum Isaac	09-OCT-1885	11-OCT-1885	Isaac St.-Antoine/Maria-Joanna Letourneau	Isaac St.-Antoine/Maria Bromhamer
St.-Antoine	Franciscum Raimundum	17-NOV-1896	30-NOV-1896	Isaaci St.-Antoine/Joanna Letourneau	Franciscus Balthazar/Philumena Letourneau
St.-Antoine	Gilbertum	10-FEB-1865	19-FEB-1865	Moysis St.-Antoine/Domitilla St.-Antoine	V. Langlois/M. Robert
St.-Antoine	Gulielmum Victorem	14-JAN-1900	04-FEB-1900	Isaaco St.-Antoine/Joanna Letourneau	Gulielmus Balthazar/Ida Letourneau
St.-Antoine	Hermengildam	18-NOV-1862	30-NOV-1862	Moysis St.-Antoine/Clotilda St.-Antoine	J. Balthazar/H. Marcou
St.-Antoine	Isaac	26-NOV-1866	02-DEC-1866	Isaaci St.-Antoine/Julia Anna St.-Antoine	J. Marcou/H. Faucher
St.-Antoine	Isidorum	31-DEC-1866	15-JAN-1867	Moysis St.-Antoine/Domitilla St.-Antoine	I. Dufresne/E. St.-Antoine
St.-Antoine	Joannes B---		24-SEP-1857	Joannes----tum St.-Antoine/Caterna Kelly	D O'conner/B. B--t
St.-Antoine	Josephum Clarentium	30-MAR-1892	03-APR-1892	Isaaco St.-Antoine/Maria-Joanna Letourneau	Josephus Dietto/Elizabeth Letourneau
St.-Antoine	Marguartam	02-FEB-1863	08-FEB-1863	Isaaci St.-Antoine/Julia St.-Antoine	F. Carboneau/A. Lemaire
St.-Antoine	Margueritam	18-JUL-1861	12-AUG-1861	Moysis St.-Antoine/Domitilla St.-Antoine	F. St.-Antoine/G. St.-Antoine
St.-Antoine	Mariam	23-MAY-1854	28-MAY-1854	Moesa St.-Antoine/Julia Benoit	M. Barasseau/M Delain
St.-Antoine	Melmam	23-MAY-1854	28-MAY-1854	Moesa St.-Antoine/Julia Benoit	I Bodreaux/P Tibodeaux
St.-Antoine	Moses	06-JAN-1852	08-JAN-1852	Moses St.-Antoine/Mathilde Benoit	L. Malheur/C. Bourassa
St.-Antoine*	Pierre	08-NOV-1850	19-NOV-1850	Isidore St -Antoine/Julie-Ann Lebeau	F. Marcou/E Cyr
St.-Antoine*	--seline	14-MAR-1858	04-APR-1858	Monsse St.-Antoine/Marie Benoit	Julien Benoit/Deli-- Mo--sept
St.-Antoine*	Gilbert				
St.-Antoine*	Gilbertum	07-OCT-1859	09-OCT-1859	Moisc St.-Antoine/Matilda Benoit	J Lebeau/F. Str
St.-Antoine*	Irene	23-MAR-1856	23-MAR-1856	Moise St.-Antoine/Matilda Benoit	E. St.-Antoine/J. Lebeau
St.-Antoine*	Isaac	23-MAR-1856	23-MAR-1856	Moises St.-Antoine/Matilda Benoit	I. St.-Antoine/J Lebeau
St.-Antoine*	Olivine	29-AUG-1859	25-SEP-1859	Issac St -Antoine/Julienne Lebeau	J ---iceau/M. Tremble
St.-Antoine*	Olivine				
St.-Antoine*	Urselinam	13-MAR-1858	04-APR-1858	Moeess St.-Antoine/Matilda Benoit	J. Benoit/D. Morrissept
St -Jean*	--delia				
St -Jean*	Cadiliam	14-MAY-1860	19-MAY-1860	Josephi St.-Jean/---- Lajulien	Francois Moquin/Josephnam Libilion
St.-Pierre	Franciscum	23-AUG-1863	06-SEP-1863	Josephi St.-Pierre/Edmira St.-Pierre	H. Pariso/O. Pariso
St -Pierre	Josephnam	25-JAN-1866	10-FEB-1866	Moysis St.-Pierre/Justina St.-Pierre	J Touchete/O Vieu
St -Pierre	Josephinam	20-MAR-1864	23-MAR-1864	Moysis St.-Pierre/Justina St.-Pierre	L. Lécuyer/J. Lécuyer
St -Pierre	Marcellinam	03-AUG-1861	18-AUG-1861	Moysis St.-Pierre/Justina St.-Pierre	T Maunville/J. Chenor
St -Pierre	Zoahm	22-AUG-1861	25-AUG-1861	Josephi St.-Pierre/Edwina St.-Pierre	F. Bellime--/Zoah Dufresne
St.-Pierre*	Rosam Mariam Delima	19-JUL-1859	15-AUG-1859	A---st St.-Pierre/Justine Dechaine	F. Meunier/M. Dechaine
Stack*	Stephen	14-OCT-1858	19-DEC-1858	M.C. Stack/Hondra Fullon	John Lyons/Helene Dogherty
Stack*	Stephen	14-OCT-1858	19-DEC-1858	Mcl Stack/Honora Fullon	John Lyons/Helene Dogherty
Stack*	Stephen				

Surname	Given Name	Birth	Baptism	Parents	Godparents
Stada	Corinnam Josephinam	04-MAR-1895	09-MAR-1895	Frederico Stada/Josephina Prefontaine	Alexius Prefontaine/Margaritta Scholl
Stada	Elizabeth		26-APR-1896		Antonius Nicholas/Cara Robidoux
Stada	Florentiam Margaritam	07-JAN-1907	20-JAN-1907	Frederico Stada/Rosam-Annam Corbeille	Aaron Raymond/Salome Baillargeon-Raymond
Stada	Josephum Clifford Ralph	21-JUN-1900	08-JUL-1900	Frederico-Antonio Stada/Rosana Corbeille	Petrus Rhael/Alphonsina Corbeille
Stade	Ruth Elizabeth	02-APR-1904	18-APR-1904	Frederico Stade/Rosana Corbeille	Eduardus Guernon/Elizabeth Stade
Stade	Violam Genovefam	06-JUN-1902	17-JUN-1902	Frederico Stade/Rosana Corbeille	Petrus Lepine/Amanda Corbeille
Stantan	Willielium	06-DEC-1859	12-DEC-1859	Thamas Stantan/Catherina Lensh	Joannis O'Bryan/Margetha Well
Stanten*	David	18-AUG-1857	23-AUG-1857	David Stanten/Tere--- Flannigan	P. -/E. -
Stanton	Bridgittam	08-FEB-1862	09-FEB-1862	Thoma Stanton/Catharina Stanton	C. Clarke/M. Vaughn
Stanton*	David	15-AUG-1857	23-AUG-1857	David Stanton/Sara Flannegan	P S----sy/M Flannigan
Stanton-Toran*	Anna	16-FEB-1858	21-FEB-1858	Thamas Stanton–Toran/Anne Mc'Ceun	Patrick Mc'Ceun/Anne–Eugenia Kesy
Stauber	Mariam	18-APR-1863	03-MAY-1863	Josephi Stauber/Edwidga Stauber	J. R-t/C. Kettler
Ste.-Marie	Elizabetham	06-MAR-1873	23-MAR-1873	Eugenii Ste -Marie/Maria Robert	Josephus Lyonnais/A. Lefève
Ste -Marie	Eugenium	05-MAR-1872	05-MAR-1872	Eugerii Ste -Marie/Maria Robert	Josephus Ste -Marie/Maria-A Chef
Ste -Marie	Mathildam Delinam	11-MAY-1882	14-MAY-1882	Eugenio Ste.-Marie/Maria-Delna Corbeile	Josephus Corbeille/Mathilda Groulx
Steada	Josephum Alfredum Dewey	13-SEP-1898	26-SEP-1898	Alfredo Steada/Rosanna Corbeille	Petrus Lepine/Josephina Corbeille
Stearns	Mariam Annam Ruth	26-JUL-1898	07-AUG-1898	Georgio Stearns/Malinda Letourneau	Gulielmus Balthazar/Ida Letourneau
Stefano*	Gertrude	14-JUL-1855	22-JUL-1855	Bartolemus Stefano/Maria-Gertruda Gunyan	A. Servatius/G. Stef----
Steffes	Catharinam Angelinam	05-AUG-1907	05-AUG-1907	Ludovico Steffes/Louisa Dame	----/Catharine Dame-Fanand
Steinbarth	Alixiam Adelam	01-JUL-1896	05-JUL-1896	Joanne Steinbarth/Marcellina Edon	Pacificus Bastien/Maria-Adela Robidoux
Steinbarth	Eduardum Andream	22-MAR-1900	01-APR-1900	Joanne Steinbarth/Marcellina Edon	Andreas Steinbarth/Emma Edon
Steinbarth	Florentiam Melinam	20-APR-1903	03-MAY-1903	Joanne Steinbarth/Marcellina Edon	Eduardus Wickert/Elizabeth Timm
Steinbarth	Mariam Gertrudem	06-MAR-1900	01-APR-1900	Andrea Steinbarth/Maria Sotz	Joannes Steinbarth/Lucreciam Robidoux
Steinbarth	Stellam Adelinam	01-SEP-1898	11-SEP-1898	Joanne Steinbarth/Marcellina Edon	Alexander Edoin/Engelbertum Edelman
Stenbert	Edwigam Mariam	29-JAN-1905	04-FEB-1906	Joanne Stenbert/Marcelna Edous	Gulielmus Steinbart/Maria Sitz-Steinbert
Stenz	Walter Eugene	17-SEP-1920	10-OCT-1920	Archibald-Martin Stenz/Amanda-Marie Boda	Joseph Pluger/Leona Boda-Pluger
Stephan	Joannem		02-MAR-1862	W. Stephan/Maria Stephan	S. Lemare/S. Pinor
Stephani	Catharinam	19-AUG-1865	20-AUG-1865	Jacobi Stephani/Anna Stephan	V. Coole/M Wagner
Stephani*	Eva Chaterina	04-JUN-1857	07-JUN-1857	Bartholimus Stephani/Marie Gedrand	P. Servatius/E. Stephani
Stephani*	Evam Catherinam	04-JUN-1857	07-JUN-1857	Bartholomei Stephani/Maria Gedrant	P Servatus/E. Stephani
Stephani*	Gertrudam	14-JUL-1855	22-JUL-1855	Bartholomeii Stephani/Maria-Gertruda Janson	A Servatius/G. Stephani
Stern	Edessam Itam	18-JAN-1900	11-FEB-1900	Georgio Stern/Melina Letourneau	Alfredus Diette/Edessa Letourneau
Stern	Gulielmum		25-MAR-1902	Georgio Stern/Melinda Letourneau	Isaacus St.-Antoine/Joanna Letourneau
Stevenson	Josephum Owenum	20-DEC-1863	27-DEC-1863	Georgii Stevenson/Sarah-Catharina Stevenson	J. Reiley/H. Reiley
Stevenson*	Mathias				
Stewart	Annam	31-JAN-1853	10-MAY-1853	Joannis Stewart/Anna Strasse	P. Vaghn/C. Gibson
Stewart	Margarethe	19-FEB-1879	14-MAY-1879	Caroli Stewart/Calist Delicer	---- --/C. P---puer
Stivens*	Angela	01-OCT-1856	12-OCT-1856	Nicolau Stivens/Catherina Smit	M. Girben/---- Kiers
Stivens*	Angelicam	01-OCT-1856	12-OCT-1856	Nicolau Strvens/Catherina Smet	M. Giben/A. Kierens
Stivens*	Elisabeh	23-AUG-1855	09-SEP-1855	Roland Stivens/Catheria Smet	D. Scheffer/E. Brown
Stivens*	Elizabetham	23-AUG-1855	09-SEP-1855	Nicola Stivens/Cath Smet	D. -he-fer/E. Brown
Stoffel	Carolinam	18-NOV-1862	18-NOV-1862	Michaelis Stoffel/Carolina Stoffel	A. Boe-ler/----- ---
Stoffel	Franciscam	18-NOV-1862	18-NOV-1862	Michaelis Stoffel/Carolina Stoffel	F. Hack/----- ---
Stoffel*	Charles				
Stoffll*	Charles	06-SEP-1857	22-NOV-1858	Mcl Stoffll/Caroline Hock	Charles Hock/Rosaline Bufs
Stophel*	Anna				
Stophil*	Annam	11-AUG-1859	09-OCT-1859	Michel Stophil/Carolina -u-k	J. -u-k/A. Rand
Story	Georgium	26-AUG-1860	12-OCT-1860	Georgii Story/Catharina Story	P. McCullen/H. McCullen
Story	Mariam Annam	21-SEP-1854	30-NOV-1854	Jacobi Story/Catharina McKelly	D. Dorn/E. McKelly

121

Surname	Given Name	Birth	Baptism	Parents	Godparents
Story	Mariam Annam	08-MAR-1853	10-MAY-1853	Thoma Story/Anna McKennan	C. Flood/R. Clark
Straatz	Emmam	18-MAR-1860	28-OCT-1860	Martini Straatz/Maria Straatz	J. Roef/B. Uhrling
Stras*	Mathas		05-OCT-1856	Matins Stras/Mary Haman	J. Bcry/M. Campert
Strass*	Matham	23-MAY-1856	05-OCT-1856	Martini Strass/Maria Haman	J. Rouf/M. Compert
Strats	Joannem	11-JUN-1852	11-SEP-1853	Martini Strats/Maria Lyman	J. Sing/M. Kampert
Strats*	Catherina	24-MAY-1857	31-MAY-1857	Joannes Strats/Chatrena Crammer	C. Hermann/------
Strats*	Catherinam	27-MAY-1857	31-MAY-1857	Joannes Strats/Catherina Crummer	------ ------/C Shermann
Stratz	Ludovicum	30-JUL-1863	25-MAY-1864	Martini Stratz/Maria Stratz	G. Fisher/M. Cambert
Stratz*	Maria Sophia	06-MAR-1858	11-JUL-1858	Martine Stratz/Maria Layman	Joseph Rouf/Maria Gambert
Stratz*	Mariam Sopham	06-MAR-1857	11-JUL-1858	Martini Stratz/Maria Leman	J. Ref/M Gambert
Straus*	Matham Bernardam	07-OCT-1858	12-DEC-1858	Ignace Straus/Cathurno Crammer	Bernard-Matthias Crammer/Catherine Millr
Straus*	Mathum Bernadum	07-DEC-1858	12-DEC-1858	Ignas Straus/Catherina Crammer	Renard-Matthias Crammer/Catherina Crammer
Straus**	Anna Catharina	03-JUL-1865	02-JUL-1865	Joannis Straus/Catharina Straus	C. Trim---e
Strauss	Annam	17-MAR-1864	10-APR-1864	Joannis Strauss/Catharina Strauss	J. Mangel/A. Rosseter
Straws*	Matthias				
Streets	Philomenam	06-JAN-1855	13-MAY-1855	Martini Streets/Maria Lyman	G Fireher/M. Courbat
Streiss	Antonum Reynardum	18-JUL-1861	04-AUG-1861	Mathias Streiss/Mara-Anna Streiss	B. Miller/R. Miller
Streiss	Augustum	18-JUL-1861	04-AUG-1861	Francisci Streiss/Catharina Streiss	A. Kinsel/R. Miller
Strong	Annam Augustum	21-JAN-1862	13-MAR-1864	Josephi Strong/Maria Strong	F. Delpée/M. Bird
Strong	Emmam		12-MAY-1867	Joannis Strong/Maria Strong	P. Borasseau/C Cummings
Strong	Georgam Annam		20-NOV-1870	Stephan Strong/Marguarita Strong	Josephus Shoe/Aurelia Trahant
Strong	Guillelmum		08-NOV-1868	Nelson Strong/Maria Gauther	Carolus Fleuret/Maria Poirier
Strong	Guillelmum Henricum	28-JUL-1873	10-AUG-1873	Nelson Strong/Maria Gautier	Antonius Gautier/Flavia Robert
Strong	Israelem	28-JUN-1867	13-AUG-1867	Josephi Strong/Maria Trahant-Strong	N. Strong/M. Strong
Strong	Ludovicam		06-MAR-1864	Narcissi Strong/Maria Strong	R. Gauthier/M Eri-ume
Strong*	Helenam	19-APR-1856	19-MAY-1856	Stephan Strong/Margcretha Crammer	J Crammer/L. Strong
Styds	Mariam Elenam Caristiam	24-MAR-1876	30-MAR-1876	Willaam Styds/Carista Lucia	C. Tramble/C. Tramble
Sullian	Joannem	22-OCT-1862	01-NOV-1862	Jacobi Sullian/Maria Sullian	E Maghar/C. Duffy
Sullivan	Annam	30-JUN-1877	05-JUL-1877	Michaelis Sullivan/Maria Kennedy	W. Corteny/M. Fitz-urrall
Sullivan	Catharinam	23-FEB-1862	01-APR-1862	Danelis Sullivan/Catharina Sullivan	T. Gough/A Rosseter
Sullivan	Joannem		12-OCT-1863	Jacobi Sullivan/Marguarita Sullivan	J. King/A. Roghan
Sullivan	Joannem Franciscum	13-APR-1862	15-APR-1862	Dyonisii Sullivan/Maria Sullivan	J. Stack/C. Sullivan
Sullivan	Marguartam	22-AUG-1862	24-AUG-1862	Michaelis Sullivan/Maria Sullivan	M. O'Brien/M Ryan
Sullivan	Marguerite Ellen	25-JAN-1852	08-JUN-1852	Daniel Sullivan/Mary McGrath	T. McGrath/M Moran
Sullivan*	Anne				
Sullivan*	Joannem	18-JUL-1858	22-AUG-1858	Joannis Sullivan/Catharina D-----	J. Lynch/H. McLaughlin
Supple	Fredericum	19-JUL-1860	29-JUL-1860	Josephus Supple/Alisena Viens	-asa- L'Enplois/Malina Ba-lait
Suprenant	Arthurem	22-NOV-1872	22-NOV-1872	Gilberti Suprenant/Zoah Barbeau	Isaïas Langto/Mathilda Barbeau
Suprenant	Dalilam	12-JUN-1871	18-JUN-1871	Gilbert Suprenant/Zoah Barbeau	Petrus Barbeau/Philomena Charon
Suprenant	Delphnam	28-OCT-1874	01-NOV-1874	Gelberti Suprenant/Soe Barbeau	Baptista Dupus/V. Belargant
Suprenant	Zoé	18-MAR-1878	21-MAR-1878	Gilbert Suprenant/Zoe Barbo	J. Lafontane/S. Barbo
Suprenant*	Rosa	19-OCT-1855	21-OCT-1855	Petrus Surprenant/Frigina F---it	F. Mortien/J Mere
Surprenand	Irenam Mariam	03-FEB-1907	10-MAR-1907	Gilbert Surprenant-Jr /Fred Singer	Emericus Gervais/Olivina Charron-Gervais
Surprenand	Zoem	01-APR-1903	19-APR-1903	Levi Surprenand/Emma Markoe	M.-Arthurus Carpenter/Zoea Surprenand
Surprenant	Antonum	02-MAR-1865	25-APR-1865	Isaaci Surprenant/Julia Gayet	M. Balthazar/I. Surprenant
Surprenant	Arthurum Harvey	25-NOV-1899	17-DEC-1899	Arthuro Surprenant/Amelia Mikie	Josephus Landerman/Marra Landerman
Surprenant	Davidem Alexandrum	17-JUN-1863	17-JUN-1863	Petri Surprenant/Ludovica Beaudin	D Doré/F. Surprenant
Surprenant	Davidem Orvilem	19-APR-1901	12-MAY-1901	Levi Surprenant/Emma Marcoe	Gulielmus Gagner/Dorthea Marcoe
Surprenant	Elismam	01-NOV-1875	14-NOV-1875	Julberti Surprenant/Zoe Barbo	P. Barbo/A. Gervais

122

Surname	Given Name	Birth	Baptism	Parents	Godparents
Surprenant	Euclidem Ludovicum	22-AUG-1899	17-SEP-1899	Levi Surprenant/Emma Markoe	Emericus Gervais/Olivina Charron
Surprenant	Eugenum	19-MAY-1867	26-MAY-1867	Isaac Surprenant/Julia Surprenant	J. Balthazar/M Balthazar
Surprenant	Franciscum Haroldum	14-SEP-1897	03-OCT-1897	Levi Surprenant/Emma Marcoe	Arthurus Surprenant/Melina Beauregard
Surprenant	Guillelmum	19-APR-1868	19-APR-1868	Guillem Surprenant/Ludovica Surprenant	Evaristus Vadney/Angela Dufraine
Surprenant	Henricum Ludovicum	24-OCT-1896	15-NOV-1896	Jospho Surprenant/Jeanetta Dake	Alexander Barbeau/Sophia Tinget
Surprenant	Josephum Clarentium	02-NOV-1895	10-NOV-1895	Levi Surprenant/Emma Marcoux	Gilbertus Surprenant/Zoea Barbeau
Surprenant	Julian Marcellinam	05-AUG-1861	11-AUG-1861	Emerii Surprenant/Euphrosena Surprenant	A Grizet/J Ebert
Surprenant	Laurentium Elmer	15-MAR-1899	19-MAR-1899	Gilberto Surprenant/Joanna Dake	Franciscus Demers/Ida-Maria Audet-Lapointe
Surprenant	Leonem Franciscum	30-AUG-1896	18-SEP-1896	Arthuro Surprenant/Amelia Mike	Levi Surprenant/Emma Surprenant
Surprenant	Ludovicum	26-NOV-1861	25-DEC-1861	Isaaci Surprenant/Julia Surprenant	F Gayet/D. Brico
Surprenant	Marguaritam	20-FEB-1864	21-FEB-1864	Isaaci Surprenant/Julia Surprenant	O. Durocher/S. Balthazar
Surprenant	Napoleonem	16-AUG-1864	04-SEP-1864	Emery Surprenant/Euphrosina Surprenant	S. Houle/M Houle
Surprenant	Sophroniam Mariam	05-JAN-1907	20-JAN-1907	Levi Surprenant/Emma Markow	Julius Pangaire/Louis Leriviere-Paingaire
Surprenant*	Josephum	19-OCT-1859	23-OCT-1859	Essau Surprenant/Julia Gayet	M Baltazar/----- Baltazar
Surprenant*	Maria Adelina	15-JUL-1857	19-JUL-1857	Emery Surprenant/Sophia Jigan	J. Marcou/J Bouchard
Surprenant*	Maria Melina				
Surprenant*	Mariam	21-JUN-1857	28-JUN-1857	Joseph Surprenant/Julia Gaÿet	J. R-yome/F. Tibodeaux
Surprenant*	Mariam Delinam	15-JUL-1857	19-JUL-1857	Emery Surprenant/Josephina Gayen	J. Marceau/J. Bouchard
Surprenant*	Mariam M-lo-rinam	14-JUL-1859	19-JUL-1859	Emerie Surprenant/Regina Garon	J. Ga-on/M. Lamer
Surprenant*	Marie	21-JUN-1857	28-JUN-1857	Joseph Surprenant/Julie Gayet	J. ---ami/F. Tibodeaux
Surprenant*	Rosam	19-OCT-1855	21-OCT-1855	Petri Surprenant/Rigena Frant	F. Shorten/J. M---
Surprentant*	Joseph				
Suster	Lousia Lisa	22-FEB-1857	07-JUN-1857	Joseh-Jorge Suster/Elissa Suster	J Marks/E. Suster
Sweet	Gulielmum Haroldum	03-APR-1906	03-JUN-1906	Gilialmo Sweet/Dora Crowley	-----/Mamie Canoboy
T-ffo-	Victorem	22-FEB-1863	15-JUN-1863	Joannis T-ffo-/Maria T-ffo-	J. ---/S. Barrett
Taf	Mariam Georgiam Alinam	23-OCT-1873	25-OCT-1873	Francisci Taf/Adelina Hurto	Olivarus Hurto/Adelina Hurto
Tanakes	Margarettam	23-AUG-1863	13-SEP-1863	Jacobi Tanakes/Catharina Tanakes	J. Pomerick/M Shefer
Tate*	Franciscus Lester Eduardum		27-MAY-1860	Joannis Tate/Maria Bertrant	Israel-C. Bodreau/Lousa Bodreaux
Tates	Arthurum Gulielmum	30-MAR-1904	28-APR-1904	Martino Tates/Olivina Marcoux	Samuel Marcoux/Gertrudis Tates
Tates	Catharnam Mariam	01-MAR-1910	17-APR-1910	Martino Tates/Lavina Marcoux	Samuel Marcoux/Maria Schreiner
Tates	Feliciam Laurettam	18-FEB-1908	29-MAR-1908	Martino Tates/Lavina Marcoux	Alexander Marcoux/Orzelia Beaudrea-Marcoux
Tates	Martinum F.		18-AUG-1902		Samuel Marcoux/Albertina Pratt
Tautge	Robert Adelbert Joseph	25-JUN-1920	27-JUN-1920	Jacob Tautge/Rachel Dupaue	Eugene Dupane/Monica Tautge
Tautges	Josephum	20-JUL-1865	30-JUL-1865	Jacobi Tautges/Catharina Tautges	J. Pomerich/S. Hamzy
Tautges	Mariam Josepham	29-OCT-1861	02-NOV-1861	Jacobi Tautges/Catharina Tautges	J Hanson/M Weber
Taylor	Mariam Joannam	06-AUG-1886	16-JUN-1866	Francisci Taylor/Marguarita Taylor	P. Rulo/L. Stier
Teller*	Mathias	21-DEC-1859	19-FEB-1860	Michelis Teller/Francisca Bisseler	Michel Serwe/Francisca Borgois
Teller*	Matthias				
Tenessee	Edmond	24-AUG-1850	16-SEP-1850	Richard Tenessee/Julia Gratton	J Murray/M. Do
Tenter	Anastasia Stacey	23-MAY-1879	08-JUN-1879	Gerhardi Tenter/A--- Tenter	-----/Ida Stacey
Terger*	Joannes	17-MAR-1860	18-MAR-1860	Mic Terger/Hanna Jorges	Joannes Lyben/Teressa Lyben
Tessier	Adelnam	15-SEP-1868	20-SEP-1868	Thoma Tessier/Leucadia Tessier	Theotimus Tessier/Maria Theresa Tessier
Tessier	Agnetem	06-AUG-1886	30-AUG-1886	Jeremia Tessier/Anna Taute	Carolum Kramer/Agnes Thorp
Tessier	Alexandrum	01-JUL-1861	27-JUL-1861	Thoma Tessier/D--- Landris	S. Brico/S. Doff
Tessier	Cleopham	15-OCT-1867	15-OCT-1867	Thoma Tessier/Leucadia Tessier	B Tessier/B Tessier
Tessier	Elizabetham	17-JAN-1864	28-FEB-1864	Thoma Tessier/Leucadia Tessier	J. Barbaut/O. Vient
Tessier	Fredcricum		17-MAR-1865	Petri Tessier/Oliva Delamagdalene	F. Miller/L Bolduc
Tessier	Georgum	01-APR-1864	17-MAR-1865	Petri Tessier/Oliva Delamagdalene	F. Miller/L. Bolduc
Tessier	Joannem Baptistam	24-APR-1871	24-APR-1871	Joannes-Thoma Tessier/Leucadia Tessier	Josephus Ochme/Maria Ochue

Surname	Given Name	Birth	Baptism	Parents	Godparents
Tessier	Joannem Guillelmum	09-MAY-1867	09-MAY-1867	Timothei Tessier/Maria Tessier	C. Blanchete/E. Blanchete
Tessier	Josephum	27-JAN-1866	27-JAN-1866	Thoma Tessier/Leucadia Tessier	D Trocquet/P Trocquet
Tessier	Josephum Henricum	01-MAY-1866	31-MAY-1866	Theo---i Tessier/Maria-Ludovica Tessier	E. Martin/---- ----
Tessier	Leucadiam	28-FEB-1865	01-MAR-1865	Theot--- Tessier/Maria-Ludovica Tessier	T Tessier/L Landry
Tessier	Ludovicum	27-JAN-1866	27-JAN-1866	Thoma Tessier/Leucadia Tessier	T. Deschènes/C. Deschènes
Tessier	Mariam Aloysiam	02-MAY-1868	19-MAY-1868	Theotius Tessier/Maria-Ludovica Tessier	Baptista Tessier/Marguarita Tessier
Tessier	Mariam Laurnam	25-FEB-1888	25-MAR-1888	Jeremia Tessier/Anna Faunter	Alfredus Bessette/Adelina Tessier
Tessier	Salome Adelinam	07-MAY-1869	27-MAY-1869	Onesimi Tessier/Maria Tessier	Antonius Brico/Salome Vadney
Tessier	Thomam Ellsworth	07-APR-1888	05-AUG-1888	Treffleo Tessier/Martha Elridge	Jeremias Tessier/Anna Tainter
Tessier*	Alfred				
Tessier*	Alfridum	19-MAR-1859	10-APR-1859	Thoma Tessier/Leocadie Landre	N. Langlois/M Bo----t
Tessier*	Josephum Guilielmum Theo	22-DEC-1904	29-DEC-1904	Henrici Tessier/Yvonne Mayrand	Gulielmus Mayrand/Winnefreda Leath-Mayrand
Tessier*	Josephum Guilielmum Theo	22-DEC-1904	29-DEC-1904	Henrici Tessier/Joanna Mayrand	Gulielmus Mayrand/Winnefreda Leath-Mayrand
Tête	Edwardum Albertum	07-MAR-1865	26-NOV-1865	Joannis Tête/Maria Bastian	E Joubert/J Leduc
Tete	Josephum Guillelmum	19-MAR-1868	29-MAR-1868	Joannis Tete/Maria Bertrand	Ludovicus Bertrand/Eulila Beaudreau
Tête*	Francis Edward	02-APR-1860	10-MAY-1860	J. Tête/M. Bertrand	
Thamas*	Ellina	18-SEP-1856	27-OCT-1856	Joseph Thamas/Maria Peron	----- Cai-/M. Lamer
Thattey	Thomam	20-NOV-1862	08-DEC-1862	Joannis Thattey/Catharina Thattey	D. Whalan/M. Ryan
The---lt	Jocobus	24-FEB-1856	11-MAY-1856	Jabob The---lt/Sophie Slaté	J. Deal/---- ----
The--ald*	Josephina Antonina		18-APR-1858	Jocab The-ald/Sophia Slater	Antonus Servatius/Josephina Craems
Theawatt	Henricum		09-FEB-1862	Jocobi Theawatt/Sophia Theawatt	C. Keesler/---- ----
Therburn	Franciscum	03-APR-1882	14-MAY-1882	Georgio Sherburn/Celina Pinguer	Moises Bastien/Adelina Bocage
Therese	Antonam	16-AUG-1877	16-SEP-1877	Joansi Werse/Rosalia Fresdesdag	-----/Sister-M. Dale
Thetro	Adelaidam Rosam	11-MAR-1872	25-MAR-1872	Hamiltons Thetro/Sophia Allar	Petrus Allar/Sophia Allar
Thetro	Mariam Virgniam	05-OCT-1870	05-OCT-1870	Felicis Thetro/Marcelina Laurin	Vitalis Laurin/Euphremia Robert
Thetro	Petronellam	16-OCT-1869	17-OCT-1869	Josephi Thetro/E---- Thetro	Maximus Bertrand/Clarissa Bertrand
Thetro	Virgniam Ludovicam	17-AUG-1869	25-AUG-1869	Dominici Thetro/Sophia Thetro	Petrus Agar/Julia Richer--
Thewald*	Josephinam Antonam	29-DEC-1857	18-APR-1858	Jocobi Thewald/Sophia Stater	A. Servatius/J. Crar--
Thibodeau	Emeritum	25-JUL-1865	25-JUL-1865	Salomonia Thibodeau/Lucia Thibodeau	G Boucher/L. Petit
Thibodeau	Henricum	26-APR-1864	28-APR-1864	Salomonus Thibodeau/Lucia Thibodeau	J Gayet/C. Thibodeau
Thibodeau	Josephum	06-DEC-1863	13-DEC-1863	Olivieri Thibodeau/Maria Thibodeau	C. Gayet/R. Thibadeau
Thibodeau*	Joseph				
Thibodeaux	Rosalie	10-APR-1851	13-APR-1851	Olivier Thibodeaux/Louse Thibodeaux	G Oualete/C Duf----
Thill	Annam Regnnam	07-APR-1861	14-APR-1861	Caroli Thill/Catharina Thill	H. Fox/A. Miller
Thill	Marguaritam	07-OCT-1864	10-OCT-1864	Caroli Thill/Catharina Thill	D Thill/M. Mangel
Thill	Mariam Josephinam	23-JAN-1863	24-JAN-1863	Caroli Thill/Catharina Thill	D Thill/M. Thill
Thill*	Anna Catharina				
Thomas	------	29-JUN-1906	29-JUN-1906	Arthuro Thomas/---- ----	Frank Beaudreau/---- ----
Thomas	Alvina Emily	02-SEP-1918	19-MAY-1919	Arthur Thomas/Rose Chartrey	----- -----/Emily Goudreau
Thomas	Augustinum	12-JAN-1874	13-APR-1881	Josepho Thomas/Maria-Anna Perron	B. Perron/C. Lemieux
Thomas	Edward	23-MAY-1861	04-JUL-1861	Josepho Thomas/Maria-Anna Thomas	T Perron/M. Gayet
Thomas	Mariam Carolinam	10-JUN-1869	13-APR-1881	Josepho Thomas/Maria Perron	J Dem---/M. Perron
Thomas	Rosanno Theotse	27-OCT-1857	15-FEB-1858	Jos Thomas/Marianne Péron	Andre Peron/Mariam Doville
Thomas*	Elnam	18-SEP-1856	27-OCT-1856	Josephi Thomas/Maria Peron	P Cha-ter/M Lamir
Thornton	Aliciam	13-JUN-1862	19-JUN-1862	Thoma Thornton/Anna Thornton	J Crowley/M. O'conner
Thornton	Annam	19-DEC-1862	20-DEC-1862	Hughii Thornton/Maria Thornton	P. Mccane/A. Mckee
Thorp	Franciscum Xavierium	17-JAN-1896	08-JUL-1896	Frederico Thorpe/Victorra Hurteau	Franciscus Hurteau/Laura Durocher
Thorp	Fredericum Guilielmum	27-MAR-1894	26-APR-1894	Frederico Thorp/Victoria Hurteau	Gulielmus Durocher/Maria Perron
Thorp	Joanem Leroy	17-SEP-1899	22-OCT-1899	Alfredi Thorp/Victoria Hurteau	Joannes Hurteau/Maria Turcot

124

Surname	Given Name	Birth	Baptism	Parents	Godparents
Thorp	Mariam Adelnam	22-OCT-1891	25-OCT-1891	Frederico Thorp/Victoria Hurteau	Ludgerius Noupré/Elmira Lefort
Thy-*	Laurentium	02-AUG-1859	04-SEP-1859	Joannis Thy-/Anna Hergaty	W ----Ity/B. Kelly
Tibeaudcau*	Louis Napolon	27-FEB-1856	28-FEB-1856	Joseph Tibeaudeau/Catherina Beauraseau	O. Tibeaudeau/D Manine
Tibodeau*	Josephi	03-NOV-1858	07-NOV-1858	Joseph Tibodeau/Philumina Tibodeau	Joseph Gayet/Phi-- Sir
Tibodeaux	Adolphum	28-JUL-1853	04-AUG-1853	Jacobi-Oliverii Tibodeaux/Maria Cyr	V Langlois/----- Langlois
Tibodeaux*	Ludovicum Napoilon	27-FEB-1856	28-FEB-1856	Joseph Tibodeaux/Catharina Beauraseaux	O. Tibodeaux/A. Manne
Tichakanorowe	Charles		18-JUN-1852	----- Tichakanorowe/Mary-Ann Chnanan	C. Juneau/C. Juneau
Tierney	Martham	01-SEP-1861	06-SEP-1861	Jacobi Tierney/Catharina Tierney	H. Th----t-/M. McCune
Tierney	Thomasum	17-FEB-1863	01-MAR-1863	Jacobi Tierney/Catharina Tierney	J Murry/M. Murry
Tierny	Annam	31-DEC-1859	01-JAN-1860	Jocobi Tierny/Catherina Turren-	Patricus McCay/Anne Tur--t--
Tiffoer	Carolum		24-OCT-1861	Joannis Tiffoer/Maria Tiffoer	J. Tiffoer/M. Fitzhenry
Tinger	Annam Mariam Sopham	16-JAN-1862	23-NOV-1890	Henrico Tinger/Maria Burgmiester	Petrus Barbeau/Exilda Moquin
Toland*	Michael				
Tompson	Mariam Suzanam		05-OCT-1879	Henri Tompson/Martha Eldridge	M Sauve/A. Tessier
Tonner	Antonium Joannem	04-JUN-1877	13-JUL-1877	Jocobi Tonner/Allena Gasselain	J Col----/M. Bolles
Tonner	Jocalum William	26-MAY-1876	30-JUL-1876	Jqcob Tonner/Dina Gosselin	W Broun/E Gosselin
Tonor	Susanam	30-SEP-1852	18-JAN-1853	Danelis Tonor/Elvira Campbel	J Murray/M. Powers
Tooney	Sarha Larha	05-NOV-1879	07-NOV-1879	Petro Tooney/Larha Cotter	M. Duggan/H. Duggan
Toran*	Annam	16-FEB-1858	21-FEB-1858	Thoma Toran/Anna Mccuen	P. Mccuen/A. Kessy
Torton	Mariam	17-MAY-1860	03-JUN-1860	Thoma Torton/M-Anna McCoen	Hugh Torton/Maria McCoen
Touchet*	Alfred	11-FEB-1858	21-FEB-1858	Joseph Touchet/A------ Viens	Antoine Grise/Olivino Malheur
Touchet*	Alfredum	11-FEB-1858	21-FEB-1858	Josephum Touchet/Micena Viens	A Grisé/O. Malh---
Touchete	Alexandrum	09-AUG-1867	25-AUG-1867	Joseph Touchete/Onesima Touchete	E Robert/V. Touchete
Touchete	Henricum	25-MAR-1865	02-APR-1865	Joseph Touchete/Aloysia Touchete	P Chef/J. Touchete
Touchete	Ludovicum Joannem	08-NOV-1862	16-NOV-1862	Joseph Touchete/Olivina Touchete	L. Landreman/C. Guérin
Touchete	Oliverum Eduardum	29-MAR-1870	11-JUL-1870	Joseph Touchete/Onesima Vient	Olivierus Papineau/Mathilda Touchete
Touchette	Almam Annam	14-DEC-1888	16-DEC-1888	Joanne-Ludovico Touchette/Julia Godin	Eugenius Robert/Philumena Marcoux
Touchette	Joannem Fredericum	07-DEC-1896	24-JAN-1897	Joanne Touchette/Julia Godin	Petrus Schef/Josephina Touchette
Touchette	Josephum Bernardum Alvin	07-MAR-1896	15-MAR-1896	Josepho-Henrico Touchette/Agnete Gervais	Josephus Touchette/Cecilia Gay
Touchette	Laverne Theodorum	27-OCT-1908	01-NOV-1908	Eduardo Touchette/Anna Roy	Arsenus-L.J. Roy/Emma Allard-Roy
Touchette	Maria		15-AUG-1857		D. Hubert/C. Maurin
Touchette	Mariam Ludovicam Onesi	14-OCT-1903	22-OCT-1903	Eduardo Touchette/Anna Roy	Philius Roy/Georgina Roy
Touchettc	Mariam Ruth Evangelinam	28-AUG-1903	06-SEP-1903	Henrico Touchette/Agnete Gervais	Alexander Touchette/Cecilia Guay
Touchette	Paulum Archibald Laurent	25-JUN-1906	02-JUL-1906	Eduardo Touchette/Anna Roy	Jeremias Gervais/Mathilda Touchette-Gervais
Touchette	Roy Edwinum	13-JAN-1900	16-JAN-1900	Eduardo-Olivero Touchette/Ludovica Roy	Petrus-Josephus Roy/Anna Roy
Tousept*	Maria Philomina	27-SEP-1855	30-SEP-1855	Joseph Tousept/Olivina Vienne	M Marcot/L. Gilon
Toutsept*	Mariam Philomenam	27-SEP-1855	30-SEP-1855	Josephi Toutsept/Olivina Venne	M- -ilo--/U. -ilo-
Towne	Gratiam	08-JUL-1881	28-SEP-1901	Ephrem Towne/Josephina Owen	Thomas Lepine/----- -----
Townsend	Lot		16-JAN-1853		J. Walters/M. Gill
Trahant	Franciscum Augustinum	02-MAY-1866	20-MAY-1866	Francisci Trahant/Maria Trahant	D.Destroismaisons/----- -----
Trahant	Josephum	16-NOV-1870	27-NOV-1870	Narcissi Trahant/Maria Trahant	Josephus Pomainville/Agnes Gau-tier
Tramble	Will Alfred	13-JAN-1877	10-FEB-1877	Caroli Tramble/Clementina Vannery	F. Moiquin/ wife
Trambly	Ludovicum	15-NOV-1874	22-NOV-1874	Charles Trambly/Clemence Phenfuff	Adolphus Deroché/-mth Randeau
Treblëy	Carolum	08-APR-1862	22-APR-1862	Moysis Trembléy/Eugenia Trembléy	J L'hussier/P. Bissonet
Trelevan	Mariam Edessam Helenam	01-MAY-1894	24-JUN-1894	Theodore Trelevan/Helena-Eleonora Bullis	Alfredus Bullis/Helena Jaubert
Tremblay	Alseam Saram	03-MAY-1885	24-MAY-1885	Josepho Tremblay/Ada Dufresne	Moises Tremblay/Sara Ste.-Marie
Tremblay	Earl Moysen	29-DEC-1883	30-DEC-1883	Josepho Tremblay/Ada-Maria Dufresne	Pascolis Dufresne/Eugenia Lussier
Tremblay	Edmundum Albertum	10-NOV-1887	20-NOV-1887	Josepho Tremblay/Adea Dufresne	Carolus Tremblay/Maria Tremblay
Tremblay	Edmundum Eduardum	24-AUG-1882	27-AUG-1882	Moise Tremblay/Eugenia Lucier	Edwardus Tremblay/Emelia Chenart

125

Surname	Given Name	Birth	Baptism	Parents	Godparents
Tremblay	Emeliam Ezildam	15-MAY-1883	20-MAY-1883	Eduardo Tremblay/Emelia Chenart	Alphonsus Chenart/Ezilda Tessier
Tremblay	Franciscum	27-JUN-1887	31-JUL-1887	Josepho Tremblay/Zoea Petit	Carolus Tremblay/Clementia Phaneuf
Tremblay	Henricam Phoebeam	16-DEC-1888	23-DEC-1888	Josepho Tremblay/Adda Dufresne	Andreus Maurice/Emma Dufresne
Tremblay	Hiram Josephum	05-JUN-1886	20-JUN-1886	Josepho Tremblay/Ida Dufresne	Stephanus Dufresne/Emelia Tremblay
Tremblay	Jacobum Dionysium	01-DEC-1889	08-DEC-1889	Josepho Tremblay/Ada Dufresne	Ernestus Tremblay/Agnes Dufresne
Tremblay	Mariam Amandam	25-NOV-1889	08-DEC-1889	Eduardo Tremblay/Arzelia Gervais	Telespharus Gervais/Ezilda Chenart
Tremblay	Mariam Exedam	16-SEP-1887	18-SEP-1887	Alexio Tremblay/Melania Edoin	Franciscus Rondeau/Flavia Edoin
Tremblay	Moise Earl	31-DEC-1883	01-JAN-1884	Josephi Tremblay/Adea-Maria Dufresne	Paschalis Dufresne/Eugenia Tremblay
Tremblay	Philiam Miner	26-JUL-1885	09-AUG-1885	Moyse Tremblay/Maria-Eugenia Lucier	Paschalis Letourneau/Maria B--mhauer
Tremble	Edwardum Isidorum	17-AUG-1874	23-AUG-1874	Edwardi Tremble/Emilia Chenart	Narcissus Bussonette/Sophia Bussonnette
Tremblé	Emiliam	14-JUN-1865	18-JUN-1865	Moysis Tremble/Virginia Lhussier	V. Graton/P. Tremblé
Tremblé	Franciscum	07-MAR-1871	01-APR-1871	Caroli Tremblé/Clementia Tremblé	Josephus Tremblé/Josephna Leduc
Tremblé	Georgium Ernestum Guille	01-MAY-1872	12-MAY-1872	Moysts Tremblé/Joanna Tremblé	Josephus Bransheau/Carolina Lucier
Tremblé	Idam Cary	29-APR-1878	05-MAY-1878	Moese Tremblé/Marie Lucie	J Lucie/wife
Tremblé	Josephmam	16-SEP-1867	20-OCT-1867	Caroli Tremblé/Clementia Tremblé	J V--nauf/T. V--nauf
Tremble	Ludovicam Israelem	05-APR-1877	22-APR-1877	Eduardi Tremble/Melie Snow-Chinard	I Besset/ wife
Tremble	Ludovicum Hurbertum	10-NOV-1875	10-NOV-1875	Josephi Tremblé/Josephina Leduc	H. Leduc/wife
Tremblé	Mariam Exildam	01-FEB-1865	05-MAR-1865	Caroli Tremblé/Clementia Tremblé	E. Tremblé/P. Tremblé
Tremblé	Mariam Joannam	12-JUL-1868	19-JUL-1868	Moysis Tremblé/Joanna Lhussier	Carolus Tremblé/Clementia Faneuf
Tremblé	Mariam Phiomenam	24-MAR-1872	02-APR-1872	Eduardi Tremblé/Emilia Chenar	Carous Tremblé/Phébé Bissonete
Trembley	Henricum Alphonsum	26-MAY-1874	02-JUN-1874	Moyses Trembley/Maria-Eugenia Lucier	Joseph Tremblé/Josephina Tremblé
Trembloy	Josephum	28-JAN-1880	16-FEB-1880	Eduard Trembloy/Emelia Schenar	M. Trembloy/M. Tremblay
Triap*	Michaelis	28-MAR-1857	29-MAR-1857	Joseph Trnap/Anna Jabas	P. Jabas/C. Jamus
Tridcnsy	Mariam Blancam	14-OCT-1895	16-OCT-1895	Isidoro Trndensy/Maria Lamonchc	Nicolaus Lamonche/Josephina Livernois
Trier	-----	05-JUN-1907	05-JUN-1907	Frank-J. Trier/Cara Barbeau	
Trier	Claram Philomenam	17-DEC-1863	20-DEC-1863	Josephi Trıer/Anna Trier	G. Rochel/C. Litze
Trier	Franklin Cornelium	23-JUN-1908	05-JUL-1908	Frank Trier/Cora Barbeau	Petrus Barbeau/Exilda Moquin-Barbeau
Trier	Joannem Franciscum	26-JAN-1866	11-FEB-1866	Josephi Trier/Anna Trier	J Gasper/A. Blum
Trier	Joannem Josephum	01-SEP-1861	08-SEP-1861	Josephi Trier/Anna Trier	J Coens/C. Jaspers
Trier*	Joannem Josephum	07-JUL-1859	07-JUL-1859	Josephi Trier/Anatra Jaspars	J Jaspars/G. Rouse
Trier*	John Joseph				
Trio*	Michaelem	25-MAR-1857	27-MAR-1857	Josephi Trio/Anna Jambus	M. Jabas/C. Jansen
Trıppe	Mariam	07-OCT-1865	19-SEP-1866	Roverti Trıppe/Solona Trippe	L. Léger/M. Léger
Tritter	Franciscum	09-JUN-1867	02-APR-1868	Guillelmi Tritter/Emilia Shina	Isaacus Miller/-------
Trocquet	Edessam	28-APR-1863	03-MAY-1863	Demasis Trocquet/Philomena Trocquet	T Rondeau/J Rondeau
Trocquet	Josephum	12-JUL-1865	25-JUL-1865	Damasii Trocquet/Philomena Trocquet	J Douville/J. Trocuet
Trocquet	Josephum	25-JUL-1864	31-JUL-1864	Damasii Trocquet/Philomena Trocquet	A Faucher/M. Pedlant
Trocquet	Mariam Agnctiam	20-FEB-1862	02-MAR-1862	Damasii Trocquet/Philomena Trocquet	F. Pedlant/J. Roi
Troquet	Aliciam	01-DEC-1860	09-DEC-1860	Damasii Troquet/Philomena Troquet	F. Roi/J. Faucher
Trotier	Mariam Jessa	06-JAN-1870	09-JAN-1870	Damasii Trotier/Philomena Pellant	Stephanus Houle/Maria Houle
Trotier	Mariam Melvinam	06-NOV-1868	18-NOV-1868	Damasii Trotier/Philomena Pellant	Joannis-Baptista Perron/Elizabetha Perron
Trotier	Petrum Franciscum	29-JUN-1872	07-JUL-1872	Damasii Trotier/Philomena Trotier	Josephus Trotier/Phébe Trotier
Trotter	Mariam	08-MAY-1871	12-MAY-1871	Damasii Trotier/Philomena Troter	Josephus Robidou/Adelina Hill
Trottier	Joannem Baptista	06-SEP-1874	08-SEP-1874	Danali Trottier/Philomena Pellan	Eusebius Trottier/Dna Trottier
Trottier	Mariam Melinam	25-SEP-1867	29-SEP-1867	Damasi Trottier/Philomena Trottier	F. Pellant/H. Pellant
Trouillete	Emmam Ludovicam	14-JAN-1869	17-JAN-1869	Teophii Trouillete/Philomena Trouillete	Israel Bassete/Julia Chenar
Trout	Guillelmum Jacobum	13-FEB-1864	02-MAR-1864	Valentini Trout/Wilhelmina Trout	J. Flatten/M. Flatten
Trout	Mariam	17-MAY-1861	16-JUN-1861	Valentini Trout/Wilhelmina Trout	G. Russell/M. Mae
Trudeau	Alva	16-MAY-1880	24-MAY-1880	Gulelmo Trudeau/Henrelia Letourneau	J. Demers/H. Trudeau

Surname	Given Name	Birth	Baptism	Parents	Godparents
Trudeau	Elizabetham	03-FEB-1872	03-FEB-1872	Guillelmi Trudeau/Auralia Trudeau	Pascal Letourneau/Maria Letourneau
Trudeau	Mariam	27-JUL-1870	07-AUG-1870	Zacharia Trudeau/Aurelia Trudeau	Christophus Létourneau/Maria Létourneau
Trudeau	Mariam Altam Phaebeam	03-JUL-1873	06-JUL-1873	Andrea Trudeau/Elinore	Vital Graton/Julianna Chef
Trudeau	Philomena	07-OCT-1873	16-OCT-1873	Zacharias Trudeau/Aurelia Letourneau	Nazarius Lapierre/Mathilda Letourneau
Trudeau	Zachariam	03-FEB-1868	01-MAR-1868	Zacharia Trudeau/Aurelia Letourneau	Julianus Demars/Lucia Letourneau
Trudell	Franciscum	01-NOV-1866	11-NOV-1866	Octavi Trudell/Flavia Trudell	A. Gauthier/F. Robert
Trudell	Ludovicam	27-SEP-1868	01-OCT-1868	Artemii Trudell/Flavia Trudell	Hubertus Foye/Julia Gauthier
Trudo	Aureliam		02-AUG-1866	Zacheria Trudo/Aurelia Trudo	C. Létourneau/N. Landri
Trudo	Jessé	05-AUG-1877	12-AUG-1877	Zaharie Trudo/Aurilia L'Etourneauu	J Letourneau/D. Pratt
Tut*	Mariam Elisabethlam	31-JUL-1858		Nicolaus Tut/Eugena Curran	Patricus McCoy/Eugenia McCoy
Turcot	Carolum Davidem	12-SEP-1887	13-SEP-1887	Eduardo Turcot/Philumena Coté	Zaticus Laporte/Leopaldina Pratte
Turcot	J Josephum	30-SEP-1878	30-SEP-1878	Eduardi Turcot/Philomena Cotté	J. Losechet/ wife
Turcot	Maria Rosalia	04-OCT-1876	08-OCT-1876	Eduardo Turcot/Philumena Coté	F. Beauchemin/R. Beauchemin.
Turcot	Mariam Juliam Phlumenam	12-AUG-1884	30-AUG-1884	Edwardo Turcot/Philomena Coté	Ludgerius Prefontaine/Julia Simonn
Turcote	Virgniam	10-FEB-1872	11-FEB-1872	Eduardi Turcote/Philomena Turcote	Stephanus Touchete/Henrica Touchete
Turenne	Georgium Ludovicum		26-FEB-1900	Ludovico Turenne/Delma Juneau	Josephus Gratton/Aurelia Lepine
Turenne	Josephum Adelardum	12-JUN-1897	19-JUN-1897	Ludovico Turenne/Delia Turenne	Harmelus Potovin/Delia Turenne
Turkotte	Edwardum	23-JUL-1873	27-JUL-1873	Edwardi Turkotte/Philomena Coté	Georgius Audette/Julia Audette
Turner*	Maria	22-AUG-1856	31-AUG-1856	Patrick Turner/Poriget Galliger	A. Galliger/M. Galliger
Turner*	Mariam	12-AUG-1856	31-AUG-1856	P-t-- Turner/Brigetha Galliger	A Galliger/M. Galliger
Turquat	Mariam Rosaliam	03-OCT-1875	03-OCT-1875	Eduardi Turquat/Phlomene Coté	F. Chemain/O. Poulain
Tut*	Joannem	13-JAN-1856	02-MAR-1856	Nicoulaii Tut/Joanna Kerran	M. Kerran/J. Cofville
Uhrling	Joannem	07-JUL-1860	16-SEP-1860	Michaelis Uhrling/Clementia Uhrling	C. Coch/M. Henshenmacher
Uhrling	Mariam Franciscam	20-JUL-1866	20-JUL-1866	Michaelis Uhrling/Clementina Koch-Urling	N Scheushen/F. Flatten
Urlins	Annam Mariam	23-FEB-1855	15-APR-1855	Michaelis Urlins/Clementina Lnam	M. Smet/A. P-ts
Van	Helena	09-MAY-1857	10-MAY-1857	James Vann/Annasthta Logan	John Devin/Maria Vain
Van	Mariam Agnetam	17-JUL-1877	17-JUL-1877	Euclid Vain/Sopha Bastian	L. Vain/ wife
Van*	Evaristum	03-MAR-1860	29-APR-1860	Adolphi Van/------	Evaristh-D Vernais/Desanges Dufraine
Van*	Jacobum Patricum	03-MAY-1859	05-MAY-1859	Jacobi Vain/Anastasia Rayan	T. Newcome/B Gill
Vane	Mariam Alexsiam	02-MAY-1875	05-MAY-1875	Eduardi Vaine/Delia Beaupré	Adulare Delaporte/Delia Vaine
Vaine	Mariam Ludovicam	20-JUN-1875	20-JUN-1875	Euclide Vaine/Sebastian Duracant	Joannes-Bastista Bastien/Rachel Vaine
Vanne	Victor	16-FEB-1876	20-FEB-1876	Ludovici Vainne/Christiana Larue	I. Do---/R. Dor----
Valle*	Amenina	28-DEC-1856	30-DEC-1856	Perre Valle/Orela Larriviere	F. Carbonet/M. Desdclain
Vallea*	Josephine				
Vallée	Adolphum	17-JUL-1864	14-AUG-1864	Petri Vallée/Aurelia Vallée	S. Marie/A. Joubert
Vallée	Clarissam Agnetiam	30-OCT-1862	02-NOV-1862	Petri Vallée/Aurelia Vallée	N. Bullis/D. Bullis
Vallée	Leonem Fabianum	10-JAN-1867	13-JAN-1867	Petri Vallee/Aurelia Vallee	P. Amry/L Bransheau
Vallec	Mariam Aureliam	18-OCT-1860	21-OCT-1860	Petri Vallée/Aurelia Vallee	L. Joubert/E. Joubert
Vallée*	Amennam	28-DEC-1856	30-DEC-1856	Petri Vallée/Aurelia Rivère	F. Corbonet/M. Dudelain
Vallée*	Josephne	21-MAR-1859	22-MAR-1859	Pierre Vallée/Orélie Larrvière	E. Brancha-d/R. Gosselin
Vallée*	Maria Lousa	16-SEP-1855	15-APR-1856	Petrus Vallée/Orilia Larrviere	J. Gosselain/M. Emery
Vallée*	Mariam Lousam	16-SEP-1855	15-APR-1856	Petri Vallée/Ourilia Rivere	J Gosselain/M. Emery
Van Blascum	Celiam	15-OCT-1872	24-MAR-1896	Ludovico VanBlascum/Lea Post	Guielelmus Lemay/Virginia Coté
Vanbrokeln	Josephinam	27-APR-1869	27-APR-1869	Martin VanBrokelin/Emila Gina	Octavus Collin/Maria Chenar
Vander Molen	Josephum	25-JAN-1905	26-FEB-1905	Hermano Van Der Molen/Maria Landerman	
Vandermolen	Annam Viviannam	03-FEB-1906	25-FEB-1906	Hermano Vandermolen/Maria-Rosa Landerman	Leo Martin/Eleonore Dumas-Martin
VanDermolen	Hermanum		17-NOV-1902	Joannes VanDermolen/Afke Vanderweg	Josephus Landreman/Ophilia Dumas
Vandermolen	Josephum Edwardum	08-AUG-1908	23-AUG-1908	Hermano Vandermolen/Maria Lauderman	Nicholas Lamonche/Marcelna Livernois-Lamonche
Vandermolen	Mariam Vidam	03-APR-1907	19-MAY-1907	Hermano Vandermolen/Maria Landerman	Hugh Hallow/Lelian-Rose Martin-Hallow

127

Surname	Given Name	Birth	Baptism	Parents	Godparents
Vandermolen	Theresam Mariam	28-APR-1910	12-JUN-1910	Hermann Vandermolen/Maria Landerman	Isidorous Landerman/Theresa Landerman
Vandersten	Adolphum	10-SEP-1870	25-SEP-1870	Caroli Vandersten/Adelaida Vandersten	Augustus Devillerse/Adelaïda Devillerse
Vaughan	Joannem	24-DEC-1855	30-DEC-1855	Jacabi Vaughan/Anastatia Gogon	P. Gag--/M. Vaughan
Vaughn	Annam	12-MAY-1862	13-MAY-1862	Jacobi Vaughn/Anastasia Vaughn	M Fitzsimmons/M Vaughn
Vaughn	Petrum	02-MAR-1861	03-MAR-1861	Jacpbi Vaughn/Anastasia Vaughn	M. Corkeran/M Lawlar
Vaughn*	James Patrick				
Veine	Josephum Franciscum	14-DEC-1867	15-DEC-1867	Euclidis Veine/Sophia Veine	F. Veine/M Paquete
Veine	Josephum Gustavum	17-AUG-1873	24-AUG-1873	Ludovici Veine/Christina Larue	Eduardi Veine/Emilia Beaupré
Veine	Ludovicum Jacobum	26-JUL-1867	28-JUL-1867	Ludovici-Josephi-T. Veine/Christina Veine	A. Veine/D. Veine
Veine	Maria Alexa Irenea	29-OCT-1879	09-NOV-1879	Ludovico Veine/Christina Larue	A Laporte/D. Veine
Veine	Mariam Ludovicam Claram	04-MAY-1880	09-MAY-1880	Eduardo Veine/Maria-Delia Beaupré	L. Veine/C. Veine
Veine	Mariam Ludovicam Emiliam	11-JUN-1871	11-JUN-1871	Ludovici Veine/Christina Veine	Zotcus Laporte/Ludovica Veine
Veine	Mariam Rosaliam Elidam	02-JAN-1870	03-JAN-1870	Euclidius Veine/Sophia Bastien	Hilarus Landreman/Rosalia Veine
Vellet	Josephum	05-MAR-1854	05-MAR-1854	Huberti Oellet/Sena Lei	L Mathew/F. Lei
Venne	Agnetem Mabel	10-FEB-1901	12-FEB-1901	Arthuro Venne/Maria Dufresne	Aldericus Venne/Olivina Fontaine
Venne	Ceciliam Elsie	18-OCT-1905	22-OCT-1905	Arthuro Venne/Ovila Dufraisne	Eduardus Desrochers/Eliza. Dufraisne-Desrochers
Venne	Claudium Stephanum	11-OCT-1889	13-OCT-1889	Henrico-Alfredo Venne/Eliza.-Ludovica Fretlnc	Ludovicus Venne/Christina Larue
Venne	Felicem Armandum	29-JUL-1890	29-JUL-1890	Alderico Venne/Maloma Fontaine	Euclides Venne/Sophia Bastien
Venne	Haroldum Patricum Mildre	17-MAR-1904	27-MAR-1904	Ludovico-Jacobo Venne/Henrica Lyonais	Cosma Lyonais/Christina Larue
Venne	Josephum Alexandrum Ed	09-SEP-1885	13-SEP-1885	Eduardo Venne/Maria-Dalila Beaupre	Isidorus Daunet/Rosalia Venne
Venne	Josephum Alphonsum	19-MAY-1882	21-MAY-1882	Josepho Venne/Maria Letourneau	Franciscus Pellant/Philumena Letourneau
Venne	Josephum Arthurum Claviu	29-FEB-1872	03-MAR-1872	Euclidis Venne/Sophia Venne	Josephus Landreman/Marguarita Venne
Venne	Josephum Avrilam	18-MAR-1888	18-MAR-1888	Josepho Venne/Maria Letourneau	Loticus Laporte/Leopoldina Pratte
Venne	Josephum Eduardum Arthu	08-SEP-1872	09-SEP-1872	Eduardi Venne/Adelia Beaupré	Agapitus Venne/Theotissa Venne
Venne	Josephum Henricum Edmu	16-JUN-1886	20-JUN-1886	Josepho Venne/Maria Letourneau	Henricus Venne/Carolina Venne
Venne	Josephum Leonem Cleopha	18-JUL-1903	26-JUL-1903	Arthuro Venne/Maria-Ovide Dufresne	Ovides Senecal/Rosa-Delima Venne
Venne	Josephum Raymondum Gil	14-MAR-1884	16-MAR-1884	Josepho Venne/Maria Letourneau	Isidorus Danne/Rosalia Venne
Venne	Josephum Victorem	29-APR-1890	04-MAY-1890	Josepho Venne/Maria Letourneau	Calixtus-E Errard/Delphina Leduc
Venne	Linum Franciscum	02-JUN-1907	16-JUN-1907	Ludovico-J. Venne/Henrietta Lynais-Lyonnais	------/Joanna Lynais-Lyonnais
Venne	Mariam Esilda	07-FEB-1877	07-FEB-1877	Leopoldi Venne/Genovefa Durocher	F. Venne/M Landreman
Venne	Mariam Florentiam	19-MAY-1898	22-MAY-1898	Arthuro Venne/Maria Dufresne	Stephanus Dufresne/Marie-Louisa Lebeau
Venne	Mariam Lousam Corrinam	09-FEB-1883	11-FEB-1883	Eusebio Venne/Maria Beaupre	Henricus Venne/Carolina Venne
Venne	Mariam Margueritam Leon	18-DEC-1896	20-DEC-1896	Arthuro Venne/Maria Dufresne	Franciscus Dufresne/Elisa Ste.-Marie
Venne	Mariam Melinam Hazel	11-NOV-1893	12-NOV-1893	Alderico Venne/Olivina Fontaine	Ovidis Senecal/Maria-Rosa-Delima Venne
Verbonlaire	Mariam Virgenem	03-APR-1877	08-APR-1877	Ludovici Verbonlaire/Vergena Class	C. Gordon/ wife
Vergan*	Michaelem	20-DEC-1857	25-FEB-1858	Mich. Vergan/Julia Clossy	T. Clossy/M. Clossy
Vergan*	Michaelis	20-DEC-1857	25-FEB-1858	Mich Vergan/Julia Clossy	Thamas Clossy/Maria Clossy
Vernais*	Evariste				
Vernais*	Reginam	12-MAY-1857	07-AUG-1858	Isais Vernais/Ma--a Hubert	Rubertus Gentier/Maria T--yat
Vernay*	Reginam	12-MAY-1857	07-AUG-1858	Isaia Vernay/Mathilda Hubert	R. Gauther/M. Turcote
Vernet	Isaiam		29-MAY-1875	Joannis Vernet/Melia Roledue	Petrus Duvraine/Chelie Vernet
Vernet	Josephum		29-MAY-1875	Joannis Vernet/Melia Roledue	Petrus Duvraine/Chelie Vernet
Vernet	Matilda	12-OCT-1876	15-OCT-1876	Joannis Vernet/Melia Boisledur	J. Boisledur/E. Bodriaux
Vernuf	Mariam	25-AUG-1855	26-AUG-1855	Josephi Vernuf/Lousa Sonnet	------/M Dulaine
Verro-*	Joannem Baptistam	01-OCT-1853	19-JUL-1857	Joannes Verro-/Maria Linsy	N Jubert/E. Doudelain
Verro-*	Joannem Michaelem	04-NOV-1855	19-JUL-1857	Joannes Verro-/Maria Linsy	D. Jubert/J. Gosselain
Verron*	Joannes Michaelis	04-NOV-1855	19-JUL-1857	John-P---/ Verron/Loreta Lnsy	D. Jubert/D. Daiselam
Verron*	Marie	10-OCT-1853	19-JUL-1857	John Verron/----- Linsy	N Hubert/E. Dendelain
Vetter	Carolum Nicholaum	06-MAR-1865	10-MAR-1865	Ferdinandi Vetter/Maria Vetter	N Christ/H Early

128

Surname	Given Name	Birth	Baptism	Parents	Godparents
Veughn	Joannes	24-DEC-1855	30-DEC-1855	Jacobus Veughn/Anastatia B-gan	P. ---e/M. Veughn
Vi--t	Carolum		14-JUL-1861	Narcissi Vi--t/Aurelia Vi--t	C. Thon/L. Thon
Vi--t	Isabellam		14-JUL-1861	Narcissi Vi--t/Aurelia Vi--t	J Chenar/M. Chenar
Vicort	Josephum	08-APR-1861	12-APR-1861	Josephi Vicort/Gertruda Vicort	J. Rost/S. Hogart
Vienne	Josephum	27-JUL-1877	26-AUG-1877	Josephi Vienne/Josephine Gothie	S. Demarsh/A. Tryant
Vient	Henricum	24-AUG-1869	19-SEP-1869	Narcissi Vient/Julia Bertrand	Ludovicus Bertrand/Eulalia Beaudrieau
Vient	Josephum Albertum	23-JUL-1872	24-JUL-1872	Narcissi Vient/Julia Bertrand	Carolus Bird/Aurelia Trahant
Vilbert*	Joanem	17-JUL-1858	19-SEP-1858	Petri Vilbert/Margaretha -----	Joanne Hansen/Marie Tau--c--
Violet	Elizabetham Helenam		14-APR-1861	Francisci Violet/Elizabetha Violet	J. Crane/B. O'connor
Violet	Marcum Josephum		30-AUG-1863	Francisci Violet/Elizabetha Violet	J Harlen/M. Harlen
Voile.*	Maria Anna	26-JAN-1857	02-FEB-1857	Augustinus Voile/Anne Dunsy	P. ---/----- Dantz
Wachs	Georgio Carlkel	27-AUG-1905	08-OCT-1905	Alfredo Wachs/Elsie-Maria Devillers	Franciscus Sweeney/Stella Devillers
Wagner	Georgium Antonium	09-DEC-1861	10-DEC-1861	Josephi Wagner/Agnetia Wagner	A Wagner/C Curry
Wagner*	Francis Joseph				
Wagoner*	Franciscus Josephus	12-MAR-1860	14-MAR-1860	Josephus-J Wagoner/Agnes Cu---	Joannis Wagner/Maria-Frances Flaten
Waller	Helenam Florentiam	12-SEP-1870	13-FEB-1871	Caroli Waller/Helena Waller	Stephanus Houle/Maria Houle
Walsh	Annam	22-JUL-1852		Edwardi Walsh/Maria Carrol	R. Adell/A. Norton
Walsh	Jacobum	21-APR-1862	04-MAY-1862	Jacobi Walsh/Catharina Walsh	T. Roach/M. Roach
Walsh	Michaelem	29-DEC-1863	17-JAN-1864	Jacobi Walsh/Catharina Walsh	P. Crowley/M. Crowley
Walsh	Thomam	17-OCT-1861	20-OCT-1861	Guillelmi Walsh/Marguarita Walsh	T. Brown/R. Borke
Walsh	Thomam Franciscum	15-MAY-1862	18-MAY-1862	Guillelmi Walsh/Marguarita Walsh	E. Wall/M Flinn
Walsh*	Ellen				
Walsh*	George	11-SEP-1859	22-MAR-1860	Jocobus Walsh/Hellena Cralen	Gulielllmus Cralen/Brigetta Cralen
Walsh*	Hellena				
Walsh*	Marie Ellen				
Walsh*	Mary Ellen				
Walsh*	Richard Edward	14-OCT-1859	14-OCT-1859	G. Walsh/M Ring	W Walsh/N. Flinn
Walsh* **	Wina				
Walsh* **	Mary Helen	18-SEP-1858	07-NOV-1858	Prick Walsh/Helen -oelen	Patrick Roden/Ann Melia
Walters	Ludovicum Cornelium	18-MAR-1861	09-MAY-1861	Francisci Walters/Emllia-Eleonora Walters	J Walters/R. Mcgennis
Walters	Margaritam		17-JUL-1874	Caroli Walters/Helena Juneau	Franciscus Juneau/Leucadia Baudoin-Juneau
Walthe-	Elizabetham Ludovicam		07-MAY-1865	Hermani Walthe-/Catharina Bla---	E Bla--/J. L---t
Ward	James	21-MAY-1851	19-JUN-1851	Thomas Ward/Mary Cavinagh	P. Baker/M. Lawlor
Ward	Mariam Juliam	01-OCT-1861	04-OCT-1861	Julii Ward/Maria Ward	J. Kenni/B. Gill
Ward*	Bridget	30-JAN-1858	31-JAN-1858	Thos Ward/Bridget Furgusson	P'trick Enley/Ellen O'Connor
Ward*	Brigetham	30-JAN-1858	04-FEB-1858	Thoma Ward/Brigetha Furgeson	P. Kelly/E. O'Coner
Ward*	Jocabum	12-MAY-1857	15-MAY-1857	Jocobi Ward/Cath. McLevy	J McLevy/----- McLevy
Ward*	Thoma Henricus	20-APR-1860	06-MAY-1860	Thamas Ward/Brigetta Ferguson	A----- Ferguson/Maria-Anna Ferguson
Ward*	Thomas Henry				
Warner	Albertum		23-AUG-1869	B. Warner/Rosalia Garo	Petrus Garo/Clementa Garo
Warner	Estherem	05-SEP-1870	06-JAN-1871	Joannis Warner/Rosalia Garo	-----/Julia Loisele
Water*	Jacobum Henricum	15-SEP-1859	18-SEP-1859	Joannes Water/----ana Kelly	- --tio--/B. Nu----
Water*	James Henry				
Waters	Catharinam	24-DEC-1855	28-DEC-1855	Joannis Waters/Sousana. Kelly	J Cavenach/A. Flury
Waters	Maria Eugenia	10-FEB-1858	13-FEB-1858	Jonh Waters/Susana Kelly	Patrick Kristel/Marie Kristell
Waters	Michaelem	05-APR-1855	15-APR-1855	Joannis Waters/Susanna Kelly	D. Waters/B. Denneys
Waters*	Mariam-Eugenam	10-FEB-1858	13-FEB-1858	Joannis Waters/Susanna Kelly	P. Kristel/M. Krstel
Watters	Cornelam		06-FEB-1864	Guillelmi Watters/Emilia Watters	V. Watters/----- ---
Watters	Joannem Edwardum		30-JUN-1861	Joannis Watters/Suzanna Watters	T. Newgent/B. O'Loughlin

129

Surname	Given Name	Birth	Baptism	Parents	Godparents
Webb	John	10-DEC-1851	24-JUN-1852	John Webb/Ellen Kief	P. Brown/A. Farley
Weber	Alicem Margaritam	23-JUL-1906	29-JUL-1906	Petro Weber/Corinna Sauve	Nicholas Weber/Eulodia Venne
Weber	Catharinam	08-APR-1861	24-APR-1861	Petri Weber/Chrstiana Weber	B. Colp/C. Stanton
Weber	Esther Mariam	24-MAY-1909	30-MAY-1909	Petro Weber/Corinna Sauve	Paulus Sauve/Barbara Weber-Keanigs
Weber	Helmerum Josephum	10-DEC-1902	15-DEC-1902	Petro-Josepho Weber/Corinna Laurie	Josephus Weber/Paulma Sauvé
Weber	Joannem	13-SEP-1864	02-OCT-1864	Petri Weber/Chrstina Weber	J. Shleier/M Konig
Weber	Charlottam Margaritam	17-FEB-1907	08-MAR-1907	Hobarto Weeks/Margarita Chagnon	Josephus Errard/Delonsa Errard
Weeks	Mariam Ednam Isabellam	23-APR-1898	08-MAY-1898	Hoberto-Owen Weeks/Margaritta Chagnon	Calixtus Errard/Delphine Leduc
Weeks	Mariam Phulumenam Adel	02-JAN-1902	30-JAN-1902	Huberto-H. Weeks/Marguerita Chagnon	Edmundus Errard/Odelia Marcoux
Weid	Thomam	25-MAR-1853	10-MAY-1853	Thoma Weid/Maria Cavanagh	B. Farel/----- -----
Weiler	Anna-Maria	04-APR-1852	10-JUN-1852	Nicholas Weiler/Elizabeth Hanson	P. Brıl/A. Everlling
Weiler	Annam Franciscam		25-SEP-1865	Nicolai Weiler/Elizabetha Hanson	J. Hanson/A. Francis
Welchs*	Richardum Edwardum	23-OCT-1859	30-OCT-1859	Will Welchs/Margeta B-n-	W. Wells/H. Flood
Welhs*	Patrıcus	17-OCT-1856	28-OCT-1856	James Welhs/Brgita Enard	B. Welsh/C Welsh
Wellan*	Joanna	13-AUG-1856	24-AUG-1856	Thamas Wellan/Margeretha Dayer	J. Whelan/B. Hogan
Wellan*	Joannam	13-AUG-1856	24-AUG-1856	Thoma Wellan/Margeretha Dayer	J Wellen/B Hogon
Welle-	Catharinam		08-JUN-1862	Nicholai Welle-/Elizabetha Welle-	M. Gibel/C. Gartner
Welle-	Marguaritam		08-JUN-1862	Nicholai Welle-/Elizabetha Welle-	W Gibel/M Gärtner
Wells*	Bernardum	05-MAY-1863	08-SEP-1863	Jacobi Wells/Bridgitta Wells	D. Mccowley/E. Wells
Wells*	M-g-niliam	07-NOV-1859	12-NOV-1859	Willim Wells/Marget Daly	T G--/A. Vae-
Wells*	Marguaret				
Wells*	Mariam Elenam	27-NOV-1858	10-JAN-1859	Michelis Wells/Elisabeth O'Kieff	James Fitzgerald/Anna Hennora
Wells*	Mariam Elenam	27-NOV-1858	10-JAN-1859	Michelis Wells/Elisabeth O'Kieff	James Fitzjarral/Anna-Honnora LeGee
Welsch	Mariam	25-DEC-1853	29-JAN-1854	Jacobi Welsch/Chaterina Fayant	H McGregory/C Haim
Welsch*	Brigta	26-JUN-1856	15-AUG-1856	James Welsch/Mary --keran	J. P--tte/S. Morta
Welsch*s	Margereta Anna	10-NOV-1855	20-NOV-1855	Jacobus Welschs/Caterina Jensen	P. Melony/M Melony
Welschs	Michae;em	05-FEB-1856	10-FEB-1856	Michaeli Welschs/Elisabetha Okeÿ	G. Legee/J. Bergin
Welschs	Michel	08-FEB-1856	10-FEB-1856	Michel Welsch/Elisabeh Okee	W -----/J Bergan
Welschs*	Brigetham	26-JUN-1856	15-AUG-1856	Jocobi Welschs/Maria Gekeran	J. Parter/S Martha
Welschs*	Joannam	22-MAR-1857	27-MAR-1857	Guelli-- Welschs/Margeretha Ring	M. Fitzsimmons/M. Kellar
Welschs*	Margata Ellena	26-APR-1858	02-MAY-1858	William Welschs/Margarta Deuly	Jeremias Loyetan/Brigeta Pier
Welschs*	Margeritham Annam	01-NOV-1855	20-NOV-1855	Jacobi Welschs/Catharina Fenner	P. Melony/M. Melony
Welschs*	Matheas	14-MAR-1858	04-APR-1858	James Welschs/Catherina --nnan	Marek -innon/Brigita Crauly
Welschs*	Patricum	17-AUG-1856	28-OCT-1856	Jocobi Welschs/Brigetha Maid	B. Welschs/C Welschs
Welsh	Brıgt	18-MAY-1852	23-JUN-1852	James Welsh/Catherine Finan	J Kelly/----- Kelly
Welsh	Catherine	11-SEP-1850	15-SEP-1850	Joannes Welsh/Catherine Finneux	M. Finneux/B Reilly
Welsh	Thomam Henricum	03-JUL-1854	24-JUL-1854	Jocobi Welsh/Brdgida Weid	J Welsh/M Welsh
Welsh*	Evınam	06-MAY-1860	19-MAY-1860	Jocabi Welsh/Catherina Fennan	Joannes Cain/Maria Welsh
Welshs*	Elisabet Delma	22-JUL-1857	26-JUL-1857	William Welshs/Maria Stanten	T. Stanten/C. -n-----
Welshs*	Elisabetham Lenam	22-JUL-1857	26-JUL-1857	Wilhelmı Welshs/Maria Stantan	T. Stantan/C. Egan
Welshs*	Jo---ss	14-JAN-1859	08-APR-1859	Jo----- Welshs/Brigetha Weed	B. Wels/M Wels
Welshs*	Margeretham Elenam	28-APR-1858	02-MAY-1858	Welhuelmi Welshs/Margeretha Daily	J Logelon/B Rici-
Welshs*	Matheam	14-MAR-1858	04-APR-1858	Jocobi Welshs/Cath Fennan	M Fennan/B. Cranly
West	Johanna	04-SEP-1851	28-SEP-1851	James West/Marguerite Connelly	W Lunhagan/M. Connely
Wethbur*	Elısabeh	04-SEP-1853	01-JUL-1855	Joseph Wethbur/Selina Sneglagen	M. Smet/E. Lendum
Wethburg*	Joannes	28-AUG-1841	18-JUL-1855	Joseph Wethburg/Elizabeth Sneglagen	M. Smet/E. Lendum
Wetstein	Mildred Josephine	14-DEC-1918	23-DEC-1918	Michael Wetstein/Josephine Marcoe	Frank Marcoe/Josphine Balthazar-Marcoe
Whalan*	Joannam	11-SEP-1856	05-OCT-1856	Danielis Whalan/Maria Nayly	P. Whalen/M. Carrol
Whalen	Michae;em	19-NOV-1859	25-DEC-1859	James Whalen/Brigetha Hagam	Joannes Whalen/Hol---- Whelan

Surname	Given Name	Birth	Baptism	Parents	Godparents
Whelan*	Cornelius	10-SEP-1858	25-SEP-1858	James Whelan/Bridget Whelan	Eduard Ward/Weifred Hogan
Whelan*	Joanna	11-SEP-1856	05-OCT-1856	Daniel Whelan/Marie Raly	D Whelan/M. Carrol
Whelan*	Margcretham	26-MAR-1857	03-MAY-1857	Jocobi Whelan/Brigetha Hogan	T Flind/B. Whelan
Whelan*	Margerita	26-MAR-1857	03-MAY-1857	James Whelan/Brigita Hogan	T. Flind/B. Whelan
Wheler*	Henricum	05-SEP-1857	04-JUL-1858	Nicholai Wheler/Elizabetha Hanson	H. Wagner/M. Engeheur
Whell--*	Henricum Felton	05-SEP-1837	04-JUL-1858	---- Whell--/Ch----- Hunjan	Henricus Wagner/M---- --gelk-se
White	Elizabetham Annam		10-MAR-1862	Joannis White/Marguarita White	J White/A. White
White	Elizabetham Marguaritam	27-OCT-1860	11-NOV-1860	Joannis White/Marguarita White	J Fagan/M. Fagan
White	Georgium Justinum	19-DEC-1860	19-DEC-1860	Justini White/Lucia White	G Wotet/L. Wo---t
White	Joseph Carolum		11-OCT-1863	Joannis White/Marguarita White	P White/S. White
White	Mary Frances	01-SEP-1850	10-SEP-1850	Henry White/Theresa Juneau	S Juneau/M. Juneau
White*	Mariam	19-AUG-1859	28-AUG-1859	Joannes White/Meregetha White	J. Du--hy/B Dwyer
White*	Mary				
Whiten	Mariam Jamantea		23-MAY-1878	William Whiten/Majie Norph-n	J Chrstoni/E. Norten
Whitmore	Floyd Vincentium	16-JUN-1899	25-NOV-1899	Gulielmo Whitmore/Vitalina Moquin	Georgius Langois/Maria Moquin
Whitmore	Georgum Bernardum	16-OCT-1903	05-NOV-1903	Gulielmo Whitmore/Vitalina Moquin	Ernest Moquin/Cordelia Moquin
Whitmore	Gulielmum Laurentium	12-JUL-1902	23-JUL-1902	Gulielmo Whitmore/Vitalina Moquin	Gulielmum Durocher/Josephina Dupuy
Whitmore	Joannem Baptistam Russell	30-APR-1901	05-MAY-1901	Gulielmo Whitmore/Vitalina Moquin	Joannes-Baptista Moquin/Eva Moquin
Whitty*	Marguerite	19-FEB-1858	16-MAR-1858	Will Witty/Mary Ryan	John McCoy/Marguerite Ryan
Wickert	Eduardum	23-MAR-1887	28-MAR-1887	Matheo Mand/Catharina Wickert	Eduardus Wickert/Anna Mand
Wilber	Petrum	03-DEC-1865	17-DEC-1865	Petri Wilber/Marguarita Wilber	P Shove/S. Hanson
Wilbert	Annam Marguaritam		21-FEB-1864	Petri Wilbert/Marguarita Wilbert	M. Giebet/A. Root
Wilbert*	John				
Wilby-Willey	Simeonem	13-JAN-1908	10-MAY-1908	Ruperto Wilby/Tessie LeTourneau	Alfredus Dictte/Edessa Letourneau-Diette
Wilcoque	Davidem	20-JUL-1869	01-DEC-1869	Francisci Wilcoque/Josephina St.-Louis	Marcelus Picor/Paulina Wilcoque
Wilcox	Carolum Henricum		30-SEP-1865	Elisha Wilcox/Joanna Wilcox	E Branscheau/M. Deshautels
Wilcox	Elmer Ludovicum		02-NOV-1878	Ludovici Wilcox/Laurentia Rassett	C. Nolan/S Wilcox
Wilcox	Guilielmum Henricum	28-NOV-1868	28-MAR-1869	Caroli-Guilelmi Wilcox/Ludovica Wilcox	Carolus-Eduardus Joubert/Edessa Bullis
Wilde	Mariam Melvinam	07-MAY-1869	31-MAY-1869	F.F. Wilde/Melvina Gagnon	Fredericus Wilde/Marguarita Gagnon
Wilbert	Barbaram	17-DEC-1860	29-DEC-1860	Petri Wilbert/Marguarita Wilbert	J Pomerich/B Giebel
Wilbert	Jacobum		03-JAN-1863	Petri Wilbert/Marguarita Wilbert	J Tautges/M. Pomerich
Willcote	Carolum Fredericum	05-JUL-1872	15-DEC-1872	Francisci Willcoque/Josepha St-Louis	Ludovicus Lecoque/Anna Bessete
Willcox	Ludovicum	12-APR-1873	12-APR-1873	Ludovici Willcox/Laurentia Willcox	Ludovicus Wilcox/Marguarita Bessete
Willcox	Carolum Edwardum	07-JAN-1867	22-FEB-1867	Caroli-Henrici Wilcox/Albina Wilcox	S. Joubert/M. Joubert
Willer*	Madulnam	11-MAY-1855	01-JUL-1855	Nicolai Willen/Elizabetha H-ndson	M. Smetz/E Sneylager
Willer*	Madalena	11-MAY-1855	21-JUL-1855	Nicolas Willer/Elizabeth Lendsun	M. Smet/E. S--glager
Willey	Almira Eve Joan	24-MAR-1919	22-AUG-1920	Rupert Willey/Lucy-Jessie LeTourneau	William Balthazar/-----
Willey	Flora Imogene Elizabeth	25-FEB-1917	22-AUG-1920	Rupert Willey/Lucy-Jessie LeTourneau	----- -----/Florence Deitte
Willey	Francis Lorraine	20-JAN-1913		Rupert Willey/Lucy-Jessie LeTourneau	----- -----/Ida Balthazar
Willey	Jessie Coral Mary	01-JAN-1915	22-AUG-1920	Rupert Willey/Lucy-Jessie LeTourneau	----- -----/Edith Deitte
Williams	Annam	15-JUN-1863	14-AUG-1863	Frederici Williams/Bridgitta Ryan-Williams	A. Mcnamara/----- -----
Williams	Mildredam Mariam Stellam	07-JUN-1907	16-JUN-1907	Benjamin Williams/Stella Devillers	Arthurus Devillers/Maria Laberge-Devillers
Williams*	Anna		03-JUL-1858	----- Williams/----- -----	
Williams*	Annam		03-JUL-1858	-ay--d Williams/Sarah Williams	T Reily/C Jacobi
Williams*	Bernard		03-JUL-1858	----- Williams/----- -----	
Williams*	Bernardum		03-JUL-1858	-ay--d Williams/Sarah Williams	T. Reily/C. Jacobi
Williams*	Joannem		03-JUL-1858	-ay--d Williams/Sarah Williams	T. Reily/C. Jacobi
Williams*	Joannes		03-JUL-1858	----- Williams/----- -----	
Williams*	Robertum		03-JUL-1858	-ay--d Williams/Sarah Williams	T Reily/C Jacobi

131

Surname	Given Name	Birth	Baptism	Parents	Godparents
Williams*	Robertus		03-JUL-1858	----- Williams/----- -----	
Williams*	Sarahm		03-JUL-1858	----- Williams/----- -----	T. Reily/C. Jacobi
Williams*	Sera		03-JUL-1858	----- Williams/----- -----	
Williams*	Wilhelmum		03-JUL-1858	-ay--d Williams/Sarah Williams	T. Reily/C. Jacobi
Williams*	William		03-JUL-1858	----- Williams/----- -----	
Willis	Harold Edwin	07-OCT-1918	13-OCT-1918	Francisco Willis/Christina Ferdinand	Leo Schmitz/Paulina Schmitz-Birschback
Willis*	Joanna	22-MAR-1857	29-MAR-1857	William Willis/Maria King	M. Fitsimmons/M. Ke-
Wilson	Marguaritam Elizabetham	29-OCT-1861	11-JUL-1869	Joannis Wilson/Christine Edouin	Julianus Edouin/Eulalia Malheur
Wilson	Mariam Odiliam		01-APR-1868	Godfredis Wilson/Paula Wilson	Joannis-Marie Marcou/Domitilla Tremblé
Winter*	Mary Eliza				
Wirtzburger	Josephinam Mariam	14-SEP-1860	16-JUN-1861	Josephi Wirtzburger/Helena Wirtzburger	B. C-i-/M. Kông
Wisen*	Theodore	16-JAN-1860	18-MAR-1860	Landelin Wisen/Coraline Mise	Jocabus Harter/Genesia Standt
Wisen*	Theodore				
Wiser	Rose Emelia	15-FEB-1858	14-MAY-1858	Lendelin Wiser/Caroline Mayer	Christopher Bach/Emelie Matthew
Wiser	Rosem Emiliam	15-FEB-1858	14-MAY-1858	Wendeline Wiser/Caroline Hayes	C. Bach/L. Matthew
Witty*	Marguerite	19-FEB-1858	04-APR-1858	Will Witty/Mary Ryan	John McCoy/Marg Ryan
Witzburger	Ferdinandum	05-OCT-1864	07-APR-1865	Josephi Witzburger/Helena Witzburger	F. Philips/M. Philips
Wolf	Annam	18-APR-1861	28-APR-1861	Joannis Petri Wolf/Catharina Wolf	C. Vildner/A. Crembs
Wolf*	Louis				
Wood	Ludovicum Nelson		02-SEP-1852	Nelson Wood/Helena Perkins	P. Harnois/L. Delaire
Wood*	Jocabus	12-MAY-1857	15-MAY-1857	James Wood/Chaterina McTevy	J McTevy/M McTevy
Woods	John	18-FEB-1851	06-MAR-1851	James Woods/Catherine McTevy	J. McTevy/M. McTevy
Woods-McTevy	Edward	25-DEC-1850	01-MAR-1851	James Woods/Caterina McTevy	J Kein/B. Forin
Woolf*	Mariam Eugeniam	13-JAN-1858	07-JUN-1858	Victoris Woolf/Anna Loghelan	J Emerson/M Doyle
Wotete	Alfredum Georgium	13-OCT-1871	15-OCT-1871	Francisci Wotete/Rosalia Dupuis	Georgius Wotete/Virginia Wotete
Wotete	Hubertum	28-APR-1873	11-MAY-1873	Huberti Wotete/Maria Wotete	Isaacus St.-Antoine/Julia-Anna St -Antoine
Wotete	Petrum Joannem	16-OCT-1872	20-OCT-1872	Petri Wotete/Carolina Wotete	Joannes-Baptista Bolduc/Lucia Bolduc
Wotett	Teophilum	12-JUL-1862	21-JUL-1862	H Wottet/Celestina Wottet	T Thibodeau/E. Molheur
Woulf*	Annam Mariam	10-NOV-1855	20-NOV-1855	Petri Woulf/Catharina Jansen	A. Servatius/A. Woulf
Woulf*	Ludovicum		13-MAR-1859	Petri Woulf/Catheria -uinlan	P. Niehart/A. -----ars
Woulf*	Maria Eugenia	13-JAN-1858	07-JUN-1858	Victor Woulf/Anna Hogelan	James Emmerson/Maria Donn
Wright	Alfredum Eduardum	23-JUN-1894	30-JUL-1894	Josepho Wright/Flora Gervais	Isaac Gervais/Virginia Geise
Wulf*	Anna Maria	10-NOV-1855	20-NOV-1855	Joannes-Peter Wulf/Chaterina Jansen	A. Servatius/A. Wulf
Wurgburger	Henricus	08-SEP-1855	12-JAN-1860	Joseph Wurgburger/Hellena Wurgburger	Gustavus White/Elisabeth Collob
Yelle	--lea Phelia	21-JUL-1879	27-JUL-1879	Josephi Yelle/Sophia Lepine	
Ying	Daniel		10-FEB-1856	Chang Ying/Andrina --gard	E Jubet/S. Ellant
Yong	Georgium	07-MAY-1868	31-MAY-1868	Francisci Yong/Carolina Yong	Baptista Channière/Aurelia Trahant
Young	Danielem	27-JAN-1856	10-FEB-1856	Joannis Young/Andrina Reg--d	E Jubet/S. Bellant
Z--d--*	Peter	28-JUN-1858	01-JUL-1858	Jacob Z--d--/Catherine -auch-	Peter Lossillion/----- Lossillion
Zacherel	Ludovicum	29-OCT-1863	29-NOV-1863	Georgii Zacherel/Magdalena Zacherel	G. Shertzinger/L. Davis
Zacherel	Rosam Mariam	24-JUN-1862	13-JUL-1862	Georgii Zacherel/Magdalena Zacherel	J. Denis/R. Denis
Zacherel	Sopham	15-FEB-1866	11-MAR-1866	Georgii Zacherel/Magdalena Zacherel	B. Serwe/S. Koepfer
Zacherel*	Willehlmina				
Zacherl*	Wilhemminam	04-APR-1859	09-OCT-1859	Georg Zacherl/Matalena Shmider	----- S-ome
Zimmerman	Dorotheam May	18-JUL-1906	22-JUL-1906	Eduardo Zimmerman/Emilia Balthazar	Martinus Balthazar/Melinda Balthazar
Zimmermann	Josephum Douglas	08-MAR-1908	12-MAR-1908	Eduardo Zimmermann/Emelia Balthazar	Jaonnes-B. Balthazar/Maria Marcou-Balthazar
Zundler*	Petrum	28-JUN-1858	01-JUL-1858	Jacobi Zundler/Catharina Loselion	P. Losselion/----- Losselion
Zunellic*	Madelaida	03-FEB-1860	15-FEB-1860	Jocobus Zunelle/Catherine Lessilyony	Joannes Lessilyony/Madilade Muldore

St. Louis Catholic Parish, Fond du Lac, Wisconsin

Marriages – Index of Grooms
1850-1920

Groom's Surname	Groom's Name	Groom's Parents	Date	Bride's Surname	Bride's Name	Bride's Parents
——	Petrus		08-APR-1861	Coke	Marguarita	
——	James		19-AUG-1860	Junsh	Maria	
——*	R.		05-FEB-1866	——	A.	
——*	Josephus		29-JAN-1866	Gauth	E-	
——*	Petrus		06-JAN-1866	Bruel	Bridgitta	
—llimeur	Franciscus	Franciscus —llimeur/Marg. —llimeur	26-NOV-1860	Dufresne	Zoah	Pascalis Dufresne/Angelica Coché
Alain	Franciscus	Jacobi Alain/Judith Guenan	26-DEC-1871	Bouchar	Josephina	Germain Bouchar/Lucia Petit
Alain	Carolum		13-OCT-1883	Pellant	Edessam	
Alar	Carolus	Georgii Alar/Adelaïda Alar	26-JUN-1868	Donet	Emilia	Josephi Donet/Emilia Donet
Allard	Gulielmum L.		24-NOV-1886	Simonin	Augustinam	
Allen	Samuel		05-JUL-1859	Cannada	Margeritham	
Amel	Eduardum		18-AUG-1904	Desvillers	Helenam	
Annen	Antoine		31-OCT-1856	Hiers	Maria	
Ardle, Richard			06-JAN-1852	Dunnevin	Mary	
Arimond	Jacobus	Petri Arimond/Judita Arimond	03-APR-1866	Dewes	Maria	Nicholai Dewes/Catharina Dewes
Atkinson	Benjamin		19-JUN-1886	Durocher	Angelam Rosam	
Atkinson	Benjamin		19-JUN-1886	Durocher	Angelam Rosam	
Auchue	Alfredum		25-AUG-1903	LeMieux	Delphinam	
Babin	Leonem	Theodori Babin/Maria Poirier	22-SEP-1908	Marcoux	Margaritam Tesse	Augusti Marcoux/Julia Leduc
Baillargeon	Josephum		07-FEB-1885	Desmarais	Jospehinam	
Baltazar	Alfredus	Joseph Baltazar/Sophia Meunier		Pratte	Delima	Joseph Pratte/Heniette Laroque
Baltazar	Martinus		14-JAN-1878	Vernet	Darselia	
Baltazare	Theodorus	Michaelis Baltazare/Rosalia Plante	17-NOV-1879	St-Antoine	Hermine	Moses St.-Antoine/Mathilda Benoit
Balthazar	Baptista		03-OCT-1865	Marcou	Herminia	
Balthazar	Joannem Baptistam		03-AUG-1904	Desmarais-Baillargeon	Josephinam	
Balthazar	Josephum		07-NOV-1899	LéTourneau	Floram	
Balthazar	Joannem Baptistam		29-JUN-1896	LeBeau	Emeliam	
Balthazar	Gegium		10-SEP-1895	Venne	Exilda	
Balthazar	Gulielmum		13-NOV-1894	LéTourneau	Adam Agnetam	
Balthazar	Baptista	Martini Balthazar/Sophia Balthazar	05-NOV-1861	Marcou	Maria	Francisci Marcou/Emilia St.-Cyr
Balthazar	Josephum	Michaelis Balthazar/Rosalia Balthazar		Goyet	Marguarita	Josephi Goyet/Magdalena Goyet
Balthazar	Julianum		08-NOV-1887	Lejeunesse	Marguaritam	
Balthazar	Baptista	Michaelis Balthazar/Ros. Balthazar	03-OCT-1865	Marcou	Herminia	Francisci Marcou/Emilia Marcou
Barbeau	Lawrence		19-NOV-1904	Touchette	Naizzon	
Barbeau	Carolum		16-NOV-1904	Touchette	Mariam	
Barbeau	Alexandrum		25-NOV-1890	Tinger	Annam Maria Sophiam	
Barbeau	Ludovicum		05-MAY-1883	Gervais	Malvina	
Barbeau	Petrum		01-MAY-1881	Moquin	Ezildam	
Baret	Eduard		14-FEB-1858	Hubert	Emilie	
Barrette	Israel	Xavierii Barrette/Sophia Barrette	02-MAR-1862	Chenar	Julie	Isidori Chenar/Sophia-Sara Chenar
Bart	Josephum		06-AUG-1887	Pinguère	Mariam	
Bartow	Charles A.	Leverett Bartow/Ella Chase	04-FEB-1920	Perron	Eldora	Joh Perronn/Cecilia Hatton
Bar†	Thamas			Galligar	Elsabuth	
Bassete	Josephus	Petri Bassete/Sophia Beaulieu	01-AUG-1869	Bré	Maria	Gilberti-Philippi Bré/Maria Molheur
Bastien	Antonius	Josephi Bastien/Angela Bastien	22-MAR-1863	Rondeau	Marguarita	Francis Rondeau/Felicitatis Rondeau
Bastien	Pacificum		25-AUG-1897	——	Mariam Adelam	
Bastien	Eugenium		23-JUN-1896	Dufrèsne	Agnetam	
Bastien	Wilfredum		03-JUL-1894	DuFrèsne	Martham	
Bathazar	Ludovicum		04-NOV-1885	Robert	Emilinam	

135

Groom's Surname	Groom's Name	Groom's Parents	Date	Bride's Surname	Bride's Name	Bride's Parents
Baudin	Guillemus	Guill. Baudin/Ludovica Normandais	26-DEC-1860	Balthazar	Julia	Moysis Balthazar/Josepha Leblanc
Bayargon	Josephus		29-SEP-1878	Landreman	Aurilie	
Bayer	Thomas	Joannis Bayer/Catherina Bayer	13-FEB-1866	Petri	Gertruda	Antonii Petri/Marguarita Petri
Beaudeault	Asa C.		15-JAN-1902	LeMieux	Ezildam	
Beaudin	Carolus	Jacobi Beaudin/Ludovica Beaudin	16-JUN-1863	Joubert	Idessa	Juliani Joubert/Ludovica Joubert
Beaudin	Julianus	Jacobi Beaudin/Ludovica Beaudin	16-JUN-1863	Joubert	Ludovica	Juliani Joubert/Ludovica Joubert
Beaudin	Joannem Baptistam		15-SEP-1896	Lucier	Mariam Mabel	
Beaudreau	Placidum Franciscum		12-APR-1904	Thériault Carrière	Leam	
Beaudriau	Laurent		03-MAR-1851	Begnier–Breau	Sophie	
Beaudriau	Franciscus Placidus	Laur. Beaudriau/Henrietta Beaudriau	19-OCT-1863	Fenet	Alpha	Michaeli Fenet/Mathilda Fenet
Beaudriau	Israel Carolus	L. Beaudriau/M–Ludovica Beaudriau	29-SEP-1861	Mulony	Catharina–Agnetia	Jacobi Mulony/Anna Mulony
Beaudry	Levi		02-AUG-1894	Bernineg	Antoniam	
Beaupré	Israel		07-FEB-1875	Bibo	Ann	
Beauprez	Armidolt		18-AUG-1878	Pedelant	Edesse	
Belanger	Petrum		28-OCT-1893	Landry	Leocadiam	
Bélanger–Baker	Petrum		24-JAN-1889	Tuttle	Mariam E.C.	
Bellanger	Petrus	Ludovici Bellanger/M–A. Bellanger	15-JUN-1864	Ebert	Lina	Joannis-Baptista Ebert/Lina Ebert
Bellehumeur	Francis		19-JUN-1851	Petit	Mary	
Bellmer	Giuliolmum	J Bellmer,/S. Dufresne	14-OCT-1905	Lemieux	Leam	Israelis Lemieux/Melina Larose
Bellmer	Henricum		20-APR-1901	Balthazar	Malvinam	
Bensinger	Michel		21-NOV-1858	Glese–	Anna Maria	
Benzer	Carolus	Caroli Benzer/Lina Benzer		Lamblot	Flora	Constantine Lamblot/Rosalia Davilas
Bergen	Michael	Timothy Bergen/Marguerite Ryan	11-MAY-1852	Closky	Julia	James Closky/Julia Cosgrain
Bernier	Eduardus	Narcissi Bernier/Electram Bernier	19-JUL-1869	Gagné	Emilia	Pauli Gagné/Cleotilda Blair
Bertrand	Joannes Napoléon	Ludovici Bertrand/Merantha Ebert	29-DEC-1872	LeClerc	Eudalia	Eusebii LeClerc/Clarissa Bérubé
Bertrand	Maximus	Ludovici Bertrand/Amarantha Ebert	02-SEP-1866	Bérubé	Clarissa	Andrea Bérubé/Mathilda LeMaire
Beryan	Michel		16-NOV-1856	Garden	Maria	
Besset	Petrus	Petri Besset/Sophia Beaulieu	17-JUN-1867	Thibodeau	Rosalia	Oliverii Thibodeau/Ludovica Cyr
Bessete	Franciscum Xaverium		10-SEP-1895	Charron	Emmam	
Bessette	Josephum		04-FEB-1882	Bessette	Sophiam Emmam	
Bird	Carolus	Petri Bird/Emilia Bird	11-MAY-1868	Bisson	Martha	Francisci Bisson/Josephina Bisson
Bisept	Celestine		20-OCT-1856	Briceau	Pliomi	
Bisson	Ludovicus	Francisci Bisson/Josephina Léveque	31-DEC-1871	Lefort	Maria	Caroli LeFort/Adelaida Lepine
Bisson	Franciscus Xaverius	Francisci Bisson/Josephina Léveque	31-DEC-1871	Loiseau Bird	Maria	Francisci Loiseau/Emilia Loiseau
Bisson	Martinus	Francisci Bisson/Josephina Bisson	30-JUL-1866	Loiseau	Julia	Petri Loiseau/Emilia Loiseau
Bissonet	Narcissus	Francisci Bissonet/Josepha Pinsoneau	20-JUL-1870	Chenar Snow	Sophia	Joannis-B. Cyr/Elizabetha Gireau
Bissonet	Noel Norbertus	Petri Bissonet/Collixtina Poudrite	10-JUL-1870	Paquete	Agnetia	Petri Paquete/Maria Paquete
Bissonnette	Narcissum		29-JUN-1885	Dandurand	Theotistam	
Blondeau	Franciscus		12-MAR-1865	Gauthier	Elizabetha	
Boddit	Josephus		12-APR-1875	Carbina	Maria	
Boivin	Joannem Baptistam		02-AUG-1882	Dufort	Josephinam	
Bonnet	Eduard		28-AUG-1857	L'Eno—	Julie	
Bonnet	Lucus	Ferdinand Bonnet/Esther Sauvé	05-JUN-1879	Jolly	Eudoxie	Caroli Jolly/Claudia Binnet
Boroseau	Michel		27-SEP-1858	Duquette	Marguerta	
Boucher	Octavus	Germani Boucher/Lucia Boucher	31-MAY-1864	Ebert	Rosalia	Caroli Ebert/Maria Ebert
Boucher	Josephus	Francisci-Jos. Boucher/Julia Laduron	06-APR-1869	Faneuf	Tharsila	Alexii Faneuf/Aurelia LeClaire
Boucher	Germanus	Germani Boucher/Lucia Boucher	03-SEP-1861	Bellimeur	Olivina	Francis Bellimeur/Marg, Bellimeur
Boulet	Josephus		01-AUG-1875	Malheur	Felicita	
Bourasseau	Carolus	Huberti Bourasseau/A–Ioïda Bourass	16-MAY-1865	Marcou	Melina	Francisci Marcou/Melina Marcou

136

Groom's Surname	Groom's Name	Groom's Parents	Date	Bride's Surname	Bride's Name	Bride's Parents
Boutet	Josephus	Petri-S. Boutet/M-Magdelena Toutan	25-OCT-1871	Linz	Rosa	Georgii Linz/Maria Linz
Bowen	Jacobum	Eduardi Bowen/Anna Caniff	25-JUN-1907	Beaudreau	Ermina	Laurentii Beaudreau/Sophia Briand
Boyer	Carolum		02-JAN-1882	LePine	Josephinam	
Brabant	Josephus	Joseph Brabant/Esthera Brabant	18-OCT-1868	Balthazar	Sophia	Josephi Balthazar/Sophia Balthazar
Brabant	Josephus		24-MAR-1868	Balthazar	Sophia	
Brackett	Nelson Ludovicus		16-SEP-1860	Pedlant	Helena	
Branchard	Norbertus	JB Branchard/Maria-Clara Primeau	29-JAN-1872	Bransheau	Maria Ludovica	Eugenni Bransheau/Maria Disautels
Brandt	Walter	E. Brandt/M. Beauregard	25-SEP-1906	Sauvé	Minnie	Joseph Sauvé/Alida Venné
Brausseau	Joannes	Joannis-B. Brausseau/Thersila Bigras	14-SEP-1869	Goulin	Ludovica	Ludovici Goulin/Agnetia Paquet
Bré	Isidore		03-JUL-1876	Malheur	Maria	
Bré	Philipus		27-JUN-1876	Boisin	Philomena	
Breister	Fredericum C.		12-NOV-1890	Charbonneau	Elisam	
Breslahan	Carolus	Patricii Breslahan/Cath. Breslahan	18-OCT-1863	Kerry	Maria	Joannis-Henrici Kerry/Julia Kerry
Brico	Ludovicus	Ludovici Brico/Genovefa Brico	01-JUL-1862	Dodelin	Philomena	Oliverii Dodelin/Sophia Dodelin
Briscoe	Amos Pollard		22-FEB-1898	Préfontaine	Mariam C—am	
Brockway	Gulielmum		27-SEP-1898	Marcoux	Melvinam	
Brown	Bernard		13-OCT-1851	Gablar	Mary	
Brown	Thomas	Edmundi Brown/Bridgitta Brown	12-JUL-1863	Bishen	Marguarita	Timothei Bishen/Elizabetha Bishen
Brown	Michael	Josephi Brown/Walburga Brown	05-MAY-1861	Steffens	Anna	Antonii Steffens/Suzanna Steffens
Brown	Joannes	Henrici Brown/Magdelena Brown	30-OCT-1866	Show	Anna	Joannis Shoe/Elizabetha Shoe
Brown	Petrus	Petri Brown/Sophia Fredet	14-MAY-1866	Flanegan	Joanna	Joannis Flanegan/Elizabeth Flanegan
Brucker	Albertum P.		23-OCT-1900	Bastien	Mariam Annam	
Bruedrle	Jacobum		12-NOV-1886	Miller	Mariam Sophiam	
Brunet	Josephum	Gedeonis Brunet/Melina Bastian	29-NOV-1906	Pratt	Mariam Stellam	Felicis Pratt/Sarah Duquette
Brunet	Adelbertum		12-JUN-1900	Bruederle	Junam	
Brunet	Josephum Ferdinand		02-JAN-1896	Potvin	Mathildam	
Brunet	Josephum Axilum		19-JUN-1895	LeBeau	Delinam	
Brunet	Gedeon	Ferdinandi Brunett/Esthera Sovie	12-AUG-1867	Bastien	Melina	Andrea Bastien/Magdelena Paquete
Brunkhorst	Georgium W.	Gulielmi Brunkhorst/Anna Lang	03-MAR-1906	Atkinson	Stellam	Benjamin Atkinson/Angie Desrochers
Buch	Josephum		14-JUN-1893	Roy	Georginam	
Buckless	Franciscum A.		13-NOV-1895	Carey	Mariam	
Bugnon	Josephius		16-JUN-1856	Paddick	Rosalia	
Bullis	Nethn		10-NOV-1851	Smith	Mary	
Burch	Jeremias		02-MAY-1859	Say	Ellena	
Burch	Michel		27-NOV-1858	Anderson	Brigitha	
Burck	William		07-JUL-1856	Poirrier	Margaret	
Burk	William	Thomas Burk/Catherine Daughaney		Karney	Mary	William Karney/Ann McCarl
Burke	Thomam		14-NOV-1852	Falvay	Ellenam	
Burns	James		07-MAY-1857	Kelly	Katerina	
Burrell	Joannes	Petri Burrell/Florence Sullivan	25-JAN-1862	McCrury	Marguarita	Joannis McCrury/Maria McCrury
Cagil	John		10-MAY-1856	McTevit	Margerth	
Cain	Michael		10-NOV-1851	Smith	Mary	
Calliger	John		26-SEP-1858	Conners	Jenna	
Camp	Richard	Alphonso Camp/Amelia Proctnow	16-FEB-1920	Schoefer	Rose	Charle Schoefer/Anna Krauss
Campbell	Walter		31-DEC-1868	Tessier	Ludovica	
Capperon	David		17-NOV-1878	Bird Oiseau	Delia	
Carbet	John		11-NOV-1855	Curan	Maria	
Carboneau	Franciscus	Petri Carboneau/Carola Jeandon	12-JUL-1869	Veine	Rosalia	Agapiti Veine/Felicitatis Montant
Carbonneau	Ricardum		22-NOV-1899	Moquin	Evam	
Cardinal	Franciscus		14-APR-1864	Coyer	Maria	

137

Groom's Surname	Groom's Name	Groom's Parents	Date	Bride's Surname	Bride's Name	Bride's Parents
Cardinal	Leo	Christ. Cardinal/Adelaide Payment	24-JAN-1864	Veine	Rosalia	Francis Veine/Marcelina Landremann
Carney	Jacobus	Mattei Carney/Bridgitta Carney	06-SEP-1863	O'Brien	Honora	Timothei O'Brien/Joanna O'Brien
Carney	Jacobus	Michaelis Carney/Maria Carney	17-APR-1863	Glenan	Maria	Luke Glenan/Maria Glenan
Carney	Jacobus W.	Michaeli Carney/Helena Carney	17-JUN-1903	Eagan	Maria-Anna	Joannis Eagan/Suzanna Eagan
Carpenter	Manley Arthurum			Surprenand	Zoeam Mariam	
Carr	Jacobum W.		02-FEB-1892	Flood	Catharinam	
Carroll	Daniel	Thoma Carroll/Bridgitta Carroll	28-DEC-1862	Larkin	Elizabetha	Danielis Larkin/Maria Larkin
Carter	Harvey		16-SEP-1851	Mullen	Mary	
Carter	Cleophus	Claudii Cartier/Angela Cartier	28-OCT-1872	Dufresne	Dulima	Petri Dufresne/Onesima Meunier
Cary	Michael	Thoma Cary/Maria Cary	31-AUG-1863	Clarke	Maria-Anna	Malachia Clarke/Anna Clarke
Cassy	William		20-OCT-1878	Durand	Hetty	
Cavanaeth	John		28-JUN-1857	Cousin	Margerita	
Cavanagh	Mcl		25-JAN-1858	Dumphy	Anna Marguerita	
Cavanagh	Jacobus	Pat. Cavanaugh/Honora Cavanaugh	03-DEC-1860	Connor	Maria	Jacobi Connor/Honora Connor
Cavanaugh	Daniel	James Cavenach/Ellen Cogilan		Hardgrove	Margeret	Henny Hardgrove/Maria Kind
Cavenach	Elias	Caroli Chagnion/Josephina Mitote	14-SEP-1869	Leduc	Philomena	Josephi Leduc/Marg. Dwire-Bundig
Chagnion	Davidem Edmundum		14-FEB-1901	LéPine	Ettam	
Chaperon	Theophilus	Theophili Chaperone/—— Surprenant	10-AUG-1874	Ouellette	Clara	Ludovici Oulette/Louisa Lea
Chaperone	Joannes-Baptista	Antonii Charete/Emilia Payer	08-OCT-1871	Fontaine	Ludovica	Mathei Amelançou/Ursula Amelançou
Charete	Josephum		27-JUL-1889	McSweeney	Franciscam Ceciliam	
Charlebois	Jacobum		16-JUL-1897	Pellant	Sophiam	
Charron	Petrus	Petri Chef/Christina Rondeau	05-JAN-1869	Touchete	Josephina	Josephi Touchete/Olesinia Vient
Chef	Alphonsus	Isidori Chenar/Sophia Cyr	17-APR-1871	Tessier	Maria Exilda	Caroli Tessier/—— Tessier
Chenar Snow	Jeremias		20-SEP-1857	N—ber	Lebodina	
Cherchinger	Germain		18-NOV-1856	Hiers	Chaterina	
Cherzinger	Joannes		17-JUL-1857	Snow	Margeta	
Chessehan	Ludovicum		26-NOV-1878	D'Anneau	Philumenam	
Chinard Snow	James		30-NOV-1851	Newcombe	Rosa	
Clark	Louis		29-SEP-1859	Dufraine	Adelphe	
Clis	Ludovicum		22-SEP-1887	Dufrèsne	Desanges	
Clish	Amatum		19-JUN-1883	Sicard	Josephinam	
Clish	Patrick		11-SEP-1851	McCoy	Mary	
Codd	Josephus	Christophi Colbs/Veronica ——	25-MAY-1865	Seiboldt	Maria	Josephi Seiboldt/Maria Seiboldt
Colbs	Samuel		22-FEB-1905	Lambert	Anna	Michael Lambert/Sophronie Barbeau
Collett	Samuelem	Samuelis Collette/—— ——	23-FEB-1905	Lambert	Annam	Michael Lambert/Sophronia Barbeau
Collett	Octovus	Vincentius Collin/Josepha Ollet	24-MAY-1863	Garro	Julia	Petri Garro/Clementia Br—
Collin	Patricium		05-DEC-1852	Norton	Saram	
Collins	Arthurum		05-APR-1894	Vass	Philumenam	
Comeau	Medardum		20-NOV-1888	Diette	Mathilda	
Comeau	Michaelem		21-NOV-1887	LeBeau	Olivinam	
Conaboy	James		08-SEP-1850	McCabe	Catherine	
Conaughty	Guillemus	Patricii Connell/Ursula Connell	06-JAN-1862	Toomey	Anna	Timotheis Toomey/Jo.-Tabon Toomey
Connell	Guillelmus	Guillelmi Cooke/Theresia Cooke	21-OCT-1861	Voght	Josephina	Antonii Voght/Josephina Voght
Cooke	Carolum Greff		21-OCT-1895	Langlois	Mathildam	
Coon	Eduardum Franciscum		03-JAN-1893	Hansel	Reginam	
Cooper	Cyrillus	Josephi Corbeil/Catharina Corbeil	21-AUG-1864	Dufort	Anastasia	Antonii Dufort/Julia Dufort
Corbeil	Zoticus	Josephi Corbeil/Catharina Couyé	22-JUL-1872	LeBeau	Melinda	Moysis LeBeau/Angela Miricier
Corbeil	Hormidas	Josephi Corbeil/Catharina Corbeil	29-OCT-1871	Chef	Maria-Anna	Petri Chef/Christina Rondeau
Corbeil	Petrum Treffié		04-AUG-1886	Maheu	Josephinam Estiam	

138

Groom's Surname	Groom's Name	Groom's Parents	Date	Bride's Surname	Bride's Name	Bride's Parents
Corbeille	Norbertum	Napoleonis Corbeille/Melinda Lebeau	14-APR-1910	Hopp	Annam	Andrea Hopp/—— ——
Corbeille	Evarist		28-JAN-1877	Duvain	Mathilda	
Corbeille	Peter H.		19-NOV-1904	Berg	Mary	
Corbeille	Fredericum Moisen		28-MAY-1902	Kinney	Mariam Josephinam	
Corbeille	Josephum Napoleonem		10-AUG-1898	Brunet	Mariam Clotildam Leonam	
Costas	Samuel	George Costas/Lulla Manzy	25-NOV-1919	Gosh	Fern Hermine	Hermin Gosh/Hermina Lesage
Coughlin	Joannes	Patricii Coughlin/Maria Coughlin	10-FEB-1861	Fuller	Marguarita	Guillelmi Fuller/Catharina Fuller
Coulomb	Marsellum	Ambrosium Coulomb/Maria C—et	26-JUN-1865	Henger	Mariam Josephinam	Joan. Henger/M.Elizabeth Zichtinger
Coulomb	Marcellus	—— Coulomb/Maria Coulet	29-JUN-1865	Henzler	Maria-Josephine	Joan. Henzler/M.Elizabeth Lichtinger
Crain	Michel		31-MAR-1856	Leng	Winni	
Crammer	Peter		31-JAN-1856	Stephani	Maria	
Crouly	James		09-FEB-1856	Fitzjurrall	Julie	
Crowley	Patricius	Jacobi Crowley/Marguarita Crowley	04-MAY-1861	Crowley	Bridgitta	Mathei Crowley/Helena Crowley
Crämmer	Nicholaus	Hubert Crämmer/Veronica Crämmer	28-FEB-1865	Wolf	Catharina	Huberti Wolf/Gertruda Wolf
Cröns	Josephus	Petri Cröns/E. Aveli-	04-JUN-1865	Marz	Apollonia	Henrici Marz/Christina Patton
Curb	Peter		08-OCT-1856	Meussen	Elisabeth	
Czarnezki	Josephium	Laurentii Czarnezki/Susanna Schmitz	25-NOV-1908	Brandt	Mariam	Henrici Brandt/Minnie Beauregard
Dalson	Harry Jacobi	Jocobi Dalson/Mellie Richard	22-SEP-1906	Desrochers	Angie Rosam	Gulielmi Desrochers/Maria Perron
Dandelain	Olivier		23-OCT-1859	Vernais	Celine	
Daniel	Franciscus	Ludovici Daniel/Maria Daniel	21-NOV-1870	Mayou	Catherina	Antonii Mayou/Angelica Malo
Daniel	Carolum		10-NOV-1896	Johnson	Josephinam	
Danos	Petrum		16-MAY-1853	Beaulieux	Clementinam	
Darigon	Patricius	Hughii Darigon/Joanna Darigon	18-MAY-1862	Lomery	Maria	Guillelmi Lomery/Catharina Lomery
Delafontaine	Franciscum		22-OCT-1876	Barajohem	Jospehina	
Deleers	Alphonsum J.	Josephi Deleers/Maria Debecker	06-JUN-1906	Corbeille	Ednam	Napoleonis Corbeille/Melinda Lebeau
Dellise	Julius	Petri Dellise/Francisca Dellise	16-FEB-1862	Mettier	Phillipina	Francisci Mettier/M-Josepha Mettier
Demarchs	Salomon		13-JAN-1878	Pommenville	Maria	
Demers	Juber–		23-OCT-1859	Leturneau	Anne	
Demers	Franciscum		17-OCT-1881	Audette LaPointe	Idam	
Demers	Solomon	Stephan. Demers/Angelica Vincelette	24-SEP-1879	Viens	Henrelie	Stephani Trahan/Ludovica Picard
Demers	Francis		28-AUG-1905	Cliche	Mathilda	Louis Cliche/Delphine Dufresne
DeNamar	Noël	Ludovici DeNamar/M-Francisca Vass	11-FEB-1872	Miné	Maria Julia Anna	Joan.-Jose. Miné/M-Theresa Nissaint
Denell	Dominic		18-FEB-1905	Rose	Mary Ann	
Denevan	Michel		16-MAY-1857	Devinun	Marie	
Deroché	Francois		24-OCT-1859	Pellant	Sophia	
Deroché	–tasse		26-MAY-1856	Defraine	Dedine	
Deschênes	Eugenius	Petri Deschênes/Mag. Deschênes	13-JUL-1863	Gervais	Josephina	Joan.-Bap. Gervais/Mathilda Gervais
Desjardins	Josephus	Dom. Desjardins/Sophia Courtemoin	03-JUL-1867	Blanchete	Marguarita	Caroli Blanchete/Isabella Blanchete
Desnoyers	Huberto		06-APR-1853	Beaudriaux	Delia	
Despas	Alfredus	Ignatii Despas/Theresa Despas	20-SEP-1863	Fontaine	Carolina	Petri-A. Fontaine/Ludovica Fontaine
Despins	Florimundus	Ignatii Despins/M.-Theresa Despins	06-OCT-1861	Delisse	Philomena	Petri Delisse/Maria-Francisca Delisse
Desrochers	Leo	Alex. Desrochers/Josepha Desrochers	04-JUL-1861	Joubert	Idalia	Julien Joubert/Ludovica Joubert
Devan	John		29-NOV-1855	Logelan	Ellen	
Devillers	Theodore	August Devillers/Felicity Doré	17-MAY-1905	Lanctot	Eliza	—aire Lanctot/Olivine Laberge
Devillers	Theophilum		12-MAY-1905	Lanctot-Devillers	Alphonsinan	
DeVine	Jacobus		13-MAY-1877	Brais Leduc	Louisa	
Devoe	Kelly Eduardum		05-AUG-1902	Boucher	Eleonora	
Diette	Alfredum		07-NOV-1893	LéTourneau	Edassam	
Diette	Josephum		08-NOV-1887	LeTourneau	Elisam	

139

Groom's Surname	Groom's Name	Groom's Parents	Date	Bride's Surname	Bride's Name	Bride's Parents
Diette	Narcissum		16-SEP-1883	Belanger	Hermeline	
Dinelle	Dominicum	Ludovici Dinelle/Maria Gervais	18-FEB-1905	Rose	Marion	
Dion	Michaelem		20-APR-1888	Barbeau	Adelam	
Ditter	Georgius Josephus	Andreas Ditter/Eva Regina Ditter	22-MAY-1866	Seibel	Maruarita	Joannis Seibel/Maria Seibel
Dodelin	Josephus	Oliverii Dodelin/Sophia Dodelin	01-JUL-1862	Brico	Adelina	Ludovici Brico/Genovefa Brico
Dodelin	Denysius	Oliverius Dodelin/Sophie Molleur	19-NOV-1879	Pariseau	Josephina	
Dolan	Joannes	—— Dolan/Maria Dolan	08-JUL-1862	Mangan	Marguarita	Eduardi Mangan/Anna Mangan
Dolton	John		18-FEB-1851	Flaharty	Catherine	
Donly	Michel		20-APR-1857	Rag--on	Margerit	
Donnais	Isidore		27-SEP-1875	Vaine	Rosalia	
Donovan	Joannum	Richardi Donovan/Marg. Cummins	21-APR-1909	Lépine	Lucretiam	Josephi Lépine/Sophie Beaudreau
Doroghty	Patricium		21-NOV-1852	Duly	Joannam	
Doune	John		13-FEB-1858	Duaire	Chaterina	
Dreikosen	Joannes Leonardus	Petri Dreikosen/Magdalena Dreikosen	15-JAN-1863	Hall	Anna-Cecilia	Guillelmi Hall/Anna-Catharina Hall
Dreikosen	Joannes Guillelmus		14-OCT-1866	Noble	Petra	
Drinkwine	Georgium Boivin		24-SEP-1903	Turcot	Juliam	
Dubois	Elmerum	Josephi Dubois/Cecilia Beaudriard	13-AUG-1907	Field	Purl Inez	Phillippi ——/Clara Clainent
DuBois	Godfroy		05-APR-1875	DeBois	Virginia	
DuBois	Georgium		15-NOV-1887	Tremblay	Emeliam	
Dubois/Alfredum		Joseph Dubois/Cecilia Beaudreau	24-FEB-1909	Braun	Ida	
Duffy	William	Hughi Duffy/Maria Duffy	10-FEB-1861	Walsh	Catharina	Jacobi Walsh/Catharina Walsh
Duford	Cyrillum		17-JUN-1893	Boivin	Salomeam	
Dufort	Josephum		28-JUL-1886	Rochell	Elizabetham	
Dufraine	Pascal		21-OCT-1858	Ste.-Marie	Seragen	
DuFrèsne*	Albertum		24-NOV-1896	Bastien	Alexinam	
DuFresne	Franciscus	Pascalis Dufresne/Angelica Dufresne	26-NOV-1860	Ste.-Marie	Elizabetha	Alexii Ste.-Marie/Sarah Ste.-Marie
Dufresne	Isidorus	Pascali Dufresne/Angelica Coch--	06-AUG-1866	St.-Antoine	Emilia	Moysis St.-Antoine/Mathilda Benoit
DuFrèsne	Sephanum		18-FEB-1890	LeBeau	Heloisam	
Dufrèsne*	Noël		20-NOV-1865	Lepine	Marguarita	
Dufresne*	Noel	Pascalis Dufresne/Angela Caye-	21-NOV-1865	LePine	Marguarita	Josephus LePine/Elizabetha Bordeau
Dumas	Maglorium		12-SEP-1887	Carley	Evam Beleau	
Dumas	J.B.		23-JUN-1884	Lines	--aty	
Dumund	Israel		07-JAN-1878	Hurto	Margereth	
Dunn	Guillelmus	Guillelmi Dun/Anna Dun	30-AUG-1863	Dalony	Sarah	Edwardi Dalony/Maria Dalony
Dunn	Jacobi	Guillelmi Dunn/Anna Dunn	22-NOV-1863	Graham	Catharina	Allen Graham/Bridgitta Graham
Dunnevan	Timothy		17-FEB-1852	B--ddan	Brigit	
Dupuis	Stanislas	Baptista Dupuis/Clotilda Agagnier	07-AUG-1871	Painguère	Eugenia	Eugenii Painguère/Hort. Lismonde
Dupuis	Lodgerius	Eusabii Dupuis/Flavia Dub--e	03-AUG-1868	Mayou	Angelica	Antonii Mayou/Angelica Malo
Dupuis	Amandus	Eusebius Dupuis/Zoe Moquin	13-JAN-1880	Prefontaine	Alphonsina	Barth. Prefontaine/Henselia Trudeau
Dupuis	Onesime	Joh.-Bapt. Dupuis/Clotilde Eugéner	15-JUN-1879	LaBarge	Albina	Francis LeBarge/Maria Telly
Dupuis	Onesimi		22-OCT-1878	Dufort	Annie	
Dupuy	Franciscum		27-SEP-1881	Clische	Rosanam	
DuRoché	Eugene		02-JAN-1856	Dufraine	Dematina	
Durocher	Isadorum	Francisci Durocher/Sophie Pellant		Holz	Lizzie	Oscari Holz/——
Durocher	Eduardum		25-OCT-1904	Rayaume	Evam	
Durocher	Ludgerium		26-DEC-1900	Ryaume	Mariam	
Durocher	Adolphum		14-SEP-1891	Prefontaine	Rosam	
Durocher	Gulielmum		09-NOV-1884	Perron	Mariam	
Durocher	Eduardum		25-DEC-1883	Dufrèsne	Elizabetha	

Groom's Surname	Groom's Name	Groom's Parents	Date	Bride's Surname	Bride's Name	Bride's Parents
Duynat	Joseph		29-JUN-1860	——	Christine	
Ebert	Moyses	Caroli Ebert/Maria-Regina Marcou	29-MAY-1865	Morin	Loisa	Josephi Morin/Julia Roi
Ebert	Napoleo	Davidis Ebert/Matilda Ebert	31-DEC-1872	Ebert	Maria	Isidori Ebert/Florentia Ebert
Edoin	Vitalem		01-SEP-1890	Seidentopf	Mariam	
Edoin	Telesporem Vitalem		22-JUL-1889	Fontaine	Mariam Deliam	
Edoin	Amatum		05-JUN-1882	Maurice	Mariam Annam	
Edoin	Leverus	Leonis Edoin/Flavia Moquin	22-SEP-1879	Morris	Maria Adelina	Josue Morris/Christina Longtin
Edwin	Julianus	Antonii Edwin/Marguarita Edwin	25-SEP-1865	Malheur	Euladia	—— Malheur/Felicitata Cyr
Ellison	Alfredum E.		16-NOV-1897	Préfontaine	Mariam Laurentiam	
Emerson	James		04-JUN-1858	Nicolus	Maria	
Emerson	Thamas		09-DEC-1855	Corrigan	Anna	
Emerson	Matthens	Thoma Emerson/Marg. Emerson	15-SEP-1861	McGrath	Sarah	Patricii McGrath/Maria McGrath
Emmerich	Jacob	Nicolai Emmerich/Anna Wendel	02-JUN-1879	May	Anna-Maria	Hilarii May/Maria Maas
Ennely	John		29-JUL-1860	Mcarnell	Althora	
Errand	Alex		29-NOV-1874	Leduc	Delphine	
Estrecher	Petrus	Caroli Estrecher/Maria Estrecher	09-JUN-1862	Loselion	Clara	Nicholai Loselion/Catharina Loselion
Evans	Guilelmum L.		25-NOV-1890	Gratton	Mariam	
Faris	Sheker		02-JUN-1902	Kalile	Mariam	
Farrel	Brian		10-NOV-1851	Donnely	Anne	
Faucher	Arthurium	Alexandri Faucher/Maria Sylvestre	17-SEP-1907	Freenor	Mathildam	Josephi Freenor/Nellie Fontaine
Faucher	Alexander	Ludovici Faucher/Josepha Bignon	10-JUL-1870	Silvestre	Maria	Petri Silvestre/Christina Coté
Fayly	Thomas	Edwardi Fayly/Maria Fayly	07-JUN-1863	Barrett	Silla	Joannis Barrett/Sabina Barrett
Fellers	Victorem		16-SEP-1883	Mangin	Catarinam Alidam	
Fenelon	Daniel	Joannis Fenelon/Marguarita Fenelon	25-DEC-1862	Gough	Maria	Joannis Gough/Anna Gough
Ferdinand	Simmon		01-JUN-1859	Scheutuels	Ellisabeth	
Fernet	Joannes	Michaelis I. Fernet/Mathilda Hubert	12-FEB-1872	Bolduc	Emilia	Joannis Bolduc/Lucia Tessier
Ferry	Gulieluium	Jacobi Ferry/Elizabeth Strong	31-JUL-1907	Marcoux	Arabella	Alex. Marcoux/Eleonora Lajeunesse
Fields	Silas	Fred Fields/Laura Haberland	03-JUL-1920	Dufrane	Emily	Alberti Dufrane/Alexina Bastien
Finnegan	Geraldum	Mathia Finnegan/Julia Crosby	19-JUN-1906	Dufrane	Sarah	Francisci Dufrane/E. Ste.Marie-Defoe
Fish	Joannes	Mathei Fish/Magdalena Fish	08-SEP-1861	Diedrichs	Annam	Francisci Diedrichs/Anna Diedrichs
Fitz-Henry	Thomas		02-JUN-1861	Hennis	Catharina	
Fitzgerald	Thomas		18-FEB-1851	Dalton	Bridgett	
Fitzgerald	Patrick		08-NOV-1850	Ro——	Mary	
Fitzgerald	Clarence Martin	Wm Fitzgerald/Nellie Martin	01-MAY-1920	Jarvis	Dora	Emery Jarvis/Levina Sharron
Fitzgerald	Patricius	Josephi Fitzgerald/Cath.-Em. Fitzgerald	16-MAY-1862	Flood	Alicia	Timothei Flood/Catharina Flood
Fitzjurrall	Patrick		03-FEB-1856	Sannal	Anna	
Fitzsimmons	Michael	Mic. Fitzsimmons/Bridg. Fitzsimmons	01-NOV-1862	Brown	Catharina	Joannis Brown/Maria Brown
Flagerty	Brian		01-NOV-1856	——igny	Honora	
Flagherty	Edmundus	Edmundi Flagherty/Honora Flagherty	09-APR-1861	Mullen. Maria		Jacobi Mullen/Helena Mullen
Flagherty	Morgan	Edmundi Flagherty/Hanna Flagherty	28-NOV-1860	Moore	Maria	Mauritii Moore/Helena Moore
Flanders	Carolum Ruel		17-JUN-1902	Turenne	Deliam	
Fleischman	Leo George	Arthur Fleischman/Emma Wagner	25-NOV-1920	Balthazar	Rose-Olivine	Julius Balthazar/Marg. Lajeunesse
Fleishman	Joannes Martinus	Adami Fleishman/Eliz. Fleishman	07-JAN-1865	C——ker	Anna	Antonii C——ker/Barbara C——ker
Flood	Thomas	Patricii Flood/Bridgitta Flood	26-JUL-1863	Duffy	Helena	Jacobi Duffy/Marguarita Duffy
Flood	Georgium		12-NOV-1902	Balthazar	Agnetam	
Flood	John		20-APR-1856	Fitsjurrall	Marie	
Florent	Albertus	Ludovici Florent/Scholastica Florent	08-FEB-1864	Beaudriau	Pranella	Laur. Beaudriau/Hen. Beaudriau
Fontaine	Narcissus	Narcissi Fontaine/Julia LeMaire	21-JUN-1866	Melancon	Ludovica	Amedei Melançon/Mathilda Melanço
Fontaine*	Josephus		09-NOV-1865	Santuaire	Maria	

Groom's Surname	Groom's Name	Groom's Parents	Date	Bride's Surname	Bride's Name	Bride's Parents
Fontaine*	Josephus		09-NOV-1865	Santuaire	Maria	Agapita Veine/Felicitatis Contant
Foret	Petrus	Josephi Foret/Magdalena Morima	05-JUL-1869	Veine	Alicia	P----elinge-/Esa Gerade
Foung	Joannes	Bartholins Foung/Madalen Dudslind		--elinge-	Catherina	
Fournier	Vitalis	B---- Fournier/Aurelia Trudeau	18-AUG-1872	LeMieux	Héléna	Petri LeMieux/Maria Samson
Fournier	Henricus	Alexii Fournier/Maria P-tr-s	09-SEP-1867	Deshautels	Olivina	Caroli Desautels/Anastasia Moquin
Fournier-Préfontaine	----ins	Bartholomi Fournier/Maria Trudeau		Ebert	Edmira	Vin--tii Ebert/Marguarita Dupuis
Fox	Joannem		12-JAN-1904	Moquin	Addeam Mariam	
Fox	Sebastian	Henrici-Petri Fox/Anna-Maria Fox	05-JUL-1866	Hiback	Anna Ludovica	Francisci Hiback/Regina Hiback
Fraem	Josephus		13-AUG-1876	Hardel	Catherina	
Frost	Guillelmus-Wallace	Guillelmi Frost/Maria Frost		Veite	Maria	Conradis Veite/Francisca Veite
Funk	Julium		18-SEP-1895	Sauvé	Paulinam	
G----	Michael Andrew		29-APR-1866	Gau	Cecilia	
Gagé	Olivier		03-JUN-1877	Parent	Sa--	
Gagné	Paulus		17-SEP-1876	Frego	Cilina	
Gagnier	Guilielmo		26-SEP-1899	Barbeau	Melinam	
Gagnier	Guilelmum		06-MAY-1891	Moquin. Liam	Josephinam	
Gagnier	Paulum		28-NOV-1883	Duquet	Elizabeth	
Gagnon	Urbanum		02-JUN-1886	Moquin	Elizabeth	
Gagnon	Urbanum		25-JUN-1886	Moquin	Edessa	
Gaigné	Edwardi		10-JAN-1876	Parriso	Katerina	
Gaigne	Franciscus			Daugherty	Joanna	
Galavan	Jeramias	Bernardi Galavan/Anna Galavan	26-NOV-1860	Harkan	Brigitte	Bernardi Harkan/Marguerita Harkan
Gallagher	John		10-OCT-1851	H----y	Rossa	
Galligar	James		16-OCT-1855	Dorethy	Maria Joanna	
Ganor	Patricius		29-MAY-1861	Casey	Rosalia	
Garron	Petrus	Petri Garro/Marguarita Garro	20-OCT-1861	Lécuyer	Maria	Petri Lécuyer/Marguarita Lécuyer
Garron	Perre		11-SEP-1858	Boroseau	Anastasia	
Gauthier	Francis		31-AUG-1850	Bourassa	Annom	
Gavigan	Jacobum Eugenium		22-AUG-1903	Rondeau	Julie	
Gay	Thamas		26-APR-1858	Coffy	Maria	
Gayan	Joannes		29-NOV-1856	Pethid	Josephina	
Gayet	Ludovicus	Joseph Gayete/Magdelena LaClaire	04-JUN-1872	Bathazar	Rosalia	Petri Balthazar/Rosalia Desautels
Gayet	-m----	Colii Gervais/Saloma Yelle	22-JUL-1873	Touchette	Maria	Josephi Touchette/Onesima Vie-
Gayet	Carolus	Josephi Gayet/Magdalena LaValie	20-AUG-1870	Plante	Florie	Petri Plante/Elizabetha Meunier
Gayet	Joseph		03-APR-1856	Chef	Amelia	Petri Chef/Christina Rondeau
Gaÿet	Alexander	Callixti Gervais/Saloma Gervais	31-DEC-1877	Touchete	Sarah	Josephi Touchete/Onesima Vient
Geelan	Francis	Callixti Gervais/Salomé Rielle	24-JUN-1851	Thibodeau	Josephina	
Gervais	Ludovicus	Joan.-Bap. Gervais/Mathilda Leclaire	03-JUL-1865	Lajeunesse	Philomena	
Gervais	Jeremias		22-JUL-1873	McGau	Philoména	
Gervais	Telesporum		07-AUG-1872	Lécuyer	Mathilda	Noeli Lécuyer/Leucadia Lécuyer
Gervais	Emericum		19-SEP-1871	Bearuregard	Melinam	
Gervais	Calese		23-JAN-1894	Charron	Olivinam	
Gervais			20-JUL-1886	Bailargon	Belanise	
Gervais			28-JUL-1878			
Gervais. Isaacus		Pauli Gervais/Marguerita Gerville	30-SEP-1860	Grizet	Virginia	Antonii Grizet/Clotilda Guerin
Gibbons	Robertum		03-JUL-1853	O'Connel	Margueritam	
Gibbons	John		21-DEC-1851	Cauffield	Brigitte	
Giebel	Wendelinus		06-JAN-1865	Ackerman	Theresa	
Gildus	Hermane	M. Archambeau/J. Archambeau	17-AUG-1869	Fernet	Julia Anna	Isaïa Fernet/Mathilda Hubert
Gillan	Christophle		26-MAY-1856	Bays	Ellisa	

Groom's Surname	Groom's Name	Groom's Parents	Date	Bride's Surname	Bride's Name	Bride's Parents
Gilliber	Joannes		06-MAY-1857	Penser	Marria	
Gillman	Narcissus	Thoma Gillman/Domitilla Groton	17-FEB-1873	Robert	Marguarita	Francisci Robert/Maria Beaudoin
Gillman	Joannes		01-JUL-1867	Marcou	Emma	
Gilmann	Joseph	Thoma Gilmann/Domitilla Graton	21-JAN-1880	Fox	Barbara	Nicolai Fox/Barbara Miller
Ginel	Ludovicus	Ludovici Genel/Maria Grou	26-SEP-1869	Gervais	Dyonisia	Narcissi Gervais/Adela Barbeau
Glazer	Petrum		21-SEP-1852	Krauss	Anna-Mariam	
Glons	Joseph		23-NOV-1856	Cudé	Elisath	
Godin	Calix	Ludovici Godin/Rosalia Marcou	14-JUL-1879	Dupuis	Emma	Eusebi Dupuis/Zoe Moquin
Gordon	Joseph H.		17-JUN-1867	Lécuyer	Aurelia M.	
Gordon	George	Caroli Gorden/Louise Gordon	29-APR-1879	Balthazar	Babie	Joseph Balthazar/Sophie Balthazar
Gores	Joannes Hubertus	Joannis Gores/Maria Gores	12-OCT-1863	Kraemer	Marguarita	Petri Kraemer/Eva Kraemer
Gosselin	Georgius	Joannis Gosselin/Eliza.-C. Gosselin	03-JUL-1870	Leduc	Elizabetha	Hilarii Leduc/Julia Leduc
Gould	Sylvester			Ezel	Elizabeth	
Goulet	Ludovicus	Ludovici Goulet/Agnetia Paquete	01-MAR-1870	Gagné	Adelina	Pauli Gagné/Clothilda Gagné
Goulet	Ludovicum		13-DEC-1880	Bérubé	Clarissam	
Goulet	Louis	Joseph Goulet/Maria Réneau	27-APR-1879	Landermann	Romella	Augustini Landermann/Ther- Joly
Goyet	Franciscus	Josephi Goyet/Magdalena Goyet	29-AUG-1864	Beaudin	Léna	Guillelmi Beaudin/Ludovica Beaudin
Goyette	Henrieum	Alexandri Goyette/Maria Lajeunesse	08-JUN-1910	Marcoux	Evam	Francisci Marcoux/Josephina Roy
Goyette	Alexandrum		23-OCT-1900	Balthazar	Herminiam	
Gr——ng	Jonumiem		27-NOV-1852	Fitzgerald	Juliam	
Graton	Vitalem		14-MAY-1884	Choinière	Maria Louisa	
Gratton	Josephum		19-JAN-1886	Lepine	Aureliam	
Gratton	Ludgerium		24-NOV-1891	Michotte	Mariam Louisam	
Gratton	Davidem		09-JUN-1891	Michotte	Malvinam	
Gratton	Josephum		19-JAN-1886	LéPine	Aureliam	
Gratton	Moisen		05-JUL-1881	LéPine	Isabellam	
Green	Irenus H.		28-APR-1861	Gardiner	Marguarita	
Grenier	Oliverius	Francisci Grenier/Emilia Gibou	15-JUL-1872	Marcou	Olivina	Francisci Marcou/Emilia Cyr
Grisé	Carolum		12-SEP-1887	Dufrèsne	Esther	
Gruin	Joseph		19-JUN-1856	Scha–	Rossa	
Gueron	Eduardum		29-APR-1896	Stada	Elizabeth	
Gutreuter	Henricum	Mathia Gutreuter/M.-Anna Hurter	28-NOV-1905	Marcoe	Della	Augusti Marcoe/Julia Leduc
Guyette	Albert	Allen Guyette/Mary Young	25-FEB-1919	Balthazor	Frances	Louis Balthazor/Emiline Roberts
Ha-kins	Patricius	Bernardi Ha-kins/Marg. Ha-kins	01-NOV-1863	O'Hagan	Marguarita	Patricii O'Hagan/Sarah O'Hagan
Hackentolf	Fredericus	Fred. Hackentolf/B—ta Hackentolf	23-NOV-1862	Büehler	Anna	Joannis Büehler/Catherina Büehler
Haff-Inger	Carolus		01-JUN-1864	Krembs	Anna	Antonii Krembs/Ludovica Krembs
Halfman	Chrysantus	Geraldi Halfman/Anna-C. Halfman	08-JUL-1866	Sontag	Eva	Joannis Sontag/Maria Sontag
Hallows	Hugonem Bernardum		14-SEP-1900	Martin	Rosaliam	
Halpen	Patrick		09-MAR-1857	Mclone	Mary	
Hamelonzon	Carolus	Fra. Hamelonzon/Anna Hamelonzon	03-SEP-1865	Lintz	Maria	Hectoris Lintz/Catharina Lintz
Hamilton	Michaelis		31-AUG-1855	Kerry	Catherina	
Hammon	Joannes			O-innen	Jeanne	
Hammon	Michaelis		06-JAN-1856	Fox	Catherina	
Hanniker	Joannes		28-OCT-1856	Liecks	Catherina	
Harlan	Jacobus	Joannis Harlan/Rosa Harlan	20-JUL-1862	Connell	Marguarita	Dyonisii Connell/Bridgitta Harlan
Hartnet	John		13-JUN-1858	Flagerty	Ellen	
Hassenfuss	Jacobus	Jos. Hassenfuss/Anna-M. Hassenfuss	31-DEC-1871	Boivin	Aurelia	Antonii Boivin/Amabilis Hurteau
Hayes	John		13-MAY-1857	Hain	Catharina	
Hénault	Moisen		01-SEP-1891	Mallette	Celissam	

143

Groom's Surname	Groom's Name	Groom's Parents	Date	Bride's Surname	Bride's Name	Bride's Parents
Henchy	Patricius	Michaelis Henchy/Maria Henchy	13-DEC-1860	Lynch	Helena	Josephi Lynch/Julia Lynch
Henker	Hermanum H.		10-JUN-1902	Pratte	Josephinam	
Henry	Michei		10-SEP-1855	Schannel	Catherina	
Herrig	Petrum	Henrici Herrig/Anna Brincus	24-FEB-1909	Lajeunesse	Levina	Gen. Lajeunesse/Levina Balthazar
Herschleb	R. Carolum		21-SEP-1902	Brunet	Olimpiam	
Hess	Joannem P.		26-JUN-1901	Gagnier	Josephinam Helenam	
Hewitt	Georgium		18-SEP-1859	Mack	Catharina	
Hicken	Henricum		02-OCT-1886	Gagnier	Melinam	
Hiers	Jannis		27-NOV-1856	Sessel	Nanne-Marie	
Higgins	Eduradi		22-JUL-1860	Mcglayelan	Bridgette	
Hippach	Joseph	Joseph Hippach/Catherina Schulder	19-JUN-1853	Ebberling	Lina	Joannes Ebberling/Maria Ge—n
Hoag	Joannem			Kief	Catherinam	
Hobbs	Enos			Simons	Elizabetha	
Hodges	Herbert	Joseph Hodges/Elizabeth Blause	27-NOV-1919	O'Malley	Charlotte	
Hoffmann	Robertum Carolum		19-JUL-1894	Boucher	Georginam	
Hofmann	Joannes		09-APR-1860	B——	Elizabeth	
Hoge	Gustavum		09-SEP-1902	Balthazar	Mariam	
Holly	Danniel		23-JUN-1857	Hennigan	Maria	
Hopper	Levi J.		27-DEC-1915	Nelson	Elizabeth	
Horicans	Joannes	Bernardi Horicans/Marg. Hofferty	27-AUG-1862	Kelly	Bridgitta	Joannis Kelly/Joanna Kelly
Houle	Etienne		08-SEP-1856	Langlois	Marie	
Hubertum	Julien		08-NOV-1852	Mallend	Mariam	
Hunsall	Augustus		12-AUG-1860	Meller	Chaterina	
Hurteau	Joannem		06-FEB-1895	Turcot	Mariam	
Jantz (Jorgenson)	Les	John Jantz/Pauline Zarnetski	24-NOV-1920	Lapine	Cecile Elodie Gladys	Joseph Lapine/Sophie Beaudreault
Jarvis Gervais	Leonem	Amabilis Gervais/Philomena Cheffe	23-DEC-1909	Abel-Nest	Ellam	Eduardi Nest/Eda Abel
Jenner	Niclaus		21-JAN-1860	Brown	Elisabeth	
Jenner	William		09-JAN-1860	Waginer	Catharina	
Jentz	Franciscum		30-NOV-1899	Corbeille	Adelina	
Job	George August		06-DEC-1904	Faris	Esther	
Job	Augustinum Georgium		07-DEC-1904	Faris	Esther	
Jocoby	Dominicus	Nicolai Jacobi/—— ——	29-OCT-1874	Akkermann	Caolina	
Johnson	Bernard		20-FEB-1851	Clarke	Elizabeth	
Jolin	Eusebius		09-OCT-1865	Beaumar	Julia	
Jolin	Eusebius	Michaelis Jolin/Maria-Rosa Jolin	09-OCT-1865	Beaumar	Julia	Abrahami Beaumar/Osite Beaumar
Joly	Carolus		16-AUG-1875	LeBerge	Jorissa	
Jongers	Henricum		18-APR-1876	Tell	Mariam	
Joubert	Xaverius	Juliani Joubert/Ludovica Talon	22-MAY-1865	Chennire	Sophia	Michaelis Chennire/Maria Filion
Joubert	Antonius	Julian Joubert/Ludovica Joubert	03-JUL-1870	Boudreau	Magdalena	Josephi Bourdeau/Octavia Bourdeau
Joubert	Carolus Edwardus	Stephani Joubert/Paulina Morin	05-APR-1869	Sco-ley	Sophia	Stephani-D. Sco-ley/Isabella Sco-ley
Jubert	Julien			Cannada	Maria	
Jubert	Franciscum		22-OCT-1876	Baltatzar	Rosalia	
Julius	Carolum Assaf		25-MAY-1905	Mansor	Terphoriam	
Kaufman*	Petrus	Nicholai Kaufman/Maria Kaufman	06-JAN-1866	Bröel	Brigitta	Petri Bröel/Anna Bröel
Keinea	Andrew		26-JAN-1852	McTivy	Marguerite	
Kelly	Thomas		05-AUG-1851	Rider	Rosa	
Kelly	Joannem		10-OCT-1858	Dwyer	Mariam	
Kelly	Peter		15-FEB-1858	Manngan	Margerita	
Kelly	Patrick		31-JAN-1858	Linschs	Margeta	

Groom's Surname	Groom's Name	Groom's Parents	Date	Bride's Surname	Bride's Name	Bride's Parents
Kelly	James		09-JUL-1856	Conly	Margeret	
Kennedy	Patrick		03-OCT-1859	Claury	Marie	
Kennedy	John		26-SEP-1859	Turvelle	Maria	
Kenney	Edward Augustin	Thomas Kenney/Mathilda LaPrairie	05-OCT-1920	Balthazar Maraga	Irene	Martin Balthazar/Tarcila Frenet
Ketchens	Joannum	Thomas Ketchens/Louisa Faber	28-NOV-1906	Lambert	Valedam	Michael Lambert/Sophronia Barbeau
Keyran	Michael	Bernardi Keyran/Elizbeth Keyran	09-MAY-1861	Brown	Marguarita	Edmundi Brown/Bridgitta Brown
Kienow	Fredericum	Augusti Kienow/—— ——	22-JUN-1910	Sénécal	Rosam DeLima	Ovidis Sénécal/Melina Venne
Kilmer	Gulielmum		14-AUG-1900	Gervais	Evam	
King	Joannium	Francisci King/Anna Solael	21-AUG-1907	Lépine	Mariam	Josephi Lépine/Sophia Beaudreau
Kinney	James	Jacobi Kinney/Rose Mcginnis	27-AUG-1919	Schuessler	Josephine	Wm Schuessler/Ida Schoefer
Kintzler	Henricum G.		23-MAY-1899	Dion	Mariam	
Korer	Edmundus	Huberti Korer/Mari-Francisca Korer	15-AUG-1864	Haas	Elizabetha	F. Haas/Catharina Haas
Kraimer	John		10-JAN-1851	Pelant	C——Catherine	
Kreiser	Petrus	Joannis Kreiser/Eva Smith	26-MAY-1863	Wilverzett	Maria	Joannis Wilverzett/Magdalena Wilver
Kremer	Bertholdum Jacobum		22-JUN-1904	Gagnier	Esther Mariam	
Krëmmer	Nicholaus	Hub. Krëmmer/Veronica Krëmmer	26-JAN-1861	Hart-isen	Clementina	Josephi Hart-isen/Carola Hart-isen
Krendwich	Matthias	J. Krendwich/G. Krendwich	04-NOV-1866	Rheinhart	Catharina	Bernardi Rheinhart/Eliza Rheinhart
Kropp	Joannum F.	Francisci Kropp/Catherina Gebel	03-JUN-1908	Cardinal	Mariam Annam	Leonis Cardinal/Rosalia Venne
Kurmal	Salimann Abo		20-FEB-1905	Cabar	Messay	
LaBassiere	Henricum		18-FEB-1878	Roy	Elisam	
Labelle	——riaus	Laurentii Labelle/Genovefa Labelle	03-OCT-1864	Rulo	H—ri-a	Petri Rulo/Ludovica Rulo
Laca	Camille	Narcis Laca/Ursula Trudell	24-AUG-1879	Ouellette	Olivine	Ludovici Ouellette/Lucia Louffe
Lacause	Ferdinand		11-JUN-1857	LeDuc	Matilde	
Lafayette	Henricum		16-FEB-1898	Rabidoux	Marcellinam	
Laing	Alexander	Jacobi Laing/Maria ——	03-SEP-1866	Lucier	Sophronia	Ludovicus Lucier/Maria ——
Lajeunesse	Petrus	Henrici Lajeunesse/Marg. Lajeunesse	30-APR-1867	Surprenant	Eleonora	Isaaci Surprenant/Julia Surprenant
Lajeunesse	Generosum		19-FEB-1889	Balthazar	Olivinam	
Lajeunesse	Josephum		26-NOV-1882	Gratton	Juliam	
Lajeunesse	Michaelem		23-OCT-1882	LeBeau	Rosanam	
Lajeunesse	Henricus		08-OCT-1877	Leduc	Lucia	
Lamb	Petrus	Jacobi Lamb/Bridgitta Lamb	27-JUL-1862	Hanegan	Helena	Patricii Hanegan/Julia Hanegan
Lamb	Thomas	Jacobi Lamb/Maria Lamb	13-JAN-1862	Carrol	Bridgitta	Thomas Carrol/Bridgitta Flanegan
Lamb	Nicholas	Nicolai-Jacobi Lamb/Bridgitta Lamb	13-JAN-1862	McDermott	Anna	Francisci McDermott/Maria McDerm
Lambert	Paula		25-JUL-1899	Barbeau	Corina	
Lambert	Michael	Bonaventura Lambert/Maria Denis	21-OCT-1867	Barbeau	Sophronia	Petri Barbeau/Marcelina Gervais
Lamblot	Michaelem			Dion	Mariam	
Landerman	Josephum Maglorium Dalorem		06-AUG-1898	Abel	Louisam	
Landerman	Hilarium		14-SEP-1891	Minier	Louisam	
Landreman	Ludovicus	Augustini Landreman/Theresa Joli	16-AUG-1863	Mocquin	Marguarita	Josephi Mocquin/Zoah Beaudeau-Mo
Landreman	Josephus	Augustus Landreman/Theresa Joli	04-FEB-1873	Dumas	Phi——	
Landreman	Ludovicum		22-OCT-1902	Duley	Elizabetham Ettam	
Landri	Josephus	Michaelis Landri/Julia Landri	26-DEC-1866	Garo	Suzanna	Petri Garo/Maria Garo
Langlois	——		21-MAY-1859	Bullet	Martinam	
Langlois	Josephum		23-SEP-1874	Moquin	Josephina	
Langlois	Edmondus	Jacobi Langlois/Ludovica Huole	11-NOV-1873	Bonette	Marguarita	Julian Bonette/Marguarite Cyr
Langlois	Josephus	Nazarii Langlois/Matilda Langlois	06-JUL-1869	Landreman	Martha	Leandri Landreman/Aurelia Molheur
Langlois	Georgium		26-NOV-1889	Moquin	Mariam	
Langlois	Vitalem		23-NOV-1887	Balthazar	Emeliam	
Langlois	Cesarium		23-NOV-1887	Gosselin	Franciscam	

145

Groom's Surname	Groom's Name	Groom's Parents	Date	Bride's Surname	Bride's Name	Bride's Parents
Langlois	Cyprianum		09-JAN-1882	Gauthier	Angelinam	
Langto	Josephus	Francisci Langto/Carola Biet	09-SEP-1872	Parent	Anna	Josephi Parent/Emilia LaBerge
Lanto	Judani		11-OCT-1875	Dufraine	Maria	
Lapine	Lawrence	Joseph Lapine/Sophie Beaudreault	11-NOV-1920	Prey	Lorraine	Albert Prey/Lillian Schwebke
LaPlante	Oliverius	Josephi LaPlante/Catharina LaPlante	15-FEB-1872	Préfontaine Robidou	Aurelia	Alexii Préfontaine/M.-L. Padenoide
LaPorte	Josephus		17-SEP-1876	Pratt	Leopolda	
LaPorte	Zotique	Leonis LaPorte/Zoe Bernard-Bouillet	19-AUG-1867	Veine	Ludovica	Agapiti Veine/Felicitatis Contant
LaPorte	Napoleon	Leonis LaPorte/Zoe Bernard	28-OCT-1879	L'Epine	Malvina	Ludovici L'Epine/Adelina L'Epine
Larenche	Jaque		06-NOV-1859	Osait	Lenise	
Larkens	John		07-JUN-1857	McGillan	Marie	
Larose	Ludovicum		01-DEC-1903	Dix	Lauram	
Larson	Josephum Axel		18-DEC-1902	Balthazar	Juliam	
Leager	Laurentius Georgius	Joannis Leager/Elizabeth Trahant	17-AUG-1873	——eau	Helena	Petri ——eau/Emilia Trahant
Leahy	Samuel		23-MAY-1859	Terry	Brigetha	
Lebeau	Josephus	——ali Lebeau/Marguarita Deble	23-MAY-1865	Faucher	Horminia	Ludovici Faucher/Josephina Dagno
LeBlanc	Henricum		24-JUL-1890	LeBeau	Georginam	
LeBlanc	August		29-AUG-1858	LeDuc	M. Luc	
LeBrecque	Josephus	Jacobi LeBrecque/Arch. LeBrecque	09-APR-1866	Deschênes	Delima	
LeClair	Jule		03-JUL-1876	Anglois	Adena	
LeCoque	Ludovicus	Ludovici LeCoque/Sophia Ric-r	11-JUN-1872	Rossete	Laurentia	Juliani Rossete/Marguarita Cyr
Lécuyer	Petrus	Petri Lécuyer/Leucadia Lécuyer	10-APR-1866	Lefort	Carolina	Caroli LeFort/Angela LeFort
Leduc	Josephus	Josephi Leduc/Marguarita Leduc	10-APR-1864	Rondeau	Philomena	Francis Rondeau/Christina Rondeau
Leduc	Ceril		10-OCT-1876	Leduc	Delima	
Leduc	Remigius Oliverius	Josephi Leduc/Marg. Devire-Bundy	29-AUG-1870	Bassete	Sophia	Xavierii Bassete/Sophia Robert
LeDuc	Eduard		03-NOV-1858	Duquette	Matilde	
LeDuc	Petrus	Josephi Leduc/Marguarita Leduc	16-JUN-1867	Bertrand	Ludovica	Ludovici Bertrand/Julia-A. Bertrand
Lee	Emory	Ellery Lee/Esther Wilson	21-APR-1920	Hurteau	Margaret	John Hurteau/Mary Turcotte
Lefeve	Elia-ar			Jubert	Elisabeth	
LeFève	Israel	Augustini LeFève/Emilia LeFève	25-JUN-1872	Langlois	Zoeh	Vitali Langlois/Flavia Langlois
LeFève	Camilus	Camili LeFève/Julia LaBarge	01-AUG-1870	Edouin	Delima	Leonis Edouin/Flavia Mocquin
LeFort	Joannis	Caroli LeFort/Angelica ——gette	06-JUL-1874	Gagné	Emilia	Eduardi Bonnier/– Gagné
LeFort	Narcissus	Caroli LeFort/Angela LeFort	29-OCT-1866	Demars	Celina	Amabilis Demars/Maria Demars
LeGault	Bellami		01-JAN-1876	Rando	Maria	
Lemaire	Josephus		01-NOV-1865	Dumas	Jana	
Lemaire	Petrus	Stephani Lemaire/Sophia Piner	03-NOV-1862	Desnoyer	Hermina	Huberti Desnoyer/Sophis Desnoyer
Lemaire	Josephus	Jul.-Steph. Lemaire/Sophia Lemaire	03-AUG-1862	Lécuyer	Helena	Noeli Lécuyer/Eleonora –-er
LeMaire	Achiles	Stephani LeMaire/Sophia P-nar	16-SEP-1866	Robidou	Exarina	Huberti Robidou/Aurelia Fournier
LeMaire	Josephus		01-NOV-1865	Dumos	Joanna	
LeMieux	Anthony	Israel LeMieux/Melina Larose	26-APR-1905	Benedict	Mable	
LeMieux	Jeremiah	Israel LeMieux/Melina Larose	08-FEB-1905	Paré	Julia	Louis Paré/Duleme Joubert
Lemieux	Antonium	Israelis Lemieux/Melina Larose	26-APR-1905	Benedict	Mable	
Lemieux	Jeromiau	Israel Lemieux/Melina Larose	31-JAN-1905	Paré	Julia	Ludovici Paré/Delima Joubert
Lenshs	John		29-AUG-1858	Mangan	Marget	
Lentz	Franciscum	Gulielmi Lentz/Maria Hemming	20-FEB-1906	Corbeille	Exildam	Napoleoni Corbeille/Melinda Lebeau
Leonard	Petrus	M. Leonard/Brigitta Clark	10-NOV-1861	Hogan	Maria	Michaelis Hogan/Maria Hogan
Lepin	Josephum		09-NOV-1874	Bodrieaux	Sophiam	
Lepine	Joannes-Baptista-Amatus		17-JUL-1864	Beaulieu	Maria	
Lépine	Thomasum	Thomas Lépine/Josephina Brunet	22-APR-1907	Corbeille	Amanda	Cyrilli Corbeille/Anastasia Lefort
LePine	Franciscus		18-SEP-1876	Gothié	Lucia	

Groom's Surname	Groom's Name	Groom's Parents	Date	Bride's Surname	Bride's Name	Bride's Parents
LePine	Josephus		30-MAR-1875	Gothier	Emma	
LePine	Franciscum		31-MAY-1881	Landermann	Philomenam	
LePine	Louis	Joseph LePine/Louise Rondeau	01-MAY-1905	Cliche	Mary	Louis Cliche/Delphine Dufresne
Lepine	Ludovicum	Josephi Lepine/Louisa Rondeau	01-MAY-1905	Cliche	Maria	Ludovici Cliche/Delphina Dufrane
LePine	Thomam		25-NOV-1884	Brunet	Josephinam	
LePine	Petrum		13-AUG-1883	Corbeille	Josephinam	
LePine	Franciscum		31-MAY-1881	Landermann	Philumenam	
Lepper	Georgium		23-NOV-1890	Turcot	Eugeniam	
Lesselyoung	Oscar L.	Henry Lesselyoung/Ida Zille	21-APR-1920	Develice	Helen	Adolph Develice/Elizabeth Langteau
Letourneau	Joannem		16-JAN-1853	Debelin	Ellena	
Letourneau	Pascal		23-OCT-1859	Bea-mure	Marie	
Letourneau	Christopherus	Christ. Letourneau/Vitalia Landris	20-APR-1862	Molhens	Maria	Ludovici Molhens/Felicitatis Molhens
Letourneau	Josephum		07-JUN-1881	Letourneau	Mathildam	
LeTourneau	Pascalem		04-APR-1903	Milquet	Mathildam	
LeTourneau	Petrus		25-SEP-1870	Bissonet	Sophia	Narcissi Bissonet/Marcelina Russeau
Létourneau	Josephus	Petri Létourneau/Lucia Sorel	21-OCT-1867	Bessete	Adelida	Petri Bessete/Sophia Beaulieu
LeTourneau	Petrum		16-SEP-1886	Perron	Catherinam	
Letourneau	Josephum		07-JUN-1881	Letourneau	Mathildam	
Lewis	Josephum C.		20-AUG-1902	Balthazar	Idam	
Linden	Thomas	Petri-Josephi Linden/Maria Linden	16-APR-1865	Stecken	Catharina	Huberti Stecken/Maria Stecken
Lisson	Jacobus	Gulielmi Lisson/Marguarita Lisson	04-JUL-1866	LeMaire	Virginia	Stephanii LeMaire/Sophia LeMaire
Logan	David	Petri Logan/Francisca Logan	30-OCT-1860	Ebert	Martina	Isidori Ebert/Florentia Ebert
Logelain	Patrick		04-OCT-1858	B--nnel	Marie	
Logelan	William		11-NOV-1855	Conderon	Theresa	
Loiseau Bird	Leonem		23-SEP-1901	Tonne	Gratiam	
Lomblat	Josephum		05-MAY-1886	Kramer	Catherinam	
Lomblat	Josephum		05-MAY-1886	Kramer	Catharina	
Lonner	Jacobus		20-AUG-1902	Gosselain	Lina	
Lorge	Franciscus	Francisci Lorge/M.Catharina Lorge	29-SEP-1861	Houssois	Adelaida	Josephi Houssois/M.Theresa Houssois
Loselion	Joannes	Petri Loselion/Elizabetha Loselion	28-DEC-1862	Cane	Catharina	Thoma Cane/Helena Cane
Losson	F—		18-JUL-1857	Jubert	L–id–	
Louiss-	Franciscus		20-AUG-1865	Miller	Carolina	
Lucier	Josephus	Ludovici Lucier/Pelagia Regnier	20-OCT-1872	Duffy	Maria-Anna	Thoma Duffy/Anna McGinty
Lucier	Baptista	Caroli Lucier/Rosalia Lucier	17-MAY-1871	LePage	Adelina	Moysis LePage/Clotilda N—
Lucier	Camillus	Ludovici Lucier/Pelagia Laquin	27-DEC-1869	Garo	Adelina	Petri Garo/Clementina Brou
Ludovicus	Joannes		12-APR-1860	Massel	Madalina	
Lumblot	Victorem		05-SEP-1904	Platte-Noupré	Albertam	
Lynks	John		05-AUG-1860	Noverty	Cathernia	
Lyon	Franciscum		20-JUN-1853	McCoy	Rosam	
Lyonnais	Claudium		27-JAN-1900	Cartier	Georgianam	
Lyonnais	Josephi Walter		11-DEC-1897	Kavel	Amanda	
Lyonnais	Gulielmum		05-JAN-1897	Bonin	Delphinam	
Lyonnais	Cosmam Edw.		27-JAN-1885	Gosselain	Edessam	
Lyonnais	Comé	Ludovici Lyonnais/Angela Lyonnais	08-JUL-1862	Beaudriau	Ludovica	Laur. Beaudriau/Harr. Beaudriau
Lyonnais	Franciscus	Ludovici Lyonnais/Angela Gamelin	18-NOV-1872	Rondeau	Marguarita	Baptista Rondeau/Julia Anna Chef
Lyonnais	Fredericus	Ludovici Lyonnais/Angela Comelin	15-APR-1872	LeFève	Olivia	Eduardi LeFève/Josephina Deneau
Lyonnais	Edwardus	Ludovici Lyonnais/Angela Camelin	06-JUL-1868	Bessete	Sophia	Petri Bessete/Sophia Beaulieu
Lyonnais	Josephus	Antonii Lyonnais/Julia Lyonnais	07-JAN-1867	Bessete	Lucia	Petri Bessete/Sophia Bessete
Lyonnais	Narcissus	Ludovici Lyonnais/Angelica Hamelin	30-OCT-1865	LeDuc	Maria	Hilarii LeDuc/Julia Beaudrieau

147

Groom's Surname	Groom's Name	Groom's Parents	Date	Bride's Surname	Bride's Name	Bride's Parents
Lyonnis	Narcissus		30-OCT-1865	Leduc	Maria	
Lyons	Patricum		29-MAY-1900	Préfontaine	Aliceam	
M——s	John			Mettendorf	-usson——len	
Magellan	Patrick			Matin	Julli	
Maide	Thomas		11-APR-1858	McGinty	Brigita	
Mairh	Joannes		12-AUG-1860	Voght	Anna Chaterina	
Malone	Petrus	Martini Malone/Elizabetha Malone	23-NOV-1862	Gough	Marguarita	Joannis Gough/Anna Gough
Managan	Michel		19-FEB-1858	Lyons	Eliz-Maria	
Manali–	John		02-NOV-1850	Kinnison	Mary	
Mangan	Michael		10-FEB-1852	Mortats	Sarah	
Mangan	Jacobus	Michaeli Mangan/——itta Mangan	27-JUL-1862	Boyce	Margurita	Georgii Boyce/Anna Boyce
Mangin	Ludovicum Lafayette		11-JAN-1881	Leduc	Mariam Louisam	
Mannon	Stiven		07-JUL-1856	Morson	Catherina	
Marcotte	Leandrum		18-JUL-1881	DuBois	Maria	
Marcou	Joannes Maria	Joannis-M Marcou/Angela Marcou	12-JUL-1862	Chenar	Helena	Isidori Chenar/Sophia Chenar
Marcou	Alexander	Francisci Marcou/Melicia Sir	19-OCT-1874	Delajeunesse	Leurda	Henri Delajeunesse/Leonanda Gayet
Marcou	Franciscus	Francisci Marcou/Maria Cyr	22-FEB-1870	Roi	Josephina	Isaïa Roi/Julianna Ebert
Marcou	Joseph	Joannis-M. Marcou/Angela Marcou	04-SEP-1866	Pellant	Elizabetha	Francisci Pellant/Josepha Pellant
Marcou	Franciscum		25-APR-1881	St. Germain	Zoeam Elmiram	
Marcou	Augustinus	Joannis-M Marcou/Matilde Tremblay	07-JAN-1880	Leduc	Julia	Joseph Leduc/Marguarita Bondi
Marcou	Alexander		30-SEP-1877	Bodrieau	Orrelia	
Marcoux	Samuelem	Samuelis Marcoux/—— ——	29-JAN-1910	Schreiner	Mariam	
Marcoux	Oliverum J.		03-JUN-1902	Webber	Catharinam	
Marcoux	Franciscum		13-JUN-1899	Balthazar	Josephinam	
Marcoux	Joannem		09-JUN-1896	LeBeau	Josephinam	
Marcoux	Napoleonem		29-MAR-1883	Dufrèsne	Sophroniam	
Marcoux	Jeremias		12-OCT-1880	Mainé	Mariam-Sophiam	
Margan	John		27-AUG-1855	Mullen	Catherine	
Marion	Felix	Ludovici Marion/Felicitata Mer-	18-JUN-1865	Thirien	Ludovica Catherina	Ludovici Thirien/Rosa Patras
Marion	Seraphinus	Ludovici Marion/Elizabetha Talis	17-APR-1870	Roi	Emma	Isaïa Roi/Julia-Anna Ebert
Markow	Franciscum Henricum		29-AUG-1899	Burnham	Leoniam	
Marlow	Gilbertum Josephum		04-NOV-1903	Dinelle	Rosannam	
Martel*	Prosper	Josephi Martel/Francisca Dolby	05-FEB-1866	Tremblé	Agla	Henrici Tremblé/Josephina Girard
Marten	Hugh		04-FEB-1856	Mangan	Anna	
Martin	Arthus C.	Leon Martin/Lenora Dumas	28-OCT-1919	Gardner	Denora Marie	Alphonse Gardner/Marie Tardif
Martin	Napoleonum L.	Leonis Martin/Eleonora Dumas	19-JUL-1910	Holtz	Annam	Oscari Holtz/——
Martin	Laurentium		14-OCT-1902	Piehl	Netam Josephinam	
Martin	Leo	Benjamini Martin/Narcissa Dumas	24-JUL-1871	Dumas	Eleonora	Josephi Dumas/Dyonisia Duquete
Martin	Xavieri	Joannis Martin/Henrica Carmel	22-JUL-1867	Joubert	Josephina	Juliani Joubert/Ludovica Joubert
Mass	Ovide	J.B. Mass/Flavia Dugas	22-JUN-1879	Demers	Octavia	Soloman Demers/Emelia LaGasse
Mathews	James		04-APR-1858	Higgens	Maria	
Mathius	Charles		14-NOV-1858	Cumminks	Brigitha	
Mathews	Louis		10-MAY-1851	Pelant	Matilde	
Maurice	Geo.	FrankMaurice/Michotte	30-DEC-1919	Schauss	Elizabeth	
Maurice	Franciscum	Francisi. Maurice/Josephina Michotte	12-JUN-1906	Robidoux	Lucretiam M	Josephi Robidoux/Ermina Pellant
Maurice	Guiellelmus	Angeli Maurice/Victoria Maurice	30-APR-1861	Mainville-Deschesnes	Rosa-Delima	T. Mainville/C. Mainville
Maurice	Andreum		12-JUN-1887	Dufresne	Emma	Francisci Dufresne/——
Maurice	Franciscum		01-OCT-1883	Michotte	Josephina	
Maurice	Josephum		24-JAN-1883	Fontaine	Agnetam	

148

Groom's Surname	Groom's Name	Groom's Parents	Date	Bride's Surname	Bride's Name	Bride's Parents
Mayer	Edwardus	Malachi Mayer/Catharina Mayer	19-APR-1863	Duffy	Maria	Hughii Duffy/MariaDuffy
Mayer	Thomas		18-APR-1858	Vaughen	Marg.	
Mcay	Turner			Milligan	Honore	
McBryon	Thamas		10-MAY-1856	Strang	Nanis	
McCabe	Michel		31-OCT-1859	Doyle	Ellen	
McCabe	Roy	James McCabe/Catherine Doyle	07-SEP-1920	Perrizo	Marie Irene	Joseph Perrizo/Melanie Dupuis
McCabe	Richard		04-JUL-1858	Grogeon	Rosanna	
McClain	James		02-JAN-1859	Nicalus	Brigitha	
McCormick	Gulielmum Henricum		03-JUN-1897	Besnah-Bazinet	Delphinam-Helenam	
McDonald	Joannes	Alex. McDonald/Helena McDonald	29-JUL-1861	Shaw	Isabella	Joannes Shaw/Anna Shaw
McDonald	Joannem		30-APR-1881	Corey	Juliana	
McDormitt	Joannes		01-OCT-1876	Gardener	Elena	
McEnetty	Patrick		03-AUG-1851	McCoy	Susan	
Mcessy	Joannem		20-JAN-1891	Robert	Josephinam	
McGay	Robert		03-NOV-1856	Cullen	Margret	
McGiffirn	Patrick			Cannada	Luca	
McGinny	James			Kelly	Marry	
McGivern	Hugh		16-APR-1857	Currans	Catherina	
McGlogen	John		29-NOV-1856	Murry	Marget	
McGowen	Mauritium		21-NOV-1880	Spe— Carbonneau	Louisa	
McGrath	John-Finly		13-NOV-1851	Duprey	Mary-Anna-Agnes-Roselia	
McGrath	Jacobus	Jacobi McGrath/Marg. McGrath	07-SEP-1862	Molton	Joanna	Roberti Molton/Maria Molton
McGree	Petrus		14-JUL-1856	Gibben	Anna	
McGregery	Own		27-OCT-1856	Melony	Maria Anna	
McKinley	Guilbertum Jacobum		25-DEC-1885	Racette	Arminam	
McKiver	John		05-MAY-1857	Bay	Marg.	
McLaughlin	Daniel		15-NOV-1863	McMonagle	Julia	Antonii McMonagle/Julia McMonagle
McLonen	Joannes	Archibaldi McLonen/Marg. McLonen	21-JUL-1861	Thornton	Anna	Jacobi Thornton/Anna Thornton
McManniker	Nick		07-NOV-1858	Harkens	Ruth	
McMullen	Joannes	Guill. McMullen/Maria McMullen	23-JAN-1871	Ebert	Maria Thersila	Davidis Ebert/Clotilda Ebert
McNiclus	John		07-SEP-1856	Gill	Anna	
McTegret	Hueh		25-OCT-1857	Dogerty	Margeta	
Mctetevy	James	Francis McTetevy/Margit -wlnn——		Gursin-Mayfort	Marie	——/Margr—— ——
Melony	Patrick		23-JUL-1856	Dollan	Anna	
Mengle	Joannem		16-APR-1883	Diette	Azildam	
Mensted	Carolus	Joannis Mensted/Maria Christenson	13-JUL-1879	LeFaure	Maria	J.B. LeFaure/Edmire Rondeau
Mertes	Mattheus Josephus	Antonii Mertes/Anna-Maria Mertes	19-MAY-1863	Vogt	Maria	Antonii Vogt/Josephina Vogt
Metlon	John		01-APR-1859	Wellon	Elisabith	
Meunier	Franciscus	Isaaci Meunier/Elizabetha Meunier	10-FEB-1861	Chenard	Sophia	Isidori Chenard/Sophia Chenard
Meunier	Nazaire		13-JUL-1877	Hébert	Felicité	
Milady	Robertus	Richardi Milady/Julia Milady	06-APR-1863	Lawlor	Maria	Joannis Lawlor/Marguarita Lawlor
Milette	Ulric		26-JUN-1859	Keblier	Mary	
Miller	Christianus		19-SEP-1870	Morris Beaudry	Maria	
Mishote	Deodatus	Francisci Mishote/M-Josepha Mishote	08-JUN-1862	Mocquin	Olivia	Josephi Mocquin/Ludovica Mocquin
Mitchell	Josephum		09-SEP-1884	Smith	Mariam E.	
Mocquin	Josephus	Josephi Mocquin/Zoah Bredeau	07-APR-1863	Odet	Vitalina	Georgii Odet/Julia Préjean
Mocquin	Issau		24-FEB-1878	Mocquin	Matilda	
Mogon	John		16-APR-1857	McGarikel	Brigita	
Molheur	Germanus	Ludovici Molheur/Felicitatus Cyr	06-JUL-1869	Landreman	Maria	Augustini Landreman/Theresia Joli

149

Groom's Surname	Groom's Name	Groom's Parents	Date	Bride's Surname	Bride's Name	Bride's Parents
Monsen	Mathias		14-APR-1860	Albert	Maria-Veronica	
Moor	Jocobus		29-NOV-1856	Done	Maria	
Moquin	Narsis		25-DEC-1876	Loussele	Philome	
Moquin	Alexander	Francis Moquin/Henriette Percheron	09-MAY-1905	Moquin	Anna	Joseph Moquin/Mathilda Barbeau
Moquin	Alexandrum	Francis Moquin/Henrietta Percheron	09-MAY-1905	Moquin	Annam	Josephi Moquin/Mathilda Barbeau
Morel	Reneum		08-SEP-1903	Venne-Hover	Carolinam	
Morgan	Michaelem		18-JAN-1853	Lunim	Elizam	
Morris	Carolus	Joannis Morris/Maria Morris	01-MAR-1864	Morris	Maria	Francisci Morris/Clotilda Morris
Morris	Gorge		07-JUL-1860	Ragame	Clemence	
Morrisson	Jacobus	Joannis Morrisson/Maria Morrisson	22-JUN-1868	Bird	Lucretia	Petri Bird/Emilia Bird-Letourneau
Mullen	Michaelem		25-APR-1853	Chrishams	Mariam	
Mullen	Hugh		01-JUL-1851	McCoy	Mary	
Mullen	John		18-SEP-1856	Galligar	Nosa	
Mullen	John		18-NOV-1855	Meller	Ann	
Murphy	Thomas		07-JAN-1857	Murphy	Ellen	
Murry	Thomas	Joannis Murry/Catharina Murry	11-AUG-1861	Atkinson	Maria-Anna	Joannis Atkinson/Anna Atikinson
Myer	Nicholaum		14-NOV-1887	McCullan	Elenam	
Neilan	Thomas	Joannes Neilan/Maria Neilan	09-MAY-1861	Haverty	Maria	Martini Haverty/Maria Haverty
Neisor	Henricus	Eberhardi Neisor/Agnetia Neisor	27-SEP-1866	Hemmer	Maria-Anna	Caroli Hemmer/Ludovica Hemmer
Nelly	John		02-MAY-1856	Hueh	Anna	
Nelson	Henricus		19-AUG-1870	Boucher	Josephina	
Nenlon	John		11-APR-1856	Leonard	Joanna	
Newman	Franciscum	Adolphi Newman/Maria Ashenbruner	20-NOV-1907	Perrizo	Maud	Josephi Perrizo/Belonisa Dupuis
Nichlas	Antonium		03-NOV-1891	Rodidoux	Mariam Claram	
Nicholson	Patricius	Jacobi Nicholson/Sarah Nicholson	15-JUN-1861	Turto	Odilia	Jacobi Turto/Elizabeth Turto
Nolli	Peter		21-SEP-1851	Provot	Julienne	
Noton	Peter		02-AUG-1857	Fendelin	Maria	
Noupré	Josephum		25-APR-1886	Pratte	Albertam	
Noupré	Josephum		25-APR-1886	Pratte	Albertam	
O'Brien	James		25-NOV-1850	Lery	Mary	
O'Brien	Jacobi	Thoma O'Brien/Catharina O'Brien	15-NOV-1863	Hagerty	Marguarita	Caroli Hagerty/Honora Hagerty
O'Brien	Patricius	Patricii O'Brien/Maria O'Brien	02-FEB-1862	Brennan	Anna	Timothei Brennan/Maria Connaughty
O'Brien	Michael	Jacobi O'Brien/Brigette O'Brien	28-OCT-1861	Burns	Anna-Nancy	Francisci Burns/Helena Burns
O'Brien	Thomas	Jacobi O'Brien/Honora O'Brien	15-APR-1861	Webb	Marguarita	Jacobi Webb/Joanna Webb
O'Kieff	John		20-OCT-1858	Hegarty	Anna	
O'Sullivan	Maurtius		20-SEP-1859	O'Connor	Brigittam	
O—	Denis		20-NOV-1659	Oconner	Brigeta	
Obryan	Thamas		03-FEB-1859	Phillips	Margetha	
Obryan	John		29-NOV-1856	Dalton	Marie	
Ochlevain	James		14-NOV-1856	McGarty	Marie	
Odentrit	Philipp	John Odentrit/Cath.-Emilie Odentrit	24-JUL-1855	Abler	Sofiah	
Odete	Baptista	Georgii Odete/Cyrila Odete	07-MAY-1870	Ralo	Mathilda Adgett	Petri Ralo/Ludovica Ralo
Odete*	Stepharius		26-DEC-1865	Dufort	Carolina	
Odete*	Stephanus	Georgii Odete/Julia Prejean	26-DEC-1865	DuFort	Carolina	Antonii DuFort/Christina Cliché
Ogé	Andreas		21-MAY-1878	Harnois	Adé	
Ottery	George T.	Herbert Ottery/Nina M. Stage	12-FEB-1919	Senecal	Angelicam	David Seneca/Rose Venne
Ouellette	Franciscum		28-NOV-1907	Balthazar	Zoam	Joannis Balthazar/Marie Marcoux
Ouellette	Alexium		19-FEB-1889	Lajeunesse	Emeliam	
Page	—	Moysis Page/Cornelia Page		Chef	Maria	Petri Chef/Christina Chef

150

Groom's Surname	Groom's Name	Groom's Parents	Date	Bride's Surname	Bride's Name	Bride's Parents
Painguère	Josephus	M.-J Painguère/M.-Josepha Sti-man	21-AUG-1870	LeClerc	Adelina	Gilberti LeClerc/Adelina Gagnier
Papineau	Oliverius	Francisci Papineau/Anastasia Ganier	05-SEP-1871	Agagnier	Alphonsina	Huberti Agagnier/Maria Mocquin
Paquet*	Israel	Ludovici Paquet/Genovefa Mans–	06-NOV-1865	Polie	Josephina	Michaelis Polie/Maria Polie
Paquete	Felix	Petri Paquete/Ludovica Plouf	13-APR-1868	Beaudrieau	Maria Emma	Joseph Beaudrieau/Cor Beaudrieau
Paquette*	Israel		06-NOV-1865	Polie	Josephina	
Paradis	Davidem		17-APR-1888	LéPine	Eleonoram	
Pariseau	Michel		13-OCT-1856	Hebbet	Masseline	
Pariseault	Eduardum		30-SEP-1896	Marcoux	Malvinam	
Pariso	Georgius	Michaelis Pariso/Pelagia Pariso	24-NOV-1862	Grizet	Maria	Antonii Grizet/Clotilda Grizet
Pariso	Josephus	Michaelis Pariso/Pelagia Pariso	08-OCT-1861	Bellanger	Sophronia	Eusebii Bellanger/Josepha Bellanger
Parizo	Josephus	Michaelis Parizo/Pelagia Parizo	21-OCT-1867	Agagnier	Maria Octavia	Huberti Agagnier/Maria Moquin
Parriso	–hte		24-OCT-1859	Belhumer	–vena	
Patrick	John		13-OCT-1855	Morgan	Catharine	
Patt	Ferdinandum		14-JUN-1892	LéTourneau	Adelam Josephnam	
Pellant	Joseph Thomas		18-JAN-1905	Robidoux	Josephine Mary	
Pellant	Franciscus Xavierius	Francisci Pellant/Josepha Faucher	30-JAN-1872	LéTourneau	Philomena	Petri LéTourneau/Lucia Sorele
Pellant	Josephum T.	Adolphi Pellant/Alphonsina Laberge	10-JAN-1905	Robidoux	Josephinam M.	Josephi Robidoux/Ermina Pellant
Pellant	Adolphum Napoleonem		22-NOV-1880	LaBerge	Alphonsina	
Pelletier	Louis		06-MAY-1852	Smith	Catherine	
Peren	John Baptista		19-FEB-1858	Ring	Sophia	
Perkins	Ephraim J.	Eduardi Perkins/Sarah Perkins	21-JUL-1869	Vancour	Martha	Isaaci Vancour/Maria Vancour
Perron	Joannes-Baptista	Andrei Perron/Maria-Auréle Perron	28-MAY-1867	Pellant	Maria	Francisci Pellant/Josephina Faucher
Petit	Joseph	Lambert Petit/Ptalina Brabe		Belhumur	Edimis	Francois Belhumur/Margerit Fillion
Petters	Albertum Emilium		14-OCT-1880	Balthazar	Sophiam	Francisco Pellant/Thoma LePine
Phelan	Jacobum K.		17-APR-1883	Meunier Miller	Josepham	
Philips	Ferdinandus	Henrici Philips/Helena Philips	20-APR-1868	Dumas	Emma	Baptista Dumas/Maria Perron
Pierron	Joannem Carolum		21-DEC-1893	Linscott	Mariam Philumenam	
Pierson	Josephum		13-AUG-1883	Pellant	Adelam	
Plouf	Thomas	Sulpitii Plouf/Adelaida Houle	28-AUG-1870	Wotete	Georgina	Ludovici Wotete/Lucia Louf
Plugers	Joseph G.	Peter Plugers/Mary Theissen	30-SEP-1918	Boda	Mariam Leonani	Louis Boda/Exilda Derwin
Pomainville	Michael	Mich. Pomainville/Sophia Desjardins	27-SEP-1873	Graton	Sophia	Vitalis Graton/Phebé Tremblé
Pomminville	Gulielmum		22-OCT-1900	Marcoux	Eleonoram	
Potrin	Joannes Bapt.		25-AUG-1875	Nolain	Maria Jean	
Powers	Arthurum		25-NOV-1896	Lambert	Mariam Dinam	
Pratt	Theodorus	Josephi Pratt/Heriette Pratt-Laroque	26-APR-1880	Deshotels	Emma	Caroli Deshotels/Anastasia Moquin
Pratte	Stanislaum		04-JUL-1886	Beauregard	Mariam	
Pratte	Alfredum		03-JUL-1883	Prefontaine	Octaviam	
Pratte	Felicem		17-OCT-1881	Duquette	Saram	
Préfontaine	Andreas	Bart. Préfontaine/Angelica Trudeau	18-SEP-1871	Mocquin	Ludovica	Josephi Mocquin/Zoeh Bourdeau
Prefontaine	Ludgerium		25-DEC-1881	Simonin	Juliam	
Prefontaine	Andreum		29-JUL-1877	Morris	Delia	
Pret	Josephus		03-SEP-1876	Prat	Francisca	
Prova	Peter		10-OCT-1855	Peron	Paulina	
Prudhomme	Josephum		12-APR-1888	Venne	Adelinam	
Rabidou	Josephus	Christo Rabidou/Eliza Dugas	07-SEP-1872	Boivin	Maria	Georgii Boivin/Emilia Boivin
Rabidou	Josephus	Huberti Rabidou/Aurelia Préfontaine	12-OCT-1869	Pellant	Hermina	Francisci Pellant/Josephina Faucher
Rabidou	Moyses	Caroli Rabidou/Elizabetha Edouin	17-AUG-1869	Fernet	Emilia	Isaïa Fernet/Mathilda Hubert
Rabidou	Alfredus	Caroli Rabidou/Anastasia Edouin	29-NOV-1868	Mocquin	Ludovica	Francis Mocquin/Henrica Percheron
Ragan	Patrick		27-NOV-1856	McIntyre	Theresa	

151

Groom's Surname	Groom's Name	Groom's Parents	Date	Bride's Surname	Bride's Name	Bride's Parents
Ramme	Christopher	Heinrich Ramme/Christiana Ramme	21-SEP-1863	Müller	Regina	Peter Müller/Antoinette Müller
Randeau	Thamas		19-AUG-1857	Pellant	Josephina	
Ransom	Arthur E.		11-APR-1887	Gilmen	Matildam	
Rayly	Patrick		24-FEB-1857	Hoegen	Marie	
Rayly	James		21-FEB-1857	Benton	Anne	
Rayly	Own		19-FEB-1857	Bennon	Ellen	
Raymond	Georgius	Gregorii Raymond/Felicita Raymond	17-APR-1880	Edouin	Exilda	Leonis Edouin/F.— Moquin
Réal	Elizius	Josephi Réal/Amarrantha Réal	17-OCT-1869	Tetro	Petronella	Josephi Tetro/A.-Tetro
Reau	Leonem		17-OCT-1852	Labade	Josephinam	
Reddenton	Antony		15-JAN-1859	Manly	Brigeth	
Rehl	Petrum		24-NOV-1887	Corbeille	Alphonsinam	
Reil	Thos		11-SEP-1859	Fitzeman	Mariam	
Reuny	James	Henry Reuny/—— ——		Hay	Chaberia	Peter Hag/Margaret Murphy
Rhodes	Gulielmum		15-JUL-1902	DuBois Woods	Coram	
Richard	Franciscus		17-APR-1865	Dolan	Celinda	
Richards	Chauncey E.		22-JUN-1898	Lucier	Claram Edessam	
Richie	Guillelmus	Thoma Richie/Emilia A——	27-OCT-1868	Joli	Eusebia	
Richly*	George		03-JUL-1876	Emerson	Maria	
Richtly*	George		03-JUL-1876	Emmerson	Maria	
Ring	Ricardum		15-APR-1898	Moran	Mariam	
Risch	Charles	Peter Risch/Elizabeth Risch	27-SEP-1864	Morning	Marguarita	John Morning/Bridget Morning
Ritchey	Joannes		26-MAY-1861	Griffin	Genovifam	Joannes Griffin/Maria Griffin
Ro-ame	Magloire		23-OCT-1877	Dumund	Maria Adelaine	
Robage	Octavius	Baptista Robage/Magd. Baillargeon	30-MAY-1871	Dupuis	Belonisia	Baptista Dupuis/Clotilda Agagnier
Robert	David	Davidis Robert/Scholastica Chennière	05-JUL-1864	Surprenant	Julia	Ignati Surprenant/Julia Goyet
Robert	Eugenius	Ignatius Robert/Ada Walterstein	15-MAY-1871	Touchete	Virginia	Josephi Touchete/Onesima Vient
Robert	Josephum		25-AUG-1892	Marcoux	Rosaliam	
Robert	Alexandrum		19-JAN-1890	Tessier	Adelam	
Robert	Georgium		18-JUN-1889	Rondeau	Josephinam	
Robert	Cyrillus	Davidis Robert/Scholastica Chennière	12-FEB-1866	Jolin	Lucina Lesima	Michaelis Jolin/Maria Brun
Robert	Franciscum		04-NOV-1885	Balthazar	Marcellinam	
Robidoux	Joannem		28-MAY-1902	Steffes	Catharinam Leona	
Rochel	Guillelmus	Henrici Rochel/Elizabetha Rochel	03-OCT-1861	Lynan	Agnetia	Petri Lynan/Lina Lynan
Rodgers	Felix	Thomas Rodgers/—— Co-om		Dunkin	Catherine	Thomas Dunkin/Bridget ——
Rodwell	Joannem H.		21-JUN-1891	Durocher	Virginiam	
Rohm	Michel		04-JUL-1858	Castello	Julie	
Romach	Henricum	Josephi Romach/Catharina Romach	08-AUG-1861	Sneyder	Annam-Ceciliam-Sybilla	P. Sneyder/C. Sneyder
Ronan	Guielmum H.		12-SEP-1893	Gilman	Luciam	
Rondeau	Andreas	Baptista Rondeau/Julia-Anna Chef	18-NOV-1872	Graton	Albina	Vitalis Graton/Phebé Tremblé
Rondeau	Franciscus	Francisci Rondeau/Eleonora Lépine	30-DEC-1867	Edouin	Octavia	Léonis Edouin/Flavia Moquin
Rondeau	Josephus	Francisci Rondeau/Eleonora Rondeau	06-AUG-1866	Dufresne	Maria	Pascalis Dufresne/Angelica Dufresne
Rondeau	Josephum		10-AUG-1885	Augé	Mariam	
Rondeau*	Franciscus Alvin--		01-JAN-1866	De—	Maria	
Rondeau*	Franciscus Aloida	Francis Rondeau/Christina Rondeau	01-JAN-1866	DesMarais	Maria	Antonii DesMarais/Adel. DesMarais
Rost	Guillelmus	Augusti Rost/Honora Rost	24-JUL-1862	Crins	Anna Marguerita	Petri Crins/Maria-Elizabeth Crins
Roy	Philippum Josephum		03-SEP-1901	Smith	Phoebeam	
Roy	Philippum Josephum		20-JUL-1897	Coon	Edeth Adellam	
Roy	Narcissum Oliverum		21-JUN-1892	Pratte	Malvinam	
Russell	Jacobus			Chresy	Rosa	

Groom's Surname	Groom's Name	Groom's Parents	Date	Bride's Surname	Bride's Name	Bride's Parents
Samuell	Cornelius		11-AUG-1850	Clare	Mary	
Sansal	Jocob		25-SEP-1857	Losselion	Catherina	
Santuaire	Octavus	Michaelis Santuaire/Eliza. Santuaire	12-JAN-1867	Henry	Abigail	Benjamin Henry/Maria-Anna Henry
Sauvé	Paulus	JM Sauvé/Emilia Pilon–Terrebonne	04-FEB-1873	Veine	Maria Marguarita	Francisci Veine/M. Landreman
Sauvé	Stanislaus	Joannis-Marie Sauvé/Elmira P-l-	20-JUL-1869	Joli	Emilia	Caroli Joli/Leucadia Binete
Sauvé	Philemon	Joannis Sauve/Cecilia Pal-man	05-OCT-1867	Bastien	Christina	Andrei Bastien/Magdelena Paquete
Sauvé	Josephum		09-APR-1883	Venne	Elodiam	
Sauvé	Magloire		19-JUN-1877	Vaine	Josephina	
Scannel	Jeriath		24-JAN-1859	Leary	Brigitha	
Schleidan	Gasporus	Petri Schleidan/M-Josepha Neld–	29-APR-1865	Schneider	Anna Sybilla	Petri Schneider/C. Nicholaus-Schnür
Schneider	Petrus	Joannis Schneider/Anna-M Schneider	26-DEC-1861	Mertz	Anna Marie	N. Mertz/M. Mertz
Schuhardt	Ulysses Samuel	A.B. Schuhardt/Amalia Wickert	18-NOV-1920	Mayrand	Virginia	W.-T. Mayrand/Winifred Le-t
Schumacher	Petrum		25-APR-1893	Lyonais	Joannam Adelam	
Scot	James		13-NOV-1859	O'Hara	Ellen	
Secord	Desere		31-JAN-1859	LaPlante	Zoa	
Seggison	Bartolomay		13-APR-1857	Curran	Marian	
Seifert	Stephen		15-APR-1852	Browning	Mary-Ann	
Seligan	Michel		16-MAY-1857	Ragan	Anna	
Senat	Francius		01-JAN-1856	Gibbens	Letia	
Sénécal	Alexandrum	Ovidii Sénécal/Melissa Venne	22-SEP-1909	Holtz	Martha	Caroli Holtz/——
Sénécal	Ovidem		26-DEC-1880	Veine	Maria-Rosam Delima	
Serke	Michel		24-FEB-1857	H--t	Br——	
Serwa	Michael		05-APR-1852	Thelan	Sibelia	
Sévérin	Emilium	Francisci Sévérin/Virginia Rome	22-OCT-1905	Harmer	Myram	Joannis Harmer/Gratia Smith
Shaeffer	Charles		03-SEP-1863	Olinger	Catharina	Nicholai Olinger/Suzanna Olinger
Shea	Josephus	Danielis Shea/Maria Shea	04-OCT-1875	Webbe	Maria	Jacobi Webbe/Joanna Webbe
Sheban	Georgius		22-FEB-1883	Paige	Selina	
Sherburne	Jefferson		22-NOV-1855	Pinguer	Alphonsina	
Sheridan	Barny		31-DEC-1872	Douthy	Maria	
Shields	Robertus	Joannis Shields/Isabella Shields	01-FEB-1859	Bellimeur	Adelaida	Francisci Bellimeur/Maria Bellimeur
Shoemaker	Peter	Mathias Shoemaker/Catherina Smit	21-AUG-1864	Allen	Margeritte	Mathias Allen/Catherina Maci
Shroevan	Joannes	Theodori Shroevan/Marg. Shroevan	16-DEC-1862	Stephans	Maria	Antonii Stephans/Suzanne Stephans
Shümmer	Franciscus	Nicholai Shümmer/Marg. Shümmer	04-APR-1888	Resh	Theresa	Josephi Resh/Theresa Resh
Sibolt	Joannem		25-JAN-1864	Pingair	Josephinam	
Siegler	Fredericus	Joannis Siegler/Bridgitta Siegler	27-APR-1907	Frietag	Anna	Henrici Frietag/Anna-Barb. Frietag
Sizer	Georgium		01-FEB-1859	Balthazar	Esther	Joannis-Bapt. Balthazar/L. Marcoux
Smet	Willian		23-JUN-1903	Lorasay	Anna Maria	
Smet	Fredericum		24-JAN-1859	Paré Perry	Emmam	
Smet	Mathias		20-OCT-1856	Bordman	Mathilde	
Smet	Jorge		20-APR-1857	Digny	Ellis	
Smet	Patrick		11-DEC-1856	Stantan	Anna	
Smet	Jocob		31-MAR-1856	Redmiller	Christina	
Smit	Joannes		24-JAN-1859	Smet	Louisa	
Smit	Joannes		20-OCT-1856	Joannes	Maria	
Smith	Moyses	Benjamin Smit/Juliana Troquet	02-SEP-1867	Bonin	Eloisa	Isaia Bonin/Julianna Ebert
Smith	Michael	Nicholai Smith/Maria Smith	25-AUG-1850	Horne	Marianne	
Smith	Paulus		24-FEB-1862	Perron	Marguarita	Andrea Perron/Maria-Aurelia Perron
Smith	Gulielmum F.		04-JUL-1902	Bird	Josephinam	
Smith	Adam		12-APR-1901	Gagnier	Josephinam	

Groom's Surname	Groom's Name	Groom's Parents	Date	Bride's Surname	Bride's Name	Bride's Parents
Smith	Georgium Joannem		14-JAN-1893	Surprenant	Lisamam	
Snow	Olivarium	Alphonsi Snow/Exilda Tessier	28-AUG-1906	Baillergeon	Phoebeam	Jose. Baillergeon/Jose. Desmarrais
Soike	Albertus	Alberti Soike/Henrietta Kraemer	14-OCT-1908	Gardner	Mable	Pauli Gardner/Josephina Cleffe
Solon	James		08-NOV-1856	Cain	Maria	
Spatore	Petrum Josephum		09-SEP-1895	Scalfe	Mariam	
St Pierre	Moses		05-JUN-1852	Deshenes	Justina	
St. Aubin	Franciscum		16-APR-1884	Allain	Clotildam	
St. Marie	Eugenium		12-JUL-1881	Corbeille	Miriam Delinam	
St. Pierre	Moises		17-MAY-1881	Auger	Georgiana	
St. Pierre	Moise-		17-MAY-1881	Auger	Georgianna	
St.-Antoine	Isaac		30-DEC-1884	LeTourneau	Mariam Joannem	
Stada	Fredericum		08-SEP-1897	Corbeille	Rosinam	
Stada	Frederum Antonium		10-APR-1894	Préfontaine	Josephinam	
Stantan	Patrick		07-NOV-1858	Leon	Louisa	
Starick	Joseph	John Starick/Mary Krall	09-JUN-1920	Young	Margaret	Jerry Young/Levina Balthazor
Stauber	Joannem		27-DEC-1883	LeBeau	Celinam	
Ste.-Marie	Eugerius	Josephi Ste.-Marie/Maria Robidou	31-DEC-1871	Robert	Maria	Francisci Robert/Maria Beaudoin
Stenten	Thamas		09-JAN-1857	Lenschs	Catherina	
Stentons	John		03-APR-1856	Smet	Caroline	
Stenz	Archibald	Augus Stenzt/Helen Braum	06-APR-1920	Boda	Amanda	Louis Boda/Exilda Derwin
Stephani	Joannes	Joannis-Pet. Stephani/Eva Stephani	01-JUL-1866	Ge-er	Agnetia	Stephani Ge-ser/Catharina Ge-ser
Stephans	Joannes	Francisci Stephans/Maria Stephans	02-MAR-1862	Pedlant	Adelina N.	Francisci Pedlant/Josepha Pedlant
Story	Georgium		28-MAR-1853	McCallan	Catherinam	
Strong	Nelson Franciscus	Stephani Strong/Elizabetha Strong	24-MAY-1863	Gauthier	Maria	Ruperti Gauthier/Maria Turcote
Sullivan	Michaelem J.		30-NOV-1897	Sullivan	Elizabetham	
Supple	Mathiam		03-NOV-1886	Charron	Celina	
Surprenant	Carolus	Emer. Surprenant/Soph. Surprenant	03-JUL-1872	Boivin	Héléna	Georgii Boivin/Emilia Boivin
Surprenant	Petrus	Petri Surprenant/Victoria Surprenan	09-JUN-1862	Beaudin	Ludovica	Guillelmi Beaudin/Ludovica Beaudin
Surprenant	Gilbertum		17-SEP-1895	Clare	Jeannettam	
Surprenant	Arthurum		13-MAY-1895	Mike	Emiliam	
Surprenant	Levi		20-OCT-1894	Markoe	Emmam Louisam	
T—-Deroque-Roque	Josephus	Josephi Deroque/Angela T——	20-JUN-1864	Lemaire	Emma	Stephani Lemaire/Sophis Lemaire
Taff	Franciscus		18-FEB-1872	Hurteau	Aurelia	
Tanges	Jacobus	Christophus Tanges/Maria Tanges	06-JAN-1861	Po—ich	Catharina	Josephi Po—ich/M-Josepha Po—ich
Tates	Martinum		24-SEP-1902	Marcoux	Olivinam	
Tautges	Jacob	Joseph Tautges/Wilhelmina Papke	25-JUN-1919	Dufrane	Rachel	Alberti Dufrane/Alesina Bastien
Tell	Michel		04-SEP-1859	Besseler	Francisca	
Tella-	Patrick		03-OCT-1858	Ludigaf	Lady	
Teschendorf	Emilem		18-MAY-1891	Pariseau	Estheam	
Thibodeau	Theophilus	Oliverii Thibodeau/M.-Ludovica Cyr	05-SEP-1865	Goyet	Rosalia	Josephi Goyet/Magdalena Lavallee
Thibodeau	Solomon	Olivieri Thibodeau/—— Thibodeau	07-OCT-1862	Boucher	Lucia	Germain Boucher/Lucia Boucher
Thibodeau	Theophilium		23-SEP-1883	LeMieux	Edwidgem	
Thield	Petrus	Carolus Thield/—— ——	29-OCT-1874	Fa-ied	Anna	
Thornton	Hughius	Jacobi Thornton/Anna Thornton	08-FEB-1862	McCue	Maria	Ewardi McCue/Maria McCue
Thouma	Thomas		04-NOV-1855	Riburnans	Maria	
Tibeaudeau	Oliverius		03-MAR-1861	Petit	Maria	
Touchet	John Fred	John Touchet/Julia Gordon	23-JUN-1920	Lynei	Ruth Eleanor	Ed-C. Lynel/Edith Gosslin
Touchette	Eduardum O.		25-DEC-1902	Roy	Mariam Annam	
Touchette	Oliverum Eduardum		11-SEP-1895	Roy	Mariam Louisam	

154

Groom's Surname	Groom's Name	Groom's Parents	Date	Bride's Surname	Bride's Name	Bride's Parents
Toutand	Alexis	Francisci Toutand/Carlotta Briette	20-APR-1874	LaBarge	Olivina	Francisci LaBarge/Maria Yelle
Tramblé	Alex	Caroli Tramblé/Clementina Faneffe	03-JUN-1879	Edoin	Malonia	Leonis Edouin/Theresia Moquin
Tremblay	Eduardum		18-FEB-1889	Gervais	Arzilinam	
Tremblay	Josephum		01-MAY-1883	DuFrèsne	Adeam	
Tremblé	Cleophi		24-DEC-1876	Bodriau	Maria	
Tremblé	Eduardus	Caroli Tremblé/Phoebé Bissonet	07-APR-1871	Chenar Snow	Emilia	Isadori Chenar/Sophia Cyr
Tremblé	Josephus	Caroli Tremblé/Phoeba Bissonet	11-NOV-1867	LeDuc	Josephine	Huberti LeDuc/Marantia Beaulieu
Tria	Joseph		17-JAN-1856	Yapas	Anna	
Tridénez	Isidorum		19-JUN-1894	LeMouche	Mariam Delphinam	
Trier	Frank	J.-J. Trier/Rosa Sperring	21-AUG-1906	Barbeau	Coram	Petri Barbeau/Exilda Moquin
Trotier	Damascus		23-JAN-1859	Pellant	Philomena	
Trudeau	Zacharias	Ludovici Trudeau/Felicitatis Trudeau	02-JAN-1865	Letourneau	Aurilia	Ch. Letourneau/Anatolia Letourneau
Trudell*	Josephus	Joachim Trudell/Emilia LaJoie	29-JAN-1866	Gauthier	Flavia	Antonii Gauthier/Flavia Robert
Turcote	Eduardus	Davidus Turcote/Sophia Bealieu	25-SEP-1870	Coté	Philomena	Antonii Coté/Marcelina Boisvert
Vain	James		10-MAY-1857	Logan	Annasthsia	
Vandermolem	Hermanum		19-NOV-1902	Landerman	Mariam	
Vanderstein	Carolus	Eduardi Vanderstein/Theresa Pinard	25-SEP-1870	Devillerse	Adelia	Augusti Devillerse/Felicitatis Dor
Vanderstein	Leopolduc	Francis Veine/Marcelina Landreman	31-AUG-1874	Desrochers	Maria Joanna	Adolphi Desrochers/Henrietta Bando
Veine	Eduardus	Agapiti Venne/Flicitatis Contant	31-DEC-1871	Beaupré	Adalia	David Beaupré/Theddista Glandurant
Venne	Ludovicum J.		25-DEC-1901	Lyonais	Henriettam	
Venne	Clovem Arthurum		18-SEP-1895	DuFrèsne	Mariam	
Venne	Aldericum		25-JAN-1887	Fontaine	Olivinam	
Venne	Josephum		17-JAN-1881	LeTourneau	Mariam	
Venns	Julius		19-APR-1875	LeClair	Josephina	
Vernay	Evariste	Joseph Vernay/Maria Prejean		Dufraine	Desanges	Pascal Dufraine/Angelique Coché
Wagner	Joannes Petrus	Petri Wagner/Maria Wagner	06-JUL-1862	Wall	Martha	Guillelmi Wall/Helena Wall
Wagner	Fredericus	Petri Wagner/Maria Wagner	30-SEP-1866	Lohmüller	Maria	Martin Lohmüller/Tharisa Lohmüller
Wagner*	Henricus		29-JAN-1866	Ronndel	Anna	
Wagner*	Henricus	Nicholai Wagner/Maria Taylor	29-JAN-1866	Reindel	Anna	Johannis-Geo. Reindel/Maria Andaly
Wall	Thamas		07-AUG-1859	Rock	Chaterina	
Walther	Julius	Julius Walther/Louisa Walther	15-SEP-1862	O'Hagan	Anna	Patrick O'Hagan/Sara O'Hagan
Walthers	Herman	Julius Walthers/Louisa Walthers	25-DEC-1864	Blosine	Catharina	Mathias Blosine/Elizabeth Blosine
Waltz	Jacobum		13-MAY-1890	Bastien	Eugeniam	
Ward	Thomas		09-FEB-1852	Fergussin	Brigitte	
Ward	Elias		21-NOV-1855	Kenna	Maria	
Warpier	Franciscus		30-APR-1861	Studeur	Maria	
Weber	Peter		01-JUL-1860	Colb	Christina	
Weber	Petrum		14-NOV-1900	Sauvé	Corinam	
Weeks	Hubertus O.		05-JUL-1897	Chagnon	Margerettam	
Weiller	Nicholas		22-JUN-1851	Hennson	Elizabeth	
Wells	Joannem	John Wells/Mary Wells	06-JUN-1905	Freenor	Mariam	Josephi Freenor/Mathilda Fontaine
Wells	John C.	John-M. Wells/Mary Thomas	06-JUN-1905	Freenor	Mayme	Joseph Freenor/Nellie Fontaine
Wertz	Joseph		04-FEB-1856	Cremmer	Marianna	
Westphall	Carolum	Caroli Westphall/Carolina Jotts	28-JUN-1906	Brunet	Rosam	Luca Brunet/——— ———
Wetstein	Franciscus		20-JUL-1860	Jihtnam	Elisabeth	
Wettstein	Michaelum	Adriani Wettstein/Catherina Mauer	09-SEP-1908	Marcoux	Josephina	Alex. Marcoux/Eleonora Lajeunesse
White	Jacobus	Patricii White/Marguarita White	31-MAY-1863	Rodgers	Sarah	Thoma Rodgers/Anna Rodgers
White	Georgius	Joannis White/Elizabetha White	15-JUN-1862	McKeets-Duffy	Anna	Thoma McKeets/Maria McKeets
White	John		04-OCT-1858	White	Margeta	

Groom's Surname	Groom's Name	Groom's Parents	Date	Bride's Surname	Bride's Name	Bride's Parents
Whitmore	Gulielmum		16-JUN-1892	Moquin	Vitalinam	
Wichert	Michaelem		24-OCT-1899	Duroucher	Mariam Vitalam	
Wickert	Franciscum		14-SEP-1891	Durocher	Elizabeth	
Wilcox	Carlus Henricus	Elisha Wilcox/Jane Wilcox	01-OCT-1865	McCarter	Albina	Jacobi McCarter/Suzanna Mo—
Willard	Eugenius M		01-JUN-1881	Dacy	Eleonora	
Willard	Eugenius W.		01-JUN-1881	Dacy	Eleonora	
Willett	Charles E.	Charles Willet/Delia Mangan	08-SEP-1919	Ronan	Lenora	William Ronan/Lucy Tilman
Williams	Benjamin	Evan Williams/Elizabeth Williams	25-JUL-1906	Devillers	Stellam	Emilii Devillers/Maria Laberge
Wilson	Olon		29-NOV-1856	Duffy	Catherina	
Wolete	Hubertus	Ovilié Wolete/Celestina Cyr	20-FEB-1871	LeBeau	Maria	Josephi LeBeau/Adelilna Morrisset
Wood Dubois	Arnold Alexander	Joseph Wood/Cedulia Beaudreault	22-SEP-1920	Balthazar	Marie Mabel	Gulielmo Balthazar/Adea Letourneau
Wright	Josephum Henricum		25-DEC-1885	Gervais	Florentiam	
Zekil	Georgium		02-JUN-1903	Lambert	Josephinam	
Zerringer	Wendelinus	Christiani Zerringer/Sidonia Fishter	08-MAY-1865	Zimmer	Maria	Gottefried Zimmer/Cath Vinande
Zimmerman	Eduardum C.		09-JUN-1903	Balthazar	Emeliam	
Zoelner	Gulielmum		29-MAY-1900	Charron	Leam	

St. Louis Catholic Parish,
Fond du Lac, Wisconsin

Marriages - Index of Brides
1850-1920

Bride's Surname	Bride's Name	Bride's Parents	Date	Groom's Surname	Groom's Name	Groom's Parents
———	Christine		29-JUN-1860	Duynat	Joseph	
———	A.		05-FEB-1866	———*	R.	
———	Mariam Adelam		25-AUG-1897	Bastien	Pacificum	
——eau	Helena	Petri ——eau/Emilia Trahant	17-AUG-1873	Leager	Laurentius Georgius	Joannis Leager/Elizabeth Trahant
——igny	Honora		01-NOV-1856	Flagerty	Brian	
—elinge-	Catherina	P.——elinge-/Esa Gerade		Foung	Joannes	Bartholins Foung/Madalen Dudslind
Abel	Louisam		06-AUG-1898	Landerman	Josephum Maglorium Dalorem	
Abel-Nest	Ellam	Eduardi Nest/Eda Abel	23-DEC-1909	Jarvis Gervais	Leonem	Amabilis Gervais/Philomena Cheffe
Abler	Sofiah		24-JUL-1855	Odentrit	Philipp	John Odentrit/Cath.-Emilie Odentrit
Ackerman	Theresa		06-JAN-1865	Giebel	Wendelinus	
Agagnier	Alphonsina	Huberti Agagnier/Maria Mocquin	05-SEP-1871	Papineau	Oliverius	Francisci Papineau/Anastasia Ganier
Agagnier	Maria Octavia	Huberti Agagnier/Maria Moquin	21-OCT-1867	Parizo	Josephus	Michaelis Parizo/Pelagia Parizo
Akkermann	Caolina		29-OCT-1874	Jocoby	Dominicus	Nicolai Jacobi/——
Albert	Maria-Veronica		14-APR-1860	Monsen	Mathias	
Allain	Clotildam		16-APR-1884	St. Aubin	Franciscum	
Allen	Margeritte	Mathias Allen/Catherina Maci		Shoemaker	Peter	Mathias Shoemaker/Catherina Smit
Anderson	Brigitha		27-NOV-1858	Burch	Jeremias	
Anglois	Adena		03-JUL-1876	LeClair	Jule	
Atkinson	Stellam	Benjamin Atkinson/Angie Desrochers	03-MAR-1906	Brunkhorst	Georgium W.	Gulielmi Brunkhorst/Anna Lang
Atkinson	Maria-Anna	Joannis Atkinson/Anna Atikinson	11-AUG-1861	Murry	Thomas	Joannis Murry/Catharina Murry
Audette LaPointe	Idam		17-OCT-1881	Demers	Franciscum	
Augé	Mariam		10-AUG-1885	Rondeau	Josephum	
Auger	Georgiana		17-MAY-1881	St. Pierre	Moises	
Auger	Georgianna		17-MAY-1881	St. Pierre	Moise-	
B——	Elizabeth		09-APR-1860	Hofmann	Joannes	
B–ddan	Brigit		17-FEB-1852	Dunnevan	Timothy	
B–nnel	Marie		04-OCT-1858	Logelain	Patrick	
Bailargon	Belanise		28-JUL-1878	Gervais	Calese	
Baillergeon	Phoebeam	Jose. Baillergeon/Jose. Desmarrais	28-AUG-1906	Snow	Olivarium	Alphonsi Snow/Exilda Tessier
Balatzar	Rosalia		22-OCT-1876	Jubert	Franciscum	
Balthazar	Rose-Olivine	Julius Balthazar/Marg. Lajeunesse	25-NOV-1920	Fleischman	Leo George	Arthur Fleischman/Emma Wagner
Balthazar	Marie Mabel	Gulielmo Balthazar/Adea Letourneau	22-SEP-1920	Wood Dubois	Arnold Alexander	Joseph Wood/Cedulia Beaudreault
Balthazar	Zoam	Joannis Balthazar/Marie Marcoux	28-NOV-1907	Ouellette	Franciscum	
Balthazar	Esther	Joannis-Bapt. Balthazar/L. Marcoux	27-APR-1907	Sizer	Georgium	
Balthazar	Emeliam		09-JUN-1903	Zimmerman	Eduardum C.	
Balthazar	Juliam		18-DEC-1902	Larson	Josephum Axel	
Balthazar	Agnetam		12-NOV-1902	Flood	Georgium	
Balthazar	Mariam		09-SEP-1902	Hoge	Gustavum	
Balthazar	Idam		20-AUG-1902	Lewis	Josephum C.	
Balthazar	Malvinam		20-APR-1901	Bellmer	Henricum	
Balthazar	Herminiam		23-OCT-1900	Goyette	Alexandrum	
Balthazar	Josephinam		13-JUN-1899	Marcoux	Franciscum	
Balthazar	Julia	Moysis Balthazar/Josepha Leblanc	26-DEC-1860	Baudin	Guillemus	Guill. Baudin/Ludovica Normandais
Balthazar	Sophia	Josephi Balthazar/Sophia Balthazar	18-OCT-1868	Brabant	Josephus	Joseph Brabant/Esthera Brabant
Balthazar	Sophia		24-MAR-1868	Brabant	Josephus	
Balthazar	Olivinam		19-FEB-1889	Lajeunesse	Generosum	
Balthazar	Emeliam		23-NOV-1887	Langlois	Vitalem	
Balthazar	Marcellinam		04-NOV-1885	Robert	Franciscum	
Balthazar	Sophiam	Francisco Pellant/Thoma LePine	14-OCT-1880	Petters	Albertum Emilium	

Bride's Surname	Bride's Name	Bride's Parents	Date	Groom's Surname	Groom's Name	Groom's Parents
Balthazar	Babie	Joseph Balthazar/Sophie Balthazar	29-APR-1879	Gordon	George	Caroli Gorden/Louise Gordon
Balthazar Maraga	Irene	Martin Balthazar/Tarcila Frenet	05-OCT-1920	Kenney	Edward Augustin	Thomas Kenney/Mathilda LaPrairie
Balthazor	Frances	Louis Balthazor/Emiline Roberts	25-FEB-1919	Guyette	Albert	Allen Guyette/Mary Young
Barajohem	Jospehina		22-OCT-1876	Delafontaine	Franciscum	
Barbeau	Coram	Petri Barbeau/Exilda Moquin	21-AUG-1906	Trier	Frank	J.-J. Trier/Rosa Sperring
Barbeau	Melinam		26-SEP-1899	Gagnier	Guilelmo	
Barbeau	Corina		25-JUL-1899	Lambert	Paula	
Barbeau	Sophronia	Petri Barbeau/Marcelina Gervais	21-OCT-1867	Lambert	Michael	Bonaventura Lambert/Maria Denis
Barbeau	Adelam		20-APR-1888	Dion	Michaelem	
Barrett	Silla	Joannis Barrett/Sabina Barrett	07-JUN-1863	Fayly	Thomas	Edwardi Fayly/Maria Fayly
Bassete	Sophia	Xavierii Bassete/Sophia Robert	29-AUG-1870	Leduc	Remigius Oliverius	Josephi Leduc/Marg. Devire-Bundy
Bastien	Mariam Annam		23-OCT-1900	Brucker	Albertum P.	
Bastien	Alexinam		24-NOV-1896	DuFrêsne	Albertum	
Bastien	Christina	Andrei Bastien/Magdelena Paquete	05-OCT-1867	Sauvé	Philemon	Joannis Sauvé/Cecilia Pal-man
Bastien	Melina	Andrea Bastien/Magdelena Paquete	12-AUG-1867	Brunet	Gedeon	Ferdinandi Brunet/Esthera Sovie
Bastien	Eugeniam		13-MAY-1890	Waltz	Jacobum	
Bathazar	Rosalia	Petri Balthazar/Rosalia Desautels	04-JUN-1872	Gayet	Ludovicus	Josephi Gayete/Magdelena LaVallée
Bay	Marg.		05-MAY-1857	McKiver	John	
Bays	Ellisa		26-MAY-1856	Gillan	Christophle	
Bea-mure	Marie		23-OCT-1859	Letourneau	Pascal	
Bearuregard	Melinam		23-JAN-1894	Gervais	Telesporum	
Beaudin	Léna	Guillelmi Beaudin/Ludovica Beaudin	29-AUG-1864	Goyet	Franciscus	Josephi Goyet/Magdalena Goyet
Beaudin	Ludovica	Guillelmi Beaudin/Ludovica Beaudin	09-JUN-1862	Surprenant	Petrus	Petri Surprenant/Victoria Surprenan
Beaudreau	Ermina	Laurentii Beaudreau/Sophia Briand	25-JUN-1907	Bowen	Jacobum	Eduardi Bowen/Anna Caniff
Beaudriau	Pranella	Laur. Beaudriau/Hen. Beaudriau	08-FEB-1864	Florent	Albertus	Ludovici Florent/Scholastica Florent
Beaudriau	Ludovica	Laur. Beaudriau/Harr. Beaudriau	08-JUL-1862	Lyonnais	Comé	Ludovici Lyonnais/Angela Lyonnais
Beaudriaux	Delia		06-APR-1853	Desnoyers	Huberto	
Beaudrieau	Maria Emma	Joseph Beaudrieau/Cor Beaudrieau	13-APR-1868	Paquete	Felix	Petri Paquete/Ludovica Plouf
Beaulleu	Maria		17-JUL-1864	Lepine	Joannes-Baptista-Amatus	
Beaulieux	Clementinam		16-MAY-1853	Danos	Petrum	
Beaumar	Julia		09-OCT-1865	Jolin	Eusebius	
Beaumar	Julia	Abrahami Beaumar/Osite Beaumar	09-OCT-1865	Jolin	Eusebius	Michaelis Jolin/Maria-Rosa Jolin
Beaupré	Adalia	David Beaupré/Theddista Glandurant	31-DEC-1871	Venne	Eduardus	Agapiti Venne/Flicitatis Contant
Beauregard	Mariam		04-JUL-1886	Pratte	Stanislaum	
Begnier-Breau	Sophie		03-MAR-1851	Beaudriau	Laurent	
Belanger	Hermeline		16-SEP-1883	Diette	Narcissum	
Belhumer	---vena		24-OCT-1859	Parriso	---hte	
Belhumur	Edimis	Francois Belhumur/Margerit Fillion		Petit	Joseph	Lambert Petit/Ptalina Brabe
Bellanger	Sophronia	Eusebii Bellanger/Josepha Bellanger	08-OCT-1861	Pariso	Josephus	Michaelis Pariso/Pelagia Pariso
Bellimeur	Adelaida	Francisci Bellimeur/Maria Bellimeur	31-DEC-1872	Shields	Robertus	Joannis Shields/Isabella Shields
Bellimeur	Olivina	Francis Bellimeur/Marg. Bellimeur	03-SEP-1861	Boucher	Germanus	Germani Boucher/Lucia Boucher
Benedict	Mable		26-APR-1905	LeMieux	Anthony	Israel LeMieux/Melina Larose
Benedict	Mable		26-APR-1905	Lemieux	Antonium	Israelis Lemieux/Melina Larose
Bennon	Ellen		19-FEB-1857	Rayly	Own	
Benton	Anne		21-FEB-1857	Rayly	James	
Berg	Mary		19-NOV-1904	Corbeille	Peter H.	
Bernineg	Antoniam		02-AUG-1894	Beaudry	Levi	
Bertrand	Ludovica	Ludovici Bertrand/Julia-A. Bertrand	16-JUN-1867	Leduc	Petrus	Josephi Leduc/Marguarita Leduc
Bérubé	Clarissa	Andrea Bérubé/Mathilda LeMaire	02-SEP-1866	Bertrand	Maximus	Ludovici Bertrand/Amarantha Ebert

160

Bride's Surname	Bride's Name	Bride's Parents	Date	Groom's Surname	Groom's Name	Groom's Parents
Bérubé	Clarissam		13-DEC-1880	Goulet	Ludovicum	
Besnah-Bazinet	Delphinam-Helenam		03-JUN-1897	McCormick	Gulielmum Henricum	
Besseler	Francisca		04-SEP-1859	Tell	Michel	
Bessete	Sophia	Petri Bessete/Sophia Beaulieu	06-JUL-1868	Lyonnais	Edwardus	Ludovici Lyonnais/Angela Camelin
Bessete	Adelida	Petri Bessete/Sophia Beaulieu	21-OCT-1867	Létourneau	Josephus	Petri Létourneau/Lucia Sorel
Bessete	Lucia	Petri Bessete/Sophia Bessete	07-JAN-1867	Lyonnais	Josephus	Antonii Lyonnais/Julia Lyonnais
Bessette	Sophiam Emmam		04-FEB-1882	Bessette	Josephum	
Bibo	Ann		07-FEB-1875	Beaupré	Israel	
Bird	Josephinam		04-JUL-1902	Smith	Gulielmum F.	
Bird	Lucretia	Petri Bird/Emilia Bird-Letourneau	22-JUN-1868	Morrisson	Jacobus	Joannis Morrisson/Maria Morrisson
Bird Oiseau	Delia		17-NOV-1878	Capperon	David	
Bishen	Marguarita	Timothei Bishen/Elizabetha Bishen	12-JUL-1863	Brown	Thomas	Edmundi Brown/Bridgitta Brown
Bisson	Martha	Francisci Bisson/Josephina Bisson	11-MAY-1868	Bird	Carolus	Petri Bird/Emilia Bird
Bissonet	Sophia	Narcissi Bissonet/Marcelina Russeau	25-SEP-1870	Letourneau	Petrus	
Blanchete	Marguarita	Caroli Blanchete/Isabella Blanchete	03-JUN-1867	Desjardins	Josephus	Dom. Desjardins/Sophia Courtemoin
Blosine	Catharina	Mathias Blosine/Elizabeth Blosine	25-DEC-1864	Walthers	Herman	Julius Walthers/Louisa Walthers
Boda	Amanda	Louis Boda/Exilda Derwin	06-APR-1920	Stenz	Archibald	Augus Stenzt/Helen Braum
Boda	Mariam Leonani	Louis Boda/Exilda Derwin	30-SEP-1918	Plugers	Joseph G.	Peter Plugers/Mary Theissen
Bodriau	Maria		24-DEC-1876	Tremblé	Cleophi	
Bodrieau	Orrelia		30-SEP-1877	Marcou	Alexander	
Bodrieaux	Sophiam		09-NOV-1874	Lepin	Josephum	
Boisin	Philomena		27-JUN-1876	Bré	Philipus	
Boivin	Maria	Georgii Boivin/Emilia Boivin	07-SEP-1872	Rabidou	Josephus	Christo Rabidou/Eliza Dugas
Boivin	Hélèna	Georgii Boivin/Emilia Boivin	03-JUL-1872	Suprenant	Carolus	Emer. Surprenant/Soph. Surprenant
Boivin	Aurelia	Antonii Boivin/Amabilis Hurteau	31-DEC-1871	Hassenfuss	Jacobus	Jos. Hassenfuss/Anna-M. Hassenfuss
Bolduc	Salomeam		17-JUN-1893	Duford	Cyrillum	
Bolduc	Emilia	Joannis Bolduc/Lucia Tessier	12-FEB-1872	Fernet	Joannes	Michaelis I. Fernet/Mathilda Hubert
Bonette	Marguarita	Julian Bonette/Marguarite Cyr	11-NOV-1873	Langlois	Edmondus	Jacobi Langlois/Ludovica Huole
Bonin	Delphinam		05-JAN-1897	Lyonnais	Gulielmum	
Bordman	Eloisa	Isaia Bonin/Julianna Ebert	02-SEP-1867	Smit	Moyses	Benjamin Smit/Juliana Troquet
Boroseau	Mathilde		24-JAN-1859	Smet	Mathias	
Bouchar	Maria		11-SEP-1858	Garron	Perre	
Boucher	Josephina	Germain Bouchar/Lucia Petit	26-DEC-1871	Alain	Franciscus	Jacobi Alain/Judith Guenan
Boucher	Lucia	Germain Boucher/Lucia Boucher	07-OCT-1862	Thibodeau	Solomon	Olivieri Thibodeau/—— Thibodeau
Boucher	Eleonora		05-AUG-1902	Devoe	Kelly Eduardum	
Boucher	Josephina		19-AUG-1870	Nelson	Henricus	
Boucher	Georginam		19-JUL-1894	Hoffmann	Robertum Carolum	
Bourdreau	Magdalena	Josephi Bourdeau/Octavia Bourdeau	03-JUL-1870	Joubert	Antonius	Julian Joubert/Ludovica Joubert
Bourassa	Anastasia		31-AUG-1850	Gauthier	Francis	
Boyce	Marguerita	Georgii Boyce/Anna Boyce	27-JUL-1862	Mangan	Jacobus	Michaeli Mangan/——itta Mangan
Brais Leduc	Louisa		13-MAY-1877	DeVine	Jacobus	
Brandt	Mariam	Henrici Brandt/Minnie Beauregard	25-NOV-1908	Czarnezki	Josephium	Laurentii Czarnezki/Susanna Schmitz
Bransheau	Maria Ludovica	Eugenni Bransheau/Maria Disautels	29-JAN-1872	Branchard	Norbertus	JB Branchard/Maria-Clara Primeau
Braun	Ida		24-FEB-1909	Dubois/Alfredum		Joseph Dubois/Cecilia Beaudreau
Bré	Maria	Gilberti-Phillippi Bré/Maria Molheur	01-AUG-1869	Bassete	Josephus	Petri Bassete/Sophia Beaulieu
Brennan	Anna	Timothei Brennan/Maria Connaughty	02-FEB-1862	O'Brien	Patricius	Patricii O'Brien/Maria O'Brien
Briceau	Pliomi		20-OCT-1856	Bisept	Celestine	
Brico	Adelina	Ludovici Brico/Genovefa Brico	01-JUL-1862	Dodelin	Josephus	Oliverii Dodelin/Sophia Dodelin
Brown	Elisabeth		21-JAN-1860	Jenner	Niclaus	

161

Bride's Surname	Bride's Name	Bride's Parents	Date	Groom's Surname	Groom's Name	Groom's Parents
Brown	Catharina	Joannis Brown/Maria Brown	01-NOV-1862	Fitzsimmons	Michael	Mic. Fitzsimmons/Bridg. Fitzsimmons
Brown	Marguarita	Edmundi Brown/Bridgitta Brown	09-MAY-1861	Keyran	Michael	Bernardi Keyran/Elizbeth Keyran
Browning	Mary-Ann		15-APR-1852	Seifert	Stephen	
Bruederle	Junam		12-JUN-1900	Brunet	Adelbertum	
Bruel	Bridgitta		06-JAN-1866	—*—	Petrus	
Brunet	Rosam	Luca Brunet/——	28-JUN-1906	Westphall	Carolum	Caroli Westphall/Carolina Jotts
Brunet	Olimpiam		21-SEP-1902	Herschleb	R. Carolum	
Brunet	Mariam Clotildam Leonam		10-AUG-1898	Corbeille	Josephum Napoleonem	
Brunet	Josephinam		25-NOV-1884	LePine	Thomam	
Bröel	Brigitta	Petri Bröel/Anna Bröel	06-JAN-1866	Kaufman*	Petrus	Nicholai Kaufman/Maria Kaufman
Bullet	Martinam		21-MAY-1859	Langlois	——	
Burnham	Leoniam		29-AUG-1899	Markow	Franciscum Henricum	
Burns	Anna-Nancy	Francisci Burns/Helena Burns	28-OCT-1861	O'Brien	Michael	Jacobi O'Brien/Brigette O'Brien
Büehler	Anna	Joannis Büehler/Catherina Büehler	23-NOV-1862	Hackentolf	Fredericus	Fred. Hackentolf/B—ta Hackentolf
C—ker	Anna	Antonii C—ker/Barbara C—ker	07-JAN-1865	Fleishman	Joannes Martinus	Adami Fleishman/Eliz. Fleishman
Cabar	Messay		20-FEB-1905	Kurmal	Salimam Abo	
Cain	Maria		08-NOV-1856	Solon	James	
Cane	Catharina	Thoma Cane/Helena Cane	28-DEC-1862	Loselion	Joannes	Petri Loselion/Elizabetha Loselion
Cannada	Luca			Jubert	Julien	
Cannada	Margeritham			McGiffirn	Patrick	
Cannada	Maria		05-JUL-1859	Allen	Samuel	
Carbina	Maria		12-APR-1875	Boddit	Josephus	
Cardinal	Mariam Annam	Leonis Cardinal/Rosalia Venne	03-JUN-1908	Kropp	Joannum F.	Francisci Kropp/Catherina Gebel
Carey	Mariam		13-NOV-1895	Buckless	Franciscum A.	
Carley	Evam Beleau		12-SEP-1887	Dumas	Maglorium	
Carrol	Bridgitta	Thomas Carrol/Bridgitta Flanegan	13-JAN-1862	Lamb	Thomas	Jacobi Lamb/Maria Lamb
Cartier	Georgianam		27-JAN-1900	Lyonais	Claudium	
Casey	Maria Joanna		29-MAY-1861	Ganor	Patricius	
Castello	Julie		04-JUL-1858	Rohm	Michel	
Caulfield	Brigitte		21-DEC-1851	Gibbons	John	
Chagnon	Margerettam		05-JUL-1897	Weeks	Hubertus O.	
Charbonneau	Elisam		12-NOV-1890	Breister	Fredericum C.	
Charron	Leam		29-MAY-1900	Zoellner	Gulielmum	
Charron	Emmam		10-SEP-1895	Bessete	Franciscum Xaverium	
Charron	Celina		03-NOV-1886	Supple	Mathiam	
Charron	Olivinam		20-JUL-1886	Gervais	Emericum	
Chef	Philomèna	Petri Chef/Christina Rondeau	07-AUG-1872	Gervais	Amabilis	Callixti Gervais/Saloma Gervais
Chef	Maria-Anna	Petri Chef/Christina Rondeau	29-OCT-1871	Corbell	Hormidas	Josephi Corbeil/Catharina Corbeil
Chef	Maria	Petri Chef/Christina Chef		Page	——	Moysis Page/Cornelia Page
Chenar	Helena	Isidori Chenar/Sophia Chenar	12-JUL-1862	Marcou	Joannes Maria	Joannis-M Marcou/Angela Marcou
Chenar	Julie	Isidori Chenar/Sophia-Sara Chenar	02-MAR-1862	Barrette	Israel	Xavierii Barrette/Sophia Barrette
Chenar Snow	Emilia	Isadori Chenar/Sophia Cyr	07-APR-1871	Tremblé	Eduardus	Caroli Tremblé/Phoebé Bissonet
Chenar Snow	Sophia	Joannis-B. Cyr/Elizabetha Gireau	20-SEP-1870	Bissonet	Narcissus	Francisci Bissonet/Josepha Pinsoneau
Chenard	Sophia	Isidori Chenard/Sophia Chenard	10-FEB-1861	Meunier	Franciscus	Isaaci Meunier/Elizabetha Meunier
Chennire	Sophia	Michaelis Chennire/Maria Filion	22-MAY-1865	Joubert	Xaverius	Juliani Joubert/Ludovica Talon
Choinière	Maria Louisa		14-MAY-1884	Graton	Vitalem	
Chresy	Rosa		25-APR-1853	Russell	Jacobus	
Chríshams	Mariam			Mullen	Michaelem	
Clare	Mary		11-AUG-1850	Samuell	Cornelius	

162

Bride's Surname	Bride's Name	Bride's Parents	Date	Groom's Surname	Groom's Name	Groom's Parents
Clare	Jeannettam		17-SEP-1895	Surprenant	Gilbertum	
Clarke	Elizabeth		20-FEB-1851	Johnson	Bernard	
Clarke	Maria-Anna	Malachia Clarke/Anna Clarke	31-AUG-1863	Cary	Michael	Thoma Cary/Maria Cary
Claury	Marie		03-OCT-1859	Kennedy	Patrick	
Cliche	Mary	Louis Cliche/Delphine Dufresne	01-MAY-1905	LePine	Louis	Joseph LePine/Louise Rondeau
Cliche	Maria	Ludovici Cliche/Delphina Dufrane	01-MAY-1905	Lepine	Ludovicum	Josephi Lepine/Louisa Rondeau
Cliche	Mathilda	Louis Cliche/Delphine Dufresne	28-AUG-1905	Demers	Francis	
Clische	Rosanam		27-SEP-1881	Dupuy	Franciscum	
Closky	Julia	James Closky/Julia Cosgrain	11-MAY-1852	Bergen	Michael	Timothy Bergen/Marguerite Ryan
Coffy	Julie		26-APR-1858	Gay	Thamas	
Coke	Marguarita		08-APR-1861	———	Petrus	
Colb	Christina		01-JUL-1860	Weber	Peter	
Conderon	Theresa		11-NOV-1855	Logelan	William	
Conly	Margeret		09-JUL-1856	Kelly	James	
Connell	Marguarita	Dyonisii Connell/Bridgitta Harlan	20-JUL-1862	Harlan	Jacobus	Joannis Harlan/Rosa Harlan
Conners	Jenna		26-SEP-1858	Calliger	John	
Connor	Maria	Jacobi Connor/Honora Connor	03-DEC-1860	Cavanaugh	Jacobus	Pat. Cavanaugh/Honora Cavanaugh
Coon	Edeth Adellam		20-JUL-1897	Roy	Philippum Josephum	
Corbeille	Amanda	Cyrilli Corbeille/Anastasia Lefort	22-APR-1907	Lépine	Thomasum	Thomas Lépine/Josephina Brunet
Corbeille	Ednam	Napoleonis Corbeille/Melinda Lebeau	06-JUN-1906	Deleers	Alphonsum J.	Josephi Deleers/Maria Debecker
Corbeille	Exildam	Napoleoni Corbeille/Melinda Lebeau	20-FEB-1906	Lentz	Franciscum	Gulielmi Lentz/Maria Hemming
Corbeille	Adelina		30-NOV-1899	Jentz	Franciscum	
Corbeille	Rosinam		08-SEP-1897	Stada	Fredericum	
Corbeille	Alphonsinam		24-NOV-1887	Rehl	Petrum	
Corbeille	Josephinam		13-AUG-1883	LePine	Petrum	
Corbeille	Miriam Delinam		12-JUL-1881	St. Marie	Eugenium	
Corey	Juliana		30-APR-1881	McDonald	Joannem	
Corrigan	Anna		09-DEC-1855	Emerson	Thamas	
Coté	Philomena	Antonii Coté/Marcelina Boisvert	25-SEP-1870	Turcote	Eduardus	Davidus Turcote/Sophia Bealieu
Cousin	Margerita		28-JUN-1857	Cavanaeth	John	
Coyer	Maria		14-APR-1864	Cardinal	Franciscus	
Cremmer	Marianna		04-FEB-1856	Wertz	Joseph	
Crins	Anna Marguerita	Petri Crins/Maria-Elizabeth Crins	24-JUL-1862	Rost	Guillelmus	Augusti Rost/Honora Rost
Crowley	Bridgitta	Mathei Crowley/Helena Crowley	04-MAY-1861	Crowley	Patricius	Jacobi Crowley/Marguarita Crowley
Cudé	Elisath		23-NOV-1856	Glons	Joseph	
Cullen	Margret		03-NOV-1856	McGay	Robert	
Cumminks	Brigitha		14-NOV-1858	Mathius	Charles	
Curan	Maria		11-NOV-1855	Carbet	John	
Curran	Marian		13-APR-1857	Seggison	Bartolomay	
Currans	Catherina		16-APR-1857	McGivern	Hugh	
D'Anneau	Philumenam		26-NOV-1878	Chinard Snow	Ludovicum	
Dacy	Eleonora		01-JUN-1881	Willard	Eugenius M	
Dacy	Eleonora		01-JUN-1881	Willard	Eugenius W.	
Dalony	Sarah	Edwardi Dalony/Maria Dalony	30-AUG-1863	Dun	Guillelmus	Guillelmi Dun/Anna Dun
Dalton	Bridgett		18-FEB-1851	Fitzgerald	Thomas	
Dalton	Marie		29-NOV-1856	Obryan	John	
Dandurand	Theofistam		29-JUN-1885	Bissonnette	Narcissum	
Daugherty	Katerina			Gaigne	Franciscus	
De———	Maria		01-JAN-1866	Rondeau*	Franciscus Alvin—	

163

Bride's Surname	Bride's Name	Bride's Parents	Date	Groom's Surname	Groom's Name	Groom's Parents
Debelin	Ellena		16-JAN-1853	Letourneau	Joannem	
DeBois	Virginia		05-APR-1875	DuBois	Godfroy	
Defraine	Dedine		26-MAY-1856	Deroché	—tasse	
Delajeunesse	Leurda	Henri Delajeunesse/Leonanda Gayet	19-OCT-1874	Marcou	Alexander	Francisci Marcou/Melicia Sir
Delisse	Philomena	Petri Delisse/Maria-Francisca Delisse	06-OCT-1861	Despins	Florimundus	Ignatii Despins/M.-Theresa Despins
Demars	Celina	Amabilis Demars/Maria Demars	29-OCT-1866	Lefort	Narcissus	Caroli LeFort/Angela LeFort
Demers	Octavia	Soloman Demers/Emelia LaGasse	22-JUN-1879	Mass	Ovide	J.B. Mass/Flavia Dugas
Deschênes	Delima		09-APR-1866	LeBrecque	Josephus	Jacobi LeBrecque/Arch. LeBrecque
Deshautels	Olivina	Caroli Desautels/Anastasia Moquin	09-SEP-1867	Fournier	Henricus	Alexii Fournier/Maria P-tr-s
Deshenes	Justina		05-JUN-1852	St Pierre	Moses	
Deshotels	Emma	Caroli Deshotels/Anastasia Moquin	26-APR-1880	Pratt	Theodorus	Josephi Pratt/Heriette Pratt-Laroque
DesMarais	Maria	Antonii DesMarais/Adel. DesMarais	01-JAN-1866	Rondeau*	Franciscus Aloida	Francis Rondeau/Christina Rondeau
Desmarais	Josephinam		07-FEB-1885	Baillargeon	Josephum	
Desmarais-Baillargeon	Josephinam		03-AUG-1904	Balthazar	Joannem Baptistam	
Desnoyer	Hermina	Huberti Desnoyer/Sophis Desnoyer	03-NOV-1862	Lemaire	Petrus	Stephani Lemaire/Sophia Piner
Desrochers	Angie Rosam	Gulielmi Desrochers/Maria Perron	22-SEP-1906	Dalson	Harry Jacobi	Jocobi Dalson/Mellie Richard
Desrochers	Maria Joanna	Adolphi Desrochers/Henrietta Bando	31-AUG-1874	Veine	Leopolduc	Francis Veine/Marcelina Landreman
Desvillers	Helenam		18-AUG-1904	Amel	Eduardum	
Develice	Helen	Adolph Develice/Elizabeth Langteau	21-APR-1920	Lesselyoung	Oscar L.	Henry Lesselyoung/Ida Zille
Devillers	Stellam	Emilii Devillers/Maria Laberge	25-JUL-1906	Williams	Benjamin	Evan Williams/Elizabeth Williams
Devillerse	Adelia	Augusti Devillerse/Felicitatis Dor	25-SEP-1870	Vanderstein	Carolus	Eduardi Vanderstein/Theresa Pinard
Devinun	Marie		16-MAY-1857	Denevan	Michel	
Dewes	Maria	Nicholai Dewes/Catharina Dewes	03-APR-1866	Arimond	Jacobus	Petri Arimond/Judita Arimond
Diedrichs	Annam	Francisci Diedrichs/Anna Diedrichs	08-SEP-1861	Fish	Joannes	Mathei Fish/Magdalena Fish
Diette	Mathilda		20-NOV-1888	Comeau	Medardum	
Diette	Azildam		16-APR-1883	Mengle	Joannem	
Digny	Ellis		20-APR-1857	Smet	Jorge	
Dinelle	Rosannam		04-NOV-1903	Marlow	Gilbertum Josephum	
Dion	Mariam		23-MAY-1899	Kintzler	Henricum G.	
Dion	Mariam			Lamblot	Michaelem	
Dix	Lauram			Larose	Ludovicum	
Dodelin	Philomena	Oliverii Dodelin/Sophia Dodelin	01-DEC-1903	Brico	Ludovicus	Ludovici Brico/Genovefa Brico
Dogerty	Margeta		01-JUL-1862	McTegret	Hueh	
Dolan	Celinda		25-OCT-1857	Richard	Franciscus	
Dollan	Anna		17-APR-1865	Melony	Patrick	
Done	Maria		23-JUL-1856	Moor	Jocobus	
Donet	Emilia	Josephi Donet/Emilia Donet	29-NOV-1856	Alar	Carolus	Georgii Alar/Adelaïda Alar
Donnely	Anne		26-JUN-1868	Farrel	Brian	
Dorethy	Rossa		10-NOV-1851	Galligar	James	
Douthy	Maria		16-OCT-1855	Sheridan	Barny	
Doyle	Ellen		22-NOV-1855	McCabe	Michel	
Duaire	Chaterina		31-OCT-1859	Doune	John	
DuBois	Maria		13-FEB-1858	Marcotte	Leandrum	
DuBois Woods	Coram		18-JUL-1881	Rhodes	Gulielmum	
Duffy	Helena	Jacobi Duffy/Marguarita Duffy	15-JUL-1902	Flood	Thomas	Patricii Flood/Bridgitta Flood
Duffy	Maria	Hughii Duffy/MariaDuffy	26-JUL-1863	Mayer	Edwardus	Malachi Mayer/Catharina Mayer
Duffy	Maria-Anna	Thoma Duffy/Anna McGinty	19-APR-1863	Lucier	Josephus	Ludovici Lucier/Pelagia Regnier
Duffy	Catherina		20-OCT-1872	Wilson	Olon	
Dufort	Carolina		29-NOV-1856	Odete*	Stepharius	

164

Bride's Surname	Bride's Name	Bride's Parents	Date	Groom's Surname	Groom's Name	Groom's Parents
Dufort	Anastasia	Antonii Dufort/Julia Dufort	21-AUG-1864	Corbeil	Cyrillus	Josephi Corbeil/Catharina Corbeil
DuFort	Carolina	Antonii DuFort/Christina Cliché	26-DEC-1865	Odete*	Stephanus	Georgii Odete/Julia Prejean
Dufort	Josephinam		02-AUG-1882	Boivin	Joannem Baptistam	
Dufort	Annie		22-OCT-1878	Dupuis	Onesimi	
Dufraine	Desanges	Pascal Dufraine/Angelique Coché		Vernay	Evariste	Joseph Vernay/Maria Prejean
Dufraine	Adelphe		29-SEP-1859	Clis	Louis	
Dufraine	Maria		11-OCT-1875	Lanto	Judani	
Dufraine	Dematina		02-JAN-1856	DuRoché	Eugene	
Dufrane	Emily	Alberti Dufrane/Alexina Bastien	03-JUL-1920	Fields	Silas	Fred Fields/Laura Haberland
Dufrane	Rachel	Alberti Dufrane/Alesina Bastien	25-JUN-1919	Tautges	Jacob	Joseph Tautges/Wilhelmina Papke
Dufrane	Sarah	Francisci Dufrane/E. Ste.Marie-Defoe	19-JUN-1906	Finnegan	Geraldum	Mathia Finnegan/Julia Crosby
Dufrèsne	Dulima	Petri Dufresne/Onesima Meunier	28-OCT-1872	Cartier	Cleophus	Claudii Cartier/Angela Cartier
Dufrèsne	Agnetam		23-JUN-1896	Bastien	Eugenium	
Dufrèsne	Mariam		18-SEP-1895	Venne	Clovem Arthurum	
DuFrèsne	Martham		03-JUL-1894	Bastien	Wilfredum	
Dufresne	Zoah	Pascalis Dufresne/Angelica Coché	26-NOV-1860	–Ilimeur	Franciscus	Franciscus —Ilimeur/Marg. —Ilimeur
Dufresne	Maria	Pascalis Dufresne/Angelica Dufresne	06-AUG-1866	Rondeau	Josephus	Francisci Rondeau/Eleonora Rondeau
Dufrèsne	Desanges		22-SEP-1887	Clish	Ludovicum	
Dufrèsne	Esther		12-SEP-1887	Grisé	Carolum	
Dufresne	Emma	Francisci Dufresne/——	12-JUN-1887	Maurice	Andreum	
Dufrèsne	Elizabetha		25-DEC-1883	Durocher	Eduardum	
DuFrèsne	Adeam		01-MAY-1883	Tremblay	Josephum	
Dufrèsne	Sophroniam		29-MAR-1883	Marcoux	Napoleonem	
Duley	Elizabetham Ettam		22-OCT-1902	Landreman	Ludovicum	
Duly	Joannam		21-NOV-1852	Doroghty	Patricium	
Dumas	Jana		01-NOV-1865	Lemaire	Josephus	
Dumas	Phi—		04-FEB-1873	Landreman	Josephus	Augustus Landreman/Theresa Joli
Dumas	Eleonora	Josephi Dumas/Dyonisia Duquete	24-JUL-1871	Martin	Leo	Benjamini Martin/Narcissa Dumas
Dumas	Emma	Baptista Dumas/Maria Perron	20-APR-1868	Philips	Ferdinandus	Henrici Philips/Helena Philips
Dumos	Joanna		01-NOV-1865	LeMaire	Josephus	
Dumphy	Anna Marguerita		25-JAN-1858	Cavanagh	Mcl	
Dumund	Maria Adelaine		23-OCT-1877	Ro–ame	Magloire	
Dunkin	Catherine	Thomas Dunkin/Bridget ——		Rodgers	Felix	Thomas Rodgers/—— Co–om
Dunnevin	Mary		06-JAN-1852	Ardle. Richard		
Duprey	Mary-Anna-Agnes-Roselia		13-NOV-1851	McGrath	John–Finly	
Dupuis	Belonisia	Baptista Dupuis/Clotilda Agagnier	30-MAY-1871	Robage	Octavius	Baptista Robage/Magd. Baillargeon
Dupuis	Emma	Eusebi Dupuis/Zoe Moquin	14-JUL-1879	Godin	Calix	Ludovici Godin/Rosalia Marcou
Duquet	Josephinam		28-NOV-1883	Gagnier	Paulum	
Duquette	Matilde		03-NOV-1858	LeDuc	Eduard	
Duquette	Marguerta		27-SEP-1858	Boroseau	Michel	
Duquette	Saram		17-OCT-1881	Pratte	Felicem	
Durand	Hetty		20-OCT-1878	Cassy	William	
Durocher	Angelam Rosam		19-JUN-1886	Atkinson	Benjamin	
Durocher	Elizabeth		14-SEP-1891	Wickert	Franciscum	
Durocher	Virginiam		21-JUN-1891	Rodwell	Joannem H.	
Durocher	Angelam Rosam		19-JUN-1886	Atkinson	Benjamin	
Duroucher	Mariam Vitalam		24-OCT-1899	Wichert	Michaelem	
Duvain	Mathilda		28-JAN-1877	Corbeille	Evarist	
Dwyer	Mariam		10-OCT-1858	Kelly	Joannem	

Bride's Surname	Bride's Name	Bride's Parents	Date	Groom's Surname	Groom's Name	Groom's Parents
Eagan	Maria-Anna	Joannis Eagan/Suzanna Eagan	17-APR-1863	Carney	Jacobus W.	Michaeli Carney/Helena Carney
Ebberling	Lina	Joannes Ebberling/Maria Ge—n		Hippach	Joseph	Joseph Hippach/Catherina Schulder
Ebert	Edmira	Vin—tii Ebert/Marguarita Dupuis		Fournier-Préfontaine	—ins	Bartholomi Fournier/Maria Trudeau
Ebert	Lina	Joannis-Baptista Ebert/Lina Ebert	15-JUN-1864	Bellanger	Petrus	Ludovici Bellanger/M.-A. Bellanger
Ebert	Rosalia	Caroli Ebert/Maria Ebert	31-MAY-1864	Boucher	Octavus	Germani Boucher/Lucia Boucher
Ebert	Maria	Isidori Ebert/Florentia Ebert	31-DEC-1872	Ebert	Napoleo	Davidis Ebert/Matilda Ebert
Ebert	Maria Thersila	Davidis Ebert/Clotilda Ebert	23-JAN-1871	McMullen	Joannes	Guill. McMullen/Maria McMullen
Ebert	Martina	Isidori Ebert/Florentia Ebert	30-OCT-1860	Logan	David	Petri Logan/Francisca Logan
Edoin	Malonia	Leonis Edouin/Theresia Moquin	03-JUN-1879	Tramblé	Alex	Caroli Tramblé/Clementina Faneffe
Edouin	Delima	Léonis Edouin/Flavia Mocquin	01-AUG-1870	LeFève	Camilus	Camili LeFève/Julia LaBarge
Edouin	Octavia	Léonis Edouin/Flavia Moquin	30-DEC-1867	Rondeau	Franciscus	Francisci Rondeau/Eleonora Lépine
Edouin	Exilda	Leonis Edouin/F— Moquin	17-JAN-1880	Raymond	Georgius	Gregorii Raymond/Felicita Raymond
Emerson	Maria		03-JUL-1876	Richly*	George	
Emmerson	Maria		03-JUL-1876	Richly*	George	
Ezel	Elizabeth			Gould	Sylvester	
Fa–ied	Anna		29-OCT-1874	Thield	Petrus	Carolus Thield/—— ——
Falvay	Ellenam		14-NOV-1852	Burke	Thomam	
Faneuf	Tharsila	Alexii Faneuf/Aurelia LeClaire	06-APR-1869	Boucher	Josephus	Francisci-Jos. Boucher/Julia Laduron
Faris	Esther		06-DEC-1904	Job	George August	
Faris	Esther		07-DEC-1904	Job	Augustinum Georgium	
Faucher	Horminia	Ludovici Faucher/Josephina Dagno	23-MAY-1865	Lebeau	Josephus	—ali Lebeau/Marguarita Deble
Fendelin	Maria		02-AUG-1857	Noton	Peter	
Fenet	Alpha	Michaeli Fenet/Mathilda Fenet	19-OCT-1863	Beaudriau	Franciscus Placidus	Laur. Beaudriau/Henrietta Beaudriau
Fergussin	Brigitte		09-FEB-1852	Ward	Thomas	
Fernet	Emilia	Isaïa Fernet/Mathilda Hubert	17-AUG-1869	Rabidou	Moyses	Caroli Rabidou/Elizabetha Edouin
Fernet	Julia Anna	Isaïa Fernet/Mathilda Hubert	17-AUG-1869	Gildus	Hermane	M. Archambeau/J. Archambeau
Field	Purl Inez	Philippi ——/Clara Clainent	13-AUG-1907	Dubois	Elmerum	Josephi Dubois/Cecilia Beaudriard
Fitsjurrall	Marie		20-APR-1856	Flood	John	
Fitzeman	Mariam		11-SEP-1859	Reil	Thos	
Fitzgerald	Juliam		27-NOV-1852	Gr—ng	Jonumiem	
Fitzjurrall	Julie		09-FEB-1856	Crouly	James	
Flagerty	Ellen		13-JUN-1858	Hartnet	John	
Flaharty	Catherine		18-FEB-1851	Dolton	John	
Flanegan	Joanna	Joannis Flanegan/Elizabeth Flanegan	14-MAY-1866	Brown	Petrus	Petri Brown/Sophia Fredet
Flood	Alicia	Timothei Flood/Catharina Flood	18-MAY-1862	Fitzgerald	Patricius	Josephi Fitzgerald/Cath.-Em. Fitzgerald
Flood	Catharinam		02-FEB-1892	Carr	Jacobum W.	
Fontaine	Carolina	Petri-A. Fontaine/Ludovica Fontaine	20-SEP-1863	Despas	Alfredus	Ignatii Despas/Theresa Despas
Fontaine	Ludovica	Mathei Amelançou/Ursula Amelançou	08-OCT-1871	Charete	Joannes-Baptista	Antonii Charete/Emilia Payer
Fontaine	Mariam Deliam		25-JUL-1889	Edoin	Telesporem Vitalem	
Fontaine	Olivinam		25-JAN-1887	Venne	Aldericum	
Fontaine	Agnetam		24-JAN-1883	Maurice	Josephum	
Fox	Catherina		06-JAN-1856	Hammon	Michaelis	
Fox	Barbara	Nicolai Fox/Barbara Miller	21-JAN-1880	Gilmann	Joseph	Thoma Gilmann/Domitilla Graton
Freenor	Mathildam	Josephi Freenor/Nellie Fontaine	17-SEP-1907	Faucher	Arthurium	Alexandri Faucher/Maria Sylvestre
Freenor	Mariam	Josephi Freenor/Mathilda Fontaine	06-JUN-1905	Wells	Joannem	JohnWells/Mary Wells
Freenor	Mayme	Joseph Freenor/Nellie Fontaine	06-JUN-1905	Wells	John C.	John-M. Wells/Mary Thomas
Frego	Cilina		17-SEP-1876	Gagné	Paulus	
Frietag	Anna	Henrici Frietag/Anna-Barb. Frietag	25-JAN-1864	Siegler	Fredericus	Joannis Siegler/Bridgitta Siegler
Fuller	Marguarita	Guillelmi Fuller/Catharina Fuller	10-FEB-1861	Coughlin	Joannes	Patricii Coughlin/Maria Coughlin

166

Bride's Surname	Bride's Name	Bride's Parents	Date	Groom's Surname	Groom's Name	Groom's Parents
Gablar	Mary		13-OCT-1851	Brown	Bernard	
Gagné	Emilia	Eduardi Bonnier/– Gagné	06-JUL-1874	LeFort	Joannis	Caroli LeFort/Angelica –gette
Gagné	Adelina	Pauli Gagné/Clothilda Gagné	01-MAR-1870	Goulet	Ludovicus	Ludovici Goulet/Agnetia Paquete
Gagné	Emilia	Pauli Gagné/Cleotilda Blair	19-JUL-1869	Bernier	Eduardus	Narcissi Bernier/Electram Bernier
Gagnier	Esther Mariam		22-JUN-1904	Kremer	Bertholdum Jacobum	
Gagnier	Josephinam Helenam		26-JUN-1901	Hess	Joannem P.	
Gagnier	Josephinam		12-APR-1901	Smith	Adam	
Gagnier	Melinam		02-OCT-1886	Hicken	Henricum	
Galligar	Elsabuth			Barý	Thamas	
Galligar	Nosa		18-SEP-1856	Mullen	John	
Garden	Maria		16-NOV-1856	Beryan	Michel	
Gardener	Elena		01-OCT-1876	McDormitt	Joannes	
Gardiner	Marguarita		28-APR-1861	Green	Irenus H.	
Gardner	Denora Marie	Alphonse Gardner/Marie Tardif	28-OCT-1919	Martin	Arthus C.	Leon Martin/Lenora Dumas
Gardner	Mable	Pauli Gardner/Josephina Cleffe	14-OCT-1908	Soike	Albertus	Alberti Soike/Henrietta Kraemer
Garo	Adelina	Petri Garo/Clementina Brou	27-DEC-1869	Lucier	Camillus	Ludovici Lucier/Pelagia Laquin
Garo	Suzanna	Petri Garo/Maria Garo	26-DEC-1866	Landri	Josephus	Michaelis Landri/Julia Landri
Garro	Julia	Petri Garro/Clementia Br–	24-MAY-1863	Collin	Octovus	Vincentius Collin/Josepha Ollet
Gau	Cecilia		29-APR-1866	G–	Michael Andrew	
Gauth	E-		29-JAN-1866	–*	Josephus	
Gauthier	Elizabetha		12-MAR-1865	Blondeau	Franciscus	
Gauthier	Maria	Ruperti Gauthier/Maria Turcote	24-MAY-1863	Strong	Nelson Franciscus	Stephani Strong/Elizabetha Strong
Gauthier	Flavia	Antonii Gauthier/Flavia Robert	29-JAN-1866	Trudell*	Josephus	Joachim Trudell/Emilia LaJoie
Gauthier	Angelinam		09-JAN-1882	Langlois	Cyprianum	
Ge-er	Agnetia	Stephani Ge-ser/Catharina Ge-ser	01-JUL-1866	Stephani	Joannes	Joannis-Pet. Stephani/Eva Stephani
Gervais	Josephina	Joan.-Bap. Gervais/Mathilda Gervais	13-JUL-1863	Deschênes	Eugenius	Petri Deschênes/Mag. Deschênes
Gervais	Evam		14-AUG-1900	Kilmer	Gulielmum	
Gervais	Dyonisia	Narcissi Gervais/Adela Barbeau	26-SEP-1869	Ginel	Ludovicus	Ludovici Genel/Maria Grou
Gervais	Arzilinam		18-FEB-1889	Tremblay	Eduardum	
Gervais	Florentiam		25-DEC-1885	Wright	Josephum Henricum	
Gervais	Malvina		05-MAY-1883	Barbeau	Ludovicum	
Gibben	Anna		14-JUL-1856	McGree	Petrus	
Gibbens	Letia		01-JAN-1856	Senat	Francius	
Gill	Anna		07-SEP-1856	McNiclus	John	
Gilman	Luciam		12-SEP-1893	Ronan	Guielmum H.	
Gilmen	Matildam		11-APR-1887	Ransom	Arthur E.	
Glenan	Maria	Luke Glenan/Maria Glenan	06-SEP-1863	Carney	Jacobus	Michaelis Carney/Maria Carney
Glese–	Anna Maria		21-NOV-1858	Bensinger	Michel	
Gosh	Fern Hermine	Hermin Gosh/Hermina Lesage	25-NOV-1919	Costas	Samuel	George Costas/Lulla Manzy
Gosselain	Lina			Lonner	Jacobus	
Gosselain	Edessam		27-JAN-1885	Lyonais	Cosmam Edw.	
Gosselin	Franciscam		23-NOV-1887	Langlois	Cesarium	
Gothié	Lucia		18-SEP-1876	LePine	Franciscus	
Gothier	Emma		30-MAR-1875	LePine	Josephus	
Gough	Maria	Joannis Gough/Anna Gough	25-DEC-1862	Fenelon	Daniel	Joannis Fenelon/Marguarita Fenelon
Gough	Marguarita	Joannis Gough/Anna Gough	23-NOV-1862	Malone	Petrus	Martini Malone/Elizabetha Malone
Goulin	Ludovica	Ludovici Goulin/Agnetia Paquet	14-SEP-1869	Brausseau	Joannes	Joannis-B. Brausseau/Thersila Bigras
Goyet	Rosalia	Josephi Goyet/Magdalena Lavallee	05-SEP-1865	Thibodeau	Theophilus	Oliverii Thibodeau/M.-Ludovica Cyr
Goyet	Marguarita	Josephi Goyet/Magdalena Goyet		Balthazar	Josephum	Michaelis Balthazar/Rosalia Balthazar

Bride's Surname	Bride's Name	Bride's Parents	Date	Groom's Surname	Groom's Name	Groom's Parents
Graham	Catharina	Allen Graham/Bridgitta Graham	22-NOV-1863	Dunn	Jacobi	Guillelmi Dunn/Anna Dunn
Graton	Sophia	Vitalis Graton/Phebé Tremblé	27-SEP-1873	Pomainville	Michael	Mich. Pomainville/Sophia Desjardins
Graton	Albina	Vitalis Graton/Phebé Tremblé	18-NOV-1872	Rondeau	Andreas	Baptista Rondeau/Julia-Anna Chef
Gratton	Mariam		25-NOV-1890	Evans	Guilelmum L.	
Gratton	Juliam		26-NOV-1882	Lajeunesse	Josephum	
Griffin	Genovifam	Joannes Griffin/Maria Griffin	26-MAY-1861	Ritchey	Joannes	
Grizet	Maria	Antonii Grizet/Clotilda Grizet	24-NOV-1862	Pariso	Georgius	Michaelis Pariso/Pelagia Pariso
Grizet	Virginia	Antonii Grizet/Clotilda Guerin	30-SEP-1860	Gervais, Isaacus		Pauli Gervais/Marguerita Gerville
Grogeon	Rosanna		04-JUL-1858	McCabe	Richard	
Gursin-Mayfort	Marie	——Margr———		Mctetevy	James	Francis McTetevy/Margit -whnn——
H——y	Brigitte		10-OCT-1851	Gallagher	John	
H——t	Br——		24-FEB-1857	Serke	Michel	
Haas	Elizabetha	F. Haas/Catharina Haas	15-AUG-1864	Korer	Edmundus	Huberti Korer/Mari-Francisca Korer
Hagerty	Marguarita	Caroli Hagerty/Honora Hagerty	15-NOV-1863	O'Brien	Jacobi	Thoma O'Brien/Catharina O'Brien
Hain	Catharina		13-MAY-1857	Hayes	John	
Hall	Anna-Cecilia	Guillelmi Hall/Anna-Catharina Hall	15-JAN-1863	Dreikosen	Joannes Leonardus	Petri Dreikosen/Magdalena Dreikosen
Hanegan	Helena	Patricii Hanegan/Julia Hanegan	27-JUL-1862	Lamb	Petrus	Jacobi Lamb/Bridgitta Lamb
Hansel	Reginam		03-JAN-1893	Cooper	Eduardum Franciscum	
Hardel	Catharina		13-AUG-1876	Fraem	Josephus	
Hardgrove	Margeret	Henny Hardgrove/Maria Kind		Cavenach	Daniel	James Cavenach/Ellen Cogilan
Harkan	Joanna	Bernardi Harkan/Marguerita Harkan	26-NOV-1860	Galavan	Jeramias	Bernardi Galavan/Anna Galavan
Harkens	Ruth		07-NOV-1858	McManniker	Nick	
Harmer	Myram	Joannis Harmer/Gratia Smith	22-OCT-1905	Sévérin	Emilium	Francisci Sévérin/Virginia Rome
Harnois	Adé		21-MAY-1878	Ogé	Andreas	
Hart-isen	Clementina	Josephi Hart-isen/Carola Hart-isen	26-JAN-1861	Krëmmer	Nicholaus	Hub. Krëmmer/Veronica Krëmmer
Haverty	Maria	Martini Haverty/Maria Haverty	09-MAY-1861	Neilan	Thomas	Joannes Neilan/Maria Neilan
Hay	Chaberia	Peter Hag/Margaret Murphy		Reuny	James	Henry Reuny/——— ——
Hebbet	Masseline		13-OCT-1856	Pariseau	Michel	
Hébert	Felicité		13-JUL-1877	Meunier	Nazaire	
Hegarty	Anna		20-OCT-1858	O'Kleff	John	
Hemmer	Maria-Anna	Caroli Hemmer/Ludovica Hemmer	27-SEP-1866	Neisor	Henricus	Eberhardi Neisor/Agnetia Neisor
Henger	Mariam Josephinam	Joan. Henger/M.Elizabeth Zichtinger	26-JUN-1865	Coulomb	Marsellum	Ambrosium Coulomb/Maria C—et
Hennigan	Maria		23-JUN-1857	Holly	Danniel	
Hennis	Catharina		02-JUN-1861	Fitz-Henry	Thomas	
Henson	Elizabeth		22-JUN-1851	Weiller	Nicholas	
Henry	Abigall	Benjamin Henry/Maria-Anna Henry	12-JAN-1867	Santuaire	Octavus	Michaelis Santuaire/Eliza. Santuaire
Henzler	Maria-Josephine	Joan. Henzler/M.Elizabeth Lichtinger	29-JUN-1865	Coulomb	Marcellus	——— Coulomb/Maria Coulet
Hiback	Anna Ludovica	Francisci Hiback/Regina Hiback	05-JUL-1866	Fox	Sebastian	Henrici-Petri Fox/Anna-Maria Fox
Hiers	Chaterina		18-NOV-1856	Cherzinger	Germain	
Hiers	Maria		31-OCT-1856	Annen	Antoine	
Higgens	Maria		04-APR-1858	Mathews	James	
Hoegen	Marie		24-FEB-1857	Rayly	Patrick	
Hogan	Maria	Michaelis Hogan/Maria Hogan	10-NOV-1861	Leonard	Petrus	M. Leonard/Brigitta Clark
Holtz	Annam	Oscari Holtz/—— ——	19-JUL-1910	Martin	Napoleonum L.	Leonis Martin/Eleonora Dumas
Holtz	Martha	Caroli Holtz/—— ——	22-SEP-1909	Sénécal	Alexandrum	Ovidii Sénécal/Melissa Venne
Holz	Lizzie	Oscari Holz/—— ——		Durocher	Isadorum	Francisci Durocher/Sophie Pellant
Hopp	Annam	Andrea Hopp/—— ——	14-APR-1910	Corbeille	Norbertum	Napoleonis Corbeille/Melinda Lebeau
Horne	Marianne		25-AUG-1850	Smith	Michael	
Houssois	Adelaida	Josephi Houssois/M.Theresa Houssois	29-SEP-1861	Lorge	Franciscus	Francisci Lorge/M.Catharina Lorge

Bride's Surname	Bride's Name	Bride's Parents	Date	Groom's Surname	Groom's Name	Groom's Parents
Hubert	Emilie		14-FEB-1858	Baret	Eduard	
Hueh	Anna		02-MAY-1856	Nelly	John	
Hurteau	Margaret	John Hurteau/Mary Turcotte	21-APR-1920	Lee	Emory	Ellery Lee/Esther Wilson
Hurteau	Aurelia		18-FEB-1872	Taff	Franciscus	
Hurto	Margereth		07-JAN-1878	Dumund	Israel	
Jarvis	Dora	Emery Jarvis/Levina Sharron	01-MAY-1920	Fitzgerald	Clarence Martin	Wm Fitzgerald./Nellie Martin
Jihtnam	Elisabeth		20-JUL-1860	Wetstein	Franciscus	
Joannes	Maria		20-OCT-1856	Smit	Joannes	
Johnson	Josephinam		10-NOV-1896	Daniel	Carolum	
Joli	Emilia	Caroli Joli/Leucadia Binete	20-JUL-1869	Sauvé	Stanislaus	Joannis-Marie Sauvé/Elmira P-l–
Joli	Eusebia		27-OCT-1868	Richie	Guillelmus	Thoma Richie/Emilia A––
Jolin	Lucina Lesima	Michaelis Jolin/Maria Brun	12-FEB-1866	Robert	Cyrillus	Davidis Robert/Scholastica Chennière
Jolly	Eudoxie	Caroli Jolly/Claudia Binnet	05-JUN-1879	Bonnet	Lucus	Ferdinand Bonnet/Esther Sauvé
Joubert	Idessa	Juliani Joubert/Ludovica Joubert	16-JUN-1863	Beaudin	Carolus	Jacobi Beaudin/Ludovica Beaudin
Joubert	Ludovica	Juliani Joubert/Ludovica Joubert	16-JUN-1863	Beaudin	Julianus	Jacobi Beaudin/Ludovica Beaudin
Joubert	Idalia	Julien Joubert/Ludovica Joubert	04-JUL-1861	Desrochers	Leo	Alex. Desrochers/Josepha Desrochers
Joubert	Josephina	Juliani Joubert/Ludovica Joubert	22-JUL-1867	Martin	Xavieri	Joannis Martin/Henrica Carmel
Jubert	Elisabeth			Lefeve	Elia-ar	
Jubert	L–id–		18-JUL-1857	Losson	F––	
Junsh	Maria		19-AUG-1860	––––	James	
Kalile	Mariam		02-JUN-1902	Faris	Sheker	
Karney	Mary	William Karney/Ann McCarl		Burk	William	Thomas Burk/Catherine Daughaney
Kavel	Amanda		11-DEC-1897	Lyonais	Josephi Walter	
Keblier	Mary		26-JUN-1859	Milette	Ulric	
Kelly	Marry			McGinny	James	
Kelly	Bridgitta	Joannis Kelly/Joanna Kelly	27-AUG-1862	Horicans	Joannes	Bernardi Horicans/Marg. Hofferty
Kelly	Katerina		07-MAY-1857	Burns	James	
Kenna	Maria		21-NOV-1855	Ward	Elias	
Kerry	Maria	Joannis-Henrici Kerry/Julia Kerry	18-OCT-1863	Breslahan	Carolus	Patricii Breslahan/Cath. Breslahan
Kerry	Catherina		31-AUG-1855	Hamilton	Michaelis	
Kief	Catherinam		19-JUN-1853	Hoag	Joannem	
Kinney	Mariam Josephinam		28-MAY-1902	Corbeille	Fredericum Moisen	
Kinnison	Mary		02-NOV-1850	Manali–	John	
Kraemer	Marguarita	Petri Kraemer/Eva Kraemer	12-OCT-1863	Gores	Joannes Hubertus	Joannis Gores/Maria Gores
Kramer	Catherinam		05-MAY-1886	Lomblat	Josephum	
Kramer	Catharina		05-MAY-1886	Lomblat	Josephum	
Krauss	Anna-Mariam		21-SEP-1852	Glazer	Petrum	
Krembs	Anna	Antonii Krembs/Ludovica Krembs	01-JUN-1864	Horicans	Carolus	
L'Eno––––	Julie		28-AUG-1857	Bonnet	Eduard	
L'Epine	Malvina	Ludovici L'Epine/Adelina L'Epine	28-OCT-1879	LaPorte	Napoleon	Leonis LaPorte/Zoe Bernard
Labade	Josephinam		17-OCT-1852	Reau	Leonem	
LaBarge	Olivina	Francisci LaBarge/Maria Yelle	20-APR-1874	Toutand	Alexis	Francisci Toutand/Carlotta Briette
LaBarge	Albina	Francis LeBarge/Maria Telly	15-JUN-1879	Dupuis	Onesime	Joh.-Bapt. Dupuis/Clotilde Eugéner
LaBerge	Alphonsina		22-NOV-1880	Pellant	Adolphum Napoleonem	
Lajeunesse	Levina	Gen. Lajeunesse/Levina Balthazar	24-FEB-1909	Herrig	Petrum	Henrici Herrig/Anna Brincus
Lajeunesse	Emeliam		19-FEB-1889	Ouellette	Alexium	
Lajeunesse	Amelia		31-DEC-1877	Gaŷet	Alexander	
Lambert	Valedam	Michael Lambert/Sophronia Barbeau	28-NOV-1906	Ketchens	Joannum	Thomas Ketchens/Louisa Faber
Lambert	Anna	Michael Lambert/Sophronie Barbeau	22-FEB-1905	Collett	Samuel	

Bride's Surname	Bride's Name	Bride's Parents	Date	Groom's Surname	Groom's Name	Groom's Parents
Lambert	Josephinam		02-JUN-1903	Zekil	Georgium	
Lambert	Mariam Dinam		25-NOV-1896	Powers	Arthurum	
Lambert	Annam	Michael Lambert/Sophronia Barbeau	23-FEB-1905	Collett	Samuelem	Samuelis Collette/——
Lamblot	Flora	Constantine Lamblot/Rosalia Davilas		Benzer	Carolus	Caroli Benzer/Lina Benzer
Lanctot	Eliza	—aire Lanctot/Olivine Laberge	17-MAY-1905	Devillers	Theodore	August Devillers/Felicity Doré
Lanctot-Devillers	Alphonsinan		12-MAY-1905	Devillers	Theophilum	
Landerman	Mariam		19-NOV-1902	Vandermolem	Hermanum	
Landermann	Philomenam		31-MAY-1881	LePine	Franciscum	
Landermann	Philumenam		31-MAY-1881	LePine	Franciscum	
Landermann	Romella	Augustini Landermann/Ther-Joly	27-APR-1879	Goulet	Louis	Joseph Goulet/Maria Réneau
Landreman	Maria	Augustini Landreman/Theresia Joli	06-JUL-1869	Molheur	Germanus	Ludovici Molheur/Felicitatus Cyr
Landreman	Martha	Leandri Landreman/Aurelia Molheur	06-JUL-1869	Langlois	Josephus	Nazarii Langlois/Matilda Langlois
Landreman	Aurilie		29-SEP-1878	Bayargon	Josephus	
Landry	Leocadiam		28-OCT-1893	Belanger	Petrum	
Langlois	Zoeh	Vitali Langlois/Flavia Langlois	25-JUN-1872	LeFève	Israel	Augustini LeFève/Emilia LeFève
Langlois	Mathildam		21-OCT-1895	Coon	Carolum Greff	
Langlois	Marie		08-SEP-1856	Houle	Etienne	
Lapine	Cecile Elodie Gladys	Joseph Lapine/Sophie Beaudreault	24-NOV-1920	Jantz (Jorgenson)	Les	John Jantz/Pauline Zarnetski
LaPlante	Zoa		31-JAN-1859	Secord	Desere	
Larkin	Elizabetha	Danielis Larkin/Maria Larkin	28-DEC-1862	Carroll	Daniel	Thoma Carroll/Bridgitta Carroll
Lawlor	Maria	Joannis Lawlor/Marguarita Lawlor	06-APR-1863	Milady	Robertus	Richardi Milady/Julia Milady
Leary	Brigitha		24-JAN-1859	Scannel	Jeriath	
LeBeau	Melinda	Moysis LeBeau/Angela Miricier	22-JUL-1872	Corbeil	Zoticus	Josephi Corbeil/Catharina Couyé
LeBeau	Maria	Josephi LeBeau/Adelina Morrisset	20-FEB-1871	Wolete	Hubertus	Ovilié Wolete/Celestina Cyr
LeBeau	Georginam		24-JUL-1890	LeBlanc	Henricum	
LeBeau	Emeliam		29-JUN-1896	Balthazar	Joannem Baptistam	
LeBeau	Josephinam		09-JUN-1896	Marcoux	Joannem	
LeBeau	Delinam		19-JUN-1895	Brunet	Josephum Axilum	
LeBeau	Heloisam		18-FEB-1890	DuFrêsne	Sephanum	
LeBeau	Olivinam		21-NOV-1887	Conaboy	Michaelem	
LeBeau	Celinam		27-DEC-1883	Stauber	Joannem	
LeBeau	Rosanam		23-OCT-1882	Lajeunesse	Michaelem	
LeBerge	Jorissa		16-AUG-1875	Joly	Carolus	
LeClair	Josephina		19-APR-1875	Venns	Julius	
LeClerc	Eudalia	Eusebii LeClerc/Clarissa Bérubé	29-DEC-1872	Bertrand	Joannes Napoléon	Ludovici Bertrand/Merantha Ebert
LeClerc	Adelina	Gilberti LeClerc/Adelina Gagnier	21-AUG-1870	Painguère	Josephus	M.-J Painguère/M.-Josepha Sti-man
Lécuyer	Josephina	Noeli Lécuyer/Leucadia Lécuyer	03-JUL-1865	Gervais	Ludovicus	Joan.-Bap. Gervais/Mathilda Leclaire
Lécuyer	Helena	Noeli Lécuyer/Eleonora —e-er	03-AUG-1862	Lemaire	Josephus	Jul.-Steph. Lemaire/Sophia Lemaire
Lécuyer	Rosalia	Petri Lécuyer/Marguarita Lécuyer	20-OCT-1861	Garro	Petrus	Petri Garro/Marguarita Garro
Lécuyer	Aurelia M.		17-JUN-1867	Gordon	Joseph H.	
Leduc	Maria		30-OCT-1865	Lyonnis	Narcissus	
Leduc	Delima		10-OCT-1876	Leduc	Ceril	
Leduc	Delphine		29-NOV-1874	Errand	Alex	
Leduc	Elizabetha	Hilarii Leduc/Julia Leduc	03-JUL-1870	Gosselin	Georgius	Joannis Gosselin/Eliza.-C. Gosselin
Leduc	Philomena	Josephi Leduc/Marg. Dwire-Bundig	14-SEP-1869	Chagnion	Elias	Caroli Chagnion/Josephina Mitote
LeDuc	M. Luc		29-AUG-1858	LeBlanc	August	
LeDuc	Matilde		11-JUN-1857	Lacause	Ferdinand	
LeDuc	Josephine	Huberti LeDuc/Marantia Beaulieu	11-NOV-1867	Tremblé	Josephus	Caroli Tremblé/Phoeba Bissonet
LeDuc	Maria	Hilarii LeDuc/Julia Beaudrieau	30-OCT-1865	Lyonnais	Narcissus	Ludovici Lyonnais/Angelica Hamelin

Bride's Surname	Bride's Name	Bride's Parents	Date	Groom's Surname	Groom's Name	Groom's Parents
Leduc	Mariam Louisam		11-JAN-1881	Mangin	Ludovicum Lafayette	
Leduc	Julia	Joseph Leduc/Marguarita Bondi	07-JAN-1880	Marcou	Augustinus	Joannis-M Marcou/Matilde Tremblay
Leduc	Lucia		08-OCT-1877	Lajeunesse	Henricus	
LeFaure	Maria	J.B. LeFaure/Edmire Rondeau	13-JUL-1879	Mensted	Carolus	Joannis Mensted/Maria Christenson
LeFève	Olivia	Eduardi LeFève/Josephina Deneau	15-APR-1872	Lyonnais	Fredericus	Ludovici Lyonnais/Angela Comelin
Lefort	Maria	Caroli LeFort/Adelaida Lepine	31-DEC-1871	Bisson	Ludovicus	Francisci Bisson/Josephina Lévèque
Lefort	Carolina	Caroli LeFort/Angela LeFort	10-APR-1866	Lécuyer	Petrus	Petri Lécuyer/Leucadia Lécuyer
Lejeunesse	Marguaritam		08-NOV-1887	Balthazar	Julianum	
Lemaire	Emma	Stephani Lemaire/Sophis Lemaire	20-JUN-1864	T——Deroque-Roque	Josephus	Josephi Deroque/Angela T——
LeMaire	Virginia	Stephanii LeMaire/Sophia LeMaire	04-JUL-1866	Lisson	Jacobus	Gulielmi Lisson/Marguarita Lisson
Lemieux	Leam	Israelis Lemieux/Melina Larose	14-OCT-1905	Bellmer	Giuliolmum	J Bellmer./S. Dufresne
LeMieux	Héléna	Petri LeMieux/Maria Samson	18-AUG-1872	Fournier	Vitalis	B—— Fournier/Aurelia Trudeau
LeMieux	Delphinam		25-AUG-1903	Auchue	Alfredum	
LeMieux	Ezildam		15-JAN-1902	Beaudeault	Asa C.	
LeMieux	Edwidgem		23-SEP-1883	Thibodeau	Theophilium	
LeMouche	Mariam Delphinam		19-JUN-1894	Tridénez	Isidorum	
Leng	Winni		31-MAR-1856	Crain	Michel	
Lenschs	Catherina		09-JAN-1857	Stenten	Thamas	
Leon	Louisa		07-NOV-1858	Stantan	Patrick	
Leonard	Joanna		11-APR-1856	Nenlon	John	
LePage	Adelina	Moysis LePage/Clotilda N——	17-MAY-1871	Lucier	Baptista	Caroli Lucier/Rosalia Lucier
Lépine	Marguarita		20-NOV-1865	Dufresne*	Noël	
Lepine	Lucretiam	Josephi Lépine/Sophie Beaudreau	21-APR-1909	Donovan	Joannum	Richardi Donovan/Marg. Cummins
Lépine	Mariam	Josephi Lépine/Sophia Beaudreau	21-AUG-1907	King	Joannium	Francisci King/Anna Solael
Lepine	Aureliam		19-JAN-1886	Gratton	Josephum	
LéPine	Ettam		14-FEB-1901	Chaperon	Davidem Edmundum	
LéPine	Eleonoram		17-APR-1888	Paradis	Davidem	
LePine	Marguarita	Josephus LePine/Elizabetha Bordeau	21-NOV-1865	Dufresne*	Noel	Pascalis Dufresne/Angela Caye-
LéPine	Aureliam		19-JAN-1886	Gratton	Josephum	
LéPine	Josephinam		02-JAN-1882	Boyer	Carolum	
LéPine	Isabellam		05-JUL-1881	Gratton	Moisen	
Lery	Mary		25-NOV-1850	O'Brien	James	
Letourneau	Aurlia	Ch. Letourneau/Anatolia Letourneau	02-JAN-1865	Trudeau	Zacharias	Ludovici Trudeau/Felicitatis Trudeau
Letourneau	Mathildam		07-JUN-1881	Letourneau	Josephum	
LéTourneau	Philomena	Petri LéTourneau/Lucia Sorele	30-JAN-1872	Pellant	Franciscus Xavierius	Francisci Pellant/Josepha Faucher
LéTourneau	Floram		07-NOV-1899	Balthazar	Josephum	
LéTourneau	Adam Agnetam		13-NOV-1894	Balthazar	Gulielmum	
LéTourneau	Edassam		07-NOV-1893	Diette	Alfredum	
LéTourneau	Adelam Josephnam		14-JUN-1892	Patt	Ferdinandum	
LeTourneau	Elisam		08-NOV-1887	Diette	Josephum	
LeTourneau	Mariam Joannem		30-DEC-1884	St-Antoine	Isaac	
Letourneau	Mathildam		07-JUN-1881	Letourneau	Josephum	
LeTourneau	Mariam		17-JAN-1881	Venne	Josephum	
Leturneau	Anne		23-OCT-1859	Demers	Juber–	
Liecks	Catherina		28-OCT-1856	Hanniker	Joannes	
Lines	--aty		23-JUN-1884	Dumas	J.B.	
Linschs	Margeta		31-JAN-1858	Kelly	Patrick	
Linscott	Mariam Philumenam		21-DEC-1893	Pierron	Joannem Carolum	
Lintz	Maria	Hectoris Lintz/Catharina Lintz	03-SEP-1865	Hamelonzon	Carolus	Fra. Hamelonzon/Anna Hamelonzon

171

Bride's Surname	Bride's Name	Bride's Parents	Date	Groom's Surname	Groom's Name	Groom's Parents
Linz	Rosa	Georgii Linz/Maria Linz	25-OCT-1871	Boutet	Josephus	Petri-S. Boutet/M-Magdelena Toutan
Logan	Annasthsia		10-MAY-1857	Vain	James	
Logelan	Ellen		29-NOV-1855	Devan	John	
Lohmüller	Maria	Martin Lohmüller/Tharisa Lohmüller	30-SEP-1866	Wagner	Fredericus	Petri Wagner/Maria Wagner
Loiseau	Julia	Petri Loiseau/Emilia Loiseau	30-JUL-1866	Bisson	Martinus	Francisci Bisson/Josephina Bisson
Loiseau Bird	Maria	Francisci Loiseau/Emilia Loiseau	31-DEC-1871	Bisson	Franciscus Xaverius	Francisci Bisson/Josephina Léveque
Lomery	Maria	Guillelmi Lomery/Catharina Lomery	18-MAY-1862	Darigon	Patricius	Hughii Darigon/Joanna Darigon
Lorasay	Anna Maria		01-FEB-1859	Smet	Willian	
Loselion	Clara	Nicholai Loselion/Catharina Loselion	09-JUN-1862	Estrecher	Petrus	Caroli Estrecher/Maria Estrecher
Losselion	Catherina		25-SEP-1857	Sansal	Jacob	
Loussele	Philome		25-DEC-1876	Moquin	Narsis	
Lucier	Claram Edessam		22-JUN-1898	Richards	Chauncey E.	
Lucier	Mariam Mabel		15-SEP-1896	Beaudin	Joannem Baptistam	
Lucier	Sophronia	Ludovicus Lucier/Maria ——	03-SEP-1866	Laing	Alexander	Jacobi Laing/Maria ——
Ludigaf	Lady		03-OCT-1858	Tella-	Patrick	
Lunim	Elizam		18-JAN-1853	Morgan	Michaelem	
Lynan	Agnetia	Petri Lynan/Lina Lynan	03-OCT-1861	Rochel	Guillelmus	Henrici Rochel/Elizabetha Rochel
Lynch	Helena	Josephi Lynch/Julia Lynch	13-DEC-1860	Henchy	Patricius	Michaelis Henchy/Maria Henchy
Lynei	Ruth Eleanor	Ed-C. Lynei/Edith Gosslin	23-JUN-1920	Touchet	John Fred	John Touchet/Julia Gordon
Lyonais	Henriettam		25-DEC-1901	Venne	Ludovicum J.	
Lyonais	Joannam Adelam		25-APR-1893	Schumacher	Petrum	
Lyons	Eliz-Maria		19-FEB-1858	Managan	Michel	
Mack	Catharina		18-SEP-1859	Hewitt	Georgium	
Maheu	Josephinam Estiam		04-AUG-1886	Corbeil	Petrum Trefflé	
Mainé	Mariam-Sophiam		12-OCT-1880	Marcoux	Jeremias	
Mainville-Deschesnes	Rosa-Delima	T. Mainville/C. Mainville	30-APR-1861	Maurice	Guiellelmus	Angeli Maurice/Victoria Maurice
Malheur	Euladia	—— Malheur/Felicitata Cyr	25-SEP-1865	Edwin	Julianus	Antonii Edwin/Marguarita Edwin
Malheur	Maria		03-JUL-1876	Bré	Isidore	
Malheur	Felicita		01-AUG-1875	Boulet	Josephus	
Mallend	Mariam		08-NOV-1852	Hubertum	Julien	
Mallette	Celissam		01-SEP-1891	Hénault	Moisen	
Mangan	Anna		04-FEB-1856	Marten	Hugh	
Mangan	Marguarita	Eduardi Mangan/Anna Mangan	08-JUL-1862	Dolan	Joannes	—— Dolan/Maria Dolan
Mangan	Marget		29-AUG-1858	Lenshs	John	
Mangin	Catarinam Alidam		16-SEP-1883	Fellers	Victorem	
Manly	Brigeth		15-JAN-1859	Reddenton	Antony	
Manngan	Margerita		15-FEB-1858	Kelly	Peter	
Mansor	Terphoriam		25-MAY-1905	Julius	Carolum Assaf	
Marcoe	Della	Augusti Marcoe/Julia Leduc	28-NOV-1905	Gutreuter	Henricum	Mathia Gutreuter/M.-Anna Hurter
Marcou	Herminia		03-OCT-1865	Balthazar	Baptista	
Marcou	Melina	Francisci Marcou/Melina Marcou	16-MAY-1865	Bourasseau	Carolus	Huberti Bourasseau/A-loida Bourass
Marcou	Olivina	Francisci Marcou/Emilia Cyr	15-JUL-1872	Grenier	Oliverius	Francisci Grenier/Emilia Gibou
Marcou	Maria	Francisci Marcou/Emilia St.-Cyr	05-NOV-1861	Balthazar	Baptista	Martini Balthazar/Sophia Balthazar
Marcou	Emma		01-JUL-1867	Gillman	Joannes	
Marcou	Herminia	Francisci Marcou/Emilia Marcou	03-OCT-1865	Balthazar	Baptista	Michaelis Balthazar/Ros. Balthazar
Marcoux	Evam	Francisci Marcoux/Josephina Roy	08-JUN-1910	Goyette	Henrieum	Alexandri Goyette/Maria Lajeunesse
Marcoux	Margaritam Tesse	Augusti Marcoux/Julia Leduc	22-SEP-1908	Babin	Leonem	Theodori Babin/Maria Poirier
Marcoux	Josephina	Alex. Marcoux/Eleonora Lajeunesse	09-SEP-1908	Wettstein	Michaelum	Adriani Wettstein/Catherina Mauer
Marcoux	Arabella	Alex. Marcoux/Eleonora Lajeunesse	31-JUL-1907	Ferry	Guileluium	Jacobi Ferry/Elizabeth Strong

172

Bride's Surname	Bride's Name	Bride's Parents	Date	Groom's Surname	Groom's Name	Groom's Parents
Marcoux	Ollivinam		24-SEP-1902	Tates	Martinum	
Marcoux	Eleonoram		22-OCT-1900	Pomminville	Gulielmum	
Marcoux	Melvinam		27-SEP-1898	Brockway	Gulielmum	
Marcoux	Malvinam		30-SEP-1896	Pariseault	Eduardum	
Marcoux	Rosaliam		25-AUG-1892	Robert	Josephum	
Markoe	Emmam Louisam		30-OCT-1894	Surprenant	Levi	
Martin	Rosaliam		14-SEP-1900	Hallows	Hugonem Bernardum	
Marz	Apollonia	Henrici Marz/Christina Patton	04-JUN-1865	Cröns	Josephus	Petri Cröns/E. Aveli-
Massel	Madalina		12-APR-1860	Ludovicus	Joannes	
Matin	Julli			Magellan	Patrick	
Maurice	Mariam Annam		05-JUN-1882	Edoin	Amatum	
May	Anna-Maria	Hilarii May/Maria Maas	02-JUN-1879	Emmerich	Jacob	Nicolai Emmerich/Anna Wendel
Mayou	Catherina	Antonii Mayou/Angelica Malo	21-NOV-1870	Daniel	Franciscus	Ludovici Daniel/Maria Daniel
Mayou	Angelica	Antonii Mayou/Angelica Malo	03-AUG-1868	Dupuis	Lodgerius	Eusabii Dupuis/Flavia Dub—e
Mayrand	Virginia	W.-T. Mayrand/Winifred Le-t	18-NOV-1920	Schuhardt	Ulysses Samuel	A.B. Schuhardt/Amalia Wickert
Mcarnell	Althora		29-JUL-1860	Ennely	John	
McCabe	Catherine		08-SEP-1850	Conaughty	James	
McCallan	Catherinam		28-MAR-1853	Story	Georgium	
McCarter	Albina	Jacobi McCarter/Suzanna Mo—	01-OCT-1865	Wilcox	Carlus Henricus	Elisha Wilcox/Jane Wilcox
McCoy	Rosam		20-JUN-1853	Lyon	Franciscum	
McCoy	Mary		11-SEP-1851	Codd	Patrick	
McCoy	Susan		03-AUG-1851	McEnetty	Patrick	
McCoy	Mary		01-JUL-1851	Mullen	Hugh	
McCrury	Marguarita	Joannis McCrury/Maria McCrury	25-JAN-1862	Burrell	Joannes	Petri Burrell/Florence Sullivan
McCue	Maria	Ewardi McCue/Maria McCue	08-FEB-1862	Thornton	Hughius	Jacobi Thornton/Anna Thornton
McCullan	Elenam		14-NOV-1887	Myer	Nicholaum	
McDermott	Anna	Francisci McDermott/Maria McDerm	13-JAN-1862	Lamb	Nicholas	Nicolai-Jacobi Lamb/Bridgitta Lamb
McGarikel	Brigita		16-APR-1857	Mogon	John	
McGarty	Marie		14-NOV-1856	Ochlevain	James	
McGau	Sarah		24-JUN-1851	Geelan	Francis	
McGillan	Marie		07-JUN-1857	Larkens	John	
McGinty	Brigita		11-APR-1858	Maide	Thamas	
Mcglayelan	Bridgette		22-JUL-1860	Higgins	Eduradi	
McGrath	Sarah	Patricii McGrath/Maria McGrath	15-SEP-1861	Emerson	Matthens	Thoma Emerson/Marg. Emerson
McIntyre	Theresa		27-NOV-1856	Ragan	Patrick	
McKeets-Duffy	Anna	Thoma McKeets/Maria McKeets	15-JUN-1862	White	Georgius	Joannis White/Elizabetha White
Mclone	Mary		09-MAR-1857	Halpen	Patrick	
McMonagle	Julia	Antonii McMonagle/Julia McMonagle	15-NOV-1863	McLaughlin	Daniel	
McSweeney	Franciscam Ceciliam		27-JUL-1889	Charlebois	Josephum	
McTevit	Margerth		10-MAY-1856	Cagil	John	
McTivy	Marguerite		26-JAN-1852	Keinea	Andrew	
Melançon	Ludovica	Amedei Melançon/Mathilda Melanço	21-JUN-1866	Fontaine	Narcissus	Narcissi Fontaine/Julia LeMaire
Meller	Ann		18-NOV-1855	Mullen	John	
Meller	Chaterina		12-AUG-1860	Hunsall	Augustus	
Melony	Maria Anna		27-OCT-1856	McGregery	Own	
Mertz	Anna Marie	N. Mertz/M. Mertz	26-DEC-1861	Schneider	Petrus	Joannis Schneider/Anna-M Schneider
Mettendorf	-usson—len			M——§	John	
Mettier	Phillipina	Francisci Mettier/M-Josepha Mettier	16-FEB-1862	Dellise	Julius	Petri Dellise/Francisca Dellise
Meunier Miller	Josepham		17-APR-1883	Phelan	Jacobum K.	

173

Bride's Surname	Bride's Name	Bride's Parents	Date	Groom's Surname	Groom's Name	Groom's Parents
Meussen	Elisabeth		08-OCT-1856	Curb	Peter	
Michotte	Mariam Louisam		24-NOV-1891	Gratton	Ludgerium	
Michotte	Malvinam		09-JUN-1891	Gratton	Davidem	
Michotte	Josephina		01-OCT-1883	Maurice	Franciscum	
Mike	Emiliam		13-MAY-1895	Surprenant	Arthurum	
Miller	Carolina		20-AUG-1865	Louiss-	Franciscus	
Miller	Mariam Sophiam		12-NOV-1886	Bruedrle	Jacobum	
Milligan	Honore			Mcay	Turner	
Milquet	Mathildam		04-APR-1903	LeTourneau	Pascalem	
Miné	Maria Julia Anna	Joan.-Jose. Miné/M-Theresa Nissaint	11-FEB-1872	DeNamar	Noël	Ludovici DeNamar/M-Francisca Vass
Minier	Louisam		14-SEP-1891	Landerman	Hilarium	
Mocquin	Marguarita	Josephi Mocquin/Zoah Beaudeau-Mo	16-AUG-1863	Landreman	Ludovicus	Augustini Landreman/Theresa Joli
Mocquin	Olivia	Josephi Mocquin/Ludovica Mocquin	08-JUN-1862	Mishote	Deodatus	Francisci Mishote/M-Josepha Mishote
Mocquin	Ludovica	Josephi Mocquin/Zoeh Bourdeau	18-SEP-1871	Préfontaine	Andreas	Bart. Préfontaine/Angelica Trudeau
Mocquin	Ludovica	Francis Mocquin/Henrica Percheron	29-NOV-1868	Rabidou	Alfredus	Caroli Rabidou/Anastasia Edouin
Mocquin	Matilda		24-FEB-1878	Mocquin	Issau	
Molhens	Maria	Ludovici Molhens/Felicitatis Molhens	20-APR-1862	Letourneau	Christopherus	Christ. Letourneau/Vitalia Landris
Molton	Joanna	Roberti Molton/Maria Molton	07-SEP-1862	McGrath	Jacobus	Jacobi McGrath/Marg. McGrath
Moore	Maria	Mauritii Moore/Helena Moore	28-NOV-1860	Flagherty	Morgan	Edmundi Flagherty/Hanna Flagherty
Moquin	Josephina		23-SEP-1874	Langlois	Josephum	
Moquin	Elizabeth		02-JUN-1886	Gagnon	Urbanum	
Moquin	Anna	Joseph Moquin/Mathilda Barbeau	09-MAY-1905	Moquin	Alexander	Francis Moquin/Henriette Percheron
Moquin	Addeam Mariam		12-JAN-1904	Fox	Joannem	
Moquin	Evam		22-NOV-1899	Carbonneau	Ricardum	
Moquin	Vitalinam		16-JUN-1892	Whitmore	Gulielmum	
Moquin	Annam	Josephi Moquin/Mathilda Barbeau	09-MAY-1905	Moquin	Alexandrum	Francis Moquin/Henrietta Percheron
Moquin	Mariam		26-NOV-1889	Langlois	Georgium	
Moquin	Elizabeth		25-JUN-1886	Gagnon	Urbanum	
Moquin	Ezildam		01-MAY-1881	Barbeau	Petrum	
Moquin. Liam			06-MAY-1891	Gagnier	Guilelmum	
Moran	Mariam		15-APR-1898	Ring	Ricardum	
Morgan	Catharine		13-OCT-1855	Patrick	John	
Morin	Loisa	Josephi Morin/Julia Roi	29-MAY-1865	Ebert	Moyses	Caroli Ebert/Maria-Regina Marcou
Morning	Marguarita	John Morning/Bridget Morning	27-SEP-1864	Risch	Charles	Peter Risch/Elizabeth Risch
Morris	Maria	Francisci Morris/Clotilda Morris	01-MAR-1864	Morris	Carolus	Joannis Morris/Maria Morris
Morris	Maria Adelina	Josue Morris/Christina Longtin	22-SEP-1879	Edoin	Leverus	Leonis Edoin/Flavia Moquin
Morris	Delia		29-JUL-1877	Prefontaine	Andreum	
Morris Beaudry	Maria		19-SEP-1870	Miller	Christianus	
Morson	Catherina		07-JUL-1856	Mannon	Stiven	
Mortats	Sarah		10-FEB-1852	Mangan	Michael	
Mullen	Mary		16-SEP-1851	Carter	Harvey	
Mullen	Catherine		27-AUG-1855	Margan	John	
Mullen. Maria		Jacobi Mullen/Helena Mullen	09-APR-1861	Flagherty	Edmundus	Edmundi Flagherty/Honora Flagherty
Mulony	Catharina-Agnetia	Jacobi Mulony/Anna Mulony	29-SEP-1861	Beaudriau	Israel Carolus	L. Beaudriau/M-Ludovica Beaudriau
Murphy	Ellen		07-JAN-1857	Murphy	Thamas	
Murry	Marget		29-NOV-1856	McGlogen	John	
Müller	Regina	Peter Müller/Antoinette Müller	21-SEP-1863	Ramme	Christopher	Heinrich Ramme/Christiana Ramme
N—ber	Lebodina		20-SEP-1857	Cherchinger	Jeremias	
Nelson	Elizabeth		27-DEC-1915	Hopper	Levi J.	

Bride's Surname	Bride's Name	Bride's Parents	Date	Groom's Surname	Groom's Name	Groom's Parents
Newcombe	Rosa		30-NOV-1851	Clark	James	
Nicalus	Brigitha		02-JAN-1859	McClain	James	
Nicolus	Maria		04-JUN-1858	Emerson	James	
Noble	Petra		14-OCT-1866	Dreikosen	Joannes Guillelmus	
Nolain	Maria Jean		25-AUG-1875	Potrin	Joannes Bapt.	
Norton	Saram		05-DEC-1852	Collins	Patricium	
Noverty	Cathernia		05-AUG-1860	Lynks	John	
O'Brien	Honora	Timothei O'Brien/Joanna O'Brien	24-JAN-1864	Carney	Jacobus	Mattei Carney/Bridgitta Carney
O'Connel	Margueritam		03-JUL-1853	Gibbons	Robertum	
O'Connor	Brigittam		20-SEP-1859	O'Sullivan	Maurtius	
O'Hagan	Marguarita	Patricii O'Hagan/Sarah O'Hagan	01-NOV-1863	Ha-kins	Patricius	Bernardi Ha-kins/Marg. Ha-kins
O'Hagan	Anna	Patrick O'Hagan/Sara O'Hagan	15-SEP-1862	Walther	Julius	Julius Walther/Louisa Walther
O'Hara	Ellen		13-NOV-1859	Scot	James	
O'Malley	Charlotte		27-NOV-1919	Hodges	Herbert	Joseph Hodges/Elizabeth Blause
O-innen	Jeanne			Hammon	Joannes	
Oconner	Brigeta		20-NOV-1659	O——	Denis	
Odet	Vitalina	Georgii Odet/Julia Préjean	07-APR-1863	Mocquin	Josephus	Josephi Mocquin/Zoah Bredeau
Olinger	Catharina	Nicholai Olinger/Suzanna Olinger		Shaeffer	Charles	
Osait	Lenise		06-NOV-1859	Larenche	Jaque	
Ouellette	Clara	Ludovici Oulette/Louisa Lea	10-AUG-1874	Chaperone	Theophilus	Theophili Chaperone/—— Surprenant
Ouellette	Olivine	Ludovici Ouellette/Lucia Louffe	24-AUG-1879	Laca	Camille	Narcis Laca/Ursula Trudell
Paddick	Rosalia		16-JUN-1856	Bugnon	Josephius	
Paige	Selina		04-OCT-1875	Sheban	Georgius	
Painguère	Eugenia	Eugenii Painguère/Hort. Lismonde	07-AUG-1871	Dupuis	Stanislas	Baptista Dupuis/Clotilda Agagnier
Paquete	Agnetia	Petri Paquete/Maria Paquete	10-JUL-1870	Bissonet	Noel Norbertus	Petri Bissonet/Collixtina Poudrite
Paré	Julia	Louis Paré/Duleme Joubert	08-FEB-1905	LeMieux	Jeremiah	Israel LeMieux/Melina Larose
Paré	Julia	Ludovici Paré/Delima Joubert	31-JAN-1905	Lemieux	Jeromiau	Israel Lemieux/Melina Larose
Paré Perry	Emmam		23-JUN-1903	Smet	Fredericum	
Parent	Anna	Josephi Parent/Emilia LaBerge	09-SEP-1872	Langto	Josephus	Francisci Langto/Carola Biet
Parent	Sa–		03-JUN-1877	Gagé	Olivier	
Pariseau	Estheam		18-MAY-1891	Teschendorf	Emilem	
Pariseau	Josephina		19-NOV-1879	Dodelin	Denysius	Oliverius Dodelin/Sophie Molleur
Parriso	Edessa		10-JAN-1876	Gaigné	Edwardi	
Pedelant	Edesse		18-AUG-1878	Beauprez	Armidolt	
Pedlant	Adelina N.	Francisci Pedlant/Josepha Pedlant	02-MAR-1862	Stephans	Joannes	Francisci Stephans/Maria Stephans
Pedlant	Helena		16-SEP-1860	Brackett	Nelson Ludovicus	
Pelant	Matilde		10-MAY-1851	Maurice	Louis	
Pelant	C——-Catherine		10-JAN-1851	Kraimer	John	
Pellant	Sophia		24-OCT-1859	Deroché	Francois	
Pellant	Hermina	Francisci Pellant/Josephina Faucher	12-OCT-1869	Rabidou	Josephus	Huberti Rabidou/Aurelia Préfontaine
Pellant	Sophiam		16-JUL-1897	Charron	Jacobum	
Pellant	Philomena		23-JAN-1859	Trotier	Damascus	
Pellant	Josephina		19-AUG-1857	Randeau	Thamas	
Pellant	Maria	Francisci Pellant/Josephina Faucher	28-MAY-1867	Perron	Joannes-Baptista	Andrei Perron/Maria-Aurèle Perron
Pellant	Elizabetha	Francisi Pellant/Josepha Pellant	04-SEP-1866	Marcou	Joseph	Joannis-M. Marcou/Angela Marcou
Pellant	Edessam		13-OCT-1883	Alain	Carolum	
Pellant	Adelam		13-AUG-1883	Pierson	Josephum	
Penser	Marria		06-MAY-1857	Gilliber	Joannes	
Peron	Paulina		10-OCT-1855	Prova	Peter	

175

Bride's Surname	Bride's Name	Bride's Parents	Date	Groom's Surname	Groom's Name	Groom's Parents
Perrizo	Marie Irene	Joseph Perrizo/Melanie Dupuis	07-SEP-1920	McCabe	Roy	James McCabe/Catherine Doyle
Perrizo	Maud	Josephi Perrizo/Belonisa Dupuis	20-NOV-1907	Newman	Franciscum	Adolphi Newman/Maria Ashenbruner
Perron	Eldora	Joh Perronn/Cecilia Hatton	04-FEB-1920	Bartow	Charles A.	Leverett Bartow/Ella Chase
Perron	Marguarita	Andrea Perron/Maria-Aurelia Perron	24-FEB-1862	Smith	Paulus	Nicholai Smith/Maria Smith
Perron	Catherinam		16-SEP-1886	LeTourneau	Petrum	
Perron	Mariam		09-NOV-1884	Durocher	Gulielmum	
Pethid	Maria		29-NOV-1856	Gayan	Joannes	
Petit	Mary		19-JUN-1851	Bellehumeur	Francis	
Petit	Maria		03-MAR-1861	Tibeaudeau	Oliverius	
Petri	Gertruda	Antonii Petri/Marguarita Petri	13-FEB-1866	Bayer	Thomas	Joannis Bayer/Catherina Bayer
Phillips	Margetha		03-FEB-1859	Obryan	Thomas	
Piehl	Netam Josephinam		14-OCT-1902	Martin	Laurentium	
Pingair	Josephinam		04-APR-1888	Sibolt	Joannem	
Pinguer	Alphonsina		22-FEB-1883	Sherburne	Jefferson	
Pinguère	Mariam		06-AUG-1887	Bart	Josephum	
Plante	Maria	Petri Plante/Elizabetha Meunier	20-SEP-1870	Gayet	Carolus	Josephi Gayet/Magdelena LaValie
Platte–Noupré	Albertam		05-SEP-1904	Lumblot	Victorem	
Po—ich	Catharina	Josephi Po—ich/M-Josepha Po—ich	06-JAN-1861	Tanges	Jacobus	Christophus Tanges/Maria Tanges
Poirrier	Margaret		07-JUL-1856	Burck	Michel	
Polie	Josephina		06-NOV-1865	Paquette*	Israel	Ludovici Paquet/Genovefa Mans—
Polie	Josephina	Michaelis Polie/Maria Polie	06-NOV-1865	Paquet*	Israel	
Pommenville	Maria		13-JAN-1878	Demarchs	Salomon	
Potvin	Mathildam		02-JAN-1896	Brunet	Josephum Ferdinand	
Prat	Francisca		03-SEP-1876	Pret	Josephus	
Pratt	Mariam Stellam	Felicis Pratt/Sarah Duquette	29-NOV-1906	Brunet	Josephum	Gedeonis Brunet/Melina Bastian
Pratt	Leopolda		17-SEP-1876	LaPorte	Josephus	
Pratte	Albertam		25-APR-1886	Noupré	Josephum	
Pratte	Josephinam		10-APR-1894	Henker	Hermanum H.	
Pratte	Malvinam		21-JUN-1892	Roy	Narcissum Oliverum	
Pratte	Albertam		25-APR-1886	Noupré	Josephum	
Pratte	Delima	Joseph Pratte/Heniette Laroque	29-MAY-1900	Baltazar	Alfredus	Joseph Baltazar/Sophia Meunier
Préfontaine	Aliceam		22-FEB-1898	Lyons	Patricum	
Préfontaine	Mariam C—am		16-NOV-1897	Briscoe	Amos Pollard	
Préfontaine	Mariam Laurentiam		10-APR-1894	Ellison	Alfredum E.	
Préfontaine	Josephinam		14-SEP-1891	Stada	Frederum Antonium	
Prefontaine	Rosam		03-JUL-1883	Durocher	Adolphum	
Prefontaine	Octaviam			Pratte	Alfredum	
Prefontaine	Alphonsina	Barth. Prefontaine/Henselia Trudeau	13-JAN-1880	Dupuis	Amandus	Eusebius Dupuis/Zoe Moquin
Préfontaine Robidou	Aurelia	Alexii Préfontaine/M.-L. Padenoide	15-FEB-1872	LaPlante	Oliverius	Josephi LaPlante/Catharina LaPlante
Prey	Lorraine	Albert Prey/Lillian Schwebke	11-NOV-1920	Lapine	Lawrence	Joseph Lapine/Sophie Beaudreault
Provot	Julienne		21-SEP-1851	Nolli	Peter	
Rabidoux	Marcellinam		16-FEB-1898	Lafayette	Henricum	
Racette	Arminam		25-DEC-1885	McKinley	Guilbertum Jacobum	
Rag–on	Margerit		20-APR-1857	Donly	Michel	
Ragame	Clemence		07-JUL-1860	Morris	Gorge	
Ragan	Anna		16-MAY-1857	Seligan	Michel	
Ralo	Mathilda Adgett	Petri Ralo/Ludovica Ralo	07-MAY-1870	Odete	Baptista	Georgii Odete/Cyrila Odete
Rando	Maria		01-JAN-1876	LeGault	Bellami	
Rayaume	Evam		25-OCT-1904	Durocher	Eduardum	

Bride's Surname	Bride's Name	Bride's Parents	Date	Groom's Surname	Groom's Name	Groom's Parents
Redmiller	Christina		31-MAR-1856	Smet	Jacob	
Reindel	Anna	Johannis-Geo. Reindel/Maria Andaly	29-JAN-1866	Wagner*	Henricus	Nicholai Wagner/Maria Taylor
Resh	Theresa	Josephi Resh/Theresa Resh	16-DEC-1862	Shümmer	Franciscus	Nicholai Shümmer/Marg. Shümmer
Rheinhart	Catharina	Bernardi Rheinhart/Eliza Rheinhart	04-NOV-1866	Krendwich	Matthias	J. Krendwich/G. Krendwich
Riburnans	Maria		04-NOV-1855	Thouma	Thomas	
Rider	Rosa		05-AUG-1851	Kelly	Thomas	
Ring	Sophia		19-FEB-1858	Peren	John Baptista	
Ro—	Mary		08-NOV-1850	Fitzgerald	Patrick	
Robert	Marguarita	Francisci Robert/Maria Beaudoin	17-FEB-1873	Gillman	Narcissus	Thoma Gillman/Domitilla Groton
Robert	Maria	Francisci Robert/Maria Beaudoin	31-DEC-1871	Ste.-Marie	Eugerius	Josephi Ste.-Marie/Maria Robidou
Robert	Josephinam		20-JAN-1891	Mcessy	Joannem	
Robert	Emilinam		04-NOV-1885	Bathazar	Ludovicum	
Robidou	Exarina	Huberti Robidou/Aurelia Fournier	16-SEP-1866	LeMaire	Achiles	Stephani LeMaire/Sophia P-nar
Robidoux	Lucretiam M	Josephi Robidoux/Ermina Pellant	12-JUN-1906	Maurice	Franciscum	Francis. Maurice/Josephina Michotte
Robidoux	Josephine Mary		10-JAN-1905	Pellant	Joseph Thomas	
Robidoux	Josephinam M.	Josephi Robidoux/Ermina Pellant	10-JAN-1905	Pellant	Josephum T.	Adolphi Pellant/Alphonsina Laberge
Rochell	Elizabetham		28-JUL-1886	Dufort	Josephum	
Rock	Chaterina		07-AUG-1859	Wall	Thamas	
Rodgers	Sarah	Thoma Rodgers/Anna Rodgers	31-MAY-1863	White	Jacobus	Patricii White/Marguarita White
Rodidoux	Mariam Claram		03-NOV-1891	Nichlas	Antonium	
Roi	Emma	Isaïa Roi/Julia-Anna Ebert	17-APR-1870	Marion	Seraphinus	Ludovici Marion/Elizabetha Talis
Roi	Jospehina	Isaïa Roi/Julianna Ebert	22-FEB-1870	Marcou	Franciscus	Francisci Marcou/Maria Cyr
Ronan	Lenora	William Ronan/Lucy Tilman	08-SEP-1919	Willett	Charles E.	Charles Willet/Delia Mangan
Rondeau	Philomena	Francis Rondeau/Christina Rondeau	10-APR-1864	Leduc	Josephus	Josephi Leduc/Marguarita Leduc
Rondeau	Marguarita	Francis Rondeau/Felicitatis Rondeau	22-MAR-1863	Bastien	Antonius	Josephi Bastien/Angela Bastien
Rondeau	Marguarita	Baptista Rondeau/Julia Anna Chef	18-NOV-1872	Lyonnais	Franciscus	Ludovici Lyonnais/Angela Gamelin
Rondeau	Annom		22-AUG-1903	Gavigan	Jacobum Eugenium	
Rondeau	Josephinam		18-JUN-1889	Robert	Georgium	
Ronndel	Anna		29-JAN-1866	Wagner*	Henricus	
Rose	Mary Ann		18-FEB-1905	Denell	Dominic	
Rose	Marion		18-FEB-1905	Dinelle	Dominicum	Ludovici Dinelle/Maria Gervais
Rossete	Laurentia	Juliani Rossete/Marguarita Cyr	11-JUN-1872	LeCoque	Ludovicus	Ludovici LeCoque/Sophia Ric-r
Roy	Mariam Annam		25-DEC-1902	Touchette	Eduardum O.	
Roy	Mariam Louisam		11-SEP-1895	Touchette	Oliverum Eduardum	
Roy	Georginam		14-JUN-1893	Buch	Josephum	
Roy	Elisam		18-FEB-1878	LaBassiere	Henricum	
Rulo	H–ri-a	Petri Rulo/Ludovica Rulo	03-OCT-1864	Labelle	–rius	Laurentii Labelle/Genovefa Labelle
Ryaume	Mariam		26-DEC-1900	Durocher	Ludgerium	
Sannal	Anna		03-FEB-1856	Fitzjurrall	Patrick	
Santuaire	Maria		09-NOV-1865	Fontaine*	Josephus	
Santuaire	Maria		09-NOV-1865	Fontaine*	Josephus	
Sauvé	Minnie	Joseph Sauvé/Alida Venné	25-SEP-1906	Brandt	Walter	E. Brandt/M. Beauregard
Sauvé	Corinam		14-NOV-1900	Weber	Petrum	
Sauvé	Paulinam		18-SEP-1895	Funk	Julium	
Say	Ellena		02-MAY-1859	Bullis	Nethn	
Scalfe	Mariam		09-SEP-1895	Spatore	Petrum Josephum	
Scha–	Rossa		19-JUN-1856	Gruin	Joseph	
Schannel	Catherina		10-SEP-1855	Henry	Michei	
Schauss	Elizabeth		30-DEC-1919	Maurice	Geo.	FrankMaurice/Michotte

177

Bride's Surname	Bride's Name	Bride's Parents	Date	Groom's Surname	Groom's Name	Groom's Parents
Scheutuels	Ellisabeth		01-JUN-1859	Ferdinand	Simmon	
Schneider	Anna Sybilla	Petri Schneider/C. Nicholaus-Schnür	29-APR-1865	Schleidan	Gasporus	Petri Schleidan/M-Josepha Neld--
Schoefer	Rose	Charle Schoefer/Anna Krauss	16-FEB-1920	Camp	Richard	Alphonso Camp/Amelia Proctnow
Schreiner	Mariam		29-JAN-1910	Marcoux	Samuelem	Samuelis Marcoux/------
Schuessler	Josephine	Wm Schuessler/Ida Schoefer	27-AUG-1919	Kinney	James	Jacobi Kinney/Rose Mcginnis
Sco-ley	Sophia	Stephani-D. Sco-ley/Isabella Sco-ley	05-APR-1869	Joubert	Carolus Edwardus	Stephani Joubert/Paulina Morin
Seibel	Maruarita	Joannis Seibel/Maria Seibel	22-MAY-1866	Ditter	Georgius Josephus	Andreas Ditter/Eva Regina Ditter
Seiboldt	Maria	Josephi Seiboldt/Maria Seiboldt	25-MAY-1865	Colbs	Josephus	Christophi Colbs/Veronica ------
Seidentopf	Mariam		01-SEP-1890	Edoin	Vitalem	
Senecal	Angelicam	David Seneca/Rose Venne	12-FEB-1919	Ottery	George T.	Herbert Ottery/Nina M. Stage
Sénécal	Rosam DeLima	Ovidis Sénécal/Melina Venne	22-JUN-1910	Kienow	Fredericum	Augusti Kienow/------ ------
Sessel	Nanne-Marie		27-NOV-1856	Hiers	Jannis	
Shaw	Isabella	Joannes Shaw/Anna Shaw	29-JUL-1861	McDonald	Joannes	Alex. McDonald/Helena McDonald
Show	Anna	Joannis Shoe/Elizabetha Shoe	30-OCT-1866	Brown	Joannes	Henrici Brown/Magdelena Brown
Sicard	Josephinam		19-JUN-1883	Clish	Amatum	
Silvestre	Maria	Petri Silvestre/Christina Coté	10-JUL-1870	Faucher	Alexander	Ludovici Faucher/Josepha Bignon
Simonin	Augustinam		24-NOV-1886	Allard	Gulielmum L.	
Simonin	Juliam		25-DEC-1881	Prefontaine	Ludgerium	
Simons	Elizabetha			Hobbs	Enos	
Smet	Louisa		24-JAN-1859	Smit	Joannes	
Smet	Caroline		03-APR-1856	Stentons	John	
Smith	Catherine		06-MAY-1852	Pelletier	Louis	
Smith	Mary		10-NOV-1851	Cain	Michael	
Smith	Phoebeam		03-SEP-1901	Roy	Philippum Josephum	
Smith	Mariam E.		09-SEP-1884	Mitchell	Josephum	
Sneyder	Annam-Ceciliam-Sybilla	P. Sneyder/C. Sneyder	08-AUG-1861	Romach	Henricum	Josephi Romach/Catharina Romach
Snow	Margeta		17-JUL-1857	Chessehan	Joannes	
Sontag	Eva	Joannis Sontag/Maria Sontag	08-JUL-1866	Halfman	Chrysantus	Geraldi Halfman/Anna-C. Halfman
Spe--- Carbonneau	Louisa		21-NOV-1880	McGowen	Mauritium	
St. Germain	Zoeam Elmiram		25-APR-1881	Marcou	Franciscum	
St.-Antoine	Emilia	Moysis St-Antoine/Mathilda Benoît	06-AUG-1866	Dufresne	Isidorus	Pascali Dufresne/Angelica Coch--
St.-Antoine	Hermine	Moses St-Antoine/Mathilda Benoît	17-NOV-1879	Baltazare	Theodorus	Michaelis Baltazare/Rosalia Plante
Stada	Elizabeth		29-APR-1896	Gueron	Eduardum	
Stantan	Anna		11-DEC-1856	Smet	Patrick	
Ste.-Marie	Seragen		21-OCT-1858	Dufraine	Pascal	
Ste.-Marie	Elizabetha	Alexii Ste.-Marie/Sarah Ste.-Marie	26-NOV-1860	Dufresne	Franciscus	Pascalis Dufresne/Angelica Dufresne
Stecken	Catharina	Huberti Stecken/Maria Stecken	16-APR-1865	Linden	Thomas	Petri-Josephi Linden/Maria Linden
Steffens	Anna	Antonii Steffens/Suzanna Steffens	05-MAY-1861	Brown	Michael	Josephi Brown/Walburga Brown
Steffes	Catharinam Leona		28-MAY-1902	Robidoux	Joannem	
Stephani	Maria		31-JAN-1856	Crammer	Peter	
Stephans	Maria	Antonii Stephans/Suzanne Stephans	21-AUG-1864	Shroevan	Joannes	Theodori Shroevan/Marg. Shroevan
Strang	Nanis		10-MAY-1856	McBryon	Thamas	
Studeur	Maria		30-APR-1861	Warpier	Franciscus	
Sullivan	Elizabetham		30-NOV-1897	Sullivan	Michaelem J.	
Surprenand	Zoeam Mariam		17-JUN-1903	Carpenter	Manley Arthurum	
Surprenant	Julia	Ignati Surprenant/Julia Goyet	05-JUL-1864	Robert	David	Davidis Robert/Scholastica Chennière
Surprenant	Lisanam		14-JAN-1893	Smith	Georgium Joannem	
Surprenant	Eleonora	Isaaci Surprenant/Julia Surprenant	30-APR-1867	Lajeunesse	Petrus	Henrici Lajeunesse/Marg. Lajeunesse
Tell	Mariam		18-APR-1876	Jongers	Henricum	

178

Bride's Surname	Bride's Name	Bride's Parents	Date	Groom's Surname	Groom's Name	Groom's Parents
Terry	Brigetha		23-MAY-1859	Leahy	Samuel	
Tessier	Maria Exilda	Caroli Tessier/----- Tessier	17-APR-1871	Chenar Snow	Alphonsus	Isidori Chenar/Sophia Cyr
Tessier	Ludovica		31-DEC-1868	Campbell	Walter	
Tessier	Adelam		19-JAN-1890	Robert	Alexandrum	
Tetro	Petronella	Josephi Tetro/A.-Tetro	17-OCT-1869	Réal	Elizius	Josephi Réal/Amarrantha Réal
Thelan	Sibelia		05-APR-1852	Serwa	Michael	
Thériault Carrière	Leam		12-APR-1904	Beaudreau	Placidum Franciscum	
Thibodeau	Florie		03-APR-1856	Gayet	Joseph	
Thibodeau	Rosalia	Oliverii Thibodeau/Ludovica Cyr	17-JUN-1867	Besset	Petrus	Petri Besset/Sophia Beaulieu
Thirien	Ludovica Catherina	Ludovici Thirien/Rosa Patras	18-JUN-1865	Marion	Felix	Ludovici Marion/Felicitata Mer-
Thornton	Anna	Jacobi Thornton/Anna Thornton	21-JUL-1861	McLonen	Joannes	Archibaldi McLonen/Marg. McLonen
Tinger	Annam Maria Sophiam		25-NOV-1890	Barbeau	Alexandrum	
Tonne	Gratiam		23-SEP-1901	Loiseau Bird	Leonem	
Toomey	Anna	Timotheis Toomey/Jo.-Tabon Toomey	06-JAN-1862	Connell	Guillemus	Patricii Connell/Ursula Connell
Touchete	Mathilda	Josephi Touchete/Onesima Vient	19-SEP-1871	Gervais	Jeremias	Callixti Gervais/Salomé Rielle
Touchete	Virginia	Josephi Touchete/Onesima Vient	15-MAY-1871	Robert	Eugenius	Ignatius Robert/Ada Walterstein
Touchete	Josephina	Josephi Touchette/Olesinia Vient	05-JAN-1869	Chef	Petrus	Petri Chef/Christina Rondeau
Touchette	Philomena	Josephi Touchette/Onesima Vie-	22-JUL-1873	Gervais	-m—	Colii Gervais/Saloma Yelle
Touchette	Naizzon		19-NOV-1904	Barbeau	Lawrence	
Touchette	Mariam		16-NOV-1904	Barbeau	Carolum	
Tremblay	Emeliam		15-NOV-1887	DuBois	Georgium	
Tremblé	Agla	Henrici Tremblé/Josephina Girard	05-FEB-1866	Martel*	Prosper	Josephi Martel/Francisca Dolby
Turcot	Juliam		24-SEP-1903	Drinkwine	Georgium Boivin	
Turcot	Mariam		06-FEB-1895	Hurteau	Joannem	
Turcot	Eugeniam		23-NOV-1890	Lepper	Georgium	
Turenne	Deliam		17-JUN-1902	Flanders	Carolum Ruel	
Turto	Odilia	Jacobi Turto/Elizabeth Turto	15-JUN-1861	Nicholson	Patricius	Jacobi Nicholson/Sarah Nicholson
Turvelle	Maria		26-SEP-1859	Kennedy	John	
Tuttle	Mariam E.C.		24-JAN-1889	Bélanger-Baker	Petrum	
Vaine	Rosalia		27-SEP-1875	Donnais	Isidore	
Vaine	Josephina		19-JUN-1877	Sauvé	Magloire	
Vancour	Martha	Isaaci Vancour/Maria Vancour	21-JUL-1869	Perkins	Ephraim J.	Eduardi Perkins/Sarah Perkins
Vass	Philumenam		05-APR-1894	Comeau	Arthurum	
Vaughen	Marg.		18-APR-1858	Mayer	Thomas	
Veine	Maria Marguarita	Francisci Veine/M. Landreman	04-FEB-1873	Sauvé	Paulus	JM Sauvé/Emilia Pilon-Terrebonne
Veine	Rosalia	Agapiti Veine/Felicitatis Montant	12-JUL-1869	Carboneau	Franciscus	Petri Carboneau/Carola Jeandon
Veine	Alicia	Agapita Veine/Felicitatis Contant	05-JUL-1869	Foret	Petrus	Josephi Foret/Magdalena Morima
Veine	Ludovica	Agapiti Veine/Felicitatis Contant	19-AUG-1867	LaPorte	Zotique	Leonis LaPorte/Zoe Bernard-Bouillet
Veine	Maria-Rosam Delima		26-DEC-1880	Sénécal	Ovidem	
Veine	Rosalia	Francis Veine/Marcelina Landremann		Cardinal	Leo	Christ. Cardinal/Adelaide Payment
Veite	Maria	Conradis Veite/Francisca Veite		Frost	Guillelmus-Wallace	Guillelmi Frost/Maria Frost
Venne	Exilda		10-SEP-1895	Balthazar	Gegium	
Venne	Adelinam		12-APR-1888	Prudhomme	Josephum	
Venne	Elodiam		09-APR-1883	Sauvé	Josephum	
Venne-Hover	Carolinam		08-SEP-1903	Morel	Reneum	
Vernais	Celine		23-OCT-1859	Dandelain	Olivier	
Vernet	Darselia		14-JAN-1878	Baltazar	Martinus	
Viens	Henrelie	Stephani Trahan/Ludovica Picard	24-SEP-1879	Demers	Solomon	Stephan. Demers/Angelica Vincelette
Voght	Josephina	Antonii Voght/Josephina Voght	21-OCT-1861	Cooke	Guillelmus	Guillelmi Cooke/Theresia Cooke

179

Bride's Surname	Bride's Name	Bride's Parents	Date	Groom's Surname	Groom's Name	Groom's Parents
Voght	Anna Chaterina		12-AUG-1860	Mairh	Joannes	
Vogt	Maria	Antonii Vogt/Josephina Vogt	19-MAY-1863	Mertes	Mattheus Josephus	Antonii Mertes/Anna-Maria Mertes
Wagiiier	Catharina		09-JAN-1860	Jenner	William	
Wall	Martha	Guillelmi Wall/Helena Wall	06-JUL-1862	Wagner	Joannes Petrus	Petri Wagner/Maria Wagner
Walsh	Catherina	Jacobi Walsh/Catharina Walsh	10-FEB-1861	Duffy	William	Hughi Duffy/Maria Duffy
Webb	Marguarita	Jacobi Webb/Joanna Webb	15-APR-1861	O'Brien	Thomas	Jacobi O'Brien/Honora O'Brien
Webbe	Maria	Jacobi Webbe/Joanna Webbe	03-SEP-1863	Shea	Josephus	Danielis Shea/Maria Shea
Webber	Catharinam		03-JUN-1902	Marcoux	Oliverum J.	
Wellon	Elisabith		01-APR-1859	Metlon	John	
White	Margeta		04-OCT-1858	White	John	
Wilverzett	Maria	Joannis Wilverzett/Magdalena Wilver	26-MAY-1863	Kreiser	Petrus	Joannis Kreiser/Eva Smith
Wolf	Catharina	Huberti Wolf/Gertruda Wolf	28-FEB-1865	Crämmer	Nicholaus	Hubert Crämmer/Veronica Crämmer
Wotete	Georgina	Ludovici Wotete/Lucia Louf	28-AUG-1870	Plouf	Thomas	Sulpitii Plouf/Adelaida Houle
Yapas	Anna		17-JAN-1856	Tria	Joseph	
Young	Margaret	Jerry Young/Levina Balthazor	09-JUN-1920	Starick	Joseph	John Starick/Mary Krall
Zimmer	Maria	Gottefried Zimmer/Cath Vinande	08-MAY-1865	Zerringer	Wendelinus	Christiani Zerringer/Sidonia Fishter

St. Louis Catholic Parish, Fond du Lac, Wisconsin

Burials 1850-1920

Surname	Given Name	Death	Burial	Age	Cemetery	Spouse	Parents
----	----		12-NOV-1876				
----	----		10-FEB-1866				
----	Edmira	07-AUG-1879	16-AUG-1879	6 -			
----	Georgius	06-AUG-1879	10-AUG-1879	18 mos		Julian Demars	
----	Ludovica Maria Victoria		14-FEB-1872			Julian Demars	
----	Victor		10-SEP-1867				
----LaJoie	Joseph		06-JAN-1880	14 mos			
-anard	Catharina	09-JAN-1891	12-JAN-1891	68 yrs	Taycheedah	Huberti Pariseau	
-orri-	-he-foria		23-FEB-1878	24 yrs			
Abraham	Catharina	01-OCT-1895	03-OCT-1895	4 mos	Taycheedah	Huberti Pariseau	Jacobi Abraham/ Maria Joanna
Ackey	Ann H.		29-MAY-1863				
Allain	Felicia	05-OCT-1895	07-OCT-1895	54 yrs	Taycheedah	Petri Brenael	
Allain	Josephina Ezilda	16-AUG-1881	17-AUG-1881	2 yrs	Taycheedah		Francisci Allain/ Josephina Bouchard
Allard-Venne	Domititila	05-JUL-1890	08-JUL-1890	65 yrs	Taycheedah	Agapiti Venne	
Allen	Jacobi	19-MAY-1887	21-MAY-1887	76 yrs	Taycheedah		
Auger	----		27-AUG-1865	14 mos			
Babeau	Melina Ironia	29-APR-1899	01-MAY-1899	3 yrs	Calvary		Levi Babeau/ Maria-Celina Levesque
Bacon	Patricius		05-SEP-1862				
Baillargeon	Clio	11-SEP-1882	12-SEP-1882	3 yrs	Taycheedah		Josephi Baillargeon/ Aurelia Landermann
Baillargeon	Josephi Ambrosii	15-MAR-1883	27-MAR-1883	15 days	Taycheedah	Agapiti Venne	Josephi Baillargeon/ Aurelia Landerman
Baker	Agnetis	15-OCT-1896	17-OCT-1896	65 yrs	Rienzi	Julii Plunket	
Baker-Belanger	Peter	24-NOV-1920	26-NOV-1920	100 yrs			
Baltazar	Micheal		10-JAN-1875	59 yrs			
Baltazar	Per-		19-JUN-1876	18 yrs, 3 mos			
Balthazar	Eduardi	19-NOV-1887	21-NOV-1887	19 days	Taycheedah		Alfredi Balthazar/ Delima Pratte
Balthazar	Isabella		09-SEP-1903	20 yrs	Calvary		
Balthazar	Levino		28-JAN-1868	10 mos			
Balthazar	Maria	12-JUL-1883	15-JUL-1883	3 mos	Taycheedah		Theodori Balthazar/ Armina St.-Antoine
Balthazar	Maria Zotiosa	08-JAN-1901	10-JAN-1901	7 wks	Calvary		Joseph Balthazar/ Flavia Letourneau
Banael	Petri Justin-	18-FEB-1888	20-FEB-1888	28 yrs	Taycheedah		Petri Brenael/ Felicia Allain
Barbay	Louis		01-MAY-1877	83 yrs			
Barbeau	Nora	10-OCT-1918	14-OCT-1918	24 yrs	Calvary		Ludovici Jarvis/ Milvina Jarvis
Barrett	Florentia Marie			4 1/2 mos			
Barrett	Isadore	31-JAN-1920	02-FEB-1920	82 yrs		Julii Plunket	
Barteau	Henricus		18-JAN-1872	29 yrs			
Basset	Julie Eldia		03-SEP-1875	3 mos		Julii Plunket	
Bassete	Julianus		01-MAR-1867				
Bastien	----		13-OCT-1868				
Bastien	Andreas		01-AUG-1868				
Bastien	Joannes Baptista			20 mos			
Bastien	John Baptist	20-MAR-1919	24-MAR-1919	85 yrs	Calvary	Eugenie Bastien	
Bastien	Melina	09-MAY-1897	11-MAY-1897	5- yrs	Taycheedah	Gedeonis Brunet	
Bastien	Sophia	30-JUN-1903	02-JUL-1903	68 yrs	Taycheedah	Euclidis Venne	
Beadrieau	Moyses Francisus		08-OCT-1866	1 yrs	Taycheedah	Euclidis Venne	
Beaubiau	Jaques		04-APR-1878	88 yrs	Taycheedah		
Beaubien	Olivier				Byron		
Beaudet	Alma	22-OCT-1886	23-OCT-1886	2 yrs	Taycheedah		Evaristi Beaudet/ Anna Carbonneau

Surname	Given Name	Death	Burial	Age	Cemetery	Spouse	Parents
Beaudet	Velina	30-AUG-1887	01-SEP-1887	4 yrs	Taycheedah		Euristi Beaudet/ Elena Carbonneau
Beaudette	Evaristi	18-NOV-1902	21-NOV-1902	54 yrs	Taycheedah		
Beaudette	Margarita	04-JUL-1888	04-JUL-1888		Taycheedah	David Beaudette	
Beaudin	Clementia		28-MAY-1866	9 yrs			
Beaudin	Guillelmus		06-MAY-1869	6 yrs			
Beaudin	Jacobus		05-MAY-1871	68 yrs			
Beaudoin	Isidori Marguerita						
Beaudreau	Laurentii	21-FEB-1904	24-FEB-1904	91 yrs	Taycheedah		
Beaudry	Benjaminis	16-JAN-1898	18-JAN-1898	9 yrs	Calvary		Johannis-Baptista Beaudry/ Ursula Charron
Beaupré	Clovis		04-OCT-1880	1 month	Taycheedah		Petri Beaupre/ Ede-a Pelland
Beaupre	David		20-OCT-1876	56 yrs			
Beaupre	Hormisda	04-JUN-1882	06-JUN-1882	25 yrs	Taycheedah	Edessa Pellant	
Beaupre	Joseph Hormidas		22-SEP-1875	6 wks		Edessa Pellant	
Beauregard							
Becquet	Josephum		25-DEC-1864	3 or 5 mos			
Bellanger	Josephina		09-NOV-1868				
Bellanger	Josephus		05-OCT-1864	18 yrs			
Benete	Marguarita			73 yrs			
Benoit	Matilde		08-SEP-1876	52 yrs		Moise St.-Antoine	
Bernier	Eduardi	22-OCT-1891	24-OCT-1891	20 yrs	Taycheedah		
Bernier	Eduardus						
Bertrand			03-JUL-1878	42 yrs			
Bertrand	Mathuri	23-OCT-1893	25-OCT-1893	15 yrs	Rienzi		Joannis-Napoleonis Bertrand/ Odelia Leclerc
Bessete	L. A.		31-DEC-1867	2 yrs			
Bessette	Adelaide	30-JAN-1880	01-FEB-1880	28 yrs			
Bessette	Petri	16-JUN-1881	18-JUN-1881	102 yrs	Taycheedah	Margueritta Michot	
Bibeau	Philonisa	23-OCT-1884	25-OCT-1884	35 yrs	Taycheedah	Michaelis Dion	
Bisson	M. Lucinda	25-APR-1885	28-APR-1885	7 mos	Taycheedah		Martini Bisson/ Julia Loiseau
Bisson	Maria			18 yrs			
Bissonet	David		13-SEP-1872				
Bissonet	Ludovicus		17-DEC-1861	44 yrs			
Blanchard	Josephine		06-SEP-1876	52 yrs		Jeremie Marcou	
Bodriau	Martha		10-MAY-1875	10 yrs 11 mos 17 days			
Boisvert			30-AUG-1865	2 yrs			
Boisvert	Paulus		12-JUL-1863	13 mos			
Bonin	Adeline		24-AUG-1867	4 yrs			
Bonin	Eduardi	26-MAR-1895	28-MAR-1895	80 yrs	Taycheedah	Julia Emery	
Boraseau	Joseph		26-SEP-1875	22 mos			
Bouchar	Carolina		07-SEP-1866	6 mos			
Boucher	Lucia		05-FEB-1871	58 yrs			
Bouchor	Rosalia		24-AUG-1867				
Boulais	Mathilda	16-FEB-1903	19-FEB-1903	71 yrs	Calvary	Nazarii Langlois	
Bourassa	Huberti	18-APR-1888	18-APR-1888	77 yrs	Taycheedah		
Bourgar	Marie	28-FEB-1875	05-MAR-1975		Taycheedah	David Albert	
Bourgmeyer							
Bozer	Catherina	19-MAY-1891	21-MAY-1891	94 yrs	Taycheedah	Ludovici Barbeau	
Branchaud	Eugenii	20-SEP-1891	22-SEP-1891	67 yrs	Taycheedah	Maria Desautels	
Brant	Maria Bertha			9 mos			
Braquette	Helena						

184

Surname	Given Name	Death	Burial	Age	Cemetery	Spouse	Parents
Bré	Phillipus		06-MAR-1861				
Brenael	Emelii	11-JAN-1887	13-JAN-1887	18 yrs	Taycheedah		Petri Brenael/ Felicia Allain
Brenael	Joannis Baptista	05-MAY-1886	07-MAY-1886	19 yrs	Taycheedah	Maria Desautels	Petri Brenael/ Felicia Allain
Brenael	Petri	21-AUG-1888	23-AUG-1888	53 yrs	Taycheedah	Felicia Allain	
Brenoel	Danielis	18-JUL-1897	20-JUL-1897	18 yrs	Taycheedah		
Brion	Maria Josepha		11-APR-1865	80 yrs			
Brisson	Pelagia		04-SEP-1897	88 yrs		Alexandri Ste.-Marie	
Brown	Patricii		27-OCT-1872	1 day			
Brunet	Gideonis	09-DEC-1900	11-DEC-1900	3 yrs	Taycheedah		Avila Brunet/ Delina Lebeau
Brunett	Sophia		10-MAR-1870				
Buch	Oliva	17-MAY-1901	19-MAY-1901	1 yr	Calvary		Josephi Buch/ Georgine Roy
Burel	Petri	14-SEP-1885	15-SEP-1885	77 yrs	Taycheedah	Maria Daniel	
Burkard	Justin		18-SEP-1872	20 mos			
Cage	Pellimoire		26-MAR-1876	3 mos			
Carboneau	Francisci			18 mos			
Carbory	Mary		05-APR-1863				
Cartier	Georgina	15-DEC-1902	17-DEC-1902	23 yrs	Calvary	Claudi Lyonais	
Cary	Bernard	15-JAN-1852	16-JAN-1852	42	Eden		
Cavanagh	Catharina	10-MAR-1904	13-MAR-1904	36 yrs	Eldorado	Petri Duquette	
Channière	Alfred		17-MAR-1863	4 mos			
Chaperon	Maria Olivina	10-AUG-1887	11-AUG-1887	3 mos	Taycheedah		Joannis Chaperon/ Rosalia Le——
Chaquate	——		18-NOV-1871	4 yrs			
Charboneau	Henricus		01-SEP-1866				
Charron	——		28-MAR-1867	1 day			
Charron	Emeri			22 mos			
Charron	Emeritus		03-MAR-1867	19 mos			
Charron	Telespori	12-JAN-1885	16-JAN-1885	22 yrs	Taycheedah		Jacobi Charron/ Delima Laguerre
Chartrand	Emeritus		30-OCT-1867	2 yrs			
Chartrand	Odilia		16-OCT-1867	33 mos			
Chaunier	Joannes Baptisa			14 mos			
Chauniere	Isaias		01-JUL-1866	21 mos		Petri Duquette	
Chauniere	Lepage	01-JUL-1866	01-JUL-1866	20 -			
Chef	Henricus		25-AUG-1861	8 mos			
Chef	Petri			4 mos			
Chef	Petri			4 mos			
Cheff **	Petri	16-FEB-1901	13-FEB-1901	79 yrs	Calvary	Petri Duquette	
Chenart	Juliae	12-NOV-1882	16-NOV-1882	37 yrs	Taycheedah	Samuelis Bessette	
Chinard	Philom—	04-JUL-1879	13-JUL-1879	23 --			
Choinière	Maria Lucovica	04-APR-1894	07-APR-1894	72 yrs	Taycheedah	Vitalis Gratton	
Claus	Emilia		10-AUG-1864	8 yrs			
Clavet	Joann Baptista	16-MAY-1899	18-MAY-1899	102 yrs	Calvary		
Clinch	Olive	20-FEB-1920	23-FEB-1920	80 yrs	Calvary		
Clish	Joannis Baptista	21-JUL-1892	23-JUL-1892	13 yrs	Taycheedah		Ludovici Clish/ Delphina Dufresne
Clish	Julia	21-DEC-1885	23-DEC-1885	18 mos	Taycheedah		Ludovici Clish/ Delphina Dufresne
Clish-Dufort	Julia-	08-MAR-1890	11-MAR-1890	63 yrs	Taycheedah	Antonii Dufort	
Cloumb	William		29-MAY-1877	8 yrs, 3 mos			
Clure	Maria Anna	06-NOV-1887	08-NOV-1887	25 yrs	Cokefield	Caroli Eton	
Collins	Delima		14-OCT-1860	12 yrs			
Comeau	Medardi	24-MAR-1893	27-MAR-1893	81 yrs	Taycheedah	Mathilda Gibeault	

Surname	Given Name	Death	Burial	Age	Cemetery	Spouse	Parents
Connell	Joannes		01-SEP-1861	19 yrs			
Conway	Catharina		29-OCT-1872	7 yrs			
Cook	A. —		27-JUL-1872	1 yrs			
Corbeil	Marguerita Maria	21-JUN-1887	22-JUN-1887	12 days	Taycheedah		Petri-Treffle Corbeil/ Ostia Maheu
Corbeille	Adolphe		19-AUG-1875	1 yr, 5 mos			
Corbeille	Joseph		19-JAN-1876	70 yrs			
Corbeille	Adelina	30-JUN-1904	05-JUL-1904	26 yrs	Taycheedah	Francisici Jentz	
Corbeille	Amanda	22-JUL-1881	26-JUL-1881	3 yrs	Taycheedah		Evaristi Corbeille/ Mathilda Venne
Corbeille	Ernesti Francisci	19-SEP-1891	20-SEP-1891	7 mos	Taycheedah	Francisici Jentz	Napoleonis-Gotici Corbeille/ Melinda Lebeau
Corbeille	Eugenia	26-AUG-1890	27-AUG-1890	7 mos	Taycheedah		Eurista Corbeille/ Mathilda Venne
Corbeille	Josephi	22-JAN-1894	25-JAN-1894	59 yrs	Taycheedah	Mathilda Groux	
Corbeille	Josephi Alfredi	09-OCT-1884	10-OCT-1884	4 mos	Taycheedah	Mathilda Groux	
Corbeille	Petri Ernesti	26-SEP-1885	27-SEP-1885	10 —	Taycheedah		Evaristi Corbeille/ Mathilda Venne
Corbett	Joannes		14-JAN-1862	20 mos			
Corriere	Davidis	21-DEC-1897	24-DEC-1897	54 yrs	Calvary	Lea- Theriault	
Costan	Joannes			8 mos			
Costello	Maria		06-FEB-1863	4 yrs		Lea- Theriault	
Coté	N.			3 mos			
Couillard	Maria	12-OCT-1881	14-OCT-1881	73 yrs	Taycheedah	Pa--agis Trottier	
Crammer	Felix		21-DEC-1862	5 yrs			
Cyr	Flavia	27-NOV-1899	30-NOV-1899	67 yrs	Calvary	Vita Langois	
Cyr	Lizette		07-MAY-1864				
Cyr	Margaritta	07-APR-1899	10-APR-1899	76 yrs	Calvary	Juliani Rasette	
Cyr	Sophia	29-MAR-1885	31-MAR-1885	66 yrs	Taycheedah	Narcissi Bissonnette	
Czarnezki	Joseph	22-NOV-1919	25-NOV-1919	70 yrs	Calvary		
D--n-- -	Maria Juliana		01-APR-1873			Narcissi Bissonnette	
Dandelin	Adeas	10-JAN-1903	14-JAN-1903	37 yrs	Calvary	Gulielmi Painter	
Daniel	Stephani	26-JUL-1888	28-JUL-1888	64 yrs	Taycheedah		
Daniels	Francisci		06-AUG-1871				
DeLajeunnesse	Bellanie		13-OCT-1875	5 wks			
Delfour	Auguste		10-MAY-1975	25 yrs			
Delfair	Maria Louisa		02-FEB-1865	65 yrs			
DeMarche	George		16-JUN-1875	4 mos			
Demarches	Martin		06-SEP-1876	5 mos, 2 days			
Demars	—			6 mos			
Demars	Ferdinius		20-MAR-1867	15 mos			
Demers	Alfredus		01-JUN-1867	20 mos			
Demers	Elizabetha		01-SEP-1866				
Demers	Juliani		17-SEP-1872				
Demers	Juliani						
Demers	Juliani	01-MAY-1887	04-MAY-1887	49 yrs	Taycheedah		
Denau	Celina	03-DEC-1887	06-DEC-1887	49 yrs	Taycheedah	Vitalis Edoin	
Deshottel	Madame		01-OCT-1877				
Desjardins	Sophia	22-FEB-1888	26-FEB-1888	78 yrs	Taycheedah	Michaelis Pomminville	
Desnoyers	Adelia		17-SEP-1866				
Desnoyers	Huberti	26-MAY-1904	29-MAY-1904	69 yrs	Calvary	Michaelis Pomminville	
Deso—	Guillelmus Georgius Michael		15-JUL-1872				
Despes	Alfredus		06-NOV-1864				
Desrochers	Alexius		23-FEB-1863				

186

Surname	Given Name	Death	Burial	Age	Cemetery	Spouse	Parents
Desvillers	Adolphi	27-JUL-1902	30-JUL-1902	32 yrs	Calvary		
Desvillers	Eduardi	25-OCT-1891	27-OCT-1891	5 yrs	Taycheedah		Emilii Desvillers/ Maria Laberge
Desvillers	Emelii	17-MAR-1902	20-MAR-1902	44 yrs	Calvary		
Desvillers	Rosalia	16-JUN-1898	18-JUN-1898	64 yrs	Calvary	Constantine Lomblot	
Devillers	Amati	10-APR-1884	12-APR-1884	4 yrs	Taycheedah		Amati Devillers/ Maria Laberge
Devillers	Desdatus Josephus		23-SEP-1861	3 yrs			
Devillers	Leonardus		29-JUN-1863	38 yrs			
Devry	Anna Catherina		28-JUN-1865	90 yrs			
Diette	Famille		11-DEC-1875	38 yrs			
Dinelle	Elizabeth	14-JUL-1886	16-JUL-1886	15 yrs	Taycheedah		Ludovici Dinelle/ Dionysia Gervais
Dinelle	Israelis	31-AUG-1883	03-SEP-1883	25 yrs	Taycheedah	Sophia Belanger	
Dinelle	Joseph	02-AUG-1879	04-AUG-1879	38 yrs	Taycheedah	Sophia Belanger	
Dinelle	Ludovici	26-MAY-1889	28-MAY-1889	14 yrs	Taycheedah		Ludovici Dinelle/ Dyonisia Gervais
Dinelle	Maria	25-SEP-1893	27-SEP-1893	20 yrs	Taycheedah		Ludovici Dinelle/ Dyonsia Gervais
Dinelle	Telespori	16-AUG-1883	17-AUG-1883	7 mos	Taycheedah		Ludovici Dinelle/ Dyonisia Gervais
Dobrinot	George T	12-NOV-1918	15-NOV-1918	33 yrs	Calvary	Sophia Belanger	Joseph Dobrindt/ Catherine Hess
Dodelin	Adiline						
Dohany	Patricius						
Dondelain	Olivier		24-MAR-1876	68 yrs			
Dougherty	Dyonisius		11-JUN-1863				
Doyle	Mauritii						
Dubois	Laurentii Henrici	17-NOV-1894	19-NOV-1894	6 yrs	Taycheedah		Josephi Dubois/ Cedulia Beaudreault
Dubois	Petri	15-APR-1901	18-APR-1901	82 yrs	Calvary		
Dubois	W. M.		17-MAR-1865	6 wks			
Duclos	Antonini			85 yrs			
Duffy	Marguarita			7 yrs			
Duford	Madame		10-JUL-1878	42 yrs			
Dufort	—			56 yrs			
DuFresne	Anastasia	09-MAR-1920	11-MAR-1920	74 yrs	Taycheedah	Cyrille Langlois	
Dufresne	Alfredi	01-JUN-1882	03-JUN-1882	19 yrs	Taycheedah		Petri Dufresne/ Onesima Meunier-LaPierre
Dufresne	Delphina	17-AUG-1886	19-AUG-1886	48 yrs	Taycheedah	Ludovici Clish	
Dugas	Adelina	15-MAR-1891	19-MAR-1891	55 yrs	Taycheedah	Oliverii Hurteau	
Dumas	Joannis Baptista	17-AUG-1894	20-AUG-1894	68 yrs	Calvary	Maria Perron	
Dumund*	Madame		02-AUG-1876	50 yrs 7 mos			
Dun—ind*	Madame		02-AUG-1876	50 yrs, 7 mos			
Dupruy	Gulielmi Arthuri	23-AUG-1885	24-AUG-1885	3 days	Taycheedah	Maria Perron	Ludgerii Dupuy/ Julia Lucier
Dupuis	Baptista						
Dupuis	Eusebius						
Dupuis	Jean B					Maria Perron	
Dupuis	Victoris	24-JAN-1894	25-JAN-1894	12 yrs	Taycheedah		Ludgerii Dupuis/ Juliana Lucier
Dupuis*	Madame Zoe		28-JUL-1876				
Dupuis*	Madame Zoé		28-JUL-1876				
Dupuy	Belonisa	24-DEC-1881	26-DEC-1881	49 yrs	Taycheedah	Octavi Roberge	
Dupuy	Guilielmi	05-JAN-1883	07-JAN-1883	2 yrs	Taycheedah		Onesimi Dupuy/ Onesiphasa Préfontaine
Duquet	Dionysia	07-APR-1884	09-APR-1884	67 yrs	Taycheedah	Josephi Dumas	
Duquette	Virginia			8 mos			
Durocher	Adolphi	13-DEC-1883	15-DEC-1883	59 yrs	Taycheedah	Henrietta Rondeau	
Durocher	Angela Rosa	11-AUG-1886	13-AUG-1886	20 yrs	Taycheedah	Benjaminis Atkinson	
Durocher	Francisci	28-OCT-1886	31-OCT-1886	52 yrs	Taycheedah	Sophia Pellan	

Surname	Given Name	Death	Burial	Age	Cemetery	Spouse	Parents
Durocher	Henrici	20-DEC-1889	23-DEC-1889	17 yrs	Taycheedah		Adolphi Durocher/ Henrica Rondeau
Durocher	Joanna	21-AUG-1886	23-AUG-1886	32 yrs	Taycheedah	Leopoldi Venne	
Durocher	Rosa	10-SEP-1895	11-SEP-1895	1 yr	Taycheedah		Adolphi Durocher/ Rosa Préfontaine
Eagan	Johannes		14-NOV-1860		Byron		
Early	Michael		05-JAN-1862	c. 45 yrs			
Ebert	Antonius		05-JUL-1861				
Ebert	Isidore		02-MAR-1863				
Ebert	Josephus		07-JUN-1861	11 mos			
Ebert	Onesimus		14-AUG-1867	16 mos			
Edoin	Adelina	05-AUG-1904	08-AUG-1904	34 yrs	Taycheedah		
Edoin	Delima	14-OCT-1881	16-OCT-1881	8 mos	Taycheedah	Severi Edoin	
Edoin	Josephi			5 yrs			
Edoin	Vitalis			2 mos			
Ellie	Victoria		29-JAN-1875	48 yrs			
Errard	Ephrem	16-JUL-1887	18-JUL-1887	33 yrs	Taycheedah		
Etier	Nelson		11-AUG-1866	6 yrs			
Etier	Peter		01-MAR-1867				
Fahy	Nicholai		08-SEP-1872				
Faucher	Flavia	07-OCT-1902	09-OCT-1902	69 yrs	Taycheedah		
Faucher	Josephte		22-OCT-1869				
Faucher	Sophia	27-JUN-1899	01-JUL-1899	76 yrs	Taycheedah		
Fee	Joannis						
Ferdinand	Jacobi						
Finnet	Isaia		01-JUN-1875	1 day			
Finnet	Joseph		01-JUN-1875	1 day			
Fitz-Henry	Anna		20-JAN-1861	33 yrs			
Foisy	Maria	13-JUN-1881	15-JUN-1881	57 yrs	Taycheedah	Alexandri Audet-LaPointe	
Fontaine	Amati	16-JAN-1881	16-JAN-1881	3 yrs	Taycheedah		Edmundi Fontaine/ Marguerita Racette
Fontaine	Eleosia	26-FEB-1881	07-MAR-1881	8 mos	Taycheedah		Edmundi Fontaine/ Margeritta Racette
Fontaine	Leon		14-JAN-1875	4 yrs			
Fontaine	Narcissus		30-MAY-1871				
Foret	Alice		14-NOV-1871	23 yrs			
Fort——	Joannes Baptista		02-SEP-1866	6 mos		Alexandri Audet-LaPointe	
Frechette	Francisci		30-OCT-1881	2 yrs	Taycheedah		Olivieri Frechette/ Helena Donahue
Freenor-Jentz	Emila	31-OCT-1918	19-NOV-1918	35 yrs	Calvary	—— Freenor	
Frenchette	Alpha	26-DEC-1901	29-DEC-1901	56 yrs	Calvary		
Frenette	Isaia	30-MAR-1888	02-APR-1888	89 yrs	Taycheedah	Mathilda Hébert	
Frenette	Theresa	23-FEB-1920	26-FEB-1920	55 yrs	Taycheedah	Martin Balthazor	
Frizette	Mathilda			5 yrs			
Gable	Felix			5 yrs	Byron		
Gagnier	Eduardi	15-JAN-1896	18-JAN-1896	23 yrs	Calvary		Francisci Gagnier/ Emilia Lepine
Gagnier	Eduardi	14-JUN-1892	16-JUN-1892	15 yrs	Taycheedah		Eduardi Gagnier/ Edessa Pariseau
Gagnier	Esther	02-MAR-1893		83 yrs	Taycheedah	Renei Surprenant	
Gagnier	Gertrudis	07-MAY-1893	09-MAY-1893	4 yrs	Taycheedah		Eduardi Gagnier/ Edessa Pariseau
Gagnier	Henrici	11-MAR-1896	13-MAR-1893	26 yrs	Calvary		Francisci Gagnier/ Emilia Lepine
Gagnier	Ludovica	25-OCT-1891	26-OCT-1891	7 mos	Taycheedah		Pauli Gagnier/ Josephina Duquet
Gagnier	Pauli	11-JUN-1891	13-JUN-1891	74 yrs	Taycheedah	Renei Surprenant	
Gaige	Clotilde		25-JUN-1875	53 yrs			
Galipeau	Maria Louisa	07-OCT-1880	08-OCT-1880	10 mos			Josephi Galipeau/ Louisa Bouchard

Surname	Given Name	Death	Burial	Age	Cemetery	Spouse	Parents
Gallaghar	Dyonisius		10-NOV-1861				
Gamelin	Angela	01-JUN-1901	01-JUN-1901	87 yrs	Taycheedah	Ludovici Lyonais	
Ganard	Rosana	10-AUG-1881	12-AUG-1881	7 mos	Taycheedah		Ludovici Ganard/ Delima Blanche
Gardner	Lawrence	04-JUL-1919	07-JUL-1919	35 yrs	Calvary		Paul Gardner/ Marie-Katherine Dobrindi
Garo	Eugenius		05-SEP-1866	13 mos			
Garo	Eustasia		05-MAY-1861				
Garren	Joannes						
Garringer	Sebastianus		16-OCT-1872				
Garro	Virginia		11-MAR-1865	2 yrs			
Gascon	Joanna	15-FEB-1899	17-FEB-1899	75 yrs	Calvary	Peter DuBois	
Gauthier	Antonia						
Gelbo	Joseph		19-SEP-1875				
Gerbay	Emmory		23-MAY-1875	21 yrs, 7 mos, 5 days			
Gerber	Elizabetha		16-OCT-1865	7 1/2 yrs			
Germani							
Gervais	Carali	16-DEC-1881	17-DEC-1881	10 yrs	Taycheedah		Isaac Gervais/ Virginia Grise
Gervais	Clara		31-DEC-1891	4 mos	Taycheedah		Emerici Gervais/ Olivina Charron
Gervais	Eliza		20-DEC-1862	3 yrs			
Gervais	Gulielmi	11-DEC-1902	13-DEC-1902	7 yrs	Calvary	—— Barbeau	
Gervais	Josephi		29-DEC-1881	12 yrs	Taycheedah		Isaac Gervais/ Virginia Grise
Gervais	Ludovici	31-DEC-1903	02-JAN-1904	57 yrs	Calvary		
Gervais	Narcissi	04-JAN-1884	07-JAN-1884	60 yrs	Taycheedah	Adela Barbeau	
Gervais	Virginia			11 yrs			
Gilbert	Delphina Elizabeth	10-DEC-1881	12-DEC-1881	-- yrs	Taycheedah		Antonii Gilbert/ Jonna Frederic
Gilbert	Emma	16-FEB-1882	18-FEB-1882	9 yrs	Taycheedah		Antonii Gilbert/ J-Anna Frederic
Gilbert	Georgii		18-OCT-1881	18 yrs	Taycheedah		Antonii Gilbert/ Jonna Frederic
Gilbert	Jane	01-MAR-1919	03-MAR-1919	83 yrs	Calvary		
Gilbert	Ludovici	02-OCT-1892	05-OCT-1892	22 yrs	Taycheedah		
Gill	Michael		25-DEC-1852	4 yrs	Bryon		
Gillis			11-NOV-1861				
Gilman	Albert		04-JUN-1876	4 yrs, 5 mos			
Gilman	Thoma	04-AUG-1889	08-AUG-1889	64 yrs	Lamartine	Domitilda Gratton	
Gireau	Addea		17-MAR-1903	43 yrs	Calvary	Carole Stamm	
Godin	Francisca	14-FEB-1880	14-FEB-1880	96 yrs			
Godin	Ludovicus	26-APR-1880	28-APR-1880	55 yrs			
Gordon	Alexander		05-NOV-1871	4 yrs			
Gordon	Caroli Acham	19-NOV-1881	21-NOV-1881	70 yrs	Taycheedah	Maria Manz	
Gordon	Eduardi	13-SEP-1890	15-SEP-1890	7 mos	Taycheedah		Georgii Gordon/ Sara Balthazar
Gordon	Joannis	12-JAN-1897	15-JAN-1897	12 yrs	Taycheedah		Georgii Gordon/ Sara Balthazar
Gores	Maria Catharina						
Gosselain	J—						
Gosselain	Jos						
Gosselin	Eva	30-OCT-1884	01-NOV-1884	1 yr	Taycheedah		Georgii Gosselin/ Louisa Leduc
Gosselin	Joannis Baptista	18-OCT-1894	24-OCT-1894	76 yrs	Calvary	Ludovici Chritien	
Gosselin	Maria	30-OCT-1884	01-NOV-1884	2 yrs	Taycheedah		Georgii Gosselin/ Louisa Leduc
Goyet	——		30-MAR-1862	4 yrs			
Goyette	Joseph	11-JAN-1902	14-JAN-1902	94 yrs	Taycheedah		
Goyette	Lina	07-NOV-1883	08-NOV-1883	18 yrs	Taycheedah		Francisci Goyette/ Delima Brandeau
Grandbois	-vidis	15-AUG-1880	17-AUG-1880	42 yrs	Taycheedah	-o- Tessa	

Surname	Given Name	Death	Burial	Age	Cemetery	Spouse	Parents
Grandbois	Georgii	11-APR-1896	15-APR-1896	22 yrs	Taycheedah		
Gratant	-o—		05-DEC-1876	15 yrs, 6 mos			
Grathan	Delphina		19-FEB-1875	19 yrs			
Graton	Pheba		11-FEB-1873				
Graton	Albina	05-APR-1881	07-APR-1881	27 yrs	Taycheedah	Andrea Rondeau	
Gratton	Laurentii	25-FEB-1901	27-FEB-1901	9 mos	Calvary	Malina Michotte	
Gratton	Vitalis	02-DEC-1898	05-DEC-1898	77 yrs	Taycheedah		
Gratton-Gilman	Domitilda	02-SEP-1895	04-SEP-1895	66 yrs	Lamartine	Thoma Gilman	
Graus			29-FEB-1864	6 yrs			Caroli Grise/ Esther Dufresne
Grise	Joannis	30-JUN-1889	02-JUL-1889	12 mos	Taycheedah	Isaaci Gervais	
Grisé	Virginia	08-APR-1895	10-APR-1895	53 yrs	Taycheedah	Josephi- Corbeill	
Groux	Mathilda	18-APR-1892	21-APR-1892	59 yrs	Taycheedah	Vitalis Gratton	
Guénard	Esther	26-FEB-1884	28-FEB-1884	55 yrs	Taycheedah	Elizabeth Stade	
Guernon	Alfredi	06-JUL-1902	07-JUL-1902	6 yrs	Taycheedah		
Hall	Stellae	08-DEC-1882	10-DEC-1882	18 mos			Alberti Hall/ Louisa Devilliers
Harndis	Carali Napoleonis	25-MAR-1903	28-MAR-1903	55 yrs	Rienzie		
Harnois	Edmira		01-NOV-1866				
Harnois	Oliveri	25-DEC-1892	28-DEC-1892	79 yrs	Taycheedah	Marg-rita Marrais	
Harnois	Triffle		14-NOV-1876				
Hébert	Juliana	10-JAN-1891	13-MAR-1891	72 yrs	Taycheedah	Isaia Roy	
Hébert	William		07-DEC-1876	25 yrs			
Hébert-Frenette	Mathilda	30-MAR-1888	02-APR-1888	77 yrs	Taycheedah	Isaia Frenette	
Hébert-Lapierrre	Felicitatis	11-JAN-1886	14-JAN-1886		Taycheedah	Nazaire Meunier-LaPierre	
Hennis	Petrus	02-JUL-1861	02-JUL-1861	22 yrs			
Heussay	Marie Ludovica	09-OCT-1903	11-OCT-1903	61 yrs	Calvary	Jacob La Rose	
Hicken	Ludovici Elm.	14-MAR-1892	16-MAR-1892	3 mos	Taycheedah		Henrici Hicken/ Melinda Gagnier
Hicken	Maud Mabel	26-NOV-1887	27-NOV-1887	9 days	Taycheedah		Henirii Hicken/ Delima Gagneau
Higgins	Margaritta Bella	08-SEP-1890	09-SEP-1890	7 mos	Taycheedah		Henrici Higgins/ Adelina Gagner
Hoge	Eleonora	09-MAY-1904	11-MAY-1904	3 days	Calvary		Gustavi Hoge/ Maria Balthazar
Houle	Genevieve	12-JAN-1881	16-JAN-1881	70 yrs	Taycheedah	Ludovici Paquet	
Houle	Louisa	17-FEB-1881	19-FEB-1881	71 yrs	Taycheedah	Jacobi Langlois-Fontaine	
Hurt—	Narcissus						
Hurteau	Emilia	17-NOV-1904	20-NOV-1904	73 yrs	Taycheedah	Antonii Boivin	
Hurteau	Oliveri	22-OCT-1886	25-OCT-1886	82 yrs	Taycheedah	Adelina Dugas	
Hurtot	Joannes Ludovicus		09-SEP-1864	22 mos			
Inna—	Lucia		31-MAR-1877	8 yrs			
Jalbert	Odelia		11-DEC-1899		Taycheedah	Francisci Carbonneau	
Jerve	Joie		01-APR-1876	10 yrs			
Joly	Eudoxia	11-DEC-1903	13-DEC-1903	48 yrs	Calvary	Luca Brunet	
Joly-Landerman	Teresia	27-APR-1890	29-APR-1890	70 yrs	Taycheedah	Augustini Landerman	
Jordan	Maria	20-APR-1888	25-APR-1888	67 yrs	Taycheedah	Lot Angelici Maurice	
Josephi	Petri		18-AUG-1899	1 yr	Calvary		Abraham Josephi/ Maria Josephi
Joubert	Lisote Elizabeth						
Joubert	Xaverius		26-SEP-1871	51 yrs			
Justin	Agnes Gertruda						
Kenni	Jacobus		09-AUG-1861		Byron		
Kierus	Helen		05-NOV-1851	15 yrs		Lot Angelici Maurice	
King	——		29-MAR-1867	6 -			
Kinztler	Lucilla	26-OCT-1900	28-OCT-1900	6 mos	Taycheedah		Henrili Kinztler/ Maria Dion

190

Surname	Given Name	Death	Burial	Age	Cemetery	Spouse	Parents
Krammer	Clementina		13-OCT-1862	27 yrs			
Krembs	------						
Krembs	------						
Krembs	Ludovicus		11-MAY-1866	33 yrs		Rosalia Devillers	
Krämmer	Catharina		27-AUG-1866	37 yrs		Alberti Liebermann	
Krämmer	Eberhard			5 -			
L'ecuyer	Petrus		28-DEC-1861				
L----eau	Constantis	27-NOV-1881	29-NOV-1881	47 yrs	Taycheedah		
La Rose	Philumena	09-NOV-1903	12-NOV-1903	36 yrs	Calvary	Alberti Liebermann	
Laberge	Alfret		22-FEB-1875	7 mos 10 days			
Laberge	Madame		15-FEB-1877				
LaBerge	Rosina		10-AUG-1877	6 mos			
Laborde	Alexander	01-JAN-1851	11-JAN-1851		St John Church, Calumet		
Ladoun	Damas		14-NOV-1858			Alberti Liebermann	
LaFontaine	Edmire-		23-FEB-1878				
LaFontaine-Roberge	Maria	03-MAR-1887	05-MAR-1887	32 yrs	Taycheedah	Octavii Roberge	
Lafort	Angela		30-MAR-1865	25 yrs			
Lafort	Joannis Baptista	11-JUN-1898	13-JUN-1898	64 yrs		Emelia Gagnier	
Laguerre-Charron	Delima	10-DEC-1895	13-DEC-1895	58 yrs	Taycheedah	Jacobi Charro	
Lajeunesse	Henrici	09-MAY-1895	12-MAY-1895		Lamartine	Eleonara Goyette	
Lajeunesse	Ludovici	11-MAY-1894	13-MAY-1894	3 yrs	Taycheedah		Generosi Lajeunesse/ Olivina Balthazar
Lajeunesse	Ludovoci	18-DEC-1900	20-DEC-1900	9 yrs	Taycheedah	Eleonara Goyette	Generosi Lajeunesse/ Ludevina Balthazar
Lambert	Alberti	21-SEP-1894	23-SEP-1894	5 mos	Taycheedah		Michaelis Lambert/ Sophronia Barbeau
Lambert	Anna		04-SEP-1881	4 mos	Taycheedah		Michaelis Lambert/ Sophronia Barbeau
Lambert	Delia		26-AUG-1875	11 mos			
Lambert	Delima		25-AUG-1881	3 mos	Taycheedah		Michaelis Lambert/ Sophronia Barbeau
Lambert	Zephiri	23-JUL-1892	25-JUL-1892	13 yrs	Taycheedah		Michaelis Lambert/ Sophronia Barbeau
Lamblat	Maria	24-DEC-1884	26-DEC-1884	24 yrs	Taycheedah	Vincentii Annen	
Lan-	Maria		29-JAN-1880	48 yrs			
Lanctot	Oscilia	02-FEB-1880	03-FEB-1880	2 yrs			
Landerman	Alberti	18-JUN-1885	20-JUN-1885	3 wks	Taycheedah		Josephi Landerman/ Ophelia Dumas
Landerman	Aurelia	09-MAR-1883	22-MAR-1883	22 yrs	Taycheedah	Josephi Baillargeon	
Landerman	Leandri	24-OCT-1880	26-OCT-1880	18 mos	Taycheedah		Hilarii La-derman/ Ros--deLima Moquin
Landerman	Leonis	07-MAR-1884	09-MAR-1884	20 mos	Taycheedah		Josephi Landerman/ Ophilia Dumas
Landerman	Marcellina	03-DEC-1885	05-DEC-1885	71 yrs	Taycheedah	Francisci Venne	
Landerman	Philia	25-MAY-1898	27-MAY-1898	54 yrs	Taycheedah		
Landermann	Augustini	20-OCT-1888	22-OCT-1888	72 yrs	Taycheedah	Teresia Joly	
Landermann	Francisci Pacifici	19-SEP-1886	20-SEP-1886	3 mos	Taycheedah	Teresia Joly	Josephi Landerman/ Ophilia Dumas
Landreman	------						
Landry	Natalia	28-MAR-1891	30-MAR-1891	84 yrs	Taycheedah	Christophori Letourneau	
Langlois	------	27-FEB-1902	28-FEB-1902	1 day	Calvary		
Langlois	Adrianus		28-OCT-1871	5 yrs			Georgii Langlois/ Maria Moquin
Langlois	Amati	05-JUL-1883	06-JUL-1883	3 mos	Taycheedah		Edmundi Langlois/ Margarita Racette
Langlois	Edmond		28-AUG-1875	10 mos			
Langlois	Isaia	28-FEB-1897	02-MAR-1897	40 yrs	Calvary	Regina Elsberg	
Langlois	Maria		31-AUG-1895	1 month	Calvary		Vitalis-David Langlois/ Emelia Balthazar
Langlois	Maria Hermina Zitta	11-SEP-1893	15-SEP-1893	9 mos	Taycheedah		Vita-is Langlois/ Emelia Balthazar
Langlois	Martie Josephine		20-MAR-1875	24 days			
Langlois	Norbor		20-JAN-1875	56 yrs			

Surname	Given Name	Death	Burial	Age	Cemetery	Spouse	Parents
Langlois	Olivina		08-MAR-1865	19 mos			
Langlois	Vital		20-JAN-1861	2 yrs			
Langlois	Vitalie		25-JUL-1872				
Lanto	------		28-DEC-1876				
Lanto	Cordilia		31-MAY-1877	14 mos			
Lanto	Madame Cristine		17-DEC-1877	73 yrs			
Lanto	Olivine		06-DEC-1877	21 yrs, 5 mos			
LaPointe-Audet	Alexandri	26-OCT-1888	30-OCT-1888	76 yrs	Taycheedah		B-tici Laporte/ Ludovica Venne
Laporte	Josephi	11-MAR-1885	13-MAR-1885	12 yrs	Taycheedah		Jacobi Larose/ Ludovica Houssait
Larose	Alfredi	08-OCT-1888	10-OCT-1888	21 yrs	Taycheedah		
Larose	Jacobi	19-APR-1904	22-APR-1904	75 yrs	Calvary		Jacobi Larose/ L-udovica Houssait
Larose	Josephi		29-SEP-1891	8 yrs	Taycheedah		
Lauzon	Felicis	08-OCT-1901	11-OCT-1901	72 yrs	Calvary		
LaVallie	Magdelina	01-APR-1899	04-APR-1899	90 yrs	Taycheedah	Joseph Goyette	
Le-uyer	------					Joseph Goyette	
Leaghy	Michael			60 yrs			
Leary	Anne		13-NOV-1875				
Lebeau	Angela	10-MAR-1920	12-MAR-1920	89 yrs			Moises Lebeau/ Angela Macier
Lebeau	Ezilda	16-JAN-1882	18-JAN-1882	20 yrs	Taycheedah		
Lebeau	Ludovicus			2 yrs			
LeBlanc	Sophia		07-DEC-1867	71 yrs			
LeBlanc	Henrici Joseph	12-SEP-1904	15-SEP-1904	39 yrs	Calvary		
Leclair	Eusebius						
Leclair	Ludovicus		11-AUG-1866	8 yrs			
Leclerc	Elizabeth		01-AUG-1870	76 yrs			
Lecoq	Mathuri Walter	28-AUG-1886	29-AUG-1886	1 month	Taycheedah	Joseph Goyette	Ludovici Lecoq/ Laurentia Racette
Ledoux	Joseph B.		01-MAR-1861				
Leduc	Margareta Josephina		26-JAN-1868	14 days			
Leduc	Petrus						
Leduc-Miles	Ludovicus Phillipus						
Lefefer	Caroli Gulielmi	21-SEP-1891	23-SEP-1891	2 mos	Taycheedah		Georgii Lefefer/ Virginia Turcot
Lefeve	Carolina		27-FEB-1864	7 yrs			
LeFort	Engelle		17-OCT-1875	65 yrs			
LeFort	Joannes		12-MAY-1871	16 yrs			
LeFort	Joseph		22-JUL-1877	6 wks			
Lefort	Josephi	11-JUL-1901	14-JUL-1901	50 yrs	Taycheedah	Josephina Dogherty	
Lefort	Maria		16-MAY-1872	16 yrs			
Lefort	Paulina	02-APR-1882	04-APR-1882	4 yrs	Taycheedah		
Lefort	Petri	24-MAR-1889	26-MAR-1889	57 yrs	Taycheedah	Victoria Johnson	
Lego	Belonisii						
Lemaire	Herminia		30-MAY-1867				
Lemaire	Petri						
Lemieux	Catherina	07-MAY-1887	10-MAY-1887	72 yrs	Taycheedah	Bernardi Peron	
Lemieux	Narcissi	16-JUL-1881	17-JUL-1881	3 days	Taycheedah		Israel Lemieux/ Amelina LaRose
Lemieux	Petrus	13-JUL-1879	15-JUL-1878	72 yrs		Bernardi Peron	
Lemieux	Victorina		13-NOV-1867	2 yrs			
Lemire	Eleonora						
Lemire	Stephanus		11-AUG-1864	5 mos			
Leoghry	Anostosia		11-MAY-1861	75 yrs			

Surname	Given Name	Death	Burial	Age	Cemetery	Spouse	Parents
Leone	Petri		29-SEP-1869				
Leonen-	Josephus		06-MAR-1861				
Lepine	——		29-AUG-1865				
Lepine	Corinne	27-FEB-1899	01-MAR-1899	2 yrs	Taycheedah		Thoma Lepine/ Josephina Brunet
Lepine	Emelia	05-MAR-1897	08-MAR-1897	50 yrs	Taycheedah	Francisci Gagnier	
Lepine	Flora	03-MAR-1896	06-MAR-1896	30 yrs	Taycheedah		Josephi Lepine/ Elizabeth Rondeau
Lepine	Isabella		28-FEB-1872				
Lepine	Josephina	10-MAY-1892	15-MAY-1892	5 yrs	Taycheedah		Petri Lepine/ Josephina Corbeille
Lepine	Louis	24-JAN-1920	27-JAN-1920	42 yrs	Calvary		
Lepine	Louisa	31-AUG-1881		8 mos	Taycheedah		Joseph Lepine/ Sophia Beaudriault
Lepine	Ludovici	25-MAR-1890	28-MAR-1890	76 yrs	Taycheedah	Emelina Rondeau	
Lepine	Luminae	19-JAN-1899	21-JAN-1899	9 yrs	Taycheedah		Thoma Lepine/ Josephina Brunet
Lepine	Marguerita	13-MAY-1887	15-MAY-1887	35 yrs	Taycheedah		Ludovici Lepine/ Emelia Lepine
Lepine	Marie		16-JUN-1875	2 mos			
Letourneau	Ada	09-JAN-1899	12-JAN-1899	27 yrs	Rienzii	Robert Scott	
Letourneau	Christophori	27-FEB-1888	29-FEB-1888	82 yrs	Taycheedah	Natalia Landry	
Letourneau	Elizabetha		17-SEP-1861	17 mos			
Letourneau	Georgii Henrici	01-MAY-1891	03-MAY-1891	17 yrs	Taycheedah		Christophori Letourneau/ Maria Molleur
Letourneau	Gratia	24-FEB-1893	26-FEB-1893	10 yrs	Taycheedah		Paschalis Letourneau/ Maria Baumhaur
Letourneau	Josephi	22-FEB-1888	25-FEB-1888	18 yrs	Taycheedah		Paschalis Letourneau/ Maria Baunhaur
Letourneau	Natalia	28-OCT-1900	30-OCT-1900	73 yrs	Taycheedah		
Letourneau	Petri	16-APR-1869		2 yrs			
Letourneau	Stella	01-JAN-1887	02-JAN-1887	8 mos	Taycheedah		Paschalis Letourneau/ Maria Boomhauer
Lismond	Hortensia	16-APR-1893	16-APR-1893	61 yrs	Taycheedah	Eugenii Pingair	
Lisote	Clemens		17-SEP-1864	90 yrs			
Loiseau	Francisci	31-MAR-1888	02-APR-1888	8 days	Taycheedah		Caroli Loiseau/ Bertha Bisson
Loiseau	Gulielmi Leonardi	24-MAY-1892	25-MAY-1892	11 mos	Taycheedah		Gulielmi Loiseau/ Sophronia McDonald
Loiseau	Leonardi		06-NOV-1880	7 mos	Taycheedah		Gulielmi Loiseau/ S·ph-onia McDonald
Loisele	Julie			1 yr 11days			
Lomblot	Auralia		01-NOV-1872	3 mos	Calvary		
Lottinville	Heloise	31-JUL-1897	02-AUG-1897	75 yrs	Calvary		
Lucie-	Ludovici	30-JUN-1889	03-JUL-1889	80 yrs	Taycheedah		
Lucifer	Camilii	21-JAN-1903	23-JAN-1904	5 yrs	Taycheedah		Ludovici Lucifer/ Adea Hilt
Lucifer	Joannis M.	20-APR-1901	23-APR-1901	50 yrs	Calvary		
Lyneis	Corin	24-APR-1920	26-APR-1920	80 yrs	Calvary		
Lyonais	Ludovici	31-OCT-1891	03-NOV-1891	80 yrs	Taycheedah	Angela Gamelin	
Manny	Sophia	01-AUG-1892	03-AUG-1892	74 yrs	Taycheedah	Josephi Balthazar	
Mansfield	——						
Marcou	Joannis Maria			3 mos		Neta-Josephina Piehl	
Marcou	Maria Olivine		16-JAN-1876	5 mos			
Marcoux	Emelia	07-MAR-1887	08-MAR-1887	4 yrs	Taycheedah		Alexandri Marcoux/ Eleonara Lajeunesse
Marcoux	Francisci	09-JUN-1889	11-JUN-1889	74 yrs	Taycheedah	Zoa St.-Germain	
Marcoux	Herminia	22-JUN-1885	23-JUN-1885	39 yrs	Taycheedah	Joannis-Baptista Balthazar	
Marcoux	Jeremia	22-JUL-1887	23-JUL-1887	2 yrs	Taycheedah		
Marcoux	Juliani	15-MAY-1888	17-MAY-1888	36 yrs	Taycheedah	—— Heine	
Marcoux	Rosalia	03-MAR-1881	10-MAR-1881	48 yrs	Taycheedah	Ludovici Godin	
Martin	——	04-DEC-1902	07-DEC-1902	3 days	Calvary	Neta-Josephina Piehl	
Martin	Gonofeva	25-NOV-1892	29-NOV-1892	18 mos	Taycheedah		Leonis Martin/ Eleonara Dumas
Martin	Maria Anna	27-JAN-1884	29-JAN-1884	8 mos	Taycheedah		Leonis Martin/ Eleonora Dumas

193

Surname	Given Name	Death	Burial	Age	Cemetery	Spouse	Parents
Mass	Adele	10-MAY-1880	12-MAY-1880	22 yrs	Taycheedah		Josephi Maurice/ Agnetia Fontaine
Maurice	—	07-DEC-1886	10-DEC-1886		Taycheedah		Andrea Maurice/ Emma DuFresne
Maurice	Elizabeth	07-OCT-1897	10-OCT-1897	3 mos	Taycheedah		Josephi Maurice/ Agnetis Fontaine
Maurice	Leonardi-Josephi	20-SEP-1884	21-SEP-1884	6 wks	Taycheedah		
Maurice	Ludovici	24-MAR-1901	27-MAR-1901	73 yrs	Calvary	Mathilda Perron	
McCabe	Petri		06-FEB-1863		Taycheedah		
McCarthy	Maria-Henrici	19-JAN-1885	21-JAN-1885	6 mos	Taycheedah		Michaelis McCarthy/ Elizabeth Tumby
McClone	Bartholomew	11-JAN-1851	11-JAN-1851		Eden		
McCormick	Anno		24-JAN-1863		Taycheedah		
McDonald	Isabella		01-SEP-1862				
McKeaver	P.			7 mos			
Meunier-LaPierre	Jesse	31-DEC-1880	02-JAN-1881	5 yrs	Taycheedah		Czriuci Meunier-LaPierre/ Agnetis Fontaine
Meunier-LaPierre	Leonis Vitalis	11-AUG-1885	12-AUG-1885	4 mos	Taycheedah	Mathilda Perron	Nazarii Meunier-LaPierre/ Felicitatis Hébert
Miller	Isaacus	23-MAR-1873					
Milleur	Francisci		30-JUL-1870				
Mine	Sophia	06-JUN-1898	08-JUN-1898	36 yrs	Calvary	Jeremia Marcoux	
Mishote	Deodati		27-AUG-1868				
Mishote	Josephina		17-JUN-1866	2 yrs			
Mocquin	Franciscus			-- yrs			
Mocquin	Joseph		24-FEB-1863				
Mocquin	Olivina			16 yrs			
Moguin	Zepherini	23-MAR-1899	25-MAR-1899	36 yrs	Calvary	Elizabeth Ferdinand	
Moignin	Hudumia Zoe		12-APR-1876			Joseph Moiguin	
Moignin	Narsis		18-DEC-1876	5 mos			
Moiguin	Joseph		17-APR-1876	61 yrs		Zoe Moignin	
Molheur	Eleonora						
Molleur	Maria	05-APR-1903	08-APR-1903	66 yrs	Taycheedah	Christaphori Letourneau	
Molleur-Dandelin	Sophia	31-OCT-1886	02-NOV-1886		Taycheedah	Oliveri Dandelin	
Mongel	—		27-AUG-1865	10 mos			
Moore	Joannes		15-DEC-1861	1 yrs			
Moquin	Annonima	09-JAN-1902	09-JAN-1902	1 day	Calvary		Nehema Moquin/ Maria Ferdinand
Moquin	Josephi	30-OCT-1901	01-NOV-1901	72 yrs	Calvary		
Moquin	Juliani	14-APR-1891	18-APR-1891	62 yrs	Taycheedah		
Moquin	Louisa	18-OCT-1887	20-OCT-1887	68 yrs	Taycheedah		
Moquin	Narcisis				Fond du Lac	Oliveri Dandelin	
Moquin	Panagii Toussaint	16-MAY-1897	19-MAY-1897	19 yrs	Calvary	Oliveri Dandelin	Joseph Moquin/ Octaline Audet
Morris	Lot	30-DEC-1872				Oliveri Dandelin	
Morris	Maria	10-JUL-1872	10-JUL-1872	36 yrs		— Beaudry	
Moses	Maria Anastasia	23-AUG-1902	24-AUG-1904	14 mos	Taycheedah	Abib Moses	
Mosher-Mangin	Edna	31-AUG-1890	02-SEP-1890	3 mos	Cavalry		Lafayette Mosher-Mangin/ Delia Leduc
Mullen	—		26-JUL-1872	c. 52 yrs			
Mulony	Jacobus						
Murphy	Ahicia	11-JAN-1862	17-JAN-1862				
Murphy	Joannes	11-JAN-1862	17-JAN-1862				
Nomprey	Ludger	15-OCT-1919	17-OCT-1919	80 yrs	Taycheedah		
O'Brien	Marguarita	13-OCT-1860	13-OCT-1860	20 mos			
O'Connel	Mary	15-FEB-1853	16-FEB-1853	c. 16 —			
O'Loughlin	Mary				Dodge County		
O'Loughlin	Michaelis						

194

Surname	Given Name	Death	Burial	Age	Cemetery	Spouse	Parents
Odete	Carolina		30-OCT-1867	21 yrs			
Odete	Petrus		03-DEC-1876				
Olgeis	Francois		18-MAR-1876			Abib Moses	
Ollet	Martin						
Ouelette	Georgi	06-MAR-1903	09-MAR-1903	74 yrs	Taycheedah		
Ouellette	Francisci	03-DEC-1884	05-DEC-1884	21 yrs	Taycheedah	Nazara -----	
Paguette	Emery						
Paquet	Ludovici	19-JUL-1886	21-JUL-1886	83 yrs	Taycheedah		
Paquet	Magdelena	12-OCT-1887	14-OCT-1887	82 yrs	Taycheedah	Andrea Bastien	
Parent	Anna	06-DEC-1880	08-DEC-1880	26 yrs		Josephi Lanctot	
Pariseau	Huberti	12-OCT-1892	14-OCT-1892	76 yrs	Taycheedah		
Pariso-Bellinger	Sophronia		06-MAY-1864				
Parizo	-----		10-OCT-1872	18 mos			
Parizo	Georgius		07-SEP-1866	c. 30 yrs			
Pefontaine	E.ma Odilia		15-JAN-1875	4 yrs			
Pellant	J. Baptista		09-AUG-1871	17 yrs			
Pepins	Joseph Alfreet		30-JUN-1876	18 mos			
Peron	Marie		10-MAY-1876	74 yrs			
Perron	Bernardi	25-OCT-1903	27-OCT-1903	82 yrs	Calvary		
Perron	Delima	01-JUN-1883	02-JUN-1883	39 yrs	Taycheedah		
Perron	Joannis Baptista	17-AUG-1898	19-AUG-1898	62 yrs	Taycheedah	Narcissi Fontaine	
Petit	Felicitas		17-JAN-1872				
Petit-St.-Pierre	Virginia	26-MAY-1884	28-MAY-1884	57 yrs	Taycheedah	Georgii Ouellette	
Petit	Henrica		01-APR-1863				
Pfistner	Maria	09-FEB-1893	11-FEB-1893	3 days	Taycheedah		Philippi Pfistner/ Melvina Duford
Picard	Marceli		26-AUG-1866				
Pierron	Joannis Caroli	26-MAY-1893	27-MAY-1893	65 yrs	Rienzi		
Pingair	Joseph Alfredi	06-SEP-1903	08-SEP-1903	40 yrs	Calvary		
Plotz	Franciscus		09-OCT-1865	4 yrs			
Plouff	Louise	26-FEB-1920	28-FEB-1920	64 yrs	Calvary	Solomon Lepine	
Pratte	Arthuri	30-MAY-1899	10-JUN-1899	25 yrs			
Pratte	Josephi Clarentii	18-AUG-1886	19-AUG-1886	3 yrs	Taycheedah	Solomon Lepine	Fabicis Pratte/ Sara Duquet
Préfontaine	-----		12-MAR-1876				
Préfontaine	-----		29-JUL-1868				
Préfontaine	Alexii		01-NOV-1867				
Préfontaine	Amelia	04-JAN-1881	06-JAN-1881	4 yrs	Taycheedah		Magliorii Préfontaine/ Olivia Desautels
Préfontaine	Anna	21-DEC-1880	23-DEC-1880	12 yrs	Taycheedah		Magliorii Préfontaine/ Olivia Desautels
Préfontaine	Aurelia	24-FEB-1904	27-FEB-1904	82 yrs	Taycheedah	Huberti Rabidoux	
Préfontaine	Barsussi	06-MAY-1898	09-MAY-1898	42 yrs	Taycheedah	Elizabeth Warner	
Préfontaine	Eudoxia	14-AUG-1887	16-AUG-1887	22 yrs	Taycheedah		Alexis- Préfontaine/ Elmiira Hubert
Préfontaine	Henrici	05-FEB-1892	06-FEB-1892	23 yrs	Taycheedah		Alexi Préfontaine/ Elmira Hubert
Préfontaine	Julia	11-FEB-1892	13-FEB-1892	20 yrs	Taycheedah		Alexi Préfontaine/ Elmira Hubert
Préfontaine	Magliorii	22-JAN-1884	26-JAN-1884	45 yrs	Taycheedah	Oliva Desaultel	
Préfontaine	Maria Nathalia	26-DEC-1880	28-DEC-1880	3 yrs	Taycheedah		Magliorii Préfontaine/ Olivia Desautels
Préfontaine	Oliveri	09-APR-1889	11-APR-1889	19 yrs	Taycheedah		Alexis Préfontaine/ Elmira Hubert
Préfontaine	Theresia	08-NOV-1894	10-NOV-1894	12 yr	Taycheedah		Ludgerii Préfontaine/ Julia Limonin
Préfontaine-Pratte **	Desiderati	21-OCT-1894	09-OCT-1894	21 yrs	Taycheedah	Oliva Desaultel	Ludgerii Préfontaine/ Cesaria Laricheliere
Préfontine	Henery Magloir	25-MAY-1891	28-MAY-1891	28 yrs	Taycheedah	Alfredi Pratte	
			12-MAR-1876	6 mos. 11 days			

Surname	Given Name	Death	Burial	Age	Cemetery	Spouse	Parents
Preister	Petri						
Préjean	Julia	24-DEC-1883	26-DEC-1883	65 yrs	Taycheedah	Georgii Audette	
Priss	Maria	06-OCT-1901	08-OCT-1902	40 yrs	Taycheedah	Vitalis Edoin	
Putz	Anna Catharina		25-JAN-1863	105 yrs			
Quin	Joannes		26-JUL-1872	12 yrs			
Raberse	Marie		21-NOV-1876	7 mos			
Rabert	Francisci	16-JUN-1904	19-JUN-1904	80 yrs	Taycheedah	Vitalis Edoin	
Racette	Laurentia	18-AUG-1886	20-AUG-1886	33 yrs	Taycheedah	Ludovici Lecoq	
Racette	Margaritta	04-MAY-1899	06-MAY-1899	44 yrs	Calvary	Edmundi Langois	
Rafferty	Joannis		17-NOV-1876				
Rando	-----		14-JAN-1876	11 yrs			
Rando	Francois						
Raymond	Francisci	25-FEB-1887	27-FEB-1887	7 yrs	Taycheedah		Isidori Raymond/ Solomee Papineau
Raymond	Georgius		12-OCT-1876	82 yrs			
Raymond	Israelis	29-APR-1901	06-MAY-1901	57 yrs	Taycheedah		
Raymond	Mamie	30-NOV-1918	03-DEC-1918	35 yrs	Calvary		
Raymond	Marie Salome		29-APR-1877	7 mos			
Reach	Margarita		13-FEB-1863	1 mos			
Real	Amarantha		09-AUG-1868				
Regnier	Pelagia	25-AUG-1887	27-AUG-1887	73 yrs	Taycheedah	Ludovici Lucien	
Reinhard	Ione	24-FEB-1919	27-FEB-1919	34 yrs	Calvary	C-H Reinhard	
René	-----		23-AUG-1872				
Rial	Joannes Alfredus		15-JUN-1863	8 1/2 yrs			
Roberge	Guillemi	25-FEB-1887	27-FEB-1887		Taycheedah		Octavii Roberge/ Maria LaFontaine
Robert	Edessa	04-OCT-1895	05-OCT-1895	3 mos	Taycheedah		Josephi Robert/ Rosalia Marcoux
Robert	George		07-SEP-1875	14 mos			
Robidou	Alexander			15 yrs, 3 mos			
Robidou	Josephi			13 mos			
Robidoux	Alexii	15-JUN-1892	18-JUN-1892	22 yrs	Taycheedah		Josephi Robidoux/ Herminia Pellant
Robidoux	Anna	02-SEP-1887	04-SEP-1887	3 yrs	Taycheedah		Josephi Robidoux/ Herminia Pellant
Robidoux	Maria- Elizabeth	29-MAR-1890	31-MAR-1890	18 yrs			Josephi Robidoux/ Herminia Pellant
Robidoux	Melania			18 yrs			
Robidoux	Louis Francis			13 mos			
Roche	June	11-JAN-1920		7 mos	Calvary		Fred Rock/ Theresa Brickner
Rock	-----	30-JAN-1882	02-FEB-1882		Taycheedah	C-H Reinhard	
Roget	Liguori		29-MAR-1873	2 yrs			Leguarius Roget/ Maria Faucher
Roi	Maria Josephina			13 mos		C-H Reinhard	
Roi	Francisci		18-NOV-1861	18 mos	Taycheedah		
Rondeau	Francisci	28-JUN-1887	30-JUN-1887	101 yrs	Taycheedah		
Rondeau	Melinda		16-SEP-1867	23 yrs			
Rondeau	Meloni-e		20-OCT-1867	3 mos			
Rondeau	Hety		16-JAN-1875	18 mos			
Rondo	Marguarita		28-DEC-1860				
Rone	Georgiana	02-FEB-1904	04-FEB-1904	33 yrs	Calvary	Joseph Buch	
Roy	Isaia	12-NOV-1902	15-NOV-1902	83 yrs	Calvary		
Roy	Ludovica Victorina	11-JAN-1901	13-JAN-1901	33 yrs	Calvary	G.-Eduardi Touchette	
Roy	Oliva	05-AUG-1899	07-AUG-1899	23 yrs	Calvary		Liguorii Roy/ Maria Faucher
Rulo	Jerimias			17 mos			
Ryan	Michelis		19-DEC-1862	15 mos			

Surname	Given Name	Death	Burial	Age	Cemetery	Spouse	Parents
Sain	Alexis		08-FEB-1876	5 mos			
Salmon	----						
Santuaire	----		28-AUG-1868				
Sauve	Clouise		01-NOV-1875	8 mos	Taycheedah		
Sauve	Petri	27-MAY-1903	29-MAY-1903	35 yrs			
Sauve	Philomene		02-SEP-1875	39 yrs			
Sauve	Victoris	15-OCT-1893	17-OCT-1893	19 yrs	Taycheedah		Pauli Sauve/ Margaritta Venne
Sauve*	Julie Marie Louise		30-MAY-1876	6 wks			
Sauvé*	Maria Lou—		30-JUL-1876	6 wks			
Schank	Leonis		17-JAN-1897	1 day	Calvary		Henrici Schank/ Anne Dupree
Schnuur	Augustus		20-FEB-1861	3 yrs	Byron		
Seager	Archibaldi	10-NOV-1883	12-NOV-1883	9 yrs	Taycheedah		Georgii Seager/ Helena Loiseau
Seing	Crescentia			42 yrs			
Senecal	Alma	19-JUL-1897	31-JUL-1897	8 yrs	Calvary		Ovidis Senecal/ Melina Venne
Senecal	Bernice	14-OCT-1919	16-OCT-1919	9 yrs	Calvary		Alex Senecal/ Martha Holz
Severin	Caroli	11-AUG-1884	13-AUG-1884	19 yrs	Taycheedah		Francisci-Petri Severin/ Virgina Rome
Severin	Emil	20-JUN-1919	23-JUN-1919	7 yrs	Calvary		Emil-P. Severin/ Myra Harms
Shambo	Francois		03-JAN-1876	14 mos			
Shambo	Madame		22-SEP-1875	25 yrs			
Shambo	Marie		09-SEP-1875	1 day			
Sheff	Juliana	03-AUG-1902	05-AUG-1902	89 yrs	Taycheedah	Joann-Baptisa Rondeau	
Sherburn	Maria Agnetis	28-NOV-1880	29-NOV-1880	8 days	Taycheedah		George Sherburn/ Celina Pinger
Shertzinger	Germani						
Sicar	Alfret		04-MAR-1876				
Smith	Helena		11-NOV-1860	18 mos	Byron		
Smith	Melina						
Smith	Rosa		26-AUG-1862		Byron		
St. Antoine	Isaaci	30-MAY-1901	01-JUN-1901	85 yrs	Taycheedah		
St.-Antoine	Marcellina			5 months			
St.-Antoine	Mary			10 yrs			
St.-Antoine	Moise		09-OCT-1877				
St.-Marie	Joseph		18-OCT-1875	76 yrs			
St.-Pierre	Josephina			7 mos			
Stacey	Gabrielimus	07-NOV-1880	26-NOV-1880	7 yrs	Taycheedah		Thoma Stacey/ Mathea ——
Stada	Corinna	17-AUG-1895	19-AUG-1895	5 mos	Taycheedah		Frederici Stada/ Josephina Préfontaine
Stada	Joseph Alfredi	27-SEP-1900	29-SEP-1900	2 yr	Calvary	Joann-Baptisa Rondeau	Alfredi Stada/ Rosa-Anna Corbeille
Stauber	Fredericus		21-AUG-1866	6 yrs			
Ste. Marie	Eliza		24-MAR-1873				
Ste. Marie	Eugenius		05-MAR-1872	1 day			
Ste.-Marie	Heloisa	26-SEP-1904	29-SEP-1904	66 yrs	Calvary	Francisci Dufresne	
Ste.-Marie	Philomena		23-JAN-1863				
Stenler	Theresia	22-MAR-1890	26-MAR-1890	76 yrs	Taycheedah	Laurentii Simonin	
Steyds	Clara		06-FEB-1875	2 days			
Strauss	Josephina		18-OCT-1864	2 yrs			
Suave	Corrine Weber	01-AUG-1919	04-AUG-1919	42 yrs	Calvary		
Sullivan	Nicolas		23-SEP-1862	9 mos			
Suprenant	Delphine		27-JUL-1875	9 mos			
Suprenant	Henrici Ludovici	30-DEC-1896	02-JAN-1897	2 mos	Taycheedah		Gilberti Suprenant/ Joanna Depre
Sween—	----		04-SEP-1872				

197

Surname	Given Name	Death	Burial	Age	Cemetery	Spouse	Parents
Taff	—		08-AUG-1872	5 mos			
Tatro	Hamilton						
Tessier	—				Taycheedah		Trefflei Tessier/ Martha Eldrige
Tessier	Hezelis	04-MAY-1892	06-MAY-1892	7 mos	Taycheedah		Jeremia Tessier/ Anna Faintes
Tessier	Maria Laurina	26-AUG-1888	27-AUG-1888	5 mos			
Tessier	Thomas		17-MAR-1871				
Tessier	Zoa	28-MAR-1891	30-MAR-1891	55 yrs	Taycheedah	Davidis Grandbois	
Thibodeau	—						
Thibodeau	Henricus		22-JAN-1866	2 yrs			
Thibodeau	Lucia		11-NOV-1866	21 yrs			
Thill	Maria Catharina		13-SEP-1860	18 mos			
Thorp	Maria Laura		26-FEB-1865				
Touchette	Joseph	15-JAN-1902	20-JAN-1902	77 yrs	Taycheedah		
Trahan	Aurelia	07-JAN-1901	07-JAN-1901	73 yrs	Calvary	Salamonis Demers	
Tramblé	Magdalene Seder—		13-JUN-1877	93 yrs			
Tremblay	Azaria	18-MAR-1887	20-MAR-1887	9 yrs	Taycheedah		MoiseTremblay/ Maria Lucier
Tremblay	Early Moysis	25-SEP-1884	27-SEP-1884	9 mos	Taycheedah		Josephi Tremblay/ Eugenia DuFrèsne
Tremblay	Edmundi E	11-MAR-1887	12-MAR-1887		Taycheedah		Moise Tremblay/ Maria Lucier
Tremblay	Mathilda	22-JAN-1883	27-JAN-1883	58 yrs	Taycheedah	Joannis-Maria Marcoux	
Tremblé	—			8 yrs			
Tremble	Louis Alfred		21-MAY-1875	6 mos, 6 days			
Tremble	Philomena		09-OCT-1866	17 -			
Turcot	Eduardi	09-AUG-1897	11-AUG-1897	10 yrs	Taycheedah		Eduardi Turcot/ Florentia Cote
Turcot-Levesque	Eduardi	14-OCT-1887	16-OCT-1887	42 yrs	Taycheedah	Philomena Coté	
Vadney	Evaristi		06-AUG-1868				
Valley	Elizabetha		16-MAY-1861	7 yrs		Philomena Coté	
Vander-Wegermister	Dora			17 yrs			
Vandervisse	Octavii	17-MAY-1889	18-MAY-1889	c. 60 yrs	Taycheedah		
Veine	Theodore		31-JUL-1867	29 yrs			
Venne	Agapiti	27-JUL-1887	29-JUL-1887	74 yrs	Taycheedah	Domitilda Allard	
Venne	Alphonsi	31-OCT-1887	02-NOV-1887	6 yrs	Taycheedah		Josephi Venne/ Maria Letourneau
Venne	Euclidis	22-NOV-1902	25-NOV-1902	68 yrs	Taycheedah		
Venne	Felicis Elm—	18-NOV-1893	19-NOV-1893	3 yrs	Taycheedah		Alderici Venne/ Olivina Fontaine
Venne	Francisci	28-OCT-1890	30-OCT-1890	82 yrs	Taycheedah	Marcellina Landerman	
Venne	Leopoldi	25-DEC-1884	27-DEC-1884	33 yrs	Taycheedah	Genovefa Durocher	
Venne	Margarita	14-FEB-1882	16-FEB-1882	36 yrs	Taycheedah	Pauli Sauvé	
Venne	Rachel	29-MAY-1895	31-MAY-1895	50 yrs	Taycheedah	Joannis-Baptista Bastien	
Verbontiere	Louis Alphonse		16-APR-1876	5 mos, 24 days			
Walsh	Michael		07-DEC-1860		Byron		
Weber	Corinne	01-AUG-1919	04-AUG-1919	42 yrs	Calvary	Peter Weber	
Wilbert	Jacobus			2 or 3 yrs			
Wolf	Petrus						
Zell	Salomie	20-MAR-1899	21-MAR-1899	79 yrs	Taycheedah	Caroli Beauregard	

Appendices

199

APPENDIX A

EXAMPLE OF ORIGINAL MARRIAGE RECORDS

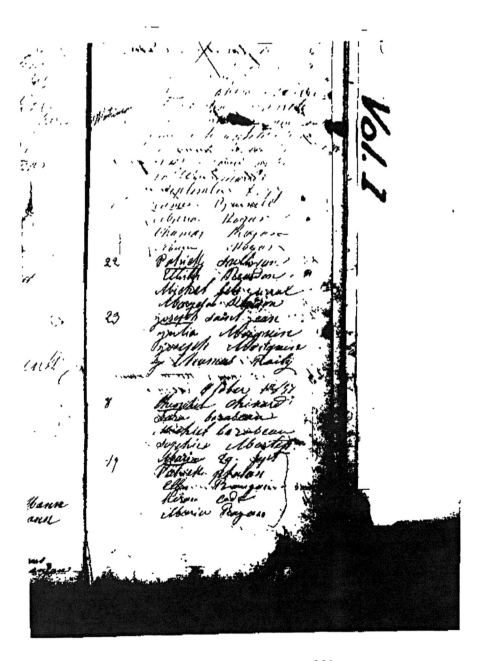

APPENDIX B

LIST OF LATIN NAMES AND THEIR FRENCH AND ENGLISH EQUIVALENTS

Latin	M/F	English	FRENCH
ADA/ADAM	F	ADA	
ADALBERTUS/ADALBERTUM/ADALBERTI	M	ADALBERT	ADELBERT
ADELA/ADELAM	F	ADEL/ADELA	ADÈLE
ADELAÏDA/ADELAÏDAM	F	ADELAIDE	ADÉLAïDE
ADELINA/ADELINAM	F	ADELINE	ADÈLE
AEMILIUS/AEMILIUM/AEMILII	M	EMIL	ÉMILE
AGNETIA/AGNETIAM/AGNETIS	F	AGNES	AGNÈS
ALBERTA/ALBERTAM	F	ALBERTA	ALBERTA
ALBERTUS/ALBERTUM/ALBERTI/ALBERTO	M	ALBERT	ALBERT
ALEXA/ALEXAM	F	ALEXIS	ALEXIS
ALEXANDRA/ALEXANDRAM	F	ALEXANDRA	ALEXANDRIE
ALEXANDRUS/ALEXANDRUM/ALEXANDRI/ALEXANDRO	M	ALEXANDER	ALEXANDRE
ALEXIS/ALEXEM/ALEXI	M	ALEXIS/ALEX	ALEXIS
ALFREDUS/ALFREDUM/ALFREDI/ALFREDO	M	ALFRED	ALFRED
ALICIA/ALICIAM	F	ALICE	ALICE
ALPHONSINA/ALPHONSINAM	F	ALPHONSINE	ALPHONSINE
ALPHONSUS/ALPHONSUM/ALPHONSI/ALPHONSO	M	ALPHONSE	ALPHONSE
AMABILA/AMABILAM	F	MABEL	
AMABILIS/AMABILEM/AMABILI	M	AMABEL	AMABLE
AMADEUS/AMADEUM/AMADEI/AMADEO	M		AMÉDÉE
AMBROSIUS/AMBROSIUM/AMBROSII/AMBROSIO	M	AMBROSE	AMBROISE
AMELIA/AMELIAM	F	AMELIA/EMELIE	AMÉLIE/EMÉLIE
ANACLITUS/ANACLITUM/ANACLITI	M	ANACLETE	
ANASTASIAM/ANASTASIA	F	ANASTIASIA	ANASTASIE
ANDREAS/ANDREAM	M	ANDREW	ANDRÉ
ANNA/ANNAM	F	ANNA/ANNE/ANN	ANNE
ANTONIUS/ANTOMIUM/ANTONII/ANTONIO	M	ANTHONY	ANTOINE
ARSENIUS/ARSENIUM/ARSENII	M		ARSÈNE
ARTURIS/ARTUREM/ARTURI/ARTURO	M	ARTHUR	ARTHUR
AUGUSTA/AUGUSTAM	F	AUGUSTA	
AUGUSTUS/AUGUSTUM/AUGUSTI/AUGUSTO	M	AUGUST(E)	AUGUSTE
AURELIA/AURELIAM	F	AURELIE	AURÉLIE
AURELIUS/AURELIUM/AURELII	M		AURÈLE
BAPTISTA/BAPTISTAM	M		BAPTISTE
BASILIUS/BASILIUM/BASILII	M	BASIL	BASILE
BEATRIX	F	BEATRICE	BEATRICE
BELONISIA/BELONISIAM	F		
BELONISIUS/BELONISIUM/BELONISII	M		
BERNARDUS/BERNARDUM/BERNARDI/BERNARDO	M	BERNARD	BERNARD

BRIDGITTAÉ/BRIDGITTAM	F	BRIDGET	
CALISTA/CALISTAM	F	CALISTA	
CALISTUS/CALISTUM/CALISTI	M		
CAMILLA/CAMILLAM	F	CAMILLA	CAMILLE
CAMILLUS/CAMILLUM/CAMILLI/CAMILLO	M	CAMILLE	CAMILLE
CAROLA/CAROLAM	F	CAROLE/CAROL	CAROLE
CAROLUS/CAROLUM/CAROLI/CAROLO	M	CARL	CAROLE
CATHARINA/CATHARINAM	F	KATHERINE	CATHERINE
CECILIA/CECILIAM	F	CECILIA	CÉCILE
CECILIUS/CECILIUM/CECILII/CECILIO	M	CECIL	
CHRISTOPHORUS/CHRISTOPHORUM/CHRISTOPHORI	M	CHRISTOPHER	CHRISTOPHE
CLARA/CLARAM	F	CLARE	
CLAUDIUS/CLAUDIUM/CLAUDII	M	CLAUDE	CLAUDE
CLEMENTIA/CLEMENTIAM	F	CLEMENTINE	CLEMENTINE
CLEMENTIUS/CLEMENTIUM/CLEMENTII	M	CLEMENT	CLÉMENT
CLOTILDA/CLOTILDAM	F	CLOTILDE/CLOTILDA	CLOTHILDE
COMAS/COMAM/COMA	M	COSMAS	COMÉ
CONSTANTUS/CONSTANTUM/CONSTANTI	M	CONSTANT	
CORNELIA/CORNELIAM	F	CORNELIA	CORNÉLIE
CORNELIUS/CORNELIUM/CORNELII	M	CORNELIUS	
CYRILLUS/CYRILLUM/CYRILLI/CYRILLO	M	CYRIL	CYRILLE
DAMASIUS/DAMASIUM/DAMASII	M		
DANIELA/DANIELAM	F	DANIELLE	DANIÈLE
DANIELIS/DANIELEM/DANIELI/DANIELO	M	DANIEL	DANIEL
DAVIDIS/DAVIDEM/DAVIDI/	M	DAVID	DAVID
DELIMA/DELIMAM	F	(ROSE) DELIMA	
DELINA/DELINAM	F	DELIN/DELINA	
DELPHINA/DELPHINAM	F	DELPHINE/DELPHINA	DELPHINE
DEODATUS/DEODATUM/DEODATI	M		DÉODAT
DIONYSIUS/DIONYSIUM/DIONYSII	M	DENNIS	
DYONYSIA/DIONYSIAM	F	DENISE	
EDESSA/EDESSAM	F		
EDMIRA/EDMIRAM	F		
EDMIUNDUS/EDMUNDUM/EMUNDI/EDMUNDO	M	EDMUND	EDMOND
EDUARDUS/EDUARDUM/EDUARDI/EDUARDO	M	EDWARD	EDUARD
ELEONORA/ELEONORAM	F	ELEONORE/LENORE	ELÉONORE
ELISABETHA/ELISABETHAM	F	ELIZABETH	ELISABETH
ELLENA/ELLENAM	F	ELLEN	
ELMIRA/ELMIRAM	F	ELMIRA	
ELODIA/ELODIAM	F	ALODIA	ELODIE
ELOISE/ELOISAM	F	ELOISE/HELOISE	ÉLOÏSE
EMERENTA/EMERENTAM	F		
EMERITIUS/EMERITIUM/EMERITII	M	EMERY	
EMILIA/EMILIAM	F	EMILY/EMILIE	ÉMILIIE
EMILIANUS/EMILIANUM/EMILIANI	M	EMIL	ÉMILIEN
ERNESTUS/ERNESTUM/ERNESTI	M	ERNEST	ERNEST
EUGENIA/EUGENIAM	F	EUGENIE/GENIE	EUGÉNIE
EUGENIUS/EUGENIUM/EUGENII	M	EUGENE/GENE	EUGÈNE
EUGERIUS/EUGERIUM/EUGERII	M		
EULALIA/EULALIAM	F	EULALIE	EULALIE

EVARISTUS/EVARISTUM/EVARISTI	M		ÉVARISTE
EZILDA/EZILDAM	F	ZELDA	
FELICITATA/FELICITATAM/FELICITATIS	F	FELICITY	FÉLICITÉ
FLAVIA/FLAVIAM	F	FLAVIE	FLAVIE
FLORENTIA/FLORENTIAM	F	FLORENCE	FLORENCE
FLORENTIUS/FLORENTIUM/FLORENTII	M	FLORENT	FLORENT/FLORENTIN
FRANCISCA/FRANCISCAM	F	FRANCES	FRANÇOISE
FRANCISCUS/FRANCISCUM/FRANCISCI/FRANCISCO	M	FRANCIS	FRANÇOIS
FREDERICA/FREDERICAM	F	FREDERICKA	FRÉDERIQUE
FREDERICUS/FREDERICUM/FREDERICI/FREDERICO	M	FREDERICK	FRÉDERIC
GENOVEFA/GENOVEFAM	F	GENEVEVE	GENEVIÈVE
GEORGIA/GEORGIAM	F	GEORGINA	GEORGETTE
GEORGIUS/GEORGIUM/GEORGII/GEORGIO	M	GEORGE	GEORGES
GILBERTUS/GILBERTUM/GILBERTI	M	GILBERT	
GODEFRIDUS/GODFRIDUM/GODFRIDI	M	GODFREY	
GRATIA/GRATIAM	F		
GRATIANUS/GRATIUM/GRATII/GRATIO	M		GRATIEN
GUILLLELMUS/GUILLELMUM/GUILLELMI	M	WILLIAM	GUILLAUME
HELENA/HELENAM	F	HELEN/ELLEN	HÉLÈNE
HENRICUS/HENRICUM/HENRICI/HENRICO	M	HENRY	HENRI
HENRIETTA/HENRIETTAM	F	HENRIETTA	HENRIETTE
HERCULANUS/HERCULANUM/HERCULANI	M	HERCULES	HERCULE
HILARIUS/HILARIUM/HILARII	M	HILLARY	HILAIRE
HONORA/HONORAM	F		HONORÉE
HONORATUS/HONORATUM/HONORATI	M		HONORÉ
HORMIDAS/HORMIDEM	M		
HUBERTUS/HUBERTUM/HUBERTI	M	HUBERT	HUBERT
HUEH/HUEHM/HUEHI	M	HUGH	HUGUES
HYACINTHA/HYACINTHAM	F	HYACINTHE	HYACINTHE
HYACINTHUS/HYACINTHUM/HYACINTHI	M		HYACINTHE
IDA/IDAM	F	IDA	
ISAACUS/ISAACUM/ISAACI	M	ISAAC	
ISAIA/ISAIAM	M	ISAIAH	
ISABELLAÉ/ISABELLAM	F	ISABELLE/ELIZABETH	ISABEL
ISIDORUS/ISIDORUM/ISIDORI	M	ISIDORE	ISIDORE
JACOBUS/JACOBUM/JOCOBI	M	JAMES/JACOB	JACQUES
JEREMIAS/JEREMIEM/JEREMII	M	JEREMY	JÉRÉMIE
JOANNA/JOANNAM	F	JOANN/JOANNA	JEANETTE
JOANNIS/JOANNEM/JOANNES/JOANNI	M	JOHN	JEAN
JOSEPHA/JOSEPHAM	F	JOSETTE	JOSEPHTE
JOSEPHINA/JOSEPHINAM	F	JOSEPHINE	JOSEPHINE
JOSEPHUS/JOSEPHUM/JOSEPHI/JOSEPHO	M	JOSEPH	JOSEPH
JULIA/JULIAM	F	JULIE	JULIE
JULIANA/JULIANAM	F	JULIANNA	JULIE
JULIANUS/JULIANUM/JULIANI	M	JULIEN	JULIEN
JUSTINA/JUSTINAM	F	JUSTINE	
JUSTINUS/JUSTINUM/JUSTINI	M	JUSTIN	
LAURENTIA/LAURENTIAM	F	LAUREN	LAURENCE
LAURENTIUS/LAUENTIUM/LAURENTII	M	LAWRENCE	LAURENT
LEA/LEAM	F	LEA	LEAH

LEOCADIA/LEOCADIAM	F		LEOCADIE
LEONIA/LEONIAM	F		LÉONE
LEONIS/LEONEM/LEONI	M	LEON	LÉON
LUCIA/LUCIAM	F	LUCY	LUCE
LUDGERIUS/LUDGERIUM/LUDGERII	M	LUDGER	
LUDOVICA/LUDOVICAM	F	LOUISA/LOUISE	LOUISA/LOUISE
LUDOVICUS/LUDOVICUM/LUDOVICI/LUDOVICO	M	LOUIS	LOUIS
MAGDELENA/MAGDELENAM	F	MADELENE	MADELEINE
MAGLIORIUS/MAGLIORIUM/MAGLIORII	M	MAGLIORE	MAGLOIRE
MARCELLIUS/MARCELLIUM/MARCELLII	M	MARCEL	MARCEL
MARCUS/MARCUM/MARCI	M	MARK	MARC
MARGUARITA/MARGUARITAM	F	MARGRET	MARGUERITE
MARIA/MARIAM	M/F	MARY/MARIE	MARIE
MARTHA/MARTHAM	F	MARTHA	MARTHE
MARTINA/MARTINAM	F	MARTINA	MARTINE
MARTINUS/MARTINUM/MARTINI	M	MARTIN	MARTIN
MATHIAS/MATHIAM	M	MATHIAS	
MATHILDA/MATHILDAM	F	MATILDA	MATHILDE
MAURITIUS/MAURITIUM/MAURITII	M	MAURICE/MORRIS	MAURICE
MAXIMUS/MAXIMUM/MAXIMI	M	MAX	MAXIME
MELINDA/MELINDAM	F	MELINDA	
MELVINA/MELVINAM	F	MELVINA	
MICHAELIS/MICHAELEM/MICHAELI	M	MICHAEL	MICHEL
NAPOLIONIS/NAPOLIONEM/NAPOLIONI	M	NAPOLEON	NAPOLÉON
NARCISSUS/NARCISSUM/NARCISSI	M	NARCISSUS	NARCISSE
NAZARIUS/NAZAIRIUM/NAZAIRII	M		NAZAIRE
NICOLAUS/NICOLAUM/NICOLAI	M	NICHOLAS	NICOLAS
NOELIS/NOELEM/NOELI	M	NOEL	NOËL
NORBERTUS/NORBERTUM/NORBERTI	M	NORBERT	
ODILIA/ODILIAM	F	ODILE	ODILE
ODILONIS/ODILONEM/ODILONI	M	ODILON	ODILON
OLIVARUS/OLIVARUM/OLIVARI	M	OLIVER	OLIVIER
OLIVIERUS/OLIVIERUM/OLIVIERI	M	OLIVER	OLIVIER
OLIVINA/OLIVINAM	F	OLIVE	OLIVIE
ONESIMA/ONESIMAM	F		ONÉSIMÉE
ONESIMUS/ONESIMUM/ONESIMI	M		ONÉSIME
OVIDUS/OVIDUM/OVIDI	M	OVID	OVIDE
PACIFICUS/PACIFICUM/PACIFICI	M		
PASCALIS/PASCALEM/PASCALI	M		PASCAL
PATRICIUS/PATRICIUM/PATRICII	M	PATRICK	PATRICE
PAULUS/PAULUM/PAULI	M	PAUL	PAUL
PERPETUA/PERPETUAM	F		
PETRUS/PETRUM/PETRI	M	PETER	PIERRE
PHILIPPUS/PHILIPPUM/PHILIPPI	M	PHILLIP	PHILIPPE
PHILOMENA/PHLOMENAM	F	PHILOMENA	PHILOMENE
PHILOMONIS/PHILOMONEM/PHILOMONI	M	PHILEMON	
PHOEBEA/PHOEBEA	F	PHOEBE	
PLACIDUS/PLACIDUM/PLACIDI	M		PLACIDE
RACHELIS/RACHELEM/RACHELI	F	RACHEL	RACHEL
RAYMONDUS/RAYMONDUM/RAYMONDI/RAYMONDO	M	RAYMOND	RAYMOND

REGINA/REGINAM	F	GINA	RÉGINE
RICARDUS/RICHARDUM/RICHARDI	M	RICHARD	RICHARDE
ROBERTA/ROBERTAM	F	ROBERTA	
ROBERTUS/ROBERTUM/ROBERTI	M	ROBERT	ROBERT
ROSALIA/ROSALIAM	F	ROSALIE	ROSALIE
RUDOLPHIS/RUDOLPHUM/RUDOLPHI/RUDOLPHO	M	RUDOLPH	RUDOLPH
SALOMEA/SALOMEAM	F	SALLY	SALOMÉ
SALOMONIS/SALOMONEM/SALOMONI	M	SOLOMON	SOLOMON
SARA(H)/SARA(H)M	F	SARAH	SARAH
SEVERUS/SEVERUM/SEVERI	M		SÉVÈRE
SOPHIA/SOPHIAM	F	SOPHIE	SOPHIE
SOPHRONIA/SOPHRONIAM	F		SOPHRONIE
STANISLAUS/STANISLAUM/STANISLAI	M	STANISLAS	
STELLA/STELLAM	F	STELLA	ESTELLE
STEPHANUS/STEPHANUM	M	STEPHAN/STEVEN	ÉTIENNE/STÉPHANE
SUSANNA/SUSANNAM	F	SUSAN/SUZANNE	SUZANNE
TELESPORUS/TELESPORUM/TELESPORI/TELESPORO	M		TELESPORE
THARSILA/THARSILAM	F		THARSILE
THEODORUS/THEODORUM/THEODORI/THEODORO	M	THEODORE	THÉODORE
THEOPHILIUS/THEOPHILIUM/THEOPHILII/THEOPHILIO	M		THÉOPHILE
THERESA/THERESAM	F	THERESA	THÉRÈSE
THOMA/THOMAM/THOMAS	M	THOMAS	THOMAS
THURSA/THURSAM	F	THURSA	
TIMOTHEUS/TIMOTHEUM/TIMOTHEI	M	TIMOTHY	TIMOTHÉE
TOUSSAINTIUS/TOUSSAINTIUM/TOUSSAINTI	M	ALL SAINTS	TOUSSAINT
VICTORIA/VICTORIAM	F	VICTORIA	VICTOIRE
VICTORIS/VICTOREMVICTORI	M	VICTOR	VICTOR
VINCENTUS/VINCENTUM/VINCENTI/VINCENTO	M	VINCENT	VINCENT
VIRGINIA/VIRGINIAM	M	VIRGINIA	VIRGINE
VITALES/VITALEM/VITALI	M	VITAL	VITAL
VITALINA/VITALINA	F	VITALINA	
WILFREDUS/WILFREDIUM/WILFREDII	M	WILFRED	
XAVIERIUS/XAVERIUM/XAVERII	M	XAVIER	XAVIER
ZEPHIRUS/ZEPHIRUM/ZEPHIRI	M		SÉVÈRE
ZOAH/ZOAHM	F	ZOÉ	ZOÉ
ZOTICUS/ZOTICUM/ZOTICI	M		ZOTIQUE

APPENDIX C

MISCELLANEOUS LIST OF NAMES
FROM ST. LOUIS CHURCH RECORDS

The list of the following persons is found in the original records in the pages immediately before the pages containing the baptisms for the year 1857. The records give no indication of the meaning of this list. The list is presented as extracted. The project team did not correlate the names on the list with other extracted information, e. g., baptisms, in an attempt to find some pattern that might indicate the significance of the list.

Melliny, Catharina
Melliny, Anna
Hill, Madelena
Marcou, Anna-Mariam
-----, Jud---
--ohy, Mageta
Connegan, Matilda
-----, Anna
Gareaux, Josephus
Maine, Sera
Fainon, Mark
Fainon, Thomas
Verbins, William
Dollony, Thomas
Faist, Anna-Maria-Agnes
McCoy, Patrick
O'Brayen, John
Brie-, Elise
Moby, Bernhard
Baden, Maria
McCulligan, Catherina
Hales, Mary
Doil-Dayl, Mathias
Douderler, Denisius

Carley, Car--irn-Anna
Moloney, Eduard-Dem
Dolans, William
Brown, William
Lienschs, Joannis
McMann, Patricius
McMann, Jocobus
O'Bryan, Anna
Ganyan, Carolus-
Christianus

APPENDIX D

St. Louis Catholic Parish, Fond du Lac, WI
Confirmations 1850-1920

Name	Year	Sponsor
-----, Hib--	1857	
-----, Maria	1857	
-nhins, William	1857	
Allain, Andreas	11-OCT-1891	
Allain, Eduardus Henricus	11-OCT-1891	
Allain, Maria Catherina	11-OCT-1891	
Allain, Philippus	11-OCT-1891	
Ann, Elisabeh	1857	
Ansel, Carolus	1857	
Atkinson, Stella	1899	
Auchue, Joseph Lavern	10-NOV-1918	Butler, Eli
Badricaux, Brinida	1857	
Baillargeon, Paulus	1897	
Baillargeon, Phoebea	1899	
Balthazar, Agnes	1894	
Balthazar, Alexander	10-DEC-1882	
Balthazar, Blanca	1897	
Balthazar, Edessea	1899	
Balthazar, Emelia	1894	
Balthazar, Esther	1899	
Balthazar, Franciscus	01-NOV-1886	
Balthazar, Franciscus	10-NOV-1918	Balthazar, Oliver
Balthazar, Fredericus	10-NOV-1918	Raymond, Aaron
Balthazar, Georgius	01-NOV-1886	
Balthazar, Gulielmus	01-NOV-1886	
Balthazar, Gulielmus	11-OCT-1891	
Balthazar, Hermina	11-OCT-1891	
Balthazar, Ida	1894	
Balthazar, Isabella	1894	
Balthazar, Joseph Alton	10-NOV-1918	Hogan, Harold
Balthazar, Joseph Walter	10-NOV-1918	Balthazar, Ed

Balthazar, Josephina	1899	
Balthazar, Josephus	11-OCT-1891	
Balthazar, Josephus	1894	
Balthazar, Josephus	1894	
Balthazar, Justina	1894	
Balthazar, Ludovicus	1897	
Balthazar, M. Zoe	10-DEC-1882	
Balthazar, Malvina	1894	
Balthazar, Maria	1894	
Balthazar, Maria	1894	
Balthazar, Maria Josephina	11-OCT-1891	
Balthazar, Martinus	11-OCT-1891	
Balthazar, Olivina	01-NOV-1886	
Balthazar, Theodorus	1897	
Balthazaz, Joannes	1897	
Barbeau, Clara	1894	
Barbeau, Cora	1897	
Barbeau, Franciscus N.	1897	
Barbeau, Joseph Normand	10-NOV-1918	Drinkwine, Geo.
Barbeau, Josephus N.	1897	
Barbeau, Laura	1899	
Barbeau, Ludovicus	10-DEC-1882	
Barbeau, Maria Azelina	11-OCT-1891	
Barbeau, Mélina	01-NOV-1886	
Barbeau, Rosina	01-NOV-1886	
Barrag-r, Maria	1857	
Bastien, Andreas	11-OCT-1891	
Bastien, Elodia	1894	
Bastien, Joannes Baptista	11-OCT-1891	
Bastien, Leona Maria	10-NOV-1918	Robidoux, Mrs. John
Bastien, M. Alexina	10-DEC-1882	
Bastien, M. Eugenia	10-DEC-1882	
Bastien, Maria Anna	11-OCT-1891	
Bastien, Pacificus	01-NOV-1886	
Bastien, Wilfredus	10-DEC-1882	
Bearuregard, M. Josephina	10-DEC-1882	
Beaudet, Benjamin	11-OCT-1891	
Beaudet, Evaristus	11-OCT-1891	
Beaudet, Henricus	1894	
Beaudette, Elida	01-NOV-1886	
Beaudreault, Asa	01-NOV-1886	
Beaudreault, Emma	01-NOV-1886	
Beaudreault, Laurentius	10-DEC-1882	
Beaudry, Anna	11-OCT-1891	
Beaudry, Clarinda	1894	
Beaudry, J.B. Levi	10-DEC-1882	
Beaudry, Marcellinus	01-NOV-1886	
Belheumeur, Melina	1857	
Bernier, Eduardus	01-NOV-1886	
Bernier, M. Edena	10-DEC-1882	
Berry, Elisabalhta	1857	
Bertrand, Florentia	01-NOV-1886	

Bertrand, Francisca	1899	
Bertrand, Ludovicus	1894	
Besset, Catherina	1857	
Bessette, Alfredus	10-DEC-1882	
Bessette, Isidorus	10-DEC-1882	
Bissonnette, Clara	10-DEC-1882	
Boden, Man--	1857	
Bodrieaux, Louisa	1857	
Boivin, Salomea	01-NOV-1886	
Bonin, Eduardus	01-NOV-1886	
Bonnin, Maris Delph.	10-DEC-1882	
Boucher, David	11-OCT-1891	
Boucher, Eleonora	1894	
Boucher, Franciscus	1894	
Boucher, Georgina	01-NOV-1886	
Boucher, Henricus	11-OCT-1891	
Bourgois, Marie Louisa	1857	
Brandt, Josephus W.	1897	
Braun, Elizabetha	11-OCT-1891	
Brenaël, Elizabetha Maria	11-OCT-1891	
Brenaël, Noe Florianus	11-OCT-1891	
Brerere, Maria	1857	
Brise, Elise	1857	
Brockway, Gulielmus	1897	
Broun, Margereta	1857	
Brown, William	1857	
Brunet, Adalbertus	01-NOV-1886	
Brunet, Alphonsus	11-OCT-1891	
Brunet, Edmundus	10-NOV-1918	Rouphen, Edward
Brunet, Emma	1897	
Brunet, Ferdinandus	10-DEC-1882	
Brunet, Honora	1894	
Brunet, Josephus	11-OCT-1891	
Brunet, Josephus	1897	
Brunet, Leonia	01-NOV-1886	
Brunet, Ludovicus Avila	10-DEC-1882	
Brunet, Olympia	11-OCT-1891	
Brunet, Rosa	1894	
Bu--jois, Elisa	1857	
Buch, Paul Alden	10-NOV-1918	Gardner, Paul
Cahy, Narsisus	1857	
Cannadieu, Tenperanere	1857	
Cannon, Mai--	1857	
Carbonneau, M. Domitilda	10-DEC-1882	
Carbory, Anna	1857	
Carbory, Sara	1857	
Carley, Anna	1857	
Cenneyan, Matild-	1857	
Chainey, Thamas	1857	
Chaperon, David	01-NOV-1886	
Charbonneau, Carolus	01-NOV-1886	
Charbonneau, Elosia	01-NOV-1886	

Charbonneau, Eusebius	01-NOV-1886	
Charbonneau, Maria Delina	11-OCT-1891	
Charron, Achilles	01-NOV-1886	
Charron, M. Celina	10-DEC-1882	
Charron, M. Olivina	10-DEC-1882	
Charron, Maria O.	01-NOV-1886	
Chasinger, Jeremias	1857	
Chef, Chrestina	1857	
Chenard, Ellena	1857	
Chenart, Arthurus	01-NOV-1886	
Chenart, Carolus	11-OCT-1891	
Chenart, Emelia Blanca	11-OCT-1891	
Chenart, Jos. Alphonsus	01-NOV-1886	
Chenart, M. Louisa Ezilda	10-DEC-1882	
Chenart, Oliverus	1894	
Chinard, Issdor	1857	
Clarek, Elena	1857	
Clish, Alfredus	1894	
Clish, Carolus	10-DEC-1882	
Clish, Josephus	11-OCT-1891	
Clish, Margaritta	01-NOV-1886	
Clish, Maria	11-OCT-1891	
Clish, Mathilda	10-DEC-1882	
Comeau, Arthurus	10-DEC-1882	
Comeau, Clara J.	10-DEC-1882	
Commo, Maxine Maria	10-NOV-1918	Errard, Mrs. Chas.
Corbeile, Josephus	10-DEC-1882	
Corbeile, Maria Joanna	1894	
Corbeille, Adelina	11-OCT-1891	
Corbeille, Alfredus	11-OCT-1891	
Corbeille, Amanda	1899	
Corbeille, Eduardus	11-OCT-1891	
Corbeille, Ezilda	1899	
Corbeille, Josephus	01-NOV-1886	
Corbeille, M. Alphonsine	10-DEC-1882	
Corbeille, Maria Mathilda	11-OCT-1891	
Corbeille, Melvina	1894	
Corbeille, Rosa Anna	11-OCT-1891	
Craney, Franciscus	1897	
Curron, Maria Anna	1857	
Dame, Gulielmus	11-OCT-1891	
Dame, Joannes	01-NOV-1886	
Dame, Ludovica	11-OCT-1891	
Dame, Rosa	01-NOV-1886	
Damer, Robertus	1857	
Dandelain, Phelomena	1857	
Dandelin, Gulielmus	1894	
Dandelin, Helena	1894	
Danderler, Denesius	1857	
Daniel, Carolus	01-NOV-1886	
Daniel, Elizabeth	10-DEC-1882	
Daniel, Emma	1894	

Daniel, Henrica	01-NOV-1886	
Daniel, Josephina	01-NOV-1886	
Daniel, Josephus	01-NOV-1886	
Decalp, Elisabet	1857	
Deitte, Maria Rosa	10-NOV-1918	Balthazar, Miss Mabel
Delisse, Laurentius	1857	
Dellise, Maria	1857	
Deneau, Petrus	1894	
DeRusha, Maria Norma	10-NOV-1918	Snow, Mrs. Phoebe
Derwin, Joseph Clarence	10-NOV-1918	Barboe, Archie
DeSois, Delaidi	1857	
Desvillers, Adolphus	01-NOV-1886	
Desvillers, Helena	1899	
Desvillers, Rosa N.	1894	
Devis, Maria	1857	
Diette, Alfredus	10-DEC-1882	
Diette, Mathilda	10-DEC-1882	
Dinelle, Ludovica	1899	
Dinelle, Ludovicus Domina	11-OCT-1891	
Dinelle, Maria	01-NOV-1886	
Dinelle, Maria	1897	
Dinelle, Narcissus	1897	
Dinelle, Rosa Anna	11-OCT-1891	
Dion, Felix	10-DEC-1882	
Dion, Georgius	10-DEC-1882	
Dion, Gulielmus	11-OCT-1891	
Dion, Israel	11-OCT-1891	
Dion, Maria	01-NOV-1886	
Dion, Maria Rosa	11-OCT-1891	
Dockry, Elisabeh	1857	
Dodelain, Phelomine	1857	
Dogerty, May	1857	
Doil-Doyl, Malachias-	1857	
Dolens, William	1857	
Dollony, Thomas	1857	
Dolton, Maria	1857	
Dondelain, Denis	1857	
Donly, Margeta	1857	
Dorothy, Anna	1857	
Dougherty, Isabella	1857	
Dougherty, Rossana	1857	
Drinkwine, Joseph Merrill	10-NOV-1918	Lyneis, Claud
Drouin, Xenophonius	1897	
Dubois, Cora	1899	
Dubois, Felix	01-NOV-1886	
Dubois, Vincentius	10-NOV-1918	Wood, Arnold
Duchaine, Catherina	1857	
Duchaine, Maria	1857	
Duchaine, Theopile	1857	
Dufort, Cyrillus	10-DEC-1882	
Dufraine, Sophia	1857	
Dufrane, Ambrosius	10-NOV-1918	Balthazar, Wm.

Dufrane, Bernardus	10-NOV-1918	Welling, Nicolas
Dufrane, Eugenius	10-NOV-1918	Morris, Andrew
Dufrane, Franciscus	10-NOV-1918	Dufrane, Steve
Dufrane, Leonora Maria	10-NOV-1918	Rondeau, Mrs. Hilda
Dufresne, Albertus	10-DEC-1882	
Dufrèsne, Eduardus	11-OCT-1891	
Dufresne, Georgius	01-NOV-1886	
Dufrèsne, Gratia	1894	
Dufrèsne, Maria	01-NOV-1886	
Dufresne, Martha	01-NOV-1886	
Dufresne, Petrus	10-DEC-1882	
Dufrèsne, Sara	11-OCT-1891	
Dufresne, Stephanus	10-DEC-1882	
Dumas, Eduardus	10-DEC-1882	
Dumas, Joseph Elmo	10-NOV-1918	Martin, Lawrence
Dumas, Margaritta	10-DEC-1882	
Dumphy, Thamas	1857	
Duphy, Anna	1857	
Duphy, Hueh	1857	
Duphy, Margereta	1857	
Dupuy, M. Adelina	10-DEC-1882	
Durocher, Alexander	01-NOV-1886	
Durocher, Carolus Adolphus	11-OCT-1891	
Durocher, Eduardus	11-OCT-1891	
Durocher, Elizabeth	01-NOV-1886	
Durocher, Georgius	01-NOV-1886	
Durocher, Gulielmus	11-OCT-1891	
Durocher, Gulielmus	1897	
Durocher, Henricus	01-NOV-1886	
Durocher, Isidorus	1894	
Durocher, Laura	1897	
Durocher, Ludgerius	11-OCT-1891	
Durocher, Maria Adela	1897	
Durosha, Edwin W.	10-NOV-1918	Durosha, Wm.
Duspeid, Margeta	1857	
Ebert, Napolion	1857	
Edoin, Adelina	01-NOV-1886	
Edoin, Alexander	10-DEC-1882	
Edoin, Marcellina Melina	11-OCT-1891	
Edoin, Maria Emma	11-OCT-1891	
Emmery, Petrus	1857	
Errard, Carolus	1897	
Errard, Edmundus	1894	
Errard, Josephus	01-NOV-1886	
Errard, Josephus	11-OCT-1891	
Evans, Gulielmus	11-OCT-1891	
Evans, Gulielmus	1894	
Evrard, Maria Melina	11-OCT-1891	
Fainan, Mark	1857	
Fainon, Thomas	1857	
Fairburn, Joseph Angus	10-NOV-1918	Sweeny, Ed.
Faist, Anna Maria Agnes	1857	

Faucher, Arsenius	1894	
Faucher, Elodia	1894	
Faucher, Felix	11-OCT-1891	
Faucher, Ludov. Alex.	01-NOV-1886	
Faucher, M. Ezela	01-NOV-1886	
Faucher, Oliverus	11-OCT-1891	
Felret, Fredericus	10-NOV-1918	Nomprey, Ludger
Fit-sammons, Thamas	1857	
Fitsjurall, Margireta	1857	
Flind, Margereta	1857	
Fontaine, Gratia	01-NOV-1886	
Fontaine, M. Delia	10-DEC-1882	
Fontaine, Maria	01-NOV-1886	
Frisque, Raymundus	10-NOV-1918	Goyett, Noah
Funk, Joseph	10-NOV-1918	Moquin, Alen
Gaaff, Maria	1857	
Gabbns, Gullielmus	1857	
Gagner, Guilielmus	10-DEC-1882	
Gagnier, Albert	1897	
Gagnier, Carolus	1897	
Gagnier, Eduardus Henricus	11-OCT-1891	
Gagnier, Esther	1899	
Gagnier, Georgius	1894	
Gagnier, Josephina	1897	
Gagnier, Josephina Helena	11-OCT-1891	
Gagnier, Laurentius	1897	
Gagnier, M. Melina	10-DEC-1882	
Galvan, Brigita	1857	
Ganyan, Carolus Christianus	1857	
Gareaux, Josephus	1857	
Gautier, Josephus	1857	
Gélman, M. Emma	10-DEC-1882	
Gentz, Gilbertus	10-NOV-1918	Corbeille, Fred
Gervais, Georgius	1897	
Gervais, Joanna	11-OCT-1891	
Gervias, Eva Jacoba	11-OCT-1891	
Gilbert, Maria Josephina	11-OCT-1891	
Gorau, Maria	1857	
Gordon, Georgius	11-OCT-1891	
Gordon, Josephus	1897	
Gordon, Lucia	1894	
Gosselain, Emilia	1857	
Gosselan, Delina	1857	
Gosselin, Francesca E.	10-DEC-1882	
Goyet, Franciscia	1857	
Goyette, Alexander	11-OCT-1891	
Goyette, Elizabeth	10-DEC-1882	
Goyette, Franciscus	10-DEC-1882	
Goyette, Henricus	1897	
Goyette, Josephina	1899	
Gratton, David	10-DEC-1882	
Gratton, Delphina	1899	

Gratton, Josephina	1899	
Gratton, Maria	01-NOV-1886	
Grey-y, Maria Anna	1857	
Gu-es, Charles	1857	
Halas, Mary	1857	
Hallows, Harold	10-NOV-1918	Martin, Emery
Harlons, Franciscus	1857	
Hebert, Imilia	1857	
Hennery, Jadueas	1857	
Hibert, Moses	1857	
Hill, Carolus	01-NOV-1886	
Hogan, Joannes	11-OCT-1891	
Huchu, Alfredus	1894	
Hurteau, Elizabeth	01-NOV-1886	
Hurteau, Joannis	01-NOV-1886	
Hurteau, Leonia	1894	
Hurteau, Victoria	10-DEC-1882	
Jarvis, Gertruda	10-NOV-1918	Pauger, Mrs. Julius
Joeger, Henricus	10-NOV-1918	Barboe, Walter
Joubert, Helena	11-OCT-1891	
Jubert, Alloisa	1857	
Jubert, Antonius	1857	
Jubert, Edicht	1857	
Jubert, Margerita	1857	
Jubert, Napolion	1857	
Jubert, Xavier	1857	
Kain, Maria	1857	
Kelly, Brigita	1857	
Kilmer, Laurentius	10-NOV-1918	Barboe, Edmund
L---, Go-oocu	1857	
Lajeunesse, M. Emilia	10-DEC-1882	
Lajeunesse, M. Margaritta	10-DEC-1882	
Lajeunesse, Maria	01-NOV-1886	
Lambert, Anna	1897	
Lambert, Josephina	1897	
Lambert, Josephus	10-DEC-1882	
Lambert, Michael	10-DEC-1882	
Lamouche, Maria	01-NOV-1886	
Lanctot, Alphonsina	11-OCT-1891	
Landerman, Albertus Dolor	11-OCT-1891	
Landerman, Isidorus	11-OCT-1891	
Landerman, Josephus	1894	
Landerman, Ludovicus	1894	
Landerman, Maria	1897	
Landreman, Bernardus	10-NOV-1918	Kinney, Jas.
Landreman, Leo	10-NOV-1918	Dooly, Earl
Landreman, Lillian Maria	10-NOV-1918	Schuessler, Miss Josephine
Langlois, Alfredus	10-DEC-1882	
Langlois, Estier	1894	
Langlois, Georgius	10-DEC-1882	
Langlois, Gertrudis	1899	
Langlois, Josephus	01-NOV-1886	

Langlois, Martha	1899	
Langlois, Mathilda	11-OCT-1891	
Langlois, Noe Vitalis	11-OCT-1891	
Lapierre, Albertus	11-OCT-1891	
LaPlante, Esorva	1857	
Laporte, Hector	10-DEC-1882	
Larose, Carolus	10-DEC-1882	
Larose, Joannes	11-OCT-1891	
Larose, Maria Josephina	11-OCT-1891	
Lauzon, -atrius	11-OCT-1891	
Lebeau, Adeline	01-NOV-1886	
Lebeau, Emelia	01-NOV-1886	
Lebeau, Josephina	11-OCT-1891	
Lecuiller, Pierre	1857	
Leduc, Josephus	1857	
Lefort, Helena	11-OCT-1891	
Lefort, M. Ezilda	10-DEC-1882	
Lefort, Narcissus	11-OCT-1891	
Lemieux, Antonius	11-OCT-1891	
Lemieux, Daphina	1894	
Lemieux, Ezilda	01-NOV-1886	
Lemieux, Israel	10-DEC-1882	
Lemieux, Josephus	11-OCT-1891	
Lemieux, Lea	01-NOV-1886	
Lemieux, Rosa Anna	11-OCT-1891	
Lépine, Avila	1897	
Lépine, Eduardus	11-OCT-1891	
Lepine, Florence Corinne Maria	10-NOV-1918	Lepine, Miss Hilda
Lépine, Ida	1894	
Lepine, Joanna	11-OCT-1891	
Lepine, Josephus	10-NOV-1918	Lepine, Thomas
Lépine, Ludovicus	01-NOV-1886	
Lépine, M. Aurelia	10-DEC-1882	
Lépine, Odilia	01-NOV-1886	
Lépine, Petrus	1897	
Lépine, Thomas	1897	
Létourneau, Ada Agnes	11-OCT-1891	
Létourneau, Elodie	01-NOV-1886	
Létourneau, Emma	10-DEC-1882	
Letourneau, Georgius	1894	
Létourneau, Josephina Adela	11-OCT-1891	
Letourneau, Josephus	10-DEC-1882	
Létourneau, Josephus	1897	
Letourneau, Lucia J.	1894	
Létourneau, M. Edessa	01-NOV-1886	
Letourneau, Maria	01-NOV-1886	
Létourneau, Mélina	01-NOV-1886	
Létourneau, Philomena	1894	
Lienchs, Joannes	1857	
Lomblot, Carolus	10-DEC-1882	
Lomblot, Constans	01-NOV-1886	
Lomblot, Josephina Henrica	11-OCT-1891	

Lomblot, Rosa	01-NOV-1886	
Lower, Chaterina	1857	
Lucier, Arthurus	01-NOV-1886	
Lucier, Clara Edith	11-OCT-1891	
Lucier, Eduardus	01-NOV-1886	
Lucier, Ludovicus	01-NOV-1886	
Lucier, Mabel Francisca	11-OCT-1891	
Lumblo, Maria Adice Olive	10-NOV-1918	Jentz, Mrs. Frank
Lyneis, Gertruda Adice	10-NOV-1918	Lyneis, Miss Ruth
Lyneis, Joseph Roman	10-NOV-1918	Plisker, Eric
Lyneis, Lloyd Joseph	10-NOV-1918	Reinwand, Leonard
Lyneis, Marjorie Francesca Maria	10-NOV-1918	Lyneis, Miss Iva
Lyonais, Claudius	1894	
Lyonais, Eduardus	10-DEC-1882	
Lyonais, Georgius	11-OCT-1891	
Lyonais, Jos. Walter	01-NOV-1886	
Lyonais, M. Henrietta	10-DEC-1882	
Lyonais, M. Ida	01-NOV-1886	
M-g-a-h, Ellisa	1857	
Maine, Sara	1857	
Maloney, Edward Dam	1857	
Marcou, Anna Maria	1857	
Marcou, Frances	1857	
Marcou, Francis	1857	
Marcoux, Alfredus Guy	1897	
Marcoux, Arthurus	1894	
Marcoux, Eleonora	1894	
Marcoux, Emelia	01-NOV-1886	
Marcoux, Eva	1899	
Marcoux, Franciscus	11-OCT-1891	
Marcoux, Franciscus	1894	
Marcoux, Georgius Henricus	1897	
Marcoux, Henricus	1894	
Marcoux, Henricus	1897	
Marcoux, Josephus Eduardus	11-OCT-1891	
Marcoux, M. Malvina	10-DEC-1882	
Marcoux, Malvina	11-OCT-1891	
Marcoux, Rosalia	01-NOV-1886	
Margru-, Olivina	1857	
Markou, Emma Ludovica	1894	
Martin, Eleonara	01-NOV-1886	
Martin, Emericus	1894	
Martin, Laurentius	11-OCT-1891	
Martin, Rosa	11-OCT-1891	
Mc---y, Anna	1857	
McCay, Jocabus	1857	
McCay, Patrick	1857	
McClene, Ellena	1857	
McClone, Margereta	1857	
McCoy, Bernhard	1857	
McCulligan, Catherina	1857	
McDonald, Sophronia	01-NOV-1886	

McKeep, Thamas	1857	
McMain, Joannes Baptista	1857	
McMann, Jacobus	1857	
McMann, Patricius	1857	
Melle-y, Anna	1857	
Melony, Catherian	1857	
Melony, Delia	1857	
Meylolur, Brigeta	1857	
Michotte, M. Louisa	10-DEC-1882	
Michotte, M. Malvina	10-DEC-1882	
Miller, Alexender	1857	
Moquin, Alfredus	01-NOV-1886	
Moquin, Andreas	11-OCT-1891	
Moquin, Anna	10-DEC-1882	
Moquin, Cordelia	1899	
Moquin, Eduardus	11-OCT-1891	
Moquin, Ernestus	1897	
Moquin, Esmeralda Anna	10-NOV-1918	Moquin, Miss Orpha
Moquin, Georgius	10-DEC-1882	
Moquin, Joannes	1894	
Moquin, Josephina	1899	
Moquin, Josephine Maria	10-NOV-1918	Moquin, Miss Genevieve
Moquin, Josephus	10 DEC-1882	
Moquin, Ludovicus	1894	
Moquin, M. Delia	10-DEC-1882	
Moquin, Maria	10-DEC-1882	
Moquin, Maria Ada	11-OCT-1891	
Moquin, Zephirus	01-NOV-1886	
Moreaw, Jerimias	1857	
Morris, Joseph Clarence	10-NOV-1918	Dufrane, Ed.
Mosher, Ludovicus L.	10-DEC-1882	
Mullin, Elisabehta	1857	
Murphy, Joannes	1857	
Nallen, Ellis	1857	
Nayen, Olivina	1857	
O'Brayen, John	1857	
O'Bryan, Anna	1857	
O'Bryan, Maria	1857	
O'Corner, Brigita	1857	
Pagel, Franciscus	10-NOV-1918	Kingsley, Wm.
Paré, Julia	1899	
Parriso, Jado-us	1857	
Pellant, Ellena	1857	
Pellant, Margeta	1857	
Peron, Maria	10-DEC-1882	
Perron, Albertus	10-NOV-1918	Deuer, John
Peters, Albertus H.	10-DEC-1882	
Pfeitner, Ruth	1894	
Pinguère, M. Josephina	10-DEC-1882	
Poirier, M. Malvina	10-DEC-1882	
Poirier, Philomena	10-DEC-1882	
Pomerville, Genovefa	10-NOV-1918	Ferry, Mrs. Arabelle

Pommeville, Maria	10-NOV-1918	Marcoe, Miss Lena
Potvin, Georgius	1897	
Pratte, Arthurus	01-NOV-1886	
Pratte, Josephina	11-OCT-1891	
Pratte, M. Emma	10-DEC-1882	
Pratte, Stella	1894	
Prefontain, Lucretia	01-NOV-1886	
Prefontaine, Carolus	1897	
Prefontaine, Desideratus	01-NOV-1886	
Préfontaine, Honoratus	10-DEC-1882	
Préfontaine, Josephina	11-OCT-1891	
Préfontaine, Julia	01-NOV-1886	
Préfontaine, M. Corinna	10-DEC-1882	
Préfontaine, Rosa	10-DEC-1882	
Préfontaine, Stella Evelina	11-OCT-1891	
Prefontaine, Theresia	1894	
Prester, Antonius	1857	
Rayain, Catheria	1857	
Rayly, Thamas	1857	
Raymond, Eduardus	1897	
Raymond, Irenaus	1897	
Raymond, Isaac	1897	
Raymond, Israel	1857	
Rebarins, Maria		
Reichling, Leo Joseph	10-NOV-1918	O'Hearn, Thomas
Reinhart, Anna	10-DEC-1882	
Roberge, Arthurus	10-DEC-1882	
Roberge, M. Dalvina	01-NOV-1886	
Robert, Josephus	10-DEC-1882	
Robert, Ludovicus	01-NOV-1886	
Robert, M. Josephina	10-DEC-1882	
Roberts, Franciscus	10-NOV-1918	Dufrane, Frank
Robidoux, Angela	1894	
Robidoux, Joannes	11-OCT-1891	
Robidoux, Josephina	1894	
Robidoux, Lucretia	1894	
Robidoux, Maglorius	1897	
Robidoux, Marcellina	01-NOV-1886	
Robidoux, Maria Adela	11-OCT-1891	
Robidoux, Maria-Clara	10-DEC-1882	
Roch, Francisca	11-OCT-1891	
Rodidoux, Cesarina	11-OCT-1891	
Roi, Josephus	1857	
Rondeau, Alfredus	10-DEC-1882	
Rondeau, Eleonara	01-NOV-1886	
Rondeau, Henricus	01-NOV-1886	
Rondeau, Josephus	11-OCT-1891	
Rondeau, M. Flora	10-DEC-1882	
Rondeau, M. Josephina	10-DEC-1882	
Rondeau, Maria Emma	11-OCT-1891	
Roy, Anna	1899	
Roy, Arthurus	11-OCT-1891	

Roy, Ludovicus	11-OCT-1891	
Roy, M. Georgius	10-DEC-1882	
Roy, Maria Oliva	11-OCT-1891	
Roy, Maximillanius	10-DEC-1882	
Roy, Oliverus	10-DEC-1882	
Roy, Petrus	11-OCT-1891	
Roy, Philias	01-NOV-1886	
Roy, Philippus	01-NOV-1886	
Ryaume, Eva	1899	
Ryaume, Ludovicus	1897	
Sauvé, Josephus	11-OCT-1891	
Sauvé, Maglorius	10-DEC-1882	
Sauvé, Maria-A.	10-DEC-1882	
Sauvé, Victor	11-OCT-1891	
Sauvé, Zeno	10-DEC-1882	
Sénécal, Ovidus	1894	
Sénécal, Rosa de Lima	1899	
Severin, Adolphus	01-NOV-1886	
Sévérin, Emelianus	11-OCT-1891	
Severin, Maximilianus	1894	
Siny, Maryeta	1857	
Smet, Ellena	1857	
St. Antoine, Eduardus	1897	
St. Antoine, Stella	1899	
Staten, Theodore	10-NOV-1918	Robidoux, John
Ste. Marie, Sara Eudelia	1897	
Strong, Joannes	11-OCT-1891	
Surprenant, Arthurus	01-NOV-1886	
Surprenant, Juliana Lizama	11-OCT-1891	
Surprenant, M. Delia	10-DEC-1882	
Surprenant, Maria Zoe	11-OCT-1891	
Surprenant, Petrus-Levi	10-DEC-1882	
Tebodeaux, Doptine	1857	
Tell, Madalena	1857	
Tessier, M. Adelina	10-DEC-1882	
Tessier, M. Elizabeth	01-NOV-1886	
Tinder, Anna Maria Sophia	11-OCT-1891	
Toner, Jacobus Gulielmus	11-OCT-1891	
Tremblay, Arthurus	01-NOV-1886	
Tremblay, Ernestus	01-NOV-1886	
Tremblay, Franciscus	01-NOV-1886	
Tremblay, M. Eugenia	10-DEC-1882	
Tremblay, Philomena	01-NOV-1886	
Turcot, Eduardus	01-NOV-1886	
Turcot, Julia	1899	
Turcot, Maria	11-OCT-1891	
Turcot, Virginia	01-NOV-1886	
Vain, Maria	1857	
Venne, Agnes	1894	
Venne, Coecilia	10-NOV-1918	Durosha, Mrs. Elizabeth
Venne, Emelia	01-NOV-1886	
Venne, Ezilda Maria	11-OCT-1891	

Venne, Ludovicus	10-DEC-1882	
Venne, M. Elodia	10-DEC-1882	
Venne, Maria	1894	
Venne, Maria Ludovica	1897	
Venne, Victor	11-OCT-1891	
Ward, Francicus	1857	
Weber, Alice Margarita	10-NOV-1918	Weber, Mrs. Barbara
Weelks-Gratton, Elva Maria	10-NOV-1918	Gratton, Rose
Wood, Joanna	1857	

APPENDIX E

LETTER FROM FEDERAL BUREAU OF INVESTIGATION

UNITED STATES DEPARTMENT OF JUSTICE

FEDERAL BUREAU OF INVESTIGATION

In Reply, Please Refer to
File No.

WASHINGTON 25, D. C.

October 25, 1956

Mr. Armand L. Singleton
155 West Johnson Street
Fond du Lac, Wisconsin

Dear Mr. Singleton:

I have received your letter dated October 15, 1956, concerning ink writing which has disappeared from church records.

The facilities of the FBI Laboratory are necessarily available only to Federal Government agencies and state, county and municipal law enforcement agencies in connection with their official investigations of criminal matters. Therefore, I regret very much that the church records cannot be examined in the FBI Laboratory.

It is suggested you may wish to try exposing the pages to ultraviolet light to determine whether the ink writing will fluoresce to such an extent that it can be read. If the fluorescence is not extensive, it may be possible to record the writing by making photographs of the pages while exposed to ultraviolet light. This would necessitate taking the photographs in a dark room. If the ultraviolet-light process does not bring out the writing, it is suggested that you have photographs made using red-sensitive negatives with either tungsten light bulbs or an arc-light as the source of light. A red filter should be used in this process. The filters most commonly used are Wratten Numbers 25, 29 and 87. The Wratten filter Number 87 produces an infrared photograph. Your local photographer should be able to assist you in connection with the photographic work.

If the photographic processes do not produce the desired results, it is suggested that you contact a chemist who may be able to make suitable tests of the ink writing to determine the proper reagents for developing the faded writing.

I hope this information will assist you in solving your problem.

Sincerely yours,

J. E. Hoover

John Edgar Hoover
Director

222

APPENDIX F

MAP SHOWING THE COUNTIES OF THE STATE OF WISCONSIN

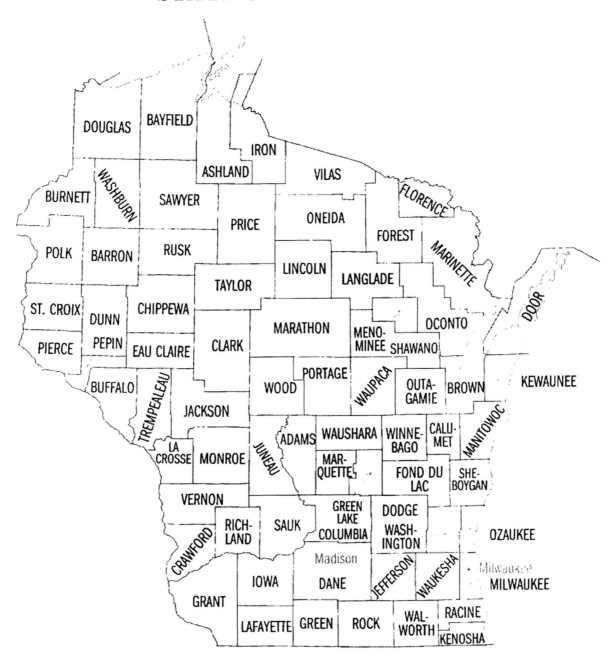

MAP SHOWING THE TOWNSHIPS OF
FOND DU LAC COUNTY

CALUMET

RIPON | ROSENDALE | ELDORADO | FRIENDSHIP

TAYCHEEDAH | MARSHFIELD

METOMEN | SPRINGVALE | LAMARTINE | FOND DU LAC | EMPIRE | FOREST

ALTO | WAUPUN | OAKFIELD | BYRON | EDEN | OSCEOLA

ASHFORD | AUBURN

LaVergne, TN USA
15 November 2010
204964LV00001B/14/P